The Rise of Asia

The Rise of Asia

Economics, Society, and Politics in Contemporary Asia

Frank B. Tipton
Department of Economic History
University of Sydney

UNIVERSITY OF HAWAI'I PRESS
HONOLULU

HC
460.5
.T56
1998

Published in North America by
UNIVERSITY OF HAWAI'I PRESS
2840 Kolowalu Street
Honolulu, Hawai'i 96822

First Published in the United Kingdom by
MACMILLAN PUBLISHERS LTD
Houndmills
Basingstoke, Hampshire, RG21 6XS

This book is printed on paper suitable for recycling and
made from fully managed and sustained forest sources.

Library of Congress Cataloging-in-Publication Data
Tipton, Frank B., 1943–
The rise of Asia : economics, society, and politics in
contemporary Asia / Frank B. Tipton.
p. cm.
Includes bibliographical references and index.
ISBN 0–8248–2055–X (alk. paper). — ISBN 0–8248–2056–8
1. East Asia—Economic conditions. 2. Asia, Southeastern-
-Economic conditions. 3. East Asia—social conditions. 4. Asia,
Southeastern—Social conditions. 5. East Asia—Politics and
government. 6. Asia, Southeastern—Politics and government.
I. Title.
HC460.5.T56 1998
330.95—dc21   97–47687
                                                         CIP

Printed in Malaysia

CONTENTS

LIST OF TABLES

PREFACE AND ACKNOWLEDGEMENTS

This book is the outcome of a number of years of teaching a broadly comparative course in economic history. I have felt the need for a text which would provide an introduction not only to the economics of growth and development in Asia, but also to the social and political contexts of growth. As a historian I have a professional prejudice in favour of a treatment which takes account of the longer term and which is sensitive to the continuities underlying the extraordinary changes taking place across Asia today. As a comparative historian I have been interested in the need for multiple disciplinary perspectives as well. As a teacher I am concerned to introduce students to history not as a body of facts, but as a problematical and contested terrain. The structure of the book reflects these concerns. It also reflects both my own range of interests and those of my students. Most of the sections within chapters began as lectures, discussion group topics, or essay assignments, and although they are very far from covering all possible areas of concern, they have proved successful in the classroom environment. As such, I hope they will prove useful to others as well.

The specific occasion for writing arose from a request from Richard Tilly that I prepare a survey of recent work on the economic and social history of Asia for inclusion in an issue of *Geschichte und Gesellschaft* devoted to 'extension of social history'. Working on that project reinforced my conviction that the shift among a wide range of Asian specialists towards an emphasis on the internal dynamics of Asian societies had significantly altered the terms in which economic development, social change, and political processes were being studied, and that these newer approaches did indeed constitute a broad underlying consensus. Within that framework, the book attempts to do a wide range of specialist fields justice, keeping in view the obvious fact that a consensus on a basic approach does not preclude vigorous and impassioned debate over facts and their interpretation. I might emphasize that this is particularly the case in economic history, where many of the 'facts' are produced synthetically. The most important 'fact' of all, the amount of goods and services produced in a country, for example, is always an estimate subject to more or less wide margins of error, and the margins increase rapidly as we move backward in time.

The University of Sydney, and the Australian academic community generally, is an exciting place to pursue Asian and comparative studies. I have benefited from the advice and assistance of a number of individuals. Some of their forthcoming work is cited as working papers. In particular, my departmental colleagues John Drabble and Lily Zubaidah Rahim have shared their knowledge of Southeast Asia with me. Haishun Sun (Economics) has informed me on recent foreign investment in China, and Michael Leigh (Government and Public Administration) on Malaysian politics. The discussion of Asian nationalism and of Indonesia in particular has benefited from suggestions made by Michael van Langenberg (School of Asian Studies), and the chapters on Japan have benefited from conversations with Elise Kurashige Tipton (also School of Asian Studies, who has borne the additional burden of being married to me). Pierre van der Eng (Economic History, Australian National University) has been exceptionally generous in introducing me to the statistical study of the Indonesian economy. I have benefited from reports produced by the Economic History of Southeast Asia (ECHOSEA) project at the Australian National Univerity, whose individual country and thematic studies will be appearing over the next two years. The 1996 meeting of the Asian Studies Association of Australia, *Communications With/In Asia: 20th Anniversary Conference of the Asian Studies Association of Australia*, held at Latrobe University, provided the opportunity to present a session on the role of the state in Asian economic development. My fellow panel members Linda Weiss (Government and Public Administration, University of Sydney), John Hobson (Politics, LaTrobe University), and Kanishka Jayasuriya (Asia Research Centre, Murdoch University) have also shared their work and their insights with me. A visit to The University Professors, Boston University, in 1994 led to discussions with Liah Greenfeld on nationalism and with Harry Gelber on the role of the state in increasing productivity which have strengthened those portions of the book. The book also incorporates research which has been supported by grants from the Australian Research Council, and the writing was speeded by leave granted by the University of Sydney. Finally, there are a number of individuals both in and out of government who have responded to my requests for information, assistance, or evaluation, who prefer anonymity. The book is better for the efforts and support of these individuals and institutions; the blame for its shortcomings is mine.

The bibliography lists works cited in the text; I have generally confined citations to secondary works in English, especially those which provide introductions into more specialized areas. I have tried to be even-handed in citing works on different sides of the various disputed areas considered. In the bibliography I have listed surnames, followed by commas, then given names. In the text names are given in the order of the language from which they come, except for migrant Asians who have adopted the Western order of given name first, for instance Kozo Yamamura. Chinese names of people and places in mainland China are given generally in Pinyin, except where this would cause confusion, for instance Chiang Kaishek, or when the place is known historically in an older spelling, for instance Dairen. People and places in Taiwan are given in the modified Wade-Giles system used in most English-language publications produced in Taiwan. The quotations from Confucius and Mencius are from the excellent translations by D.C. Lau (London: Penguin, 1970 and 1979). Everyone interested in social and economic history owes an immense debt to B.R. Mitchell's *International Historical Statistics* (Mitchell 1992, 1993, 1995).

And finally but not least importantly, the book is dedicated to my two daughters, Lee and Christine.

FBT
Department of Economic History, University of Sydney
February 1997

1

PROLOGUE: EAST AND SOUTHEAST ASIA AND THE CHANGING BALANCE OF WORLD ECONOMIC FORCES

The Changing Balance

Head to Head: The Coming Economic Battle Among Japan, Europe, and America
Lester Thurow, 1993

'Asia, A Civilization in the Making'
Masakazu Yamazaki, *Foreign Affairs*, 1996

The explosive growth of the economies of Asia is shifting the balance of world economic power eastward, away from Western Europe and the United States and towards East and Southeast Asia. Five of the ten largest holders of foreign exchange in the world today are Asian nations, and the trend shows no sign of slowing. This is very possibly the most important change taking place in the world today, although the ultimate significance of Asian development is a matter for dispute. For some, Asian growth appears an impending apocalypse, and for others, an approaching millennium. Looked at from the dark side, the world appears to pessimists to be dividing into huge competitive economic blocs, in North America, in Western Europe, and in East Asia, destined to strive against each other for supremacy (Thurow, 1993). However, it appears to more optimistic observers not only that Asia, 'a civilization in the making', might 'take the entire Pacific Basin as the sphere of the emerging civilization', but also that 'it will have to collaborate with the Atlantic sphere of civilization that is sharing its experience' (Yamazaki, 1996).

Taking a cooler view, the shift in part reflects predictable changes in the 'core' regions of the world economy and a convergence in the economic

1

productivity of the United States and European nations (Hugill, 1988; Nelson and Wright, 1992), as well as the dramatic growth in Asia (Maddison, 1987, 1989). Hegemonies, whether diplomatic or economic, do not last forever. Britain, the first industrial nation, displaced France in the late eighteenth and early nineteenth centuries, and established a pre-eminence which lasted for nearly a century. In the late nineteenth century the spread of industrial technologies to Western Europe, the United States, and Japan led to a relative decline in Britain's position and the rise of Germany in Europe, the United States in the Americas, and Japan in East Asia. The United States especially advanced in productivity, applying mass production techniques to supply a domestic market unmatched in breadth and depth by any other country. The Second World War – the 'Pacific War' in Asia – led to a period of competition between two superpowers, the Soviet Union and the United States, and the collapse of the Soviet Union left the United States as the single pre-eminent power. In the meantime, however, industrial technologies have spread once again, this time to other nations in East and Southeast Asia, and Japan and Western Europe have moved towards American levels of productivity, also based on previously unprecedented levels of personal income in their domestic markets.

Most observers do not take the cool view, however. Although no industrial country has ever 'de-industrialized', and even declining powers have continued to grow and advance, the loss of position *relative* to newer industrial powers has always proved traumatic. A series of wars between Britain and France culminated in the Napoleonic wars and Britain's victory in 1815. In the late nineteenth century Germany became Britain's rival in Europe and overseas. That rivalry contributed to the outbreak of the First World War, which in turn paved the way for the Second World War (Tipton and Aldrich, 1987). As we will see later in Chapter 7, the rise of Japan destabilized the balance of power in Asia and led to the Pacific War. In Chapters 8 and 9, we will look at Asian development in the postwar era that was marked by the Cold War between the United States and the Soviet Union. In the United States today, serious proposals are being made for the defence of America's 'hegemony' against any threat, from whatever direction (Kristol and Kagan, 1996).

Today, Asia is 'hot', and so are the emotions it arouses. Economic growth translates directly into power, and this has prompted a search not only for explanations of Asian growth, but most urgently for those explanations which might be lessons for competitors and potential imitators. Fashion has changed with the changing fortunes of the Asian economies. Japan's rapid growth in the 1950s and 1960s led scholars to pronounce solemnly that Japan was 'number one' and to ponder possible 'lessons for America' in industrial organization and education (Vogel, 1979). As we will see in Chapters 12 and 13, the emergence of the 'four tigers' has led to intensive debate over the lessons of the success of South Korea, Taiwan, Hong Kong, and Singapore, particularly the proper role of the state in economic development (Chowdhury and Islam, 1993). The emergence of further 'newly industrializing economies' and the recent rapid growth of the larger nations of Southeast Asia and China has been accompanied by an 'Asian triumphalism', the assertion by Asian intellectuals and political leaders that the ultimate lesson of Asian success is the role of 'Asian values' in economic development (Berger, 1996).

The transformation of the world economy is also transforming the way Westerners view their own economic past. Gunnar Myrdal's classic *Asian Drama* (1968) presented a gloomy vision of the prospects for economic development in Asia, in which the hindrances to growth were numerous and intractable, anchored in the institutional structure of Asian societies. The problem as Myrdal and others writing in the 1960s saw it was to translate the radical discontinuity of the English Industrial Revolution and the subsequent dynamism of Europe and America into terms compatible with essentially static 'traditional' societies. A generation later, economic and social historians are no longer confronted with widespread backwardness, from which isolated cases of 'development' emerged, but with widespread development emerging from extremely diverse social and historical contexts. For some historians this implies a devaluation of the European experience. Eric Jones, who began his career as an economic historian with studies of England during the Industrial Revolution, now argues that the central problem of economic history is no longer to explain the unique breakthrough in England and then ask why other regions could follow or not, but rather to understand the negative forces – especially rent-seeking 'distributional coalitions' – which frustrated a very widespread potential for growth in many other regions (Jones, 1993). For Jones and others, eighteenth-century English society now appears much more traditional, English economic development much more gradual, and Europe and America merely one of many cases of 'growth recurring'.

To explain growth, whether in any of the countries of Asia or in any of the countries of the West, requires an integrated approach to economic, social, and political development. Although there is no single cause or secret of development, there is a common core to the development process. Although the forms and timing of development have depended on specific circumstances, the underlying relationships have been similar across the nations of East and Southeast Asia, and these relationships resemble those found in Western development as well. And, although the underlying processes have been similar, the explanation of the timing and pattern of development in each case needs to take account of the specific circumstances of the historical period, economic possibilities, social structure, and political system. Into the 1980s various versions of 'modernization theory' contended with Marxist analyses of capitalist development and imperialism in explaining the patterns of Asian development. As we will see in Chapter 2, more recent empirical work has argued that rather than simply responding to development in the West, Asia possessed its own internal dynamic. In addition, and this is explored further there and in Chapter 11, the assumptions underlying both modernization theory and Marxism have been challenged by interdisciplinary approaches, especially by feminist social scientists and historians.

This book approaches Asian development from three perspectives, distinct but overlapping. The economic view concentrates on the development of aggregate structures and relationships, on consumption, supplies of natural resources, the development of the labour force, savings and investment, and technology. An underlying theme is the astonishing variety of ways in which an economy can develop. The social view considers the same phenomena, but from the perspective of individuals and groups of individuals, and looks at them as women and men, as families, as local communities, as workers, and as entrepreneurs. An underlying theme is the remarkable flexibility of ordinary people in their responses to potential opportunities. The political view, lastly, looks at the interaction of individuals and groups, whether in cooperation or conflict, at the imposition of colonial regimes, at the creation of national states, at the structures of government, and at the role of elites. Here the underlying theme is the continuity of elite groups and their dogged pursuit of power.

Recent research has demonstrated the inadequacy of the traditional Western view of Asia as essentially static before the intrusion of the imperialist powers in the nineteenth century. These were dynamic, market-oriented economies, although the lack of industrial technologies placed limits on their growth potential. The concerns of Asian specialists parallel many of the developments in European social history (see Tilly et al., 1991). In particular, the newer approach in Asian studies matches the newer view of early modern economic development in Europe, where 'protoindustrialization' – the manufacture of goods for interregional trade – was widespread (Ogilvie, 1993; Ogilvie and Markus, 1996). However, the newer approach which emphasizes the internal dynamics and the inherited strength of indigenous traditions in Asian development, if pushed too far, runs the risk of falling victim to the nationalist fallacy of crediting all good things to indigenous traditions, and blaming all bad things on foreigners. Thus, as argued in Chapters 8 and 12, the various attempts to claim that Asian development has resulted from essentially 'Asian' values, whether 'national' traditions or a supranational 'Neo-Confucianism', are as one-sided in their way as the old 'modernization' theory which attributed growth to the adoption of 'Western' values (see Tipton, 1996; Berger, 1996).

Sustained economic development has never been easy. Pre-industrial farmers and artisans were connected to markets, but these markets were competitive. Before the industrial age regions developed, but they often declined as well. Not all cases of 'early modern' or 'protoindustrial' development led to later industrial development. However, when industrial technologies became available, economic agents, which might be individuals, families, local communities, or governments, adopted them as soon as they were able. This was not always a pleasant process, for those with power over others exploited their position to gain economic advantage. Women, those with the least power, tended to be the most exploited, and the gendered nature of development needs to be recognized as a consistent pattern, a theme underlying economic, social, and political transformations alike.

Resources and Technology

It is said that once, an old economist and a young economist were walking along the street, and the young economist saw a twenty-dollar bill lying on the sidewalk.
Young Economist: There is a twenty-dollar bill lying on the sidewalk. Why don't you pick it up?
Old Economist: There is no twenty-dollar bill lying on the sidewalk.
Young Economist: But how can you say that?
Old Economist: Because, if there *had* been a twenty-dollar bill lying on the sidewalk, someone would already have picked it up.

Asian development seems to support the view that the absence of natural resources does not hinder growth. Japan and the four tigers are obvious cases in point. In addition, the presence of valuable mineral resources or fertile agricultural land made Asian areas more likely to be colonized by the imperialist powers in the late nineteenth century, which may have delayed development. It is not resources, but what you do, or are allowed to do, with them which matters. Technology is the crucial variable, but here as well technologies must be used to be effective. Certainly, for better or for worse, many of the former colonial nations are now launched into modern economic growth and development, which provides at least implicit support to the common claim that colonialism retarded indigenous development.

Why did Asia not industrialize *before* the intervention of the West, however? Especially in the case of China we confront the 'Needham paradox', after Joseph Needham's voluminous *Science and Civilization in China* (Ronan, 1980–94). China was clearly technologically more advanced than Europe over a wide range of fields in the late medieval and early modern period. In fact, as Needham and his students have shown, many Chinese techniques were exported and adopted by European producers, where they became the basis for later European advances. Yet, this early technological superiority did not lead to sustained economic development in China. For instance, Chinese silk technology stagnated during the Qing dynasty after a period of continuous advance during the Ming (Li, 1981).

'The paradox of growth without development' in China has challenged scholars, both specialists and students of comparative development (Fairbank, 1992; Mokyr, 1990). Many, including Mao Zedong, have blamed Western imperialism for crushing China's 'capitalist sprouts'. In several cases in the later nineteenth century Chinese enterprises were able to import new technologies, and it can be argued that in the absence of foreign intervention after 1897 China could have industrialized (Thomas, 1984). Others, following Max Weber's lead, argued that 'Chinese' or 'Confucian' values inhibited the growth of a capitalist ethos and therefore retarded growth. More recent attempts to resolve the paradox often refer to underlying structures within China, for instance the 'high level equilibrium trap' of rice culture (Elvin, 1973), the complex relations between large and small farmers which led to 'involution' (Huang, 1985, 1990), or rent-seeking by distributional coalitions whose predatory activities choked off the potential for growth (Jones, 1993; see Hamilton, 1985, 1990).

Whatever their preferred approach, Chinese historians now look for the explanation of China's delayed development in the internal dynamics of Chinese society. Similarly, Japan's internal dynamics, internal trade and protoindustrial development seemed for a time to explain Japan's successful early industrialization. Here, however, more recent studies of proto-industrial development both in Europe and elsewhere in East and Southeast Asia suggest that Japan's experience was not unique. In both Europe and

Asia protoindustrial development was widespread, but not all protoindustrial districts later became industrial regions. This leads again to the idea that Asia is not in fact so very much different from Europe. But this does not mean that all types of economic growth are the same. In particular, the pre-industrial economies of both Europe and Asia were just that – pre-industrial. The progressive accumulation typical of modern societies requires modern – meaning Western – technologies. To be even more specific, until the very late nineteenth century, the technologies required for modern economic growth were British. Only the emergence of modern industrial technology in Britain in the late eighteenth century made it possible to move beyond the bounds imposed by reliance on muscle tissue, wind, and water (Landes, 1969). It is not true that any sort of development could or should have led to industrialization, and it is not true that industrial growth is merely another example of 'growth recurring'. Rather, industrial growth is the defining characteristic of the modern world.

For all countries in the modern world, therefore, industrialization has required a process of technology transfer. Once the new techniques were known, they could be copied (even an economist will pick a twenty-dollar bill up off the sidewalk), but the process has never been easy and may rely in part on luck as well as design. The timing and conditions of each country's integration into world markets played a role. As we will see in Chapter 5, Japan, the first Asian nation to experience modern economic growth, was an 'early-comer' in the use of modern technology. The Japanese could draw on widespread experimentation in industrial techno-logy before the Meiji Restoration. They learned to operate simple steam-driven machines – virtually all imported directly from Britain – in the closing decades of the nineteenth century. They subsequently learned the newer, more arcane technologies emerging one by one in the early twentieth century. Some of the innovations which aided Japan's success were not mechanical technologies at all. Japan's silk industry won markets not because of better machines, but as a result of careful quality control. Japanese cotton firms developed a blend of short- and long-fibre cotton, which enabled them to shift from mule to ring spindles, running at higher speeds and operated by inexpensive female workers, which gave them a decisive advantage in Asian markets in the early twentieth century.

Japan's industrialization, therefore, did not serve as a simple 'model' to be emulated by other nations. The technology then was relatively simple, compared to the much more complex technologies (electricity- and gas-driven and electronically guided) of the second and third industrial revolu-tions confronting less developed countries after the Second World War.

Despite what appear at first to be increasingly difficult circumstances, (examined in Chapters 10, 12, and 13) many other regions of Asia have succeeded in introducing modern techniques across a broad spectrum of industries, but conditions have varied from decade to decade and place to place. Therefore, systematic explanations of the resulting patterns of technology transfer over the past generation have proved elusive.

Politics and Society

I have always asked God to guide me in each of my tasks. And thank God, to this day...I have never felt that I have failed. And if people think I have been wrong, I think: 'Who is it who can rightfully gauge my mistakes? Who decides if something is wrong?' I believe that whatever I do, after I've asked for guidance and direction from God, that whatever the results, these are the results of His Guidance.

Soeharto, *My Thoughts*, 1991

How are the technologies which make modern economic growth possible transferred? One set of answers lies in the role played by the state. For many of the countries of Asia until recently, this was either a colonial state, or a state subject to severe pressures from foreign powers. The heritage of colonialism and imperialism might be negative; indigenous peoples were certainly exploited (Dixon, 1991; So and Chiu, 1995). The heritage may have been positive; indigenous peoples were also given opportunities for economic advance. The European powers possibly neglected the crucial area of education, but they also created important elements of physical and institutional infrastructure which have benefited their former colonies. As we will see in Chapters 8 and 9, at the same time as examining the origins and development of Asian nationalisms, and the origins of later economic development, the heritage of the age of colonialism and imperialism needs to be recognized. Among the former colonial areas, Korea, Taiwan, and Manchuria are interesting special cases, for they were colonies of another Asian power, Japan, and as we will see in Chapter 7, the Japanese colonial governments in Korea and Taiwan may have laid the foundations for rapid growth. The difficulties and ambiguities found there seem to typify the problems inherent in any interpretation of the colonial experience.

In all societies gender differences are one of the key dividing lines, and rapid Asian development has had profound effects on gender relations

(Papenek, 1984). Development has sometimes paradoxically been supported by the 'surprising tenacity' of traditional beliefs, such as the widespread opinion among Chinese women that 'at the time they reach puberty their brains become less focused and they are henceforth less intelligent than men' (Honig, 1985). However, as will be argued in Chapter 11, gender identities are constructed, and sometimes the act of construction is quite deliberate. Pre-industrial and pre-national gender relations allowed women to work for the benefit of their family, and this could involve a wide variety of roles. Most of the Asian nationalist movements mobilized women in support of their claims, and in doing so created new 'national' female identities. Once in power, however, new national governments attempted to redefine gender roles once again, in ways which would confine women politically to a circumscribed domestic sphere while allowing them to be mobilized for work in an expanding industrial sector.

Looking at both gender relations and the course of economic development, we can attribute much of Asia's success to the efforts of a great many hardworking individuals and families, but as we will see in Chapter 9, through the 1950s and 1960s the successes tended to be outweighed by the failures. The influence of the Cold War can still be seen in discussions of this difficult period in Asian economic development. The relatively slow growth of the postwar and early independence periods are often blamed on policy failures – an 'inward looking' approach, attempts to achieve 'self-sufficiency', programmes of 'import substitution', and in particular the 'excessively' large role played by the state. The later period of rapid growth in turn is attributed to a shift to 'export orientation', deregulation, market forces, and especially to a reduced role for the state (World Bank, 1993). But as we will see in Chapters 12 and 13, 'statist' approaches contest this interpretation. The continued large role of the state is obvious even after the shift to export orientation, and 'statists' argue that government action is important and possibly essential in continuing growth (Weiss and Hobson, 1995).

Government policy is an important part of the story, but there seems no single policy which succeeds in all contexts. Even genuinely independent states have not always been successful in their attempts to foster economic growth. Policy choices, however, do reflect the interests of the leadership. Elite groups in Asia have proved remarkably durable over time. Sometimes the continuity is direct: leaders in the Philippines belong to or rely on the support of a landed oligarchy rooted in the Spanish colonial period; descendants of the Malay aristocracy continue to exercise influence in Malaysia; and Hosokawa Morihiro, briefly prime minister of

Japan in 1993, had served as governor of the same prefecture where his family had ruled as *daimyô* before the Meiji Restoration. Sometimes the continuity is imagined: as we see in Chapter 10, in Singapore Lee Kuan Yew made strenuous attempts to inculcate a Confucian morality among his subjects, and Soeharto, the ruler of Indonesia since 1965, clearly believes himself to be acting in the manner of traditional Javanese rulers (see Ricklefs, 1993, pp. 258, 286–7; van Langenberg, 1993; Schwarz, 1994, ch. 2). The debate between neo-classical approaches emphasizing the market, and statist analyses which look to the role of government, sometimes misses this context, which is so important for the historical explanation of rates and patterns of change.

Elites always play an important role in economic development, but their behaviour often seems arbitrary and contradictory, in that their actions encourage development in some ways and restrict it in others. Further, their actions often seem to undermine their own best interests. Some of these inconsistencies can be explained by looking at the values held by elite groups, and some by looking at the structure of the state or the colonial regime within which elites could act. The leaders and ruling groups that emerged from the colonial period and gained power with independence were frequently more concerned with their own position or with opposing Western 'imperialism' than with economic development. In addition, there are two sorts of tradition. One is inherited and pervasive, a metasystem which determines the structures of thought and action. But within this metasystem there are many elements, not all of them consistent, and some of them contradictory. Therefore, there can also be created traditions, composed of elements selected from the inherited tradition to serve a particular purpose. Chapters 5 and 8 will argue that these are not tradition but ideology – but they will claim to be traditions, and will claim that their selection of elements from the inherited tradition is in fact the only possible variant of the tradition (Chatterjee, 1986).

But above all the members of the emerging national elite want to gain and retain power. Individual leaders from left to right – Mao, Sukarno, Chiang Kaishek, Syngmann Rhee, and their successors – have seen themselves as indispensable and irreplaceable. Social elites across Asia have proved remarkably resistant to the notion that they should share power with other groups. Potential elements in the new national identity which do not contribute to their power have been suppressed. Not surprisingly, new national elites also brought some of the preconceptions of their old traditional elite status with them, firstly into the new nationalist movements, and eventually into the new national governments. This remains true, and at lower levels as well, especially in the definition of the basis of recruitment into state bureaucracies. The continual pressure on women to conform to stereotyped roles, and the assertion that central governments must play a leading part in economic development, both have their origins here, not in the inheritance of a mythical tradition, for instance 'Korean Confucianism' or 'the ideal of the unity of life' which Indonesian nationalists claimed constituted 'the inner spirit and spiritual structure of the Indonesian people'.

Economies: How Much Growth?

... research findings show that China's social and economic indicators are associated with a much higher level of per capita income than the current levels recorded by international agencies.

Yanrui Wu, 'How Wealthy Is China?' 1995

Analysing and explaining the recent rapid growth of the Asian economies poses all of the problems – measurement of aggregate and per capita incomes, regional variations, estimating the weight and role of 'traditional' and 'modern' sectors, the role of agriculture, supplies of capital, labour, and technology, and the foreign sector – which occupy students of European and American economic history. In addition, for most countries, systematic data of any sort were not available until quite recently, and the historical pattern of growth must be estimated from scattered information often collected for very different purposes. The interests of the Dutch colonial administration in Indonesia, or the scholar-gentry who administered the nineteenth-century Qing state, were not the same as those of the regimes which succeeded them, or those of later generations of economic historians.

The efforts of specialist scholars have provided us with estimates of rates of growth since the late nineteenth century for most countries. Some of these results are presented in Table 1.1 and offer some reasonably certain conclusions. Some growth in per capita product, accompanied by the structural changes associated with modern economic growth (Kuznets, 1966), did take place before the First World War, not only in Japan but also in Korea, Taiwan, and several Southeast Asian countries. The depression of the 1930s and the Second World War obviously devastated many of these countries. Following the war, Japan of course grew spectacularly. Korea and Taiwan grew as well, however, and in Southeast Asia Thailand also grew rapidly from the 1950s and was joined by Malaysia and Indonesia from the 1970s; war-ravaged Indochina and Myanmar (Burma) lagged behind.

More detailed studies seem to show periods of decisive spurts of growth of the sort predicted by Alexander Gerschenkron, possibly connected with the advantages of a backward country in introducing advanced technologies in the process of catching up with the previous

Table 1.1   Growth of Per Capita Incomes
A. Per capita gross domestic product in 1980 international dollars, 1870–1950

	1870	*1900*	*1913*	*1929*	*1950*
Burma	–	431	369	492	276
Indonesia	413	439	552	719	522
Japan	425	696	819	1184	1141
Philippines	–	640	878	972	801
South Korea	–	504	559	687	516
Taiwan	–	398	415	580	482
Thailand	506	425	598	565	604

B. Per capita gross domestic product in 1985 international dollars, 1950–90, and recent rates of growth

	1950	*1960*	*1973*	*1990*	*Rate of growth of per capita product, 1991– 1996, %*
Burma/Myanmar	304	437	446	562	–
China	417	–	924	2594	8 to 9
Indonesia	727	957	1253	2118	4 to 6
Japan	1208	2631	7133	13197	−1 to +1
Malaya/Malaysia	1828	1748	3088	5775	3.5 to 5.5
Philippines	943	1280	1629	1934	0 to 1.5
Singapore	–	2276	5372	14441	3 to 4
South Korea	565	816	1782	6012	6 to 7
Taiwan	595	921	2226	6574	5.5 to 6.5
Thailand	652	883	1559	3694	5.5

Source: Per capita product from Van der Eng, 1992, p. 359; 1994a, p. 102. Purchasing power parities, expressed as the ratio of the values of standard baskets of goods in international and national activity. Data from the International Comparison Project, reported and discussed in R. Summers and A. Heston, 'The Penn World Table (Mark 5),' *Quarterly Journal of Economics*, 104 (1991): 327–68, and A. Heston and R. Summers, 'What Can be Learned from Successive ICP Benchmark Estimates?' in A. Szirmai, et al., eds., *Explaining Economic Growth: Essays in Honor of Angus Maddison* (Amsterdam, 1993), pp. 353–73. Recent growth of total product, ranges of estimates from various sources.

leaders (Gerschenkron, 1952; Malinvaud, 1986). Japan is the classic case, though whether the truly decisive spurt took place before the First World War or during the 1950s and 1960s, when Japan's gross domestic product grew at over 9 per cent per year, is a matter of judgement. Other well-known spurts include Korea's 'sustained rapid economic growth' beginning in 1963 (Moskowitz, 1982, p. 63; Amsden 1989), Indonesia's very rapid growth in the 1970s (Dapice, 1980; Hill, 1996), and Malaysia's burst from 1973 to 1985 (Bowie, 1991). And, possibly most significant of all, since 1978 China's national product has risen at over 10 per cent annually.

Although there is a diversity of hypotheses to explain growth, no single synthesis has emerged from the study of aggregate economic statistics. The extensive statistical study of the Japanese economy has not resulted in a generally accepted explanation for Japanese development. Econometric modelling requires estimation of parameters and arbitrary judgements about which variables to include; it is conceptually possible to create many models with quite different basic assumptions and specifications which still produce results closely consistent with 'reality' as measured by the incomplete historical record. Although these techniques have produced valuable estimates of the pattern of past development, they do not explain the development which they describe. (Ohkawa et al., 1979; Kelley and Williamson, 1974). The same basic objections can be made about econometric models of each of the other Asian economies. The best models based on current data have been quickly outdated, overtaken by events as rapidly changing economic structures alter the basic parameters of the economy. In addition, even among neoclassical economists there are quite different approaches to economic development, and each study therefore reflects its author's preferences. For those not sharing the neo-classical assumptions, of course, the entire attempt to explain growth and development through the application of macroeconomic models appears circular and tautological at best.

There are further problems. Comparable figures are not always available. Index number problems arising from changes in the relative prices and varying proportions of goods entering markets make international comparisons hazardous even with the best of data, and the problems are magnified the further back in time one goes. If we are to make judgements about either early 'pre-modern' growth or about the course of later development, we must know where the countries of Asia started, relative to Europe and the United States. Thus Hanley and Yamamura's argument that growth was substantial throughout the Tokugawa period and laid the foundation for modern growth in the Meiji period depends on the estimated level of income in the 1850s and 1860s (Hanley and Yamamura, 1977).

Conventional methods of comparison of present to past incomes using monetary deflators are subject to the same problems as the comparison of present incomes of rich and poor countries using international exchange rates. Exchange rates do not reflect the domestic purchasing power of currencies, and usually past incomes, and the present incomes of poor countries, are seriously understated. It is now common to make comparisons of current incomes in terms of 'purchasing power parities', ratios of the cost of a standard 'basket' of goods, and the United Nations International Comparison Project has developed estimates of contemporary incomes in Third World countries which are generally substantially higher than previous estimates (see Hanson, 1988, 1991).

China is a good example, because of its size, its actual and potential political importance, and especially because evaluation of its economic

Table 1.2 Estimates of Per Capita National Product in China

Source	Period	Per capita product using purchasing power parity	Per capita product using US$ exchange rate	Ratio of PPP estimate to exchange rate estimate
Gordon, et al.	1987	1689	278	6:1
Summers & Heston	1988	2472	341	7:3
Chen, et al.	1989	3426	377	9:1
Garnaut & Ma	1990	1100	327	3:4
United Nations	1991	2946	328	9:0
Garnaut & Ma	1993	1300	465	2.8:1

Sources: Table taken from Wu, 1995. The estimates are:

Myron J. Gordon, Fei Luo, and Zhenping Wang, 'International Comparison of China's GNP', in William C. Wedley and Nigel Campbell, eds., *Advances in Chinese Industrial Studies*, vol. 3 (JAI Press, 1992). Gross national product. Estimates of output by sector, with further estimates of product generated by government services, education, and research.

R. Summers and A. Heston, 'The Penn World Table (Mark 5)', *Quarterly Journal of Economics*, 104 (1991): 327–68. Gross domestic product. Model based on an identical 'basket' of goods and services available in countries participating in United Nations project.

Haichun Chen, M. J. Gordon, and Zhiming Yan, 'The Real Income and Consumption of an Urban Chinese Family', *Journal of Development Studies* 31 (1) (1994): 201–13. Gross national product. Household surveys used to estimate food and other products, purchased services, and services provided by the government.

Ross Garnaut and Guonan Ma, 'How Rich is China: Evidence from the Food Economy', *Australian Journal of Chinese Affairs*, No. 30, pp. 121–46. Gross national product. Based on social and economic indicators, including life expectancy, daily caloric intake, food consumption, and trade ratios, compared with other East Asian Chinese communities such as Taiwan and Hong Kong.

growth is inevitably bound up with judgements about the governmental regime which is to receive the credit − or the blame − for economic performance. Table 1.2 shows some recent estimates of Chinese national product. They diverge widely, with the highest more than three times the lowest. As the notes suggest, these experts disagree on a range of definitional and methodological questions. Virtually the only point where they do agree, is that all of the purchasing power parity estimates are far higher than estimates which convert Chinese income using international exchange rates. The debate over Chinese development in the late Qing and Nationalist periods is considered in Chapter 6, the Maoist era in Chapter 8, and the period since Mao's death in Chapter 13.

These are technical issues, but they are important. The hotly disputed 'facts' of Chinese growth crucially affect our understanding of the Marxist notion of autonomous 'capitalist sprouts' independent of the intrusion of the West, the role of the Qing state, the development of Chinese capitalism, the role of foreign investment and hence of 'imperialism', the role of government during the Nationalist period, development under Mao, and not least the question of whether sustained growth is possible under his successors. Note for instance that if the recent higher estimates of income in the early twentieth century are accepted, then growth under the Qing must have been greater, and growth in the Nationalist period less, than some scholars have thought. Similarly, if recent studies which show the Chinese economy grew during the Nationalist period, rather than stagnating as earlier writers argued, then growth during the early years of the People's Republic cannot have been as impressive as previously thought. Finally, measures of income today affect our estimate of the degree of success of the market reforms since Mao's death.

Outline

A journey of a thousand li begins with a single step.

Mao Zedong

The following chapters are arranged chronologically, but also thematically. The theories deployed to interpret the 'facts' are often as contentious as the facts themselves, and chapters and sections have therefore been framed around the disputes over these interpretive frameworks. The story of each individual country can be followed across chapters as well.

China usually comes first and receives the most extended treatment because of its size and complexity. Japan usually follows, with Korea and Taiwan treated according to their role in the given period. The sections covering Southeast Asia usually move from the mainland to the archipelagos, again giving more coverage to large countries and more coverage in particular periods to the smaller countries as their importance demands. The bibliography contains complete references for the works cited by author and date in the text. These have generally been limited to English-language publications, and especially to those which represent important interpretative positions or which can serve as introductions to specialized areas of study.

Chapters 2, 3, and 4 cover the period of confrontation between Asia and the West. Chapter 2 considers political, social and gender relations, and the internal social and political dynamics of Asian societies in the nineteenth century, and the attempts of Asian leaders to come to terms with the expansion of Western power. Chapter 3 looks behind this story to examine the role of markets and the efforts of Asian women and men, as family members and as farmers, artisans, and merchants, to improve their lot in life. Chapter 4 moves up the social scale from the 'little' people to consider the role of Asian elites in politics and economic life, both before and during the imperialist period.

Chapter 5 looks at the most important case study of early industrialization, that of Japan during the Meiji period. The patterns of Japanese development – the role of force in the creation of the new government, the deliberate creation of a new 'national' identity, and the state's attempts to foster and guide economic development – have been repeated by other Asian countries. However, Japan's role in Asia was not so much as a model, though many hoped to emulate Japanese success, but as a destabilizing force in the economic and political equilibrium of the colonial era. Chapter 6 sets the scene by considering the interwar international economy and the impact of the depression. The cases of Indonesia and China are considered in detail, both for their intrinsic importance and because they exemplify the issues and the difficulty of achieving a consensus in our views of Asian development during this difficult period. Chapter 7 returns to Japan, to the general problem of Japanese imperialism, the role of Japan as an imperialist power, the development of Taiwan, Korea, and Manchuria, and the Pacific War. Chapter 8 overlaps somewhat; it looks at the earlier histories of Asian nationalisms, and then at the impact of the war on nationalist movements and the achievement of independence.

Chapters 9 to 13 consider the postwar experience. Chapter 9 tells the story of the postwar era chronologically, to the point in each country where some sort of political stability was achieved, or the postwar regime changed significantly. A recurrent theme is the continued elusiveness of both political stability and economic growth into the 1960s and beyond. Chapter 10 looks at growth over the entire postwar era thematically, considering the factors which economists emphasize in explaining growth, population and especially the 'demographic transition' in Asia, the availability of resources such as labour and capital, their quality, and the efficiency with which they are used. Although the role of gendered structures and the exploitation of women is a repeated theme, Chapter 11 concentrates specifically on the role of women in Asian development in the economic, social, and political spheres. Building on the material in Chapters 10 and 11, the next two chapters consider the Asian economies in the contemporary world, focusing on the role of the state. Chapter 12 looks at Japan and the four tigers – South Korea, Taiwan, Hong Kong, and Singapore – as 'developmental' states, and Chapter 13 takes up the story of China and Southeast Asia, the states which have attempted to replicate the success of Japan and the four tigers. Chapter 14 briefly considers the prospects for the future.

2

THE AGE OF COLONIALISM AND IMPERIALISM: FROM AN EXTERNAL TO AN INTERNAL DYNAMIC

Changing Images

From an external to an internal dynamic

Images of the economic, social, and political landscape of Asia have changed dramatically over the past generation, and at an accelerating pace. In the 1960s scholars fought bitterly over the impact of the West on Asia – modernization theorists argued the West had affected Asia in ways that were essentially benign and progressive, while Marxists replied that the intrusion of Western capitalism into Asia had brought misery and exploitation. Still, virtually all agreed that 'the great tradition' of Asia had been essentially unchanged before the arrival of the Westerners, and that signposts such as the Opium War in China in 1839, the arrival of the American fleet in Japan in 1854, and the Bowring mission to Thailand in 1855 marked the beginning of 'the great transformation' for those parts of Asia which had not previously been in contact with the West. In 1958 and 1960 two of the early leaders in Chinese and Japanese studies in the United States, John King Fairbank and Edwin Reischauer, collaborated on a standard text whose two volumes were entitled *East Asia: The Great Tradition* and *East Asia: The Great Transformation*. Current work, in contrast, argues that Asian societies were diverse, dynamic, and changing before the intrusion of the West. In the case of China, for instance, Fairbank argued in his last book that 'this new view has rendered obsolete the old sinologue's all-about-China approach to the country as a single entity inhabited by "the Chinese"' (Fairbank, 1992, p. xv; see Evans, 1988).

Asian societies have never been static societies, any more than Europe was a static society in the pre-modern period. Discussions among Asian specialists parallel recent developments in European economic and social history: 'as economic and social historians, responding to the multiple mobilities of our own time, turn away from fixation on the world of fixed capital and settled labour, they begin to notice flux everywhere'. European social historians now argue that the unprecedented changes of the nineteenth century misled both contemporaries and subsequent scholars into believing they were witnessing 'the breaking up of a previously immobile European population' (Tilly et al., 1991, pp. 656–7). So it is in Asian studies. Periods of fundamental social change and vigorous intellectual debate preceded the arrival of the Westerners. The new emphasis on change has led in some cases to new periodizations, and in others to the revival of older views. For example, the recent rapid growth of Asian economies seems to some to lead backwards, to an explanation based on the internal values and structures of Asian societies inherited from their distant past.

However, the conservatism of those inherited structures and value systems also needs to be recognized. Even a brief survey of Confucian or Buddhist views of the economy and of economic activity reveals the static world view and hostility to innovation of officially sanctioned attitudes. Change was imperative. Western power was based on industrial technology, and all the nations of East and Southeast Asia were forced to confront the implications of the fact that the world had entered the industrial age. To retain or regain one's independence, to achieve wealth and power, indeed to survive, Asians needed modern – meaning Western – technologies, both in industry and in agriculture. The tensions between the need for change and resistance to change, and the divisions between individuals and groups over who would benefit from change, form key themes in the histories of all Asian countries.

The role of colonialism and imperialism

Appreciation of the internal dynamisms of Asian societies inevitably has led to a re-evaluation of the impact of the West. In particular, periods of colonial rule or imperialist pressure are now seen as much less significant. Along with the newer emphasis on internal sources of change in Asian societies, theories of imperialist exploitation, dependence, and the 'development of underdevelopment' have been subjected to searching criticism. This critique has focused on the empirical evaluation of the early theories of imperialism on which more recent approaches rest. Early in the twentieth century John Hobson asserted that imperialism resulted from the low wages paid to European workers, which caused 'under-consumption' and therefore limited the profits that European manufacturers could earn at home. V. I. Lenin argued on Marxist lines that an inevitable decline in the rate of profit would force capitalists to seek 'supernormal profits' in overseas areas, and Joseph Schumpeter attributed imperialist expansion to the 'atavistic' influence of pre-capitalist elites in European politics. All of these approaches rest on contemporary critiques of European society. All implicitly assume that the rest of the world was simply passive. Most importantly, none has survived empirical testing. Real wages were rising in Europe during the age of imperialism, the average rate of profit has not declined over time, and the motives of imperialist politicians varied. Rather than a simple process of expansion resulting from internal European developments, imperialism now seems the outcome of a complex interaction between Europe and overseas areas, with the balance of forces varying from case to case (Fieldhouse, 1984; Doyle, 1986).

In addition, however, Asian specialists have been re-evaluating the impact of imperialism and colonialism on Asian societies. The results generally show that the direct effects on Asian economic development were less than previously imagined. Westerners forced themselves into Asia, but once there, they were often obliged to fit themselves into pre-existing market frameworks. Where they failed to do so, their visions of wealth and glory were disappointed. In addition, the more general effect of new periodizations in Asian history 'was to put colonialism into a position that was subordinate to the domestic history of the region or individual countries ... Colonialism became one influence among others that were at work in southeast Asian societies' (Van Neil, 1990b, pp. 113–14).

Nevertheless, although it can no longer be argued that the intrusion of the West simply 'awakened' East and Southeast Asia, the impact of the West was important and needs to be evaluated in each case. The timing of a region's integration into world markets often had a decisive impact on its subsequent history, but the indigenous population was given no choice in the matter. International trade remained firmly in the hands of Westerners; only in 1912 did Japanese merchants handle more than half of Japan's foreign trade, for instance. Further, some regions were unambiguously directly affected by colonialism, especially districts where international demand led to the development of export-oriented agricultural or mineral production. This could lead to massive shifts in population and relocation of entire social groups, and it could have further enduring social effects through its impact on education or the distribution of income.

In addition to plantations and mines, railways are often cited among foreign investments in Asia as prime examples of Western capitalist exploitation of Asians, because of the repatriation of excessive payments to foreign investors. This view has been criticized on quantitative grounds. Beyond the question of returns to foreign investors, however, the development of modern transportation, especially railways, was the source of potentially destructive and redistributive effects. And, as with international trade, control over railway development lay almost entirely in the hands of Westerners, and here again the indigenous population had no choice. That lack of choice created another tension, a resentment which became another of the key forces propelling the histories of Asian peoples. It became one of the main sources of the appeal of the nationalist movements and remains potent today. If the ultimate impact of colonialism and imperialism was more political than economic, this would not make it less important, but it would alter our view of its impact, of the processes of change, and of the relations between economy, society, and politics more generally.

Inherited Structures and Traditions

China under the Qing

> Those who labor with their minds rule others, and those who labor with their physical strength are ruled by others.
>
> Mencius

The first impression Westerners had of China, and the one fact that continued to impress them, was China's sheer size. This is still true. China is so large and so diverse, that the proper comparison might be with Europe as a whole rather than with any single European nation. China's total population rose from around 100 million in the sixteenth century to 150 million in the early seventeenth century, and then from 150 million in the late seventeenth century to 500 million in 1900. Finally, in the twentieth century, an increase from 500 to 600 million between 1900 and 1950 was followed by a doubling to over 1.1 billion in 1990 (Lavely et al., 1990).

Further, scholars examining China's early development discovered a society whose level of technology in the fourteenth century was significantly higher than that of Europe across a broad range of industries, but China's early technological advance was followed by a long period of stagnation, the 'Needham paradox', after Joseph Needham's *Science and Civilization in China* (Ronan, 1980–94). Why? Most of the answers have revolved around that immensely large population. One key factor is an improvement in rice cultivation, which supports a dense population, but which at the same time requires very large increases in inputs of labour to raise yields (Perkins, 1969, pp. 23, 51, 186–7). Mark Elvin argues that this large, dense population led to stagnation in technology, a 'high-level equilibrium trap' (Elvin, 1973). Another possible answer is the symbiotic relationship between rich and poor farmers in the north and the exploitation of female family labour in the south (Huang, 1985, 1990). Until the end of the eighteenth century the Qing government could divert food supplies from one region to another to reduce the effects of poor harvests. Ironically, however, this effective famine relief may have led to overpopulation, reduced average incomes, and contributed to the rebellions of the mid-nineteenth century (Will, 1980; Li, 1982).

But how could a 'stagnant' society grow? As Ramon Myers asked in 1980, 'what kind of economic system enabled China to more than double its population between the late seventeenth century and the mid-nineteenth century to reach a total of nearly half a billion people?' (Myers, 1980, pp. ix–x). That is, why did the Chinese population increase so dramatically before the intrusion of the West? The answer many Westerners gave was that China was a traditional society with a high birth rate; locally confined, family-centered patterns of production and consumption, state encouragement of family ties, equal inheritance among sons, the focus of religious practice on household and lineage units, and a dearth of intermediate organizations on which individuals could rely, all seemed to encourage families to have as many children as they could (for example Rozman, 1981, pp. 146, 182). This is inaccurate. The increase was not the result simply of high birth rates. Marital fertility in China was moderate compared to pre-industrial Europe, between five and eight children for a woman who married at age twenty and remained in an unbroken union until age forty-five, compared to figures ranging from seven to eleven for Europe in the seventeenth and eighteenth centuries. Chinese families of all social classes practised infanticide as a means of controlling the number and sex of their children. A revealing study of the imperial clan during the eighteenth and nineteenth centuries discovered a female mortality rate of 260 per thousand during the first month of life, four times the male mortality rate of 70 per thousand (Lavely et al., 1990, p. 817).

The growth of the Chinese population, then, must have resulted from a general expansion of the economy. The way in which the economy grew will be examined in Chapter 3. As seen there, there was not one 'Chinese' economy, but a number of regional economies, and therefore attempts to determine the total population or the average birth rate are in a sense irrelevant and misleading. One problem which arises immediately, however, is the question of whether the evidence of *growth* is to be explained in terms of Mark Elvin's 'high-level equilibrium trap' or Philip Huang's notion of 'involution', or whether it should be interpreted as *development* – as 'capitalist sprouts' – as argued by Chinese Marxists. Was the Chinese economy and therefore Chinese society essentially unchanging, or were they undergoing a structural transformation? The answer to this question will determine our answers not only to questions about the internal dynamics of Chinese society, but also to the question of the importance of the Western impact on China.

The second aspect of China which impressed Westerners was its government. Confucian tradition prescribed the proper relations of a ruler to his ministers, and of government officials to their subjects. The emperor and his advisers in Beijing presided over a hierarchical bureaucratic organization. Functional ministries in the capital passed their orders to the eight governors-general and the governors of eighteen provinces. They in turn passed them to nearly 200 regional and finally to some 1500 district officials for implementation. The district magistrate, the 'father-mother official', was responsible for the care and well-being of an average of 200 000 people.

Entry to and promotion within the bureaucracy was achieved by merit. Candidates were judged by their performance in written examinations, set on topics drawn from the rich trove of 'classics' by authors in the approved Confucian tradition. Mastery of the written language and the classical texts was fundamental. Written language was the crucial tool of administration, for the dialects spoken in different regions were mutually incomprehensible. The inherited tradition was crucial as well, for the bureaucrats were generalists who might be called on to solve a broad range of problems, especially at the local level of administration. They generally assumed that if a problem arose, then someone among the classical authors would have already written about it and discovered a solution, and in addition they could refer to a large number of handbooks and memoirs written by their predecessors. They were essentially civilians, who believed that the use of military force was evidence of a failure of administration.

But things were not as simple as this idealized picture made them appear. The Qing dynasty which had ruled since 1644 were in fact not Chinese, but Manchu, a people from the northeast who had invaded and displaced the previous Ming dynasty. They had adopted Chinese culture, but were not integrated. They made up a small ruling stratum with a separate military, a law forbidding intermarriage with the Chinese majority, and a further law forbidding Chinese migration into Manchuria. The bureaucracy was divided between Manchu and Chinese, sometimes intentionally, as when Chinese governors-general were placed over Manchu governors and vice versa. In addition, the 'Chinese' majority were themselves divided along regional, linguistic, and ethnic lines. At the local level, the district magistrate relied on an extra-legal group of unpaid assistants in the administration of his district, who might regard him as a foreigner. In the far south in particular, it was never clear how effective the authority of the central government was.

Further, the Qing had inherited a longstanding tradition of tension between the bureaucracy and the emperor. The imperial institution was hereditary and essentially military, rooted in conquest. An emperor needed to grant lands to his supporters, but in order to prevent them becoming too independent, he needed the centralized bureaucracy. The bureaucrats in turn considered themselves much more than mere tools of the emperor's will. The bureaucrat brought his status as an educated and cultured individual to his office; holding office did not itself confer status. At any moment there were over a million degree-holders, but only some 27 000 of them would be employed in an official position. Their monopoly of administrative expertise and their connections with regional gentry families meant that the bureaucracy continually threatened to undermine direct imperial authority. Yet, as Joseph Levenson has expressed it, though the bureaucracy ate away at central authority, it required central authority to eat, and therefore worked to maintain both the imperial institution and the non-hereditary and non-military essentials of the civilian examination system (Levenson, 1968, pp. 27–35).

The third major aspect of Chinese tradition which has continued to impress observers is the role of the family. The sociologist Max Weber, whose work continues to influence the direction of Asian studies, referred to China as a 'familistic state' (Fairbank, 1992, p. 20). The family and the state were closely linked in Confucian thought:

Yu Tzu said 'It is rare for a man whose character is such that he is good as a son and obedient as a young man to have the inclination to transgress against his superiors; it is unheard of for one who has no such inclination to be inclined to start a rebellion. The gentleman devotes his efforts to the roots, for once the roots are established, the Way will grow therefrom. Being good as a son and obedient as a young man is, perhaps, the root of a man's character.' (Confucius, *The Analects*, I.2).

The family was the fundamental unit of society. The father ruled as head of the family, making all decisions and disciplining the disobedient. He arranged his children's marriages, and he had the right to sell them into slavery if necessary. Families in turn were commonly organized into lineage groups, which claimed descent from a common ancestor. Their organization varied from region to region, but in the south in particular they held estates in common, maintained ancestral halls, celebrated a cycle of rituals, and in consequence could exercise powerful social and political influence in and beyond their district: 'Tseng Tzu said, "Conduct the funeral of your parents with meticulous care and let not sacrifices to your remote ancestors be forgotten, and the virtue of the common people will incline towards fullness."' (Confucius, *The Analects*, I.9).

Confucian tradition again focused on proper relationships, of husband to wife, parent to child, older brother to younger brother. The legal code reinforced status differences within the family by treating members differently; it was far more serious for a nephew to strike his uncle than for the uncle to strike the nephew, for instance. Property law and inheritance were framed in terms of acceptable family structure. Sons continued the family line, and adoption became a component of the 'Confucian' family system because the practice of ancestor worship had become the core of the religious belief of most Chinese – the specific practices were not the rites portrayed in the classics, but a popular religion, outside official control, but tolerated by the state and the gentry elite because it reinforced social stability (Ebrey, 1991 p. 80). Further, a man who succeeded in a bureaucratic career could make the fortune of his district. Lineage groups therefore often supported promising boys during the years of study leading to the examinations.

As with so much else in China, the key elements in the family system originated in the Han period, roughly contemporaneous with the Roman Empire. The family head received greater authority than he had possessed previously. Family names became universal as a result of the systematic recording of population by the Qing government, and the existing names were frozen and then passed down to subsequent generations, which made identification of (and with) ancestors easier. Inheritance of office and title were greatly reduced, and the principle of partible inheritance (equal division among all sons) was encouraged and reinforced, at first among the elite to prevent the rise of large nobles who could challenge central authority, and then becoming more widespread as an accepted 'tradition'. The 'tradition' was spread and reinforced by the publication of texts, not only the classics but also popular literature. By the Qing period a substantial share of the population could read well enough to use books, and the publishing industry was highly developed, so this official and semi-official indoctrination was effective (Ebrey, 1991, pp. 51–2, 59–60).

The Chinese family unit depended on its women. Oppression began with birth, as unwanted girl babies were disposed of. It continued through childhood in the practice of footbinding. From age five to eight, until adult growth was reached, girls' feet were continuously bound with strips of cloth. As the bones of the feet grew, the pressure of the cloth strips broke the arches of the feet and forced the heels and balls of the feet from horizontal to vertical, so they almost touched. In theory the incredible pain this caused was welcomed, for the resulting 'three-inch golden lotuses' would ensure a good marriage. The shared memory of pain defined the female condition, as mothers who had passed through it in turn taught their daughters how to cope – to apply the bindings evenly to avoid gangrene, to clip the nails of the bent-over toes to prevent punctures and infection, to use massage to maintain circulation and reduce the pain. Mothers informed and literally shaped their daughters for survival in their male-dominated world (Blake, 1994). The practice began at the imperial court in the tenth century, and spread among all classes. The Qing government opposed footbinding and forbade it among the Manchu. It was also not practised among other minority groups and was less common in the south, but it was nearly universal in the central and northern provinces until around 1900. In the early 1930s every 'farmer's wife over the age of thirty' had bound feet (Fairbank, 1992, p. 173).

Adult women were the property of their families, but because women left their natal families and their native villages to live with their husband's family, most of the benefits of raising a female child would accrue to the husband's family. Thus infanticide could become a rational family strategy, and investment in a girl's education would seem a waste of resources. Commonly names were not registered in the ancestral halls for daughters, only numbers, for they would be given a name by their husband's family.

Poor families sold their daughters, sometimes in advance, and poor men often remained unmarried because the price of a wife was too high.

A new daughter-in-law came under the authority of her mother-in-law, and could be beaten and starved into submission, to provide whatever labour services were needed. She literally could not run away, so her only defence was to produce male children, and wait until they grew up and married, providing her in turn with daughters-in-law to relieve some of her burden. Finally, tradition held that widows were not to remarry, regardless of their age. The development of this 'tradition' reflected increased pressure from larger numbers of degree-holders and candidates for office than the economy could comfortably support. Those aspiring to high status wanted to distinguish themselves by exemplary behaviour, and they needed to manage their family property very carefully, so they 'were only too happy to assign a younger son to be the heir of a cousin and his widow'. Accordingly, a young widow might be called upon to follow her husband in death. Widow suicide was especially prevalent in Anhui and coastal Fujian, highly commercialized areas with many degree-holders, and therefore a very competitive environment (Mann, 1987b; Ebrey, 1991, p. 76).

Japan under the Tokugawa

From of old the rule has been to practise 'the arts of peace with the left hand, and the arts of war with the right'; both must be mastered.
Laws Governing the Military Households, 1615

In 1600 Tokugawa Ieyasu and his allies won a decisive victory over their rivals at Sekigahara. Possibly 150 000 soldiers fought on each side in the battle, and a substantial fraction of them were armed with firearms. Even allowing for later exaggeration, the comparison with the Thirty Years' War of 1618–48 in Europe, during which the largest armies had only just over 30 000 soldiers and were often raised by private entrepreneurs, demonstrates that as in the case of China, Japan too was far from being a simple, backward society before the intrusion of the West.

As part of his attempt to consolidate his power, Ieyasu ordered all foreigners to leave the country, outlawed the practice of Christianity among the Japanese, and in 1607 closed the country to foreign contact. The firearms were locked away. Except for certain Dutch, Chinese, and

Korean merchants, foreigners were forbidden to enter Japan. The Japanese people in turn were forbidden to leave Japan, on pain of death. Ieyasu's descendants ruled Japan for the following two centuries, but the Japan of the early nineteenth century was a very different country from the Japan of the early seventeenth century.

The rule of the Tokugawa government was justified by a sophisticated theory, a variant of neo-Confucianism drawn from Chinese sources. The social structure envisaged by Japanese neo-Confucian intellectuals had four elements. At the top was a class of hereditary military aristocrats (the *samurai*), centred around the castles of their lords (the *daimyô*) and receiving an annual stipend of rice according to their rank. They made up some 10 per cent of the population. The distinguishing mark of the aristocracy remained the right to practise with and bear arms. However, over the two centuries of peace they evolved into an administrative bureaucracy responsible for tax collection, record keeping, and an elaborate cycle of ritual observances. Next came the farmers, making up 80 per cent of the population. Honoured as the source of wealth, they were of course also the source of tax revenue, and intellectuals and officials alike frequently reiterated their belief that it was evil for farmers to possess more than bare subsistence, lest they become fat. Rice was the chief of the 'five grains', and cultivation therefore was labour-intensive, organized at the village level. The third recognized group were the artisans, a small class concentrated with the *samurai* into the towns surrounding the castles. Organized into hereditary guilds, they supplied the rest with manufactured goods.

At the bottom of the official hierarchy were the merchants, despised as unproductive and parasitic, but nonetheless necessary. Because of the difficulty of managing the collection and distribution of the taxes and stipends, merchants were employed as intermediaries. They advanced credit to the aristocracy in anticipation of the harvest, and they marketed the crops after the harvest to the concentrated populations of the castle towns and cities. Merchants also provided for the exchange of manufactured goods produced by the artisans. Neo-Confucian scholars regularly denounced them, and occasionally the government would simply cancel the debts owed to the merchants by the aristocracy.

But, as in the case of China, things were not so simple. First, although the Tokugawa ruled, they did not reign. Ieyasu and his successors bore the title of *shôgun*, a military commander appointed by the emperor. The symbolic head of the Japanese state, but deprived of real power, the emperor was kept carefully isolated in his palace in Kyôtô, surrounded by officials appointed by the Tokugawa and watched over by a governor and garrison assigned to guard the city. Secondly, the Tokugawa did not rule directly over the whole country. The *shōgun* and his retainers controlled about 25 per cent of the total revenue derived from the marketing of the tax imposed on the rice crop. Junior branches of the Tokugawa family and descendants of vassals who had joined the Tokugawa before the battle of Sekigahara together controlled something over a third. However, the 'outside' *daimyō* and their retainers, descendants of former enemies who had submitted only after the defeat, controlled 40 per cent of the total tax revenue.

The Tokugawa developed an elaborate set of regulations to ensure their control over potential threats to their power. The highest offices were reserved for the Tokugawa family and retainers. Ieyasu restructured and redistributed the domains. Rice was designated as the basis of wealth and status. The tax assessed on each village, the annual stipend paid to each *samurai*, and the ranking of each domain, all were measured in terms of a stipulated number of *koku* of rice (a *koku* was about five bushels, and the number of *koku* produced in a district was considered roughly equivalent to the number of people). The Tokugawa family and their allies were given administration of the strategic areas around the Tokugawa capital of Edo (modern Tokyo), around the imperial capital Kyōtō, and along the major highway linking Edo with Ōsaka and Kyōtō, the 'Tōkaidō' or 'eastern sea road'. The 'outside' *daimyō* were isolated and generally confined to the south and west. All *daimyō* were strictly regulated, their marriages approved, their inheritance confirmed, and all their construction projects (especially, of course, castles) scrutinized by the government. They were obliged to reaffirm their allegiance periodically. Most importantly, every *daimyō* was required to reside in Edo in alternate years, and in those years when he was permitted to return to his domain, his wife and children remained in Edo as hostages. Every year lords and their retainers moved in procession day by day along the Tōkaidō and the other officially designated highways, from one of the approved 'stages' to the next.

The domains ruled by the *daimyō* each repeated many of the features of the central government. The *daimyō* controlled their retainers in much the same way that they were controlled by the Tokugawa. An elaborate etiquette governed the lives of the *samurai*, divided into a dozen or more grades according to the size of their annual stipend. Each peasant village yielded up a sum of taxes assessed by their assigned local official, the artisans laboured within their guild structures, and the merchants provided the necessary financial and marketing services. This was a stable system, but one which combined centralized authority with a very high degree of local autonomy, and therefore a system which could change in quite complex ways. Domain governments wished to increase their revenue if possible, and therefore took an interest in the regulation and improvement of their economies. Levels of literacy were relatively high in Japan compared to other pre-industrial societies, and significantly temple schools provided education to commoners as well as the elite.

The population of Japan grew substantially in the seventeenth century, from perhaps 18 million in 1600 to 26 million in the 1720s. It then remained constant for nearly a century, growing again from the 1780s and certainly from the early nineteenth century, and had reached 33 million by 1870. In the seventeenth century population growth resulted from political stability and extension of arable land following the end of a generation of civil war and the establishment of the Tokugawa regime. In the eighteenth century population was held in check by delayed marriage, migration which separated husbands and wives for periods of time, and the spread of infanticide (Smith and Eng, 1977; Cornell, 1996). The family structures within which this occurred reflected the conservative authoritarian framework of the polity, and women were subordinate. The age and sex distributions revealed in surviving village records leave little doubt that it was girl babies who were sacrificed when necessary for the family's well-being. As in China, officially sanctioned Confucian precepts placed women under male authority, first their fathers, then their husbands, and finally their sons. On the other hand, the father's authority was not so absolute and families were not organized into lineage groups as in China. Japanese women were not crippled by footbinding. Many of them could read and write, not only aristocrats but the wives and daughters of merchants, artisans, and farmers as well, which suggests a willingness to invest in female family members which seems almost totally lacking in Chinese society.

Southeast Asia

Penghulu [village headmen] must make themselves well acquainted with the following subjects, otherwise their functions are thrown away upon them: first the *Hukum Shera* [religious law]; second, the *Hukum Akl* [principles of natural justice]; third, the *Hukum Faal* [principles of right

conduct]; and fourth, the *Hukum Adat* [custom, and customary law].
This done, they may be termed men.

Malacca Code, sixteenth century

Among Southeast Asian specialists the move away from 'colonial' history
and towards an 'autonomous history' began in the 1950s. The social forms
established around 1300 with the spread of Islam and Buddhism, and the
concurrent creation of larger political units, rather than the arrival of
Europeans after 1500, were now seen as crucial. The significant impact
of the West on Southeast Asia began only in the nineteenth century
(Smail, 1961; Van Niel, 1990b, pp. 111–14). Even in the nineteenth
century it is now argued that much important development antedated
the Western intrusion, or took place outside the range of Western control
(Gullick, 1987; Reynolds, 1995). And, as we will see in Chapter 8, in the
twentieth century the new nationalist movements emerged out of intellectual and social processes with roots in the pre-colonial past.

The pastel colours on the maps of eighteenth- and nineteenth-century
Europe are often deceptive. The powers of central governments did not
extend evenly to the borders; as one moved further away from the capital,
a complex range of regional and local conditions diluted the state's
authority. So too in Southeast Asia. In the Philippines, in the Dutch
East Indies, and on the mainland in the Burmese, Thai, Cambodian
and Vietnamese monarchies, there were core areas where central governments exercised fairly consistent control, areas in which they claimed
authority but ruled only indirectly if at all, disputed areas claimed by
other states, and large areas outside the control of any central government.
Even in the core areas, villages were often autonomous in many respects,
under the authority of a hereditary headman advised and assisted by a
council of local notables.

The Philippines were ruled by a governor appointed by the King of
Spain, typically a royal favourite who expected to profit from his time in
office. Government down to the provincial level was exclusively foreign,
men either from Spain or elsewhere in the empire, who only rarely spent
their entire lives in the Philippines. Laws explicitly forbade intermarriage
or other long-term commitments to the region. The position of provincial
governor, though usually short-term, could also be very lucrative. The
difficulty of communication among the islands muted any desire the central
administration might have had to prevent the exploitation of the indigenous population. Over time the one permanent foreign institution,
the Catholic Church, became the largest landholder. Village life reflected

inherited kinship structures similar to the Malay peninsula and islands. The indigenous chief (*datu*) was renamed 'village headman' (*cabeza de barangay*) by Spanish authorities. District authority evolved into a rotating system of selection of the 'petty governor' (*gobernadorcillo*) from among the local notables. This was the highest office attainable by natives, and since it carried responsibility for tax collection it was a potential source of profit but also the point at which the local native elite defended themselves against the exactions of the Spaniards.

The small numbers of Dutch had exercised much less influence on indigenous society than the Spanish. Well into the nineteenth century, the core of Dutch influence lay around Batavia (Jakarta) on the island of Java. The indigenous kingdom which had claimed to rule over the entire island had been supplanted in the 1750s by three successor states whose rulers had become tributary vassals of the Dutch East India Company. Both in these states and in the Dutch East India Company's own territory, however, central authorities exercised only nominal control over the local aristocracy (*priyayi*). These lords ruled and extracted labour power from the farmers in their own localities, insulated from the capital by the difficulties of communication across the mountains. In their social structure and virtual independence their small realms differed only in size from those of the Malay sultans scattered through the archipelago wherever rivers ran into the sea.

In Java, and in the mainland monarchies of Burma, Siam (Thailand), and Cambodia, the monsoon climate and mountainous geography made extensive agriculture difficult with the available technologies. Political power therefore rested on control of manpower rather than land, and diplomacy aimed to control trade in order that it could be taxed. Provincial governors and district chiefs were required to collect taxes and mobilize local farmers for labour services demanded by central government. But these official positions were quasi-hereditary, partly because only a man with extensive family and patronage connections in the district would be able to provide the central government with the manpower it required. On the other hand, these men were also expected to provide protection for their clients, so the exactions of the central governments had an inherent limit. Although they were literate, their position depended on these webs of obligation and service, not on scholarly accomplishments as in Vietnam. Their position could be reinforced, but also complicated, by the extensive networks created by the practice of polygamy by those men wealthy enough to afford it. Simply being the oldest son did not guarantee succession, and competition among rivals for office could become bitter.

At the local level, central authority was even more tenuous. The Malay village headman (*penghulu*) was appointed by the ruler, but was in fact the hereditary leader of a local kinship network. In central Burma the headman (*ywa thu-gyi* or *myei-taing*) was a hereditary official, confirmed after a search of written records. In the core area he administered a complex tax system, under the authority of a district or township headman, also a hereditary official. In lower Burma, Thailand, Laos, and Cambodia, headmen were elected from among the older village notables and relied on their age and persuasion to achieve their goals. The need for personal contacts, good relations with officials in the urban centres of the province, and patronage, repeated the position of the provincial governors on a smaller scale.

Vietnam's heritage was largely Chinese. China ruled Vietnam, the 'protectorate of the pacified south' (Annam) from the second century BC to the tenth century AD. Attempts to reimpose Chinese rule were defeated in the fifteenth and eighteenth centuries, heroic moments kept alive by Vietnamese intellectuals. From the eleventh century onwards Vietnam possessed its own hierarchical bureaucratic structure modelled on the Chinese system, with governors-general, governors, prefects, and district magistrates, who qualified for their offices by passing written examinations based on classical Chinese Confucian texts. In contrast to China, however, these degree-holders belonged to a hereditary aristocracy, and in contrast to other areas in Southeast Asia, their position was based on the ownership of land. In each province, and especially in the south, the elite possessed land, leisure, and classical learning. In addition to wealth and academic attainment, local notables possessed the experience of age. These men and their families were not clients of urban officials depending on their favour and patronage. Rather, they served the ends of the central government to preserve the good reputation of their village and to help to ensure success for their sons and grandsons in the bureaucratic examinations. Even when they did not hold official positions, they served as links between government and local community. The village headmen or 'chiefs' (*xa truong*) were elected from among these local notables. Their election had to be confirmed by the central government, and their main function was to collect taxes, but legally they were also servants of village councils consisting of their fellow notables and including former chiefs.

Vietnam displayed the same tension between the interests of a bureaucracy based in the regional gentry and the interests of the ruling dynasty as seen in China. Although regional elite families relied on their connections with the central government for an important part of their inherited status, periods of weakness and decline in the central government provided them with their greatest opportunities. Unchecked by the ruler, they could extend their landholdings at the expense of less powerful members of their communities, encroaching on the communal lands which in theory were reserved for periodic redistribution to ensure that no farmer would be without land. This was an ideal way to provide for younger sons. Dynastic decline in Vietnam was always accompanied by an increase in the numbers of very wealthy large landowners, a much larger increase in the number of landless labourers, and a decline in the number of independent small-holders.

Across Southeast Asia, informally and at the lower levels of society, women were valued for the same reason as men, for their contribution to the labour force in what was often a very difficult environment. Formally and among the upper classes, women were subordinate. In Muslim regions, upper-class women could be entirely excluded from public life, and wealthy men could take more than one wife. Christianity offered a base for a critique of patriarchal values, but as practised in the Philippines it supported the inherited status of men. Despite official Confucianism, women did enjoy a higher status in Vietnam than in China. The Vietnamese law code in effect from the sixteenth through eighteenth centuries allowed daughters to inherit family property almost equally with sons, and specified that family property was not simply the property of the husband but should be managed on a basis of equality between spouses.

Crises and Responses

War and rebellion in China

I have heard that the smoking of opium is very strictly forbidden by your country.

Commissioner Lin to Queen Victoria, 1839

The Opium War in 1839–42 and the Taiping Rebellion of 1851–64 mark the double crisis confronting the Chinese government in the middle decades of the nineteenth century, the increasing pressures from outside and from within. The origins of the Opium War lay in the pattern of trade connecting Britain, India, and China. Britain, through the East India Company, controlled India. Indian economic historians argue that British policy systematically 'de-industrialized' India to open a market for British cotton cloth. As a result, India had a negative trade balance with Britain. Britain in turn had a negative trade balance with China, for as the Chinese emperor had written to George III in the eighteenth century, 'we possess all things'. The one product for which there was a demand in China was opium, which in turn was produced in India. Here was the product which could create a balanced trade triangle. The East India Company established a monopoly of opium cultivation and marketing in 1773. Demand in China spread, from being a fad among the sons of wealthy urban families to embracing large sections of the population in southern China. In 1834 the abolition of the East India Company's monopoly of trade between India and China brought many new traders into the business. Chinese opium imports rose from 10 000 to 40 000 chests (each of some 70 kilograms) annually in 1838–9, which supplied possibly 2.1 million addicts and as many as 10 million smokers altogether.

The cultivation, sale, importation and smoking of opium were illegal in China, under edicts issued in 1729 and 1796. The East India Company had evaded the ban by licensing ships to carry the opium while publicly denying complicity. The move to free trade, however, led the British government to send an official representative to oversee British trading interests in China. He demanded treatment as a diplomatic equal, which the Chinese government refused, for to accede would have undermined the entire basis of China's relations with foreigners. The British saw trade and diplomatic equality as rights to be enjoyed by all, but the Chinese saw trade and recognition as privileges granted to inferior 'barbarians' by themselves. The emperor had charged a reforming official, Commissioner Lin, to continue his campaign of suppression of the opium traffic by shutting down the trade at Canton. Lin destroyed 21 306 chests of opium which had been surrendered to him by the British representative, who had taken possession of them from the traders in the name of the British government. For the Chinese this was a decision to destroy illegal goods taken by the emperor's chosen representative, but for the British, it was an act of war.

The war itself was a lesson in modern technology (Headrick, 1981). The four small steamers the British possessed could be used to tow their sixteen sailing ships with their 540 guns upriver. On the Chinese side, one provincial governor discovered that his only cannons were seventeenth-century antiques left over from the previous Ming dynasty. When the British occupied the town at the junction of the Yangzi River and the

Grand Canal, where they could cut off the flow of foodstuffs from south to north, the imperial government yielded.

The treaty imposed by the British in 1842 was equally a lesson in imperialist pressure: a large indemnity, abolition of the guilds through which the Chinese had regulated trade, possession of Hong Kong, opening of further ports, residence rights for British consuls and British merchants, the right of British consuls to try legal cases involving British subjects ('extra-territoriality'), and fixed tariffs which averaged 5 per cent. Further short wars followed in 1856 and 1859–60 and saw further concessions to the British, and to the French, Americans, and Russians as well. The 'treaty century' lasted until 1942, when the British and Americans formally surrendered their rights of extra-territoriality. China had been humiliated, its position as unique 'middle kingdom' and centre of the civilized universe stripped away by foreign barbarians. The Manchus bore the blame, and in the long run the resulting loss of face contributed to the end of the dynasty and became part of a new Chinese national identity.

The Qing government also faced an even greater crisis of internal unrest. In the background of the mid-century rebellions were natural disasters, such as the drought in Henan in 1847, floods in the Yangzi Valley in 1849, and the shifting of the mouth of the Yellow River from south to north in 1852. The government failed to cope effectively. Corrupt officials, many of whom had purchased their offices, siphoned away much of the available revenue. The hereditary military units of the Manchu, the bannermen, were no longer an effective force. Further, as a consequence of the Opium War, opium imports rose to 53 000 chests in 1850. The resulting outflow of silver raised the exchange rate of copper to silver coins, which injured those farmers who sold their crops for copper but paid their rent in silver, all at fixed rates. Finally, some artisan industries suffered as foreign manufactured goods began to arrive in quantity.

The leader of the Taiping rebellion was Hong Xiuquan, one of the bright boys who were supported by their family and community in the hopes of success in the imperial examinations. However, his studies were interrupted, and then he failed the examinations four times. After his third attempt he suffered a breakdown and had a series of visions which incorporated portions of Christian tracts he had received from Western missionaries. After his fourth failure in 1843 he interpreted his visions as justifications for a new religious movement in which he identified himself as the younger brother of Jesus. The God Worshippers Society destroyed temples, shrines, and idols, but regional officials considered them a Christian sect and therefore allowed under the new treaties. The famine which struck Guangxi in 1849–50 created disorder and unrest, and in 1850 Hong declared himself the new emperor, the 'Heavenly King' of a 'Heavenly Kingdom' of 'Great Peace' (*Taiping*). His followers defeated the imperial forces sent to suppress them, and three years later he was carried in triumph into Nanjing, and the Taipings had gained control of much of the fertile Yangzi Valley in central China (see Spence, 1996). The Taipings introduced a series of reforms in the areas they controlled, but they made errors which eventually doomed them. They did not establish firm administrative control over the areas they conquered. They did not bother to attempt to gain control of the trading centre of Shanghai until 1860. They dissipated their forces by sending inadequate expeditions to the north and west. Their theology of course mortally offended possible supporters among both conservative Chinese and Western missionaries, and they treated the representatives whom Western governments tentatively sent with traditional Chinese contempt. A power struggle in 1856 decimated the original leadership, and Hong retreated to theological contemplation and the pleasures of his harem. Without leadership they could not defeat the new army which had been raised and trained by Zeng Guofan, a Chinese official from Henan who eventually earned the trust of the Manchu government. The Taiping attack on Shanghai in 1860 prompted a foreign counter-attack and eventually intervention on the side of the Manchus. Nanjing was besieged in 1862, and two years later Hong committed suicide, the movement collapsed, and former supporters were executed wherever they could be found.

If the Manchus failed to meet the challenge of external pressure, they did surmount the challenge of internal unrest. They successfully suppressed not only the great Taiping rebellion of 1851–64, but also the Nian movement in the north in 1853–68, and two revolts of Chinese Muslims, in the southwest in 1855–73 and in the northwest in 1862–73. In examining this double crisis, two problems emerge. The first is to assess the origins of the mid-century rebellions and the effectiveness of the government's response. Here traditional views have regained popularity. Periods of imperial decline, accompanied by peasant rebellion, are recurrent themes in Chinese history. In responding to crisis, Chinese leaders can draw on a rich and varied intellectual tradition. Among Western scholars, Levenson in particular emphasized the creative tensions within Confucianism out of which reform could emerge. Levenson in fact believed that creative tension had been exhausted in the mid-nineteenth century, but more recently commentators on post-Mao China have again emphasized the theme of authoritarian reform in Chinese history (Cohen, 1988).

The second problem is to assess the impact of the Opium War and subsequent Western commercial penetration of Chinese markets. Here again emphasis has swung towards more traditional views. The two millennia of imperial China's history seem to possess an autonomous dynamic which might be disturbed but whose essential features could not be altered by the impact of the West. In the late nineteenth century, commerce and industry developed in response to 'the internal logic of China's own socioeconomic development' (Rowe, 1984, p. 341; Thomas, 1984). In the twentieth century, despite civil war and foreign invasion, the sheer size of the internal market ensured that industry flourished or declined in response to conditions within China rather than due to trends in international markets, for instance in the important case of the coal industry (Wright, 1984).

Nevertheless, the two crises were real, and they were related. The Qing central government suffered a financial collapse sometime in the nineteenth century. The losses caused by the rebellions were enormous. The rise in population mentioned above was interrupted catastrophically, and the total population may have declined from 410 million in 1850 to 350 million in 1873. By the late nineteenth century the government could no longer intervene to alleviate famines, as it had done so effectively in the eighteenth century (Li, 1982). The Taiping rebellion seems to mark a dividing line in this respect (Will, 1980, pp. 97–100), but did the declining abilities of the state result from the strains of the rebellions, from the population having finally grown beyond the bounds of available technologies, or from Western pressure? The distinguished Chinese economic historian Peng Zeyi, operating in a Marxist framework, locates the origins of the fiscal crisis in the decade of the Taiping rebellion, but places the blame on the drain of specie brought about by reparations and the negative balance of trade resulting from the Opium War. That is, the crisis of the nineteenth century was indeed unique, but was caused by Western imperialism, not by internal Chinese developments. In contrast, Susan Mann argues that only the fiscal crisis brought on by the great mid-nineteenth-century rebellions forced the Qing government to turn to the taxation of commerce for revenue more than for regulation. The new taxes grew, spread, and persisted as a serious impediment to China's internal commerce for nearly an entire century. Mann argues, in addition, that the accumulation of indebtedness to foreigners in the late nineteenth century reinforced but did not create this situation. That is, the unique crisis of the nineteenth century was the result of internal developments, but the dynasty could no longer respond effectively and ended by stifling development (Mann, 1987a).

The suppression of the Taiping rebellion was followed by a period of reform, of the sort which had many precedents in Chinese history. The successful leaders of the struggle, Zeng Guofan and his junior colleagues such as Li Hongzhang, rose to prominent positions in the government. Schools were reopened, new ones created, the regional quotas of degree-holders raised, and the imperial examinations revised to give more attention to current problems. The bureaucracy was placed under stricter discipline, sale of offices reduced, and corruption punished. A new office was created to handle foreign affairs, to import Western naval and military technologies, and to support a new school of Western studies. This was the institutional basis of the 'self-strengthening movement' which aimed to create the means for China to defend itself against the West.

Mary Wright (1957) argued that mid-century reforms showed the resilience of Chinese institutions. We cannot know this for sure, as China no longer existed in isolation. In contrast to previous successful restorations, however, there was no strong ruler. The death of the emperor in 1861, followed by a *coup d'état*, brought to power the dowager empress Cixi. Although it violated both Qing family law and historical precedent for an empress to act as regent or administer state affairs, with the support of her chief minister Prince Kung and the British representative she remained in control of the imperial government until her death in 1908. When her son the emperor died in 1875, aged only eighteen, she manipulated the succession to bring to the throne her three-year-old nephew with herself again as regent. In 1889 she 'retired' to the Summer Palace. The emperor and his father reconstructed the palace at a cost of 30 million taels (equivalent to £10 million) in the hope that she would in fact retire, but she did not. Intensely conservative herself, she supported reformers but at the same time encouraged conservatives to attack them, in order to maintain her own power. In 1898 she sabotaged a further attempt at reform by the emperor by throwing her support to his conservative opponents.

The self-strengthening movement registered a number of successes during the next decades, especially the military and civilian enterprises and training institutes founded under the leadership of Li Hongzhang. However, the programme lacked coordination and the central vision which stronger leadership at the centre might have given it. Government-sponsored enterprises remained isolated enclaves without contact with the broader economy. Capital was scarce, and there were some spectacular cases of waste. The emperor's father was the head of the Board of Admiralty, and the 30 million taels spent on the dowager empress's Summer Palace had been diverted from the navy budget.

China lost the tributary state of Annam (Vietnam) to the French after an inconclusive war fought in 1884–5. Facing annexation, the Vietnamese court called on China to intervene. The Chinese leaders were divided, and their failure to concentrate all their forces ensured defeat. The French caught the Fujian fleet in harbour at Fuzhou, sank or damaged eleven ships, destroyed the dockyards, and imposed a naval blockade which interfered with grain shipments to Beijing. The Chinese inflicted defeats on the French on land, and it appears the French government was unprepared for the expense of a long war, but those advocating peace and withdrawal prevailed. In addition, China lost its tributary sovereignty over Burma when the British invaded the remains of the Burmese state in 1885.

It is significant that the true failure of the self-strengthening movement was revealed, not through China's defeat by the West, but through China's defeat by another Asian power, Japan, in 1894–5. The internal dynamics of Asia provided the opportunity for the West to intervene. Coveting warm water ports themselves, the Russians protested the cession of the Liaodong Peninsula to Japan and orchestrated a joint protest with France and Germany. A treaty with Russia yielded concessions in the north. Germany first asked for and then seized Kiaochow in 1897, Russia leased Port Arthur and Dairen on the Liaodong Peninsula in 1898, Britain leased Weihaiwei and Kowloon, and France leased Kwangchow Bay. In addition, through 'non-alienation' agreements, Britain, France, and Japan established protected spheres of influence in the Yangzi Valley, the Guangdong–Guangxi–Yunnan region, and Fujian respectively – the 'scramble for China' had similarities with the 'scramble for Africa' twenty-five years before.

Nevertheless China was not divided among the imperialist powers. The open door policy enunciated by the United States at British instigation, and the mutual suspicions of the imperialist powers, brought a pause to the rush for concessions. Although the nadir was still to be reached with the occupation of Beijing and the huge indemnity exacted after the Boxer rebellion, China survived. Drawing a balance on specifically Western imperialism, it now seems clear that the effect on China was small. Further, as will be seen in Chapter 6, it seems likely that in the economic sphere the effect was on balance positive. As we will see in Chapter 7, the more significant impetus for change in China came not from the West, but from Japanese expansion on the mainland of Asia – first penetration into Korea, then the wars with China in 1894–5 and Russia in 1904–5, the Twenty-One Demands of 1915 and economic domination, and finally territorial annexations and war in the 1930s.

Tokugawa Japan in crisis

> Western foreigners, spurred by the desire to wreak havoc upon us, are daily prying into our territorial waters. And within our domains evil teachings flourish in a hundred subtle ways.
>
> Aizawa Seishisai, *New Proposals*, 1825

Japan too faced a double crisis of external pressure and internal disorder. The American fleet commanded by Commodore Matthew Perry anchored off Uraga in 1853 and delivered a formal request for the opening of the country to contact and trade, along with a promise to return the next year with a larger force. This they did, and in 1854 the Tokugawa government agreed to open ports for the supply of provisions and to allow consular representation. However, the Japan which the West encountered was already in a state of crisis. The Japanese were well aware of Western incursions into China, and there was an intensive debate over the best means to meet this obvious and immanent threat. Options ranged from the very minimal concessions to the foreigners advocated by some Tokugawa officials, to the active measures to defend against the West advocated by many outside the government, such as the coastal fortifications proposed by Sakuma Shôzan. As we will see later in Chapter 5, the crisis led to the creation of the new regime following the Meiji Restoration of 1868. But at the time Perry's arrival was a shock, even for those who were prepared. The famous westernizing intellectual Fukuzawa Yukichi, having strained to learn the foreigners' language in preparation for their eventual arrival, went to the recently opened port of Yokohama and attempted to converse with them – in Dutch:

> To my chagrin, when I tried to speak with them, no one seemed to understand me at all. Nor was I able to understand anything spoken by a single one of all the foreigners I met... I had been striving with all my

powers for many years to learn the Dutch language. And now when I had reason to believe myself one of the best in the country, I found that I could not even read the signs of merchants who had come to trade with us from foreign lands. (*Autobiography*, ch. 5)

In addition to the intellectual ferment and debate, there was what appeared to many to be a social and economic crisis. It is now generally accepted that significant changes were taking place in the Japanese economy before the intrusion of the West. The question is what the turmoil of the years preceding the arrival of the 'black ships' signified. Evaluations of the Meiji period colour interpretations of late Tokugawa development. Japanese Marxists argue that Japanese 'feudalism' was undergoing a crisis which laid the basis for the 'half-feudal' Meiji regime, for the militarism of the 1930s, imperialism in China, and war with the United States. Among Western scholars during the 1960s the earlier belief that Japanese 'modernization' had begun with Perry's 'opening of Japan' was replaced by an interpretation which emphasized the dynamism and importance of the Tokugawa period in laying the foundation for rapid economic growth in the Meiji era (Smith, 1959; Smith, 1988; Hanley and Yamamura, 1971). The progressive development of the Tokugawa economy could be seen as the linear ancestor of the 'economic miracle' of the 1950s and 1960s, with militarism and war as an unfortunate interruption to an otherwise unbroken success story (Patrick and Rosovsky, 1976).

Population reflects economic development, and therefore population studies have been one of the main areas of contention in the debate over the Tokugawa 'crisis'. Japanese Marxist scholars argue that the feudal regime stifled growth, that population was pressing against the means of subsistence, and therefore that numbers were held constant by Malthusian 'positive' checks of high mortality. There were in fact severe famines in the 1730s, 1780s and 1830s, and during those periods the total population did decline. However, some regions gained population even during these crisis periods. Further, as noted above, the demographic evidence suggests that overall population was held in check not by famine or epidemic diseases, but by late marriage, labour migration, and the spread of abortion and infanticide (Smith and Eng, 1977; Janetta, 1987; Cornell 1996). Infanticide could on the one hand be interpreted as an act of desperation in response to poverty. On the other hand, the elimination of unwanted children, generally girls, could also be seen as merely one rational strategy among others for maximizing the position of the family unit, and the preferred interpretation depends on one's view of the growth of the economy. American scholars led by Susan Hanley and Kozo Yamamura contend that expanding markets led to economic growth over the entire period, and that the slow growth of the population during the eighteenth century reflected low fertility resulting from the operation of 'preventive' checks. This might mean infanticide and abortion, but as in Europe it could also include late marriage and possibly the decision not to marry at all (Feeney and Hamano, 1990).

Japan experienced nothing like the great rebellions in China, which killed more people than the entire population of Japan. However, there were large and increasing numbers of local peasant uprisings – some 400 from 1813 to 1868. Further, the rising numbers of outbursts were concentrated in those areas which had experienced the greatest economic change, districts where some farmers were extending their holdings and possibly acting as money-lenders to others, or where farmers objected to official monopolies on cash crops which domain governments imposed to increase their revenues. For Japanese Marxists peasant uprisings in the early nineteenth century are evidence of the crisis of the feudal economy, and unrest in the later nineteenth century reflects the exploitation of the peasants by the new class of capitalists. They argue that the old peasant community had been breaking down and dividing, with a few large farmers facing a mass of poor small peasants. For non-Marxist historians, however, the operation of the market is by definition not exploitative. As Richard Smethurst states flatly, 'the rural market economy did not destroy the farmer: it freed him' (Smethurst 1986, p. 229; see Bowen, 1988).

A final aspect of the internal dynamic of Japanese society was the decline of the aristocracy, compared to the merchant class. Again, this can be interpreted either as another aspect of the crisis of feudalism, or as another aspect of the progressive development of the Tokugawa economy – a matter for dispute. By the middle decades of the nineteenth century, many *samurai* were heavily indebted to merchants. Some families declined into poverty, and some actually surrendered their *samurai* status because they could no longer maintain the required style of life. However, the income of the aristocratic class as a whole does not seem to have declined, except possibly in relative terms, compared to the merchants. There is much evidence of a sense of crisis, and domain governments extracted 'loans' from merchants as a disguised tax on their wealth. On the other hand, the merchants sometimes received a grant of *samurai* status in return, and in other cases they purchased aristocratic rank outright. The *samurai* class of the Meiji period therefore contained a substantial admixture of former merchant families.

Internal and external pressures in Korea

Western barbarians invade our land. If we do not fight, we must then appease them. To urge appeasement is to betray the nation.

Marker commemorating the defeat of French and American forces, 1871

Korea, the 'hermit kingdom', was closed in theory to foreign contact except for tribute missions to China, and until quite recently scholars accepted this view of an essentially static society awaiting 'opening' and 'modernization'. However, more recent views are in some ways parallel to the change in perceptions of Tokugawa Japan. There is clear evidence of economic development from the seventeenth century onwards – improved rice cultivation, double cropping with barley, improved irrigation and dryfield techniques, all leading to 'enlarged scale farming' of food crops and commercial agriculture, especially ginseng, tobacco, and cotton. Accompanying social and intellectual changes saw the rise of wealthy farmers and decline of some sections of the aristocracy, and the spread of 'practical learning', through the eighteenth and into the nineteenth century.

Along with economic development went an internal political crisis. During the period of 'in-law government' beginning in 1800, power alternated among powerful clans related to the royal house by marriage. Corruption marked the administration of the land tax, military service tax, and state granary system, for the bribes paid to secure office had to be recouped by embezzlement of state revenues. Local elites escaped from central government control and attempted to extract more from the farmers. Some farmers in turn moved to unoccupied upland areas to become 'fire-field people', and others became bandits. Disorder led to uprisings against local authorities, and serious revolts in 1811 and 1862 were led by members of fallen aristocratic families. This was the background of the 'eastern learning' (*Tonghak*) movement. The founder, Ch'oe Che-u, asserted he had drawn on the best from Confucianism, Buddhism, and Taoism to combat 'Western learning', meaning the Catholicism being propagated by French missionaries, but he included popular elements of both Christianity and native shamanistic beliefs, insisting on the equality of all human beings, but also chanting magical formulas and worshiping local mountain deities. *Tonghak* was a social movement which called for reform of the corrupt government, and which asserted in millenarian fashion that the day of retribution was at hand. The government became alarmed, arrested Ch'oe Che-u, and executed him in 1864.

King Kojong came to the throne at the age of twelve in 1864 and reigned until 1907. For a decade power was held by his father Yi Ha-ung, known as the Taewon'gun. Aware of Western intrusions in China, he rejected Western demands for trade in the belief that continued isolation would preserve the inherited Confucian system. An anti-Catholic campaign began in 1866, and nine French missionaries and possibly 8000 Korean converts were killed. Attempted French and American invasions were repulsed in 1866 and 1871. At the same time the Taewon'gun attempted to achieve a dynastic restoration modelled on the reforms taking place in China. Over the opposition of Confucian scholars and the aristocracy, he introduced measures to combat corruption, appointed officials on merit, widened the tax base, and strengthened the military. But there were also arbitrary assessments of money and labour, and waste, for instance in reconstructing the royal palace which had been destroyed during the Japanese invasion of the sixteenth century.

The Taewon'gun was forced from power by King Kojong and his new queen in 1873. The Japanese government took the opportunity of the change in regime to impose a commercial treaty in 1876. Along with the opening of ports to trade and provisions for Japanese settlements and extra-territoriality, the treaty declared Korea a sovereign nation, which for the Japanese implied that China no longer had any right to interfere in Korean affairs. Li Hongzhang, in his capacity as Chinese minister for the northern ports, became alarmed and recommended that Korea adopt his policies of self-strengthening to defend against the Japanese. General anti-foreign sentiment and some particularly flagrant corruption led to the Soldiers' Riot of 1882. The Japanese embassy was burned, and the Japanese and Chinese both moved troops into Korea. An attempted coup in 1884 was supported by the Japanese, but put down by Chinese troops, and in 1885 both agreed to withdraw their troops.

Through the 1880s political control remained in the hands of the corrupt ruling clique dependent on the Chinese. The queen supported Li's representative Yuan Shikai (later president of China and would-be emperor) in increasing Chinese influence. However, extensive Japanese economic penetration dislocated and injured Korean interests. Further peasant uprisings and anti-foreign hostility became focused around the *Tonghak* movement. A call for the legal exoneration of Ch'oe Che-u in 1892 was followed by a mass demonstration in 1893, and finally by an armed uprising in 1894. The government called on the Chinese, but the Japanese intervened as well, and the Japanese seizure of the royal palace in fact opened the hostilities in the Sino–Japanese War. The Japanese installed a new ministry, the 'Kabo reformers' of 1894–6, made up of opponents of the Chinese-oriented clique, many of whom had studied in Japan. They and their reforms, particularly the order to cut off the traditional male topknot, aroused hostility, and a new series of uprisings broke out. In a confused series of events, the pro-Chinese queen was murdered, the king took refuge in the Russian embassy, and then several pro-Japanese ministers in turn were killed. Having defeated the Chinese, the Japanese insisted that China recognize Korean independence, a concession which the Japanese intended to use as a basis for their penetration into Korea. As seen above, the intervention led by Russia forced the Japanese to surrender some of their gains in China, and in Korea a period of increasing Russian influence formed part of the background to the Russo-Japanese war. As we will see in Chapters 6 and 7, the defeated Russians in turn conceded Japan's rights in Korea, which paved the way for the Protectorate Treaty imposed on the Koreans by the Japanese in 1905 and the final annexation of 1910.

Dynastic cycles and imperialist expansion in Southeast Asia

I am determined to place the relations between the two countries on precisely the same footing as they were previous to the reign of the late King who committed a blunder in going to war with you, and all of those acts I wish to have annulled and forgotten.

Tharrawaddy, King of Burma 1838–46, to the British Resident

As in China, Japan and Korea, indigenous elites in Southeast Asia had to confront increasing pressure from outside, and indeed by the early twentieth century all of Southeast Asia except for Thailand had been incorporated into the British, French, Dutch, and Spanish-American empires. However, rather than searching for the causes of Western expansion within the West, we can observe that as in China, Korea and Japan, it was disorder resulting from changes within Asian societies which provided opportunities for the extension of Western power. Southeast Asia had been part of the world economy for a long time, and therefore it was not the *economic* 'penetration of the capitalist world system' which led to the extension of direct European control, as argued by Immanuel Wallerstein and his students (Wallerstein, 1974–89). Rather, the *political* weakness of states on the periphery, combined with competition among states at the core, provided the impetus (Fieldhouse, 1984). The example of the Opium War showed that the disparity in armaments, based on the industrial revolution spreading across Europe, was unprecedented (Headrick, 1981). Nevertheless, as we will see in Chapter 5 the example of Japan showed that a strong state could acquire the new armaments and maintain its independence, though the Thai example showed that this would require a bit of luck as well.

Upheavals in the core areas of the states of Southeast Asia from the early nineteenth century allowed the British and their new competitors the French to extend their empires. In Vietnam the decline of the Lê dynasty in the eighteenth century and a struggle among regional leaders had led to the impoverishment of the peasantry and a series of uprisings which culminated in the revolt of the Tayson brothers in 1771. One of the brothers proclaimed himself emperor under the name of Quang-trung in 1788. He defeated the remnants of opposition within Vietnam, and then defeated an army which the Chinese had sent to occupy northern Vietnam. He began the reconstruction of his kingdom, allied himself with oppositional secret societies in southern China, and planned to conquer the southern tier of Chinese provinces, if not more. However, he died in 1792 without having firmly established a new dynasty.

The Taysons were replaced in 1802 by a new dynasty, the Nguyen, which continued until 1945. A large number of peasant uprisings documented by Marxist scholars suggests that they too failed to consolidate their power successfully. The large numbers of converts to Catholicism gained by French missionaries also points to deep dissatisfaction. The Emperor Minh-mang launched a modernization program in the 1830s. Although the factory he established to build steamships could reproduce the form of western ships, the production of the engines proved too difficult for Vietnamese artisans, but we should remember that at this early date the construction of steam engines was also beyond the capabilities of virtually all Europeans except for a few select firms in Britain, Belgium, France, the Rhineland, and Saxony.

Minh-mang also attempted to annex Cambodia and remodel it on Vietnamese Confucian lines. This led to a war with Siam (Thailand) in the 1840s, which devastated Cambodia. Internally Minh-mang banned the Catholic Church and began the persecution and execution of converts and both French and Vietnamese priests. Through the 1840s and 1850s conflict with France over Catholic conversions intensified. In 1859 the French seized Saigon and the surrounding provinces, in 1863 they established a protectorate over Cambodia as 'heirs' to Vietnamese rule, and in 1867 they rounded out their new colony of Cochin China with further annexations. The Nguyen dynasty had begun to fracture, and there were attempted coups in 1851–3 and 1864–5, the latter including anti-Catholic violence and protests against yielding territory to France. In 1873 the French invaded the north, but the Vietnamese defeated them with the assistance of Chinese veterans of the Taiping rebellion who had fled south after their defeat. In 1882 the French invaded again, and the Vietnamese, as a 'tributary' or client state of China, requested Chinese aid. As noted above, the Chinese were defeated, and the French annexed the remainder of Vietnam, although the central portion remained under the nominal rule of the Nguyens.

New dynasties emerged in Burma and Siam in the late eighteenth century. In Burma a generation of crisis led in 1752 to the foundation of the Konbaung dynasty which ruled until 1885, but existed in almost continual conflict with its powerful neighbours over control of the small states and territories between them. The Burmese captured and sacked the Siamese capital in 1767. The Chinese governor of Yunnan invaded Burma four times in the 1760s in response to Burmese attempts to extend their power over the Shan states in the north. Wars with a revived Siam extended from 1785 to 1805. Finally, conflict with the British East India Company over control of territories in the west led to war in 1823–6. This time, however, the outcome was a humiliating defeat, loss of territory, an ongoing internal crisis, and coups in 1837 and 1846. One constant in the British pressure on Burma was the desire to open up a 'back door' into China. In 1851 the British invaded again, in response to Burmese mistreatment of their merchants. In 1853 another coup brought Mindon Min to the throne, but he was unable to regain the territory annexed by the British, which included ocean ports and crucial rice-producing areas in the south. Mindon reformed the financial system, appointed new salaried officials and based tax assessments on residence and ability to pay. He also developed new industrial and commercial enterprises, including factories with European machinery to process local products and steamships on the rivers.

Although he refused to recognize the previous British conquests, Mindon signed trade treaties with Britain in 1862 and 1867, partly in the hope of obtaining arms. However, the British refused to honour their agreement to permit Burma to import arms and proceeded to integrate 'British Burma' into their Indian empire. Attempts to gain recognition from France and Italy in the 1870s resulted in commercial treaties, but also aroused the suspicious hostility of the British, who would not tolerate any other European power gaining influence along the borders of India. Burmese internal divisions continued; Mindon's designated heir was killed in an attempted coup in 1866, and when Mindon died in 1878, his widow arranged the succession of a weak junior prince and ordered a number of her rivals killed. British interests pressing for complete annexation seized on these murders as a pretext; they were delayed by the Afghan war, but then stimulated by Burmese attempts to obtain arms from the French, and the final invasion took place in 1885.

Alone among the states of Southeast Asia, Siam (Thailand) survived. A new 'Bangkok' dynasty founded by successful generals arose from the defeat by the Burmese. Rama I was named king by rebels in 1782 and ruled until 1809. He took over and adopted traditional institutions, gaining support among the aristocracy with offices in return for service, winning the Buddhist clergy by commissioning a complete revision of the scriptural texts, and demonstrating his cultural leadership by composing the *Ramakian*, a monumental 3000–page poetic epic which remains a landmark in Siamese literature. He also successfully maintained and extended Siamese power against the Burmese. Most fortunately of all, he was succeeded by two capable successors, Rama II (1809–24) and Rama III (1824–51). Rama III was the son of a concubine of Rama II, but his half-brother, who was the son of a queen, had recently become a monk, and the succession crisis which might have occurred was avoided. The Siamese turned down a British request to join the war against Burma in 1824. However, in the aftermath of the Burmese defeat, Rama III negotiated a treaty which exchanged British recognition of Siamese rights over the Malay states for liberalization of trade in Bangkok. The gamble paid off; the loss of revenue was made good by a rapid increase in trade, and security on the western border allowed Siam to concentrate on wars against the Lao in the 1830s and the Vietnamese in the 1840s.

Siam was lucky again in 1851 as another succession crisis was barely avoided through a compromise joint kingship. The government under the new king Mongkut and his chief minister Suriyawong was therefore relatively well prepared when Sir John Bowring, British governor of Hong Kong and minister to China, arrived in Bangkok with new demands for trade and diplomatic relations. The treaty signed by the Siamese in 1855 conceded almost exactly the same terms as the treaties Britain had imposed on China – including consular representation, extra-territoriality, low tariffs, abolition of government monopolies, and a provision that property owned by foreigners would be taxed at a low rate, which had the effect of limiting the taxes that could be charged on Siamese property as well. The Siamese were well aware of events in China, and closer to home in Burma, and felt they had no choice but to concede the treaty and then attempt to reform government finances to regain the lost revenues. Opium, gambling, lottery, and alcohol monopolies were created and farmed out to Chinese entrepreneurs, and the excise revenues became a major source of government income. Trade was encouraged, the number of foreign ships calling at Bangkok increased dramatically, and Siam became a major exporter of rice and teak. The increased revenues went to purchase arms and to hire Westerners to drill Siamese troops in their use.

Under the reign of King Chulalongkorn (1868–1910), however, Siam again relied on luck to maintain its independence. An early attempt at further reforms created a crisis which very nearly led to British and French intervention in 1875. The French in fact did move into the area east of the Mekong in the 1880s, and when the Siamese attempted to force them out, the French imposed a devastating naval blockade which forced the Siamese to yield the disputed territories in 1893. Subsequent treaties with France established the present eastern border of Thailand by 1907, and in 1909 the British detached four of the dependent principalities in the Malay peninsula. However, the reluctance of Britain and France either to share a border or to see the other gain too great an influence in the remaining territory of Siam prevented complete dismemberment.

Within all these territories new bureaucratic administrations came into being. The impact of the new administrations varied, and large areas were not brought under effective control until the 1920s and 1930s. In Siam the reformers were a small group concentrated in Bangkok, and regional authorities remained largely autonomous until the 1890s. This was true in the colonial territories as well. The Dutch had begun to extend their authority outward from Batavia in the 1870s, but were bogged down in a guerilla war in northern Sumatra for nearly a quarter of a century. Unable to afford initiatives elsewhere, the Dutch continued to rely on indigenous vassal rulers for another generation. In Vietnam, the French system of dual administration, one for Vietnamese and another for French and others, meant that most of the country was in fact ruled by officials trained and chosen on the basis of the traditional Confucian examination system. The Philippines passed from Spain to the United States in 1898, but despite their imperial enthusiasm and more efficient army, the Americans faced a bitter struggle with the frustrated Filipinos who had hoped for independence, and they were still obliged to compromise with the Sultan of Sulu to gain control over the southern islands. In the Malay peninsula and North Borneo the British ruled through indigenous elites. In Burma, resistance to the British annexation, and an uprising in British Burma, meant that even nominal control over the entire area within the new borders was not achieved until the mid-1890s.

3

THE ROLE OF MARKETS: PEASANT FAMILIES, COMMERCIAL AGRICULTURE AND PROTOINDUSTRIALIZATION

The Role of Markets

Markets play a crucial role in economic development. Adam Smith, the father of modern economics, argued in 1776 that human beings possess an innate propensity to 'truck, barter, and exchange', but he also recognized that humans could exercise their trading propensities only within functioning market systems. We require the cooperation of many other people, but we each have only a few friends on whose 'benevolence' we can rely. Therefore, 'it is not from the benevolence of the butcher, or the brewer, or the baker, that we expect our dinner, but from their regard to their own self-interest'. The instinct to trade leads individuals to specialize, to produce the goods they can make most easily. It then proves convenient to trade with others, and to widen the circle of exchange through the use of money. The degree of specialization depends on the extent of the market. Given these minimum requirements, as markets expand, producers will find it in their interest to specialize further, and the resulting increases in efficiency will lead to 'opulence' (Smith, *Wealth of Nations*, Book I, Chapters 1–4).

However, 'Smithians' who analyse market relations in terms of pure self-interest have sometimes misunderstood the way in which markets in fact operate. Smith argued that in important respects markets are cooperative rather than competitive, and they will not function if self-interest rules over prudence. Successful exchange requires a certain type of behaviour, and in particular the butcher, brewer, or baker must be satisfied that they have received adequate remuneration for their services. Individuals are not isolated, and neither are their exchanges.

Human beings exist in a web of ongoing relationships. As Smith put it, each individual is 'a member of the vast commonwealth of nature' and must expect that immediate self-interest will occasionally yield to the interests of others or to the common good (see Sen, 1987, pp. 1–28).

It has been tempting for Westerners to assert that markets were a uniquely Western phenomenon, and to attribute Asian development to the penetration of Asia by modern market relationships as a result of contact with the West. The English, French, Americans, and Russians who pushed into China, Japan, Korea and Southeast Asia at gunpoint in the middle decades of the nineteenth century claimed to be opening these countries to trade. They pictured Asian societies as backward, stagnant and unchanging. In the late nineteenth and early twentieth centuries this view of Asia served as a justification for imperialism. After the Second World War and into the 1960s and 1970s the belief that traditional Asia had been stagnant and unchanging remained one of the main assumptions of modernization theorists. Development they argued, would require Westernization and the integration of isolated, self-sufficient peasant communities into regional, national and international markets. Western Marxists and adherents of world systems theory generally agreed, although they saw the intrusion of the West as essentially exploitative rather than beneficial.

However, students of the history of market relations in the West are now less certain that *Western* markets functioned as smoothly and effectively as modernization theorists and their Marxist opponents believed. Perceptions of 'the market' varied substantially among different Western societies. Although the markets for European government securities were linked in sophisticated ways in the eighteenth century, corporate financial markets did not begin to assume their modern forms until late in the nineteenth century (Neal, 1994; Baskin, 1988; Haskell and Teichgraeber, 1994). For individual firms in the market, double entry book-keeping had been developed in the fourteenth and fifteenth centuries and popularized during the sixteenth and seventeenth centuries, and was long regarded as one of the defining characteristics of 'modern' management. Nevertheless, historians of business enterprise in Europe and the United States now argue that it was not a necessary precondition of rational business enterprise. Until late in the nineteenth century, even large firms continued to use single entry systems, and many leading firms did not have any precise notion of their costs of production. Only the massive capital investments required by the 'second industrial revolution' made double entry book-keeping mandatory, because heavy initial investments, interest on borrowed capital, and depreciation of plant and equipment all needed to be precisely identified and measured in order to set output prices and predict profitability (Gardella, 1992, pp. 318–20).

Further, as was seen in Chapter 2, the societies of Asia were *not* stagnant or unchanging before the intrusion of the West. But were they *market* economies? Some scholars, both Western and Asian, have argued that Asian markets operate on different principles from Western markets, whether a 'Japanese ethos' (Morishima, 1982), Confucian values (Dore, 1973), or village solidarity (Scott, 1976; Huang, 1985, 1990). Smith himself saw nothing mysterious in the pattern of Asian development:

> The improvements in agriculture and manufactures seem likewise to have been of very great antiquity... in some of the eastern provinces of China... several great rivers form, by their different branches, a multitude of canals, and by communicating with one another afford an inland navigation much more extensive than that either of the Nile or the Ganges, or perhaps than both of them put together. It is remarkable that neither the antient Egyptians, nor the Indians, nor the Chinese, encouraged foreign commerce, but seem all to have derived their great opulence from this inland navigation. (Adam Smith, *Wealth of Nations*, 1776, Book I, Chapter 3)

And, in addition, recent work makes clear that the economies of Asia have been market economies – in Smith's sense – for a very long time. For centuries in fact before the Westerners arrived, the peasants and artisans of Asia had been integrated into market networks. Local village economies were linked together by complex systems of regional markets, and regional commercial centres were linked to each other by long-distance trade. There were no extensive areas of purely self-sufficient villages or subsistence production. Even the migratory peoples of the steppes required exchange with settled societies to survive (Waldron, 1990). Sophisticated credit arrangements provided capital for peasants and artisans as well as for merchants and larger scale manufacturers. Significantly, land was a commodity to be bought, sold, or mortgaged – there was no equivalent of the European 'feudal' pattern of a lord granting the use of a plot of land to a vassal in return for service.

Markets and mercantile agrarianism in China

In Gaotang there is more land sown under cotton than under food-grains. The rich do not store grain, and the poor rely entirely on hiring out and the board that comes with wage labour.

Magistrate of Jining, Shandong province, second quarter of nineteenth century.

To repeat Ramon Myers' question, 'what kind of economic system enabled China to more than double its population between the late seventeenth century and the mid-nineteenth century to reach a total of nearly half a billion people?' As we saw in Chapter 2, the answer cannot simply be a high birth rate. Rather, the answer must lie in the general development of the economy. It is now clear that China did not have a simple subsistence economy. In fact, an enduring feature of Chinese life dating from the Han dynasty was an economy of mercantile agrarianism – an agrarian society integrated into a market network (Hsu, 1980). For nearly two thousand years Chinese farming families produced both food and cash crops. In addition they engaged in a broad range of non-agricultural activities in slack seasons, producing goods both for home consumption and for sale in the market. In times of peace and plenty they could devote most of their efforts to the production of market goods, whereas in times of war or scarcity they could switch to producing for their own consumption. This alternation explains why the Chinese rural economy could appear highly commercialized at one time but close to self-sufficiency at another.

Farmers and artisans bought and sold goods in local markets, and these in turn were linked to district markets and integrated into a complex structure of regional economies. In an immensely influential study published in the mid-1960s, William Skinner argued that,

Anthropological fieldwork on Chinese society, by focusing attention almost exclusively on the village, has with few exceptions distorted the reality of rural social structure. Insofar as the Chinese peasant can be said to live in a self-contained world, that world is not the village but the standard marketing community. The effective social field of the peasant, I will argue, is delimited not by the narrow horizons of the village but rather by the boundaries of his standard marketing area. (Skinner, 1964–5)

Using data from the late nineteenth and early twentieth centuries, Skinner identified a hierarchy of marketing systems. The standard marketing area was the lowest, within which all the normal trade needs of the peasant household would be met. It contained about 1500 households in about eighteen villages, covering a hexagonal area of about 50 square kilometers. This was the effective social field of peasant families, the area within which marriage partners would be sought, over which secret societies and religious fraternities would recruit their members, and in which dialect speech would be uniform. It could also form the lowest unit of effective government. In the nineteenth century, in Baodi county in northeastern Hebei province, east of Beijing, the *xiangbao* was the lowest quasi-official for tax collection. Nominated by the village and supra-village elite, and confirmed by the district magistrate, the *xiangbao* each were responsible for delinquent taxes and special levies in an area containing about twenty villages (Huang, 1985, p. 50).

Connections among standard marketing areas depended on transport costs, with the most intense relations among marketing areas located along navigable waterways. Goods produced in one district would be exchanged for goods produced in others. Skinner extended his scheme to a tiered hierarchy of central places culminating in eight macroregions with relatively densely populated lowland core areas surrounded by peripheral areas or hinterlands. In the northwest the core area extended along the navigable rivers from Xi'an up the valleys of the Yellow and Fen Rivers. The North China plain, from Beijing south to the middle reaches of the Yellow River's southern route, made up the core of the north macroregion. The plains of the Upper Yangzi River including Chengdu and Chongqing, the Middle Yangzi River including an arc from Hengyang and Changsha through Wuhan and Nanchang, and the Lower Yangzi River including Nanjing, Hangzhou, Suzhou, and Shanghai, each made up the core of a distinct macroregion. In the southwest macroregion the core included an arc from west of Kunming to northeast of Guiyang. The far south core extended from the Leizhou peninsula to the plain around Guangzhou, and the southeast coast core extended along the coastal plain centered on Fuzhou (Skinner, 1977a, 1977b).

Skinner argued that each of the macroregions was a functionally integrated entity, centred on regional metropoles. His model was derived from central-place location theory, and he assumed that the hierarchies of subregions and regions were defined by transport costs. The shape of the standard marketing area is derived from the mathematical fact that if a flat surface is divided into equal units, the hexagon is the geometric form which minimizes the distance between the centre of each unit and all other points within its boundary. The definition of urban hierarchies rests on the assumption that goods and services form a hierarchy and that there is some optimum size for the units (firms or government agencies) which produce every product and service. The numbers of urban places of any given size will therefore be determined by a definite ratio, with larger places supplying goods and services to smaller places. However, the assumptions are questionable for industrial economies and almost certainly do not hold for pre-industrial economies. Skinner also tended to assume that each of the macroregions would be self-sufficient, but in fact the core and periphery areas were not always distinct, and regular core–periphery relations (exchange of raw materials or food in return for finished products and services) did not exist within every macroregion (see Sands and Myers, 1986; Little and Esherick, 1989).

Nevertheless, the macroregions were economic units, in the sense that commerce within them was more intensive than commerce among them. Thus the work of Wu Chengming (1985; cited in Huang, 1990, p. 101) shows almost universal exchange of food crops for cotton products within regions, but when we look at China as a whole, Dwight Perkins' estimates show that, until the early twentieth century, on average 30 to 40 per cent of all farm output was marketed and 7 to 8 per cent entered long-distance trade (Perkins, 1969, pp. 136–7). As Smith was arguing in the passage cited above, water transport was the cheapest means of shipping bulky goods, and where water transport existed or could be created, long-distance trade was extensive. Along the water routes, core–periphery exchange relationships did develop between districts belonging to different macroregions. In the eighteenth century the southern provinces shipped some 400 000 metric tons of food grains annually along the Grand Canal to northern provincial capitals and Beijing (Myers, 1980, p. 82). In the late eighteenth and early nineteenth centuries a fleet of 3500 ships (*shachuan* boats) with 1500–3000 *shi* capacity traded between the northeastern ports and Shanghai. A *shi* equals about 108 litres, and *a shi* of rice would weigh about 80 kilograms, so these ships each could carry from 120 to 240 metric tons, and each made three or four trips per year (Huang, 1990, pp. 88–90).

Interregional trade led to high levels of commercialization and specialization of individual peasant families and of districts along the southern and southeastern coasts, in the Upper Yangzi basin, in the Lower Yangzi delta, and on parts of the North China plain. The southern coastal provinces produced 85 per cent of China's total output of salt, which they exchanged with other provinces, for instance Guangxi, Hunan and Hubei, which produced none at all (Sands and Myers, 1986, pp. 724–5). The North China plain exported large amounts of soybean cake to the Lower Yangzi region, where it was used as fertilizer. Raw cotton produced in the northern province of Shandong passed though the Lower Yangzi (which also produced cotton in surplus) onward to the southern provinces of Fujian and Guangdong (Huang, 1985, p. 118; Huang, 1990, pp. 88–90). The Lower Yangzi imported grain from the north and from inland provinces, a total of 1 to 3 million metric tons annually. The parallel movements of grain prices in surplus areas and consuming areas shows the integration of widely separated markets. Thus the fluctuations in rice prices in Changsha, in the Middle Yangzi region, were highly correlated with those in Shanghai, one thousand miles away in the Lower Yangzi region (Brandt, 1985, 1989).

There is no question that the Chinese economy had grown and developed. The development of the Qing economy had been marked throughout by urban growth. In 1660 Beijing contained 1 million residents. In addition there were three centres of 'interprovincial or interregional commerce' of over 300 000 and a further 42 provincial or district centres with populations ranging from 30 000 to 300 000, and these 45 cities contained a total of 3.6 million people. In 1830 the population of Beijing was still around 1 million, but there were nine cities with populations over 300 000, and another 100 with populations over 30 000, and these 109 cities possessed a total population of 13 million. To put the figures in perspective, in 1660 Beijing contained 40 per cent of all residents in cities of 300 000 or more, but in 1830 Beijing's share of the population of large cities was only 20 per cent. Gilbert Rozman concludes that by 1830 'the commercial centrality of other cities enabled them as a group to dwarf the capital in total population' (Rozman, 1973, pp. 102, 283). In 1843 possibly 7.4 per cent of the population of the Lower Yangzi region lived in towns of 2000 or more, and 4.2 per cent in the North China region (Skinner, 1977a, p. 229). This is low compared to the figure of 27.5 per cent of England's population in towns of 5000 or more in 1801, or the 25 per cent of the Prussian population in towns of 2000 or more between 1816 and 1852, and it is also lower than Japan, but it is not very much lower than Europe as a whole.

The economy grew particularly rapidly in the later decades of the nineteenth century. The rebellions and natural disasters of mid-century may have reduced the total population from 410 million in 1850 to 350 million in 1873, but the population then rose again, to 500 million in 1900. But what does this growth mean? Following Mao Zedong's 1939 article 'The Chinese Revolution and the Chinese Communist Party',

Chinese Marxists interpret early development as 'incipient capitalism'. They cite the commercialization of the economy and the development of capitalist wage relations as evidence that capitalism had 'sprouted' in China long before the intrusion of the West. Western imperialism then crushed this incipient capitalism and reduced China to 'semi-feudal, semi-colonial' status (Mao 1939). Western scholars such as Perkins and Elvin dismiss these claims and emphasize the pernicious effects of population pressure. Elvin in fact insists that 'It was the historic mission of the modern West to ease and then break the high-level equilibrium trap in China', and argues that Western imperialism had a positive effect because it allowed international markets and technology transfer to operate (Elvin, 1973, p. 315; see Huang, 1985, p. 18).

However, the accumulation of evidence of trade and development points to a different interpretation of the impact of imperialism on the Chinese economy. Rather than the imposition of a new economic system, the intrusion of the West resulted in Chinese farmers and artisans using their *existing* market systems to take advantage of the opportunities for production and sale which the expanding world economy offered. Exports from the Han River basin, for instance, rose in the 1870s in response to foreign demand and included a broad range of specialized agricultural products such as sesame seed, turmeric, and tobacco, along with manufactured goods such as varnish, paper, and silk. Significantly, the Han region simultaneously increased production of food and export goods and did not need to import food until the 1910s (Liu, 1980).

Korea

Korea might be considered a 'macroregion' within the broader Chinese system, for it was largely closed to foreigners except for tributary trade relations with China. Many developments parallel those seen in regions of China. Surplus produce was marketed, and by the eighteenth century there were over a thousand regular markets located throughout Korea. By the end of the eighteenth century 'enlarged scale farming' was widespread. Farmers moved on from selling surplus food crops to producing specialized cash crops, especially ginseng, tobacco (first introduced in the early seventeenth century), and cotton. Previously, dependent tenant farmers had been employed on a shared-costs, shared-return system, but this changed with more intensive commercialization. Sharecropping was supplanted by payment of rent, and tenants now made their own decisions about crop selection and methods of cultivation rather than working under the direct supervision of their landlords.

Over the century from 1608 to 1708 the Korean government gradually shifted to a single tax system, the Uniform Land Tax Law, and a regular coinage was introduced in 1678. The government now purchased the goods it required rather than relying on collection of tribute goods. The former tribute collectors (*kongin* or 'tribute men') became the purchasing agents for the government, and many became merchants in their own right. The *kongin* and the private merchants of Seoul and Kaesong provided wholesale trading and banking services which connected local markets to each other. The merchants of Kaesong in particular established branches in the district market towns, known as 'Kaesong shops'. In the larger market towns branches of the wholesale merchants passed goods on consignment to itinerant peddlers, and provided warehousing, transportation, and some- . times temporary accommodation, as well as lending money, issuing checks and money drafts, and accepting deposits (Eckert, 1990, pp. 159ff).

In addition to the trade carried on as part of the annual cycle of tribute missions to China, there was extensive 'private' trade, some of it illegal. A large amount of tobacco was exported to China. Korean merchants of Uiju near the mouth of the Yalu exchanged with Chinese merchants on island market sites in the river, and at designated markets inside Manchuria. Korean merchants from Tongnae in the Pusan region traded with the Japanese, with legal trade limited to contacts on Iki Island off Honshu. Later a triangular trade developed in Korean ginseng and other products in exchange for Chinese silver on one end and Japanese copper on the other (Eckert, 1990, p. 162).

Internal trade in Japan

Rice fields, mountains, the sea, gold, rice, and everything between heaven and earth, are commodities. The realization of rice from rice fields is no different from the realization of profit from gold.

Kaiho Seiryo, *Lessons of the Past*, 1813

After the final seclusion edict issued in 1639 Japan was almost completely closed to foreigners for 250 years. The only exceptions were the Korean traders permitted to exchange goods with Japanese merchants on Iki Island, and the Dutch and Chinese, who were allowed to trade on the small island of Deshima in Nagasaki Bay. At first there was no limit on the amount of trade permitted with China. Then in 1685 the government limited the amount of silver that could be shipped to China each year to 6000 *kan* (about 49 620 pounds), compared with the 3000 *kan* permitted to the Dutch. In 1715 the government limited the number of Chinese ships to thirty each year and the number of Dutch ships to only two, and the export of copper was restricted. Finally in 1813 the number of Chinese ships was limited to ten each year (Hane, 1991, p. 128).

The Tokugawa government attempted to freeze social relations as it did foreign trade; but as was seen in Chapter 2, population growth and the outbursts of unrest in the early nineteenth century demonstrate the growth of the economy despite the conservative thrust of government policy. To this may be added the evidence of urban growth. In the late sixteenth century Kyôtô was the only substantial city in Japan, with about 250 000 inhabitants. The nearby port of Sakai contained 50 000 persons, Ôsaka somewhat fewer, and another half-dozen small cities possibly 20 000 each. By the middle of the eighteenth century the Tokugawa capital of Edo (present day Tokyo), a fishing village in 1590, had a population of over 1 million and rivalled Beijing as the largest city in the world. Kyôtô and Ôsaka each had nearly 400 000 inhabitants, and together with Sakai and Fushimi they made up another urban agglomeration of over 1 million. Nagasaki, the centre of the Dutch and Chinese trade, Nagoya and Kanazawa each had between 50 000 and 60 000 inhabitants. In addition there were over 200 'castle towns', the capitals of domain governments, and 30 to 40 of these contained 10 000 or more inhabitants. Altogether, 16 to 17 per cent of Japan's population lived in towns of 3000 or more inhabitants in the eighteenth century, a ratio exceeded only by England and some regions in Western Europe.

To support this large urban population Japan developed an intensive interregional trade, and this in turn provided opportunities for farmers and artisans to produce goods for export outside their home districts. Certain districts became highly specialized, particularly when they possessed some geographic advantage. Silk production concentrated in the cool, moist mountains to the north of the road connecting Edo and Nagoya, cotton growing in the relatively dry area of the Kinai between Nagoya and Ôsaka, sugar in the warm, rainy southern districts of Kyûshû in the region of Kagoshima and on the neighbouring islands (Smith, 1959, p. 69). As development proceeded commercial fertilizers were applied.

The herring fishing industry of northern Hokkaido grew up to supply fish-meal fertilizer to the commercial farmers of central Honshu (Howell, 1992).

In addition, the system of alternate residence, which was intended to place the *daimyô* under government observation and control and to weaken them financially because of the expense involved, had the effect of further monetizing and commercializing the economy. The system increased the population of Edo directly, the *daimyô* were forced to transfer large amounts of money to the capital, and they of course travelled in the company of their retainers and servants. Particularly along the Tôkaidô, the highway connecting Edo with the Kyôtô–Ôsaka region, towns grew up to service the movement of people to and from the capital. Along the Tôkaidô and to a lesser extent along other main highways, a very modern pattern of ribbon development appeared, with a nearly continuous strip of shops fronting directly on to the road.

The need for increasing amounts of money led many domains to undertake development projects to take advantage of market opportunities in trade and agriculture. The domain of Tsushima, officially valued at only 20 000 *koku*, produced revenues of 200 000 *koku* because of its trade with Korea. Many domain governments created monopolies to buy and sell commercial crops, notably the sugar monopoly of Satsuma. Satsuma and Chôshû have additional importance because of their role in overthrowing the Tokugawa government. Between 1833 and 1848 Zusho Hiromichi reorganized the sugar monopoly operated by the Satsuma domain government, and substantially increased revenues. In Chôshû, Murata Seifu was equally successful, although his programme involved reducing the number of domain monopolies while supporting agricultural development. How-ever, many other domains also worked to enhance the quality of local products, both commercial crops and artisan manufactures. The search for new revenue led to coordinated development programmes. The north-ern domain of Yonezawa had opposed the Tokugawa, and lost most of its land. Bankrupt and facing famine and unrest by the mid-eighteenth century, Yonezawa borrowed money from merchants in Edo to develop both agricultural and craft production. Silk producers were invited to settle and teach their skills to local producers. The domain government lent money to farmers to finance planting of mulberry trees, set up twelve nurseries to produce seedlings, and published a handbook summarizing the latest techniques (Morris-Suzuki, 1994, pp. 28–9).

As its population grew Edo became the major centre of consumption, while Ôsaka emerged as the financial and commercial focal point of the system. Functional differentiation between the two market centres led to and was in turn further reinforced by the creation of national markets in a number of commodities, from food staples such as rice to precious luxury fabrics. The Ôsaka rice market has been identified as the world's first well-established market in commodity futures. The rice collected by the domain governments was shipped to Ôsaka, where it was stored in their warehouses before being sold and then shipped to consumers. The domain warehouses issued 'rice tickets' which promised the delivery of a specified amount of rice to a specified person on a specified date. These tickets obviously had a value, and merchants began to buy and sell not only tickets for 'genuine rice', but also tickets for 'rice on book' or rice futures. The Tokugawa government granted an official permit for the operation of the futures market in 1730, giving legal sanction to these operations. The year was divided into three marketing periods, and the maturation date for futures extended only to the closing date of each market period. The market period from 8 January to 28 April primarily involved transactions for rice already in Ôsaka, while the period from 7 May to 9 October allowed merchants to hedge against the risk of a poor harvest. The period from 17 October to 24 December allowed hedging against the risks involved in shipping the harvested rice to Ôsaka. The market operated efficiently in the technical sense that movements in futures prices remained stable over the transaction period, while future and spot prices moved together. In the May–October market the spread between spot and futures prices widened in a regular pattern, indicating that the market was in fact used to hedge against risks (Wakita, 1994).

Local, regional and long-distance trade in Southeast Asia

[In Chiang Mai there were] many merchants who had travelled thither from China.

Ralph Fitch, 1587

[The daughter of the King of Chiang Mai] told me that from 700 to 1000 laden mules and ponies come yearly from Yunnan, and from 7000 to 8000 from Kiang Tung, Kiang Hung, and other places in the British Shan states; 1000 elephants are employed in carrying goods to and from Kiang Hsen, chiefly for transhipment to Luang Praban and elsewhere;

5000 porters travel into Lower Burmah, and 4000 to the neighbouring states, and to the British Shan states lying to the north; 3000 oxen ply between Zimme [Chiang Mai] and Lakon, and from 500 to 600 to Lower Burmah...A considerable boat traffic existed on the river, particularly in the rainy season. One thousand boats plied between Zimme and Raheng [Tak], many of them proceeding to Bangkok.

Holt Hallett, *A Thousand Miles on Elephant in the Shan States*, 1890

Southeast Asia has been a trading zone since prehistoric times – long before Europeans arrived, the coastal and riverine districts were 'an integral part of the shipping link between the Indian Ocean and the China Sea' (Van Niel, 1990b, p. 110; see Reid, 1988; Warren, 1981). This may have fostered a shared general 'outward-looking attitude and openness' among Southeast Asians, and it has even been argued that for Southeast Asians 'the possibility of being "up-to-date" was often linked to and sustained by the sense of being an integral part of the whole of the known "world" rather than merely belonging to one's own patch of territory' (Reynolds, 1995, pp. 434–5). Early and widespread use of money facilitated the development of markets. In Java, Chinese copper cash was in regular use as a medium of exchange from the thirteenth century, and Thai coinage dates from the thirteenth century as well. In the Melaka strait, Islamic gold coinages appeared in the fifteenth century. The two main coinage regions – the straits and the routes linking the Southeast Asian uplands with southern China and eastern India – were separate, but connected at their margins (Wicks, 1992).

Europeans forced themselves into these pre-existing patterns. One reason for the Spanish conquest of the Philippines was to obtain Manila as a base from which to trade with China. In order to protect the position of merchants and manufacturers in Spain, the Spanish government limited trade to a single annual galleon, calculated to provide enough income to enable the colony to survive but no more. Financing this transit trade had the effect of draining capital out of the colony, and no encouragement was given to internal development or to trade with the rest of Southeast Asia. Chinese merchants handled both the supply of goods from China to be shipped on the galleon, and trade among the Philippine islands. The Dutch East India Company had seized control of coastal shipping routes and centralized the production of cloves and other spices on certain easily controlled small islands. This had the effect of reorienting trade away from China and towards Europe. However, Dutch naval power declined from the late seventeenth century onwards, as the Company extended its power over the island of Java. By the late eighteenth century the Company was a territorial rather than a naval power, and trade relations tended to return to their previous north–south axis, again under the control of Chinese merchants. The eclipse of the Dutch was also a consequence of the rise of British naval power. The British established trading centres at Penang in 1786, Singapore in 1819, and Melaka in 1824. The trade of the British East India Company linked ports in India with Burmese ports on the Irrawaddy delta and Siamese and Malay ports on the Malay peninsula and Sumatra.

Though Europeans were a significant presence, much of the pattern of Southeast Asian trade remained outside European control. In Malaysia there was an industrially organized export economy involving both agriculture and industry from quite early times (Brookfield, ed., 1994; Gullick, 1987). Even in areas which nominally appeared under the direct control of the colonial powers, an ubiquitous trade among village communities linked those specializing in fishing or handicrafts with those producing rice. Thus, in the first decades of the nineteenth century, Java was quite sparsely populated, and peasants lived in small and often isolated villages. But these villages were not undifferentiated, self-sufficient, and self-contained units, as traditionally argued. Rather, they were diverse economically, and engaged in extensive intra-island trade (Fernando, 1993). Further, individual peasants were much more mobile than is often supposed (Elson, 1994). For example, the trade in salt, produced in huge salt pans constructed along the coast of the island of Madura off the east coast of Java, linked up districts. By the eighteenth century large-scale commercial agriculture was developing. In West Java, Chinese entrepreneurs paid local lords for use of the land, forced peasants to grow sugar cane, and exported the processed sugar through the Dutch East India Company. In the early nineteenth century, other Chinese made similar arrangements around Singapore and Johur to produce and export pepper and gambier (used as a medicine, for tanning leather, and in dyeing), through the British East India Company (Jackson, 1968). In Vietnam, sugar was also produced for export, and here the government forced the producers to sell them their output in order to export it at a profit.

Tin was mined in Malaya from an early period. The original miners were Malays, and the mines were either directly owned by local lords or else part of the tin was exacted as tribute. The Dutch attempted to monopolize the trade in tin but failed because the producers were too scattered. Chinese miners appeared in Malaya in the late eighteenth century. Khaw Soo Cheang arrived in the region from China in 1822.

He saw an opportunity in the Ranong district because there was no existing competition, so he bid for a monopoly in tin mining, and also gained a right to farm taxes. Chinese miners were brought in to work the tin deposits. Khaw and his heirs enjoyed a double identity as business entrepreneurs and as local representatives of the Bangkok court, and their court connections helped them expand their interests into land, trade and coastal shipping, linking markets in China with Malaya and the Netherlands East Indies. The Khaws' local reign lasted until the late nineteenth century, when the Thai central government began to concentrate power in its own hands and their tin-mining monopoly was threatened by Western firms (Cushman, 1991). Chinese miners also opened the gold deposits in Borneo, where their operations employed possibly tens of thousands of miners, and the Philippines government also contracted iron mining rights to an entrepreneur who imported Chinese miners (Steinberg, 1987, pp. 49ff).

Trade routes were well-established by the late eighteenth century. In addition to sea lanes, inland caravan routes connected centres in peninsular Southeast Asia such as Chiang Mai with the southern provinces of China (Bowie, 1992). Cotton, tobacco, silver, and forest products were exchanged for Chinese horses, silk, copperware, and salt. Trade with China took place partly within the tributary system, with contacts at specified intervals to reaffirm Chinese overlordship. 'Tribute' from the 'vassal' states was exchanged for Chinese goods of equal or greater value. Southeast Asian governments established monopoly organizations which extracted goods from their subjects in order to trade with the Chinese within this system. From 1770 to the 1840s each decade saw a total of ten to twenty tribute missions to China from Siam, Vietnam, Laos, Burma, and Sulu. The Chinese central government was generally hostile to private sea trade because of the political danger of possible naval development in southern China. Nevertheless, the South China Sea maintained its position as the most important trading network in the region, linking ports along the coast of southern China with Vietnam, Siam and Malaysia on the one hand, and with the Philippine and Indonesian archipelagos on the other. Alongside the official tributary trade, the 'private' trade of Chinese merchants expanded, and by the early nineteenth century this trade was far larger than official tributary exchanges. In 1821 the Chinese merchants in Siam operated a fleet of 136 ships, 82 in trade with China and 34 sailing between Siam and Vietnam, Malaya, and Java (see Reid, 1996).

Similarly, the economic impact of Western penetration in the midnineteenth century seems less than it did before. These were dynamic economies before the arrival of the West. In Thailand, for example, although increased trade and a general growth of economic activity followed the Bowring Treaty of 1855, a substantial expansion of trading activity, division of labour, emergence of entrepreneurs in light industry, growth of wage labour, and changes in elite attitudes towards economic activity had already occurred in the generation preceding Sir John Bowring's visit (Hong, 1984; Hewison, 1989). Later in the nineteenth century and into the twentieth the internal dynamic of the expansion and closure of the rice frontier provided the main impetus to Thai development (Feeny, 1982). Similarly, in the Philippines, 'to shift Filipinos to the foreground, to emphasize their active role, necessitates a socioeconomic perspective with its own, quite different periodizations based on the growth of indigenous society' and, as in Thailand, the internal dynamic of frontier settlement determined the pace and direction of development (Larkin, 1982, pp. 595, 597–8).

The extension of Western control created new economic frameworks in the final decades of the nineteenth century. Transportation improved, especially with the spread of steamships. In the islands, steamships were crucial in suppression of piracy, and they tied isolated localities into world market networks. The steamship also allowed much more intensive use of inland waterways for commerce – the Irrawaddy Flotilla Company began operations in the 1860s. In some respects these more regular and consistent systems benefited commerce, but the new borders often interfered with existing trade relations. Rather than creating markets, the imperialist powers interfered with and sometimes destroyed existing market structures.

Peasants

Within these market economies the peasants of Asia responded to economic opportunity. However, they frequently might have preferred not to have been obliged to respond. Change was unpleasant, and often the 'responsiveness' of peasants was simply forced by stark necessity. One group of scholars holds that Asian peasants were rational in the economist's sense of purposefully attempting to maximize output from a given supply of inputs. Another group holds that to a significant extent their behaviour was constrained by an inherited 'moral economy' based on traditional values. Interpretation is difficult, because we cannot ask these people why they did what they did. In one sense all behaviour must be subject to a 'technical' rationality of physical necessity – if you do not plant the right crops, you will not earn enough money to feed your family. And yet, as seen both below and in Chapter 4, the 'purposeful' rationality of profit maximization may have been absent – families are not entrepreneurial firms, and an economy organized on family lines will not behave in the same way as one in which impersonal firms are the primary actors (Sen, 1983).

The debate over peasant rationality is not a debate over the accepted fact of dynamic social change in Asian societies, but over the sources and meaning of change. In particular, Western scholars have been concerned with the origins and extent of peasant unrest and rebellion, and frequently their concern has been to reinterpret or minimize unrest in order to refute Marxist interpretations of the course of Asian history. The debate has spread from Southeast Asian to Japanese history. In the case of China, Western historians contested the 'Maoist depiction of Chinese history as perennial class struggle' of 'an immiserated peasantry...ruthlessly exploited by a venal landlord class', and suggested instead that 'there were long periods of plenty when relatively affluent farmers benefited from rising agricultural prices, and negotiated rental contracts to their own liking with accommodating landlords' (Wakeman, 1977, p. 202).

There is one important respect in which many Asian peasants were ahead of their European counterparts. The 'agricultural revolution' which spread from the Low Countries to England beginning in the late seventeenth century, and then from England to Central Europe in the late eighteenth century, had two aspects, firstly the change from field rotation to crop rotation and secondly the use of increased amounts of labour. Rather than leaving one of three large fields fallow each year, food crops were alternated with legumes (nitrogen-fixing plants) and root crops to restore nutrients and aerate the soil. More intensive cropping required more labour for cultivation, weeding and drainage as well as for planting and harvesting, and the labour was provided by small-holders and wage labourers. The new system spread slowly, taking over a century to become dominant in England. Field rotation was still common in Eastern Europe in 1900.

Many regions of Asia had already experienced an agricultural revolution, sometimes centuries before Europe, with sophisticated systems of crop rotation, fertilization, and the intensive use of wage labour. One obvious difference was the size of farms in the most advanced areas, England compared to the Lower Yangzi in China or the Kinai in Japan for instance, which reflected the far greater pressure of population in Asia. Another crucial difference was the impact of the industrial revolution on European agriculture. The 'industrialization of agriculture' led to the introduction of labour saving machines for planting and harvesting in the 1830s, and to power tractors and chemical fertilizers in the 1880s and 1890s. Without the Industrial Revolution, European agriculture would have reached a barrier similar to the situation in Asia. What could have happened in Europe as a whole was seen in Ireland and Central Europe in the 1840s and in Southeastern Europe in the 1920s and 1930s – growth of population which resulted in a division of holdings and a process of involution with the threat of famine.

China

The peasants here get only three winter months' of food from their rice fields. After they pay off their rent, they hull the rest of the rice, put it in a bin, and turn it over to the pawnshop to redeem their clothing. In the early spring, the entire household spins and weaves in order to exchange cloth for rice, because the family no longer has any grain left. By the busy fifth month, they take their winter clothing and pawn it for rice ... In the fall, whenever it rains, the sound of the shuttle of the loom again fills all the villages, and [they] carry their cloth to trade for rice to eat. It is in this way that the peasants of our country, even in times of poor harvests, manage to eke out a living so long as the cotton ripens in other places.

Gazetteer of Wuxi county, 1752

China was not simply a 'rice' economy, for the only areas suitable for double-crop rice farming were in the south. But the further distinction of a northern 'wheat' economy and a central area of 'mixed' crops also did not do justice to the complexity and sophistication of the mix of crops and techniques available to Chinese peasants. The Guangzhong plain in the northwest and the Yellow River plains were areas of dry farming, with crop rotation systems of three crops over a two-year cycle. A spring crop of sorghum, millet, or maize could be planted in May/June and harvested in September/October. It could be followed by winter wheat, sown before the frost and harvested in the next July. By then it would be too late to sow spring crops so the wheat would usually be followed by a summer-sown crop such as soybeans which would be harvested in October/November. If weather conditions dictated, farmers could overlap the seasons by interplanting different crops in alternate rows – though this required large amounts of labour. Farming in the north remained difficult. Ge Shouli, a sixteenth-century commentator, said, 'land in the south... is irrigated and can yield two or three crops of several *shi* [a volume measure, here just under 100 kilograms or about 200 pounds in weight] each year. The land in the north, whether of medium or lower grade, is very different in value and in produce. Even the best land cannot be compared to the land in the south' (Huang, 1985, p. 59).

Crop rotation in the southern regions was not necessarily a double rice crop. In the Lower Yangzi region, early-ripening long-grain rice was not popular, and peasants planted it only as an emergency crop in drought periods until the 1960s, when the government forced its widespread use. The preferred second crop was winter wheat. Wheat prices were generally high, and since tenant farmers usually paid rent only on their fall harvest, this spring-harvested crop was a bonus. But wheat is a dry crop which does not flourish in the soggy soil of rice fields. So in the nineteenth century the peasants in the most densely populated rice-growing areas actually built up their fields after harvesting rice, planted wheat, harvested it, and then lowered the fields again before planting rice. In cotton-growing districts, the second crop was usually barley rather than wheat because it had a shorter growing season (Huang, 1985, 1990).

The magistrate reporting on conditions in Shandong province quoted above was reflecting, first, on the fact that the Chinese economy was a market economy, but he also knew that production of goods for the market was risky:

> Once confronted with natural disaster and bad harvests, they are at a complete loss... Nowadays there is sometimes drought in the spring. Confusion follows: the poor have no place to turn for loans; the rich are afraid of robbers, of litigation for the fair distribution of grain. The entire area is disturbed. (Huang, 1985, p. 114)

Chinese farms were very small, with high output per unit of land, but very low output per worker. Large farms were not more productive than small farms. The use of draft animals, for instance, could bring benefits, but involved high costs and increased risks. To maintain draft animals, a farmer would need to purchase feed, and holding draft animals also limited the amount of fertilizer produced ('The hog is the king of fertilizer production', as the village saying went). Finally, the farmer using draft animals would still need to hire human labour as well. In the 1930s, the daily wage of a labourer was about the same as the cost of maintaining a donkey for a day's use, and these low wage rates set upper limits to the use of draft animals (Huang, 1985, pp. 140, 147–8).

Cotton production in Shandong expanded during the peaceful decades following the establishment of the Qing regime. Cotton was very profitable, but required a heavy capital investment. For a peasant family, a failed cotton crop meant contracting a loan with their land as collateral, which could lead to the loss of the land and the beginning of the downward spiral to tenant or wage labourer. However, population growth increased the pressure to move to cash crops. Increasing commercialization therefore led to the spread of rent relations and wage labour and to a split between managerial and family farming. Although not more productive in terms of output per unit of input, large farms possessed an advantage over small farms, because they hired only as much labour as they required, while small farms were obliged to feed and employ all family members regardless of their productivity. The growth of an underemployed labour force led to the development of cotton cloth manufacture in the north in the late eighteenth and early nineteenth centuries, almost always household handicraft production on small farms where families had surplus labour compared to their land, and therefore more people to feed than could be maintained by farming alone. Cotton spinning and weaving developed in lowland areas with good water transportation, which stimulated the extension of cotton growing into new 'peripheral' areas (Huang, 1985, pp. 106–20).

Although managerial farming brought the best returns because the owners were able to regulate their labour costs, there was an upper limit of 200 *mu* (1 *mu* = one fifteenth of a hectare or one sixth of an acre) because of the difficulty of supervising hired workers on widely scattered parcels. Wealthy farmers would not hire foremen, because the expense would cut into the fine margin which large farms held over small ones, and because if the foreman were a wage worker, he would not be motivated to extract the same effort from the other workers as the owner. Renting land did not require supervision, and therefore if one were fortunate enough to acquire more land, then it was more efficient to rent it to small farmers. Landlords who leased land, leased it in small parcels which were no more efficient than small farms cultivated by their owners (Huang, 1985, pp. 72, 155–68, 172–7).

The resulting stratification was shown in surveys conducted in the 1920s and 1930s. The Guomindang Land Commission survey of Hebei and Shandong provinces in 1937 counted 391 170 farms, of which 4122 or just over 1 per cent were 100 *mu* or above. They covered just under 10 per cent of the area. Managerial rich farmers had 100–200 *mu* of land, they were located in relatively commercialized villages, and in the north they were more common than landlords. Other surveys showed that 10–12 per cent of the population worked as long-term agricultural labourers, and that 14–17 per cent of all labour was performed by wage workers. However, not only the minority of large farms employed wage labour, for around 12 per cent of households employed long-term labourers, and 36 per cent employed short-term workers. The risks were evident as well: in one village the rich farmers of the 1930s could recall the purchases which had extended their holdings above the middle levels, usually made with profits from cotton, but of nineteen households which were identified as having been rich in the 1890s, only three had rich descendants in 1930s. The typical reason for a family's decline was the traditional practice of division of property among all sons (Huang, 1985, pp. 78–80).

In the south a different pattern emerged. The Yangzi delta, with a warmer and more consistent climate than the North China plain, was already highly developed by the early sixteenth century. Since there was little chance for increased frequency of cropping, improvement had to come from switching to more profitable cash crops, especially silk (mulberries, worms, and reeling), and cotton (growing raw cotton, spinning, and weaving). The spread and increased commercialization of cash crops forced further commercialization of other crops, because of the accompanying regional specialization of production. Thus farmers could choose between rice and cotton, both of which were commercial crops. Rice prices showed high seasonal fluctuations, whereas cotton prices showed no seasonal pattern but could rise or fall drastically from one year to the next. Rice required less labour input, so the choice depended on the relative price of cotton being high enough to justify the risk. Sometimes ecological change dictated to the farmers; in the 1660s in Shanghai county, silting in the local rivers reduced water flow so rice could not be grown, the farmers switched to cotton and beans, and the district began to import its rice from other districts in the region (Huang, 1990, pp. 78–83; Bernhardt, 1992).

Phillip Huang argues that these changes meant increased family income and increased output per unit of land, but not increased output per workday. Production for distant markets, local markets, or the family's own consumption reflected the structural preconditions of 'involution', a process of development without subsequent industrialization. He argues further that markets were imperfect, that peasants exchanged for survival, not to maximize profit, and that those with power exploited their position to extract 'surplus' from their neighbours. He further disagrees with Smithians who argue that exchange is mutually beneficial, and leans toward the substantivist argument that village communities were tied together by bonds of kinship, gifts, reciprocity, and morality (Huang, 1985, pp. 23–4; 1990, pp. 102–14; see Geertz, 1963; Scott, 1976). In addition, restrictions on employment of girls and women outside the home inhibited the development of larger enterprises, both in agriculture and in industry (Goldstone, forthcoming).

On the other hand, there was no dualism between a small capitalist sector and a large feudal or semi-feudal economy. Rather, all regions and all classes in China were involved in market relationships, and changes in the cotton industry in particular had the effect of linking Chinese peasants to world markets via pre-existing market relations. European markets were also imperfect (Wong, 1992), but also as in Europe, certain groups and certain regions in China demonstrated a quite striking responsiveness. The merchants and industrialists of Shanghai have been particularly closely studied, but they were not alone (see Rowe, 1984). In the later nineteenth century Chinese enterprises were able to import new technologies, and large numbers of young women were recruited from rural areas to work in urban factories (see Thomas, 1984).

Japan

Immediately after the winter wheat is planted between the 10th month and the year's end, paper making begins, and continues through the winter until the harvest begins in the spring. After the new rice crop is planted and during the following months there are periodic weedings. Then, in the eighth month, paper making is started again and continues until the middle of the following month when it is time to commence the fall harvest . . .

Ôkura Eijô, early nineteenth century

In Tokugawa Japan it was illegal to buy and sell land. In theory this made Japan an exception to the rule that land was a commodity. However, in the late Tokugawa period the recorded complaints of villagers came to be directed against village headmen, and peasant uprisings took place against headmen and wealthy villagers. This differs from the early Tokugawa period, when most complaints were against Tokugawa government policies or local domain officials. The split opening up within village communities was between landowners and tenant farmers. Despite the official prohibition on land sales, land did change hands. Some merchants purchased agricultural land. More commonly, though, wealthy villagers lent money to poor farmers who offered their land as security. If they could not repay the loan, the land was forfeit, despite the law. By the end of the Tokugawa era the ratio of tenant farmers had reached 50 per cent in most of the highly commercialized districts close to urban centres (Hane, 1991, pp. 144–5, 195). Like the Chinese official quoted above, Ôkura Eijô recognized the operation of the market, the link with non-agricultural production, and also the risks involved. He continues,

> In recent years the prices [of raw materials] have so increased that paper cannot be made at a profit. The paper makers have suffered so that over half have been ruined, and as a result out of more than 265 *koku*'s worth of land [in this village] nearly half has fallen into the hands of merchants. (Smith, 1959, pp. 130–1)

One important social aspect of economic change was an alteration in the status of dependent workers. In the early Tokugawa period in most regions the typical relationship was hereditary servitude, but with the ameliorating aspect that the servants lived virtually as part of the employers' families. Over time, hereditary servitude was replaced by various forms of wage labour. The period of employment might be fixed from a few days to a period of years, and payment might be made in advance, at intervals during the period, or upon completion of the employment contract. In some districts there were regular labour markets, whereas in others the worker appears more as an indentured servant, bound to the employer in return for a loan. In one small village west of Ôsaka, where cotton growing was introduced in the late seventeenth and early eighteenth centuries, in 1659 the village registers recorded 31 hereditary servants and six wage labourers, and even these had employment periods of as long as ten years. In 1728 the village reported 43 wage labourers and no hereditary servants (Smith, 1959, pp. 109–10).

On the other hand, the rise of wage labour did not originally mean freedom for individual workers, for until the beginning of the nineteenth century the labour contracts were typically negotiated between the employer and the head of the worker's family. For example,

My son, Takezô, age 19, I hereby put in pawn for a money-secured-by-person loan from you. Takezô is to work for you for three full years, from the twelfth moon of this year to the twelfth moon of the Year of the Rabbit. If during this time he serves you well, it is agreed that 15 *kan* of the total debt of 35 *kan* will be cancelled. (Smith, 1959, p. 113)

Surviving contracts show that such workers were rarely under 20 years of age and might be as old as 35 or 40, and they included wives, younger brothers, sisters, aunts, grandchildren, and daughters-in-law as well as sons and daughters. Finally, in the early nineteenth century, farmers came to employ individual workers for a day or a season, in return for an agreed wage. Employers complained of a chronic labour shortage: ' "*hôkônin*" [wage labourers] have become exceedingly short, and wages (*kyûkin*) are consequently so high that . . . large holders have recently been unable to make a living from farming alone' (Smith, 1959, pp. 110–11).

Japanese Marxists have argued that the spread of commercialization and development of wage labour was evidence of the penetration of capitalist modes of production into the countryside. The resulting divisions within village communities then led to the contradictions of the Meiji period and eventually to the rise of militaristic fascism. However, rather than a simple split between capitalist landowners and proletarians, Japanese villages showed a gradation very similar to the Chinese villages studied by Philip Huang. The most common form of day labour, for instance, was provided by small-holders working part-time for other farmers. Within villages there could be a circulation of families over the generations similar to that seen in China, although the absence of mandatory division of inheritances may have helped keep wealthy Japanese families wealthy over longer periods.

Southeast Asia

Far from being a pre-monetary society operating with a commerce based upon simple exchange, Javanese peasant society was thoroughly enmeshed in and was an integral part of a wider money economy.

Robert Elson, 1994

The modernization theory approach, with its assumption of a static traditional society, retreated in the 1970s under sustained attack. Interestingly, one of the main alternatives to modernization theory, the 'moral economy' approach to peasant societies, also came under fire. In a widely discussed book published in 1976, James Scott argued that all peasant societies found themselves continually on the margin of subsistence, 'constrained by the vagaries of the weather and the claims of outsiders'. Peasant families therefore avoided any risks that would threaten their basic subsistence. Rather than attempting to maximize incomes for themselves or their families, they elected to pursue a 'moral economy' predicated on two principles 'firmly embedded in both the social patterns and injunctions of peasant life: the *norm of reciprocity* and the *right to subsistence*' (Scott, 1976, pp. 4, 167, emphasis in original). It followed that peasant politics and particularly peasant rebellions aimed to restore inherited traditional relationships.

Samuel Popkin insisted, however, that 'there are many occasions when peasants do have some surplus and do make risky investments'. He stressed the individual rationality of Vietnamese peasant decisions and investment strategies, and saw peasant rebellions in Vietnam as attempts to alter village institutions, reduce the power of local oligarchs, and tame the market economy, rather than to restore traditional values (Popkin, 1979, p. 18). Peasants could exploit the market. Around the Red River delta in Indochina, for instance, small-holding villages managed to resist complete pauperization, and thus to keep their traditional social base intact, by providing migrant labour for modern mines and plantations (Murray, 1980, ch. 9). More generally, virtually all peasant societies were required to hold back part of their annual produce for rent, as well as additional amounts for religious and ceremonial purposes, and accumulated further reserves for investment, for instance in cattle or water buffalo in Siam or Burma, or for the education of a child to prepare him for a career in the bureaucracy in Vietnam or China. Therefore the assumption on which Scott's argument rested, that peasants possessed no surplus, could not be sustained, and neither could his assertions about peasant behaviour or motivation (see Keyes, 1983, pp. 756–7).

Among Southeast Asian specialists the effects of the Vietnam War can be seen in the background of the debate over peasant rationality, but as in the case of Chinese, Korean and Japanese specialists, the crucial sources of change are seen *within* the Asian society, not coming from outside. Thus the decline of independent farmers in Vietnam in the late eighteenth century, Burmese and Thai organization for warfare, and the Cambodian disaster of the 1840s, may be seen as the last of the internally generated 'traditional' cycles, not responses to the West. Similarly in the Philippines, the crucial social processes remained outside the range of colonial government policy. In the late eighteenth century the Church began to grant concessions to individuals to clear and improve its land in return for rental in the form of a specified amount of crops. These entrepreneurs in turn sublet the cleared land to sharecroppers in return for a share of the yield. However, since the sharecroppers bore the risk of harvest fluctuations, they tended to fall into debt, and were forced to surrender more and more of their crop to their employers, descending over time to the status of landless labourers. The resulting stratified social structure, population pressure, and expansion into uncleared areas created a dynamic frontier and a search for market crops.

The cultivation system introduced in Java by the Dutch in the early 1830s is particularly contentious. The Dutch colonial state worked through the indigenous Javanese power structure to mobilize the labour of peasants to produce crops for export. This coerced labour, pressed into service by inherited claims of overlordship and new claims backed by force, was employed to grow coffee, sugar, or indigo. Clifford Geertz argued that by 'freezing' Javanese villages into its traditional pattern, the cultivation system was to blame for Java's structural backwardness. Geertz's analysis became the basis of the 'involution argument', which has been influential both in Southeast Asian studies and beyond, notably in Philip Huang's studies of Chinese development. In his classic statement of the involution argument, Geertz argued that in Javanese rice farming, population pressure on family farms led to a decline in the marginal product of labour to zero or negative levels (Geertz, 1963). However, R. E. Elson argues that the cultivation system did not 'freeze' village structures as Geertz thought, but had a large impact on peasant life, work practices, and relations between peasants and local lords. The increase in the power of village chiefs resulted in the creation of a much more complex mode of labour organization. The new system made heavy demands on workers and resulted in obvious exploitation, but on balance the villagers made better use of resources available to them and more than held their own in respect to per capita food production. Elson agrees that substantial benefits flowed to the Netherlands treasury, but insists that the system was not merely evil and exploitative; rather, it changed village structures beyond recognition, and those changes were essentially progressive. The system opened Java to the outside world, stimulated commodity production, and brought greater prosperity to the peasants (Elson, 1984, 1994).

Protoindustrialization

The link between expanded artisan production and population growth which Franklin Mendels discovered and labelled 'protoindustrialization: the first phase of the industrialization process' (Mendels, 1972) seemed to provide answers to many of our questions about the origins of industrialization. In the impoverished upland areas of Europe, young couples might seize the opportunity to produce handicraft goods for export, to marry, to eke out their existence with a small plot of agricultural land, and to have children who could help in both the artisan and agricultural enterprises. Population increased, but the skills of the labour force could be transferred to an emerging factory system. The initial burst of studies showed that all industrial nations contained protoindustrial regions, that certain proto-industrial districts had been centres of early industrial development, and that under certain circumstances an inherited protoindustrial tradition might contribute to industrial development in a later generation. Neo-Marxists adopted the concept as defining the means by which capitalist relations of production had penetrated previously isolated traditional communities (Kriedte et al., 1981).

However, regional studies have since shown that in Europe protoindustrialization has not typically proven to be the 'first phase' of industrialization. What we can observe from regional histories across Europe from the late medieval period until the twentieth century, is that in both agriculture and industry, periodic phases of expansion and contraction resulted as agents responded to opportunities from outside the region. In particular in all regional histories there are indeed repeated phases of protoindustrialization, defined as the production of handicraft manufactured goods for export. Rather than providing the springboard to further growth, development, and industrialization, however, the more typical pattern is a dramatic expansion of an industry, followed by decline and hardship. It is important that there has been no single reason for industrial decline. A drop in exports could result from the exhaustion of raw materials or environmental degradation, consumer goods were subject to abrupt changes in fashion, competition from other regions with cheaper labour or higher quality raw materials was always a threat, and there loomed the possibility of political interference with the conditions of trade (Ogilvie, 1993; Ogilvie and Markus, 1996).

Protoindustrialization was widespread in Asia. The responses of peasants and artisans resulted in periodic increases and declines in the production of agricultural and handicraft products in the histories of all regions. As in Europe, these changes in market conditions could have social consequences, particularly on the rate of family formation. What is of interest are the conditions under which industrial production could expand substantially without increases in the scale of producing units, whether this process led to population increase and/or impoverishment, or whether it led to a region becoming the later site of large-scale industry. Asian specialists have tended to be pessimistic. Huang assumes that there was some point before which capitalism did not exist, and that it was capitalism which then led to industrialization in Europe. In China, involutionary development led to 'semiproletarianization', which was not a stage but an end result of differentiation, and would not lead to progressive 'capitalist' development (Huang, 1985, p. 17). Protoindustrial development did not always lead to industrial development, either in Asia or in Europe. Even so, although nothing is ever certain in history, we can say that once industrial technologies were available, both Asians and Europeans used existing market networks to seize the new opportunities if they could.

China

The women work especially hard. During the silkworm feeding period ... they must get up six or seven times a night. Mulberry leaves with morning dew are especially good for the silkworms; the women therefore pick the leaves early in the morning, with no time to comb their hair or wash their faces. The leaves cannot stand fog; on cloudy days, therefore, they pick the leaves at night. The leaves cannot stand sand and dust ... or heat ... They must be spread evenly on the straw trays ... As for the men, they are faced with the start of the busy farmwork season and cannot attend much to the silkworms. Thus from beginning to end, the women account for 90 per cent of the work.

Huzhou prefectural gazetteer, 1874

Raising silkworms and harvesting cocoons cannot be done with two empty hands. All the implements, feed, and living expenses come from loans and credit.

Shimen county gazetteer, 1673

Following Mao and subsequent Chinese Marxist scholars, a common argument holds that the destruction of indigenous Chinese handicrafts by western and Japanese competition in the late nineteenth and early twentieth centuries destroyed the basis for industrialization. The destruction of native handicrafts emphasized by the 'Bielefeld school' and others may be viewed as an important determinant in the timing and rate of growth (Hartmann, 1981). In contrast, in the case of the Chinese silk industry, Li argues that the organizational forms which developed were not 'capitalist sprouts', but rather resembled earlier forms of government-sponsored putting-out industry, and that in particular they did not resemble the British model which evolved into industrial capitalism (Li, 1981). Both the level of development attained by 1911 and the rate of population growth are topics of current debate, partly because of their political significance, but building on the tradition of protoindustrial development, China had begun to develop a modern industrial sector by the beginning of the twentieth century. The evidence thus seems to favour those who believe there was substantial growth in both aggregate and per capita terms before 1911.

Growth has a long history. Huang's outline of developments in the Yangzi delta is an outstanding example. Cotton spinning and weaving was introduced in the late thirteenth century. The standard bolt or *pi* was 1.4 feet wide by 23.3 feet long and weighed 1.32 standard catties or about four fifths of a kilogram. In the 1830s exports averaged 40 million bolts – Songjiang prefecture exported 15 million bolts to the northeast and Beijing, 10 million to Guangdong, and 1 million to Fujian, as well as another 10 million through Changshu and 3 million through Wuxi. Each bolt of cotton required about 7 workdays to produce: 2 for fluffing and sizing the cotton, 3.6 to 4 for spinning, and 1 for weaving. That implies 280 million workdays, or some 120 workdays per year for each of the 2.4 million households in the region in 1816. Silk production centred in Suzhou prefecture east and south of Lake Tai. The demand of the expanding commercial classes led to the development of more durable and cheaper varieties of silk cloth. Raising mulberries, raising silkworms, and reeling silk remained peasant occupations, but spinning and weaving became specialized occupations of workers in workshops in towns. In the late eighteenth century there were 20 000 silk looms in the Suzhou area. The workshops were small – in Suzhou city in 1913 the average weaving workshop had 1.5 looms and 7.7 employees. The growth of the cotton and silk industries transformed the area from a grain surplus area to a deficit area. The Yangzi delta imported 15 million *shi* (close to 200 000 metric tons) of rice via the Yangzi River from Sichuan, Hunan, Anhui, and Jiangxi, and 10 million *shi* of wheat and soybeans from the northeast via coastal shipping to Shanghai (Huang, 1990, pp. 44–8).

Production and trade were both financed by sophisticated credit arrangements. In the early seventeenth century a magistrate in the lower Yangzi region noted that 'raising silkworms and harvesting cocoons cannot be done with two empty hands', that is, peasants must raise capital before beginning silk production. Farm families combined subsistence farming, cash crop production, and handicraft production, and they moved from one to another through the use of credit. They 'obtained capital on the rural credit market to invest in production . . . many so-called consumption credits were, in fact, an integral part of the production process' (Pan, 1996, pp. 95, 102–3). The individuals and firms which provided them with credit and supplies, and others which marketed their output, used native techniques of calculation which demonstrate equally systematic and rational approaches to their enterprise. The Chinese numerical system did not preclude rational calculation, the use of the abacus did not hinder tabular reckoning, and nineteenth-century textbooks show solutions to problems such as calculation of exchange rates or distribution of profits very similar to European methods. In fact, late Ming early Qing Chinese businessmen also developed an indigenous double entry system, but as in the case of Western businesses, it was not always necessary and therefore was not always employed (Gardella, 1992).

As with Chinese history generally, one line running through the story of protoindustrial development is the systematic exploitation of women. The key difference between north and south China seems to be one of gender. Dry farming work was done almost exclusively by men, so in the dry farming areas of the north, families did not mobilize women to the same extent as in the rice and silk areas of the south. In the south, where women were mobilized exclusively by their own families, their low cost meant that managerial farming that depended on hired male labour could not compete. Increased commercialization led to greater involvement of family members in production. In north China women watched over the irrigation ditches while men operated the pumps from wells. Close to towns women and children helped with vegetable farming, for instance transplanting cabbage plants. Cotton required large amounts of labour for harvesting, but since it was spread over a fairly long period it was defined as 'light' work and therefore became 'women's work'. Indoors, women provided most of the labour for spinning and weaving cotton.

In the Yangzi delta women did not assist with rice farming in the 1930s and 1940s, except for helping pull shoots at transplanting and sometimes with threshing. Rich and middle-class peasant women did almost no work in the fields. Huang suggests that footbinding may have contributed to prejudice, because of the need to remove shoes to plant rice in paddies (Huang, 1990, pp. 55–6). But their bound feet did not prevent women from being employed in other heavy work, if there was sufficient demand for it. Crop rotation required more labour. Both wheat and barley increased the use of family members in production, as did cotton, where women worked both in harvesting and in cloth production as in the north. And silk production, especially when combined with double-cropping of rice and winter wheat, loaded women with responsibility for feeding the worms and reeling the cocoons. Silkworms feed over a 28–day period in the spring, and the intensity of labour rises rapidly as the worms grow and require more and more mulberry leaves. The trays weighed 30 to 40 catties (15 to 20 kilograms), and the worms on each sheet consumed 200 catties of leaves per day (Huang, 1990, p. 51–5).

On balance, both female employment and the wages of male workers were high in the Yangzi delta compared to north China. Living standards were higher in the south, and men enjoyed the possibility of other employment in towns. Hired workers had to be supplied with wine every day, and meat every other day, whereas workers in the north were given wine and meat only at seasonal feasts at the beginning and end of the season. Surplus male labour from the family farm sector supplied labour to managerial farms in the north. In the south a two-tiered structure of labour appeared, with women and children supplying what would have been lower-paying work, but only to their own family households. This may have reflected their productivity; women were considered to be worth less than the cost of their board, so that a worker who hired out with his wife was paid less than a single male worker. But in addition there was an active prejudice against wage work and especially against women working for wages. 'It was bad enough for a man to have to hire out himself; for his wife or daughter to do so marked him as being at the bottom of the social ladder.' It was very difficult for wealthier farmers to hire women for low wages, but women did supply labour on small family farms, in addition to textile and other industrial production. Survey results showed women performed 19.1 per cent of all farm work, but only 6.3 per cent of all hired labour (Huang, 1990, pp. 63–70).

The pressure of competition is evident. By the early eighteenth century returns from cotton spinning would not buy enough rice to support an adult, so spinners were in fact mainly children and the elderly. For a peasant household which had to feed all of its members in any case, the only relevant consideration was the cost of raw materials and tools; any return above this was worthwhile. Weaving in contrast returned enough to purchase about twice as much rice' as an adult needed to survive, which made it barely acceptable for an adult male and desirable for an adult female, but still barely adequate and providing no chance of savings accumulation and advance (Huang, 1990, pp. 84–5).

Japan

The first great market of the year in Fukushima opens on the 14th of the sixth month. During the night of the 13th peasants gather with their silk from a distance of many miles around and wait for the market to open at dawn. Buying and selling begins on the 14th and continues for two watches. During this time, about one hundred horseloads of silk amounting to 3,600 *kan* weight are sold for fifteen or sixteen thousand *ryô*... The sellers, who number several thousand, have their silk examined for quality and weighed and are paid accordingly. Nowhere in the country is there a market where so much money changes hands as here.

Local gazetteer, 1818

The discovery of protoindustrial development in Japan was an important part of the reinterpretation of Tokugawa economic development which took place in the 1960s and 1970s. The textile trade in particular passed through an evolution which strongly resembled European patterns (Houser, 1974). Almost as soon as it was developed by European historians, Japanese scholars adopted the concept to make explicit comparisons between Japanese and European growth in the period immediately preceding industrialization (Saitô, 1983). At the time, this seemed to point the way towards an explanation of Japan's success in becoming the only non-Western industrial nation. And yet, it is now less clear how significant this is for Japan, firstly since modern economic growth has now obviously spread elsewhere in Asia, and secondly since there now appear to have been periodic phases of protoindustrial development both in Europe and in Asia which did not lead to development in this sense. Current claims are more modest; although rural industry certainly provided a window of opportunity for emergent capitalism in Japan, there does not seem to be any firm linkage with demographic developments, nor does protoindustrial development seem to represent a distinct stage in the movement from pre-capitalist to capitalist forms of economic organization (Howell, 1992).

The patterns traced in Thomas Smith's classic study of agrarian development in Japan resemble those which emerge from Huang's studies of north and south China. In Japan, Smith argues, the 'triumph' of the small farm over the large farm was based on the ability of the family unit to take advantage of the opportunities to supplement farm income with earnings from handicraft production. Commentators complained of the waste of labour during the slack seasons on both large and small farms in the early Tokugawa period. With the rise in demand for artisan products, however, small family farms were better able to extract additional labour to produce them. All the income produced by family members belonged to the family. Large farmers were at a disadvantage, because they did not control the individual earnings of wage labourers to the same degree as a family. Long-term contracts obligated employers to hold workers. In addition (and in contrast to Huang), Smith argues that large farmers could not throw workers off in the slack season, because the shortage of labour meant they might not get them back when they needed them. Further, large farmers could not employ these workers profitably in handicrafts, because there were no scale economies and, Smith argues, the necessary 'tradition of skill' could be developed in a family setting but not among the ten or twelve changing workers the large farmer might employ (Smith, 1959, pp. 129–30).

Southeast Asia

> During the spring months there are always more sales than during the latter part of the year, owing to the natives generally wearing new clothes at the Siamese and Chinese New Year Holidays.
>
> British Foreign Office Report, 1862

Southeast Asian scholars are also turning their attention to protoindustrial development. Written records for earlier periods are often sparse, so the analysis often rests on backward extrapolation, but the results reinforce the new view of extensive specialized production for markets. There is evidence of a general expansion of commercial non-agricultural production in Java during the middle decades of the nineteenth century, that is precisely during the period of the cultivation system, when the Dutch authorities were forcing the production of agricultural crops for export (Fernando, 1993). Irene Nørland's study of textile production in Nam Dinh province in the Tonkin Delta of northern Vietnam in the years around 1900 shows a rapid development of both handicraft and industrial production, and even more significantly an extensive interaction of the two modes of organization. The industry clearly built on earlier traditions. Its continued development was contrary to the intentions of the French colonial government, which wanted to reserve the Vietnamese market for French manufactured products and did not support local industrial development. The pattern of development also refutes stage theories and dependency theories of development. Nørland argues that in this instance handicraft production was not merely a stage of development to be super-seded, and small producers were not simply ruined by competition from cheaper industrial goods from the metropoles (Nørland, 1991).

Katherine Bowie's study of the cotton industry in northern Thailand is an outstanding Southeast Asian example of specialized handicraft produc-tion integrated into a sophisticated market framework. Based both on archival evidence and interviews conducted with elderly villagers in the early 1980s, the results demonstrate that the production of cotton textiles was divided among households, villages, and regions at each stage. Cotton was grown in upland regions; villages in the fertile irrigated lowlands planted rice, tobacco, and a variety of other cash crops. Villages in the lowlands traded with the upland villages, exchanging both agricultural produce and specialized finished goods such as mosquito nets. Although some upland cotton-growing villages also produced woven cloth, many did not. In the manufacturing villages, carding, spinning, weaving, dyeing and sewing all were specialized occupations. Spinning was a specialized occu-pation, because of the skill required to produce a consistent, fine, continu-ous thread. Spinners might produce thread for their own weaving needs, for sale to others, or on contract, in which case they typically received half the spun thread as payment. Similarly, weavers sometimes wove their own thread, sometimes purchased thread, and sometimes wove thread for others. The cloth they produced might be for the use of their own family, for sale on their own account, or to be sold by their employer. Dyeing was more specialized still, with certain villages known as dyeing centres and some itinerant dyers moving regularly through the weaving villages. Finally, sewing too was a specialized occupation, a skill sought out by those with finished cloth to be made up into clothes.

Distribution of finished cloth and clothing took place through trading networks. At the local level, both women and men sold cloth, though men travelled greater distances. Peddlers could sell their own cloth, they might take cloth on credit and repay the owner after the cloth had been sold, or they might be hired by large manufacturers to market the cloth or to transport it to wholesale dealers in other districts. Porters could be hired by the day or according to the weight carried, and might be engaged for as long as two months on a single trip – shippers preferred human porters over oxen, because they did not have to rest in the heat of the afternoon sun. Itinerant peddlers travelled regular circuits, and in addition there were more permanent sellers in local markets and district towns.

Bowie also notes the existence of some surprisingly large producers, mostly located along the navigable waterways. One villager recalled his father purchasing lots of 2000 to 3000 kilos of cotton and transporting the finished goods downriver by raft. Pak Pong, on the Ping River, had three or four cloth-weaving factories, each with 20 to 30 full-time weavers in the factory itself and hundreds of weavers employed on a part-time piecework basis in the surrounding villages. These large producers had connections via their merchant contacts with markets in Bangkok, Burma, Laos, and southern China (Bowie, 1992; see also Hong, 1984; Hewison, 1989).

Entrepreneurship

There have always been entrepreneurs in Asia. But did Asian societies allow scope for all possible entrepreneurial activity? Were some groups more entrepreneurial than others? The question of minority and especially Chinese entrepreneurship takes on particular relevance in Southeast Asian development, where minority ethnic groups and especially the Chinese repeatedly appear as the source of apparently disproportionate amounts of entrepreneurial expertise (McVey, 1992). However, the traditional 'Confucian' firm of China – authoritarian, family-centred, cautiously conservative, and inefficient – has been blamed for retarding China's growth. Chinese family firms relied on the marketplace to handle their 'transaction costs': they hired brokers to provide market information, paid middlemen to arrange contracts and underwrite them, and joined and paid fees to guilds to control quality. They did not develop the capability to handle these costs within the firm. Even large Chinese enterprises such as manufacturing firms or banks in the treaty ports were still individually or family-owned. They generally did not expand into other markets by establishing separate divisions with impersonal, bureaucratic teams of managers. Instead, successful families diversified their investments in their own home city or region by purchasing urban property, shares in other companies, and government bonds, or by investing as silent partners in other businesses (Myers, 1989).

Outside of China, it seems Chinese entrepreneurs may have behaved differently. It has been argued that even though in China merchant families made use of their wealth to gain imperial honour, rank, and gentry status, nevertheless among emigrant Chinese families throughout Southeast Asia wealth became an end in itself. The primary goal for many emigrant Chinese was to be 'sojourners' making as much money in as short a time as possible (Godley, 1981). But many Chinese stayed, to become 'settlers'. Many never attained wealth, but some did, and their importance has remained to the present (Reid, 1996; EAAU, 1995).

Was there such a difference between the Chinese in China and the Chinese overseas? In defence of the 'traditional' Confucian firm, it must be remembered that there is conflicting evidence from China itself. Some areas such as the silk industry show the concentration of China's routine managers on short-term profits at the expense of industry-wide improvements which would have permitted them to compete more effectively with the Japanese (Li, 1981), but other areas such as the merchant communities of Hankow (Hangzhou) (Rowe, 1984) and Shanghai (Bergère, 1989) were outward-looking, certainly capitalist, and broadly entrepreneurial in their response to new opportunities. Further, the convulsions of Chinese history meant that any prudent manager would place a premium on the safety of the firm's assets and on personal or family control. Firms such as these did not become corporations with outside shareholders, bureaucratized management, or multiple divisional structures. Such complex, regulated corporate forms require trust, both that government will provide a stable environment for firms, and, on the side of government, that firms will obey the law and pay their share of taxes. Neither the late Qing nor the Nationalist governments provided this sort of environment. Suspicion of government inhibited expansion above the size of a single family's assets, and may explain the preference for dealing through intermediaries rather than establishing new branches and separate divisions. This was the tradition Chinese migrants took to Southeast Asia, and it must also be remembered that these forms of organization have been successful in Taiwan, Hong Kong, and most recently in Guangdong and Fujian. Families and lineages can resemble corporations, as can local governments in contemporary China (Kirby, 1995).

Another point to remember is that Chinese firms in Southeast Asia were not always successful, and that some of the failures resulted from traditional Confucian management practices. The death of a businessman often resulted in an inheritance battle, and the firm's holdings often did not survive. Here the tradition of division of inheritance may have conflicted with the needs of the firm as such. For many Chinese, 'capital was a tool of circulation rather than for accumulation... Chinese merchants often used investments to maintain their links with merchant networks and not necessarily to maintain profits' (Brown, 1994, pp. 255–6). Chinese banks were often simply cash-cows for their owners, and expansion was often based on poorly secured loans. Above all, accounting methods were primitive, and business interests overlapped and sometimes conflicted with personal and family concerns. For example Tan Kah Kee failed in 1932, less because of the depression and low rubber prices than because he had 'no proper system of book-keeping... no depreciation reserves or fire insurance... property and land assets were not continually revalued... expansion was thus spurred on by a capital surplus rather than simply by market opportunities and market discipline'. He had been able to borrow heavily, but he diverted funds from his businesses to philanthropic and political interests, and lost some to fraud (Brown, 1994, p. 107).

Overseas Chinese shared characteristics with migrant communities across the world. Self-selected, migrants tend to be energetic and flexible. They often possess resources, not only capital but training and a circle of relatives, friends, and acquaintances with whom they share their 'ethnic' identity. This leads first to trust in business relations, and secondly to possible ostracism if that trust is violated. Ease of communication, a broad circle of contacts, and the assurance that obligations will be honoured create conditions for successful business activities. This is as true of Irish business firms in Boston as it is of Chinese business firms in Jakarta, but it is particularly the case 'where economic and legal institutions are either embryonic or not fully effective'. In such conditions transactions costs are high, and those who can minimize their costs will have an advantage. 'Successful ethnic Chinese businesses minimize transactions costs. This it achieved in the first instance by choosing primarily to do business with one another' (EAAU, 1995, p. 123).

A further point is that successful minority entrepreneurs often depended on patrons within the local elite or the favour of colonial authorities – that is, their success did not depend on their inherited values or even on their individual talents, but on their connections to powerful friends. Chinese frequently inserted themselves as middlemen between Westerners and 'natives'. The British in Malaya and the Dutch in Indonesia, although they more or less actively discriminated against the Chinese, nevertheless left them broadly free to trade with the indigenous populations. Their success in this competition can be attributed to their resources and contacts among themselves and overseas. In addition the colonial authorities tended to regard the Chinese as a 'merchant race', to whom that portion of commerce and industry which Westerners did not themselves want could be left. During the colonial period in the Philippines,

> Spain did not intend to form, or succeed in creating, a class of native entrepreneurs... The Spaniards monopolized existing trade, setting a pattern for the mingling of political and economic power that has characterized Philippine government to the present. The internal trade that Spain did not control was left largely to the Chinese and their mestizo descendants. The *indios* had only their labour to offer.
> (Larkin, 1982, p. 606)

And, in the most cynical terms, the hostility of the indigenous populations towards the Chinese meant that it was unlikely that wealthy Chinese would ever become a political threat, whereas if Malays, Javanese, or Filipinos acquired industrial and commercial interests, they might become dangerous.

Immigrant Chinese played a particularly important role in the early development of Thailand (Hong, 1984). By 1855 there were 200 000 Chinese already living in Siam. Their numbers continued to increase through the nineteenth century, and they dominated the rubber, spice, and tin industries. Discriminated against during the interwar period, the Chinese community further increased following the Communist victory in China, and has continued to play an important role in the economy. A high rate of intermarriage and assimilation has blurred the edges of ethnic identification, and the Sino-Thai elite has even been seen as merging with the Thai army and bureaucracy into a 'bureaucratic capitalist class' (Suehiro, 1989, p. 138). However, all minority entrepreneurs have depended on the favour of elite patrons. In the late nineteenth century A. E. Nana, a Bengali Muslim with British citizenship, traded in opium, rice, and sugar, and then moved to property development in Bangkok. His connections within the Thai aristocracy allowed him to acquire land in central Thailand, from which he evicted the local farmers, many of whom held legal title to the land in question (Brown, 1994). As noted above,

Khaw Soo Cheang and his descendants not only acquired land, trade, coastal shipping, and tin mining interests, but also collected taxes for the Thai government at the fringes of Thai power on the Malay peninsula (Cushman, 1991). This continues to the present, with apparently fully assimilated wealthy Sino-Thai families cultivating their connections with politically influential 'ethnic' Thais in order to smooth the path of their business operations – the eldest son of the Chirathivat family, which controls the Central Group, recently married a niece of the queen, for instance (EAAU, 1995, pp. 74–6).

And finally, although entrepreneurs are often identified as Chinese, this is not usually the way they have seen themselves. The backgrounds and the experience of the 'Chinese' migrants to Southeast Asia varied (see Reid, 1996). The Chinese immigrants to Malaysia, for instance, though they were virtually all han Chinese, came from different regions with different spoken languages, not mutually intelligible. They established organizations (*pang*) based on their regional and linguistic identifications, which among other functions maintained separate burial grounds for their members. They saw themselves not only as distinct but also as rivals with each other, and their rivalry could become violent. A riot in Penang in 1867 involved 35 000 people and lasted for ten days. These groups were 'rigidly divided' by economic competition, and by the fact that China itself was not a single nation. The leaders of these competing Chinese communities in Malaya 'did not foresee a homogeneous Chinese society with one dialect, nor did they see the need for such a society' (Yen, 1986, p. 179; Lubeck, 1992, pp. 185–7).

4

ASIAN ELITES IN The ECONOMY
AND IN POLITICS

Moving up the social scale from peasants and artisans, this chapter examines the role of elite groups in Asian societies, their relationship to the state, their response to economic opportunities, and their contacts with the West. Much of the history of state activity and of elite behaviour makes depressing reading, but it needs to be kept in mind that development means change, that change is uncomfortable, and that change threatens existing interests. Elite groups by definition are the existing interests in any society. Therefore elites do not support change or development which does not serve their own interests. Further, their own interests can be very narrowly defined, focused on themselves personally, their families, their friends, other members of their own class, members of their religious, ethnic, or regional community – and only lastly on an abstract notion of the general good, or on the overall development of the economy.

But 'progressive' elements also often behave in ways which restrict development. Those farmers, artisans, or merchants who become wealthy seem to aspire, not to continued development, but to membership in the elite. Further, there seems no particular virtue inherent in such individuals, no matter how progressive their economic activities may be. Joseph Schumpeter, the foremost theorist of entrepreneurial behaviour, insisted that entrepreneurs are not virtuous or motivated by a desire to contribute to the common good, but are marked only by 'a certain narrowness which seizes the immediate chance and *nothing else*' (Schumpeter, 1934, p. 89, emphasis in original). Adam Smith worried that self-interest was continually threatening to win out over 'prudence'. Although markets require an ongoing fair-minded cooperation to function properly, Smith recognized that if given the opportunity, participants will attempt to gain an unfair advantage, and indeed if any three merchants sit together, they are probably plotting against the public interest.

In the terminology of contemporary economists, 'rent' is income obtained in excess of one's marginal product, usually through 'non-economic' means, and 'rent-seeking' is activity intended to secure this 'excess' income. Rent-seeking activity encompasses a broad range, from invasion and conquest, to extortion and bribery, through discriminatory legislation, to asking favours from a friend in the business. Eric Jones (1993) argues that rent-seeking coalitions continually form to extract surplus from the economy, and that the economic growth which we observe in history is in fact the net result of the struggle between productive activity and rent-seeking behaviour. The activities of rent-seeking coalitions continually work to offset the gains to the economy resulting from the efforts of those striving for material betterment. Jones goes too far in asserting that all examples of intensive growth have been essentially the same; the industrial era is unique. However, rent-seeking definitely hampers development, by diverting resources away from their most productive use. In the specific historical situation of the late nineteenth and early twentieth centuries, rent-seeking could prevent mobilization of resources and inhibit the adoption of industrial technologies at precisely the moment when the deadly threat from already-industrialized powers was at its peak.

In addition, values are important to development. As argued in Chapter 3, the hardworking farmers, artisans, and merchants of East and Southeast Asia behaved in ways which we recognize as 'modern' – open to change, responsive to economic opportunity, mobile, and flexible. The values which we call 'traditional' or 'pre-modern' were not those of the majority of the population; rather, they were the values held by the elites, adopted to justify and maintain their status. In addition, they were the values embedded in state structures, and as Jones says, 'the political context is and was crucial' (Jones, 1993, p. 129).

The role of native elites in development also raises the question of continuities between pre-modern and modern elite groups. The contrasts among the *samurai* bureaucrats of Meiji-era Japan, the scholar officials of late Qing China, and the variety of groups in Southeast Asia, suggest patterns which have persisted to the present. Intellectual and institutional rigidities prevented the Chinese elite from responding effectively to the double challenge posed by internal development and the intrusion of the West. In Japan many of the same rigidities operated as well, but as will be seen in Chapter 5 they did not have the same effect. The result was an apparently paradoxical combination of traditionalism and openness to change. In Southeast Asia the extension of effective Western control drastically reduced the number of formal centres of authority and severely restricted the formal role of native elites. Nevertheless, despite the extension and development of the colonial states, traditional groups continued to exercise substantial influence under the colonial regimes and, as we will see in Chapters 6 and 7, they often provided the leadership for new nationalist independence movements. Similar continuities can be seen in the Chinese case, and together, the more recent work on the histories of elite responses in Southeast Asia and China suggests that Japan's experience may not have been so unusual or paradoxical as it appeared to earlier observers.

The Role of the State

The history of the modern state is bound up with the histories of taxation and the development of markets. If taxes are collected in money, then taxpayers must sell their products to raise money to pay taxes. This can lead to a contradiction, because the markets in which producers sell their goods operate on principles different from those professed by the elite which controls the state. In Europe, two patterns have been identified:

> [On the one hand] the attempt to extract money from relatively uncommercialized agriculture depended on driving producers into markets, and tended to produce both bulky tax-collecting apparatuses, extensive involvement of tax farmers and other middlemen, and political understandings in which landlords received considerable autonomy, power, and/or fiscal exemption in return for their collaboration in squeezing the peasantry... [On the other hand] where cities, bourgeois, and commercialized production throve... merchants and financiers tended to accumulate great political strength, and to block royal bids for absolute power. (Tilly, 1991, p. 664)

In the first case, central authority could be undermined by the power of regional aristocracies, and in the second by the power of urban communities.

The European experience may at first seem only tangentially relevant to East and Southeast Asia. In Asia, states, taxation systems, commercialized agriculture, cities, and merchants had all existed for centuries.

Nevertheless, the progressive operation of markets outlined in Chapter 3 did work to restructure social groups in ways which would not fit into existing definitions, and the resulting tensions undermined central authority and contributed to the internal crises examined in Chapter 2. In this Asia and Europe show similar, recurrent patterns of economic growth and development followed by periods of crisis and collapse. Throughout the pre-industrial period, the role and strength of Jones' rent-seeking coalitions determined the potential for intensive growth. Then, in the industrial period, they significantly affected the ease and rapidity with which new technologies could be introduced.

Understanding the impact of elite behaviour requires an examination of the structure of the state and its rule-making activities. Whether the state worked to secure property rights, its role with respect to ownership and use of land, and its degree of tolerance for market relationships, all influenced the responsiveness of the economy. So too did the state's fiscal activities – not only the weight and incidence of taxation, but also its willingness and ability to deliver services in return for taxes. The state – government of any sort – serves elite interests. However, the state also exists in tension with elite groups. Their private interests can conflict, not only with an abstract public interest, but also with the interests of those directly involved in state administration. The conflict can be embodied in a single individual, for public officials often have powers which can be used for personal enrichment, for the benefit of members of their own class, to increase their own personal power, to increase the power of all government officials, or for 'reasons of state' which may serve none of these interests directly.

China

Po Kuei said, 'I should like to fix the rate of taxation at one in twenty. What do you think of it?'

'Your way', said Mencius, 'is that of the Northern barbarians. In a city of ten thousand households, would it be enough to have a single potter?'

'No. There will be a shortage of earthenware.'

'In the land of the Northern barbarians, the five grains do not grow. Millet is the only crop that grows. They are without city walls, houses,

ancestral temples or the sacrificial rites. They do not have diplomacy
with its attendant gifts and banquets, nor have they the numerous
offices and officials. That is why they can manage on a tax of one in
twenty. Now in the Central Kingdoms, how can human relationships
and men in authority be abolished? The affairs of a city cannot be
conducted when there is a shortage even of potters. How much more so
if the shortage is of men in authority?'

Mencius, VI, B, 10

There was one obvious difference between China and Europe – the existence of the single Chinese state. A more subtle difference, however, was the
coordinated interdependence of government and markets. As we have seen
in Chapter 3, local and regional markets had been operating in China for
2000 years, and Chinese farmers since the beginning of the Christian era
had regularly combined agricultural with handicraft production, received a
large fraction of their income from non-food products, and exchanged
much of their total output directly for money. This was true of medieval
and early modern Europe as well. In China, however, farmers, artisans, and
merchants usually operated under the supervision of representatives of a
single, centralized government. Until the end of the nineteenth century,
their transactions took place under the watchful eyes of local officials, the
district magistrate or his designate, whose responsibility for maintaining
public order included supervision of markets – the frequency of market
days, quality guarantees, price regulations, control of merchant guilds, and
resolution of disputes (Hsu, 1980; Mann, 1987a).

Local officials also collected taxes, and the taxes paid for public works.
The Ming elite were a classic rent-seeking coalition, and much of the
money went to waste. In 1561 the emperor and his current favourite,
drunk and excessively enthusiastic, overturned an oil lamp and set fire to
the bedding. The fire spread and destroyed the entire palace, and the
expense of rebuilding required substantial increases in taxes. The Ming
also suffered from an edifice complex, and much revenue was consumed
in the construction of elaborate tombs, including the famous ceramic army
of Zhu Yuelian, and the tomb of the Emperor Wanli (d. 1620), built over a
decade at a cost of 227 metric tons of silver. In the early fifteenth century
the Ming government sponsored large seaborne expeditions to India and
East Africa, but these ceased in 1433 and the Ming turned inward,
possibly because of the anti-foreign prejudice of Confucian scholar-officials
(Dreyer, 1982), but also possibly because of the expense (Huang, 1974).
Trade was forbidden in the south except for tributary missions (Viraphol,

1977), and the government attempted to relocate population inland. In the late sixteenth and early seventeenth centuries the Ming government constructed the massive fortifications now known as the Great Wall to defend themselves against the migratory peoples of the northern steppes (Waldron, 1990).

Their walls did not protect the Ming from internal rebellion, however, nor did they protect them from external invasion. The Ming dynasty dissolved in a welter of violence which depopulated much of northern China and left a quarter to a third of the land in Zhili (Hebei) and Shandong provinces vacant. Their successors, the Manchus, were northerners themselves, and their new boundary lay far to the north of the Ming walls. The new Qing dynasty was relatively untroubled by foreign threats, and through the late seventeenth and eighteenth centuries Qing officials mobilized labour to maintain and extend the systems of river dikes, highways, and canals. Two crucial examples were the massive dikes along the banks of the Yellow River which prevented the annual flooding from interfering with agriculture on the North China plain, and the Grand Canal from the Yangzi River valley in the south to Beijing in the north which ensured food supplies for the capital. The new government encouraged resettlement by granting land which had belonged to members of the former Ming aristocracy to small farmers, and issued decrees in 1649, 1651, and 1652 which gave titles of ownership to 'drifters' living on farmland.

The motives of the Qing central government were political, however, not economic. As we have seen in Chapter 3, the northern regions which the government strove to repopulate were in fact difficult to farm: 'even the best land cannot be compared to the land in the south', harvest and sowing had to be finished before the frost began, and wide variation in rainfall led to alternate drought and flooding. Historical records show that the Yellow River has burst its dikes 1593 times, and the floods lead to marshy conditions in which locusts breed. But these provinces were crucial to the security of the capital, and therefore in addition to small farmers the government granted land to members of the imperial clan, allies, officials, and soldiers. The government intended to create a system of estates based on serfdom. The typical grant was 720 *mu* (120 acres or 48 hectares), ten serfs under a headman, and six to eight oxen – sufficient to support a mounted warrior who could be called quickly to the capital in time of need. To protect this crucial region, the government regularly mobilized tens of thousands of labourers to extend and maintain the dikes holding the Yellow River within its raised bed.

The attempt failed. By 1700 much estate land was already being leased to free tenants, and in the mid-eighteenth century the government granted permission for serfs to become commoners, which transformed them into rent-paying tenants. As seen in Chapter 3, the small-holder sector became increasingly commercialized, and the previously equal small-holders divided into managerial farmers on the one hand, and poor peasants and agricultural labourers on the other. In the estate sector, the pressures of population increase and commercialization led to a further decline in serfdom and the introduction of wage labour and rent relations similar to, and eventually virtually indistinguishable from, those which had developed in the small-holder sector (Huang, 1985).

Things were different in the south. In the north, the water used for irrigation came from wells dug and maintained by single families or small groups of households. In the south, however, on the Yangzi or Pearl River deltas, the irrigation and drainage systems consisted of networks of canals, whose construction could involve hundreds or thousands of workers, but was within the means of well-organized lineage groups. Lineage groups, rather than the state, therefore provided these services. Philip Huang notes that it was in the regions of the Yangzi and Pearl deltas that lineages were most developed and suggests that social structures may have reflected natural environments and corresponding agricultural technologies (Huang, 1985, 1990).

But politics was crucial here too. This was the last region to be con-quered by the Qing, and the government's direct military control was always relatively weak. The south had the most intensive connection with the growing foreign trade, particularly the importation of opium. Local society in the south was dominated by the large lineage groups with extensive collective land holdings. Competition among them was often violent. They maintained their own armed forces, and during periods when central authority was weak, they waged feuds with each other. In particular, during the early nineteenth century parts of the southern provinces were in a state of virtual civil war (Wakeman, 1966).

A single provincial governor who could command the resources of an entire macroregion – particularly the crucial Lower Yangzi – could easily become powerful enough to pose a threat to the central government. To counter this possibility, provincial boundaries were always drawn to cut across the economic macroregions. The Lower Yangzi region's core area was split among three provinces, Jiangsu, Anhui, and Zhejiang. Obviously provincial boundaries were not established to correspond to economic divisions. Rather they were intended to counter the possible political influence of economic factors. To reduce the danger further, officials were set at odds with each other and encouraged to undermine any initiative which might further a rival's career. The Qing played on ethnic differences as well, by appointing senior officials in such a way that a Chinese governor would always have Manchu subordinates, and a Manchu governor-general would always have Chinese governors serving under him.

In the mid-nineteenth century the temporary loss of the central provinces to the Taiping very nearly destroyed the dynasty. A combination of monetary instability, lower agricultural prices, higher taxes, and declining land values led to attempts by landlords to increase rents, which led in turn to the social unrest which provided the background for the Taiping and other rebellions (Bernhardt, 1992). The Qing survived, but the suppression of the rebellions required armies and money. The armies were raised by provincial authorities, and the provincial authorities were also responsible for new taxes intended to support the armies. The most important of the new taxes was known as the *likin* (*lijin*, 'a tax of one thousandth'). Introduced in 1853, it was a tax on trade, levied on goods in transit or in stock. Networks of collection stations were established along roads and in towns and cities. The *likin* grew and spread into every province. Collections increased with the rise in domestic trade (foreign-owned goods were subject to separate taxes and transit duties prescribed by treaties), and the total collected equalled the amount derived from the old salt taxes, as reported in central government accounts (Mann, 1987a).

However, the central government had no idea how much was collected by the new taxation system, because the collection, accounting and disbursement of *likin* revenues remained under regional control, and reporting was never detailed. The central government received only a summary account of receipts and expenditures. That is, this major source of tax revenues, together with the militia system, and the regional armies, although they were nominally part of the central administrative apparatus, in fact created a new balance between central and regional governments which shifted steadily in favour of the regions. Further, the complexities of definitions, conflicting exemptions, and inconsistent applications of the *likin* persisted and, as they restricted the reach of the market and hampered the flow of goods, they constituted a serious impediment to China's internal commerce for nearly an entire century.

By the late nineteenth century, the Qing state was unable to generate sufficient resources to support the economy. At the same time, the social cohesion of the countryside was dissolving. In the Jiangnan district, until the Taiping rebellion, the Qing state had remained outside rent relations between landlords and tenants. When the Taipings occupied the area, 'guided more by expediency than ideology' (Bernhardt, 1992, p. 109), they appointed new officials from outside the scholar elite and imposed heavier taxes on landlords. The changes they implemented may therefore have been more extensive, and their control over countryside more effective, than previously thought. Furthermore, after the defeat of the Taiping, the resurgent Qing state became involved with landlords in rent collection. The increasing tendency for landlords to use more impersonal bursaries and rent-collection bureaus further widened the social distance between landlords and tenants. This closer alliance of the state and the landlords led to an increase in the real burdens on tenants, and led in turn to a new cycle of tax protests, rent resistance and unrest in the late nineteenth and early twentieth centuries.

Some see the decay of the Qing as a reflection of the pre-existing Chinese class system, while others argue that late nineteenth-century imperialism – the foreign debt, foreign concessions and monopolies, and loss of sovereignty – fatally weakened the Chinese state and rendered it incapable of fostering modern economic development as the Japanese government did. In the late eighteenth century the central government may have had an annual surplus of 8 or 9 million taels from a revenue of 43 to 44 million and after expenses of 35 million. By 1862–74 the budget showed annual deficits of 10 million taels, with 60 million income against 70 million expenditures, reflecting the cost of suppressing the rebellions. Deficits were covered by foreign loans, but the immense size of the Japanese war and Boxer rebellion indemnities took the deficits and foreign borrowing to new heights. Japan demanded 200 million taels under the Treaty of Shimonoseki in 1895. In 1899 the income of the Chinese central government was 88.4 million taels, but expenditures were 101 million, and the cost of foreign loans alone 24 million. In 1901 the Boxer Protocol levied indemnities of 450 million taels (££67.5 million), to be paid over 39 years at 4 per cent interest, with customs, *likin*, and salt tax revenues as security. Tariffs were raised and taxes extended to help meet payments, but in 1911 China was faced with a net foreign debt of £139 million (Hou, 1965).

Korea

The Korean state, though complex in its formal structure, was not well-developed. From the lowest level to the highest, officials in effect purchased their offices with bribes, and then spent their time in office attempting to recoup their expenses and if possible turn a profit. In addition to the modest official rates of taxation, farmers, artisans, and merchants were therefore subject to a variety of surcharges, handling fees, and outright extortion. The main sources of revenue, the land tax, the military service tax, and the state granary system (intended for famine relief), and of course the government's purchases as well, were all subject to this sort of abuse. During the nineteenth-century period of 'government by royal in-law families', each reign was marked by an ascendancy of unstable coalitions of members of the current queen's clan, who monopolized official positions and tried to squeeze as much as they could before they were ousted by their rivals.

The economy escaped the government's attempts at control, some of which have a farcical air to them. Through the seventeenth and eighteenth centuries the economy expanded and became increasingly commercialized. These changes and the response of farmers to expanding opportunities resulted in an extension of market relationships with which the government was poorly prepared to cope. In the mining industry, in order to produce silver for the technically illegal trade with China, the government licensed private silver miners, but it then imposed a tax which was so heavy that the number of licensed mines declined. The copper-mining industry developed in the same way, with the government first licensing mines because of the need for copper currency, then imposing heavy taxes. Again the number of officially sanctioned mines declined. This did not mean that the industry declined; mining continued, but without government authorization or control, and without the government benefiting by way of tax revenue (Eckert et al., 1990, p. 164).

During the nineteenth century attempts at reform were hamstrung by their identification with one or another of the parties contending for power. During the late 1860s the king's father-in-law introduced a series of reforms parallel to those being instituted in the aftermath of the Taiping rebellion in China, but his attempt to centralize power and to eliminate the tax exemptions enjoyed by the *yangban* aristocrats encountered strenuous opposition. In the 1880s and again in the 1890s, there were further reform efforts, which demonstrated a recognition by some elite groups of the need to resist the West through changes in inherited social structures. Again, however, they encountered resistance, in the 1880s largely in the form of a hostility to all foreigners and opposition to the opening of the country to outside contacts, and in the 1890s focusing on specific hostility to the Japanese. A long list of progressive, modernizing measures was announced during 1894–6 by the reform party, but the fact that they were sponsored and supported by the Japanese meant that the flight of the king from the royal palace to the Russian legation meant not only the temporary eclipse of Japanese power but also the end of the reforms.

Japan

The Way is an all-embracing term. It takes rites, music, law enforcement, and political administration – everything the early kings established – and brings them under one designation. There is no such thing as the Way apart from rites, music, law enforcement, and political administration.

Ogyû Sorai (1666–1728)

The Japanese central government had extensive resources, for the Tokugawa family and their allies controlled approximately 60 per cent of the officially defined revenues derived from the rice harvest. In addition, the government exercised control over the *daimyô*, whether members of the ruling family, allies, or the 'outside' domains, through an elaborate set of regulations, specifying which of them could hold offices in the central government, stipulating how many retainers they could maintain, reinforcing the ban on firearms, and requiring them to reside in Edo in alternating periods, and to leave their wives and children as hostages during the periods when they were in their home domains. Each of the domains in turn operated along lines similar to the central government, with retainers allocated stipends denominated in rice according to their status. Each domain was a 'little *bakufu*' in that the central government did not interfere so long as its spies did not report any violations of its rules.

The combination of centralized control and local autonomy operated at the local level as well. There was no tax-collecting apparatus. In some cases the higher-ranking retainers of the Tokugawa were assigned revenues from specific villages; more commonly officials were assigned by the domain governments to collect a percentage of the harvest. The tax might be assessed either in kind or in money, but villages were simply ordered to pay a set sum, which the designated village leaders allocated themselves among the families in the local community. There was little other interest taken by the central government in village life.

The enforced policy of peace inadvertently created the conditions for the expansion of commerce described in Chapter 3. The Tokugawa government separated the *samurai* warrior class from the land and centralized them in the castle towns of each domain, where they and their families had to be fed. The resulting increase in urban population inevitably led to a corresponding increase in trade. Sophisticated national markets emerged, notably the Osaka rice market. In addition, the requirement of alternate residence of the *daimyô* in Edo meant extensive travel. This contributed to the growth of Edo, and to the growth of towns to provide services to the *daimyô* and their retainers as they travelled. The expense of multiple residences, intended to weaken the *daimyô*, provided one motive for the development programmes pursued in many domains. This was particularly true of the 'outside' domains, in part because these suspect *daimyô* had been allocated the least remunerative lands following the Tokugawa victory. These development projects reinforced the tendencies toward commercialization and protoindustrial development.

The Tokugawa did not take advantage of this economic development. The shogunal government was effectively bankrupt from early in the eighteenth century. Although they felt threatened by the *daimyô*, however, they were unable to carry through any reform of the system which would have increased central government revenues. To have done so would have upset the delicate balance they themselves had created. That balance, George Wilson (1992) has argued, depended further on the continued agreement of the *daimyô* to recognize the Tokugawa as 'first among equals'. When dealing with foreigners, the Tokugawa government could speak for 'Japan'. In its development projects, however, it did not act like a central government at all, but rather seems merely one domain among many others.

Attempts to improve the government's financial position included interventions in the operation of the market. In 1695 the government undertook the first of twelve recoinings lowering the metal content of money. Programmes of 'reform' almost always included sumptuary laws restricting the consumption of luxury goods. In the early eighteenth century the *shôgun* Yoshimune attempted to reduce government expenses, encourage frugality, and improve agricultural production. He worried about declining moral standards, issued decrees restricting consumption of 'luxuries', and censored 'lewd' passages in published books. Yoshimune's programme became the standard pattern. His grandson Matsudaira Sadanobu, who served as chief councillor from 1787 to 1793, ordered reductions in expenses, greater frugality, and the creation of a rice reserve for famine relief. In 1789 he cancelled the debts owed by Tokugawa vassals to merchants. He also attempted unsuccessfully to impose price controls, and issued equally unsuccessful decrees restricting 'wasteful' consumption by the peasants and ordering peasants in the cities to return to the countryside. He too worried about the people's morals, and he attempted to reduce the attractions of the cities by reducing the numbers of unlicensed prostitutes, censoring immoral books, and banning mixed bathing of persons above the age of six.

The last such programme, that of Mizuno Tadakuni in 1841–3, again denounced excessive luxury and imposed new restrictions on bathhouses and hairdressers. Again, the government placed ceilings on commodity prices, and on interest rates as well. However, the government was unable to enforce the new regulations, and the last two decades of Tokugawa rule were marked by an especially rapid increase in prices. Significantly, Mizuno's additional proposal to increase the amount of land administered directly by the central government aroused so much opposition that it had to be abandoned, and he lost office in 1843 (Hane, 1991, pp. 187–8). Finally, even in the face of the Western threat and an unprecedented domestic crisis, the Tokugawa still could not envisage any source of increased revenue. The expenses of the major military reforms instituted in 1862 were to be met by penny-pinching economies in ceremonial expenditures and the elimination of a number of higher officials through enforced retirement and reassignment of duties (Totman, 1980, pp. 21–2).

Southeast Asia

> Damn, damn, damn the Filipino
> Pock-marked khakiac ladrone
> Underneath the starry flag,
> Civilize him with a Krag
> And return us to our own beloved home.
>   American marching song, c. 1900

Up to the mid-nineteenth century the economic role of the state in Southeast Asia had centred on control over trade. Even within their core areas, the major centres of power typically ruled indirectly through quasi-hereditary local notables, and outside of these areas they exercised only minimal control. Their main economic concern was to ensure the flow of products from the interior regions, goods which could be taxed as they passed through commercial and administrative centres. In addition, rulers attempted to secure and maintain control over trade routes in order to take advantage of international trade. The Spanish, Dutch, and more recently the British, of course, monopolized trade across the Pacific and on the Indian Ocean, but Chinese merchants with connections in southern China controlled most of the trade in the South China Sea.

Control was exercised through state monopoly organizations. The Manila Galleon, the Dutch East India Company, and the British East India Company all attempted to centralize, restrict, and control trade to their own benefit. Indigenous rulers did so as well. Southeast Asian governments established monopoly organizations which extracted goods from their subjects, both for their own benefit and in order to trade with the Chinese within the tributary system. In the early eighteenth century the Siamese state received a quarter of its revenue from these royal monopolies. In the later eighteenth century, an elaborately developed government bureaucracy collected goods in Siamese provinces, processed and stored them, shipped them to centres in southern China, and then arranged for the wholesale distribution of Chinese goods received in return. The Vietnamese government regulated trade in the same way, though the history of Chinese occupation and subsequent invasions kept the relationship ambivalent. To the south, the Malay sultans also attempted to organize export industries such as pepper and tin to benefit from Chinese markets.

Before the middle decades of the nineteenth century, Western power had merely competed with the outermost eddies of Chinese influence among a very large number of local rulers. The subsequent extension of Western control reduced the number of centres of power to six: the expanded Spanish and then American Philippines, the expanded Dutch East Indies, French Indochina, British Burma, the British-controlled Malay peninsula and northern Sarawak, and finally Siam (Thailand), the only state to remain independent of Western control. Further, these new and expanded centres defined themselves differently from the ones they had annexed or replaced. Rather than a core area from which power and influence radiated outward in diminishing waves, the new states defined themselves as uniformly sovereign across the entire area within defined geographical boundaries. In Thongchai Winichakul's formulation, the imposition of the new concept of sovereignty which associated it with territorial boundaries created a new definition of the 'geo-body'. So, in the case of Thailand, by laying claim to absolute sovereignty within a territory defined by a map, the Bangkok elite could create the mythic community which validated their power. For example, territory could not be 'lost' before there were maps with precisely delimited boundaries, and therefore the maps themselves became the source of claims to territory and to claims to absolute sovereignty within that territory. As part of this process, the geo-body contributed to the fetishism of the new 'national' state, and took on a 'diabolically generative' life of its own (Winichakul, 1994, p. 135).

Winichakul's study of the Thai 'geo-body' relates to the creation of a national myth, but the fetishism of territorial acquisition and definition had been derived from the manner in which the national states of the West were coming to conceive themselves, and their imposition of that conception on their colonial possessions. In addition, these were secular states which dispensed with the inherited tradition of sacred authority. This was obviously true of the colonial territories, but was equally the case with Thailand. When he became king of Siam in the 1870s Chulalongkorn ordered his officials not to prostrate themselves before him, but 'he was not thereby abdicating power; like the colonial rulers in neighbouring lands, which he visited in his youth, he was setting forth toward a much more comprehensive kind of authority' (Steinberg, 1987, p. 176).

The establishment of these new regimes was not peaceful. Geographical knowledge expressed on maps was translated, by military force, into social reality in the creation of centralized states. The French conquered their empire in wars fought against the Chinese, Vietnamese, and Siamese states. After British annexation, the 'pacification of Burma' lasted from 1887 to 1895. The collapse of Burmese royal authority was followed by continued armed resistance, led by royal pretenders, former military commanders, Buddhist religious communities, and rulers of Shan states. A parallel uprising in British Burma arose partly in response to the introduction of centralized administration on the Indian model which disrupted inherited local power structures. The British deployed 40 000 troops and Indian police as well as a locally raised Christian militia. Villages were burned, and there were mass executions of so-called rebels. The Dutch moved to subdue the Sultanate of Aceh in central and northern Sumatra in 1873, but after achieving their initial objective of seizing the sultan's capital, the Dutch found themselves involved in an expensive guerrilla war which did not end until 1902. The United States, having seized the Philippines from Spain, inherited the wars which the Spanish had been fighting against the emerging independence movement and against the Muslim rulers in the southern islands. The United States Army adopted the 45-calibre automatic as its officer's sidearm because experience with the Philippine rebels convinced the Americans that they required a weapon which would knock an onrushing attacker backwards, safely out of reach. There were specific atrocities; 600 Muslims were massacred at Bud Dajo in 1906. Many more died from the indirect effects of the fighting. The Americans extended the Spanish practice of removing villagers to concentration camps where they could not support the rebels. Planting, harvesting, and distribution were disrupted, and disease spread in the camps. One American commander estimated that 600 000 persons had died on Luzon alone, and total deaths may have reached 1 million, before the islands were 'pacified' (SarDesai, 1994, p. 146; Trocki, 1992, p. 105).

As they expanded and consolidated themselves, the new states created bureaucratic systems to administer a new and broader range of functions than rulers in the region had ever undertaken before. The resulting political structures defined the role native elites could play, and these structures often reflected the differences of policy and style among the colonial powers. The colonial states claimed absolute power, of course, and they also claimed that it was the Westerners who wielded that power. Nevertheless, their power was often less absolute than claimed, and in addition 'the colonial administrations and western entrepreneurs worked with or through local power figures and elites', especially when they aimed to develop large-scale commercial agriculture (Van Niel, 1990b).

There had still been no fundamental reforms in the Siamese kingdom by the mid-nineteenth century. The bureaucracy consisted largely of an unsalaried hereditary nobility. There had been no change in the education of the elite, and no change in recruitment patterns, neither for instance in the army nor in provincial administration. The legal system was unchanged, and slavery remained. The central government tattooed men it considered liable for labour service. The local aristocracy, who had their own uses for the men in question, opposed this, and the conflict led to a 'stockpiling' of men who became slaves voluntarily to avoid government service. In some districts these slaves may have made up half the male population by the 1850s.

Chulalongkorn, when he became king in his own right in 1873, announced the abolition of slavery, a reform of the legal system, a new system of finances, and the creation of a council of state and a privy council to 'advise' him on legislation. But he faced opposition and a threatened coup, which he survived – apparently at the cost of giving up his reform programme. A decade later in the mid-1880s there was a fresh burst of reform as older ministers died and the king replaced them with his brothers. New functional ministries, each with one of the king's brothers as minister, were established in 1888, and a new cabinet government in 1892. The provinces were reorganized into larger units (*monthon* or 'circles'), under commissioners who often were also brothers of the king. The old compulsory labour service was abolished. From 1890 onwards the commissioners began to organize local military units based on regular conscription, to introduce regular taxation and consistent financial administration, and to reform the judicial systems. Enrolments in the new school system rose from 5000 to 84 000 from 1898 to 1910. Railway construction began with a line to the east in 1892. As described later in Chapter 6, Chulalongkorn and his successors designed all these measures to defend the kingdom against foreign threats, and to centralize and reinforce power in the hands of the government.

In the Malay Peninsula the representatives of the British government generally followed the wishes of Singapore commercial interests, and extended the British sphere of interest steadily from 1874 onwards. A series of convenient 'fictions' (Steinberg, 1987, pp. 197–9) – among them that Malays could not govern themselves and had requested British 'advice and assistance' – masked the seizure of power. Opposition was put down by force, in Perak in 1875 and in Pahang in the 1890s. In outward form the states which the British recognized were larger versions of the traditional sultanates, but in each the British appointed a resident supported by a British bureaucracy. The original four sultanates became the Federated States in 1895 and were joined by another four in the north and one in the south, the Unfederated States, between 1909 and 1914. Malays exercised more power in the Unfederated States than in the Federated States, but all recognized that the British were paramount.

French Indochina was divided into five distinct regions. Only Cochinchina (southern Vietnam) was a formal colony directly under the administration of Paris. The others – Annam (central Vietnam), Tonkin (northern Vietnam), Cambodia, and Laos – were protectorates. Then in 1887 all five were placed under a governor-general located in Hanoi. The governor-general was advised by a council of around 20 senior French officials and five 'indigenous high functionaries' whom the governor-general himself selected. The central government controlled customs and therefore trade and commerce, and also the new postal, telegraph, and forestry administrations. The central government's budget rested on indirect revenues, such as customs, and taxes on opium, alcohol, and salt. Regional governments paid their expenses from direct taxes on land and a poll tax on people.

Although theoretically centralized, the French territories were not in fact unified. The division of Vietnam into three units, for instance, was unprecedented. The most significant French cultural influence occurred in the area of direct rule in the south, and the least in Annam where the old' court at Hue still exercised some power until 1897. Further, the French multiplied the number of regional units from 31 to 60, but they never had the personnel to staff their administrative apparatus. They first attempted to do away with all native degree-holders, then reinstated them, then gradually replaced them at the highest level with some thirty French naval officers known as 'inspectors of indigenous affairs'. Below that level, officials were Vietnamese, and the French extended their authority by taking over indigenous institutions. In the south, all administration was directly under the French. In the central and northern regions local government consisted of two parallel administrations, one French, under a 'province chief' with authority over Europeans, foreign Asians, and Vietnamese with French citizenship, and the other Vietnamese, with a governor-general, governors, regional prefects, and district magistrates. French control over the Vietnamese system was ensured in the north by senior officials set above both French and Vietnamese administrations, and in the central region by direct control over appointments and promotions in the Vietnamese administration. However, Vietnamese officials continued to be chosen on the basis of the old Chinese Confucian examination system. The reforming official Nguyen Truong To had advocated abolition of the system in the 1860s, but the French retained it until 1919.

In Cambodia and Laos, the establishment of French control meant that both were kept from falling under Siamese rule. Within Cambodia, in addition to the elimination of threats from the Siamese and Vietnamese, the problems of provincial autonomy and dynastic warfare disappeared. The French introduced regular taxation systems, systematized the existing royal monopolies, and imposed a consistent administration to suit their own needs. Laos was rather peripheral to French interests, and its inaccessibility ensured that it remained largely rural, with only 30 000 out of 1 million living in provincial towns. Nevertheless the borders established have remained to the present.

In the Dutch East Indies as late as the 1870s administration still centred on Java, with a population of over 17 million ruled by around 100 Dutch officials and the native *priyayi* administration headed by about 80 quasi-hereditary regents. Circles of power radiated outwards in the traditional pattern, with the Dutch exercising influence through local sultans and chiefs. The Dutch began their extension into Sumatra with the annexation of Toba, whose inhabitants had recently converted to Christianity, areas of plantation development, and the conquest of Aceh. On Java, the expansion of export agriculture, transport development, and modern communications seemed to require changes in administration more on European lines. New government offices appeared, for instance for irrigation and forestry. Both the Dutch and native administrations were reorganized in 1874, and in 1882 the *priyayi* regents lost their right to requisition labour services from farmers.

The development of the 'Ethical Policy', a Dutch version of the 'white man's burden', accelerated change after 1900 by providing a justification for more extensive intrusion into native life under the guise of reform. Dutch language training became mandatory for all *priyayi*, and new administrative functions were gradually extended down to the village level. Higher and more complete tariffs and the imposition of new taxes eliminated the previous budget shortage, and revenues doubled from 1899 to 1912. Victory in Aceh in 1902 meant an end to the expense of that war, and also that effective and experienced soldiers could be used elsewhere when necessary. Between 1898 and 1909 over 200 sultans and chiefs signed the 'Short Declaration' accepting Dutch rule and agreeing to obey Dutch orders. Control also extended through the activities of the semi-official shipping line, which also worked to route trade through Batavia rather than rival British Singapore.

During the 1880s the Spanish rulers of the Philippines had attempted a sort of modernization and expansion of their area of administration similar to the Dutch, abandoning the old system of monopolies and introducing more regular taxes, reorganized provincial administrations with separate finance departments, and new town councils at the local level. In 1896, however, they faced the outbreak of a nationalist revolution, two years later Spain was at war with the United States, and in 1898 the United States acquired the Philippines for US$ 20 million as part of the peace settlement. The Americans completed the extension of the Philippines southwards by concluding a treaty with the Sultan of Sulu in 1899 and followed this with military occupation after 1900. In addition to a new administration, the Philippines was incorporated into the American system of protective tariffs. This encouraged expanded sugar production, although at prices generally higher than world levels. In contrast to other colonial regimes, the Americans explicitly intended that their period of rule would be temporary, and as seen below this led them to a much more open cooperation with indigenous elites than the Dutch, French or British.

The Role of Elites

Elites control the majority of resources. In explaining their effect on the pattern of economic development, it is useful to begin with such questions as: Who are they? How are they recruited? How much chance does a person or a family from outside the elite have of rising to elite status? How did they behave? For instance, in China roughly 1 million degree-holders would have constituted less than 1 per cent of the male population in late Qing, and the small number of official positions provided employment for only a few of these fortunate men. Nevertheless, though the chance of success might be vanishingly small, if one could master the subjects set for the official examinations, it was possible in theory to rise into the bureaucracy on one's merits. In contrast, unless one were born a *samurai*, one theoretically could never aspire to an official position in Japan, and yet the theory could be modified by purchase of *samurai* status or by adoption into a higher ranking family. In Korea and in Vietnam, one had to be born into the aristocracy but also succeed in the Confucian examination system to qualify for office. In contrast again, in Muslim Southeast Asia, one might in theory have good title to an inherited position of authority, and yet be forced to contend with the potentially murderous claims of siblings and half-siblings, which could alter and dilute the content of authority in complex ways.

Confronted with the challenges of external pressure and internal crises, the leaders who emerged from these very different systems reacted in different ways. In Southeast Asia, the expanding and increasingly intrusive colonial regimes seemed to provide little opportunity for native elites and yet all depended to some extent on the cooperation of native elites. To some extent the colonial administrations trained those same elites, explicitly to exercise power within centralized bureaucracies, and implicitly to resent colonial rule, to desire real power for themselves, and to seize power when the opportunity finally arose. This again could lead to apparently paradoxical continuities even within revolutionary demands for change.

China

The gentry class forbids the local people to use Western methods and machines, so that eventually the people will not be able to do anything... Scholars and men of letters always criticize me for honouring

strange knowledge and for being queer and unusual. It is really difficult
to understand the minds of some Chinese.

Li Hongzhang

Philip Huang's studies (1985, 1990) outline a model of the process by which
the elite separated themselves from the poor families in the countryside. As
noted above, the attempt by the Qing government to create a landowning
nobility based on serfdom failed. Nobles who fell in debt had to pawn or sell
their land, and by 1750 some 50 to 60 per cent of the original grants had
already passed from Manchu and Mongol bannermen to Chinese merchants. Huang argues that from the late eighteenth to the twentieth century
the resulting social structures remained unchanged, but families could move
upwards or downwards over the course of generations. One family which
succeeded were the Bi of Lijiazhang village, Zichuan country, in Shandong
province. Bi Fenglian began his career in the late eighteenth century with
less than 30 *mu* of land. He became wealthy through silk-weaving. When he
died in 1840 his weaving enterprise had expanded to over 20 looms
operated by hired workers, and his landholdings had risen to over 300 *mu*.
His grandson Bi Yuanrong (1814–96) expanded the family's landholdings to
900 *mu*. The largest parcel of 600 *mu* lay in the family's original village and
was operated as a single managerial farm with over 30 long-term and 50
day-labourers. The family also owned a hat-making plant in addition to the
weaving plant, and employed around 100 workers in each (Huang, 1985,
pp. 96–7).

But the Bi family was unusual in their success. In the north over 80 per
cent of the land was owned and farmed by families. Most of the 'rich' in
the northern villages were not landlords, but resident farmers. The small
number of landlords who owned some 13 to 18 per cent of the land rented
it in small parcels and lived in towns or nearby villages. In the south,
landowners who did not farm land themselves owned 42 per cent of
cultivated land, but as in the north, they rented it to small tenants rather
than farming it themselves with hired labour. These elite landowners lived,
not in neighbouring villages, but in regional centres or provincial capital
cities.

It has often been noted that the practice of dividing the inheritance
among all sons could easily transform a wealthy family into several poor
families, and further, in comparison with Japan and England, that division
of inheritance prevented younger sons from seeking their fortune elsewhere and therefore reduced social mobility (Fairbank, 1992, p. 21).
However, the Bi were unusual not only because of their continued success

and the absence of division, but also because they remained a major presence in their original village. Renting land did not require supervision, so it paid better returns to rent excess land to small farmers. In the wealthier south, where wages were higher, Huang argues that no one could afford to rent land and farm it with hired labour, since the net return would be zero. Larger landowners often had other sources of income, although in contrast to the Bi family's manufacturing plants, the more common sources were money-lending and commerce. In addition, those who made money in commerce or office-holding could and did purchase land and then rent it to small farmers.

Most rich farmers who became landlords withdrew from the village, and notoriously, absentee landlords took little interest in villages where their land was located. Huang is emphatic that the lands leased by the landlords were farmed on the same basis as the small farms of poor peasant households. Landlords made no attempt to improve agricultural technology. Rather they devoted themselves to their money-lending or commercial enterprises, and to the pursuit of culture. The state protected the rights of landlords to extract rents, and the surplus permitted members of the landlord class to enjoy 'the luxury of careers divorced from farming'. And of course the state offered the opportunity of joining the elite through the examination system, with the possibility of income and wealth far beyond the possibilities open to a commoner landlord – the annual income of a district magistrate was 30 000 taels, and a provincial governor 180 000, in the nineteenth century, compared to possibly 100 taels for a landlord who owned 100 *mu*. 'The truly successful landlord was one who became a member of the gentry, and the truly successful degree-holder was one who became an official' (Huang, 1985, p. 247).

Such successful landlords could support their sons in study for official degrees, but if he succeeded in obtaining a degree, the fortunate young man was drawn away from the village towards the major market towns and county seats, with their circles of gentry contacts, government offices, big merchants, and luxury goods. These was no reason to remain in the village and concern oneself with its governance. Therefore, regular contact between the village and the elite and government was in fact indirect, through commoners appointed to quasi-official positions.

The values of this distant Confucian scholar gentry were unbendingly conservative, as seen above in the despairing outburst by the modernizing official Li Hongzhang. Despite being continually involved in the market economy, the gentry absorbed an anti-profit, anti-merchant bias. The framework of their inherited tradition equipped Confucian scholars with a mechanism for considering new challenges by a process of analogy with what had gone before. It was not a framework which encouraged innovation, however, nor was it one which endorsed Adam Smith's propensity to truck, barter, and exchange. Max Weber argued that Confucian values were inherently anti-capitalist. This has been disputed by advocates of contemporary 'Neo-Confucianism', who contend that Confucian values can indeed provide the basis for modernization and industrialization (see Tu, 1989 and Chapter 12). However, if we look at the texts memorized by successive generations of students, we see for instance that there is no mention of merchants in *The Analects*. There are only a few references to profits or markets, and those references are negative:

> The gentleman seeks neither a full belly nor a comfortable home. . . . The gentleman understands what is moral. The small man understands what is profitable. . . . If wealth were a permissible pursuit, I would be willing even to act as a guard holding a whip outside the market place. If it is not, I shall follow my own preferences. (Confucius, *The Analects*, I.14, IV.16, VII.12)

Further, as Li also complained, there was no encouragement in Confucian tradition for technological inventiveness:

> Even minor arts are sure to have their worthwhile aspects, but the gentleman does not take them up because the fear of a man who would go a long way is that he should be bogged down. . . . The artisan, in any of the hundred crafts, masters his trade by staying in his workshop; the gentleman perfects his way through learning. (Confucius, *The Analects*, XIX.4, XIX.7)

Students were encouraged, in addition to the filial piety noted in Chapter 2, to sacrifice their own desires and to work for the good of the people and the state. There are injunctions in the *Analects* and in *Mencius* to 'enrich the people'. However, the essence of good government was to maintain the 'city walls, houses, ancestral temples . . . sacrificial rites . . . diplomacy with its attendant gifts and banquets [and] the numerous offices and officials' which set civilized China off from the uncivilized barbarians (Mencius, VI, B, 10). As Confucius' disciple Tzu-chang put it, 'One can, perhaps, be satisfied with a Gentleman who is ready to lay down his life in the face of danger, who does not forget what is right at the sight of gain, and who does not forget reverence during sacrifice nor sorrow while in mourning' (Confucius, *The Analects*, XIX.1).

As argued above, these were not the commercial, profit-seeking values which guided the actions of the vast majority. Further, even at the elite level, some scholars did attempt to cope with the challenge posed by the West. Wei Yuan, a reforming official who had compiled an account of foreign countries for Commissioner Lin, certainly recognized the importance of Western technological power. A generation later, Zhang Zhidong, the modernizing governor of Wuhan, coined the formula 'Chinese learning for the substance and Western learning for the function'. Zhang thus attempted to fit modern technology into a Confucian framework. His attempt, however, has been dismissed as 'slick but inconsistent' (Fairbank, 1992, p. 258), because in Chinese philosophy *ti* (substance) and *yong* (function) referred to correlative aspects of any single entity, and therefore Chinese and Western learning each possessed both its own substance and its own function. With this formulation it is difficult to hold the balance, because a conservative could point to the inconsistency and argue that introducing any Western learning would necessarily undermine China's inherited values, while on the other hand more radical Westernizers could see the inconsistency as grounds for rejecting all inherited tradition.

In contrast to the Japanese formulation 'Eastern ethics and Western science' to be discussed in Chapter 5, Zhang's 'Chinese learning for the substance and Western learning for the function' provides no philosophical ground for introducing Western technology unless and until this inconsistency has been eliminated, or until the 'substance' of the Chinese tradition has been reinterpreted in a way which makes it compatible with Western 'function'. In the meantime no action can be justified. In practical terms this made it difficult to introduce the military technologies China needed to defend itself against the imperialist powers. In philosophical terms it meant that any action needed prior approval of the classes who acted as custodians of Chinese tradition – the literate scholar-gentry. If their values or their material interests were threatened, they would find it easy to oppose the modernization programme, and many of them did so.

It was this intellectual challenge which led Kang Youwei to his attempt to reinterpret Confucian classics in a way which would present Confucius as a social reformer, open to radical transformations of social life. Kang's efforts were impressive, impressive enough for the emperor to call him to the head of the famous '100 Days' reform ministry in 1898, but they were unconvincing to the majority of scholars. In consequence, any attempt at reform depended on power, and when the emperor lost power in a coup supported by the dowager empress, the reform programme failed and Kang had to flee for his life (Spence, 1982).

The inability of the Qing state to provide the services which it had provided in the eighteenth century, such as flood control and famine relief, suggest that the inherited pattern of government by scholar officials was no longer adequate. The Qing state survived the rebellions of the mid-nineteenth century, partly through traditional modes of reform, but later attempts to reform the system along Western lines encountered bitter opposition, and modernization movements remained limited and isolated. Thus the self-strengthening movement was essentially confined to particular provinces and to individuals generally regarded as second-rate. As with Li, the other leaders of the self-strengthening movement were provincial governors. In the absence of firm central leadership, they were rivals with each other, rather than colleagues in a coordinated programme. Li's main rival was Zhang Zhidong, who served for eighteen years at Wuhan. His efforts duplicated many of Li's projects. They included iron and coal mines, an iron foundry, a steel mill, and cotton spinning and weaving plants. They also included an independent military academy, and technical schools for mining, railways, telegraphs, and industrial technology. Li, Zhang, and other provincial leaders also sent their most able students to Japan to study the accomplishments of the Meiji government.

But the self-strengthening movement continued to attract the conservative opposition of local gentry, and the modernization programme never obtained grass-roots support as in Japan. All programmes were organized from the top down, the leaders displayed the traditional contempt for merchants, and private enterprise was discouraged. Lillian Li's study of the silk industry is one of many suggesting that the weakness of the Chinese state resulted from the interests of an elite which oppressed rather than promoted development (Li, 1981).

Leadership and individuals do matter, and the long period of power enjoyed by the dowager empress deprived China of the opportunity to respond to the threat posed by the West. The corruption of the system began at the highest levels. The 30 million taels (£ £10 million) diverted from the navy budget by the emperor's father to reconstruct the Summer Palace for the dowager empress effectively exhausted the department's resources. The lake in the Summer Palace was equipped with a boat made out of marble, but no new ships were purchased for the navy after 1888, and the Chinese navy was decisively defeated by the Japanese off the Yalu River in September 1894. A British adviser had urged the Chinese to purchase two new faster ships, but because there was no money available nothing was done. Instead, the British sold the two ships in question to the

Japanese, and one of them (the *Yoshino*) contributed to the Japanese victory in the battle.

The palace administration was thoroughly corrupt. One of the secrets of the dowager empress' power was her alliance with the chief of the eunuchs who maintained the daily administration of the Palace. The influence his position gave him over the lives of members of the imperial family, combined in turn with his connection with the formidable dowager empress, made the chief eunuch a man whose goodwill was sought by members of all parties, conservatives and reformers alike. Officials embezzled funds to pay bribes to him, and in turn he helped them conceal their thievery.

The leader of the self-strengthening movement, Li Hongzhang, defended himself following the defeat by the Japanese by arguing that he was only allowed command over limited regional forces, pitted against the entire Japanese nation. This was true; his provincial army fought alone, and of the 65 ships the Chinese possessed in 1894, Li only controlled 25 – the other three provincial fleets remained 'neutral'. But Li was not blameless. In 1884 when the French moved to annex northern Vietnam, Li had argued against military intervention. When his rivals who favoured war were made governor of Guangzhou and commander of the Fujian fleet, Li did not support them, and the resulting failure of the Chinese to concentrate their forces had ensured their defeat. The self-strengthening movement was as prone to bureaucratic inefficiency, nepotism, and corruption as their conservative opponents. Li left a huge fortune at his death, not all of it virtuously acquired. There were rumours that the Russians had paid him a bribe of $1.5 million in 1896 during the negotiation of a treaty which gave Russia the right to construct a railway along a straight route from Chita to Vladivostok, ceded land for building and operation of the railway, and granted the railway corporation complete authority including the right to maintain a police force in the ceded land, in return for a Russian guarantee of mutual defence against Japanese attack. Sergei Witte, the Russian chief minister, denied this rumour in his memoirs, but he did say that two years later in 1898 he had paid Li a bribe of 500 000 rubles to accept the occupation of the Liaodong peninsula, a 25–year lease of the ports of Dairen and Port Arthur, and a further railway concession connecting these ports with the Chita–Vladivostok line.

Further, Li recruited his colleagues primarily on the basis of their personal loyalty to him, not necessarily because of their ability or honesty. Even so, his trust was often misplaced. Many of Li's army and navy officers were notorious for their attempts to gain the favour of palace officials, especially the chief eunuch. This was a defensive tactic to protect them from attack by the conservatives who opposed the self-strengthening movement, but again the chief eunuch's favour had to be purchased, and the bribes were diverted from the funds with which they had been entrusted. Possibly the most embarrassing case of corruption related to the ammunition for Li's navy. Following the battle with the Japanese, it was said that the ten-inch guns on the largest ships had been allocated only three shells each, that some of the small guns had been given the wrong size shells, and that some shells were filled with sand. The officer in charge of supply was ironically the same man who had commanded the Fujian fleet destroyed by the French in 1884, formerly Li's enemy, but now his son-in-law (see Chu and Liu, 1994).

The habit of corruption – nepotism, favouritism, embezzlement, and bribery – penetrated from the centre through the provinces and districts, down to the local level. This can be seen as another aspect of the dynastic cycle in Chinese history, as an example of the tension between rent-seeking and intensive growth, or as a response to the historically specific impact of Western imperialism. Looking back, reforms instituted in the early eighteenth century had separated public and private funds handled by the bureaucracy, standardized fees and taxes, banned the traditional system of gift-giving, and in theory placed local finances on a firm and rational footing. But these reforms had been gradually undone, and by the 1820s corruption and inefficiency had seriously undermined government finances (Zelin, 1984). Nevertheless, only the fiscal crisis brought on by the great mid-nineteenth-century rebellions forced the Qing government to turn to taxation of commerce (Mann, 1987a). But the notoriously corrupt administration of the new taxes was paradigmatic of the further decline of central control. Local and regional authorities not only retained control over collections and disbursement, but also sold exemptions as well as accepting bribes in individual cases, so their exactions are more properly seen as extortion.

Korea

In theory the sole duty of the aristocracy of Korea, the *yangban*, was to devote themselves to the study of the Confucian classics and the self-cultivation which would suit them for the holding of public office. The *yangban* elite was a hereditary class, however, and one which placed great stress on legitimate descent. They lived in separate quarters of Seoul and other towns and married only among themselves. Access to office was limited to those holding degrees, as in China, but in Korea access to the examinations was not only restricted to members of the *yangban* class, but also largely excluded *yangban* who were the sons of secondary wives and *yangban* from the north. Public office was seen as the means of inculcating virtue in the people. Holding office, however, was not to involve this fortunate minority among the aristocracy in the application of technical knowledge, let alone the mundane tasks of administration or record-keeping. Medical officers, interpreters and translators, astronomers and astrologers, accountants, law clerks, scribes, and government artists were almost exclusively drawn from another virtually hereditary class, the *chungin* or 'middle people' (Eckert et al., 1990, pp. 108–9).

Practice diverged widely from theory, particularly in periods of dynastic weakness. As seen above, the nineteenth century was such a period, and bribery rather than virtue became the means of obtaining office. In addition, over time the impact of commercialization had undermined the traditional social structure in several ways. Many *yangban* families had fallen, unable to maintain the required lifestyle despite impeccable pedigrees, while provincial gentry and even wealthy peasants aped that same lifestyle and aspired to the power and perquisites of public office as well. The distinction between legitimate and illegitimate descent also broke down progressively. And finally the technical experts in the government, members of the *chungin* class, increasingly found opportunities to enrich themselves, either legitimately as merchants or illegitimately by appropriating government funds. The 1894–6 reformers included a large number of men who were either the sons of 'illegitimate' *yangban* aristocrats borne by secondary wives, or members of the *chungin* class (Eckert et al., 1990, p. 225).

Japan

It is a ridiculous thing that the aristocracy and military class in Japan should disdain profit, or that they should say that they disdain profit. When a man does not disdain profit, he is called a bad person. Such is the perverse practice of the times.

Kaiho Seiryô, *Lessons of the Past*, 1813

So long as Japan was the only country in Asia to have succeeded in the race for economic growth, scholars looked for aspects of Japanese society which differed from the rest of Asia and might therefore have explained Japan's success, and this included the *samurai* elite. The *samurai* class possessed some distinctive features. They were removed from the land and became salaried bureaucrats during the Tokugawa period. In contrast with much of Europe and with China, they did not own land. Compared to aristocratic elites elsewhere in the world, the approximately 1.3 million upper-class and 500 000 lower-class *samurai* and their family members were a rather large group, and both Tokugawa and domain governments often resorted to part-time work or job-sharing in order to provide employment for them. In addition, Japan is a country with a tradition of primogeniture, similar to England, and since only the oldest son would inherit the father's position, younger sons would have to seek their living elsewhere or become a parasitic burden on their older brothers. As we will see in Chapter 5, unemployed lower *samurai* violently opposed the intrusion of the West, a group of *samurai* from the 'outer' domains led the Meiji Restoration and established the new government, many other *samurai* subsequently found employment in the new government's bureaucratic offices, and some *samurai* became industrial entrepreneurs.

But did the elite and their *samurai* values 'lead' Japan's modernization and industrialization? As with other aspects of the Japanese experience, rapid growth elsewhere in Asia sheds a light which illuminates some of the other aspects of the Japanese elite. The Tokugawa shogunate sponsored the development of a neo-Confucian orthodoxy to support its rule, and as seen in Chapter 2 that orthodox vision pictured Japan as an eternally static society. The government was quite pragmatic in selecting the values it adopted, however. *Daimyô* and *samurai*, now confined to castle towns and typically employed as officials, were encouraged to emulate Confucian models. This increased the value placed on literacy and education, but the Tokugawa combined this with a very un-Confucian emphasis on military prowess. Further, the discipline of loyalty to one's lord was generally preferred to the Confucian emphasis on filial piety and family loyalties (Collcutt, 1991, pp. 128–46).

At the very top of the pyramid, the extravagance of the court posed a recurrent problem, depending on the personality of the reigning *shôgun*. Tsunayoshi (1680–1709) was lavish in his personal tastes, spent large sums renovating shrines, and debased the currency to cover the resulting deficits. Reforms and economy followed under Yoshimune (1716–45), but Ieharu (1760–86) was weak, and corruption became common under the rule of his chamberlain. Ienari (1786–1837) at first supported the reforms of Matsudaira Sadanobu, but after Sadanobu left office in 1793, Ienari's self-indulgent nature predominated – Ienari himself had forty wives and concubines – and government policy drifted into the 1840s.

As suggested above, periodic 'reform' attempts aimed as much at moral regeneration as financial solvency. The Tokugawa and domain governments alike were alarmed by static tax revenues, rising prices, a shortage of labour, rising wages, and indeed the spread of wage labour and commercialization generally. The cultural and social values of the elite appeared to be under attack. However, although the economic position of the elite required increasingly sophisticated management, it is not clear just how financially competent the hereditary aristocracy was. The *daimyô* and *samurai* were supported by taxes levied on the farming villages in rice, but which in fact were largely converted to money terms and marketed through merchants located in the towns and cities. The expenses of individual aristocratic families and of domains, not to mention the central Tokugawa government itself, were incurred largely in the urban centres. Prices here could fluctuate widely and appear to have risen generally during the Tokugawa period. In addition, the revenues from the tax on the rice crop were of course received just after the harvest, while expenses continued throughout the year. It was difficult to match revenues and expenses exactly over an entire year in the best of circumstances. As a result, aristocratic families and domain administrations turned to the merchants for advances against future revenues, usually by entering into a regular relationship with a particular merchant. By the early eighteenth century most domain administrations were already regularly indebted to merchants for large sums.

The austere ideals of the *samurai* warrior were progressively subverted by the demonstration effect of urban life, the entertainments of the 'floating world' of the merchant class, and by the example of the increasingly luxurious lifestyle of the upper aristocracy. Indulgence and luxuries had to be paid for, though. When they found themselves in difficulty, *daimyô* could either reduce expenditures or increase revenue. Economy was difficult, but so was an increase in the taxes on the villages, which could and frequently did result in violent protest. The Tokugawa government debased its coinage several times, and *daimyô* also could issue money for use within their own domains to cover their deficits, but these were temporary expedients. The *daimyô* might press the government to reduce or cancel debts to merchants, as happened in 1789 as one of the 'reforms' of Matsudaira Sadanobu, but this too provided only momentary relief, for subsequent loans would only be made at correspondingly higher interest rates. More subtly, merchants could be encouraged to 'lend' money in return for favours, particularly the offer of *samurai* status. Domain officials could also gamble in the market in rice futures, buying and selling not rice itself but the promises to deliver rice at particular prices in the future. Such 'derivative' instruments are leveraged in both directions; both profits and losses can be enormous.

Ultimately the pursuit of luxury meant that the revenues from their domains had to be increased, and this was perhaps the most common motive for sponsoring development projects. The *daimyôs'* motives were narrowly fiscal, however, and their methods inherently restrictive. The techniques for producing local specialty products were jealously guarded, for instance by the restrictions which Saga domain placed on the famous potters of Arita. Saga authorities subdivided production so that no individual would be familiar with the entire process, isolated the specialized colour glazers in a guarded village, and insisted that only one son in each family be taught the secrets of the craft. Trade was seen in mercantilist terms as beneficial to only one of the parties, for instance in a silk-weaving manual published in 1813:

It is a natural consequence that states which sell their produce to other domains, and so bring in gold and silver, should become rich, while the people of countries with little produce, which thus allow gold and silver to flow out of their lands, become poor. By increasing the production of commodities one enhances the flow of precious metals into the country while suppressing their outflow. (Morris-Suzuki, 1994, p. 29)

Individual *samurai* and their families did not have the range of expedients open to governments. Their debts could be intractable for a number of reasons. They complained of high interest rates, and they complained that the merchants took advantage of the fact that the portion of their tax revenues received in rice always had to be sold immediately after the harvest when prices were at their lowest. In the late eighteenth and early nineteenth centuries the price of rice remained generally low, but prices of other commodities appeared to be rising dangerously. Kozo Yamamura's study of the incomes of the elite class of some 6000 shogunal retainers (*hatamoto* or bannermen) shows that their incomes did not decline in real terms. However, their incomes had never been high compared to the lifestyle expected of them, and it seems clear that those expectations increased, and therefore their expenses did rise. There was very little mobility within the *samurai* class and therefore little opportunity to increase income through diligence or brilliance (Yamamura, 1974).

The difficulties which could beset a *samurai* may be seen from a letter received in November 1856 by a senior Tokugawa retainer, a man descended from a *daimyô* and with a stipend of 700 *koku* per year derived from certain stipulated districts. The letter was from three peasants, 'village leaders' from one of the districts from which he drew his revenue. It read in part,

1. Because of your promise to reduce expenditures, we have, during the past years, advanced tax rice and made loans. However, we see no sign of any efforts to achieve necessary reductions in expenditures; 2. Your brother is an immoral idler. As long as such a person is supported by your household, there is little chance of reducing expenditures. Last winter, we asked that some action be taken against your brother. What is your plan? 3. You have more than six servants, including maids and horsemen. Some should be dismissed; 4. Your representative asked us if we could assist in negotiating a further loan. Even if a low interest loan were to be made to you, it would be of little use as long as you have your useless brother. The temple from which you hope to borrow does not know that you already have 200 *ryô* of debt, but you know that you already have a large debt; 5. What is the purpose of your debt? As far as we can determine, you are sufficiently provided for; and, 6. To keep your brother is uneconomical. If no action is taken, we intend to resign our post as village leaders. (Yamamura, 1974, pp. 47–8)

On the one side, we see the burdens of office, lifestyle, and primogeniture borne by the head of an aristocratic family; on the other, the forces of the market, the money economy, and the self-confident farmers who were more than willing to dictate terms to their social superior.

If hopelessly in debt, *samurai* might arrange a marriage with a merchant family, in effect capitalizing on their aristocratic status. Alternatively they could surrender their status and escape the expenses that went with it. Becoming a farmer or a merchant was humiliating. It also required capital which an impoverished *samurai* might not possess, and it required skills which he might not have acquired. Many declining *samurai* therefore capitalized on the knowledge and skills they did have, and became teachers of martial arts, Confucian and Neo-Confucian classics, and in some cases the foreign 'Dutch learning'. Yoshida Shôin, whose pupils included several later leaders of the Meiji government, had inherited his school from his adoptive father, a military instructor who eked out a living by farming. Ogata Kôan's school of medicine and Western science in Ôsaka, founded in 1837, had some 600 regular students (Morris-Suzuki, 1994, p. 27). Thus the *samurai* might indeed have contributed to the Restoration and to Japan's modernization, but not in the direct way traditionally pictured.

Southeast Asia

While they [the Philippine *ilustrados*] deal in high sounding phrases concerning liberty and free government they have very little conception of what that means. They cannot resist the temptation to venality, and every office is likely to be used for the personal aggrandizement of the holder thereof in disregard of public interest.

United States President William Howard Taft

As in the case of Japan, the picture we have of elites in Southeast Asia depends on our standpoint and perspective. In the case of Siam, Chula-longkorn's twenty-seven brothers in fact have been seen as the only reliable group of 'modernizers' in the kingdom, because most of the aristocracy did not attempt to obtain a Western education. On the other hand, members of the aristocracy certainly used their inherited position to exploit economic opportunities. Northern Thai society was divided among the *cao* or lords, *phraj* or freeholders, and *khiikhaa* or slaves. Social hierarchy was clearly denoted by dress, with the lords wearing more and finer cottons, and in particular silk, since most silk thread was imported from China and woven into fabrics in specialized towns and at royal courts. The lords engaged in production and sale of cotton textiles on a large scale. However, rather than purchasing their raw materials and labour, they extracted raw cotton, woven cloth, and dyestuffs as tribute. And, rather than purchasing labour in the market as the commoners did, they employed slaves. A British Foreign Office official reported in 1875 that one of the major sources of income of the ruling lord in Chiang Mai was 'the sale of wearing apparel, etc., made by his several hundred slaves' (Bowie, 1992).

Corruption also in part depends on one's perspective. Early in the nineteenth century the British East India Company wanted to take over local trade in Burma and use the profits as a source of capital to finance its operations in China, and professed to be outraged by the treatment of British merchants in Rangoon. However, Burmese royal officials saw these merchants as a threat to their own monopoly privileges. The outbreak of war in 1852 also resulted from Burmese officials attempting to restrict British trade – the local governor appointed in 1850 had followed established practice in bringing criminal charges against foreign merchants to benefit his own trading connections, and in order to increase his income from the resulting court fees and from bribes extorted from the merchants to avoid prosecution. Britain used the particular case of two British ship-masters accused of murder, imprisoned, and forced to pay a bribe for their release, as justification for the naval expedition which began the conquest finally completed between 1887 and 1895. Nor was corruption, however defined, merely an Asian habit. The Philippines under Spain was a notorious case in point: 'The whole system was predicated on presumed malfeasance; before an outgoing governor could depart for home, he had to undergo an official investigation, or *residencia*. Bribery was endemic to the system, and each outgoing official knew that he would have to use a certain percentage of his profit to buy his way out' (Steinberg, et al., 1987, p. 91).

The administrations of the Dutch, Spanish, and early British possessions had adapted of necessity to the realities of distant and uncertain communication with their superiors in Europe. Until late in the nineteenth century Europeans were unable to administer the areas they claimed and ruled in partnership with indigenous elite groups. In general, the early colonial regimes ruled through local notables. In the Philippines village headmen became *gobernadorcillos*. 'Spaniards wanted labour rather than indigenous commercial produce, and they enlisted elements of the native ruling class to organize that work force. This arrangement early on determined the bifurcated social structure that has predominated to the present' (Larkin, 1982, p. 599). The British in the Straits Settlements ruled through a migrant elite, the Chinese, particularly those who controlled the opium revenue 'farms'. These private companies exercised public power in their responsibility for the marketing of opium and the collection and delivery of the profits to the colonial governments. They often had their own parallel networks of spies and enforcers, which gave them power over the local populations.

The Dutch East India Company employed regional chiefs in Java to organize the delivery of trade produce. A close relation developed between the Dutch and the native *priyayi* aristocrats. The Dutch were superior, but over time certain *priyayi* families came to exercise a substantial amount of power. Control over land and labour, despite the shift from indigenous use of tributes, taxes, and patron-client relationships towards Western legal formulas, did not alter the fundamental features of the structure of Javanese society. The persistent theme has been the survival of the *priyayi*, an administrative class with inherited family connections. Sutherland emphasizes the continual give and take of bargaining between the Dutch and local notables. The *priyayi* saw themselves as inheritors of traditional aristocratic values, the custodians of local cults and family tradition, and the guarantors of the necessary harmony between the spiritual and physical worlds. As such they were bound to respect the 'power' represented by the Dutch, and as such they evolved into an administrative caste during the nineteenth century (Sutherland, 1979; Breman, 1983; Van Niel, 1990b, p. 113).

As the new colonial regimes developed, these older groups lost status. Western regimes deliberately attempted to deprive traditional elites of their sources of patronage and private spheres of power. They also sometimes imposed much more rigid racial barriers than had existed previously. In the Dutch East Indies, for instance, this had the effect of disenfranchizing and marginalizing the Eurasians (Taylor, 1983). From the 1880s onwards colonial regimes worked to restrict the activities of the old opium farms, and they were finally abolished and replaced by government monopolies, first in the French possessions, then in the Dutch and American, and finally in British territories and Siam. But Western regimes still required natives, and their need for native administrators grew as colonial government became more ambitious in their attempt to govern the subject populations directly. New groups of native administrators appeared at the lower levels of the expanding bureaucracies. They could be members of traditional ruling groups, new groups, or migrants. In the Philippines the mixed mestizo groups maintained their power base, and the Spanish government's attempt to modernize its regime without sharing power with them led many to support the revolutionary nationalist movement. The Chinese who had been involved in opium farms often moved into the colonial bureaucracies – and their 'cultural descendants' inherited Singapore (Trocki, 1992, p. 89).

The new imperial bureaucracies employed new kinds of technical specialists, for instance in medicine, public health, and engineering. This opened a greater intellectual distance between Westerners and natives than had existed before, because the Westerners now were men with specialized technical training acquired before they arrived in the colonies. There also opened a greater social distance between Westerners and natives than before, because the Westerners now brought their wives and children with them, and in addition did not remain in any one colony more than a few years. They required the entire panoply of enclave life in the form of housing, domestic servants for their wives, schools for their children, and paid leave at 'home'. They were therefore separate and distanced from the natives in several ways, most significantly perhaps in that they conceived of themselves as a natural governing class whose duty was to do things on behalf of the natives, things which they were convinced the natives could not do for themselves. Rudyard Kipling warned Westerners that 'the silent, sullen peoples/ Shall judge your gods and you'.

But they also needed native subordinates. Members of the old elites were recruited and remolded into an administrative class of 'government officials', their preferred designation. In the Dutch East Indies, the *priyayi* regents' personal powers were progressively reduced, and they were integrated into the bureaucracy. Begun in the 1870s, the process was completed during the era of the 'Ethical Policy' in the years immediately before the First World War. In the years 1910–15 *priyayi* officials were reduced to paid functionaries of the central bureaucracy, dependent on the Dutch rather than on their local status. Some families benefited from new large-scale enterprise, but others lost wealth and status (Sutherland, 1979). In French Vietnam the old Confucian degree-holders in the Vietnamese administration were gradually replaced by men with an essentially French schooling. In the Philippines the Americans hoped to train the natives to govern themselves, but as in the case of President Taft quoted above, they often despaired. The Philippines passed from Spanish to American rule, but the very unequal distribution of property remained intact. The Americans, in order to have some chance of maintaining themselves against both a popular nationalist uprising and the resistance of the Muslims in the southern islands, 'found it expedient to allow the co-operative elements of the Filipino elite an increasingly larger role in government and to look the other way as they enriched themselves at the expense of the peasants and increased their traditional power within the local communities' (Trocki, 1992, pp. 90–1).

Eventually, native elites inherited much more centralized governments and much more effective bureaucratic institutions than the region had ever known before. And their role models, both for behaviour and for lifestyle, were the previous generation of imperial bureaucrats. They also inherited the ambiguous legacy of 'collaboration'. Colonial regimes were based on superior military force, but they required the cooperation of native elites. This provided opportunities for individuals and families, but to later nationalists, cooperation with Westerners and accommodation to the realities of Western power appeared as 'indigenous collaboration' with an alien regime (Trocki, 1992, p. 87).

In addition there is again the question of the values of the native elites. Bureaucrats they may have become, but the Javanese *priyayi* remained an aristocracy. Similarly, the Vietnamese Confucian degree-holders remained in office into the 1930s. In Cambodia French administration had the effect of confirming the local elites in power. King Norodom of Cambodia probably enjoyed a higher income under French administration than any other Cambodian ruler in the nineteenth century. Norodom did not rule; at the same time, stability, combined with maintenance of symbolic aspects of kingship, had the long-term effect of increasing the prestige of the monarchy. The Malay aristocracy enjoyed the perquisites available to them both as recipients of stipends from the British Civil List and as traditional authority figures within the carefully maintained traditional structures. In the Philippines it has been said bluntly that in the nineteenth century, 'more than colonial rule in itself inhibited industrial growth'. Although the Spanish did little to encourage development and British and American investors repatriated their profits, nevertheless 'native entrepreneurs whose fortunes remained in the Philippines, with rare exception, showed little desire to change their pattern of investment in land . . . a safe and familiar line of endeavour [which] brought with it social prestige and political power along with easy profits' (Larkin, 1982, p. 621).

5

THE FIRST ASIAN TIGER: THE TRANSFORMATION OF JAPAN

Perspectives on the Miracle

Japan's rapid rise seemed a 'miracle' to scholars writing in the 1950s, 1960s, and 1970s. Now it seems less miraculous, or perhaps one miracle among many. Changes in interpretation reflect the perspectives of the observer. Viewed from the West, as suggested in Chapter 1, interpretations of Japan's rise have been very much a product of developments in the West. This is true of Asia as well, and viewed from Asia, as will be seen in Chapters 6 and 7, interpretations of Japan's transformation reflect the fact that the emergence of an industrial economy in Japan destabilized the balance of power in Asia. In this chapter we will attempt to maintain an internal view, and look at Japanese development as experienced by the Japanese.

'Dualism' seems a principle which might encapsulate the paradoxical relations of opposites in Japanese development. Western observers of Japanese economic growth have employed it in the form of the 'Lewis model' in which labour flows from a low-wage traditional to a high-wage modern sector. But it has also framed the perspectives of Japanese scholars, in the contrast of agriculture and industry, of large-scale industry and the small-scale and part-time subcontracting sector, of the great trading companies and small shops. Dualism marks social relations as well, in the persistence of traditional forms alongside modern elements, for instance in the familial structure of business enterprises. In the realm of values too, a mix of inherited or traditional values – loyalty, group orientation, self-sacrifice, diligence – confronts Western or modern values, such as recruitment on formal educational criteria. In social structure the family and neighbourhood or village communities stand opposite large bureaucratic organizations. Government policies – education, low wages, high savings, mobilization of resources in the national interest – seem to reinforce these contrasts but in a way which results in social harmony and rapid growth.

But if Japan had *failed* to develop, the same set of economic relationships, social structures, values, and government policies which are commonly used to explain Japanese success, would be used to explain Japanese failure. In the economic sphere, such an argument would cite the monopoly position enjoyed by large firms, and the persistence of grossly inefficient small farms, industrial firms, and retailers. In the social realm it would emphasize the lack of individual initiative of the Japanese, petty jealousy, rote learning, and mindless credentialism. Hierarchy and deference would also be cited, for instance in the domination of Tokyo University graduates. The rigidity of government policy would be mentioned, along with restrictions on the domestic market, and the history of foreign aggression.

A deeper level of dualism resolves these paradoxes. Japanese development in the late nineteenth and early twentieth centuries did in fact have two aspects: first, the production of consumer goods for domestic and foreign markets, continuing the pattern of protoindustrial development and undertaken by private interests, and secondly the creation of heavy industries by the government for military purposes. The activist government legislation of the Meiji era has been cited as a model for economic development many times in other countries in East and Southeast Asia, and many of the institutional changes introduced by the new government have persisted to the present. However, an explanation of the rapid growth of the Japanese economy requires us to examine the private sector as well. This involves on the one hand the role of private entrepreneurs, and on the other hand the recruitment of a labour force. Japan relied on continuities outside the state sector, in the growth of markets, commercial agriculture, and protoindustrial development.

Dualism was maintained and deepened in the division between male and female. The industrial labour market in Japan segmented along gender lines. One of the less pleasant aspects of the Japanese 'model' of economic development was the exploitation of young women in the silk and cotton mills. The men employed in the government-subsidized heavy industrial sector, however, received much more favourable treatment. These relationships all suggest patterns which have since repeated themselves.

One crucial aspect of Japanese development was the creation of a new national community. Traditional values were not inherited; rather, they were selected to support the power of a new elite. Further, the new national community was a gendered community. If women were to be fitted into new economic relations, then the public sphere had to be redesigned in a way which would accommodate them as well, but not interfere with the authority of the government elite. Accordingly, women ceased to be *samurai*, peasant, artisan, or merchant women, and became 'Japanese women', assigned a role which would bolster the regime and support its goals.

But economic development undermined the new cultural structures even as they were being created. In the 1920s divisions in the countryside, divisions in industry, and divisions in urban society presented the government with new challenges, and as we will see in Chapter 7, the response was tragic.

Towards Restoration?

The collapse of the Tokugawa bakufu

Political affairs are drifting. Ostentation is condoned, *samurai* indolence increasing, and the élan of the Tokugawa house collapsing. Mindful of the new foreign contacts, we must make military preparation and undertake reforms in accord with the time. The system must be simplified and a true *samurai* spirit revived. Because we wish the *samurai* spirit to gleam, you should be of strong resolve and present to us such suggestions as you may have.

Shogunal Notice to Tokugawa Vassals, 1862

It is easy, and tempting, to construct an account of the Meiji Restoration which makes it seem inevitable. George Wilson reminds us of Claude Lévi-Strauss's assertion that 'the French Revolution as commonly conceived never took place', and then proceeds to detail the confusion, incoherence, and even insanity which accompanied the transition from Tokugawa to Meiji (Wilson, 1992, p. 43). It was not clear in advance what would appear to replace the Tokugawa, but there were certainly reasons for the collapse. Chapters 3 and 4 outlined the extensive economic change taking place within Japan before 1867, and ironically the peace and social order maintained by the Tokugawa ultimately undermined their position. The intensive development of internal commerce, foreign contacts and trade despite prohibitions, and development programmes sponsored by domain governments all worked to weaken the system. To many, the class structure defined by officially sponsored neo-Confucian values seemed to be breaking down. The *daimyô* and *samurai* were declining, though the decline may have been relative rather than absolute. Conversely, the merchant class was rising. In a pattern similar to Europe, Japanese merchants employed wage labour in rural areas on a putting-out basis to escape the restrictions of urban guilds, for instance in the use of the 'tall loom' in silk-weaving. Though the rise of the merchants did not threaten the existing order, there were many cases of merchants and even wealthy farmers whose incomes were large enough to excite the worried envy of the *samurai*.

To many, as well, the Tokugawa seemed to be losing control. The weakness of the central government, the inadequate fiscal system, the absence of an articulated bureaucratic structure, the dependence on indirect measures of control, and institutional and ideological rigidity, left the Tokugawa poorly prepared to cope with the ongoing economic crisis of the early nineteenth century, seen in the rural and urban uprisings. During the Ôshio Rebellion of 1837, directed against wealthy farmers and rice merchants, one quarter of the city of Ôsaka was burned to the ground. Japanese Marxists have cited social unrest as evidence of a crisis in Japanese feudalism, which led to the Meiji Restoration and the establishment of a half-feudal political system which sponsored capitalist economic development while maintaining much of the old absolutist system. For Western scholars the same evidence indicates the progressive aspects of the Tokugawa economy which laid the foundations for modern economic growth. Despite their differences, however, both schools suggest that these changes would have led to a breakdown of the Tokugawa regime even in the absence of Western intrusion.

In addition there is the evidence of genuine intellectual ferment in late Tokugawa. Domain governments maintained several hundred schools, primarily for the children of their *samurai*, and some 10 000 temple schools taught the children of merchants, artisans, and farmers. Together these became the basis of the Meiji elementary school system. In addition the number of private academies increased in the first half of the nineteenth century to several thousand. Many were Confucian, but many also specialized in 'Western studies', or in the anti-Confucian 'national learning' fostered by the Mito School, and some were dedicated to 'revival' or 'reform', for instance the school operated by Yoshida Shôin in Chôshû (Collcutt, 1991, pp. 137–8; see Wilson, 1992). Late Tokugawa thinkers had developed new approaches to the economy. Traditionally, the problem of the economy was conceived as a search for ways to maintain the position of the *samurai* class in the face of a pervasive money economy and the increasing wealth of the merchants. Early thinkers wanted to turn back the clock, but the discussion became progressively more sophisticated. In 1813 Kaiho Seiryô published his analysis of commodities and profit quoted in Chapters 3 and 4. In the 1830s Satô Nobuhiro wrote a 'confidential memorandum on government' which no longer viewed the ruler as a benevolent Confucian exemplar of virtue, but rather saw government as an active source of economic change. Satô envisioned total state control of society, but he emphasized that the state's role involved education, training, and development – not only 'managing the nation', but also 'developing its products' in order to enrich the country.

Yokoi Shônan advocated the opening of the country to foreign trade and a government programme to sponsor technical improvements to enhance Japanese exports. His 'three principles of national economy' formulated in 1860 were the principle of the rich country, the principle of the strong army, and the way of the warrior. The concept later epitomized as *fukoku kyôhei* (rich country, strong army) was already common among late Tokugawa economic thinkers. Yokoi was an adviser to Matsudaira Yoshinaga, *daimyô* of Echizen and a key figure in the Restoration, and his disciple Yuri Kimimasa played an important role in the early Meiji administrative and financial reforms. Yokoi himself was assassinated in 1869 by a conservative extremist because he had not worked to 'expel the barbarian' (Morris-Suzuki, 1989, pp. 34–43).

There is also evidence that some officials were willing to place greater reliance on the market. In Chôshû the domain government had pursued a policy of sponsoring development by creating monopolies in various products, but had nonetheless fallen further and further into debt. An attempt in 1830 to erect a system under which five privileged groups would handle all trade led to riots by farmers and artisans and was dropped. Murata Seifu, called to office by the new *daimyô* in 1838, repudiated some debts, cut expenditures, improved accounting procedures, and announced new sumptuary laws to encourage the Chôshû *samurai* to concentrate on their military duties. In addition, he ended the government's unpopular monopolies, reduced taxes, and sponsored general measures to raise agricultural output. The balance was favourable enough to permit reduced *samurai* stipends to be restored and still leave a surplus, which Murata placed in an emergency fund later used to finance Chôshû's military expenses. The question of how best to confront the West added a sense of crisis to these developments. In 1842 Sakuma Shôzan, an advocate of modern artillery and coastal defences, hit on the slogan 'Eastern ethics and Western science'. Sakuma knew of the outcome of the Opium War and in fact had read Wei Yuan's work which advocated 'learning the superior techniques of the barbarians to control the barbarians', although he claimed that they had arrived at their positions independently. Wei's ideas were later epitomized by Zhang Zhidong as 'Chinese learning for the substance and Western learning for the function', but as argued in Chapter 4 this did not provide a secure philosophical grounding for the Chinese reformers. Sakuma's formulation, however, separated *dôtoku* (ethics) from *gakugei* (science). Thus the West might possess its own ethics, which could be rejected, while its science could be adopted without sacrificing traditional Eastern values.

Note that the way Sakuma posed the problem meant that the introduction of Western technology could proceed unimpeded even while the Japanese continued to debate what precisely the essence of Japanese 'ethics' might be. It may be true that certain values are inherent in modern industrial technology, but in the context of the nineteenth century, this formula provided Japan's leaders with an unproblematic justification for a programme which allowed them to develop sufficient military power to hold off the West, while at the same time creating a unity of purpose and action based on recognized common traditions. Such a programme could be popular, in the sense of not violating the sense of propriety of important groups in society, but it did not have to be popular in the sense that all initiatives undertaken by the government required those groups' prior approval. It was difficult to oppose such a programme on either philosophical or practical grounds.

Nevertheless there were limits to these responses to the economic, political, and intellectual crises. Political power still ruled over economic power. Merchants still required permission from Tokugawa or domain officials to engage in business. Their most reliable source of profit continued to be lending to *daimyô* and *samurai*. Merchants never threatened the existing order, and within their family firms they replicated the official neo-Confucian values. The famous Family Constitution of the House of Mitsui, written around 1700 and widely imitated, had as its first three articles:

1. This Family Constitution being based on the written testament of the founder must be observed by all descendants.
2. Always bearing in mind the many benefits received from the ancestors, everyone must work diligently for the greater prosperity of the House.
3. The laws of the *bakufu* must be carried out to the letter, by family members and employees alike. (Hirschmeier and Yui, 1981, p. 63)

Also the prestige of traditional forms remained overwhelming, as seen very concretely in the eagerness of wealthy commoners to purchase *samurai* status when they could.

Furthermore, political power still rested with the Tokugawa. The government dealt firmly with opposition among officials and *samurai*. Sakuma was imprisoned when his disciple Yoshida Shôin attempted to stow away on one of Commodore Perry's ships and was duly arrested for violating the law against attempting to leave the country. Both would have been executed if highly placed friends had not interceded, and Yoshida later was executed for plotting the assassination of Tokugawa officials. Another of Sakuma's students, Katsu Awa, became navy minister and 'father of the Japanese navy', several of Yoshida's disciples were leaders in the Restoration movement, and Yoshida himself became a symbol of the 'spirit' which the leaders of the Meiji government claimed as their own. Still, if the pressure from the West had not been both unprecedented and increasing exponentially because of the development of industrial technologies, neither Sakuma nor Yoshida would have had the impact they did. There might have been civil war, there might have been a change in political leadership, but there would not have been the Meiji Restoration.

It was the foreign policy crisis which precipitated the collapse of the Tokugawa (see Totman, 1980). News of the Opium Wars in China spread. The leaders of the government and of potential opposition movements knew what was happening and recognized the threat posed by the West. The question was, what to do? All agreed that Japan would have to adopt Western military technology, and all wanted at the same time to retain Japanese culture. But what exactly was to be retained, and who was to lead the effort? Strenuous efforts were made by the Tokugawa government, beginning with a new financial reform and a series of consultations with its own retainers and with the *daimyô* as to the best policy. Students were sent to Europe – two of them, Nishi Amane and Tsuda Mamishi, returned to become leading advocates of free trade. A school was opened for the collection, translation, and study of foreign texts – this 'school for barbarian studies' was later absorbed into Tokyo University. With French assistance, a shipyard and iron foundry were set up in Yokohama and a new dockyard at Yokosuka – all later taken over by the Meiji government. The Tokugawa also brought in French advisers to assist in a reorganization of the military and civilian bureaucracies – again anticipating later Meiji policies. The *shōgun* adopted a western-style military uniform.

But the Tokugawa were still only a single family, 'first among equals' (Wilson, 1992), and as such represented Japan but did not command all the resources of Japan. They could and would be blamed for failure, but were limited in the actions they could take to ensure success. Opposed to them, lower *samurai* such as Yoshida, who exclaimed that Japanese should 'revere the Emperor and expel the barbarian', were appealing to a general symbol in the emperor, a symbol which could unite all Japanese. However, violence against foreigners led only to foreign retaliation, and in all such confrontations the Japanese lost out to superior Western military technology.

The Restoration movement

A country does not have two monarchs, a home does not have two masters; government devolves on one ruler. . . . The full authority to rule the land rests in the court.

Treaty Between Satsuma and Tosa, 1867

Finally, of course, the crisis was resolved by the overthrow of the Tokugawa by an alliance of non-Tokugawa domains led by Satsuma and Chôshû. Both had confronted the foreigners and been decisively defeated. During 1862 and 1863 Satsuma refused to hand over retainers who had killed an Englishman, and an English punitive force destroyed half of Kagoshima; Chôshû shelled foreign ships and closed the Shimonoseki straits, and a combined Western fleet in turn destroyed some of its shore batteries and landed a force to dismantle the remaining guns. In both cases, however, it was the Tokugawa government which was forced to pay the indemnities levied by the foreigners.

The failure of attempts to 'expel the barbarian' led to the emergence of new leaders, notably Ôkubo Toshimichi and Saigô Takamori in Satsuma and Kido Kôin in Chôshû. They set about acquiring the military technology necessary first to defeat the Tokugawa and then to assert Japanese power against the foreigners. As Ôkubo wrote in 1865 to two Satsuma *samurai* studying in England,

> Since the Chôshû war the so-called extremists have generally had their eyes opened and now discern the impossibility of maintaining an 'expel the barbarian' position.... there is no alternative but to aim for the fundamental policy of protecting the court and establishing imperial prestige abroad by resorting to the energetic execution of 'rich country, strong army'. (Iwata, 1965, p. 88)

Satsuma purchased arms from Britain and Belgium in return for licences to develop mineral resources and trading rights, and brokered similar deals for Chôshû. These programmes were almost exact duplicates of those being undertaken by the Tokugawa government, and of course they directly flouted the government's monopoly on diplomatic and trade relations with foreign countries. Kido led an anti-Tokugawa coup in Chôshû in 1865. Satsuma signed an alliance with Tosa in July 1867 and with Chôshû in October. Chôshû rejected a Tokugawa ultimatum and Tokugawa forces attacked, but the invasion was called off when the *shôgun* died. In 1868 the emperor died and the new *shôgun* resigned, hoping that as lord of the Tokugawa domains he would retain substantial power as a senior member of a proposed new ruling council. Instead, Satsuma and Chôshû forces seized the Imperial Palace and declared that the direct rule of the emperor had been restored. An attack by Tokugawa forces was defeated, and the Satsuma and Chôshû army, now calling themselves the 'imperial forces', marched virtually unopposed from Kyôtô to Tokyo. The former *shôgun* was stripped of most of his lands and eventually pensioned.

An apparent paradox of Japanese history is that Satsuma and Chôshû were far from being the most 'modern' domains or the most 'modern' regions. They did possess modern weapons, however, and leaders intent on using those weapons to gain power. Their intransigence, rather than any inherent logic in the situation, was the key factor responsible for the Restoration which actually occurred. Alternatives were brutally rejected. Sakuma was murdered in 1864 by assassins from Chôshû. He had been travelling from Tokyo to Kyôtô in the service of a compromise party whose leaders hoped for a 'union of civil and military' — a reformed shogunal government which would uphold the policy of opening the country but also grant a greater voice to the imperial court and the outer *daimyô*. The Chôshû extremists, however, were seeking to overthrow the Tokugawa and opposed any attempt to achieve a compromise between *shôgun* and emperor.

The success of the anti-Tokugawa forces in developing modern weapons also raises the issue of the technological response of the Japanese to the West. Tessa Morris-Suzuki argues that it was not simply the 'opening' of Japan which led to the importing of Western industrial technologies. Rather, the inherited pattern of competition among domains, combined with the general perception of the threat posed by the foreigners, led to a multiplicity of attempts to adapt new techniques to local conditions. A large number of competitors increased the likelihood of success and also ensured the rapid spread of successful approaches. Iron smelting and the construction of steamships were two crucial examples. The Japanese found they could not cast large cannon because existing methods of smelting did not yield large enough amounts of uniform iron. The *daimyô* of Saga (whose duties included the defence of Nagasaki), concerned both to improve his domain's finances and with foreign threats, commissioned a group to smelt iron in large enough quantities to cast cannon. The problem was impurities in the fuel. In 1850 the group succeeded in building a reverberatory furnace, which kept the burning fuel separate from the iron ore, according to descriptions in a translated Dutch text. By 1853, the year of Perry's arrival, Saga was already casting cannon both for itself and to fill orders from the Tokugawa government.

The success of Saga, says Morris-Suzuki, 'created a predictable chain reaction' in the competitive Tokugawa system. Satsuma began to develop an adaptation of the smelting technique in 1851, and Mito, the centre of the 'school of national learning', launched its own programme shortly after. The Tokugawa government sent a technician to study at Saga and built its own furnace in 1854 at Nirayama on the Izu peninsula. By 1868 there were eleven reverberatory furnaces in operation or under construction and another three planned. As for shipbuilding, Perry's two steam ships were the first seen in Japan, but the idea of steam power was known from Dutch textbooks. The shogunate abolished the previous ban on the construction of large ships, but retained for itself a monopoly of the right to import foreign ships. The domains responded by attempting to build their own, and Satsuma was the first to succeed, in 1855. Japan had no naval vessels in 1854, but by 1868 the shogunal government had 45 and the domains a total of 94 (Morris-Suzuki, 1994, pp. 57–8, 61–3).

Japan's technological response, therefore, not only did not require the opening to the West, it also did not require the 'Restoration'. The response built on a longstanding tradition of development projects, and this tradition included vitally not only the eventual victors in the power struggle such as Satsuma and Chôshû but also the losers, the Tokugawa shogunal government. Those looking at the Japanese story from the perspective of European studies may be struck by the comparison with England in the eighteenth century – the competitive emulation among regions and firms such as the Derbys, Cort, and Wilkinson to produce first cast and then bored cannon, efforts which paved the way to the steam engine. From an Asian studies perspective, competition among the domains may be compared to 'regionalism' in China – competition among provincial governors in the self-strengthening movement is usually seen as negative, an indication of a lack of central control. This is important, for although from the standpoint of the Tokugawa this sort of development was threatening, after the Meiji Restoration all of the significant sources of development were focused on the goal of strengthening the new state. The new government, for instance, dismantled the machines in Saga's experimental industrial plant and moved them to Tokyo (Morris-Suzuki, 1994, p. 88).

The Meiji Regime

The reforms

Every action, whether progressive or conservative, should be taken in response to the occasion, and if it develops unfavourably should be abandoned. This may entail shame, but it is to be endured.

Ôkubo Toshimichi, 1873

Changes in social structure legislated by the Meiji government seem like another of the paradoxes of Japanese development, for the government's leaders were *samurai*. Most indeed came from particularly conservative backgrounds. Yet after gaining power, they abolished the traditional signs of *samurai* status. The early acts of the government included banning the carrying of swords and outlawing the wearing of the traditional *samurai* topknot. In 1872–3 the army reform and conscription law laid the basis for a mass army and ended the *samurai* monopoly on the military profession. *Daimyô* and *samurai* also lost their control over local government. In 1871 the domains were abolished and replaced by prefectures with centrally appointed governors. Their number was then reduced to 72 in 1872, and later to 43. A new Home Ministry was established in 1873, which further centralized government administration, especially the police force. In 1870 commoners were given the right to take family names, and in 1871 they were given the right to marry *daimyô* and *samurai*. In 1871 the *daimyô* and *samurai* in turn were formally given the right to engage in agriculture, industry, and commerce without loss of status.

The stipends of *daimyô* and *samurai* were the largest expense of the new government, and the government moved to reduce them. In 1871 stipends were made subject to taxation, and in 1873–4 *daimyô* and *samurai* were offered the opportunity to convert their stipends into cash. Finally in 1876 the stipends were eliminated and replaced with interest-bearing bonds. Payments were reduced by about one-third overall, though on a sliding scale which favoured those at the bottom, so that a *daimyô* with 100 000 koku dropped to 25 000 while a lower *samurai* with 100 koku dropped to 66. The average grant of bonds, the *samurai* complained, did not provide an income sufficient for a family.

The 1872 land reform granted private ownership to farmers who cultivated their land and to the existing village landlords, recognizing the fact that land had been held by individuals for a long time. Ownership was combined with a tax levied in money, assessed on the basis of land value. Conservatives had argued that the old system of land ownership and taxation should not be altered, because the introduction of free buying and selling of land would lead to greater inequality of property ownership. They were opposed by Kanda Takahira, an early popularizer of the Western notion that inequality was rooted in native abilities, and that therefore any attempt to eliminate it would only penalize virtue and reward vice. Kanda advocated a free market in land, combined with a tax on the market value of the land. Western nations, he said, had solved the problem of tax revenues by reducing their reliance on agricultural taxes and increasing taxes on commerce; Japan was not yet advanced enough to do this, but needed to establish a simple principle of taxation.

The government's policy reflected Kanda's ideas. Matsukata Masayoshi, from Satsuma, finance minister and later prime minister, argued that this combination of measures would increase production and government revenue together, combining national wealth with the means to gain military strength. Land was not granted to the *daimyô* and *samurai* – Japan acquired a class of landlords and a class of small farmers, but not a class of landed aristocrats. The new owners were given freedom to sell their land, freedom to grow whatever crops they chose, and freedom to export their produce, even foodstuffs. However, the Meiji land tax rested on an assessed value, not on market value, and the government worked to ensure the highest possible assessed values, which increased the real burden of the new tax. Additional levies were imposed to support local governments, and later new assessments were added to support local schools (Morris-Suzuki, 1989; Sugiyama, 1994).

The new government's actions aroused the opposition of conservative *samurai*, another of the ironic paradoxes of the Restoration, since their support had been critical in the early stages of the Restoration movement. The pace of reform and its direction were too much for many conservatives. There were revolts in Chôshû in 1869–70, Hizen in 1874, and again in Chôshû in 1876. Saigô Takamori had left the government in 1873 when his plan to invade Korea was rejected. Retreating into retirement, in 1877 he was persuaded by friends to lead the so-called 'Satsuma Rebellion'. The rebels gained control of southern Kyûshû for six months, but were eventually crushed, and some 20 000 died, along with 10 000 government troops, while Saigô and other leaders committed suicide.

The government's reforms also excited a desire for further reform and the introduction of Western-style parliamentary government. The 'people's rights movement' in fact began among the disaffected and defeated conservative *samurai*, who denounced the government as a clique from Satsuma and Chôshû. However, the agitation spread widely and included many farmers who formed study groups to draft possible constitutions for the country. These demands contributed to another crisis within the government in 1881, and the group of 'liberals' who supported the early introduction of a constitution and representative assembly were ousted.

The remaining members of the ruling oligarchy were united in their commitment to military strength supported by long-term economic development. The catchphrase 'rich country, strong army' meant to them that the wealth of the country was to be directed to ensuring that the country was strong. It also meant that only they and their friends would rule. Following the 1881 crisis, official positions were even more closely restricted to *samurai* from Satsuma and Chôshû. Complaints over the continued domination of the 'Sat-Chô clique' and foreign pressure for a more modern administration contributed to the decision to introduce an examination system for recruitment of officials in 1887. The new system, as revised in 1893 and 1899, gave preference to former officials and to the graduates of the new Imperial University in Tokyo established the previous year. The oligarchy's continued control of government appointments was partly concealed, and the foundation laid for the domination of Japan's bureaucracy by Tokyo University law graduates, which continues today.

Following the 1881 crisis the government also moved to introduce a formal constitution and a representative assembly. After careful consideration of possible foreign models, the oligarchy selected the one which would ensure their continued domination. Japan's new constitution was based on the constitution which had been in force in Prussia since 1850. Introduced in the aftermath of the defeat of the 1848 revolutions, the Prussian constitution, among other things, was a grant from the ruler which reaffirmed his divine right to rule, placed the army directly under the ruler's command and outside any parliamentary control, gave the ruler the right to appoint the government, provided that only the government could initiate legislation, and provided as well that the representative assembly's right to approve legislation could be suspended in time of emergency. The Meiji Constitution included these features, but eliminated the references to the direct role of emperor which had been suggested by the government's German advisers. Instead, the Constitution defined the 'national polity' (*kokutai*) as resting on 'a line of Emperors unbroken for ages eternal', which was symbolized but not ruled by the 'sacred and inviolable' person of the reigning emperor.

The Meiji government and the economy

> 80 to 90 per cent of these commodities are luxuries, imitating foreign products, and made with imported raw materials. The manufacture of these contributes but little to national power.
>
> > Government comment on rural industries producing
> > Western consumer goods

The amount of compensation to the former *daimyô* and *samurai* may have seemed meagre to them, but the total was still very high – 173 million yen. The interest and amortization on these bonds absorbed one-quarter of the government's entire revenue to the end of the Meiji period in 1912. Government leaders hoped the *samurai* would go into business to help 'enrich the country', but they did not. Many *samurai* simply failed and sold their bonds for what they could during the depression. The bonds were bought by bankers such as Yasuda Zenjirô, founder of the Yasuda *zaibatsu* combine, who made substantial profits when economic conditions improved. The banks formed under the new banking law of 1876 were mostly established by commoners (Yamamura, 1974, chs. 7–8), and the same was true of the new industrial enterprises which began to emerge. Many former *samurai* found positions in the army and in the police. Many also joined the new government bureaucracy – hardly surprising, given that this was their main employment before the Restoration. In the 1920s half of the serving prefectural governors were from *samurai* families.

In the countryside the new taxes were not popular. There were 177 peasant uprisings between 1868 and 1873, more in fact in the decade after the Restoration than in the decade before. However, the revolts were unfocused, and the army and police units – paid for by the new taxes – were able to prevent any serious threat to the government's position. Keeping in mind that on average a quarter of the government's revenue was being paid to the former *daimyô* and *samurai*, the government can be seen as buying political stability on one side, but at the cost of instability on the other.

Through the 1870s, though, many farmers had reasons to be happy. The government's expenses – for the military and infrastructure such as railways and telegraph, for the commutation bonds, and for a number of mining and manufacturing enterprises – exceeded its income, and the deficit was covered by paper money. The rapidly rising supply of money caused an increase in prices. Even so, the farmers' new taxes were fixed, and their net real incomes therefore rose. Many merchants, landlords, and wealthy farmers invested in artisan shops and small factories to make consumer goods, particularly Western-style clothing, furniture, and the umbrellas which soon became ubiquitous.

On the other hand, the real income of the government, and of the former *daimyô* and *samurai*, declined. The 'liberals' in the government, led by Ôkuma Shigenobu, in addition to arguing for some form of representative government, also argued in favour of a foreign loan to overcome the government's financial crisis. The 'conservatives', led by Ôkubo Toshimichi and supported by Matsukata, opposed representative government and argued against a foreign loan. Matsukata insisted that the government should reduce its expenditures and cut the money supply to reduce prices and restore the value of its revenues. Matsukata won the economic argument, and the conservatives defeated the liberals, who left the government.

Under Matsukata's leadership the government reduced the money supply by 20 per cent in one year. The government's bullion reserves rose from 7 million yen in 1880 to 42 million in 1885. Prices dropped, while fixed commitments such as taxes and interest payments remained constant. The deflation caused a large number of bankruptcies, depression, and unemployment, especially among the small firms established to supply consumer goods. Matsukata was unconcerned. He argued that if Japan were to

> continue increasingly to buy foreign products with specie, and, while the government and people together rush forward in superficial progress... we continue to be swayed by and propagate the evils of easy living, the importation of western goods will rapidly increase day by day until finally we will not even know where to begin to bring it to an end.

Matsukata's concern for the trade balance was legitimate, but his disapproval of 'superficial progress' and 'easy living' shows his very selective perception of the situation. As seen above the government denounced rural industries producing Western consumer goods. These might have provided a base for import substitution, but the government worried about the need to import raw materials. At the time Japan imported sugar, a consumer good and clear evidence of 'easy living', cotton yarn, which the government tried unsuccessfully to produce in its own factories, and woollen cloth, which led the government to a futile attempt to stimulate sheep-raising (Tipton, 1990; Francks, 1992, pp. 31–2).

One of the largest categories of imported goods was military hardware, but the contribution of weapons to national power exempted them from Matsukata's concern with the balance of payments. Total military expenditures rose by half, despite the price decline and the end to resistance to the new regime, from 10.6 million yen per year in 1876–80, to 15.8 million in 1881–5. In 1883 the government introduced a new conscription law with three years of active duty followed by nine in the reserves, and increased the size of the army from 30 000 to 73 000 in peacetime and to 200 000 in wartime. By 1894, in addition to smaller craft, the navy had 28 large modern warships, mostly imported.

The deflation raised the real burden of taxes on the farmers. Taxes remained fixed in money terms while agricultural prices declined and markets for artisan products contracted because of the depression. Marxists argue that this dispossessed small farmers and concentrated land in the hands of capitalist landlords, who continued to exercise a 'semi-feudal' control in the countryside. Smethurst has argued that the deflation did not hurt progressive farmers and regions (Smethurst, 1986, pp. 57–60), but many did suffer. Between 1883 and 1890 some 368 000 farmers lost their land because they had failed to pay their taxes; they had owned an estimated 110 000 acres, which indicates that most were small farmers. The hardship contributed to the new upsurge of unrest and uprisings in the countryside in the late 1880s. Again, the government suppressed overt opposition by deploying the army and police as necessary.

Government policies and economic growth

... to construct within Japan all kinds of mechanical equipment on the western model, including shipbuilding, railways, telegraph, mines and buildings, and thus with one great leap to introduce to Japan the concepts of enlightenment.

Itô Hirobumi, on the mission of the Ministry of
Industry

To evaluate the success of the Meiji government in fostering economic growth, we need to know the level at which Japan began. Estimates of national income which begin in 1885 show quite rapid growth. Earlier figures also showed very rapid growth, which seemed to indicate that the Meiji government had created the conditions for Japan's rapid economic modernization. However, early Meiji statistics were incomplete, so that, for instance, the reports showing rises in agricultural output reflect more complete coverage rather than increased production. Therefore it is not clear when Japan's rapid growth began.

Susan Hanley has attempted an indirect approach by looking at evidence of living standards. She discovered that in terms of life expectancy, diet, housing, and urban environment, the Japanese were better off than most West Europeans in 1850. Real wages had been rising. Even poor Japanese, in addition to a mix of grains, ate soybean paste (*miso*) soup, seasonal vegetables, bean curd, dried fish, and pickles – not lavish, but 'nutritionally, the diet must certainly have been better than that of the poor working classes in the industrial cities of England where the staple food was white bread, accompanied by margarine and tea for most meals'. Housing improved, from single-room dwelling with earthen floors, to multiple-room houses with *tatami* floors. Japanese money wages in 1850 were comparable to English money wages around 1800, and may have afforded the average Japanese a higher quality of life than English workers enjoyed at the beginning of England's industrialization (Hanley, 1997).

If Japan's income was already relatively high before the Restoration, compared to European countries before the onset of industrialization, then rather than causing growth, the Meiji regime must have built on existing foundations. As seen above, Japan's technological response to the West was already well advanced before the Restoration. In addition, the shogunal government had always been a military hierarchy, and the new government followed this pattern. The government's primary goal was to strengthen Japan in order to resist the West and to increase Japanese influence in Asia. This led them to favour those kinds of economic development which led to increased military power, and this might lead to rapid aggregate growth and increased welfare, or it might not. Again, in comparison with the regional centres of the self-strengthening movement in China, the difference between Japan and China may be that in Japan one of the competing groups managed to seize effective control of the central government, and then create an ideology which concealed their control.

Traditionally, many scholars have argued that the Meiji government played a crucial role in economic growth by introducing modern Western technologies into Japan, and many still argue that Japan was feudal before the arrival of Perry and that contact with the West stimulated 'modernization' (for instance Sugiyama, 1994). This 'state-centred' view (Morris-Suzuki, 1994, ch. 4) holds that the Meiji state's policies acted as a substitute for a long period of preparation preceding industrialization in the West. This was certainly the view the government itself had of its efforts. The Kôbushô (Ministry of Industry), founded in 1870 and headed by Itô Hirobumi from 1873, aimed 'with one great leap to introduce to Japan the concepts of enlightenment'. Railways were built from Tokyo to Yokohama, Kobe to Ôsaka and to Kyôtô, and a rail and boat connection from Kyôtô to Tsuruga. The national telegraph network was completed in the early 1880s. The railway became a specialized genre subject for printmakers. Modernization here became both symbol and substance, and directly linked with political power, for centralization was enforced by information and orders passed over telegraph lines, and backed by military force deployed by railways if necessary.

The Kôbushô also established industrial enterprises using imported Western machinery, and they were often cited as the origin of modern industry in the country. Now, given the widespread responsiveness of individuals which has been discovered in the Tokugawa era, their role in transferring technology seems less important. Further, in both mining and manufacturing these state-sponsored factories were not commercially successful. This may not be relevant, for the state-centred argument holds that they provided important models for Japanese entrepreneurs. In introducing new techniques they may have absorbed the costs of experimentation and adaptation to Japanese conditions, and thereby reduced the risk to subsequent private entrepreneurs. The state enterprises were sold in the early 1880s as part of Matsukata's program to reduce the government's deficit. The Kôbushô was abolished in 1885 and combined with the agricultural sections of the Interior Ministry to form the new Ministry of Agriculture and Commerce (Nôshômushô).

The state enterprises were sold at low prices to businessmen with close connections to the oligarchy, particularly the Mitsui merchant house, the Furukawa mining family, and Iwasaki Yatarô, whose companies formed the basis of Mitsubishi combine. The sale of these enterprises laid the foundation for the later *zaibatsu*, but the low prices may simply have reflected the enterprises' unprofitability. In addition, advocates of the state-centred approach argue that these private firms not only acquired Western machinery at bargain prices, but also that they inherited the Western experts employed by the government. This allowed them to establish connections with Western firms which continued to supply technological expertise over the next generation.

The state-centred argument also holds that the government continued to play a crucial role in economic modernization even after the abolition of the Kôbushô, and points to the role of the government in introducing the technologies of the 'second industrial revolution': steel, advanced precision machinery, and electricity. Military spending and subsidies to strategically-important areas such as private dockyards and the merchant marine played a key role. The arsenals and state dockyards using these advanced technologies employed 50 000 workers in 1903. The government placed direct orders to private firms, possibly critical to the first period of development in advanced machinery industries. Finally there were spillover effects as government enterprises sold advanced equipment to private firms, and workers trained in government enterprises were later employed by or established their own private firms.

In the case of the automobile industry, Japanese engineers could produce automobiles, but the limitations of the market meant that gigantic mass-production plants on the American scale were not possible. Ishikawajima Shipyards launched a passenger car following the First World War, but the price was 10 000 yen, while American imports could be sold for 6000 to 7000 yen. The government saw motor vehicles as critical to war in the modern world, however, and so the Military Automobiles Assistance Law of 1918 offered large subsidies to producers of vehicles to government standards. Ishikawajima shifted to the production of trucks, and survived.

The 'revisionist approach' qualifies the state-centred argument. Rather than emphasizing the positive results, it highlights the overlapping jurisdictions, the abrupt changes in policy, the crooked deals by entrepreneurs with government connections, and the outright failures (Yamamura, 1974, ch. 7; Tipton, 1990). The government returned to direct investment in industrial enterprise at the end of the century, and built the first integrated iron and steel plant in Japan. The Yawata steelworks was financed with part of the indemnity from the Sino-Japanese War. Opened in 1901, it was, nevertheless, unsuccessful. The technology imported from Germany was unsuitable for Japanese coal and iron. The plant was poorly laid out and suffered from a shortage of skilled workers and raw materials. The plant was closed after less than a year to correct design faults, and costs which had been planned at 5 million yen eventually rose to 25 million. Although the works finally began to make a profit in 1910, runs were not long enough for economies of scale. The plant was intended to reduce Japan's dependence on imported steel products, and therefore was forced to produce an excessively wide range of items, which made it difficult to achieve economies of scale even in products demanded by the military. Workers trained at Yawata moved on to establish their own steel firms, but found it more profitable to import pig and scrap iron than to establish integrated plants, and this created a fateful imbalance in the 1930s (Morris-Suzuki, 1994; Yonekura, 1994).

Combined with the state-centred view of government's role in development was the belief that the *samurai* class had provided the bulk of entrepreneurial talent. However, among historians of Japan the traditional picture of *samurai* moving into roles as business leaders has also been modified. Many of the *samurai* entrepreneurs of the Meiji period were from families who had purchased noble status in the generation before the Restoration, reinforcing the picture of a dynamic Tokugawa economy. As noted above, many of the old *samurai* found employment in the government. In addition many of the Meiji business leaders were from non-noble backgrounds, some from very humble beginnings and some from traditional merchant families, for instance the House of Mitsui. The famous Japanese firm, variously known as a family, community, or group oriented, with its long time horizons and correspondingly cavalier treatment of its shareholders (see Dore, 1986), in fact does not differ so very greatly from large corporations elsewhere in the world. Although Japanese business leaders have been eager to portray themselves as exemplars of distinctively 'Japanese' values, the emergence of successful large corporations combines the appreciation of new technologies and markets with the ruthlessness in dealing with competitors and workers which marks corporate histories in Europe and the United States over the past century. Structurally as well, the organizational changes Japanese firms have undergone as they grow and develop resemble well-known patterns in Western firms (Fruin, 1983; Wray, 1984).

The crucial point may not be whether the government was right or wrong, but rather that technological change was not confined to government enterprises or to government-influenced sectors of the economy. The widespread search for better ways to do things often improved and extended existing handicraft techniques. Important in this 'bottom up' or 'social network' approach to development are private entrepreneurs and the role of the market, although their activities did not necessarily reflect the stereotype of ruthless competitive behaviour. In fact, if there is a lesson in Japan's experience, it may be that cooperation is as much a part of the market as competition. A key example is the adoption of ring-spindle machines in cotton spinning mills, along with a mix of long and short staple cotton. The machines could be operated by unskilled female workers, and the plants produced a relatively coarse thread suitable for use by the existing pool of skilled female handloom weavers. The All-Japan Cotton Spinners Federation published a journal including the latest technical and market information, sponsored trips by members to observe overseas firms and markets, and actively encouraged the exchange of ideas for improvements among its member companies.

It is also important that the search for better ways of doing things was not confined to the large, capital-intensive 'upstream' producers of basic raw materials such as cotton yarn or steel. Small factories and workshops often adapted simplified versions of machine technologies, and 'disaggregated' their production processes to utilize cheap labour and artisan skills. Firms in these 'downstream' sectors producing intermediate products and final consumer goods tended to be small and labour-intensive, but some sectors became major exporters, for instance, the bicycle industry. Japan produced a third of the world trade in bicycles in 1937, and bicycles were the leading export of the entire machinery industry. Matsushita Electric began as a small shop producing bicycle lamps. In some branches the average size of firm declined, and there are some remarkable cases where 'modern' mechanized factories were driven out of business by competition from firms relying on labour-intensive putting-out methods. Output per worker increased – labour was cheap, but highly, and increasingly, skilled as workers became more adept and machinery was adapted to specialized functions. This pattern challenges the conventional wisdom that industrialization leads to the displacement of small labour-intensive units by large capital-intensive units (Takeuchi, 1991). Adam Smith could have explained the process, however; just as in the case of his famous pin factory, the manufacturers divided production into smaller and simpler stages, which could be assigned to small producers specializing in a single sub-process or component.

Building on the pre-Restoration tradition of economic competition, regions and localities created organizations to ensure they did not miss out on the new technologies. Kyôtô City's Lake Biwa project, begun in 1881 to improve the water supply and provide power for waterwheels, evolved to include Japan's first hydroelectric power station. The Kyôtô City government was also desperately concerned about the fate of its traditional silk-weaving industry, and sponsored an overseas mission which brought back an example of the flying shuttle and a Jacquard loom. Morris-Suzuki argues that many similar attempts by local interests to upgrade speciality handicraft products frequently resulted in the development of 'intermediate' technologies, machines that could be produced by local craftsmen which improved the productivity of other local craft workers, but which did not require the 'one great leap' envisaged by Itô – a leap which might have been beyond Japan's capabilities (Morris-Suzuki 1994).

A bit of luck helps as well. The First World War cut Japan off and provided an opportunity for electrical and chemical firms in particular to introduce new technologies (and to make mistakes) in the absence of potentially destructive foreign competition. Hitachi succeeded in 'reverse engineering' numerous advanced types of electrical equipment, and Mitsui sponsored research which eventually replicated the recent Western discovery of viscose, the basis of the products of the Imperial Artificial Silk Company (Teikoku Jinken, better known by its abbreviation Teijin) beginning in 1918. Japan was also particularly well placed to take advantage of a rapid expansion of electric power in the interwar period. Power was provided cheaply to industrial users because new hydroelectric plants were often built ahead of consumer demand. Many small plants simply bypassed the steam age and moved directly from manual to electric power. Consumption rose from 277 million kilowatt hours in 1907 to 1.8 billion in 1914, 9.1 billion in 1925, and 32.4 billion in 1938, when Japan was the fourth-largest user of electric power in the world (Mitchell, 1992, 1993, 1995).

The Creation of an Imagined Community

Ressentiment, despair, and contempt

We are no more than crawling worms, whereas they have wings to fly
with. How can we rival them with their industry and trade, with their
forces and tactics? We have never been in greater danger. This is why
the construction of railways is now such an immediate necessity.

Fukuzawa Yukichi, *Popular Political Economy*, 1878

Ressentiment is a term coined by Nietzsche to describe a psychological state
resulting from suppressed feelings of envy and hatred which cannot be
satisfied. The subject believes that there is a fundamental equality between
the subject and the object of envy, but this belief is combined with an
objective situation of inequality so great that it is impossible that the
theoretical equality can ever be realized. This 'existential envy' can be
overcome through a 'transvaluation of values', a reversal which rejects and
denigrates the original object of envy, and which asserts that certain of the
subject's characteristics are not only opposite from but superior to those
which characterize the object of envy. Liah Greenfeld has applied the
concept to elite groups in emerging national communities:

Ressentiment felt by the groups that imported the idea of the nation and
articulated the national consciousness of their respective societies usually
resulted in the selection out of their own indigenous traditions of
elements hostile to the original national principle and their deliberate
cultivation. (Greenfeld, 1992, p. 16)

Public discussion of the economy in Japan during the 1870s repeatedly
displayed the despairing humiliation felt by Japanese intellectuals when
they gazed at the immense gap between Japan and the West. In 1871
Wakayama Norikazu argued against free trade, which he said was not yet
practicable for Japan, because the majority of the people were still poor,
unfamiliar with manufacturing and commerce, and too unenlightened to
understand the public interest. In 1874 the free trader Nishi Amane said,
'in our talk among friends we often make comparisons with European
countries, when we envy them and lament how unenlightened we are.
Eventually, after concluding that nothing can be done about the ignorance
of our people, we can only heave a deep sigh'. Tsuda Mamichi in 1874
scoffed that only the Japanese are so unenlightened as to believe in

mythical creatures such as 'long-nosed goblins' whereas nations which have reached a certain stage of civilization are free from such 'nonsensical' beliefs. Tsuda hoped that enlightenment, for instance through newspapers, would lead to the growth of Japanese wealth and power, but many were not so optimistic (Sugiyama, 1994, pp. 8, 20, 27). In 1875 Nishimura Shigeki wailed:

> The British opened their foreign trade of their own accord, whereas we were forced to do so by America. They are smart in mind and skilled in manufacture, whereas we are simple-minded and untrained in manufacture. With them land is used to the full and people are industrious, whereas this is in no way the case with us. (Sugiyama, 1994, pp. 9–10)

Fukuzawa Yukichi, the most famous advocate of 'enlightenment' of the age, wrote in 1870 that, 'Since our foreign trade has started, there are many among the foreigners who want to enrich themselves by keeping us poor and ignorant.' Fukuzawa opposed allowing foreigners to travel freely in Japan, because this would lead to them residing among Japanese, and then to trade, which is a one-sided benefit to the more advanced foreigners. If foreigners were allowed to travel freely, 'the Japanese could not fail to be placed under their control because the foreigners are enlightened and skilled, whereas the Japanese are unenlightened and unskilled'. And finally in anguish Fukuzawa cried in 1878: 'We are no more than crawling worms, whereas they have wings to fly with' (Sugiyama, 1994, pp. 5, 25, 48, 50).

Greenfeld argues that the crucial moment in the emergence of national identities is the point at which members of the elite extend their definition of the 'nation' to include 'the people' whom they have previously despised (1992, pp. 6–7). Through the 1870s Japanese officials and intellectuals displayed an obviously distant and disdainful attitude toward the common people. Despite 250 years of economic advance under the Tokugawa and the ferment of technological experimentation in progress as they wrote, they continued to assert that 'the people' were unenlightened, unskilled, backward, and stupid. They were patriots, but not as yet nationalists. Ôkubo argued in a famous memorial on the economy in 1874 that the volume of production depended on the industriousness of the people, but 'more fundamentally' on government guidance, because of the 'weak spirit' and lack of talent of the Japanese people. In 1871 Wakayama wrote of the need,

> to prohibit the export of agricultural products and thereby to recover the fertility of the soil, to prevent the activities of cunning merchants

and thereby to rescue trade from decay, to prohibit the import of, or levy heavy duties on, foreign goods, and thereby to encourage useful industries. (Sugiyama, 1994, p. 8)

Amane said in 1874 that, 'There have indeed been countless good policies and fine plans and yet they have not successfully reached the people at large. The reason is that it has not been long enough since the Restoration to achieve inward renewal, in spite of the outward show of progress.' Tsuda was concerned that if foreigners were granted the right to travel in Japan, in the unenlightened condition of the nation, there might be Japanese who would attack the foreigners, but there might also be Japanese who would be cheated by them – although again he was optimistic about the rapid spread of enlightenment (Sugiyama, 1994, pp. 20, 31).

Fukuzawa's *ressentiment*, his close equation of economic and military power, and his sense of threat and struggle were all present in a speech he delivered in 1880 to mark the opening of a trading company:

> When I look at the foreigners who have arrived by ship, who are selling their commodities to us and then buying our products to export, I cannot help saying that they are always the merchants and we are always the customers.... How do foreigners live who reside in our trading ports? From where does their subsistence come? Riding beautiful horses, sitting in fabulous coaches, they spend millions or else take back the money to their home countries. That money... is nothing less than the outcome of the sweat of our brow. What else do we have to lament?... The exclusionists of the old days wanted to resort to violence to expel from Japan foreigners whom they despised as lower creatures. The difference between them and us... lies only in that we want to fight in business and trade... Postponing a military battle with foreigners to some future day, at the moment we merely want to fight a trade battle.
> (Sugiyama, 1994, pp. 54–5)

Fukuzawa was desperate to enlighten the country as rapidly as possible, for instance by translating foreign works quickly rather than accurately, since translations would soon become unnecessary as Japanese learned foreign languages. He compared Japanese backwardness with Indian 'culture' and Turkish 'military prowess'; neither had been saved by their superior qualities from domination by the West, because they were absorbed with internal conflicts and did not learn from the West. He advocated 'peace inside and emulation outside'. He opposed government enterprise and favoured competition, but he also argued that Japan needed military strength first, because without strength Japan could not achieve wealth, and he wrote in 1879 that 'the private profit of each merchant will eventually be gathered and accumulated to contribute to Japan's victory in the business world' (Sugiyama, 1994, pp. 40–63). In partnership with Mori Arinori, Fukuzawa was instrumental in founding the Commercial Training School in 1875, the forerunner of Hitotsubashi University. Mori, who later became Minister of Education, had been ambassador to the United States, and he had been impressed by the commercial training available in America. Fukuzawa was proud of his ability with a sword (*Autobiography*, chs 12, 15), and the school's prospectus emphasized the similarity between learning to use the sword before going into battle, and learning the principles of business before going into 'battles by means of business' against foreigners (Sugiyama, 1994, pp. 64–75).

The state and nationalism

Our Imperial Ancestors have founded Our Empire on a basis broad and everlasting, and have deeply and firmly implanted virtue; Our subjects ever united in loyalty and filial piety have from generation to generation illustrated the beauty thereof. This is the glory of the fundamental character of Our Empire, and herein also lies the source of Our education. Ye, Our subjects, be filial to your parents ... pursue learning and cultivate arts, and thereby develop intellectual faculties and moral powers ... should emergency arise, offer yourselves courageously to the State; and thus guard and maintain the prosperity of Our Imperial Throne coeval with heaven and earth.

Imperial Rescript on Education, 1890

During the early Meiji period, despite their sense of humiliation and frustration, most intellectuals advocated a policy of 'civilization and enlightenment' (*bunmei kaika*), the introduction of Western civilization and especially British models of free trade and representative political institutions. In 1872 the Ministry of Education moved away from Confucian ethics and introduced translations of Western works, particularly those based on British utilitarianism. But this was temporary. Already in the early 1870s members of the Iwakura mission to Europe and America had been genuinely astonished and offended by Western males' excessive deference toward women and their disregard for filial piety. One of them, Kido Takayoshi, wrote that 'the path of loyalty and piety will be imperilled by *bunmei kaika*' (Collcutt, 1991, pp. 147–8).

The political crisis of the early 1880s forced liberals out, and left conservatives in control. The late 1880s saw a new upsurge in peasants' disputes in the countryside, strikes by industrial workers such as the women at the Tenma Cotton Spinning Company in September 1889 (Tsurumi, 1990, pp. 112–14), and opposition to the government from those excluded from office by the 'Sat-Chô clique' and by liberals who called for the introduction of representative government. The government responded with new laws, on the negative side with extensions of the 1875 Press Law in 1877 and 1880, and on the positive side with the new examinations for entry into the bureaucracy of 1887 and the Constitution of 1889. Generally the government turned away from liberalism and English models, and towards conservatism and German models. In 1882, Law 270 prohibited all agricultural and industrial workers from using 'stratagem or force against their employers' for the purpose of 'increasing wages or changing the conditions of their labour'. In 1887 the Peace Preservation Law gave the police power to ban any person from the area around the capital 'who is judged to be scheming something detrimental to public tranquillity'.

The government did not merely repress opposition, however, and it did not merely change from one foreign model to another. Government leaders set about creating a new identity for Japan, and in doing so created a national identity in Greenfeld's sense, one which selected among elements of indigenous tradition, which included all Japanese in the new 'nation', and which asserted that the new 'national identity' was not only different from but superior to the West (Greenfeld, 1992). However, this 'imagined community' (Anderson, 1991) did not emerge by accident. The government deliberately selected from among both 'foreign models' and 'inherited traditions' those elements which happened to suit the interests of those who had won power. In the case of the Constitution, the model was German. However, in the case of the new public ceremonies with the emperor as their focus, the models were often Chinese. The name of the Ministry of Industry, Kôbushô, had been taken from the name of the ancient Chinese bureau responsible for supervision of state-owned craft workshops (Morris-Suzuki, 1994, p. 85). Chinese rituals were adopted for the new imperial ceremony, and the new peerage took their titles from the ancient Chinese Chou dynasty (Collcutt, 1991).

Foreign models were combined with elements drawn from Shinto myths of Japan's past. On the one hand the emperor became the father and moral preceptor of the nation. Government leaders did not want to give up Confucian values, especially deference to parents and respect for the 'parental' authority of the emperor and those who ruled in his name. However, as noted above, the 1889 Constitution defined the Japanese nation as unique because its essence was 'a line of emperors unbroken for ages eternal'. This adaptation of Shinto myth removed Japan from the this-worldly Confucian realm, where the mandate of heaven might be lost, and asserted that the government's authority was inviolable because it was eternal and holy.

Rather than despair, the government said, the Japanese people could be proud. Rather than 'crawling worms', the Japanese were in fact superior to Westerners. Motoda Eifu, lecturer to the Meiji emperor, criticized technical education on Western lines:

> Outstanding in imagination and technical accomplishments, they [Westerners] are deficient in the spirit and soul of our country, their foundation in morals and in courage for righteous causes is shallow and one would try in vain to make pillars of the nation out of them... Efforts are being made to convert Japanese into facsimiles of Europeans and Americans. All this is due to a confusion between the root of education and its branches. (Collcutt, 1991, p. 189)

The process continued. Frequently, concepts and arguments which in fact were Confucian were reinterpreted as essentially 'Japanese', either as 'Shinto' or '*samurai*' values. The range of permissible ideas narrowed from the 1890s onwards, with an increasing emphasis on loyalty, filial piety, belief in the emperor system, and belief in the unique and superior Japanese nationality (Irokawa, 1985, pp. 301ff.; Gluck, 1985; Hardacre, 1989; Ikegami, 1995).

The creation of this new national identity was not inevitable, any more than the Restoration itself. The narrow group which had come to power selected from a broad range of available models to create an ideology which supported their interpretation of events and which justified their continued monopoly of power. But the crucial next step was that these values were then propagated through the expanding education system. The plan for universal education announced in 1872 built on existing domain and temple schools, which had enrolled perhaps 1 million pupils in 1860. In 1880 there were 28 000 primary schools with 2 million pupils, or 40 per cent of children of school age, and the compulsory period was raised from two to three years. In 1886 attendance had risen to 46 per cent, and the compulsory period was raised to four years. In 1895 attendance was 60 per cent overall, with 90 per cent of boys and 30 per cent of girls enrolled. In 1900 attendance was 90 per cent overall, and by 1910 it was close to 100 per cent for both boys and girls, with the compulsory period now set at six years.

As education minister from 1885 to 1889, Mori Arinori set the pattern of detailed central control over the content and process of teaching in the schools. The government prescribed all texts and supervised local schools through government offices. Motoda helped draft the Imperial Rescript on Education of 1890, with its mix of Confucian values and Shinto myth, which became the capstone of the system. Each school had its framed copy of the Rescript, to which teachers and pupils bowed. It was read aloud in every classroom and memorized by the children. Its message was reinforced by instructions to teachers, for instance the handbook published by Hibino Yutaka in 1904, *On the Way of the Subject in Japan*, which described Japan as beset by foreign enemies 'like raging tigers'. The nation, said Hibino, depended on the willingness of the people 'to serve the Emperor with their last breath'. Loyalty to the emperor, in turn, rested on loyalty to parents, for 'filial piety in the child results in true loyalty in the subject'. And loyalty to parents rested on the family:

> The vigorous and unimpeded advance of our culture, the constant increment of our wealth and power, our supremacy in the east, our equality with the other great powers, our imposing part upon the stage of human affairs, all depend upon the establishment of a healthy home life, wherein husband determines and wife acquiesces. (quoted in Beasley, 1990, p. 83)

The new national community therefore was defined by gender. If all Japanese were to be included in the nation, then women would have to be included as well. However, these were not to be the *samurai*, peasant, artisan, or merchant women defined by neo-Confucian orthodoxy under the Tokugawa. Rather, they were to become uniformly 'Japanese' women. This was done by imposing a definition of what it meant to be a woman on the female half of the population, and as in the case of the Constitution, although the government claimed to be acting in the name of 'traditional' values, the definition was in fact new. Women had always been subordinate to the head of their household, whose authority had been absolute, extending in theory to the right to kill a disobedient wife or child. In addition, domain governments had generally not interfered in the internal life of village communities. Now, however, rather than stopping at the boundaries of the village and the household, the state's authority would penetrate into the family, framing and limiting the things left to the husband to determine and regulating the wife's acquiescence as well.

The Meiji school system aimed to include all girls at the primary level, and a law passed in 1899 called for the establishment of at least one secondary school for girls in each prefecture. The curriculum designed for girls uniformly inculcated the virtues the government considered appropriate to the 'good wife, wise mother'. In primary school, in addition to practical subjects shared with boys, girls' education emphasized 'female modesty'. Girls' secondary school training did not prepare them for further academic study, but rather encouraged them to acquire the 'refined taste' appropriate to middle-class households. There was little emphasis on motherhood as such (the Japanese birthrate had not yet begun to decline), but there was an overwhelming emphasis on duties to the extended family, to the economy, and to the state. A former minister of education said in 1908:

> Our female education, then is based on the assumption that women marry, and that its object is to fit girls to become 'good wives and wise mothers'. The question naturally arises what constitutes a good wife and wise mother, and the answer to the question requires a knowledge of the position of the wife and mother in the household and the standing of woman in society and her status in the State ... [The] man goes outside to work to earn his living, to fulfil his duties to the State; it is the wife's part to help him, for the common interests of the house, and as her share of duty to the State, by sympathy and encouragement, by relieving him of anxieties at home, managing household affairs, looking after the household economy, and, above all, tending the old people and bringing up the children in a fit and proper manner.

In 1910 the Ministry of Education announced that the fundamental aim of primary education was instruction in morals and ethics. However, the phrase 'good wife, wise mother' (*ryôsai kenbo*) was not a Confucian text at all, but originated with Nakamura Masanao, a Christian intellectual, who had derived it from the writings of American moralists advocating a 'cult of domesticity' in the United States (Smith, 1983, p. 75, note 7). Nevertheless, the phrase became the epitome of 'Confucian' values inculcated in the Meiji education system and remains current in Japan today.

The new patterns were given legal form by the Civil Code introduced in 1898, which defined the household as the basic unit of Japanese society. For the first time all marriages and divorces had to be registered. The male head of household disposed of all property, including assets owned by the wife before marriage, and children required permission to marry until age 25 for daughters and 30 for sons. Divorce was made more difficult – a wife could be divorced for committing adultery, but a husband could only if he had been convicted for 'unlawful' carnal knowledge. The Criminal Code punished both a woman guilty of adultery and the 'other party' with penal servitude up to two years. The new patterns again were asserted to be traditional Japanese values, in this case those of the *samurai*. One of the framers of the Civil Code said that 'the customs of the farmers are not to be made general customs – instead we must go by the practice of *samurai* and nobleman' (Smith, 1983, pp. 72–3). However, the new regulations defining the family were as foreign to *samurai* as they were to farmers, being based largely on German models.

In addition to the school curriculum, the new patterns were propagated through the national Women's Association, Young Women's Association, and Young Men's Association, all with programmes determined by government officials in Tokyo. Meiji leaders were convinced the West would take Japan seriously only if standards of decorum matched Western expectations, and therefore phallic images and depictions of sexual intercourse were removed from public places, festival dances were modified to eliminate sexual imagery, and public near-nudity and mixed bathing were discouraged. In the 1930s rural Japanese asserted that premarital intercourse, pregnancy, early marriage, divorce, and remarriage all had been far more common before around 1910. Older women said younger women were far less likely to engage in premarital sex than their generation. The new and very strong emphasis on chastity before marriage inculcated by the schools was reinforced by magazines, novels, and films. Women's age at marriage rose from 17 to 21 between 1900 and 1920 in one group of villages. The divorce rate declined steadily compared to population, from 3.0 per 1000 in 1885 to 0.7 in 1935, and the ratio of divorces to marriages declined dramatically, from 1:2.71 in 1884–8 to 1:11.80 in 1934–5 (Smith, 1983).

One of the village informants in the 1930s also mentioned the increased expense of weddings:

...the present elaborate wedding ceremony is more or less an innovation. Formerly they were very simple, and one could get married for five yen. That is why divorce was so frequent, for for five yen you could go to a restaurant, visit a whorehouse, or get married. As a result, one broke up marriages without too much thought. Now, however, so much money goes into them that one thinks a long time before getting a divorce. (Smith, 1983, p. 80)

Under the laws governing public organizations, all women were expressly forbidden to participate in politics, because they were women. It was sometimes argued that political meetings were disreputable places of temptation, or that women's organizations could become dangerous, but these arguments do not explain the exclusion of all women without exception. The government never argued that women were too weak or that they were intellectually incapable of political activity. Rather, the ban 'placed women in the same category as public figures, including military men, public and private school teachers and students, and shrine and temple officers'. Wives were like public servants, above and outside politics, with duties to the state which precluded their participation in political activity. Those duties were firstly in the home. In 1887 the Ministry of Education sponsored a work entitled *The Meiji Greater Learning for Women* which stated bluntly that 'the home is a public place where private feelings should be forgotten'. Further publications repeatedly emphasized that in addition to wise and frugal household management, women were to work in whatever employment would best serve their families and society – they were to nurse their babies according to the latest scientific principles, and they were to deposit their earnings in the national postal savings system (Nolte and Hastings, 1991).

The government used force to impose its new value system, and repressed all signs of dissent. Although theoretically compulsory, education was not free until 1908, and the imposition of school fees and new school taxes sometimes led to riots, which were suppressed. In the intellectual sphere, the government's hostility to 'liberal' ideas led many economists to turn to protectionist trade policies and conservative political models (Morris-Suzuki, 1989, p. 58). Historians produced histories which showed that the Meiji Restoration had been inevitable, the reflection of Japan's 'imperial essence' and the outcome of central 'Japanese' values, especially 'loyalty' (Beasley, 1972, pp. 2–7). Foreign observers reported in 1880 that police officers had to force people to fly the national flag on the government's newly designated holidays (Hardacre, 1989, p. 33). For those who did not conform, direct pressure could be exercised through the press laws, which restricted the range of opinions which could be publicly expressed.

The police closely watched suspected radicals. In 1901 the first socialist party in Japan was banned within hours of its foundation.

The Balance

Economic growth

As in Europe, so too in Japan, war stimulated industrialization.

Linda Weiss and John Hobson, 1995

In the context of the late nineteenth and early twentieth century, Japan grew and developed rapidly. Measured in constant prices, total output roughly doubled from 1885 to 1910, and then rose another 50 per cent to 1920, and output per capita doubled. Agriculture declined from 42 per cent of total employment in 1885 to 27 per cent in 1920, while manufacturing employment increased from 7 to 19 per cent. Within the rapidly growing manufacturing sector, textiles increased their share from 10 per cent of output in 1877 to 25 per cent in 1900 and 28 per cent in 1920, and then levelled and declined slightly to 24 per cent in 1938. The metals and machinery branches rose from 2.5 per cent in 1877 to 4.3 per cent in 1900, but then began a rapid rise, to 22 per cent in 1920 and 35 per cent in 1938 (Ohkawa, Shinohara, and Meissner, 1979; Francks, 1992, chs. 2–3).

Exports played an important role. Japan benefited from the same rapid growth of world trade which led to the expansion of agricultural and protoindustrial output elsewhere in Asia. Textile products – raw silk, cotton thread, and finished textiles – made up the bulk of Japanese exports. Total exports rose from 7 per cent of national product in 1880s to 20 per cent in 1910. For a generation Japan remained on a silver standard, and because world gold output declined and silver output rose from the 1870s to the 1890s, the Japanese currency steadily lost value relative to gold-standard currencies. This made Japanese products progressively cheaper in world markets, and private entrepreneurs thought the silver currency had acted as a kind of protective tariff. However, Japan moved to the gold standard in 1896, using the indemnity extracted from China. Matsukata, now prime minister, carried through the new policy over the opposition of private interests. He blamed the silver standard for inflation, although the main cause of rising prices had been increased military expenditures caused by the decision to go to war. The gold standard could have been a disaster, for it lowered the prices Japan received for the key textile exports, and growth in fact did slow for five years. Fortunately for Japan, the discovery of gold in South Africa in the 1890s and a general easing of world credit launched the world economy into a boom which lasted until 1914.

However, Japan's domestic market was at least as important, particularly to textile producers, as export markets. Raw silk exports rose from 14 million yen in 1880 to 382 million in 1920, but domestic consumption increased from 6 million to 188 million yen. Japan exported none of the 1 million yen worth of cotton yarn produced in 1880; by 1920 exports were 152 million yen, but domestic consumption was 554 million. Japan also exported none of the 18 million yen of finished fabrics produced in 1880; exports in 1920 were 501 million yen, but again domestic consumption had risen even more rapidly, to 939 million (Francks, 1992).

Many observers have attributed Japan's rapid growth and structural transformation to high levels of investment. During the Meiji period Japan saved and invested around 13 per cent of national product, or perhaps 18 per cent if military investment is included. Francks notes that this is not a high rate compared to developing countries today (1992, p. 38), and it is only half the rate maintained in Japan during the 1950s and 1960s. Even so, it is about the same as Germany in the late nineteenth century and is high compared to other countries of that era. Private investment was far larger than government investment, and private savings were the main source of investment funds. The Japanese may have been savers even before the onset of industrialization. Budget studies indicate that already in the 1850s Japanese tended to save increases in income rather than consuming more (Hanley, 1997).

Government investment was closely connected with the military, and this included windfall gains such as the 200 million taels indemnity levied on China under the Treaty of Shimonoseki in 1895. The government used the money to finance the shift to the gold standard, to increase the size of the army, and to construct the Yawata steel works. Marxists and neoclassical economists agree that Japanese growth, though rapid, was marked by severe instability. Until the 1930s the cycles in the Japanese economy were always connected with military expenditures and war. Deficit financing to increase military spending led to excess purchasing power and economic expansion, but heavy indirect taxes hurt those on low incomes, which increased inequality, with effects which could extend past the end of the war. The end of the war in turn led to lower government expenditure, declining purchasing power, deficient aggregate demand, and a depression aggravated by continued heavy taxation. On the other hand, the government emphasis on military technology and technical education may have had important spillover effects on the rest of the economy.

It is also significant that agricultural productivity rose substantially. This did not reflect the introduction of new technologies or the 'industrialization of agriculture' as in Western Europe and the United States. Rather, Japanese farmers benefited from the spread of previously existing best practice. Such improvements built on the longstanding habit of regional development. They were relatively cheap, involving seed selection and better methods of irrigation. They did not require any change in the social relations of production in the countryside. The government was active in promoting change of this type, and in organizing small-scale public works, such as local roads, dams, and small harbours for coastal shipping (Francks, 1984; 1992, ch. 7). Both from the standpoint of the economy as a whole and from the standpoint of political stability, it is important that farmers did benefit and that their incomes did not decline too far, even in depressions and despite heavy taxes.

The industrial labour force

28 December: On this day I demanded the rents in Kuwado. Motegi Heijirô was out. I warned his wife who said, 'On the 30th we will receive wages from the silk factory where our daughter works and as soon as we get them we will pay you some'. . . . Nagasawa Yokichi, Kawai Sadatoshi, and Okuta Chôhei of Kamimanriki all said that as soon as they received their daughters' wages they would pay immediately, or at the latest, by 10 January. They beseeched me to wait until then.

Diary of Tenant Affairs kept by the Nezu family,
landlords in Yamanashi Prefecture, 1911

Meet him often and the factory gets upset.
Don't meet him and the master gets upset.

The company is like a brothel;
We are whores who live by selling our faces.

In Suwa geisha get thirty-five sen.
Common prostitutes get fifteen sen.
Silk reelers get one potato.

Stanzas from factory girls' songs

These two quotations, taken from Patricia Tsurumi's *Factory Girls* (1990), encapsulate the role of labour in Japan's early industrialization. The wages of a daughter employed in a distant factory might be the difference between paying the rent and losing one's land for a poor family, but the girls themselves were exploited both economically and sexually. As seen above, textiles were of overwhelming importance both for export earnings and to supply the expanding domestic market. The labour force was overwhelmingly female. Silk reeling, in which over 90 per cent of the workforce was female, employed 120 000 women in 1902 and 278 000 in 1919. Cotton spinning, in which 80 per cent of the workforce was female, employed 62 000 women in 1902 and 176 000 in 1919. Both silk reeling and cotton spinning were concentrated into mechanized factories. The factory girls lived in adjacent dormitories.

The heritage of high levels of literacy, and the especially high levels of female literacy, suggest a relative flexibility in social and gender relationships which may explain some of Japan's responsiveness to new opportunities. We do not know how many of the 1 million students in elementary schools in 1860 were girls, but many domain schools enrolled daughters of *samurai*, and many temple schools enrolled commoner girls. There was a large increase in the number of books intended for women in late eighteenth and early nineteenth centuries (Collcutt, 1991, p. 140). As seen in Chapter 3, Japan also began the industrial era with a well-established tradition of hiring out both sons and daughters on long-term labour contracts. The skills developed in specialized commercial agriculture and handicraft production were then reinforced by the expanding Meiji educational system.

But the system was also new. As detailed by Tsurumi, recruitment was far more commercialized and impersonal than inherited hiring practices. In the dormitories the girls were subjected to a detailed regimentation which many found hateful (Tsurumi, 1990, chs. 7–8). The compulsive need of employers to control their female workers repeated earlier experiences in Britain and the United States. In Japan the temptations of a concentration of many young women under the authority of relatively few men were reinforced by the great distances from the girls' homes, and the lack of a local community to judge the behaviour of supervisors and owners. Commercial considerations also encouraged recruiters and owners to misrepresent working conditions, to withhold pay, and frequently to commit outright fraud. Brutal punishments, especially of runaways, included beating and starvation.

Outside the factories, weaving, a craft requiring a four- to five-year apprenticeship, changed its technology very slowly by comparison with silk reeling and spinning, because its mostly female labour force was skilled, but also cheap. Therefore the new and much heavier capital investment in advanced technology in spinning and silk reeling made it possible to hire young, unskilled female workers and reduce labour costs, while capital investment in weaving was slowed by the existence of older, skilled female workers. The effects of gender on wages are obvious. These skilled workers were not receiving the wages they did because they were skilled, but because they were women and therefore had no other employment options (Nakamura, 1994).

Women made up a significant fraction of the labour force in the coal mining industry as well. Improved conveyors introduced in the 1890s created a need for faster loading of coal from the relatively narrow coal faces at which miners worked at that time. Foremen found that they could work best with husband and wife teams, with the husband picking coal off the coal face, and the wife hauling it to the conveyor. This arrangement duplicated the older 'badger hole' mines operated by individual families, in which the husband dug himself into the ground along the seam, passing coal behind him to his wife and children. In addition to being married to a notoriously brutal class of men and performing all household work after the day in the mine finished, underground female workers had little education and low social status, but they earned high wages. Above ground female workers were younger, more likely to be literate, and unmarried, but earned less.

But in the 1920s the decline in coal prices led firms to introduce new technologies which made work in large teams more efficient than pairs of workers. In addition, new protective legislation barred women from working in deep shafts – one of many cases where new government legislation restricted female employment because it built in assumptions about gendered roles. The owners shifted women to other jobs, but at lower salaries. In turn, with the loss of or lower income for their wives, many male miners left the industry, and they were often replaced by Koreans (Nakamura, 1994).

Women workers were then and often since have been portrayed as 'docile' and accepting of the treatment they received. Tsurumi argues that this was not the case, that the fatuous attempts to appeal to national pride, to convince the factory girls that 'reeling thread is for the country too', failed, and that the records of strike activity, runaways, suicides, and the sad and bitter songs the girls have left behind all present a truer picture of their real feelings (Tsurumi, 1990, ch. 5). Barbara Maloney continues the story into the 1920s, detailing the activism of women textile workers.

Much of this took place in the absence of formal organizations – it is relatively easy to organize in a dormitory, as a number of employers learned to their cost. The cooperation of firms described above did not extend to their labour relations. Firms did not 'cooperate' with their workers, but with each other to control their workers. They exchanged information on potentially troublesome employees and called in the police to suppress strikes (Maloney, 1991).

The area of modern industry where male workers dominated numerically was the heavy industrial sector of metals, machinery, and chemicals. Looking at factories with over ten employees, in 1902 textiles employed 260 000 mostly female workers, and this rose to 794 000 in 1919. The machinery and chemical industries employed 116 000 mostly male workers in 1902 and 388 000 in 1919, still only half the employment in textiles. In the 1950s the relatively high wages and favourable treatment of these skilled male workers were portrayed as, on the one hand, an inheritance from Japan's feudal past, and on the other a source of Japan's postwar lifetime employment system. As in the case of the alleged docility of women workers, such explanations minimized the conflict which actually occurred. In reality, employers in heavy industry confronted a chronically intractable labour force and tried almost every possible strategy to deal with the problem *except* paying high wages and guaranteeing steady employment (Gordon, 1985).

Social change and instability

Labour struggle, tenancy struggle, household struggle, struggle between man and woman, all are inevitable.

Kitamura Kaneko, 1927

In the 1920s Japan was an industrialized nation, a world power with extensive imperial possessions, and a stable constitutional monarchy. Nevertheless, divisions seemed to be opening up even as the system was being completed. There was a new upsurge of unrest in the countryside. Tenant farmers formed associations to represent their interests. The resulting confrontations with landlords led to disputes which the government considered serious and persistent enough to justify a new series of annual reports, beginning in late 1910s. Recorded tenants' disputes rose from 17 in 1917 to totals of over 2000 in some years during the 1920s (Waswo,

1977, p. 100). In the modern industrial sector, too, conflict between workers and employers escalated. The number of labour unions increased rapidly, and the number of strikes rose from 50 in 1914 to a peak of 497 in 1919, with 282 in 1920 and 246 in 1921 (Large, 1981, pp. 19, 29).

Many equated unrest and the sense of cultural crisis with urbanization. Japan's population had risen from 35 million in 1873 to 46 million in 1900 and nearly 60 million in 1925, and virtually the entire increase had flowed into towns and cities. In 1920, 30 per cent of the population lived in cities of over 100 000 inhabitants. Greater Tokyo had 3.4 million, Ôsaka over 2 million. Along with mass urban populations there emerged a new mass culture, fostered by and reported on by a new mass media. The 1100 newspapers and their 6 to 7 million readers engaged in an intensive public discussion despite censorship.

The centrality of gender in the national identity, and its problematic nature, is demonstrated by the widespread concern over the female identity and how it might be changing. Debate over the 'new woman' began following the Tokyo opening of Ibsen's *A Doll House* in 1911 and continued as the newspapers reported the real and imagined activities of the women connected with the magazine *Seitô* ('Bluestockings') (Rodd, 1991). In the 1920s the terms changed, and public concern focused on the 'modern girl', envisioned as dressed in the latest Western fashions, militantly autonomous, and with money of her own to spend, earned in a Tokyo office, restaurant, or retail store (Silverberg, 1991).

If one or two symbols could encapsulate Japanese society in the early twentieth century, they might be the department store, the centre of modern consumerism, and Christmas, the imported holiday devoted to gift-giving. Also, the department store was the place of employment for the archetypal liberated 'modern girl' – the female sales assistant. Sales clerks before 1920 had been almost exclusively male. Their replacement by female staff was welcomed by some who advocated expanded employment opportunities for women as the next step in Japan's modernization, and denounced by others as emblematic of an excessively permissive society. Shop girls, and their morals or lack of them, were widely debated as part of the broader concern with the impact of modernity on Japanese life.

On 16 December 1932 a fire began in the toy department of the Shirokiya department store, when a technician repairing Christmas tree lights set fire to a tree. Symbolically, the store was a modern eight-storey building, but located between traditional narrow side streets which made it impossible to set up ladders to rescue sales staff from the upper floors. Since ladders could not be set up, workers on the upper floors of the

Shirokiya building dropped ropes and improvised lines made from kimono fabric.

However, shop girls still wore traditional Japanese dress, and traditional Japanese underclothing, thin wraparound skirts, the number varying with the season. They did not wear underpants. Despite advertising campaigns urging them to purchase Western underwear, they only wore underpants when wearing Western dress. Older women, it was said, lowered themselves safely, hand over hand. Younger women tried to lower themselves and hold their skirts down at the same time, and thirteen of them fell to their deaths. In the aftermath, the newspapers played on the deaths as a demonstration of the lamentably backward condition of Japanese women, and launched a campaign for the adoption of Western underpants. The novelist Kawabata Yasunari noted shortly after the Shirokiya fire that all the little girls on the slides in Hama Park wore underpants (Seidensticker, 1991, pp. 32–5).

As seen below, the responses of the Japanese to the dilemmas posed by the intrusion of the West and by the imperatives of industrialization provided patterns and models for the other countries of Asia. Further, tragically, the costs of Japanese modernization would be borne by many other women and men throughout Asia, and not only by the unfortunate thirteen Shirokiya shopgirls.

6

ASIAN ECONOMIES, THE INTERNATIONAL ECONOMY AND DEVELOPMENT IN THE INTERWAR ERA

Controversy over the levels of economic development reached in Asia before the First World War and over the amount of growth during the interwar period focuses on the experiences of two large countries, China and Indonesia. The analysis of Chinese growth and development has obvious political implications, because the conclusions affect judgements of the degree of success or failure of the Republican and Communist governments in the economic sphere, and hence of the effectiveness of market and planned economies today. The debate over Indonesia is equally significant, for here we confront directly the question of the impact of colonialism on economic development. Again the political stakes in the answer are high, because the conclusions affect judgements as to the true origins of current economic growth and development, and therefore whether the credit should be given to the nationalist governments which emerged after independence, or to their colonial predecessors. And, in addition to their intrinsic interest and importance, both cases are fascinating opportunities to 'step into the kitchen' and observe economic and social historians at work as they attempt to overcome problems of incomplete and biased data, or measure the impact of changes in terms of trade on an export economy.

No matter how they evaluate the record of growth, all students agree that Asian economies benefited from expanding international markets before 1914, that the 1920s were difficult, and that the depression of the 1930s was a disaster. The impact of declining export prices brought hardship to tens of millions of individuals and families across Asia. As elsewhere in the history of Asia, however, even where the facts are agreed, their interpretation remains contentious. Economic historians continue to debate why growth should have been so difficult in the 1920s and 1930s compared to the two decades before the First World War. Social historians in turn debate how continued imperialism and colonialism affected growth in Asia. Finally, as we will see in Chapter 8, political historians debate the connection between economic development and the rise of nationalism.

The Legacy of Imperialism: East and Southeast Asia in the World Economy

The problem of exploitation

... historically capitalism has been able ... to shift the main burden of unfreedom outside the national boundaries of the metropoles and on to the then subjugated peoples of today's Third World, and to permit thereby, however reluctantly, a degree of relative empowerment of their working class. ... [The] characteristics and processes in the metropoles as opposed to the colonies ... form the two poles of an antagonistic unity.

Utsa Patnaik, 1995

The Market, God Bless It, Works.

Donald McCloskey, 1978]

Despite the new emphasis on the internal dynamics of Asian societies, students of the economies of Asia agree that movements in the international economy became increasingly important for Asia in the late nineteenth century. Further, they agree broadly that expansion before the First World War brought opportunities for Asian producers, but that the instability of the interwar period had severe negative consequences for Asian economies. However, as with the dispute over the dimensions of growth and development, the contentious discussion of the impact of the international economy on Asia reflects differing perspectives on the processes at work. For Marxists and for non-Marxist nationalists, trade during the colonial period by definition reflected the unequal power relations between Westerners and Asians. For contemporary colonial apologists and for neo-classical economists, the existence of trade by definition means that all parties improved their well-being. Politics affects these judgements; the Marxist/nationalist view neglects the very real benefits which Asians derived from trade and economic development, while the apologist/neo-classical view overlooks that Westerners derived additional benefits from the fact that their governments were able to interfere in Asian markets in ways which ensured that the benefits of trade were not shared equally.

The general theory of imperialist exploitation derives from the final chapter of the first volume of Marx's *Capital* and Lenin's classic pamphlet *Imperialism*, and continues to exercise influence today through the work of Marxist scholars and adherents of the world systems theory of Immanuel Wallerstein (Wallerstein 1974–89). According to Lenin's theory of imperialism, capitalists in industrial countries are forced to open new markets in which they can earn 'supernormal' profits in order to offset the inevitable decline in the rate of profit in their home markets. Capitalists, said Lenin, maintain political stability at home by using a portion of these excessive profits to raise workers' wages in their home countries. In the formulation of Indian Marxist scholar Utsa Patnaik:

> The triumph of the market and its equalizing, democratizing function was accomplished in the metropoles on the basis of its antithesis, or a diametrically opposite process, namely the systematic use of state power by the same metropolitan countries, to ensure that external markets, sources of raw materials, and unfettered labour mobility were secured. One might say that the operation of the invisible hand of the market has been historically conditional upon the very visible exercise of state power, and this continues to be the case today. (Patnaik, 1995, p. 84)

Patnaik argues that this had far-reaching consequences for both European and world history. In Europe, the 'early industrializers' and colonial powers such as the Netherlands, Britain, and France have been politically relatively stable, compared to 'late industrializers' such as Germany, Italy, and Spain, because the latter could not exploit colonial resources to provide a surplus. Also, although in the early nineteenth century exploitation in the early industrializers such as Britain created terrible conditions, this nevertheless provided 'excess' funds which could be invested overseas, especially in 'regions of temperate European settlement... creating the conditions for the migration of European labour to better opportunities' (Patnaik, 1995, p. 85). For Britain, the high rates of migration made possible by the expansion of the United States, Canada, Argentina, and Australia created trade opportunities abroad and increased the bargaining power of labour in the metropoles. However, in the colonies it was a different story.

In proportion as domestic labour in the metropoles became more free in the capitalist sense, acquired a higher social value and successfully struggled for democratic political rights, it would appear that in the same proportion colonized labour was subjugated, enslaved, indentured, uprooted and transported thousands of miles away to serve the interests of globalized European capital. . . . A system of global apartheid emerged . . . The same rapid expansion of economic frontiers which created the conditions for the greater freedom of labour within European domestic economies was associated with an historically unprecedented assault on the freedom of the direct producers in the non-European economies. (Patnaik, 1995, p. 85)

It was, however, not always Westerners who forced others to do their bidding. As seen below, wealthy families in China took advantage of the decline in central authority to exploit their neighbours. In traditional Southeast Asia, in contrast to China, it was the scarcity of labour which determined social relationships. Because labour was scarce, war and bondage systems developed in particular ways. 'It was the object of warfare to increase the available manpower, not to waste it in bloody pitched battles.' Further, since wage rates were very high, bondage was the only feasible method of securing labour without warfare. Compared to the European slavery system, 'the Southeast Asian system was both more personal and more monetary. Money was necessary to buy men's loyalty through debt' (Reid, 1988, pp. 123, 136). These patterns persisted into the colonial period in the recruitment of agricultural labour. Despite their increasing integration into the Dutch administrative system, the *priyayi* aristocrats and village chiefs of Java continued to demand labour services from poor villagers (Breman 1983; Elson, 1984). In North Sumatra, the most important estate crop centre of the Dutch Indies, from 1879 to 1942 foreign capitalists developed an indentured labour system to obtain labour from China and Java. Use of force and fraud were common, as were the sexual harassment of women, collusion among employers, and penal sanctions to hamper workers' organizations (Stoler, 1985). In Indochina a combination of powerful landlords, surplus labour, and Chinese merchants acting as middlemen meant that 'the expansion of strictly capitalist social-productive relations . . . remained fixed within the definite limits set by noncapitalist forms of production and exchange' (Murray, 1980, p. 467).

Thai development also reflected the exploitation of the mass of the population by the aristocratic elite, a kind of 'internal imperialism' exercised by the Bangkok elite over the remainder of the 'national body'. The gradual decline of slavery, debt-slavery, and corvée labour from 1874 to 1905 may have occurred not because of Chulalongkorn's reforms, but because a large influx of Chinese migrants transformed the region from one of labour scarcity to one of labour abundance (Feeny, 1982). Railways played an important role in the relations between Bangkok and the provinces. The first of the three major lines was begun in 1892, and reached Khorat (Nakhon Ratchasima) in 1900. It was built to counter the French advance through Laos. It was extended toward the Mekong in the 1920s and 1930s, northwards to Udon and Nongkhai (opposite Vientiane), and eastwards to Ubon. The second line ran northwards, reached the foothills at Uttaradit in 1909, and was extended to Chiang Mai in 1921. The third line, to the south, was begun 1909 and connected Bangkok with Penang in 1922. Political and strategic motives were paramount throughout. The anti-French orientation of the first line is obvious, and railways allowed the government to impose its authority throughout the kingdom by moving troops if necessary. Diplomatic motives are evident as well, particularly the determination of the Thai government to maintain its independence. Chulalongkorn insisted that the early projects all be paid for out of current revenue, and German advisers were employed in the railway department in preference to British or French. The only exception was the southern line, but the British loan contracted in 1909 came in conjunction with the final division of the Malay states between Thailand and Britain (Hong, 1984; Hewison, 1989; Suehiro, 1989).

Analysis of the economic impact of the railways remains contentious. They have been blamed for the centralization of Thai economic life in Bangkok with effects which persist to the present day. They certainly reinforced the political domination of the central government, as the government intended. It is often argued that the railways opened large 'frontier' areas to rice cultivation and export. However, the development of lands along the railways often fell into the hands of individuals and corporations with government connections. Further, the government preferred investment in railways to more extensive large-scale irrigation projects over the period from 1880 to 1940, despite advice to the contrary, because the benefits of irrigation would have been more widely dispersed among rural farmers and more difficult for the government to capture through taxation or user fees – in short because the interests of the Bangkok elite differed from those of the country as a whole (Feeny, 1982).

Officially, Western representatives favoured open markets, and in Southeast Asia the colonial regimes generally worked to reduce the traditional exploitation of unfree labour by undermining the authority of native elites and forcing the adoption of waged labour. Yet there is certainly much evidence of the use of force, compulsion, and fraud by Westerners and by colonial states to achieve their economic ends. The foreign intervention in China relied on the threat of force (Thomas, 1984). The expansion of Chinese tobacco production was actively encouraged with information, supplies of seeds, and guaranteed markets by the British-American Tobacco Company, which then withdrew the subsidies when producers had become dependent on the crop, leaving them exposed to violent fluctuations in prices (Cochran, 1980, pp. 142–4, 202–7). Both governments and private entrepreneurs used hundreds of thousands of indentured labourers on the plantations of Malaya (Jackson, 1986) and Sumatra (Stoler, 1985). Forced corvée labour was abolished in Vietnam and the outer islands of the Dutch East Indies only in the late 1930s. On balance, Robert Elson concludes that 'to the end of the colonial period, there was little real evidence of a transition to a system of free wage labour' (Elson, 1992, pp. 175–7).

The facts of exploitation need to be considered in any evaluation of the impact of the West on Asia. As was seen in Chapter 3, explanations of the reasons for Western expansion and the extension of colonial empires have become more complex and contingent. There was no single reason for the extension of Western control in Southeast Asia and no single reason for the failure of the West to establish colonial empires in China. Similarly, when we attempt to measure the impact of imperialism on Asian economies, a very complex picture emerges.

We can follow the debate over Western exploitation of Asia in the two cases of China and Indonesia. Some Marxists have argued that trade between industrial and non-industrial economies is inherently exploitative, an 'unequal exchange' in which the non-industrial country must surrender disproportionate amounts of labour to receive a given value of manufactured goods. China was clearly at a disadvantage in this regard, and did have a consistently negative trade balance in the exchange of its labour-intensive agricultural and artisan products for Western manufactured goods. Marxists and nationalist historians argue that 'imports continuously exceeded exports, causing a steady outflow of capital' (Hsü, 1995, p. 431). However, neo-classical economists argue that the negative trade balance must have been covered by imports of long-term capital investment, which should have both earned profits for foreign investors and helped develop the Chinese economy (Hanson, 1980).

Lenin also saw foreign investment as another way of earning supernormal profits, and the railways are often criticized for their disruptive effect on the economy and for the repatriation of 'excessive' payments to foreign investors. Nationalist historians agree: in China, it is claimed, 'the frenzied scramble for railway concessions after the Japanese war was probably the most blatant form of economic imperialism...Added to the insult of imperialism was the injury of economic loss' (Hsü, 1995, p. 435). However, Ralph Huenemann argues on the basis of extensive quantitative analysis, first that the railway system was small, but secondly that despite its small size it created net social savings equal to 0.5 per cent of gross national product in 1933, thirdly that foreign bondholders did not receive 'unduly' high interest payments, and finally that the railways cannot be blamed for worsening China's terms of trade or adversely affecting Chinese income distribution (Huenemann, 1984). Predictably, the extension of modern transport did alter marketing patterns and stimulate development unevenly. In Shandong, for example, the new railroad lines accelerated the restructuring of the cotton industry and contributed to the dominance of Japanese firms.

The imperialist powers' ambitions sometimes exceeded their grasp. French efforts to use railway concessions to extend their control northwards into Yunnan, for instance, failed dismally. Potential markets for French manufactured goods proved illusory, for France did not produce goods in demand by the Chinese, French prices were too high, and attempts to establish retail outlets in port cities were mismanaged. Promoters of railway projects consistently overestimated potential traffic and underestimated costs. By the time the line from Haiphong to Kunming was completed in 1911 it was already Chinese-owned, a victim of the Chinese Rights Recovery policy (Lee, 1989). Also, although during the early 1920s the 'China Consortium' of British and American bankers attempted to force the Chinese government to devote its customs revenue to servicing foreign loans rather than stimulating domestic development, the Chinese in fact successfully resisted the Consortium's proposals, which therefore had little effect on the Chinese economy (Dayer, 1981).

In the case of Indonesia, the 'colonial drain' was not a trade deficit, but rather a trade surplus. This was the reverse of China's situation – although it seems intuitively that a surplus should have benefited Indonesia, in fact a persistent trade surplus must have been balanced by an outflow of capital. An independent country would expect this outflow to be in the form of investment which would earn income in the future, but Indonesia was not independent. Anne Booth has argued that over the period from 1900 to 1940 the large surplus in Indonesia's balance of trade reflects a movement of capital out of the country which did not benefit Indonesia. This 'unusually' large 'unrequited export surplus', Booth insists, must have reduced resources available for domestic investment and consumption, and therefore the colonial 'drain' was one of the primary reasons for 'the failure of trade to promote growth' in Indonesia (Booth, 1990, pp. 286–94; 1991, p. 31; 1995, p. 359).

As discussed below, if Indonesia did in fact grow, then of course the importance of the 'colonial drain' cannot have been as significant as Booth believes. In addition, Pierre van der Eng notes that the positive balance of trade cannot be a measure of the 'drain', because it must include payments to foreign labour and capital. The United States, for instance, had a positive balance of trade twice as high in per capita terms as Indonesia in the late 1920s, balanced by capital outflows which reflected the large foreign investments in American railroads, mines, and farms. The problem in Indonesia was whether there was too much foreign labour and capital, and whether their compensation was too high. Van der Eng argues that payments to foreign workers cannot have resulted in a significant drain. Foreigners working in Indonesia received much higher salaries than native Indonesians, but this reflected their education and training, and they would have received the same salaries if Indonesia had been independent. Only about 10 per cent of public employees were Europeans. Overall, ethnic Europeans were a very small share of the population, and by 1931 some 71 per cent of them had in fact been born in Indonesia.

Most of Indonesia's trade balance was accounted for by remitted dividends, profits, and interest. However, Indonesia had very little foreign investment on a per capita basis in 1929 compared to Canada, Australia, and New Zealand – all high income countries. Compared to other countries in Southeast Asia, Indonesia ranked second behind Malaya, and it appears that these were the two most rapidly growing countries in the region. Van der Eng comments, 'it is therefore possible to explain underdevelopment on the assumption that not enough, rather than that too much foreign capital was invested'. Interest payments after 1915 went overwhelmingly to repay loans, raised mostly in the Netherlands to be sure, but used in Indonesia for public infrastructure such as transportation, utilities, and irrigation. The major portion of foreign investment was direct investment in plantation agriculture, mining, manufacturing, trade, transport, and banking. The evidence, van der Eng argues, 'does not suggest that dividend rates were extremely high compared to the interest rates paid on government bonds...The forces of competition tended to press exceptional profits down to what used to be normal rate of return, allowing for risk.' For these and other reasons he reduces the measure of the drain significantly, and in addition notes that when the drain is compared to his estimates of Indonesia's gross domestic product, those periods when the drain was greatest are precisely the periods when the economy was growing most rapidly (Van der Eng, 1993).

Asia in the world economy

However we evaluate the exploitation of Asia by the West, we need to remember that although the international economy was important for Asia, Asia was not yet a large factor in the international economy. It is not clear that Asia could have provided the resources needed to ensure social stability in the West, as argued by Patnaik; at the same time, Western countries felt no need to consider Asian desires when they made decisions which affected Asia severely. In 1870 the exports of all the countries of East and Southeast Asia (except Indochina) together made up only 3.3 per cent of total world exports; despite the rapid growth of trade that proportion had not increased by 1913, and despite Japan's expansion it rose only to 4.8 per cent in 1929 (calculated from figures in Maddison, 1995; the shares of all of Asia and Latin America together were 13.2 per cent in 1870, 11.1 per cent in 1913, and 11.8 per cent in 1929).

The main trading partners of the Western industrialized countries were other Western industrialized countries, not Asian countries. Asian countries generally did not appear among the major trading partners of any Western country. There were two exceptions, United States trade with Japan and Netherlands trade with Indonesia, and these exceptions confirm the rule that Asia was less important to the West than the West was to Asia. In the case of the United States and Japan, a large developed country was trading with a developing country half its size. The population of the United States was 62.9 million in 1890 and 132 million in 1940, while the population of Japan was 39.9 million in 1890 and 71.9 million in 1940. Further, the United States was a relatively 'closed' country whose imports and exports constituted only a small fraction of its total national product. As Table 6.1 shows, trade with Japan was only a small fraction of total United States trade. Japanese exports to the United States in 1913 exceeded those of Mexico, but were less than United States imports from Canada, France, and Germany, and only one third of United

Table 6.1   United States–Japanese Trade, 1895–1938
A. United States trade with Japan
(Current prices, US$ million)

	Imports from Japan	Imports from Japan as % of total imports	Total imports as % of national product	Exports to Japan	Exports to Japan as % of total exports	Total exports as %of national product
1895	24	3.2	5.4	5	0.6	6.2
1913	92	5.0	4.7	58	2.3	6.4
1920	415	7.8	5.9	378	4.5	9.1
1929	432	9.7	4.3	259	4.9	5.1
1938	127	5.8	2.6	240	7.7	3.6

B. Japanese trade with the United States
(Current prices, million yen)

	Imports from USA	Imports from USA as % of total imports	Total imports as % of national product	Exports to USA	Exports to USA as % of total exports	Total exports as % of national product
1895	9.3	7.2	8.3	54	39.7	8.8
1913	124	15.6	15.9	184	25.7	14.3
1920	873	32.6	16.9	565	25.7	13.8
1929	654	23.7	17.0	914	35.1	16.0
1938	915	24.1	14.2	425	10.8	14.7

Source: Calculated from figures in Mitchell, 1993, 1995.

States imports from Britain. And they constituted only a tiny proportion of United States national product.

The case of the Netherlands is even more revealing, for here we have a very small country with a very large colony. The population of the Netherlands was 4.5 million in 1889 and 8.9 million in 1940, but the population of Indonesia, the Dutch East Indies, was 19.8 million in 1890 and 60.7 million in 1930. What's more, the Netherlands was a very 'open' economy, with a large re-export trade in addition to domestic exports and imports for domestic consumption. Yet Table 6.2 shows clearly that trade with Indonesia did not dominate the trade of the Netherlands. Indonesian exports to the Netherlands in 1913 were greater than Belgium, Russia, Britain and the United States, but less than half Netherlands imports from Germany. Before the First World War Indonesia took only a small share of

Table 6.2   Netherlands-Indonesia Trade, 1900–1938
A. Netherlands trade with Indonesia (Current prices, million gulden)

	Imports from Indonesia	Imports from Indonesia as % of total imports	Total imports as % of national product	Exports to Indonesia	Exports to Indonesia as % of total exports	Total exports as % of national product
1900	202	14.0	110.0	52	4.4	94.4
1913	529	13.5	140.0	163	5.3	136.0
1920	240	7.2	53.2	264	15.3	27.4
1929	147	5.3	42.6	187	9.3	30.9
1938	102	7.0	27.1	100	9.3	20.0

B. Indonesia trade with the Netherlands
(Current prices, million guilders)

	Imports from Netherlands	Imports from Netherlands as % of total imports	Total imports as % of national product	Exports to Netherlands	Exports to Netherlands as % of total exports	Total exports as % of national product
1902	54	27.8	na	78	30.6	na
1913	145	31.3	na	173	25.8	19.0
1920	263	21.5	na	355	15.9	23.7
1929	187	16.9	na	231	16.0	23.7
1938	106	23.6	na	134	19.5	17.5

Source: Calculated from figures in Mitchell, 1992, 1995, and Booth, 1995.

the Netherlands' exports, and in the interwar period, only in the single year 1920, when the Netherlands' trade with other partners such as Germany was particularly depressed, was Indonesia as important to the Netherlands as the Netherlands was to Indonesia.

Viewed from Asia the situation was dramatically different. By 1914 the industrialized West, and especially Britain and the United States, had become crucial markets for Asian countries. Chinese figures show that in addition to exports to Hong Kong (most of which passed on to Western markets), China's main markets were Japan, Germany, Britain, and the United States. The share of France in Indochina's exports rose from around 25 per cent before the First World War to some 50 per cent in the 1930s. Indonesia's main markets, in addition to neighbouring Malaya and small but rising exports to Japan, were the Netherlands, Britain, and the United States. Malaysia's main markets, in addition to Indonesia and India and again small but rising exports to Japan, were Britain and the United States. Figures for Burma (Myanmar) were only kept separately from 1937, and they show India, Japan, and Britain as the main markets. Philippines exports went overwhelmingly to the United States, but also to Japan and again Britain. Thailand's main markets were neighbouring Malaya, China, Japan, and yet again Britain and the United States (Nørland, 1991; Mitchell, 1995).

Note in particular the importance of the United States to Japan, compared to the relative unimportance of Japan to the United States. From Table 6.1 we can see that the decline in the dollar value of Japanese exports to the United States from 1929 to 1938 would have represented nearly 4 per cent of Japanese national product, but the increase in the yen value of United States exports to Japan would have added only one tenth of 1 per cent to United States national product. As we will see in Chapter 7, Japan in the 1920s and 1930s became the centre of its own imperial system, including Taiwan, Korea, Manchuria and Kwantung, and Japan also penetrated markets in Southeast Asia and India. Japanese expansion was at least in part a response to discrimination against Japanese exports by Western countries. Nevertheless, Western countries – the United States and Australia in the Pacific, and Britain, France, and Germany in Europe – remained among Japan's major trading partners even in the 1930s (Mitchell, 1995).

Asia in the world economy before 1914

Before the First World War, widespread economic development extended Asia's pre-existing market networks to integrate Asian farmers, miners, artisans, and a new class of industrial workers into the world economy. Table 6.3 shows the uniform increase in exports from Asian countries from 1895 to 1913. As we saw in Chapter 3, Chinese peasants and artisans were able to take advantage of the opportunities presented by the upswing in international markets. In the Han River basin, exports of both specialized agricultural products and manufactured goods began to rise in the 1870s, and the Han region simultaneously increased production of food and export goods. The higher level of commercialization was accommodated within the existing system by an increase in the number of periodic markets (Liu,

1980). Examples can be multiplied. Tea production expanded in the central and northern provinces, and exports reached 2 million piculs (1 picul = 133 pounds or 60.5 kilograms) in 1880, half of total Chinese production. Sugar exports from the southern provinces reached 1.6 million piculs in 1884. In 1920 China produced 80 per cent of the world's output of soybeans, processed as before into beancake fertilizer. Some 60 to 70 per cent of Chinese output was concentrated in Manchuria and about three-quarters of this was exported. Similarly, silk exports rose from 10 000 piculs in 1840, to 102 000 in 1890, to 139 000 in 1910, and to 168 000 in 1925. This benefited the lower Yangzi and southern China, and specialization reached extraordinary levels in some cases. Shunde county in Guangdong province had 70 per cent of its arable land planted in mulberry trees in 1923 (Li, 1981; Huang, 1985, pp. 122–3; Eng, 1986).

Christopher Baker has conceptualized the impact of the West on Southeast Asia as one aspect of a general tripartite framework of interdependent regional development. From the middle of the nineteenth century 'industrial' areas emerged, not only plantations and mines but also port cities,

Table 6.3   Value of Exports from China and Southeast Asia, 1895–1938 (Current prices, millions of indicated currency)

	1895	1913	1920	1929	1933	1938
China (*haikwan taels to 1912, then Chinese dollars*)	143	371 (1912)	844	1582	1417 (1931) 612	705 (1936)
Indochina (*francs*) (changed definition 1930)	96	345	1076	3175 1932 (1930)	1031	1947
Indonesia (*guilders*)	224	671	2228	1446	471	687
Philippines (*pesos*)	37	96	302	329	211	233
Sabah (*Straits dollars to 1913, then pounds*)	2.1	7.4	1.- 4	1.- 3	0.7	1.1
Sarawak (*Straits dollars to 1913, then pounds*)	2.4	6.9	2.- 0	4.- 0	1.6	2.9
Straits Settlements (*Straits dollars*)	173	342 (1911)	na	na	na	na
Malaya (*Malay States and Straits Settlements*) (*Straits dollars*)	na	na	821	930	388	587
Thailand (*baht*)	42	113	90	220	144	204

Source: Calculated from figures in Mitchell, 1995. Figures for 'China' exclude Manchuria after 1932.

where European capital dominated and massive immigration created plural societies. Colonial governments possessed physical as well as political power; the French used mechanized dredges to open some 2 million hectares of virgin land in the Mekong delta to rice production (Murray, 1980, p. 419), and demand for rubber, tobacco, palm oil and sugar led to expansion of estate production in Malaya (Kaur, 1985), and in North Sumatra and east Java (Elson, 1984; Stoler, 1985). In addition to these 'industrial' areas, expanding 'food-supply' areas, especially the rice-producing deltas of Burma (Adas, 1974), Thailand, and southern Vietnam, were often controlled by Asian capital, and migration came from other regions in these same societies. Finally, the 'ancient' areas in eastern India, southern China, Java, upper Burma, and northern Vietnam and Thailand maintained persistent traditional structures while also providing large amounts of migrant labour to the other areas (Baker, 1981).

The trade of the Philippines provides an example both of the increasing interdependence of Asian economies and of the effects of imperialist power. Despite his insistence on the necessity of an autonomous Philippine history, John Larkin argues that the most dynamic elements in Philippine economic history have been 'the gradual attachment of the island economy to the world marketplace and the related spread of the native population onto the archipelago's vast interior frontiers' (Larkin, 1982, p. 595). The opening of the island of Negros and of central Luzon to sugar production is an important case in point (Kerkvliet, 1977). So too is the rise of the market for the abaca plant, used for 'Manila hemp' rope, and hence for rigging on sailing ships, pulleys for oil rigs, and lariats for cowboys, which attracted migrants into the Kabikolan region where the plant grows (Owen, 1984). By 1875 the Philippines' volume of trade was fifteen times larger than in the 1820s; sugar, along with abaca, tobacco, and coffee, made up 90 per cent of the exports.

Land clearing and population growth expanded the islands' productive capacity, but since Spain consumed sugar and tobacco from its Caribbean colonies, the products of the Philippines had to find other markets. In order to balance these exports, the Spanish government was forced to open the Philippines to 'foreign' imports. This trade was handled by Chinese merchants, some of them mestizos whose families had lived in the islands for generations. Great Britain was the source of machinery and consumer goods such as textiles. Traditionally, the Philippines exported rice, primarily to China, but around 1870 began to import rice from the expanding production areas elsewhere in Southeast Asia (Steinberg, 1987 pp. 164–5).

The Philippines also provide an example of the way in which the colonial powers continually interfered with the operation of the market to benefit themselves. Spanish authorities only reluctantly liberalized trade during the nineteenth century. The American conquest had little economic impact until 1909 because the treaty between Spain and the United States prohibited any discrimination against Spanish interests, and other countries had demanded the same treatment. Therefore Britain continued to supply 90 per cent of Philippine cotton imports, the main import item. However, under the Payne–Aldrich Tariff passed by the United States Congress in 1909, all United States products except rice were permitted into the Philippines free of tariffs, and all Philippines products except rice and quotas of sugar and tobacco were permitted free into the United States. Other countries' goods were subjected to tariffs in the Philippines – at the same time the United States was campaigning for an 'Open Door' in China. The quotas on sugar and tobacco were removed in the Underwood Tariff of 1913, and 'a classic colonial economy developed' with exchange of Philippine agricultural products for manufactured goods produced in the United States. As was seen in Chapters 2 and 4, the benefits went largely to the elite whose support allowed the Americans to maintain their rule, often old gentry families with extensive landholdings dating from the Spanish era. A law which limited landholdings of individuals to 355 acres and corporations to 2530 acres proved ineffective, as did provisions for homesteading. Only 35 000 homesteaders gained land, but the number of tenant farmers increased by 700 000 during the American period. However, the limits did prevent plantation-style development as in the sugar and rubber estates in Vietnam and Eastern Cambodia, or the rubber estates as in Sumatra and Malaya. The American administration also did not permit importation of 'foreign' labour as the British did in Myanmar and Malaya, and there were no opium concessions, as in Indonesia, Indochina, and Malaya.

Still, the market did continue to exert its influence. The threat of early independence reduced potential United States investment, which in 1940 still only totalled $140 million predictably concentrated in sugar, tobacco, and hemp. The Manila–Degupan railway, the best route on Luzon, was bought out by the Morgan banking conglomerate in 1906, but of a planned 1233 miles of new line, only 866 had been constructed by 1954, even with a 4 per cent guaranteed return. The Philippines market absorbed only a very small share of United States exports. The British continued to control transport, handling 60 to 70 per cent of Philippines shipping. An attempt by the railway magnate James Hill to exclude British shipping interests was blocked in Congress by the American cordage industry located on the East Coast, which could import hemp from the Philippines via London at half of American freight rates (SarDesai, 1994, pp. 151–3).

The failure of the interwar economy

Explanations for why the world economy functioned so well before 1914, and what went wrong during the 1920s and 1930s, fall into the categories of cyclical theories, evaluations of government policies, and analyses of the specific historical situation and particularly of the role of Britain. National economies and the international economy have not grown at simple constant rates. Through most of the modern period, industrial economies have experienced three main types of cyclical behaviour: three- to four-year trade or inventory cycles, seven- to eleven-year investment cycles, and long cycles of some fifty years. In the early 1920s the Russian statistician Nikolai Kondratieff argued that 'long waves' in production and prices extending back into the late eighteenth century belonged 'to the same complex dynamic process' as the shorter cycles and were connected to major sectoral shifts in investment (Kondratieff, 1926). Kondratieff's methods and conclusions have attracted much criticism (See Solomu, 1987), but the notion that there are underlying long cycles in economic development has continued to find adherents. Joseph Schumpeter argued in the 1930s that the introduction of crucial new technologies stimulated the upswings of the long cycles; Simon Kuznets claimed in the 1950s that 'long swings' in economic activity were connected with investment required by expanding populations; and Walt Rostow in the 1970s argued that the 'lumpiness' of large-scale investment in natural resources lay behind the long cycle. Joshua Goldstein has linked the peaks of long economic cycles with periodic outbursts of warfare and the subsequent depressions with the destruction and exhaustion following in the wars' aftermath (Goldstein, 1988; see Tylecote, 1993). Angus Maddison has argued that rather than recurrent cycles, the world economy has passed through distinct 'phases' of development since the 1820s, marked by substantial variations in rates of growth of output, and even larger variations in the rates of growth of foreign trade (Maddison, 1982; 1989; 1995).

  For Asian producers and traders, the cyclical up- and downswings of the major Western economies became increasingly important, as they became more closely integrated into patterns of regional and world trade. Maddison's 'Phase II', from 1870 to 1913, was marked by an acceleration of growth. In particular, the long 'Kondratieff' upswing from 1895 to 1914 saw rising incomes in Western Europe, especially Britain, and in the United States. As noted above, these two countries provided crucial markets for Asian producers. British national product, measured in constant prices, increased at a rate of 5.45 per cent yearly, and United States national product rose at 3.53 per cent yearly. British imports, measured in current prices, increased from £417 million in 1895 to £769 million in 1913, and United States imports from $752 million to $1.85 billion.

Conversely, Maddison sees 'Phase III' from 1913 to 1950 as a 'bleak age, whose potential for growth was frustrated by a series of disasters' (Maddison, 1995, p. 65). The downswing of the 1920s and especially the 1930s meant stagnant or declining incomes in Western Europe, especially Britain, and in the United States. British national product measured in constant prices grew at only 1.81 per cent yearly from 1920 to 1938. The United States boomed through the 1920s, but the depression saw a massive contraction of the American economy, and national product declined an average of nearly 1 per cent yearly from 1929 to 1938. British and United States imports declined precipitously. In current prices, British imports were £1.93 billion in 1920, but only £920 million in 1938, while United States imports were $5.37 billion in 1920 and only $2.19 billion in 1938 (figures from Mitchell, 1992; 1993).

Policy-oriented explanations focus on the operation of the international gold standard before 1914 and the failure of attempts to re-establish the gold standard system in the 1920s. Although all responsible officials in the interwar years thought that the gold standard had fostered growth and that they understood its operation, specialist scholars today do not agree on exactly how the gold standard worked its magic (see Bordo and Kydland, 1995). Partly as a result of this, there is also widespread disagreement as to what could or should have been done to promote growth in the 1920s and most importantly to avoid the collapse following 1929. Most students agree that above all, government officials in Europe and the United States failed to cooperate effectively in solving a range of problems – inter-Allied war debts and reparations to be paid by Germany, appropriate exchange rates, currency speculation, tariffs and other protectionist measures, and the technical aspects of currency stabilization programmes, to name a few.

The responses of Western countries to the crisis of the depression were essentially deflationary and protectionist. Restrictions on output imposed by cartels and reductions in wages, it was hoped, would maintain profits while making exports more competitive. Tariffs and quotas were imposed to shut foreign competitors out, and finally the gold standard was abandoned as countries devalued their currencies to make their goods cheaper than their competitors' products. The adoption of the highly protectionist Hawley-Smoot Tariff by the United States set off a chain reaction by other countries, and President Franklin Roosevelt's denunciation of 'the old fetishes of so-called international bankers', effectively wrecked the World Economic Conference in 1933 (see Eichengreen, 1992; James, 1992).

Finally, structural explanations suggest that the gold standard was not the reason for the smooth operation of the international economy before 1914. Rather, the unique position of Britain, with its large and open market, its positive balance of payments which permitted massive international lending, and the overwhelming dominance of sterling and of the London money market, both facilitated the growth of international trade and investment and worked to minimize fluctuations and instability. Following the war, Britain grew slowly and suffered a chronic negative balance of payments, and its role as a lender declined. Britain held over 40 per cent of the world's total foreign investment in 1914, but only 29 per cent in 1929. The role of sterling and of London declined relative to other 'key' currencies and other centres, and because exchange rates were fixed but not stable there was far more opportunity for speculation. Finally, increased competition in both agriculture and industry led to worldwide 'excess capacity' in a broad range of products (see Tipton and Aldrich, 1987a).

In the 1920s Britain continued to export raw materials and 'traditional' manufactured products, such as coal, iron goods, and cotton textiles. Britain lost markets to Germany in northeastern Europe, to France in Africa, to the United States in South America, and to Japan in Asia. Exports peaked at only one-fifth their 1913 level, and Britain's share of world trade declined 11 per cent. Awareness of Britain's decline led significant groups to protectionism. The Federation of British Industry called not for American-style mass production systems, but for safeguarding traditional industries in the home market and expanding those industries through 'trade-preference' principles in the colonies and other traditional markets. Bankers abandoned free trade because of tensions in world capital markets. Labour unions moved to protectionism to defend jobs and wages. Against the background of both structural weaknesses in production and increased international competition, Britain rationed international credit and attempted to exploit its bargaining power over markets for primary products and financial services. On balance these efforts failed, and the lack of success reinforced the relative decline of British exports and therefore damaged the domestic economy. Britain did not regain its position as the centre of international trade and capital flows, and could not restore the position of its staple industries (Rooth, 1993; Meredith, 1996).

Asia in the world economy between the wars

The problems of the Western economies, particularly the difficulties facing Britain in the 1920s and the depression in the United States in the 1930s, affected Asia in two ways. Because Western governments' primary concern was to protect their home industries, markets for Asian products declined, and less capital was available for investment. Even if trade and investment are seen as aspects of imperialism, this decline still limited growth and therefore limited opportunities for Asian producers. Further, when they could, Western governments attempted to impose frankly discriminatory measures on Asian countries. The pressure brought by the 'China Consortium' was one example, and quotas on Japanese products were another. In addition, some of the specific errors in policy for which Western leaders have been blamed were reflected in Asia. For instance, following the wishes of the home government in the Netherlands, which belonged to the remaining gold bloc countries, the Dutch colonial government in Indonesia did not devalue its currency until 1936, and therefore part of the spectacular collapse in the value of Indonesian exports resulted from the fact that they were forced to compete in world markets where other producers had already devalued their currencies substantially.

For Asia, exposure to the opportunities of world markets had also meant exposure to international competition and political upheaval, even in the upswing before 1914. Chinese sugar was virtually destroyed by new competition from plantations in Indonesia and tenant farmers in the Philippines, and from sugar beet producers in Europe. Exports declined to 780 000 piculs in 1894, and in 1906 exports were only 170 000 and imports 6.5 million. Chinese tea suffered from Ceylonese, Indian, Japanese, and Javanese competition. Warfare and natural disasters disrupted trade in the Han River basin from the 1910s onwards.

Competition increased in the interwar period. Chinese tea exports declined to an average of 651 000 piculs in 1918–27. The depression drove the price of tea down by more than half again, and Chinese exports sank further. Chinese soybean output continued to increase through the 1920s, but dropped behind large increases in beancake fertilizer in the United States and began to lose markets to chemical fertilizers. The depression and the collapse of the market for soybeans brought crisis to peasant farmers in specialized districts. Silk markets were lost to Japanese producers, and Japanese silk already had 60 per cent of the world market in 1925. Silk prices declined 30 per cent in 1931–2, and the value of silk exports dropped two-thirds. The mulberry trees of Shunde county went unpicked because the wages of pickers exceeded the value of the crop.

The effects of the decline in export markets for Asian products can be clearly seen in Table 6.3. These figures are in current prices, so they take no account of changes in the price level. Nevertheless, they show a striking contrast of the uniformly rapid growth of Asian exports from 1895 to 1913 with the mixed experience of the 1920s and the collapse of the 1930s. The one exception, as will be seen in Chapter 7, was Japan's trade with its imperial dependencies. The decline in imports by Western countries particularly affected producers and processors of agricultural and mineral products. In the Kabikolan district in the Philippines, the collapse of demand for hemp and therefore for abaca meant poverty. Incomes in Kabikolan were not much higher in the 1970s than in the mid-nineteenth century (Owen, 1984). The decline in the total value of exports did not necessarily mean declining volumes of goods exported. It was possible for Asian producers to export many thousands of tons more of products and receive less for their efforts, because of the drop in world prices for staple commodities. One example, exports of sugar from Indonesia, is examined below. There were many others. As rubber and tin prices dropped in London, the value of rubber exports from the Federated Malay States declined from 202 million Straits dollars in 1929 to 37 million in 1932, and tin from 117 million to 31 million.

In Southeast Asia colonial governments and private firms reacted to the depression by cutting employment and reducing the wages of those who remained by up to half. Massive shifts of population resulted. Tens of thousands of workers in cities and towns, plantations and mines, returned to the countryside to eke out an existence as best they could. Interregional migrant workers were repatriated, sometimes voluntarily and sometimes not. Between 1930 and 1934, 170 000 estate workers returned from Sumatra to Java, a quarter of a million more Indians left Penang than arrived, and a quarter of a million more Chinese left Singapore than arrived. The social consequences could also be severe. Small-holders were not protected by the various international schemes established to restrict and rationalize production, and many of them lost their land, particularly in Vietnam and in Burma. In lower Burma the proportion of land held by non-agriculturalists increased from 31 to 50 per cent from 1930 to 1935, and because many of the new owners were Indian money-lenders, violence against Indians increased. It has been argued that the impact of the depression, though severe, was no more and possibly less than typical levels of distress in poor harvest seasons caused by the failure of the monsoon (Brown, 1986). Nevertheless, the depression was perceived as man-made and as will be seen in Chapter 8, the focus of hostility had become the colonial states.

How Much Growth? The Examples of China and Indonesia

China's economy in the Republican period

The sustained expansion of output per head became a regular feature of Chinese economic life in the early decades of the present century.

Thomas Rawski, 1989

Rawski's attempt to arrive at precise quantifications for the 1910s to the 1930s does not convince.

Philip Huang, 1991

Did the Chinese economy grow in the late Qing and Nationalist periods, and if there was growth, did it constitute development? Extending his view of the Qing economy into the Republican and Communist periods, Philip Huang argues that growth was very limited, and that until the 1980s such growth as there was constituted not modern economic growth but economic 'involution'. As they had for centuries, large farms hired labour from poor households up to the point where economies of scale disappeared and rented their surplus land to the poor households. Population pressure increased the supply of cheap labour, driving down wages and depressing incentives to use more draft animals or otherwise improve economies of scale. Further, the spread of commercialization and the opening of more distant markets only increased the risk-taking and vulnerability of the small households, as they produced goods for local, regional, and international markets by extracting ever-increasing hours of labour from their members at rates of return close to zero. 'Peasant households marketed more for rent payments and survival needs than for enterprise; and peasants borrowed more for emergencies and survival than for productive investment' (Huang, 1985; Huang, 1990, p. 112). That is, China remained caught in Mark Elvin's 'high level equilibrium trap' (Elvin, 1973; see Chao, 1986).

Huang's macroeconomic argument rests on his assertion that marginal physical product per workday declined, that is, as family members worked increasing numbers of hours per day and days per year, the value of what they produced each hour and each day dropped, finally reaching a point where working additional hours brought virtually no additional income. His evidence has been disputed by Ramon Myers. Myers notes that real wages for rural workers increased from 1870 to 1937, and cites studies which show that at a number of points during this period the value of the marginal physical product of workers on farms was roughly equal to the wages paid to hired workers. Further studies indicate a high national rate of capital formation and a high marginal savings rate among rural households, showing that peasants were not pressed to the level of subsistence, but rather were able to save a large fraction of any additional income they received. That is, not only did the Chinese rural labour market function efficiently in the economist's sense of equalizing wages and marginal product, but also productivity, wages, and welfare increased. In Myers' words, 'while off-farm wages rose, household productivity kept up with them ... generally speaking, peasants choosing to stay at home and put more work into their chores enjoyed the same amount of increased income as did peasants putting the same amount of work into off-farm jobs' (Myers, 1991, p. 620).

Myers draws on a number of quantitative studies which contend that substantial growth and development did occur in the late Qing and Nationalist periods. Loren Brandt traces a pattern of rising farm wages to the 1880s and suggests that sustained growth of agricultural productivity in China, as in Japan, extends back well into the nineteenth century (Brandt, 1989). Thomas Rawski details the rapid growth of the heavy industrial sector (Rawski, 1980). Tim Wright analyses the development of the coal industry, and notes that although many large mines were owned by Western or Japanese firms, the output of Chinese-owned mines grew as rapidly as that of the foreign firms (Wright, 1984). Heavy industry grew in response to domestic Chinese demand, which suggests that broadly-based improvements in agricultural productivity raised the incomes of many Chinese, and that the resulting 'deepening' of the market provided the crucial opportunities for industrial entrepreneurs. Finally, Rawski extends and synthesizes these studies, revises previous estimates of both agricultural and non-agricultural output upwards, and concludes that total output in constant prices grew 1.8 to 2.0 per cent annually from 1914–18 to 1931–6, and that despite the substantial rise in population, output per person increased 1.1 to 1.2 per cent each year. Thus, in Rawski's view, the growth of investment and of per capita output in China during the period from 1914 to 1952 was not markedly different from the experience of Japan (Rawski, 1989, pp. 330, 356).

Huang has defended himself vigorously. He accuses Myers, with some justice, of misrepresenting his arguments (Huang, 1991, p. 629). He discusses Rawski's evidence of increasing agricultural output in the early twentieth century in some detail and concludes that Rawski's results are 'utterly unconvincing' (Huang, 1990, pp. 137–43). Regarding the possibility that the productivity of agricultural workers was rising before 1900, Huang is more than sceptical. He dismisses Brandt's figures as 'an exercise of faith, in which the results are entirely predictable from the assumptions with which he begins' (Huang, 1991, p. 631).

Politics plays a role in these interpretations. Myers has long advocated what he calls an 'accommodative' approach to Chinese development, which 'emphasizes free enterprise and the compatibility of the Confucian heritage with economic modernization', and has opposed the 'transformative' approach of Marxists who reject China's inherited culture. He insists that Huang belongs in this transformative Marxist tradition (Myers, 1991, pp. 621–3; see Myers, 1980; Jones, 1981, pp. 547–50; Wong, 1992, pp. 603–6). The answers to two related questions are at stake. The first is the question of which system produced higher rates of growth – private enterprise or socialist planning – and which is therefore to be judged superior. If substantial growth took place during the Republican period, then the People's Republic receives less credit. Thus Rawski and Wright argue that the development of the coal and producer goods industries laid the foundation for the growth achieved under the new Communist government. The second question is the role of traditional cultures and inherited values in economic development. Myers believes that Confucian values support economic development, but he also prefers free markets and private enterprise and does not believe that any reform of the Communist system from within, such as the production responsibility system of 1980, could possibly succeed (Myers, 1989; 1991, p. 612). Huang thinks Myers has either missed or misrepresented his fundamental point, which is that 'modern economic development... eluded both the free-market cum private property rural

China of 1350 to 1950 *and* the planned, collectivist rural China of the 1950s to the 1970s', and more fundamentally, that 'the classical models of Smith and Marx are both wrong with respect to China' (Huang, 1991, pp. 632–3).

Compounding the problem of the values of the author are further problems of data and method. Complete, systematic, consistent information does not exist. Much of the discussion of pre-industrial Chinese economic development rests on surveys and interviews conducted in the 1930s by the American sociologist John L. Buck, by Japanese scholars working under the sponsorship of the Japanese semi-official South Manchurian Railway, and by the Nationalist Guomindang Land Commission. The importance of these surveys extends beyond the realm of purely economic development to affect our whole understanding of peasant society in China. For instance, our knowledge of the level of marital fertility in rural China rests on the reliability and analysis of data collected by Buck's assistants from 2640 farm families (Hanley and Wolf, 1985). All three surveys have their weaknesses, and all are suspect because of the motives of their sponsors. Buck, for instance, opposed social revolution and collectivization as a means of improving the lot of poor peasants – he favoured American style 'family farms', birth control, and improved marketing – and his assistants systematically overstated the level of affluence and the degree of commercialization in the villages they studied. Huang notes the care needed in the interpretation of the data collected by the Japanese (Huang, 1985), and he in turn is accused by Brandt of 'selective and misleading' use of that same data (Brandt, 1987, p. 712).

What is known – however doubtful – must then be extrapolated backwards to what is unknown, using proxy variables, estimates, and plausible assumptions. In the case of agricultural incomes and output – crucial because of the small size of the modern industrial sector – this means using the data collected in the 1930s to construct estimates extending back in time. Huang links landholding patterns in the 1930s with earlier information to construct his picture of agricultural development beginning in the seventeenth century. Brandt and Rawski both interpolate between known figures and extrapolate backwards to estimate rates of growth and change in the late nineteenth and early twentieth centuries. For instance, Brandt's estimate that marketed agricultural output rose 'at least' 2 per cent per year depends on estimates of the non-agricultural population, their grain consumption, and the marketed proportion of cash crops, assuming that 'roughly half the cash-crop output was marketed in the 1890s, but that in the 1930s, it was nearer to two-thirds'. His estimate that labour productivity increased 40 to 60 per cent rests on information on wages from 1889 compared to reported wage rates in the 1930s, and the assumption that in a 'competitive market economy such as China's', wages will reflect marginal product (Brandt, 1989, pp. 73–6, 106, 132–3).

There is, on balance, much evidence of growth and development in China in the late nineteenth and early twentieth centuries. Systematic estimates of the output of the large agricultural sector show that output grew, and that it grew more rapidly than population. Exports of agricultural goods and protoindustrial handicrafts increased. Industrial output rose in the first three decades of the twentieth century. Coal output trebled from 1913 to 1936, pig iron output rose six times, steel ten times (figures in Mitchell, 1995). Rawski and Brandt claim that this growth was 'substantial'. In evaluating that claim we need to keep our standards of comparison clearly in mind. At 1.2 per cent per year, per capita output would require 58 years to double. This is much slower than China's recent growth. But should China's performance in the 1920s and 1930s be compared with the 1980s and 1990s, or with what had gone before? And was this growth different enough from what had gone before to constitute 'development', or was it, as argued by Huang, merely another period of 'involutionary growth', and therefore doomed to exhaust itself in the absence of fundamental changes in social organization?

How does China compare with Japan, the paragon of Asian development? Japan grew very rapidly in the decade before 1914, slowly in the 1920s, very rapidly in the 1930s, but then on balance not at all to 1950 as output boomed, collapsed, and recovered in the war and its aftermath (Ohkawa, et al., 1979). Comparing growth over the period from 1914 to 1952, as Rawski does, therefore includes two 'slow' periods and lowers Japan's performance. If we restrict the comparison with Japan to the 1920s and 1930s, when Japanese per capita domestic product rose at over 2.2 per cent per year, it appears that China could have grown only half as rapidly as Japan. Further, as seen in Chapter 5, Japan had become an industrial economy, and China as yet had not. China's population of over 400 million was possibly six times larger than Japan's, but coal output was slightly less, pig iron output only one third as large, and steel and electricity output only one tenth as large in 1936 (figures in Mitchell, 1995). But should China's performance be compared with that of Japan, the country which subjugated and conquered large parts of China, and which therefore exploited resources which would otherwise have contributed to Chinese growth? This leads to the problem of how 'normal' the interwar years were, and to consideration of the continuing impact of Japanese and Western imperialism and of the depression.

Since Adam Smith, economists have agreed that economic development proceeds best in normal times. The Republican period was not normal, and the lack of leadership and consistency in the economic sphere was a political factor of great importance. The Nationalist state inherited many of the problems which the Qing had failed to surmount, and it too has been seen as too weak to foster development (Myers, 1980; Jones, 1981). The foreign debt of £139 million in 1911 imposed a large burden on the new Nationalist government. Western governments forgave much of the sums owed them under the Boxer indemnity, but the Nationalist government failed to increase and centralize revenues and remained burdened by fixed expenses, especially on loans and indemnities. In the early 1930s the total taxes collected by all levels of government may have amounted to only 5 to 7 per cent of total output (Rawski, 1989). Little was left for positive economic initiatives; for instance, the Chinese government did not support the silk industry in the 1920s and 1930s, while the Japanese government did. Lillian Li sees this as the crucial element in the decline of the Chinese industry, with particularly bad effects on the lower Yangzi region and in southern China (Li, 1981; Eng, 1986).

These serious structural problems, however, seem minor compared to the near collapse of central power from 1916 to 1927, the emergence of some 50 regional warlords, and civil war among the warlords and then between the emerging leader of the Nationalists, Chiang Kaishek, and his former Communist allies. The confusion, and the need of regional warlords for local supporters, created new opportunities for affluent families to exploit their neighbours. The writer Shen Congwen thought the most significant change brought by the 1911 revolution had been that local elite families now held office as both civil magistrates and military garrison commanders, whereas under the Qing officials were forbidden to hold office in their home districts. Local studies have tended to confirm his insight, and document how the wealthy used their new combination of military, political, and economic power to exploit their less fortunate neighbours, take their land, and drive them sometimes to desperate acts of resistance. Shen also drew on his own experience as a soldier to recreate the cycle of casual violence into which local society slipped. Torture and execution of 'bandits' provided the chief recreation for the soldiers. Women prisoners were especially prized, but best of all were army deserters because of the bounty paid for their capture. Food served at the party held after the eventual death of the prisoner supplemented the soldiers' meagre rations. There might be 20 or 30 such killings in a quiet month in this small provincial town, rising to hundreds and even peaks of two or three thousand during a major outbreak of 'banditry' or as the result of a 'pacification' campaign (Spence, 1982, pp. 128, 139–40; see Esherick and Rankin, eds. 1990).

The new Nationalist government established at Nanjing in 1928 faced further challenges from powerful regional commanders known as the 'new warlords', internal factional divisions, the still undefeated Communists, and above all the Japanese. But would the Nationalist government have supported economic development even if it had been more able to do so, or was it dominated by Jones' rent-seeking coalitions? An ongoing debate over the complex relations among groups of businessmen on one side and divided government interests on the other revolves around these questions. In Shanghai, the Nationalist Party developed its constituency among middle-class merchants in the late 1920s, while the central government courted support among wealthy Shanghai capitalists, but by 1935 with the nationalization of the banking industry, the central government, exemplified by Chiang himself, revealed its intent simply to control private capitalists, and senior government officials moved to create personal economic empires. Parks Coble argues that the growth of 'bureaucrat-capitalism' – private firms owned and dominated by top government officials – was 'not an aberration but the re-emergence of a traditional pattern of official domination' (Coble, 1980, p. 260; see Fewsmith, 1985; Bergère, 1989). Wright's study of the coal industry shows that 75 per cent of identifiable shareholders, directors, and chief managers of Chinese coal mines between 1912 and 1927 came from the civilian and military bureaucracies (Wright, 1985, p. 146).

Was there a process of modernization, or capitalist transformation, taking place despite the malfeasances of these corrupt government officials? Richard Bush emphasizes the weakness of the Nationalist government in its dealings with industrialists in the expanding textile industry (Bush, 1982), but what were the values of this class of capitalists? As seen in Chapter 3, the values of Chinese capitalists are disputed. Myers argues that 'Confucian' traditions are clearly evident in the structure and behaviour of Chinese firms in the 1920s, as most preferred to remain small, simple in organizational form, family-owned and managed, centred around a family authority figure, with customs based on highly personal relations. Even in successful areas such as tea, silk, and rural-based handicraft manufactures, the management and organization of firms did not change, and in the 1920s they failed to reduce their transactions costs, particularly by continuing to rely on agencies to handle their relations with suppliers and customers. As a result they lost market share to new competitors with lower transaction costs, especially Japan. Myers' point is that these values can support very rapid assimilation of new techniques and therefore very rapid growth – *if* government policy is oriented towards 'instrumental rationality' (Myers, 1989). This was evidently not the case in the view of many Chinese business leaders, and they avoided government regulation when they could, for instance by not registering their firms as joint stock corporations (Kirby, 1995).

Huang in turn concludes that the pattern of 'involutionary growth' worked to 'snuff out' technological innovation. So as long as technology did not give an advantage to large-scale producers, enterprises which paid wages to adult males could not compete with households employing unpaid females. For instance, a three-spindle spinning wheel was known in the early nineteenth century in the lower Yangzi region, but it required an adult male worker to operate, and was only 50 to 100 per cent more efficient than the simple single-spindle wheel which required much less physical strength to operate and which all peasant households could afford. This manifestly was not enough of a differential to overcome the competition of households using the unpaid labour of their female members (Huang, 1990, pp. 77, 86).

However, when true industrial technologies became available, they were adopted. In 1860, 45 per cent of peasant households wove cloth, and 80 per cent of those grew their own cotton and spun the yarn. Nearly half of all cotton cloth was home-supplied. Only 0.6 per cent of yarn used by village weavers was machine spun and only 3.2 per cent of cotton cloth was machine woven. Two generations later, in 1936, 30 per cent of peasant households wove cloth, and home-supplied cloth was still 28.7 per cent of consumption. However, handwoven cloth was only 38.8 per cent of total consumption, and 75.9 per cent of all yarn used in village handwoven cloth was machine spun. In addition, 87.1 per cent of all cotton grown was marketed (Huang, 1990, p. 98). This is not to say that the adoption of industrial technologies is inevitable, easy, or painless, but merely that, as in Japan, if large numbers of agents are attempting to introduce a technique, success is likely to come to one of them, and that success will be imitated.

Further, when the central government did support regional authorities effectively, the results could be impressive. In Shaanxi province Nationalist-supported local government agencies were able to create significant irrigated areas and introduce improved seed varieties into the region's agriculture, as well as leaving behind a pool of skills and administrative expertise which laid the basis for the steady development of the region

under the People's Republic (Vermeer, 1988). In the lower Yangzi, contrary to the usual picture, Kathryn Bernhardt's sources show the Nationalist government intervened frequently on the side of tenants to reduce
rents. Despite this state intervention favouring tenants against landlords,
unrest increased. However, Bernhardt interprets unrest as the result of
organized political resistance, not an immiseration of the peasantry caused
by the exactions of parasitic landlords. In this district at least the landlords
found themselves caught between tenant resistance to rents on the one
hand, and increasing state power on the other, and by the 1940s their
'economic plight' was already severe:

> In the end what destroyed landlordism in the lower Yangzi region was
> the interrelated processes of state-strengthening and growing tenant
> political power. When the People's Liberation Army conquered Jiang-
> nan in 1949, rent relations were already on the verge of collapse. Land
> reform just dealt the final blow. (Bernhardt, 1992, p. 232)

Indonesia's economy in the colonial period

> It is now possible to conclude that the period 1900–1929 was a period
> of almost continuous growth of per capita output . . . It is therefore likely
> that the average standard of living improved during the first three
> decades of the 20th century.
>
> Pierre van der Eng, 1992

> . . . if the GDP data are adjusted to allow for changes in the terms of
> trade, the growth in the years from 1913 to 1940 was slower than van
> der Eng shows . . . the living standards of the mass of the population did
> not improve greatly, and could have declined.
>
> Anne Booth, 1995

As with China, reliable figures for the economic growth of Indonesia in
the late nineteenth and early twentieth centuries are not available. The
statistics kept by the Dutch colonial authorities concentrated on those
aspects of the economy which concerned them, not necessarily the ones
which interest today's historians. Estimates therefore depend on the backward extrapolation of relationships derived from later figures, combined
with the earlier colonial statistics. For example, although they recorded the
population of Java fairly accurately, the Dutch authorities did not attempt

to count the number of people on the other islands until 1920. They were very interested in the quantities of export crops produced. They were also interested in the amount of land planted in rice, the main food crop, because that land competed with land for export crops, and because serious food shortages could lead to unrest. However, they were much less interested in the production of other food crops, or of other cash crops which were not exported. They were interested in foreign trade, but much less concerned with domestic commerce. Whole areas of the indigenous economy – most artisan production and all cottage manufacturing, food processing, retail sales, personal services, private residential construction, market gardening – were not recorded at all.

The gaps in the statistical record left by the colonial authorities have led to an incomplete and biased view of the colonial economy. As Pierre van der Eng says,

> The general opinion is that the country's economy was dominated during the colonial period by large Western agricultural estates, sugar factories, and mining companies, which produced raw materials for export. Most students distinguish therefore between the 'indigenous' and the 'colonial' economy, and assume the two developed divergently. They presume that the 'colonial' economy flourished, while the 'indigenous' economy hardly changed or even progressed. Their conclusion is that the rural population was forced to play a passive role in the process of economic development and that during the colonial period average income and the standard of living declined, or at best stagnated.
> (Van der Eng, 1992, pp. 343–4)

Van der Eng attempts to fill this gap. He begins with an estimate of the population of the islands outside of Java and Madura, assuming a somewhat lower rate of growth than that shown in the censuses after 1930. He combines this with a further estimate of food consumption per person to obtain a figure for food production on these islands. For Java and Madura, he supplements figures for rice production with estimates of the production of other food crops. These estimates are added to figures for export crops to give total agricultural production. Van der Eng then constructs seventeen separate series for the annual output of various categories of non-agricultural production. Sometimes this can be done fairly simply, as in construction, where imports and production of cement and the output of the forestry industry can be used as indicators. Sometimes the procedure must be more complex, as in manufacturing output, where gross value added per worker is first observed to depend on the share of full-time employment in total employment and the share of employees in large and medium-sized establishments in the 1970s, and then that relationship assumed to hold in earlier decades as well (Van der Eng, 1992, appendix).

The results are dramatic. First, output appears substantially higher than previously thought, and in addition the estimates show a rapid increase. However, although total output grew from 1880 to 1900, per capita output stagnated. That is, the Aceh War in Sumatra and the extension of the empire to islands outside of Java and Madura seem to have contributed little to development. Following the end of the war, van der Eng's figures suggest that the new policy which emphasized infrastructure development encouraged growth by stimulating internal trade. From 1900 to 1929, population increased 38 per cent, but total product more than doubled, and per capita product therefore rose at 1.6 per cent annually for three decades. Further, the main sources of growth were in the 'indigenous' sector. The sectors of the economy dominated by Western firms played a relatively minor role in achieving this growth. The growth of production of 'estate crops', mining, banking and finance, and oil and gas together only explain 15 per cent of total growth in the period 1900 to 1913, and 19 per cent from 1913 to 1929.

As with China, these figures have political significance. Both defenders and opponents of the colonial regime have assumed that per capita output stagnated because the traditionalism of the indigenous sector inhibited technological change and led to a rapid increase in population. On the one hand, if the Western-dominated colonial portion of the economy was the only source of growth and development, then apologists for the Dutch could argue that their impact had been beneficial, even if limited. On the other hand, if average incomes had stagnated or declined under the Dutch, then contemporary critics and later nationalist writers could argue that the colonial economy had drained resources out of the indigenous sector and created the conditions for chronic underdevelopment.

In addition, the measurement of trends in the per capita output in the indigenous or 'small-holder' sector of Indonesia's economy has more general importance, because of the work of Clifford Geertz (1963) and the immense influence of his notion of 'agricultural involution' – for instance in Philip Huang's studies on China. According to Anne Booth,

Geertz . . . was seeking essentially cultural explanations for Java's failure to develop along the lines of Japan in the late 19th and early 20th centuries. An important 'stylized fact' that motivated Geertz's work was that small-holder agricultural output and population in Java grew at roughly equal rates over the century or so from 1860 to 1960, so that little agricultural surplus was generated which in turn could have been used to fund an industrial takeoff, as happened in Japan in the latter part of the 19th century. (Booth, 1995, p. 351)

And, Booth continues, 'subsequent scholarship, based on a more detailed examination of the statistical record, indicates that broadly this assumption was correct' (Booth, 1995, p. 351). Again as with China, Japan becomes the standard of comparison, and again the supposed failure of Indonesian farmers to raise their levels of productivity above the rate of population growth explains the underdevelopment of the economy into the 1960s.

What is at stake here is therefore the origins both of Asian under-development and of subsequent Asian growth. With regard to the mechanisms of growth, Booth's and Geertz's comparison with Japan is oversimplified (Geertz, 1963, pp. 130–43). As we saw in Chapter 5, although increases in agricultural productivity played a significant role in Japanese development, the land tax imposed by the Meiji government was not simply 'used to fund an industrial takeoff', but to compensate the former *daimyō* and *samurai* and to import military hardware. With regard to the agricultural surplus, if van der Eng is correct, then the assumption that Indonesian farmers in the indigenous small-holder sector did not improve their productivity is wrong. This would undermine the basis of Geertz's approach, for if productivity increased, then native farmers, artisans, and merchants must have been far more flexible than he thought. Van der Eng's study of the first three decades of the twentieth century links here with Elson's work on the period of the Cultivation System which demonstrates the responsiveness and flexibility of the Javanese in the middle decades of the nineteenth century (Elson, 1994). That is, if indeed Indonesia was 'underdeveloped' in the 1950s, this cannot have resulted either from traditional patterns of 'culture' or from economic 'involution' experienced in the nineteenth and early twentieth centuries.

Figures for 'real per capita small-holder agricultural output' – the value of agricultural products produced outside the export or 'estate' sector, expressed in constant prices and divided by population – show stagnation or a slight decline from 1880 to 1905. Then follows a rapid rise to 1920. The 1920s and 1930s show fluctuations, but each of the peaks in 1913, 1920, 1929, and even 1940 is higher than the one before. There follows a horrible decline to 1950. From that trough the figures rise to a plateau in 1955 to 1965, but only to a level below the 1880s, and they then decline sharply in the late 1960s. Then, beginning from a trough in 1970, there is an uninterrupted rise, with the levels of the 1880s reached in the late 1970s and the levels of the late 1930s passed in the early 1980s (Booth, 1995, p. 352, using figures from van der Eng, 1992, Table A4 columns 1–3).

The small-holder sector therefore progressed through the 1930s, but with fluctuations, and this advance was followed by a decline which wiped out the gains of half a century. Interpretation of these figures, however, depends on the perspective of the observer. Van der Eng emphasizes the period of growth from 1900 to 1929. Booth selects the years 1913 and 1940, which omits the period of rapid growth before 1913 but includes the period of decline during the depression, and insists that growth was slow. Geertz, it seems, did his fieldwork in Java during a very unusual decade. Table 6.4 shows that aside from the Second World War, the output of the small-holder agricultural sector has consistently risen

Table 6.4   Indonesia: Small-holder Agricultural Output, Manufacturing Output, and Population, 1880–1989 (constant prices, 1983 rupiahs)

	Small-holder agricultural output,* in billions	Manufac- turing output, in billions	Population, in millions, and % rate of increase	Small-holder agricultural output per capita, in thousands	Manufac- turing output as % of total
1890	2603	654	37.0	70.4	10.5
1900	3109	768	43.4 (1.6)	71.6	9.6
1910	3738	946	48.2 (1.1)	77.6	9.5
1920	4245	1283	52.9 (0.9)	80.2	10.0
1930	4897	1816	60.6 (1.4)	80.8	10.6
1940	5984	2208	70.2 (1.5)	85.2	11.5
1950	5563	2371	79.0 (1.2)	70.4	14.7
1955	6204	3199	86.8 (1.9)	71.5	16.0
1965	7620	3877	105 (1.9)	72.5	15.9
1970	8522	3784	116 (2.0)	73.5	13.4
1980	12693	7293	147 (2.4)	86.3	13.3
1989	16634	19836	179 (2.0)	94.5	20.9

*3-Year Average.

Source: Calculated from data in van der Eng, 1992, Table A.4. Total output refers to Gross Domestic Product. Because of the five-fold increase in oil prices from 1973 to 1983, van der Eng values oil at a constant shadow price of 20 per cent of the actual 1983 price. If oil is valued at its 1983 price, the share of manufacturing in GDP in 1965 is 13.3 per cent, and in 1989 is 18.5 per cent.

more rapidly than population throughout the twentieth century, but the decade from 1955 to 1965 was an unusually poor one in this respect, because of an increase in the rate of growth of population. Further, the output of the manufacturing sector began to rise rapidly in the 1920s and 1930s, and rose again in the late 1940s and early 1950s, but it then remained constant from 1958 to 1970. Therefore the demographic and economic structures which Geertz labelled 'involution' – accelerating increases in population, little or no increase in per capita agricultural output, and little or no growth in the manufacturing sector – which he argued had resulted from inherited traditional cultural patterns and the negative effects of Dutch rule (Geertz, 1963, pp. 80, 124–5, 142–3), may in fact have been unique and limited to the single decade of his personal experience in Indonesia.

Even if there was substantial growth, though, there remains the problem of instability and what this implied for living standards. Table 6.5 gives one example, Indonesian sugar exports. The inflationary effects of the First World War and the subsequent collapse of prices are obvious. However, the effect these fluctuations had on the Indonesian economy depends not only on the price of sugar, but also on the cost of imports. The United States Commerce Department publishes a measure of 'command GNP', which is the figure for real Gross National Product, but with exports divided not by the export price index, but by the price index for United States imports. That is, it values United States exports by what Americans can purchase with the money exports bring and therefore gives an indication of the volume of goods and services the United States economy can 'command'. If the 'terms of trade', the ratio of prices received for exports to prices paid for imports, declines, then command GNP could decline even if the volume of exports increased. This is not usually a problem for industrialized countries trading with each other and exchanging a broad

Table 6.5   Indonesia: Sugar Exports, 1895–1938

	Exports in thousands of tons	Receipts in millions of guilders	Guilders received per ton
1895	576	81	140.63
1913	1469	153	104.15
1920	1510	1050	695.36
1929	2403	312	129.84
1938	1071	45	42.02

Source: Calculated from data in Mitchell 1995.

range of products, since price movements either are coordinated or cancel each other out. It is also not a great problem for an economy such as the United States, in which foreign trade makes up only a small proportion of total product. However, for an economy which has a high share of foreign trade in national product, and which depends on earnings from only a few commodities, fluctuations in the prices of those commodities can have very important consequences.

Booth thinks van der Eng underemphasizes the terms of trade. She argues that in the 1920s and 1930s Indonesian exports averaged about 20 per cent of total output, a high ratio for a country as large as Indonesia, and she estimates that during this period Indonesia's terms of trade declined by 50 per cent. This meant that although the real value of Indonesian exports rose substantially, the 'import capacity' generated by those exports declined. In the disastrous year 1932, exports in 1913 prices were 1.6 billion guilders (over twice the 1913 value of 704 000 guilders), but because of the decline in the relative prices of exports compared to imports, when the value of exports in 1932 prices is deflated using the price index for imports, the 'import capacity' in 1913 prices generated by these exports was only 662 million guilders, substantially less than 1913. Booth argues that the total of real domestic product therefore must be adjusted downwards, from 5.1 to 4.1 billion guilders. That is, instead of gross domestic product, the proper measure is command GDP, and instead of per capita product in the late 1930s being substantially above the level of 1913, it was in fact still 'well below' (Booth, 1995, pp. 355–8).

To compare van der Eng's gross domestic product from 1900 to 1929 with Booth's command GDP from 1913 to 1940 comes close to comparing two lots of apples with two lots of oranges. Both writers have chosen the measures which make their preferred case, van der Eng for growth and Booth for stagnation. However, as in the case of China, the evidence that there was substantial growth appears compelling. Clearly Indonesian farmers continued to increase the amount of output they obtained per unit of input, even in the difficult 1930s, and once the value of exports began to move up once again, Indonesia would benefit. Further, although the manufacturing sector was still very small, the increase in manufacturing output in those same difficult 1930s suggests that, despite the impact of the depression and the possible negative effects of colonial dependence, Indonesia's modern transformation may have begun.

7

JAPANESE IMPERIALISM AND THE PACIFIC WAR

You've committed one of the classic blunders – the best known is 'never
fight a land war in Asia'.
> Vizzini to Wesley (disguised as the Great Pirate
> Roberts), in *The Princess Bride*, 1987

The Second World War is known in Japan as the Pacific War, a designation now widely accepted by Western specialists as well (Ienaga, 1968;
Beasley, 1987). The name is important, for it reflects the realization that
this war was separate from the one fought in Europe, North Africa, and
the Middle East. As with other aspects of Asian history, the Pacific War is
now seen as having emerged out of the internal dynamics of Asian social
development. However, the identification and analysis of those dynamics
is complex and highly contentious. A Marxist/Leninist explanation, for
instance, would see the war as essentially imperialist. Diplomatic historians
would emphasize the altered balance of power and see the war as a Great
Power conflict. Historians looking critically at the internal workings of the
Japanese social and political system might see the war as fascist. Finally,
those historians who emphasize the failings of individuals could see the
war as a tragic mistake.

Japan played a central role in the war, and therefore any interpretation
of the war depends on one's views of Japanese economic growth, expansionism, imperialism, and militarism. In addition, the emergence of the
'tiger' economies of Taiwan and Korea, and more recently the rapid
growth of China, has sparked interest in the role of Japan in the economic
development of these regions. This chapter begins with the question of
Japanese imperialism, Japan's annexation of Taiwan and Korea, the

reasons the ruling elites in Japan felt compelled to continue to expand into China, and then into Southeast Asia, and the way in which this led to the confrontation with the United States. The growth and development of the Japanese imperial system is analysed, and the economic impact of Japanese rule on Taiwan, Korea, and Manchuria is examined – the failure of the Japanese to suppress Korean nationalism foreshadows the collapse of the colonial empires in the aftermath of the war. The chapter considers the economic effects of the war, first on China and then on Southeast Asia, and the human cost of the war. The political impact of Japanese rule on the emerging nationalisms of the peoples of China and Southeast Asia is examined in Chapter 8.

The Problem of Japanese Imperialism

Japanese tradition and imperialism

...if we send troops first...the Koreans will unquestionably demand their withdrawal...We shall then have fomented a war in a manner very different from the one you originally had in mind. Would it not be far better to send an envoy first? It is certain that if we did so the Koreans would resort to violence, and would certainly afford us the excuse for attacking them. If it is decided to send an envoy officially, I feel sure that he will be murdered. I therefore beseech you to send me.

Saigô Takamori, 1873

I consider such a venture entirely beyond comprehension, as it completely disregards the safety of our nation and ignores the interests of the people.

Ôkubo Toshimichi, 1873

Following the Meiji Restoration, elements within the new government argued that Japan needed not only to reform itself internally, but also to expand externally, to defend itself against the West and to provide employment for the *samurai* displaced by the abolition of the domains. Saigô Takamori insisted that Japan must seize Korea immediately in order to forestall Russian expansion, but also noted that the plan to invade Korea was 'a far-reaching scheme which will divert abroad the attention of those who desire civil strife, and thereby benefit the country'. He volunteered as an emissary in the expectation that the Koreans would kill him and thereby give Japan a justification for the invasion. When the plan was rejected in 1873 he withdrew from the government, but then re-emerged from retirement to lead the Satsuma Rebellion in 1877 and committed suicide when the uprising was defeated.

Ôkubo Toshimichi, the victor in the 1873 crisis, rejected the proposed Korean invasion on pragmatic grounds. As we saw in Chapter 5, he insisted that 'every action, whether progressive or conservative, should be taken in response to the occasion'. At the moment, he said, 'His Majesty's reign is still young and the foundations of his reign are not yet firmly laid'. The recently inaugurated reforms were still unfamiliar, and it would require many years before the 'ignorant, uninformed people of the remote areas' realized the benefits of wealth and power which the new regime hoped to bring. The possible opposition of Russia and China, England's control of the seas, and the fact that 'our country has been largely dependent on England for its foreign loans', added to the risks of the Korean adventure. Ôkubo also worried about the cost of the invasion and argued that even if it were successful, 'considering the cost of the campaign, and of occupation and defense of Korea, it is unlikely that it could be met by the products of the entire country of Korea'.

Ôkubo's memorial repays careful reading; one wishes Japan's leaders had considered its arguments more carefully in the 1930s. However, Ôkubo's purely pragmatic and sensible opposition to Saigô's scheme was precisely that, and no more. Pragmatic, sensible arguments had no moral foundation and carried no emotional force. Ôkubo did not consider the wishes of Koreans in his calculations, only the interests of Japan. If 'the situation makes it unavoidable or because there is no other way' or if it were necessary for 'the safety of our nation', then implicitly he was willing to assent to the expense and danger of foreign war. The tension between those who demanded expansion whatever the risk and those who would support expansion only if the rewards promised to be greater than the costs was a constant theme in Japanese politics and diplomacy for the next seventy years.

Japan did not invade Korea in 1873. But in 1875 an 'incident' between Japanese surveying vessels and Korean shore batteries provided Japan with an excuse to send a squadron of ships and several thousand troops to demand an apology and the opening of Korean ports to foreign trade. As noted in Chapter 2, the treaty signed in 1876 described Korea as an independent state with 'sovereign rights', which had the implicit effect of detaching Korea from the Chinese tributary system. The following two decades of Japanese expansion and conflict with China culminated in the Sino-Japanese War in 1894. Japan annexed Taiwan, but Russian intervention prevented Japanese annexation of the Liaodong peninsula. As compensation the Japanese increased the amount of the indemnity levied on the Chinese, and spent a large portion of the money strengthening the army and navy in order to forestall similar intervention in the future (Beasley 1990, pp. 147–8). Subsequent competition with Russia in Korea and Manchuria led to the decision to attack Russian forces in 1904. Victory in the Russo-Japanese War paved the way for a protectorate over Korea in 1905 and annexation in 1910 (Duus, 1995).

The Chinese revolution in 1911 and then the outbreak of the First World War in Europe in 1914 gave Japan the opportunity for further expansion in northern China. The infamous 'twenty-one demands' of 1915 in effect placed Manchuria under Japanese control. The extension of Japanese economic interests, the army's concern with the protection of Korea, and conflict with the Nationalist Chinese government, led in 1931 to a manufactured 'incident' and the creation of a puppet state of Manchukuo with the last Manchu emperor Pu Yi as president. In the early 1930s Japanese control was extended southwards in order to protect the Manchurian border. In 1933 Japan withdrew from the League of Nations and asserted that in view of its chaotic condition China could not be regarded as 'an organized state', and that therefore 'the general principles of international law' would have to be 'considerably modified' in the case of China (Beasley, 1987, p. 200). In 1937 another 'incident' led to full-scale war and extension of Japanese control southwards to Shanghai and the Yangzi valley.

Japan gained possession of Germany's Pacific island colonies as League of Nations Mandates following the First World War. During the 1920s and 1930s Japanese interests expanded in the Pacific and in Southeast Asia. The outbreak of the Second World War in Europe again gave Japan the opportunity to extend its sphere at the expense of other imperialist powers. An agreement with the French Vichy government in May 1941 opened Indochina to Japanese economic penetration and turned it into a potential military base from which Japan could expand into the rest of Southeast Asia. In response, during July and August the United States froze Japanese assets and placed an embargo on oil and scrap metal exports to Japan, Britain cancelled Japan's commercial treaties with India and Burma, and the government of the Dutch East Indies imposed restrictions on trade with Japan and banned oil and bauxite shipments. Following fruitless negotiations, on 7 December Japan attacked the United States naval base in Hawaii and launched offensives throughout Southeast Asia, and by April 1942 had conquered Hong Kong, the Philippines, the Malay peninsula, Singapore, Burma, Indonesia, and other islands in the Pacific. As even this brief outline makes clear, Japan's relations with the rest of Asia were marked by continual expansion and the repeated use of military force. It is easy to see a pattern here, and to conclude that expansion resulted from a plot laid by Japan's leaders. Korean and Chinese historians are particularly suspicious of Japanese motives. According to a team of Korean specialists, 'as early as 1873 . . . the Japanese desire to invade Korea was apparent, the only remaining question being that of a suitable opportunity' (Eckert et al., 1990, p. 198). According to a distinguished Chinese historian, Japan had 'coveted' Manchuria 'ever since its defeat of China in 1895 . . . With the annexation of Korea in 1910, many Japanese came to regard Manchuria as the next "logical" target for conquest' (Hsü, 1995, p. 545). Some Western Japanese specialists agree. Donald Calman asserts that understanding the 1873 crisis requires us to recognize a continuous tradition of Japanese imperialism, directed particularly against Korea, dating from as early as the fourteenth century. Calman argues many scholars of the 'national learning' who emphasized the emperor system and Japanese superiority justified Japanese imperialism from the 1790s onwards, but he insists that the real motives have always been narrowly economic. The debate over Korea, he says, was not over whether to invade, but over which of the factions within the Japanese elite would benefit financially. The entire policy of expansionism 'was debated and planned for many years, and then carried out with extreme ruthlessness and cynicism' (Calman, 1992, p. xviii).

On the other hand, it is important to recognize that until 1931 each stage of Japanese expansion was achieved in cooperation with Western powers and in accordance with the currently accepted diplomatic principles. In 1875 the Japanese government had informed the United States and Britain of their proposed action in Korea, and sent an ambassador to reassure China. An alliance signed with Britain in 1902 provided that Britain would defend Japan in a war with any two other powers. Britain further recognized that Japan was 'interested in a peculiar degree politically as well as commercially and industrially' in Korea, and therefore in effect granted Japan a free hand against the Russians. Japan consulted both Britain and the United States in 1904 before establishing the formal protectorate over Korea, and the final annexation had been explicitly approved by Britain and Russia and unopposed by the United States. In 1910 a secret agreement with Russia divided Manchuria into spheres of influence. As an ally of Britain during the First World War, Japan occupied the German concessions in China as a matter of course. In 1915 Japan had Britain's support for the twenty-one demands, and through the 1920s none of the Western powers opposed the extension of Japanese interests in Manchuria.

In the context of the world depression, many Japanese saw British and United States opposition to the establishment of Manchukuo in 1931 as hypocritical. A disingenuous American proposal at the end of the First World War, for instance, had suggested that the entire 'Chinese' railway system, including Japanese lines in the north, be centralized under the supervision of American engineers and that American equipment be purchased using a loan raised in the United States (Dayer, 1981, p. 78). Naval disarmament conferences in 1921 and 1930 had systematically reduced Japanese power relative to Britain and the United States. Now, when Japanese interests in Manchuria were threatened by Chiang Kaishek's government and by a new Soviet build-up of forces, Britain, the United States, France, and the Netherlands all placed restrictions on Japanese exports, but did not give up their own imperial possessions in Asia. In response, Japan sought new Western allies. In 1936 Japan signed the Anti-Comintern Pact with Germany. Italy joined in 1937, and the treaty was extended into a defensive alliance in 1940. Expansion into Southeast Asia followed the German defeat of France and occupation of the Netherlands, and Japan had the Vichy government's assent to bases in Indochina. Japan viewed the United States military build-up in the Philippines as 'a pistol aimed at Japan's heart', and considered the embargoes hostile acts which violated international law.

Accordingly, most Western Japanese specialists have argued that the explanation of Japanese policy did not rest on a single incident which determined subsequent actions, and also did not rest on a conspiracy or 'evil plan'. Nor was Japanese imperialism the expression of a 'deep-seated historical urge'. Rather, each action needs to be understood in terms of the specific policy-makers influential at the time, and in terms of the specific historical circumstances of the decision. Thus the 1873 conflict between 'idealists' led by Saigô and 'pragmatists' led by Ôkubo led to the triumph of Western-style 'realism' in foreign policy, and each of the subsequent actions leading to the annexation of Korea can be interpreted within the same framework (Conroy, 1960; Duus, 1984, p. 129).

Similarly, the extension of Japan's 'informal empire' in China reflected the shifting balance between army leaders who believed the collapse of China to be inevitable, and civilian leaders who thought China would remain intact (Duus, 1989, pp. xxii–xxiii). Each decision, therefore, was not a step on a 'road to war', but rather reflected the changing estimation by Japan's leaders of the world situation and of how Japan's place in the world could best be defended and improved. The decision to ratify the establishment of Manchukuo in 1931 was taken by authorities in Tokyo in part because they feared 'that the Kwantung Army was itself not far short of becoming a separate political entity', but both military and civilian leaders were surprised when the conflict begun in 1937 'did not quickly end' (Beasley, 1987, pp. 195, 203) – that is, the risks and the costs proved greater than either the idealists or the pragmatists had estimated.

Japanese economic development and imperialism

In Asia, the European example was partially replicated only by Japan, which launched a successful colonization and after defeating Russia was admitted to the exclusive club of European imperialists; they became the honorary Europeans imbued with a racialist ideology *vis-à-vis* the Asians of the mainland. However, the pre-war imperialist growth phase in Japan was far too short, nor was permanent migration on a large scale possible; there was no domestic democratization.

Utsa Patnaik, 1995

Marxists of course see a direct link between economic development and imperialism. However, Japanese Marxists contend that the special nature of capitalist development in Japan also left its mark on the pattern of Japanese expansion. As we have seen in Chapters 3 and 5, although Japanese Marxists credit the rise of capitalist enterprise with undermining the stability of the Tokugawa system, they see the new Meiji regime as a half-feudal system resting on an alliance between the emerging capitalist bourgeoisie on the one hand, and the remnants of the aristocracy and the military on the other, with the ideology of the 'emperor system' giving legitimacy to the new structure. A strategic emphasis on military invest-ment, and on products and markets where there was little competition and therefore high profits, allowed a growth of the industrial sector first in cotton and silk textiles, then in the heavy industrial and chemical sectors, then in new technologies and advanced industries. The sale of the state enterprises in the early 1880s laid the foundation of the *zaibatsu*, and Japan therefore moved exceptionally rapidly through the stages of development – the stage of 'primitive accumulation' coincided with the Meiji era, the stage of 'classical industrial capitalism' was completed in the decade from the Russo-Japanese War to the First World War, and the 1920s saw the formation and development of 'monopoly capital' (Seiyama, 1989, pp. 28–9, 31–3).

However, Japanese Marxists continue, although Japan grew rapidly, workers did not benefit. Further, they assert, these patterns have persisted. Japanese development has been marked by low wages and by the 'underdeveloped state of its welfare provisions' compared especially to Western Europe and the United States. The incomplete bourgeois revolution has meant that the civil rights of the working classes remain restricted. Japanese capitalists continue to rely on 'traditional methods of accumulation' – low wages and poor working conditions, enforced by the police and the army. Wage costs per unit of production have been exceptionally low, and therefore the rate of exploitation has been exceptionally high, and capital for investment has accumulated exceptionally rapidly.

Japanese Marxists have emphasized that this rapid transition from 'feudalism' to 'monopoly capitalism' left the government in the hands of a pre-modern elite, and they argue that the contradiction between a half-feudal ruling oligarchy and the requirements of a developing industrial society led Japan into imperialist expansionism and to the policies which resulted in the war in China and eventually with the United States. In addition, Japanese Marxists argue that Japan, as a latecomer and as an Asian power, found itself in 'a world structure dominated by capitalism and imperialism'. It was also a world structure dominated by advanced capitalist powers whose imperialism was 'mature' in the sense of being more concerned with the export of capital, in contrast to Japan's 'immature' imperialism which continued to emphasize trade and direct control over sources of raw materials. Japan was therefore forced to cooperate with those powers. Prewar Japanese imperialism was not only 'feudal and militarist', but also 'dependent'. Japanese economic aggression has been accompanied by 'cooperation with, reliance on, and subordination to other major powers' – England in the Meiji period, Germany and Italy in the 1930s, and the United States in the postwar era (Seiyama, 1989, p. 35; Beasley, 1987, pp. 6–9).

Western and Japanese non-Marxist historians would agree with this analysis, in part. The emergence of an industrial economy in Japan certainly destabilized the balance of power in Asia. Further, in the context of competitive imperialist expansion, Japan could be expected to aim for the acquisition of colonies and extension of spheres of influence. As Marius Jansen puts it, 'in the climate of the times Meiji Japan had every reason to pursue an imperialist path' (Jansen, 1984, p. 62). However, as in the cases of European and United States imperialism, Western and Japanese non-Marxist historians have repeatedly emphasized that the smoking gun – the direct evidence linking capitalist economic development and imperialist expansionism – is often absent. The motives for specific decisions, in Japan as elsewhere, often were not economic. Even when economic arguments were advanced to justify expansion, they were often not made by capitalists but by generals, diplomats, and politicians. When decisions were taken, the role of capitalists in those decisions was often peripheral at most. Thus most historians would still accept Conroy's judgement that diplomatic and strategic motives predominated over economic interests in the series of decisions to increase Japanese influence over Korea until after 1900 (Conroy, 1960), and most would agree with the thrust of Beasley's argument that local military commanders played the most important role in expanding Japanese influence from Korea to Kwantung and Manchuria and from there into northern and central China. Japanese imperialism, in short, was not unique, but reflected the climate of the times and the efforts of local 'sub-imperialists' extending and defending a 'moving frontier' (Beasley, 1987).

There is also another range of arguments advanced by Marxist scholars, linking the internal patterns of Japanese economic development with external expansion. As seen in Chapter 5, the creation of a new state and a new economic system resulted in overlapping economic and cultural crises in Japan. Marxists, as noted above, argue that Japanese capitalism remained locked in 'traditional modes of accumulation'. Low wage costs per unit of production made Japanese products competitive in international markets. At the same time low wages limited the size of the domestic market. Japanese producers were therefore forced to find expanding markets overseas for their very survival. And further, because their success was based on outmoded 'traditional methods of accumulation', Japanese capitalists needed to maintain the system of domestic repression. When international competition increased, either wages in Japan had to be pressed down even further, or new markets had somehow to be opened. 'Japanese capitalism has therefore acquired aggressive, militaristic, and dominating characteristics' (Seiyama, 1989, pp. 34–5).

Despite continued growth and development, the interwar years were not good ones for ordinary Japanese people. Increasing international competition and restrictions on Japanese exports caused hardship among urban and rural workers in the 1920s. In the depression of the 1930s, in common with other Asian producers, Japanese farming and industrial families suffered disastrously. Wage cuts, shortened hours and unemployment meant many urban workers and their families went hungry. For those who had work, average wages in manufacturing declined by over 20 per cent from 1929 to 1932. In addition, some of the hardship in the cities was in effect exported to the countryside, as hundreds of thousands of distressed and discouraged workers returned to their home villages. Declining prices, particularly for silk, brought hardship and hunger to the countryside. To pay their rent, to save their land, and sometimes simply to eat, tens of thousands of rural families sold their young daughters to brothel-owners. Their sons, unable to find work in the villages, often joined the army.

Already during the First World War an upsurge of unrest in the industrial sector saw protests, strikes and repeated attempts to form unions. The number of strikes rose from 50 in 1914 to a peak of 497 in 1919, and the number of labour unions rose from 49 to 187, with some 100 000 members. Protests over rising food prices culminated in the 'rice riots' of 1918. The industrial labour movement developed close relations with radical intellectuals. The Japan Communist Party was founded in 1922. Despite constant police surveillance and harassment, the union movement grew, from 432 unions with 126 000 members in 1923, to 630 with 331 000 members in 1929. There were 270 strikes in 1923, 522 in 1929, and a peak of 823 in 1932. Whether this is evidence of a 'crisis of Japanese capitalism' depends on the position of the observer; even in 1929 unions still represented only 6.8 per cent of the industrial labour force, individual unions remained small, and the strikes of 1932 involved a total of only 47 000 workers. In the 1930s both radical and moderate organizations collapsed under police repression, as waves of arrests decimated their leadership (Large, 1981, pp. 19, 29, 52, 81; Garon, 1987, p. 249).

Unrest stalked the countryside as well. The relatively easy gains in agricultural productivity made by extending existing best practice into new districts during the Meiji era had been exhausted (Francks, 1992). Increasing numbers of disputes between tenant farmers and their landlords marked the 1920s. This may have reflected the increasing separation of elite affluent landowners from their village communities during the early twentieth century. If Meiji landlords had acted as economic protectors and social leaders of local communities, they had lost their function and therefore their rapport with their tenants by the 1920s (Waswo, 1977). Here non-Marxist and Marxist historians find common ground in identifying the 1920s and 1930s as years of crisis for Japanese agriculture, and in agreeing that the crisis resulted in increased polarization between rich and poor in the countryside. However, Richard Smethurst has disputed this interpretation. He notes that tenant disputes occurred frequently in the most prosperous districts, suggesting not that landlords were failing to provide tenants with traditional support, but that increasingly affluent and entrepreneurial tenants were organizing to seek still better rental agreements and even higher profits. He asserts first that 'the growth of the market economy between 1870 and 1940 brought Japanese farmers, rich and poor alike, great benefits', and secondly that the tenant farmers' movement of the 1920s and 1930s 'was both entrepreneurial and reformist in nature and highly successful' (Smethurst, 1986, pp. 32–3).

Again, the passion of scholars reflects the urgency of the issues. Could anything have been done to avoid the Pacific War? If Japan could have overcome the contradictions resulting from rapid development, then the position of Japanese workers would have been improved and conflicts between Japan and the other nations of Asia, and between Japan and the West, could have been resolved. It is the core of Marxist thought, however, that such contradictions cannot be overcome within a capitalist framework. Stephen Large's study of the workers' movement reflects the approach of Marxist studies in its tendency to judge the leaders of the urban workers' movement on the basis of whether or not their actions were 'correct' in terms of leading to a revolution which might have over-turned the existing political system (Large, 1981). Smethurst's assertions that living standards for farmers may have improved from the Meiji period onwards, and that urban intellectuals played little role in farmers' organ-izations or tenant disputes, which challenge both Marxist and non-Marxist analyses, have proven particularly controversial (Nishida, 1989). His asser-tion that 'the rural market economy did not destroy the farmer; it freed him' has been characterized as a 'Reaganesque . . . epiphany of rhetorical excess' (Bowen, 1988, pp. 828–9). He has vigorously defended himself and his work in return (Smethurst, 1989). Calman asserts that the Japanese have a 'native talent for hypocrisy' and attacks the work of Japanese and Western scholars who reject his preferred argument that Japanese imperi-alism was the inevitable outcome of an ancient historical tradition as 'a grotesque and dangerous distortion which might be compared to that of the lunatic fringe which maintains that there was no holocaust in Europe' (Calman, 1992, pp. xxi, 195).

The position and role of Japan has also not escaped the attention of non-Japanese Asian Marxists. As seen in the quotation above, Indian economist Utsa Patnaik sees the same link between internal and external developments in Japan as in the latecomer countries of Europe. She agrees with Japanese Marxists in seeing Japan as subordinate to the Western imperialist powers. However, in common with East and Southeast Asian nationalist writers, she also emphasizes the racist ideology developed in Japan to justify Japanese domination over other Asian peoples, an aspect which Japanese specialists, whether Marxist or not, tend to ignore.

Japanese nationalism and imperialism

Japan should be persuaded that the defence of Asian countries is its responsibility.

Fukuzawa Yukichi, 1881

Japanese imperialism and the Japanese national identity developed together, and as Japanese nationalism changed, so did Japan's relations with the other countries of Asia. As seen in Chapter 5, the shift in the values inculcated by the schools beginning in the 1890s led to a new emphasis on Japanese 'uniqueness' and on the central importance of reverence for the emperor. Alternative visions of the Japanese polity were ruthlessly suppressed, but in the 1920s a new element was added when some Japanese thinkers began to assert more strongly that the Japanese were 'unique' because they were racially distinct and different from other Asians. In addition, interwar Japanese nationalism, militarism, and expansionism were related to the 'dilemmas' posed by rapid economic development, although the connection was not as direct as Marxist authors have argued. The Meiji government had displayed a nervous combination of paternalistic concern for the health and well-being of the population and unwillingness to countenance any organized political opposition. This tradition continued in the interwar period. In this context the arguments by the army and navy that Japan required colonies could become credible in periods of economic hardship, and the belief in Japanese uniqueness and racial superiority provided justification for Japan's rule over other Asian peoples.

There are continuities here, for Japanese thinkers drew on previous authors for their arguments. Thus, for instance, Calman emphasizes the role of the school of 'national learning' in creating arguments for expansion during the nineteenth century. Some of those arguing for the Korean invasion in 1873 did use the ideas of these scholars. However, the emphasis on continuity can be overdone. Calman undermines his case with overstatement, as in the passages cited above. Where he does not have documentary evidence, he relies on 'the logic of the situation' and 'constant speculation' (Calman, 1992, p. 100). Calman returns to the earlier conspiratorial history which Conroy rejected. He assumes, plausibly enough, that those with power attempted to shape policy to suit their interests; but he also assumes that those interests reflected nothing more than personal greed, and that the actual policies in fact reflected what he believes the interests of the ruling elites to have been.

Calman has been harshly criticized by reviewers for his tenuous arguments, often resting on supposed connections without supporting evidence. Nevertheless, there are continuities, and there was a kind of 'logic of the situation'. First, all countries which could pursue imperialist policies in the late nineteenth and early twentieth centuries certainly did so. In addition, Japanese political life was burdened both with the leftover business of the Meiji Restoration and with the consequences of the subsequent growth of nationalist ideology. The new emperor took the reign name Meiji or 'enlightened rule'. But the Meiji 'restoration' was not a restoration of the emperor's 'direct rule'. Rather, a small group of men, centred on the leaders from Satsuma and Chôshû, ruled in the emperor's name. As they aged they became the *genrô* or 'oligarchs'. They did not establish a new shogunate, however, and one of the problematic legacies they left modern Japan was the absence of a clear method of choosing leaders who could act in the name of the emperor or the nation. When they died they left a vacuum, and Japan drifted.

It was not the passing of the last of the Meiji oligarchs which plunged Japan into crisis, however, or even the world depression. It was the army, 'authoritarian and irrational' in the phrase of Saburô Ienaga, in one of the best-known books on the Pacific War (Ienaga, 1968, ch. 3). As we saw in Chapter 5, the Meiji leaders followed Bismarck's example in placing the army directly under the emperor, and outside of parliamentary control. In addition, the policy of 'rich country, strong army' meant military concerns always weighed particularly heavily in their thoughts. The military emphasis of government policy is intimately connected to the aggressive polity of expansion and imperialism pursued by Japan from the 1890s onwards. However, from the perspective of political scientists, the Meiji oligarchs proved incapable of designing institutions which would protect their power. Their inability to agree among themselves on how to rule prompted them to cut the military loose from civilian control. In the absence of institutional constraints, power slipped away from the oligarchs in the 1910s, but in the inherited institutional context the emerging leaders of parliamentary parties also could not rule effectively, and by the 1930s power had fallen to independent military leaders (Ramseyer and Rosenbluth, 1995).

From the perspective of the army, their position as 'His Majesty's soldiers' placed them outside of and above politics. They could easily come to feel themselves charged with a special mission to protect and preserve the 'national essence'. As the ideology of the imperial system, of Japanese uniqueness, and of the superiority of the Yamato race spread and intensified, so did these feelings. The hardships of common people and the sense of panic and crisis in the depression further reinforced the conviction among army officers that something had to be done. Ordinary soldiers might be treated brutally, as if they were worth no more than the cost of their draft notice postcard (Ienaga, 1968, p. 52), but those with families broken by the loss of a farm, with hungry parents, or with sisters sold into prostitution, agreed with their officers. Assassinations of political and business leaders and attempted coups destabilized public life within Japan. Hawkish elements in the army pushed forward projects of expansion from Korea into Manchuria and northern China, and they led the final leap into an unwinnable Asian land war. By the time Japan attacked Pearl Harbor, 185 000 Japanese soldiers had already died fighting in China since 1937, and there was no end in sight.

Since the army claimed to act in the emperor's name, both Japanese and non-Japanese scholars have sometimes blamed the Shôwa emperor, Hirohito, for not intervening to restrain the army. Through the educational system, the religious image of the emperor as the descendant of the sun goddess had become one of Japan's most potent 'modern myths' (Gluck, 1985), and through the 1920s and particularly during the 1930s, extremists calling for a 'Shôwa Restoration' insisted that the emperor was an absolute ruler unconstrained by common political or material concerns. Nevertheless, by the time Hirohito ascended the throne in 1925 it was not clear even to constitutional experts exactly what role the emperor could or should play in governing the country. In military matters, in particular, it was unclear whether the emperor himself could decide policy, or whether his role was to ratify policies developed by the army and navy chiefs of staff. In fact Hirohito considered himself a constitutional monarch. He opposed and argued against many of the specific measures of expansion and aggression, but he believed himself to be required to sanction those measures formally when his 'responsible' advisers insisted that their policies were the only ones possible. And when the war he had tried to avoid was lost, it was he who decided to submit to the Allies' demand for an unconditional surrender (Large, 1992).

One of the main constraints on moderates and constitutionalists in the government and surrounding the throne, was quite simply the threat of assassination by extremist nationalists if it became known that they opposed Japanese expansion (Large, 1992, p. 207). It seems therefore that we must examine the development of Japanese nationalism in general, rather than the ideas or actions of individuals and groups, to approach an understanding of imperialism and war. Again, there are both continuities and transformations. In the 1880s expansionism seemed to go hand in hand with the creation of a new national identity. Fukuzawa Yukichi, the famous Westernizer, not only suffered pangs of *ressentiment* towards the West, but also felt the thrill of a special mission for Japan in Asia. Japan, he said in 1881, is destined to be the country which leads the defence of Asia against the West:

> Japan should be persuaded that the defense of Asian countries is its responsibility.... It is like the spread of fire when Western countries force themselves on us Eastern countries. The Eastern nations, particularly the Chinese and Koreans, are so slow and dull that they are no more capable of stopping the Westerners than wooden houses are able to withstand the force of fire. Therefore it is not merely for the sake of others but for our own sake that we must help them militarily. We must strive to protect them with force of arms and to lead them by cultural example, so that they too may enter the sphere of modern civilization. And, if there is no alternative, we may forcibly urge them to progress.
>
> (Sugiyama, 1994, pp. 51–2)

Also during the 1880s and 1890s a genre of popular novel emerged which portrayed heroic Japanese as the saviours of innocent Southeast Asian peoples and Pacific Islanders. Though such entertainment for the emerging mass market of readers created by the expanding education system might seem harmless enough, as in Europe and the United States the images and characterizations deployed in these novels reinforced feelings of superiority and gave credence to claims that the 'imperial races' had both the right and the duty to rule over the 'colored peoples'.

As we saw in Chapter 5, the schools effectively propagated the government's eclectic mix of Shinto, Confucian, and Western elements, moulded together and presented as a unique 'Japanese' identity. After a period of relative openness, the limits of public discussion and debate narrowed from the late 1920s onwards as the army's influence increased and the international environment became more threatening. In 1937 the *Fundamental Principles of the National Essence of Japan* combined Shinto myth with a Confucian-style benevolent ruler served by a filial, harmonious population, and this 'unique' and superior Japanese identity was cited as a justification for Japan's conquests. In Korea, Manchuria, and China, in turn, the Japanese attempted to portray themselves as restorers of Confucian tradition in cooperation with their indigenous 'younger brothers' (Collcutt, 1991, p. 152).

As the Japanese empire expanded, the problems of administering large numbers of non-Japanese subjects and further problems posed by the increasing numbers of non-Japanese workers – especially the Koreans – in Japan intersected with the increasingly narrow nationalist ideology. Explicit racism emerged in the idea of a hierarchy of racial groups, with Japanese, the 'Yamato race' at the top, and the other peoples of Asia in subordinate positions, ranked according to their ability. This posed predictable problems in the colonies, as attempts to convert colonials – Taiwanese, Koreans, Manchurians – to the state Shintô religion were hampered by their exclusion from full participation in the cult. Koreans who had died serving in the Japanese army, for instance, could not be enshrined because they were not Japanese, meaning born in the home islands of Japanese parents (Hardacre, 1989, p. 95).

The 'New Order' of Japanese imperialism may have come to differ from Western models, in the need to create some new form of governing machinery which was neither a traditional dynastic change nor a modern informal empire, and to formulate a set of ideas which would reconcile the realities of Japanese power with the often sincere desire for 'coexistence and co-prosperity' and 'Sino-Japanese accord' (Beasley, 1987, p.199). However, even if they were anything more than cosmetic, these differences only emerged after the empire had come into existence. Japan participated in an international discourse revolving around the 'race problem'. During the 1920s Japanese scholars and publicists knew and worked with members of the eugenics movement in Western Europe and the United States; during the 1930s and especially during the war there was much discussion of German theories of national identity and Nazi racial theory. A grandiose six-volume document produced by the Ministry of Health and Welfare in 1943 bore the title *An Investigation of Global Policy with the Yamato Race as the Nucleus,* and not only envisaged Japanese conquests extending all the way through India and the Middle East, but also detailed the settlement of specially selected Japanese colonists (2 million in Australia and New

Zealand, for instance) and the leading role they would be expected to play in their new homes (Dower, 1986, pp. 262–75).

Although the racist sentiments of Japanese imperialists strike us as repugnant today – intermarriage of Japanese colonists with native peoples was to be prevented, because mixed-blood children were regarded as inherently inferior, and because intermarriage would 'destroy the psychic solidarity of the Yamato race' (Dower, 1986, p. 275) – the Japanese did not simply adopt Nazi theories. Whereas Nazi racial dogma saw races as competitive entities struggling with one another until one or the other had been exterminated, Japanese leaders saw racial groups as complementary, with each to be employed in those tasks for which it was best suited by its 'nature'. Nazi leaders saw relations between races as predatory; over 6 million Jews perished in the Holocaust, and Heinrich Himmler planned to relocate Slavs from Eastern Europe into the interior of Russia, where they could be hunted by future generations of Aryan boys. The Japanese in contrast hoped that cooperation among the races under their leadership would bring benefits to all. In this they resembled not so much their German allies, but their British, Dutch, and American enemies, all of whom maintained strictly segregated hierarchies of 'racial' groups in their colonies.

Japan's Imperial System

Trade

Table 7.1 shows that Japan in the 1920s and 1930s became the centre of its own imperial system. Taiwan, Korea, Kwantung and Manchuria all became important sources of food and raw materials and equally important markets for Japanese manufactured goods. However, despite the difficulties of the depression, international competition, and discriminatory restrictions placed on Japanese exports by other powers, the pattern of exports shows that Japan's products remained competitive even in markets outside of its empire (Mizoguchi, 1989). The Japanese continued to have extensive trade with India and Indonesia in Asia, and among Western countries, the United States and Australia in the Pacific, and Britain, France, and Germany in Europe, were among Japan's major partners (Mitchell 1995). As discussed in Chapter 6, it is especially important to note the importance of the United States to Japan, compared to the

Table 7.1   Japanese Trade with Main Trading Partners, 1895–1938
(current prices, million yen)
A. Japanese exports to main trading partners

	1895	(% total)	1913	(% total)	1920	(% total)	1938	(% total)
Australia	1.3	1.0	8.6	1.2	58	2.6	69	1.8
China (total)	27	19.9	218	30.4	598	27.2	1183	30.0
Kwantung	–	–	37.1	5.2	102	4.6	509	12.9
Manchuria	–	–	–	–	–	–	319	8.1
France	22	16.2	60	8.4	72	3.3	37	0.9
Germany	3.3	2.4	13	1.8	1	–	33	0.8
India	4.4	3.2	30	4.2	192	8.7	188	4.8
Indonesia	–	–	5.1	0.7	107	4.9	104	2.6
Korea	–	–	40	5.6	143	6.5	921	23.4
Taiwan	–	–	42	5.9	110	5.0	327	8.3
UK	7.9	5.8	33	4.6	98	4.5	135	3.4
USA	54	39.7	184	25.7	565	25.7	425	10.8
Total	136		716		2200		3939	

B. Japanese imports from main trading partners

	1895	(% total)	1913	(% total)	1920	(% total)	1938	(% total)
Australia	1.0	0.8	15	1.9	62	2.3	83	2.2
China (total)	31	24.0	93	11.7	417	15.6	565	14.9
Kwantung	–	–	34.4	4.3	208	7.8	68	1.8
Manchuria	–	–	–	–	–	–	350	9.2
France	5.2	4.0	5.8	0.7	14	0.5	14	0.4
Germany	12	9.3	68	8.6	12	0.4	171	4.5
India	12	9.3	173	21.8	395	14.7	172	4.5
Indonesia	–	–	37	4.7	69	2.6	88	2.3
Korea	–	–	25	3.1	169	6.3	710	18.7
Taiwan	–	–	42	5.3	178	6.6	420	11.1
UK	45	34.9	123	15.5	235	8.8	63	1.7
USA	9.3	7.2	124	15.6	873	32.6	915	24.1
Total	129		795		2681		3794	

Source: Calculated from figures in Mitchell, 1995 and Mizoguchi, 1989.

relative unimportance of Japan to the United States. No Japanese action could damage the United States in aggregate terms, but United States restrictions on Japanese trade could damage Japan severely, and the specific embargoes on oil and scrap metal posed deadly threats to Japan's transportation system and to the strategically critical steel industry. 'Without oil and steel, Japan could not fight a war; and as the stockpiles ran down, war seemed to be the only way of renewing them' (Beasley, 1987, p. 232).

There is not much question that Japan benefited from the possession of colonies and informal empire, particularly in the 1930s. Reorientation of trade to the empire enabled Japan to escape the collapse of world demand; the Japanese trade figures may be compared with those of other Asian countries shown in Table 6.3. However, as seen above this expanding trade did not save Japan from the ravages of the depression. There has been extensive debate over the question of whether the costs of empire were less than the benefits, even before the impact of the war is taken into account. The direct costs of administration and defence were heavy. In addition, the 'moving frontier' continually involved new commitments. Kwantung was required to defend Korea, and Manchuria to defend Kwantung. Arguments for expansion into northern China rested on the assertion that further territory had to be seized in order to protect the territory already acquired. The rapid development of heavy industry in Korea, Manchuria, and Taiwan was given priority in order to create defence industries. Japan did not have the industrial capacity to defend Manchuria, but it also did not possess the capital to fund this development. New industries were competitive with Japanese 'home' industry in two respects, as users of capital and as producers of goods which took away potential markets.

Ôkubo, it seems, had been correct in 1873 when he worried that 'considering the cost of the campaign, and of occupation and defense of Korea, it is unlikely that it could be met by the products of the entire country of Korea'. Although the colonial administration of Taiwan regularly produced a surplus beginning in 1904, the Kwantung and Korean governments required large direct subsidies until the end. Throughout the 1920s and 1930s the Korean government was forced to borrow to cover from 15 to 30 per cent of its annual expenditures, and as much of 20 per cent of its expenses went to service the accumulated debt (Ho, 1984, p. 358).

Economic development in Taiwan and Korea

... the Japanese were unusually development-oriented. ... For economies in their early stages of economic transition, these are respectable rates of development and represent a break from the traditional pattern of development in Korea and Taiwan.

Samuel Ho 1984

... the well-being of the ordinary Koreans worsened in absolute terms. In other words, gross *domestic* product per capita increased remarkably, but gross *national* product per capita for Koreans actually decreased.

Byung-nak Song, 1994

Drawing a balance on Japanese imperialism in Taiwan and Korea once again poses the question of the origins of Asian economic growth. There is much evidence of Japanese exploitation during the colonial period, but both countries are today senior members in the club of Asian 'tigers'. At the very least, therefore, the Japanese did not destroy the potential for development, and there is ample evidence that Japanese policies laid the foundations for later growth. On the other hand, in both countries there were pressures and programmes working to promote modern economic development already emerging or in place before the Japanese arrived. Taiwan had become a separate province of China in 1885, following the war with France, and the first governor immediately launched a modernization programme. The Taiwanese opposed the transfer to Japan in 1895, declared independence on 25 May, established a Republic of Taiwan, and offered to make the provincial governor their president. The Qing government sent Li Hongzhang's son to supervise the transfer, and the Japanese sent large numbers of soldiers, but even so armed resistance continued for two years.

In the case of Korea, the question of whether capitalism had 'sprouted' in Korea before the period of Japanese domination is still disputed. Recent work does show the important role of native Koreans in industrial development during the period of Japanese rule (Eckert, 1991). The Japanese 'were able to undertake most of their reforms and institution building on a base of Korean precedents' and these reforms 'actually enjoyed a wide base of Korean cooperation and support... even from the numerous groups bitterly opposed to the Japanese invasion' (Moskowitz, 1982, pp. 76, 84–5). The elite demonstrated an interest in banking, possibly because of the traditional aristocratic practice of depositing money with innkeeper-merchants. In 1896 the royal family founded the Chon-il Bank with the crown prince as president; in 1897 a group including a cousin of the king and senior government officials founded the Hansong Bank, and in 1905 a group of businessmen founded the Han'il Bank, with backing from Queen Min's family. On the other hand, at the end of the Yi dynasty's rule not very many industrial enterprises in Korea could be classed as 'modern' – in 1903 there were six owned by Koreans and four by Chinese, with a total of 134 workers (Juhn 1973, p.115). Further, as we saw in Chapter 2, some of these reform proposals had originated with the Japanese. Japanese economic penetration into Korea was already extensive in the decade before formal annexation, with mining and manufacturing companies, an electric power company established in 1898, the Seoul–Pusan railroad opened in 1900, and the Korean branch office of the Daiichi Bank which served as the *de facto* central bank for Korea (Song, 1994, p. 38; Duus, 1995).

Once established, the Japanese colonial administrations made efforts to win the support of local elites, the scholar gentry in Taiwan and the aristocratic *yangban* classes in Korea. Members of the Korean aristocracy used 'imperial gift bond' money granted to them by the Japanese to purchase shares in the Hansong Bank following annexation, and both the Hansong and Chon'il banks enjoyed substantial government subsidies (Juhn, 1973, p. 115). The curriculum of the schools in Taiwan was substantially modified to appeal to the gentry, but government officials also lectured the gentry on the need for their children to obtain 'modern' learning as well as knowledge of the classics (Tsurumi, 1984, pp. 283–4). Similarly, the Japanese likened Koreans to Confucian younger brothers within the 'single body of Japan and Korea'. Not all Koreans believed in this, but for those who profited, it was appealing (Robinson, 1991, pp. 216–17). In particular, the large numbers of Korean landlords who retained their land, and the small numbers of Korean entrepreneurs who managed to develop large-scale commercial and industrial enterprises, could see themselves as junior partners with the Japanese.

Among students of the Korean economy, it is something of a sociological cliché that the industrial elite which led rapid growth in the 1960s and 1970s descended from traditional aristocratic classes. Further, virtually the entire bureaucracy and most of the army officers in South Korea had begun their careers under the Japanese. Education often provided the critical link in producing entrepreneurial talent among well-connected members of the elite. However, it remains unclear whether these men's families first rose to prominence during the Japanese colonial period or in the pre-colonial era (Jones and SaKong, 1980, p. 288; Moskowitz, 1982, p. 74; Cumings, 1984; Eckert, 1991). It is clear that during the colonial period most large modern enterprises continued to be Japanese, but it is also clear that the government discriminated against Korean enterprise. The Company Regulations in force from 1910 to 1920 required official approval for the establishment of new corporations, and the 'agriculture first' policy of the government hindered Korean entrepreneurs. The repeal of the regulations made the environment more favourable, but the Japanese still regarded the 'desirable' areas for Korean business as those related to traditional economic activities, for instance mats, lacquerware, willowware, bambooware, and foodstuffs. In 1921 the 1276 private Japanese firms in Korea produced gross output worth 138 million yen, while 1088 Korean firms produced a total of only 24 million yen. In 1937 there were 2307 Korean-owned industrial plants which employed fewer than 50 workers, but only 14 with over 200 workers (9 in chemicals, 4 in textiles, and 1 in food processing). Among incorporated establishments in 1944, the 17 Korean firms had a total paid-up capital of 38 million yen, and the 195 Japanese firms a total of 1.3 billion yen (Juhn, 1973).

We possess fairly accurate estimates of growth for the three decades from 1910–14 to 1935–9. They show that total product in constant prices rose at over 4 per cent annually in Taiwan and over 3 per cent annually in Korea. By the mid-1930s total output was three times as high in Taiwan and twice as high in Korea as it had been a generation before. Population also rose rapidly, from 3.3 to 5.9 million in Taiwan, 2 per cent annually, and from 14.8 to 23.3 million in Korea, or 1.6 per cent annually, from 1910 to 1940. Per capita product therefore increased 2.0 per cent per year in Taiwan and 1.5 per cent per year in Korea. The share of industry in employment increased significantly, especially in the 1930s. That is, there was substantial growth and development, 'a break from the traditional pattern' (Ho, 1984).

The Japanese of course managed their colonies for their own benefit – just as the European powers and the United States did. Japanese perceptions of their needs changed as the structure of the Japanese economy changed, and colonial policies reflected these changes. Thus in the early 1900s Japanese leaders saw colonies as a way to overcome a persistent balance of payments deficit. As we saw in Chapter 5 the leaders of the Meiji government worried about Japan's balance of payments, particularly imports of consumer goods which 'contributed little to national power'. From 1896 to 1904 Japan spent an annual average of 22 million yen on sugar imports, equal to over half of the deficit in the balance of trade. Taiwan appeared to offer a solution, and Japan adopted an import substitution policy, with tariffs on foreign sugar while the colonial administration encouraged a rapid expansion of Taiwanese sugar production.

Increasing urbanization and industrialization in Japan led the Japanese to view colonies as a source of agricultural products. In the 1910s the exhaustion of 'traditional' means of improving agricultural productivity by extending best practice led to rising food prices in Japan, culminating in the 'rice riots' in 1918. The government could have shifted resources to agriculture, or imported food from foreign sources, but this would have diverted capital away from industry and hampered continued imports of machinery from the West. Japanese leaders found it easier to draw food from the colonies. Taiwan and Korea were already rice-producing areas, but their techniques were less productive than Japan's, so there appeared room for improvement along traditional Japanese lines. And of course both could become markets for Japanese manufactured goods. Programmes to increase rice production were launched in the 1920s in both Taiwan and Korea. In Taiwan the new policy was relatively successful because much of the necessary infrastructure was already in place, especially irrigation. The Korean programme was less successful, for Korea was twenty years behind Taiwan in the proportion of irrigated land, and as noted above the Korean colonial government suffered a chronic financial shortage.

The further growth of Japanese industry led to concern for sources of raw materials and for secure export markets, and finally in the 1930s the colonies played an important role in preparations for war. Japanese farmers complained of the hardship caused by competition from Taiwanese and Korean rice. Their representatives demanded a tariff on colonial agricultural products, but they were opposed by industrialists who argued that tariffs would increase food prices and wages. The government compromised by abandoning programmes to improve productivity in the colonies in 1934, which did not affect Taiwan, where the improvements were already in place, but which did hurt Korea. The autarkic vision of the 1930s envisaged both self-sufficiency of the entire empire and increased self-sufficiency of all colonies. Japan's leaders now viewed Korea and Taiwan as military and naval centres, and this concern led to an additional push to develop strategic industries in each of the colonies in addition to their previous role as markets and suppliers of food and raw materials. Japanese planners intended to coordinate these programmes both to prevent competition and also to reduce the pressure on Japanese industry. Thus, for instance, a programme to move light, relatively labour-intensive textile industry to Taiwan was begun just before the war.

The resulting pattern avoided some of the aspects of 'dualistic' or 'enclave' development of other colonized areas. The 'unusually development-oriented' Japanese sponsored agricultural development, but did not encourage plantation agriculture, and they also actively encouraged industrial development and reinvested a very large share of the profits earned in the colonies. Public health improved dramatically. Waste removal, compulsory testing, quarantine measures, vaccination programmes, and improved medical services reduced infectious diseases. The death rate in Taiwan declined from 33 to 19 per 1000 from 1906 to 1940, and in Korea from 35 to 23 from 1910 to 1935–40. Education expanded. In Taiwan about one-third of all children were in school in 1930–1, and 71 per cent in 1943–4. There were 20 000 schoolchildren in Korea in 1910, 90 000 in 1920, and 901 000 in 1937, although this was still only 17 per cent of school age children in Korea. Also, since most of the increase came in the 1930s, the benefits would only be seen in the next generation, after independence (Ho, 1984).

Development throughout remained in the hands of the colonial administrations, working in cooperation with military authorities. Semi-government corporations were established and grew into giant conglomerates – the South Manchurian Railway in Kwantung and Manchuria, in Korea the Oriental Development Company and Nihon Iron (Korea), and the Taiwan Electric Power Company and the Taiwan Development Company. Infrastructure was central to Japanese policy, and there was heavy investment in transportation and communications. Government authorities extended agricultural irrigation, established credit and cooperative associations, introduced the use of chemical fertilizers and improved seed varieties, and sponsored research and development of new fertilizer-sensitive rice and sugar-cane varieties. Indeed, it has been argued that the Japanese created the infrastructure for the later 'green revolution' in both Taiwan and Korea, and that the experience of industrial and agricultural development under Japanese rule was crucial in providing Taiwan with an industrial base on which to build (Ho, 1984; Wade, 1990).

Ho thinks this repeated the pattern of 'state-led development' during the Meiji period in Japan – it might be better to say that Japanese colonial authorities in the 1920s and 1930s thought the state should play the leading role, and therefore found it convenient to believe that Meiji economic development had resulted from state actions. Ho notes that colonial industry was intended to cater to Japanese needs; although Japanese direct investment was encouraged, it was guided away from areas which would compete with Japanese manufacturing, and native entrepreneurs were actively discouraged. Further, development often depended on subsidies and protection within the Japanese imperial system. For instance, the Taiwan sugar industry was much larger than it would have been in a competitive international system (Ho, 1984).

Certain individuals and groups benefited enormously from colonial development. The favoured semi-government corporations were not economic but political entities, and the profits flowed into the pockets of insiders in the colonial administrations and of favoured *zaibatsu*. Particularly in Korea, the 'colonial' pattern of development led to excessive exploitation of natural resources. Japanese logging companies used their connections to gain rights to fell timber, and clearfelling without replacement led to widespread deforestation, erosion, and flooding. Japanese fishermen gained access to Korean waters, which led to severe declines in fish stocks. Mineral rights went to Japanese companies, especially the gold and tungsten reserves in the north. Many Japanese saw Korea as a place to settle Japan's excess population. The number of Japanese in Korea rose from 170 000 in 1910 to 770 000 in 1945. Japanese settlers were favoured in their access to public institutions – agricultural irrigation, credit agencies, health facilities, and education. The expanding schools systems catered first to the children of Japanese families and discriminated against natives.

Levels of living did not improve much – in particular the availability of food was not much better at the end of the colonial period than at the beginning. Korean historians and economists insist that the incomes and living standards of Koreans actually declined. 'Liberation from the Japanese left Koreans with little more than dire poverty' (Song, 1994, p. 39). The export of rice to Japan is a particular grievance of Koreans. Infrastructure built for agriculture, such as irrigation and reservoirs, they argue, benefited Japanese landlords, and was intended to enable them to grow rice for the Japanese market – as much as half of Korea's total output of rice from 1912 to 1937. The aggregate statistics in Table 7.2 show that as rice production increased, exports increased even more rapidly, and Korean consumption actually fell.

Korean scholars also blame the Japanese for the large increase in tenancy, shown in Table 7.3. A land survey and new registration laws deprived many Korean farming families of title to their land. Those who resisted were expelled, or shot. Taking over the holdings of the royal family and state, the Japanese colonial government emerged as the largest landowner, with 8.9 million chongbo (21.8 million acres; 1 chongbo = 2.45 acres),

Table 7.2   Production, Consumption, and Export of Rice from Korea, 1912–36

	Production million sok	Production Index	Consump- tion, million sok	Consump- tion per capita sok	Exports, million sok	Exports index
1912–16	12.3	100	11.24	0.72	1.06	100
1922–6	14.5	118	10.16	0.59	4.34	409
1932–6	17.0	138	8.24	0.40	8.76	826

Source: Song, 1994, p. 40. 1 sok = 180.39 litres, or 5.01 bushels.

Table 7.3 Tenancy in Korea, 1913–45 (percentage distribution)

	Landlords	Self-cultivators	Self-cultivator/ Tenants	Tenants
1913	3.1	22.8	32.4	41.7
1918	3.1	19.7	39.4	37.8
1924	3.8	19.4	34.6	42.2
1930	3.6	17.6	31.0	46.5
1932		16.3	25.3	52.8
1936		17.9	24.1	51.8
1939		19.0	25.3	55.7
1943		17.6	15.0	65.0
1945		14.2	16.8	69.1

Source: Eckert et al., 1990, p. 307.

nearly 40 per cent of Korea's land area in 1930. Much of this land was sold at low prices, and many of the sales were to Japanese investors. The role of the Oriental Development Company was particularly notorious – by 1930 it held 110 000 chongbo of agricultural land and planned to settle 30 000 Japanese migrants annually on its holdings. Koreans found themselves working as tenants or 'semi-tenants'. By 1931, 2.3 million farm households or 12 million farmers 'had been reduced to such a status' (Song, 1994, p. 40). The number of 'fire people' engaged in slash-and-burn farming in the marginal uplands rose from 100 000 to 300 000 (Eckert et al., 1990, pp. 307–8). Poor farmers, 'many on the verge of starvation', migrated to Manchuria, Siberia, and Japan. Today there are over 2 million Koreans in China, half a million in Russia, and over half a million in Japan (Song, 1994, p. 40).

However, the vast majority of landlords continued to be Korean. Japanese corporations and individuals did not simply grab land at cheap prices as the feudal system of land tenure collapsed. Only in the largest category (over 100 chongbo) did Japanese outnumber Koreans, and this resulted from the presence of the large development corporations. Korean landlords in general could prove their ownership during the land survey, and in fact could use the survey to expand their holdings at the expense of their poorer neighbours. In addition, wealthy and well-connected Koreans as well as Japanese insiders benefited from the government's land sales. The increase in tenancy also reflected the rise in population (Eckert et al., 1990, pp. 167, 307). Local studies show a striking continuity of landownership. The Japanese confirmed Korean landlords in their possession of land, privileged the claims of landlords against tenants, limited opportunities of tenants to dispute ownership claims, and protected landlords against claims of tenants whose rights to permanent tenancy had been taken away. However, the large rise in tenancy, the alienation of Korean land, and the mass flights of Koreans to Manchuria and Siberia did not result from these Japanese policies, but rather were consequences of the depression, which caused many bankruptcies and very large numbers of land transfers in the early 1930s. The connection with Japanese overlordship and with Japanese development remains, however, for the worst effects were seen in villages which were closely tied to the Japanese rice market (Gragert, 1994).

The outbreak of full-scale war in China led Japanese authorities to redouble their efforts to increase industrial production in Korea. Employment in the manufacturing industry in Korea jumped from 586 000 in 1938 to 1.3 million in 1943. Hundreds of thousands of workers were shifted from south to north to support the war effort, and further hundreds of thousands were mobilized to work outside Korea. By 1944, some 4 million people, or 16 per cent of the Korean population, were outside the borders of Korea, and possibly 70 000 died while working as forced labourers in Japan, Manchuria, and elsewhere. The wartime boom was followed by shortages, rationing, and a final collapse of output amid increasingly desperate and bizarre attempts to maintain production – even destroying film prints, the entire output of the early Korean film industry, for their silver content (Eckert, 1990, pp. 325–6).

The effects of the war on Taiwan paralleled Korea. An initial expansion of output was followed by a decline, particularly after Japan lost control of the sea routes. The true disaster, however, occurred in 1945 when the Nationalist Chinese government seized control from the defeated Japanese. Treating Taiwanese as enemy collaborators, Nationalist politicians and senior military officers confiscated goods and land for their personal profit. In 1947 unarmed protesters were shot down by soldiers, and reinforcements called from the mainland then launched a pogrom in which 8 to 10 000 people died, including many educated leaders of the Taiwanese community.

Korean nationalism

The fostering of loyalty and filial piety shall be made the principle of education and the cultivation of moral sentiments shall be given special attention. It is only what may be expected of a loyal and dutiful man, who knows what is demanded of a subject and a son – that he should be faithful to his duties.

Office of the Governor-General of Korea, Education Bureau, *Rules for Teachers*, 1916

From the mountains, tears of evening are rising
On the grass the grief of the dew is long
The painful cries of the hunted man
Across the plains and waters
Spread out to a nameless grey country

Pak Chong-hwa, *A Song of the Hunted Man*, 1920

Now this land occupied by others
    Even onto the lost field
A spring is coming!

Yi Sang-hwa, *Even Onto the Lost Field Spring Comes!* 1926

There was little effective Korean resistance to the Japanese following annexation. The Japanese authorities at first planned to restrict Koreans to basic levels of primary education, appropriate to their subordinate position in the empire. The Japanese selected aspects of Confucianism which would bolster their rule, especially filial piety and subservience of subject to ruler. However, although Korean leaders had been trained in the Confucian educational tradition, Korean nationalist reformers, for instance those active in the Independence Club in 1896–8, rejected Confucianism because of its association with foreign Chinese domination (Robinson, 1991, pp. 207–16). The 'watershed' Kabo reforms of 1894, the attempt to create a modern educational system, and the 'rapid, fundamental change' in Korean society in the decade *before* the Japanese seized control (Moskowitz, 1982, pp. 69–70, 84–5) played a role in an emerging national consciousness, as did the heritage of the Tonghak rebellion in the later nineteenth century.

The Japanese, believing that their administration represented 'modern' development and that their system was unquestionably superior to the Korean state it replaced, assumed that their rule would continue to meet with acquiescence and even acceptance. They were therefore caught unprepared by the 'March First Movement' in 1919. A widespread network of Korean nationalist organizations with roots in the Tonghak rebellion saw the end of the First World War and the declaration of United

States President Woodrow Wilson's Fourteen Points as an opportunity to press for independence. Although foreign missionaries themselves attempted to remain neutral, the nationalists made use of Christian religious organizations as well (Baldwin, 1973). Demonstrations demanding independence began on 1 March 1919 and persisted to mid-April. The Japanese, embarrassed and threatened by the obvious failure of their colonial endeavour, repressed the demonstrations brutally, attacking peaceful meetings and torturing prisoners. The Koreans responded in kind. The Japanese counted 553 killed, 1409 injured, and 12 522 arrests; Korean nationalists estimated over 7500 killed, 15 000 injured, and 45 000 arrested (Eckert et al., 1990, p. 279). In the aftermath the Japanese government adopted a more lenient policy towards the purely religious activities of Western Christian missionaries, which alleviated one source of opposition among foreigners. Higher levels of education, encouragement of culture, and economic development on the one hand, and increasing trust, guidance, and repression of dangerous dissent on the other, were intended to alleviate the sources of opposition among Koreans.

The Japanese policy of assimilation of Koreans into a harmonious but subordinate partnership with Japan failed. There were some successes. Along with the development of the economy, literacy rose, and the use of Japanese became widespread. The number of Koreans 'conversant' with Japanese rose from less than 100 000 in 1913 to 5.7 million in 1943, or from less than 1 per cent to over 22 per cent of the population (Dong, 1973). However, literacy in Korean also increased, and during the 1930s the number of Korean language publications began to expand rapidly. Permits for Korean language publications increased from fewer than 1000 each year in 1920–3, to some 1500 per year in 1929–31, and to over 2300 per year in 1937–9. Korean language newspapers, beginning from virtually zero in 1920, had reached a total daily circulation of 100 000 in 1929, and 160 000 in 1939. Korean authors became adept at exploiting loopholes in the censorship laws, for instance by taking advantage of the censor's ignorance of Korean, submitting manuscripts with series of xs in place of offending words, or publishing works in Japan for export to Korea. The simple use of Korean was a political act, and the expanding presence of Korean language works of all types served to reinforce the notion of a Korean identity separate from the one propagated in the schools and in the official ideology (Robinson, 1984).

Even under the censorship regime a literature of resistance emerged, particularly the 'proletarian literature' movement which produced numbers of works from the mid-1920s to the mid-1930s, when censorship and suppression drove the last remnants of radical organizations underground. An important example is the novel by Cho Myong-hi, *The Naktong River* (1927). The novel opens with a sentimental evocation of a golden age before the arrival of the Japanese, and the story of the dispossession of Korean farmers frames the story of a Korean revolutionary, his attempts to organize the farmers, the failures of the nationalist movement, his migration to Manchuria and return, his attempts to strengthen the Communist movement through coalitions, his arrest and torture, the collapse of his health, and finally his death. At his funeral a long procession of villagers follows his casket along the river, bearing banners and brightly coloured placards, the stream of people reflecting the eternal flow of the river. At the end of the novel, following the funeral, the main female character leaves her home on a northbound train, determined to continue the revolutionary work of the dead hero. Despite being heavily censored by the Japanese authorities, Cho's work was widely influential, for both its nationalist and its socialist messages (Chee, 1973, p. 242).

'Incidents' continued, even among the privileged elite. The minority of Korean students in Kwangju went on strike in November 1929 to protest against racial discrimination. They were supported by a strike of female students in Seoul in June 1930 which demanded that 'all the students who were victims in the Kwangju student's case shall be released', but also that 'the colonial educational policy shall be liquidated'. As usual the leaders were arrested, but further protests led to nationwide riots. In the north along the Manchurian border, Communists organized Red Peasant Unions and attacked landlords and government forces. Because of the ethnic divisions in industry, with Korean workers often confronting Japanese management, strikes and labour stoppages took on a political and nationalist colouring, notably the Wonsan general strike in 1929.

It is an article of faith among Korean historians that the Japanese colonial regime failed to suppress a rising tide of nationalism among the Korean people. In North Korea Cho Myong-hi and other 'proletarian' authors of course were particularly celebrated as harbingers of the eventual victory of socialist ideals as well as of Korean nationalism. However, the repression exercised by the Japanese colonial state was effective. The Japanese state was far more intrusive and efficient than the Yi state had been (Robinson, 1991, p. 215). An attempt in 1926 to repeat the 1919 uprising (the 'June Tenth Incident') failed. The extensive bureaucracy and the very large police force employed many Koreans. Many members of Korean landowning and business classes did well under Japanese rule. The nationalist movement never became a mass organization, and probably could not have while a majority of the population remained illiterate. Repression meant that most nationalist leaders spent most of the 1920s and 1930s outside the country. The Japanese tolerated moderate expressions of nationalist sentiment, but no avowedly revolutionary statements. The most prestigious intellectual journal in Korea, *Kaebok* ('Creation') was suppressed in 1926 after refusing to change its editorial policy favouring independence. As in Japan itself, left-wing radicals were the most likely to be censored or arrested. Four waves of arrests, in November 1925, June 1926, February 1928, and August 1928, decimated the Korean Communist Party (Robinson, 1984, pp. 340–1).

Economic development absorbed the energies and blunted the nationalist feelings both of the elite who profited as landowners and industrialists, and of the workers moving from agriculture to industry and country to city. The Korean press became much more commercial, and therefore more cautious (Robinson, 1984). In addition the Japanese increased the pressure of assimilation over the course of the 1930s. In 1937 the government decreed that instruction in school would be given only in Japanese, and that Korean students would not be allowed to speak Korean, in and out of school. Public communication and record-keeping were to be exclusively in Japanese. Beginning in 1939 Koreans were coerced into adopting Japanese family names.

It has been suggested that 'in the long run' the adoption of Japanese names 'would have facilitated a faster rate of assimilation' (Dong, 1973, p. 160). However, the assimilation policy was combined with continued discrimination. Koreans were required to maintain two sets of names on public documents, domicile registration, school records, and job applications, in order to prevent any Korean from passing as Japanese. Ethnic quotas remained in higher education and recruitment into the government bureaucracy, and the percentage of Koreans in higher level government positions actually declined as the bureaucracy expanded (Eckert et al., 1990, pp. 318–19). As elsewhere, then, colonial policy continued to offend the subject people, and when the pressure was removed – though not before – that resentment led quickly to the collapse of the regime.

The Japanese sphere in China

In view of the evils of an uncontrolled capitalist economy, we will use whatever state power is necessary to control the economy.

Outline for Economic Construction in Manchukuo, 1932

If you want to get your hands on these Chink broads, you better keep
up with the march. Right? Keep your eyes on those Chink bitches and
keep going.

                                        Japanese NCO to his unit, in China

The Japanese presence in China can be measured in terms of population –
2400 in 1899, 80 000 in 1914, and 255 000 in 1931, compared to, for
instance, 13 000 British citizens. Already in the late 1920s Japan had made
huge investments of 966 million yen in Manchuria, compared to 434
million in Korea and 408 million in Taiwan. The semi-governmental
South Manchurian Railway and its many subsidiaries in mining and
industry accounted for much of the total, although, there were in addition
dozens of private Japanese-owned cotton textile mills in China, compared
to virtually none in Korea and Taiwan. As seen above, the motives for
expansion were largely strategic. Kwantung was not important for its own
sake, but as a base for the defence of Korea and expansion into Manchuria, and Manchuria in turn was viewed as a huge potential source of
agricultural and industrial raw materials, particularly in the 1930s with the
new emphasis on strategic control and self-sufficiency of the entire empire.
Similarly, Japanese planners argued that possession of North China would
secure supplies of cotton and replace imports from the United States and
India. A twelve-year plan for the development of North China called for
expansion of the cotton-growing area from 5 to 6 million *mu* in 1939 to 30
million *mu* in 1950 (Huang, 1985, p. 125–37).

Manchukuo, despite the pretence of independence, was completely sub-
servient to Japan. The commander of the Kwantung Army also served as
Japanese ambassador. In 1932 the Board of General Affairs (Sômuchô)
became the centre of administration, with a Japanese official as its head.
All decisions and official appointments were made after consultation with
the Kwantung Army under the principle of 'internal guidance'. A 1935
document stated bluntly that 'the authority to make any selection of non-
Japanese officials is to be made only by the Commander'. Fixed ratios of
Japanese and non-Japanese officials were set for each branch of government,
and the proportion of Japanese was increased over time. In 1932 three large
native Chinese banks were merged into a new central bank, and new banknotes and coins replaced the multitude of currencies which had circulated.
In 1933 the Manchurian yuan was pegged to the Japanese yen to insulate the
Manchurian currency from the Chinese monetary system.

Japanese authorities intended Manchuria to act as a buffer against
the Soviet Union and against Nationalist China. However, this led the

Japanese to a policy of 'forced' industrialization, 'at a pace unprecedented in mainland China's economic history'. In the 1920s growth had been based on staple goods, especially soybeans and derivatives. Manchuria was a 'frontier' economy, with land still being cleared by an expanding agricultural sector of family farms using traditional methods of cultivation. One-third of the farms in Manchuria grew soybeans, which were purchased by Japanese firms and used for the manufacture of beancake fertilizer and oil. However, in the depression, world demand for agricultural products declined, and production of staples dropped. In addition Manchuria needed to serve as first line of defence for Japan, and therefore required sufficient industry to defend itself. Accordingly from 1934 the Japanese 'advisers' of the Manchukuo government pushed the introduction of new industries.

The army had always favoured direct state control over the economy. A draft plan for the development of Manchuria and Mongolia in 1931 proposed placing all transportation and communications, all strategic industries, and all important export industries under direct control. Other areas might be left to private enterprise, but only under strict supervision and only if operated in the interests of the Japanese economy. The army requested the South Manchurian Railway's Economic Research Organization to examine the first phase of economic construction, and the SMR mobilized a planning staff of 300 to produce its reports. The Five-Year Plan was produced in 1936 by a similar group, and promulgated in January 1937. A Key Industries Control Law placed 21 industries under direct government supervision, later increased to 86.

Full-scale war with China led to increased mobilization and an increase in the share of investment in heavy industry from 55 per cent to 78 per cent. In 1938 a Planning Commission was formed to review allocations of labour, raw materials, and capital among enterprises. In addition the government established 'special-companies' directly under the government, and 'semi-special companies' subject to government control and supervision. They increased from 35 in 1937 to 70 in 1941 and they controlled over half of all invested capital. The funds had come mainly from the Manchukuo government, the South Manchurian Railway, the Japanese government, and certain *zaibatsu*. Most private capitalists were very hesitant to invest in Manchuria, despite encouragement, because of the army's heavy handed intervention.

Statistically, the results were impressive. The Manchurian growth rate rose from 5 per cent annually in 1924–7 to 8.5 per cent in 1934–41. The share of agriculture in Manchurian gross domestic product declined from

51 per cent in 1929 to 34 per cent in 1941, and the share of manufacturing rose from 13 to 20 per cent. The share of total product invested rose from 9 per cent in 1924 to 17 per cent in 1934 and 23 per cent in 1939. By comparison, China proper had 65 per cent of total product in agriculture and 12 per cent in manufacturing in 1933, and invested only around 5 per cent.

Nevertheless, despite meeting or exceeding planned increases in pig iron, coal, energy, and salt, planners found that shortages and bottlenecks caused other sectors to fall short by substantial margins. Further, 'forced industrialization' did not involve the entire economy. Japanese investment created a very large heavy industrial enclave within the Manchurian economy. Most of the agricultural sector remained unaffected, for instance, and industrial investment did not use the savings of Manchurian agricultural households, but rather siphoned capital away from Japan (Nakagane, 1989). Finally, not only did the Japanese lose their entire investment with the war, but much was lost to China as well. In addition to destruction resulting from the fighting, the retreating Japanese destroyed some mines and factories, and during their occupation of Manchuria from August 1945 to May 1946, Soviet authorities dismantled industrial equipment worth US\$ 2 billion, according to an American estimate (Hsü, 1995, p. 623–4), and shipped it to the Soviet Union to use in their own reconstruction programme.

To the south of Manchuria, the Japanese impact was negative. The Nationalist government moved its capital from Beijing to Nanjing, and then from Nanjing to Chongqing, but they continued to control the southwestern interior provinces, and their Communist opponents continued to control their mountainous base areas in the north. The war went on. In combat zones military operations disrupted normal economic life. Advancing Japanese troops often did not distinguish between military and civilian. One regimental commander said, 'our policy has been to burn every enemy house along the way as we advance. You can tell at a glance where our forward units are' (Ienaga, 1968, p. 170). This could easily have degenerated into looting and murder. The rape of Chinese women was common and widely accepted as a 'prerogative of the Imperial Army', with captured women hauled along to serve as a reward at the end of a day's march (Ienaga, 1968, p. 166). On several notorious occasions Japanese soldiers rampaged out of control. Following the fall of Nanjing (Nanking) in December 1937, thousands of surrendering Chinese soldiers and over 100 000 civilians were slaughtered, and tens of thousands of women were raped.

Acceptance of the crimes committed in China and especially the 'rape of Nanking' remains difficult for conservative Japanese. The Education Ministry has frequently censored passages in proposed textbooks, and in 1995 the Liberal Democratic Party sponsored a commemorative history of the war which claimed flatly, against all the documentary and eyewitness evidence, that the atrocity of Nanking was 'a fabrication based on photo montages'.

Japanese military authorities established Chinese puppet governments in Mongolia, at Beijing, and at Nanjing. Japanese private and semi-government firms such as the South Manchurian Railway moved to secure access to confiscated 'enemy' property. But no firm basis for control could be established. Effective occupation of all the territory nominally under their rule was impossible, and the Japanese concentrated in the central urban areas and along the railroad lines. In large measure Japanese army units attempted to live off the land, supporting themselves with food seized from farmers in the areas in which they were stationed. Many of the observed cases of looting and killing of Chinese civilians had their origin in these food seizures. Hostility and resistance to the harsh Japanese administration continued, although the division between the Nationalists under Chiang Kaishek and Communists under Mao Zedong loomed in the background.

The human cost was enormous. Official Chinese figures list 1.3 million soldiers killed in action against Japan from 1937 to 1945, but the total was undoubtedly higher. Civilian deaths are impossible to measure accurately. Chinese estimates range from 11 to 15 million civilian dead. United Nations officials estimated 9 million civilian deaths, but noted that an additional 'enormous number' had perished as a result of the famine caused by the final – and pointless – Japanese offensive in late 1944, which devastated the rice-producing regions of Guangdong, Hunan, Jiangxi, and Guizhou provinces.

The Japanese in Southeast Asia

I have always said the mission of Japan is to proclaim and demonstrate the Imperial way throughout the world. Viewed from the standpoint of international relations, this amounts, I think, to enabling all nations and races to find each its proper place in the world.

Foreign Minister Matsuoka Yôsuke, 1940

By 1938 the Japanese had advanced to Guangzhou, and hoped to cut supplies flowing inland to the Nationalist government. France ignored Japanese pressure to close the Haiphong–Kunming railway line, but following France's defeat by Germany in 1940 the new French Vichy government granted Japan permission to maintain an army in northern Indochina and yielded effective control over the economy. Although French administration remained, power lay with the Japanese. When Japan's new ally Thailand also attacked Indochina to regain the provinces lost in 1903–7, Japan sponsored an agreement favourable to the Thais. Then when Germany attacked the Soviet Union – without informing Japan – the Japanese moved troops into southern Indochina, which threatened Singapore and the oil fields in Borneo and Sumatra, and this led to the economic embargo imposed by the United States, Britain and the other Dominions, and the Netherlands, and to war.

Japanese plans to replace the French as suppliers of manufactured goods exchanged for Indochinese raw materials proved illusory, for by 1942 shortages of manufactured goods in Japan meant none were available for export. The worsening shipping shortage brought economic dislocation. By 1944 crucial raw materials lay piled high in warehouses in Saigon because of the lack of shipping. Despite extensive concessions extracted from the French, the Japanese made little investment, except for key areas such as chromium and phosphate, previously unprofitable but now essential at any price. However, Japan did need agricultural products. Mitsui operated a rice monopoly which set quotas each year. Since prices were fixed below market rates and inflation further eroded the money actually received by producers, farmers became reluctant to sell. Small-holders and tenants found themselves pressured by an 'unholy coalition of Japanese exporters, French administrators and Chinese wholesalers'. Landlords and rich peasants often found it more profitable to push tenants off their land; small-holders tried to grow enough for their own use and hide it. Rice exports peaked at 1.02 million tons in 1943, then dropped to half that amount in 1944. Rubber production held up, but the Japanese could use only half the total, so stockpiles accumulated. The Japanese forced farmers to cultivate jute, hemp, peanuts and caster oil plants, a risky policy, especially in northern areas where there was already a food deficit.

French authorities tried to preserve normality, but this was difficult by 1944 and impossible by 1945. The Japanese charged the French for the costs of maintaining their army. The French, still in control of the money supply, created credit to meet the Japanese demands, and prices rose.

There was no kerosene and therefore no lighting in rural areas for the duration of the war. Although cotton acreage increased, 100 000 textile workers were unemployed, cloth was rationed, and children generally went naked by the end of the war. The rice ration was cut from 15 kilograms per month in mid-1943, to 7 after March 1945. The official price in Hanoi was 0.53 piastres per kilogram, but that only applied to the official ration, and even that depended on availability. The remainder (an adult required at least 12 kilograms) had to be purchased on the black market at up to 7 piastres per kilogram.

Vietnam was spared actual combat. However, attacks by American submarines, then air attacks from Kunming, and finally strikes by carrier task forces, destroyed coastal shipping, which made shipment of rice from the Mekong delta to the north impossible. In 1944–5 a cold winter led to a crop failure in the north and 1 to 2 million people died in the ensuing famine. The French claimed that 5.5 per cent of the European and 2.5 per cent of the native population died from the hardships of the war (Marr, 1980).

During the 1920s and 1930s there had been some expansion of Japanese interests in the Philippines in timber, hemp, copra, and mining. Indeed, the Philippine leader Manuel Quezon favoured Japanese interests and advised Filipinos to adopt a 'Japanese industriousness'. In 1941, however, the Japanese found a changed situation in the Philippines. The depression had led to a new alliance of United States economic interests in favour of Philippine independence. Producers of sugar, tobacco, cotton-seed oil (which competed with Philippine coconut oil in soap), and the dairy industry (butter competed with margarine, also made from coconut oil) allied with labour unions opposed to Filipino workers, who were not prohibited under the Oriental Exclusion Act of 1924. Following the election of Franklin Roosevelt in 1932, the 1934 Tydings–McDuffie Act provided for a Commonwealth form of government and for independence in 1946, as well as placing quotas on imports of sugar and coconut oil, which were to be replaced by a tariff on Philippine exports to the United States of 5 per cent 1941, rising to 25 per cent 1946.

Following the Japanese invasion Quezon fled and established a government in exile. The Japanese found themselves confronting a guerilla resistance. They established a puppet government, and granted them 'the honour of independence' in 1943, but resistance continued, including contacts with the Americans, which became more extensive following the American recapture of Leyte 1944. At the end of the war the guerrillas controlled large areas of northern Luzon and most of Mindanao. Many provincial cities and towns were virtually empty, as the population moved to the villages to obtain food and to avoid the Japanese. The fighting claimed some 30 000 Filipino soldiers, and at least 90 000 civilians, most of whom died in another atrocity, the sack of Manila by the already-defeated Japanese in 1945.

Thailand's prewar commercialized export sector – rice, rubber, tin, and teak – lay in the hands of Chinese or Western firms, except for the actual growing of rice. Thailand suffered in the depression because the government remained on the gold standard, competing against countries which had left it. This hurt exports of rice and teak, and declining government revenues led to budget cuts, especially the salaries of officials and the military. Disaffected elements combined with unemployed foreign-educated youth in a bloodless coup on 24 June 1932 which led to a constitutional monarchy on the British pattern. Western interests suffered from Japanese competition in imports of textiles, petroleum products, and other manufactured goods in the 1930s. This economic situation and the rise of a militaristic, aggressive nationalism in Thailand led to alliance with Japan, and to territorial gains which restored previous losses to the French and British, but as in Indochina power lay with the Japanese.

A Japanese document in 1944 referred to 'Thailand's three basic economic policies of supplying food to Japan and other areas of Greater East Asia, establishment of a self-sufficient economy, and stabilization of the people's livelihood', but again the plans proved impossible to implement. Imports from Europe and the United States were cut off, and could not be made good by Japan. This lead to shortages, rising prices, attempts at rationing, and a black market. The decline in shipping meant Thailand could not export. The government was forced to make large loans to Japan, and the fixed exchange rate in effect devalued the baht compared to the yen, with inflationary results. By early 1944 the cost of living had risen fourfold and was accelerating. The price of rice remained stable, because exports were impossible, but this did not help farmers who wished to purchase manufactured goods (Batson, 1980).

In Malaya the Japanese found a population of roughly half Malays, slightly over one-third Chinese, and one-sixth Indians. The British considered Chinese and Indians transients who would return home, but the 1931 census indicated that about one-third of Chinese and Indians had been born in Malaya and therefore were probably permanent. Some Malays had organized a pro-Japanese underground before the war, and the British therefore had looked to the Chinese, including Communist party members, as a more reliable source of support. Following their victory over the British, the Japanese treated the Malayan Chinese as an extension of the enemy in China proper. A massacre of Chinese began in Singapore, and then extended to the mainland. There were between 6000 and 40 000 executions of accused Communist and Nationalist sympathizers, but there were also thousands of other killings, as well as systematic rape of Chinese women by Japanese soldiers. In addition the Japanese forcibly relocated thousands of city dwellers to the countryside, especially Chinese. Malay villagers viewed these newcomers as a threat. Alienated from the Japanese, the Malays, and the British, many of these families became the Chinese 'squatters' who supported the Communist insurgency of the postwar period (Kheng, 1980).

British, American and Dutch property in Malaya was expropriated and taken over by Japanese companies, as was that of Chinese suspected of ties with the Nationalist government. However, many small Chinese producers, retailers, and suppliers continued to work for Japanese firms. Mitsubishi secured a rice monopoly, and Mitsui monopolies of sugar and salt. They formed syndicates with military units and were accused of creating shortages to raise prices (Kheng, 1980). Again, Japanese policy aimed to transform Malaya into a self-sufficient economy. An attempt to introduce new rice varieties which required new patterns of cropping failed, and the food situation went from bad to worse when Japan transferred Perlis, Kedah, Kelantan and Trengganu to Thailand in October 1943, because these included the most important Malay rice-producing areas. In addition the Japanese requisitioned rice, which both created opposition directly and made villages dependent on government rations. Some 73 000 Malayans of all ethnic groups were sent for labour on the Burma–Siam railway, and 25 000 died (Akashi, 1980).

Japanese planners had hoped to exploit Indonesian raw materials, but by mid-1943 the shortage of shipping forced them to order each region to aim for self-sufficiency. Food production was forced in every deficit area, and cotton production and other manufactures were to be produced locally as well. The Japanese allowed no contact by Indonesians among the three main regions (Java, Sumatra, and the other islands), and they permitted no shipments between regional or even sub-regional divisions without a licence. The authorities requisitioned an increasing fraction of the rice crop, at very low prices. This interference in the civilian economy gave great power to officials, both Japanese and Indonesian, but the administration was inefficient and quickly became corrupt, with an extensive black market and smuggling between districts.

The suspension of exports disrupted the plantation sector of the economy – and in contrast to the Philippines, no local elite had an interest in maintaining export production. Small-holders preferred to grow food crops in preference to sugar, rubber, tobacco, or tea, so this shift was politically popular and therefore permanent, even though it would have benefited the Indonesian balance of payments to resume their production after the war. Nevertheless, output declined, particularly of rice. Forced labour on roads and airfields caused a shortage of labour. Towards the end of the war, the Japanese attempted to stockpile rice as a reserve for a possible guerilla war in the event of an Allied invasion. This meant they attempted to requisition more than their actual current needs. In response, farmers either concealed rice for sale on the black market or did not cultivate it at all rather than give it up to the Japanese. In 1945 possibly only 60 to 65 per cent of wet rice fields were planted.

The result was mass 'semi-starvation'. Most people could not obtain cotton cloth, so thousands simply sat along the roads in rags, 'waiting for death'. But the Indonesian elite did well. The same officials who had served the Dutch continued to serve the Japanese, and they enjoyed greatly increased opportunities to enrich themselves. Some of those whose depredations were too well known paid the price in 1945. The Japanese interned 130 000 Europeans, and 30 000 died in prison. From 300 000 to 1 million Indonesians, and many Chinese, were mobilized as labourers. Many were sent outside the country, particularly to work on the Burma–Siam 'railway of death'. United Nations officials estimated 300 000 deaths among Indonesian forced labourers, but the total may have been as high as 500 000, and UN reports noted that many remained so debilitated by their experiences that they were unable to work after the war. United Nations estimates further indicated that total deaths from hunger, disease, and lack of medical attention resulting from the occupation were 3 million for Java alone and another 1 million for the other islands (Reid, 1980).

The impact of the war on Japan

Due to the nationwide food shortage and the imminent invasion of the home islands, it will be necessary to kill all the infirm old people, the very young, and the sick. We cannot allow Japan to perish because of them.

Senior army officer, Ôsaka, June 1945

Strategically the war was lost when Japan lost control of the seas in 1942 in the battles of the Coral Sea and Midway. By 1945 three-quarters of Japanese shipping tonnage had been sunk, and the shortage of steel meant that Japanese shipyards could not replace the losses. There were a few cases in which the war stimulated technological change. For instance, the Tokyo Electric Company had produced vacuum tubes under licence from the United States General Electric Company. During the war demand exceeded Tokyo Electric's capacity, and the army forced them to licence other manufacturers. This diffusion of technology to other firms created a highly competitive situation in the immediate postwar period and laid the basis for the rapid growth of Japan's electronics industry. In contrast, the American electronics industry was only opened to increased competition a decade later, by a series of antitrust suits in the mid-1950s (Morris-Suzuki, 1994). But this would have been difficult to predict in 1945. Ordinary Japanese at first experienced a boom period with full employment and high wages, then increasing inflation, then increasing shortages, ever-harsher rationing, and finally rapid economic decline as raw materials and replacement parts disappeared.

The human cost, again, was enormous. To the 185 000 military deaths in China between 1937 and 1941 were added another 1.1 million deaths in the army and 415 000 in the navy. Tragically the majority of the deaths came in 1944–5, after the outcome of the war was no longer in doubt – most notably over 300 000 in the pointless defence of the Philippines from October 1944. Civilian mortality was high in Manchuria, possibly 100 000 during the winter of 1945–6. In Japan, the Battle of Okinawa killed 150 000 persons – one third of the island's entire population. Most civilian deaths occurred after March 1945 when the United States began incendiary bombing raids on Japanese cities. Some 86 000 civilians died in raids on 63 cities. The atomic bomb dropped on Hiroshima on 6 August killed 140 000, and the one dropped on Nagasaki on 9 August killed 70 000. A further 97 000 civilians died in the incendiary raid on Tokyo of 14 August. Intended by United States General Henry H. Arnold to be 'as big a finale as possible', it involved over 1000 planes, with not a single one lost, and was totally unnecessary. Some planes had not yet returned to their bases before Japan's unconditional surrender was announced.

As seen in the quote above, despite these losses elements in the army remained committed to a last supreme effort to resist an Allied invasion, even if it meant scorched earth in Japan to match that of so much of the rest of Asia. When the emperor intervened to insist on accepting the Allied demand for an unconditional surrender, a number of senior officers committed suicide.

Finally, although it elicited little sympathy, the condition of ordinary Japanese troops was very poor by end of the war. Malnutrition, sickness, injuries, and wounds affected the vast majority of the 4.5 million troops who returned to Japan. Some 81 000 actually died after the cease-fire but before they could be repatriated. This figure does not include the troops taken prisoner by the Soviet army. Japanese authorities estimated 1.3 million troops had been taken prisoner by the Soviet forces, but over the next four years only 1 million returned to Japan (Dower, 1986, pp. 295–301).

8

ASIAN NATIONALISM

We live in a world of nationalism – of national states and national movements demanding statehood. We also live in an industrial world, of industrial
economies and developing economies demanding growth. And yet the
connection between nationalism and industrialism is often disputed. Indeed,
the very definition of 'nations' and 'nationalism' is a matter of scholarly
controversy. These debates have their origins in the West, in the histories of
Europe and the United States. The protagonists in the debates have applied
their definitions and approaches to the study of national movements elsewhere in the world, in Latin America, Africa, and of course in Asia. In these
areas the debate has taken on a new colour, conceptually in the claim that
Latin American, African, or Asian nationalisms are essentially different from
those of Europe and the United States, and sometimes literally in the claim
that such differences arise from values and traditions held by 'people of
colour' which have led them to definitions of their national communities
which differ from those of the West. Further, since the new national states of
Asia are the ones which have presided over the period of rapid economic
growth, the questions of their values, the particular sort of nationalism they
possess, and of their impact – the way nationalism may have fostered
development – have taken on a particular urgency.

This chapter considers the relations between economic development
and the emergence of national movements in Asia. Because so much of
Asia was subject to the West either through direct colonization or informal
empire, these movements became ones of resistance to external control. In
addition, Asian nationalists looked to Japan as a model of an Asian nation
which had successfully defended itself against the West. There is a double
irony here. First, although as we saw in Chapter 5, the Japanese national

245

identity was an artificial creation, many other Asian nationalists accepted the myths the Japanese had created about themselves, and then proceeded to create similar artificial myths about their own nations. Secondly, although Japan played the role of an admired model, Japanese aggression – Japan as colonial power and enemy invader – created the conditions for the establishment of new 'national' states in the rest of Asia.

Within the Japanese colonial empire, as we saw in Chapter 7, opposition continued and intensified, particularly in Korea. In China, hostility to the Japanese provided a focus for something much closer to a national identity than had existed previously. Rather than the unique centre of culture, China became one nation among many, although only after a further destructive civil war was it decided who would control this new nation. In Southeast Asia, resistance to colonial states had also spread before the war. The displacement of colonial authorities by the Japanese had the effect of promoting indigenous leaders to much higher positions of authority than they would otherwise have held; the Japanese also trained indigenous armies, and these soldiers opposed the return of the colonial powers.

These new nationalisms can be analysed using the conceptual tools developed in the study of Western nationalisms. However, once again developments in Asia reflect the internal dynamics of Asian societies. Thus the defeat of Japan and the period of occupation raises the question of how much really changed as a result of American influence. The Communist victory in China, aside from its intrinsic importance, also raises the question of how much influence the West had on developments in Asia. Finally the period of decolonization, with Indonesia figuring as a paradigmatic example, raises the same question from another angle. Even the tragedies of Vietnam and Cambodia may be considered special cases of delayed decolonization. Looking at the new regimes allows a balance to be drawn on the colonial period, and provides some perspective on the later period of rapid economic development.

Nationalism and Modernity

The idea of nationalism

An essential characteristic of any identity is that it is necessarily the view the concerned actor has of himself or herself. It therefore either exists or does not; it cannot be asleep and then awakened, as some sort of disease.

Liah Greenfeld, *Nationalism*, 1992

What is a nation? Any nationalist will insist that their nation rests on a primordial, enduring ethnic basis, an amalgam of race, culture, and rootedness to a particular place. This can pose problems for the student, because national myths are often presented as unproblematic 'facts', even by reputable scholars. Nationalist historians often project the contemporary consciousness of nationhood back into the distant past. Take, for example, the question of the Japanese influence in Korea, a sensitive subject for Korean nationalists. A text by a team of Korean specialists claims that when the Japanese invaded Korea in 1592, 'the populace at large was infuriated at the government's incompetence and irresponsibility', and that 'at Japan's request Korea entered into friendly relations with the Tokugawa shogunate from 1609, but the animosity of the Korean people toward Japan remained alive long thereafter' (Eckert et al., 1990, pp. 144, 148). Given the social structure of sixteenth- and seventeenth-century Korea, these statements are not credible. What is true is that in the twentieth century the Japanese invasion three centuries before was portrayed by Korean nationalists as evidence of the depths of Japanese perfidy.

In addition, nationalist historians tend to blame the imperialist powers for their country's problems, while asserting that despite the period of oppression, the national 'essence' remained unchanged. Byung-nak Song, a distinguished economist and adviser to the South Korean government, asserts that,

The Japanese used Koreans mainly in lower positions in organizations. As a result, Koreans had few opportunities to accumulate experience as leaders, managers, or negotiators. Forced into a 'sergeant's' role, they developed a disgruntled sergeant's mentality. This legacy persists, and modern Korea needs badly the mentality of committed 'officers' or 'generals', self-sacrificing leaders, and risk-taking entrepreneurs and innovators. (Song, 1994, p. 41)

However, three paragraphs further, Song assures us that,

There were many other negative impacts as well, even though basic Korean cultural values changed little despite the massive Japanese effort to mold Koreans into second-class Japanese subjects. For example, neither Japanese Shintoism nor Japanese-style Zen Buddhism gained ground in Korea, despite Japan's efforts to implant belief systems and discourage Korean beliefs – as well as Christianity. The Koreans remained Korean in spite of everything. (Song, 1994, pp. 41–2)

Some students of nationalism agree that there is some basis for the claim that nations rest on an inherited identity. Anthony Smith has argued that national identity rests on an *ethnie*, an ancient grouping of people residing in a particular area (Smith, 1986). Paul Kratoska and Ben Batson seem to agree, in arguing that despite the 'instability of language and racial distinctions', each of the ethnic groupings of Southeast Asia 'did form an "imagined community" that perceived itself as a nascent nation-state' (Kratoska and Batson, 1992, pp. 290–1). Other scholars such as Liah Greenfeld disagree, and point to the very arbitrary selection of possible elements as national identities emerge. In this view there is no single identity which must necessarily be derived from the inheritance of the past, nor is there any single 'ethnic' basis for nations. Rather, there are many competing elements for inclusion, some of them contradictory, and 'ethnic' identities are themselves social constructs. In this the formation of modern national consciousnesses in Asian nations shares many characteristics with European nationalism. Both Western and Asian studies of the emergence of focused national identities – 'imagined communities', in Benedict Anderson's phrase – out of previous cultural, ethnic, or regional identifications reveal the emphasis on some elements and the suppression of others. As argued in Chapter 5, Japanese nationalism, for instance, was not simply the outgrowth of an inherited Japanese tradition, but rather was constructed from a mix of elements taken from Japanese, Chinese, and Western sources.

Has the emergence of nationalism been related to 'modernization' and the development of industrial economies? It has been frequently argued that nationalism has everywhere been a response to modernization and economic development, the extension of market relationships into new areas. Western European historians have tended to see their nationalisms as the result of economic development, and the assertion that modern economic growth, representative parliamentary governments, and nationalism were all part of a single broader process was perhaps the central tenet of modernization theory. In turn, historians of Central and Eastern Europe argued that the 'latecomer' nations of those regions failed to modernize as the Western European nations had. Instead they developed 'reactive' nationalisms and adopted dictatorial forms of government. In response to the threat posed by the industrialization of Western Europe and particularly England, they might sponsor rapid industrialization as in Germany, or they might remain locked in a condition of semi-dependency as in Italy or Russia.

Partha Chatterjee has taken the approach of Central and Eastern European historians in his analysis of the emergence of nationalism in the colonial world. He draws on the work of the Italian social thinker Antonio Gramsci to argue that the subjection of native elites to the cultural and political 'hegemony' of imperialist domination resulted in a 'passive revolution' which led them to an essential contradiction. Nationalists in colonial societies had to address their texts to two audiences simultaneously, 'both to "the people" who were said to constitute the nation and to the colonial masters whose claim to rule nationalism questioned'. The problem for nationalists arose from the fact that their messages to both audiences was the same: 'To both, nationalism sought to demonstrate the falsity of the colonial claim that the backward peoples were culturally incapable of ruling themselves in the conditions of the modern world'. Therefore, on the one hand, 'nationalism denied the alleged inferiority of the colonized people', while on the other hand 'it also asserted that a backward nation could "modernize" itself while retaining its cultural identity'. In both denying and accepting that their culture was 'backward', colonial nationalism 'produced a discourse in which, even as it challenged the colonial claim to political domination... also accepted the very intellectual premises of "modernity" on which colonial domination was based' (Chatterjee, 1986, p. 30).

For Chatterjee, the results appear deeply tragic. Although colonial nationalists were able to defeat the 'blatantly ethnic slogans' of colonial domination, 'this was achieved in the very name of Reason'. The weakness of colonial nationalism, according to Chatterjee, has been that it has not confronted the continued economic domination of the former imperialist powers. 'Nowhere in the world has nationalism *qua* nationalism challenged the legitimacy of the marriage between Reason and capital', and indeed colonial nationalism 'does not possess the ideological means to make this challenge'. Rather 'the conflict between metropolitan capital and the people-nation it resolves by absorbing the political life of the nation into the body of the state'. This is the essence of the 'passive revolution' – 'the national state now proceeds to find for "the nation" a place in the global order of capital, while striving to keep the contradictions between capital and the people in perpetual suspension' (Chatterjee, 1986, p. 168).

Chatterjee is also pessimistic about the possibilities for economic development in the former colonial world, precisely because of the sort of nationalism and the sort of state which has emerged there. 'The state now acts as the rational allocator and arbitrator for the nation'. All political life is subsumed under the activities of this 'state-representing-the-nation', and any questioning of the assertion that the 'people-nation' and the 'state-representing-the-nation' are identical, is simply denied legitimacy. But the politically independent former colonial state remains economically dependent on global capital. 'Protected by the cultural-ideological sway of this identity between the nation and the state, capital continues its passive revolution by assiduously exploring the possibilities of marginal development, using the state as the principal mobilizer, planner, guarantor and legitimator of productive investment' (Chatterjee, 1986, pp. 168–9).

Chatterjee's analysis can be faulted at a number of points. Western European nationalisms are now seen as more problematical than before; the connection of imperialist expansion with capitalism is less close than he imagines; Asian economies before the intrusion of the West were already highly sophisticated; in the decade since he wrote, economic development has proceeded much more rapidly than he seemed to think possible. Nevertheless, Chatterjee's analysis is important in several respects. He argues forcefully that the new identities emerged from the internal dynamics of Asian societies. However, they were not simply outgrowths or resurgences of pre-existing national cultures or characters, suppressed, say, by foreign domination, or waiting in Greenfeld's phrase 'to be awakened, as some sort of disease'. Rather, they both built on existing historical traditions and reflected the new facts of economic development. The new nationalist movements also were new in that they were a response to the facts of imperialist domination, and they therefore resulted not from 'modernization' or economic growth in themselves, but emerged as responses to the particular state structures and patterns of economic development possible within the imperialist context.

Keeping in mind both Chatterjee's arguments and the material of preceding chapters, this chapter will explore a series of related hypotheses. Nationalist leaders emerged from pre-existing native elites which had not only continued to exist but had often actually prospered under foreign domination. However, following Smith, it seems that there must be some pre-existing *ethnie* which can become the basis of a plausible appeal to nationalist sentiment. Further, following Greenfeld, the elite needs to redefine the nation to extend it to all the 'people' including the lower classes the elite has previously despised. As seen in the case of Japan, the 'people' now must also include women, previously invisible in public life, and this will inevitably lead to attempts to redefine gender roles. In order for the new national identity to spread and become a political force, the emerging elite requires modern communications and an audience of literate persons to whom they can direct their appeal. Following Anderson (1991), the result is an 'imagined community' of individuals who may never meet but who can believe themselves to belong to a single 'nation'. The final element is that, above all, the members of the emerging national elite want to gain and retain power. Elements of Chatterjee's 'derivative discourse' therefore continue in the politics of the newly independent states, in the continual pressure on women to conform to stereotyped roles, in the assertion that central governments must play a leading part in economic development, and in the arbitrary selection among elements in inherited traditions.

Imperialism and nationalism

To colonize is to establish contact with new countries in order to benefit from their total range of resources, to develop these resources for the benefit of the national interest and at the same time to bring to the native peoples the intellectual, social, scientific, moral, cultural, literary, commercial and industrial benefits of which they are deprived and which are the prerogative of the superior races. To colonize, therefore, is to establish an advanced form of civilization in a new country in order to achieve the twin aims we have just mentioned.

From a French *Outline of Colonial Legislation and Economics*, 1912

What was the role of the colonial state in the emergence of nationalism? Colonial administrators such as the French author cited above believed that Westerners had brought 'modern' economic relations to Asian societies for the first time. If we accept that claim, and if in addition we believe that nationalism arises out of modern economic development, then the imperialist powers can be seen ironically as having created the conditions for the rise of nationalism and therefore for undermining their own position. However, as seen in previous chapters, market economies predated the Western intrusion, and Asian producers were well aware of and able to exploit the varying opportunities of local, regional, and interregional trade. Indeed, the actions of colonial governments often interfered with these market relationships, and on balance Western imperialism may not have had much identifiable economic impact at all.

However, although the direct economic impact of the imperialist regimes may be contested, where economic development shades over into social transformation, their effects were profound. As we saw in Chapters 4 and 7, the role of state was fundamentally transformed. In Europe, the United States, and Japan during the late nineteenth and early twentieth centuries, central authorities attempted to extend the areas of social life over which they exercised direct control, and this movement was reflected in their empires. The colonial states expanded educational systems, standardized languages, imposed common legal codes (including commercial regulations), extended systems of communication and transportation, and recruited 'natives' to serve in the lower levels of their bureaucracies and armies. Above all, of course, they increased tax revenues. In Japan, China, and Thailand the money was intended firstly for defence; in the colonial territories it went to subdue districts where resistance had not yet been crushed. Additional sums went for transportation, for education, and for the infrastructure required by expanding cities.

A philosophy of imperialism emerged to justify these actions. The imperial powers argued that both the colonizers and the native peoples would benefit. Americans referred to Filipinos as their 'little brown brothers', Japanese to Koreans as their 'younger brothers', and the French, British, and Dutch to their native subjects in similar terms. They all claimed that the 'intellectual, social, scientific, moral, cultural, literary, commercial and industrial benefits' of an 'advanced form of civilization' were 'the prerogative of the superior races'. They all claimed that the native peoples would not be able to attain this advanced form of civilization by themselves, and that therefore they would require the tutelage of colonial authorities. Even in the Philippines some American administrators continued to believe that the Filipinos would never be ready to govern themselves. The imperialist powers also claimed that government intervention in the economy was necessary because native peasants and artisans were 'traditional', meaning unsophisticated, backward, and irrational. This, as we have seen above, was not true; rather, it was an ideological justification for the imperial governments to remain in control. However, it is important that this portion of imperialist ideology was frequently adopted by the new nationalist leaders, thereby becoming a justification for old elites to transmute themselves into new elites.

The creation of a 'national' community requires an expansion of communications. Thus, for instance, the world of the Chinese peasant may have been broader than a single village, but in most cases did not extend beyond Skinner's 'standard marketing area'. Now, regular contacts through interregional trade became more frequent. Before the First World War, economic expansion had already led to more intensive contacts with a broader range of people, and this development continued during the 1920s and 1930s, despite the difficulties of those decades. New forms of transportation played a crucial role. Over water, vastly improved sailing ships and then steam-powered ships tied port cities together. On land, railways linked commercial urban centres with their hinterlands. Together, the steamship and the railway made it possible to ship much larger volumes of goods, much faster, and much more regularly, than ever before. Table 8.1 gives figures for the length of railway line open from 1880 to 1938. Japan's surge forward to the status of an industrialized country is clear, as are the Japanese colonial government's continued efforts in Korea and Taiwan during the 1930s, compared to the Dutch in Indonesia, the British in Malaysia, or the United States in the Philippines. The crucial point is that by the 1930s all the countries of Asia possessed at least the outlines of a modern rail system. Freight and passenger traffic increased dramatically. In Indonesia, for instance, freight shipments rose from 5 to 19 million tons, and passengers from 50 000 to 147 000, between 1905 and 1929 (Mitchell, 1995).

Table 8.1 Asia: Length of Railway Line Open, 1880–1938 (kilometers)

	1880	1890	1900	1910	1920	1930	1938
China	–	–	1516[1]	8601	10 973	13 441	na
Indochina	–	71	182	1717	2063	2395	3383
Indonesia	385	1593	3574	5145	6566	7395	7388
Japan	158	2349	6300	8661	13 645	21 593	24 928
Korea	–	–	–	1031	1863	2793	3831
Malaya	–	56	417	867	1545	1723	1719
Myanmar	na	na	na	na	na	na	3314
Philippines	–	–	196	206	1212	1306	1358
Taiwan	–	–	97	436	2404	3069	3397
Thailand	–	–	125	896	2215	2862	3100

Notes
1 This figure is for 1901.
Source: Mitchell, 1995.

The creation of a national community requires not only the movement of goods and people, however, but also that large numbers of people be able to read the appeals of would-be nationalist leaders. Colonial states all expanded education. Chapter 7 gives figures showing the growth of primary school enrolments in Korea and Taiwan. The Japanese model influenced education in Thailand as well. The reforming king Chulalongkorn sent several missions to Japan to study Japanese education. In 1910 an official recommended promulgation of a royal decree on education, and Chulalongkorn suggested that it be modelled on the 1890 Imperial Rescript on Education. The project of the royal decree was delayed by the bureaucracy, and then dropped when Chulalongkorn died (Batson, 1980), but the system which emerged imposed a uniform syllabus taught from uniform texts, with all instruction conducted in Central Thai rather than any of the many local variants and dialects. As in Japan, students learned that the Thai people were a uniform ethnic group who had lived under a single line of kings for many, many centuries, which 'neatly glossed over the ethnic muddle of Lao, Khmer, Mon, Vietnamese, Malay, and Chinese in Siam's cosmopolitan society, and elegantly submerged the Sino-Mon origins of the dynasty' (Pasuk and Baker, 1995, p. 233).

Figures for primary school enrolments in Southeast Asia are given in Table 8.2. Colonial administrators and later apologists pointed with pride to these educational efforts. Thus in the Philippines the original group of American teachers had been mostly repatriated by 1927 and replaced by Filipinos, and by 1940 literacy was approaching 50 per cent. However, the numbers of pupils remained small as a share of the potential school age

Table 8.2 Southeast Asia: Enrolments in Primary Education, 1900–38, in thousands

	1900	1910	1920	1930	1938
Indochina	na	na	130	360	617
Indonesia	172	366	863	1801	2270
Malaya	15	46	65	166	333
Myanmar	276	349	415/323[1]	465	532
Philippines	150	607	924	1144	1732
Thailand	na	115[2]	169	657	1475

Notes
1 Changed definition.
2 This figure is for 1913.
Source: Mitchell, 1995.

population – even in the Philippines primary enrolments were just over 40 per cent of the 5 to 14 age group in 1938. Further, as we will see in Chapter 10, the largest increase in enrolments in the former colonies came after independence. This was especially true of secondary education, which remained very undeveloped in the colonial era. The imperial powers, Japan included, intended that the overwhelming majority of their subject populations would receive a primary education at most.

Nevertheless the numbers were significant in their large absolute increase. Success in Western academic subjects proved the native peoples were capable intellectually. This undermined the paternalistic arguments of the colonial powers. Further, because the majority of the schoolchildren came from elite families, education reinforced the position of native elites. Children from non-elite families who gained admittance were absorbed into the elite. As leaders both of 'traditional' native society and of the new 'modern' native society, these educated men and women grew increasingly indignant at being shut out of the political process and discriminated against in economic opportunities. They were well aware of movements elsewhere in Asia, and looked particularly to the examples of Meiji Japan, of China under Sun Yatsen, and of the Indian independence movement under Gandhi. In a scene set in 1898, Minke, the high school student who is the hero of Indonesian writer Pramoedya Ananta Toer's great novel *This Earth of Mankind*, remarks 'I don't know why but I liked to seek out reports about Japan. It pleased me to find out that their youth were being sent to England and America to study. You could say I was a Japan-watcher' (ch. 2, p. 31). Their indignation led some to join in nationalist and opposition movements. A large fraction of the Chinese intellectual leaders coming to maturity from the 1890s onwards had visited or studied in Japan (Spence, 1982). Over the years many Southeast Asian nationalists attended the annual meetings of the Indian National Congress (SarDesai, 1994, p. 138). In Myanmar the British introduced new secular schools which competed with Buddhist organizations, the traditional sources of education. In 1906 a Young Men's Buddhist Association was founded, patterned on the YMCA. Religious organizations were a safe cover for nationalist agitation, and members of the YMBA later became leaders of many political parties (SarDesai, 1994, pp. 164–5).

Finally, would-be nationalist leaders require an audience, and the audience must be concentrated for nationalist texts to have significant impact. Urban centres therefore provide the most promising ground for nationalist agitation. Here again nationalism and imperialist economics intersect, for many have asserted that for instance in Southeast Asia 'the commercial urban centres are one of the major legacies of colonialism' (Van Niel, 1990b, p. 121). Urban centres expanded to handle trade, and large immigration into these centres followed. All were complex, multi-ethnic entities, yet they shared similarities in their role as nodes of development and administration. All of the 'treaty ports' in China included large enclaves where foreigners resided and where both foreign and Chinese entrepreneurs opened modern factories. In Southeast Asia, Kuching in Sarawak (Lockard, 1987), Jakarta, (Abeyasekere, 1987), Manila (Doeppers, 1984), Bangkok, and of course Singapore, are all examples.

Within these centres ever-larger numbers of people interacted with one another, read the reports in the expanding native-language press, and experienced first-hand the discrimination practised by the imperial powers. The imperialist nations excluded natives from senior positions in the public service, transportation, large-scale industry, lucrative service sectors such as insurance, and international trade. There were some exceptions: native elites frequently continued to control extensive tracts of land, in Southeast Asia some Chinese entrepreneurs amassed huge fortunes, and in Korea a number of Korean industrial firms emerged. Overwhelmingly, however, native entrepreneurs – including the majority of Indian and Chinese businesses in Southeast Asia – were confined to highly competitive small-scale trade. Further, in conflicts between members of different ethnic groups, the members of the imperialist communities always enjoyed a large advantage. In some areas there were completely separate legal and administrative systems for 'natives', as in Vietnam or Indonesia, or parallel systems for 'native communities', as in Malaya. In China and Thailand foreigners enjoyed extra-territorial rights which exempted them from the authority of the native courts. Even where all were in theory subject to the same law, natives discovered that the law always worked in favour of the imperialists.

Tables 8.3 and 8.4 give population figures for capital cities in Southeast Asia and for major cities in the coastal provinces of China, and include some figures which indicate the percentage of the national or regional population which lived in those cities. As with education, the absolute increases are impressive. Many of these cities moved from being small to being large during the early decades of the twentieth century. Note in particular, Jakarta, Singapore, and Yangon in Southeast Asia, and Tianjin and Shanghai in China.

On the other hand, urban concentration not only continued but accelerated after the departure of the imperial powers. Therefore urban growth may simply have reflected the general thrust of economic development, rather than the specific effects of imperialism. Politics played a role as well. The emerging nationalist movements all created highly centralized governing systems, and these political patterns found their physical reflection in the dominance of capital cities, for instance, Jakarta in Indonesia and of course Beijing in China. This continues to be important, for these massive urban centres may also have hampered development in other ways. Thai economic development since 1945 has been epitomized as a continual tension between the 'centre' in Bangkok and the 'periphery' (Pasuk and Baker, 1995, pp. 404–12). Manila, in particular, has been criticized for its negative role in Philippines because of its contribution to over-centralization, the lack of an economically rational hierarchy of urban centres, deterioration of conditions in the metropolis, and the spillover of the city's problems into adjoining areas (Caoili, 1988).

Table 8.3   Urbanization in Asia: Population of Capital Cities in Thousands, and Shares of Total Population, 1880–1980

	1880	(%)	1910	(%)	1930	(%)	1960	(%)	1980	(%)
Seoul, Korea	na		223	1.7	343	1.8	2445	9.8[1]	8364	21.9[1]
Taipei, Taiwan	na		102	3.1	230	4.9	799	7.0	2220	12.5
Manila, Philippines	154	na	234	2.8	325	2.5	1139	4.2	1630	3.4
Bangkok, Thailand	400	5.7	629	7.6	490	4.3	1330	5.1	4697	10.5
Jakarta, Indonesia	97	0.5	139	na	437	0.7	2907	3.0	6503	4.4
HoChiMinh, Vietnam	81	na	182	na	256	1.4	1251	7.9[2]	3420	6.5
Hanoi, Vietnam	na		114	na	135	0.8	415	na	2571	4.9
Singapore, Malaya	139	na	303	13.0	558	14.7	1687	na	2414	na
Kuala Lumpur, Malaysia	na		47	na	114	na	316	3.9	920	6.7
PhnomPenh, Cambodia	17	na	62	na	96	na	394	7.3	500[3]	7.8
Yangon, Myanmar	134	1.5	293	2.4	400	2.8	922	4.1	2513	7.5

Notes:
1 South Korea.
2 South Vietnam.
3 1 586 000 (22.5 per cent) in 1970.
Source: Computed from data in Mitchell, 1995. Years are not always exact; the figures are generally estimates subject to substantial error, and the territories included in the city boundaries sometimes changed between censuses.

Table 8.4   Urbanization in China: Populations of Coastal Provinces and Major Cities in Thousands, 1900–82; Percentage of Population in Major Cities, 1953 and 1982

	1900	1930	1953	(%)	1982	(%)
Hebei	na	na	41447[5]	15.8	70001[5]	27.8
Beijing	700	811[3]	2768		9231	
Tianjin	750	1389	2694		7764	
Tangshan	na	149[4]	693		1408	
Shijiazhuang	na	217[4]	373		1069	
Shandong	na	na	48877	2.5	74419	6.4
Zibo	na	na	1847		2198	
Qingdao	121	na	345		1209	
Jinan	100	437[4]	680		1359	
Jiangsu	na	na	47456[6]	16.2	72381[6]	20.2
Nanjing	150[1]	561	1020		2091	
Suzhou	500	260	474		670	
Shanghai	651[2]	3124	6204		11860	
Zhejiang	na	na	22866	3.0	38885	3.0
Hangzhou	350	590	697		1171	
Fujian	na	na	13143	4.2	25873	4.3
Fuzhou	624	323	553		1112	
Guangdong	na	na	34770	4.3	59300	5.4
Guangzhou	900	812	1496		3182	
Hong Kong	na	821	2242		5265	

Notes:
1   This figure is for 1890.
2   For 1904.
3   For 1936.
4   For 1935.
5   Including districts of Beijing and Tianjin.
6   Induding district of Shanghai.
Source: Calculated from data in Mitchell, 1995. Population figures for cities relate to administrative districts and may therefore include substantial rural areas; some of the declines recorded from 1900 to 1930 may reflect boundary changes.

Imperialism, Native Elites and National Movements

In contrast to the economic and social effects of Western and Japanese imperialism, which are often difficult to trace clearly, the political impact of outside intrusion was direct and important. *Ressentiment* – the terrible humiliation of being dependent in a world where self-worth depends on being independent – burned in the hearts of educated members of the elites of Asia, and the pain became worse the more they learned about the

West, about Japan, about movements to gain independence elsewhere in Asia. Drawing on foreign examples and indigenous traditions, leaders of early nationalist movements attempted to create new categories of thought and new identities which would enable their countries to become 'nations' and win respect in the world.

China: from culture to nation?

Expel the Manchus, restore the Chinese rule, and establish a federal republic.

Oath of the Revive China Society, 1895

As we saw above in Chapter 4, the leaders of the self-strengthening movement failed to gain control of the central government. Further, their argument that China required fundamental reforms in order to defend itself against foreign pressure failed to persuade the majority of the Confucian scholar gentry class, who remained convinced that Chinese civilization was simply civilization itself, and that the foreign barbarians would go away, destroy each other, or adopt civilized manners and be absorbed, as the Manchus, the Mongols, and other invaders had. The final attempts at reform by the Qing central government foundered on 'insoluble systemic problems' (Fairbank, 1992, pp. 247–9), an inherited passive and parasitic conservatism, corruption and fiscal incompetence, and, perhaps most important, the increasing power of provincial governments. Following the suppression of the great rebellions of the mid-nineteenth century, regional armies gradually became regular provincial forces. The new military academies of the self-strengthening movement built on this tradition, and added a new element, because the young officers trained there also acquired the prestige of being traditional scholars as well as soldiers. As governor of Shandong, Yuan Shikai – the 'father of the warlords' – trained a new generation of military leaders after the Japanese war, the officers of China's modern 'new army', many of whom later became contenders for regional and national power.

The political bankruptcy of the Qing government was revealed in 1900. The Imperial Court supported the Boxer uprising and declared war on the imperialist powers, but provincial leaders ignored the government's declaration. Yuan Shikai (Shandong), Li Hongzhang (Guangzhou), Liu Kunyii (Nanjing) and Zhang Zhidong (Wuhan) made an informal agreement with foreign representatives that they would undertake to suppress the Boxers and protect foreigners, if the foreign powers agreed not to send troops into their provinces. An international army rescued the foreigners besieged by the Boxers in Beijing, and looted the city; and the ensuing Boxer Protocol imposed a list of humiliating conditions as well as a large indemnity.

China remained as it had been, with a cultural identity but divided along regional lines. A growing number of intellectuals, many of them students sent to Japan by the modernizing provincial governors, dreamed of a revolutionary overthrow of the Qing which would establish a new, modern state. They began use new words taken from Japanese authors such as *minzu*, literally 'clan people' but now used in the sense of 'nation', and modified them as *Zhonghua minzu* (Chinese people or nation) and *Zhongguoren* (people of the Middle Kingdom, or Chinese people) (Kim and Dittmer, 1993, pp. 251–2). Sun Yatsen founded the Revive China Society in 1894 and attempted to organize an uprising in Guangzhou the next year, but the plot was discovered and he fled abroad. Similarly Kang Youwei fled following the suppression of the attempted reforms of 1898. Sun and Kang competed over the next years for support from overseas Chinese, Sun advocating revolutionary republicanism and Kang supporting a reformist regime under the emperor. With the support of highly placed Japanese well-wishers such as Ôkuma Shigenobu, who believed that Japan 'must repay its ancient cultural debt to China by assisting it to reform, modernize, and gain freedom from foreign imperialism' (Hsü, 1995, p. 460), Sun gradually won the political support of Chinese students in Japan and eventually the financial support of overseas Chinese communities as well.

In 1897, Sun enunciated his famous 'Three People's Principles' of Nationalism, Democracy and Socialism, or more precisely 'people's national consciousness, people's rights, and people's livelihood'. This 'threefold revolution' would firstly replace China's monarchical system with a republic, and thereby break the ancient cycle of disorder, civil war, unification and despotism. Secondly, however, the revolution would guarantee both freedom of individuals internally and the freedom of China as a whole from foreign interference. And finally, Sun argued that the revolution would avoid the strikes, inequality in wealth, and other social problems created by industrialism in the advanced imperialist countries. The people's livelihood would be guaranteed by the careful regulation of capital to prevent its concentration, and by an equal division of land among those who worked it – the ancient dream of 'land to the tiller'.

Sun's arguments reveal his *ressentiment*, and show as well the transvaluation of values in his assertion that by drawing on its traditions China could not only gain independence, but also improve on the West, that is, that there was a Chinese 'essence' which not only was not inferior to, but actually was superior to the West.

A unified revolutionary organization under Sun's leadership was founded in 1905, and eight attempted uprisings followed. The final 'revolution' in 1911 arose from an attempt by the government to nationalize the railway system. Gentry and merchant investors in Sizuan felt themselves wronged by the government's arbitrary action and by the inadequate compensation they were offered. Protests and riots in August led the government to move troops into Sizuan, which left other districts vulnerable. Police discovery of a list of revolutionary supporters in the army led to certain military units rising in revolt in October. Fifteen provinces had declared themselves independent of the Qing by the beginning of December, and the revolutionaries had gained control of Nanjing and Shanghai as well. In January 1912 Sun, hurrying home from the United States, became the provisional president of the new republic. The Qing government had called on Yuan to suppress the revolution, but he, still smarting from an involuntary 'retirement' forced on him in 1908, vacillated. Among the revolutionaries were many who felt Yuan to be the only leader who could prevent a protracted civil war. A series of compromises followed, the Qing emperor abdicated, Sun resigned, and Yuan became president in March 1912.

As president, Yuan appointed his own subordinates to key ministries. Following the victory of the new Nationalist Party in the elections in late 1912, Yuan had the party's leader assassinated. To gain financial independence from the new parliament, in early 1913 he negotiated a loan from a foreign banking consortium, and when parliamentary leaders protested he surrounded the parliamentary building with troops and declared 'there is no need for further discussion'. He put down a 'second revolution' in six southern provinces and installed his own generals as provincial rulers. Nevertheless, a series of 'modernizing' reforms to legal and educational systems remained on paper, because Yuan's government never gained control of provincial tax revenues. Finally, he attempted to make himself emperor but encountered widespread opposition. To forestall foreign intervention, in 1915 he signed agreements with Britain and Russia securing their interests in Outer Mongolia and Tibet, and agreed to Japan's twenty-one demands which recognized the Japanese position in Manchuria, Inner Mongolia, and Shandong. His actions aroused widespread hostility, but when he died in 1916, China slipped into the chaos of the warlord period (see Young, 1977).

Yuan was no democrat, and neither were the army officers who became provincial warlords, all of whom recreated the pattern of Yuan's dictatorship on a smaller scale. Yet despite his commitment to 'the people', Sun too remained in many respects a traditional authoritarian. His detailed plan for implementing his revolution envisaged three stages. The first stage was a military dictatorship during which the military would control all public life down to the district level. Political and social evils – slavery, foot-binding, opium-smoking, and corruption in the civil bureaucracy – would be eliminated. The second stage was a period of 'political tutelage'. Local self-government would be introduced gradually, with elections for local assemblies, but the military would remain in control of the central government. Sun planned the first stage to last for three years, and the second for six years. Only after the period of tutelage would the final stage, of national constitutionalism, be reached. Following the defeat of the 'second revolution' Sun fled to Japan, where he reorganized the Nationalist Party into a highly centralized body whose members swore personal allegiance to him and fingerprinted their written pledges. As leader Sun appointed all officers of the party's central and branch organizations, and he adopted the military title of generalissimo as well.

Hostile demonstrations greeted the announcement of Yuan's agreement to the twenty-one demands, and on 4 May 1919 the news that the Western Allies had confirmed Japan's position in Shandong as part of the Versailles peace settlement brought 5000 students into the streets of Beijing. The protests of the 'May Fourth Movement' forced the Chinese representatives in Paris to reject the peace treaty; they have been cited as the first modern mass political movement in Chinese history, directed not only against foreign incursions but also against the corruption and feebleness of the warlords' government. Organized boycotts of foreign goods followed, supported by Chinese factory owners and an expanding workers' movement.

The Russian Revolution added a new factor, a foreign government committed to combating imperialism. Representatives of the Comintern encouraged intellectuals from the May Fourth Movement to found the Chinese Communist Party in 1921. Sun reorganized the Nationalist Party along Communist lines, further centralizing power, and in 1923 signed an agreement with the Soviet Union, seeking help, as he wrote to Chiang Kaishek, where he could get it. Chiang visited the Soviet Union and returned to head the new Nationalist military academy. Nationalists and

Communists both hoped to use the other to achieve power, and most historians see the ensuing split as inevitable. Following Sun's death in 1925, Chiang used his control over the new generation of army officers to secure power over the Nationalist Party. A new Nationalist government was proclaimed in July 1925, in July 1926 Chiang launched his 'northern expedition' against the warlords who controlled the provinces to the north of the Yangzi, and in April 1927 he ordered a brutal massacre of the Communists in urban centres. In 1928 the Nationalist central committee adopted 'An Outline of Political Tutelage' intended to put Sun's second phase into action and named Chiang president of the republic.

However, as we have already seen in Chapters 6 and 7, Chiang and the new republic were not left in peace. A second generation of 'new warlords' had to be confronted and suppressed. Japanese aggression continued and intensified. Although Chiang was able to dislodge the new rural-based Communist Party under Mao Zedong from its stronghold in the southern province of Jiangxi and drive them on the famous 'Long March' to northern Shaanxi in 1934–5, he was unable to defeat them. Throughout the war with Japan Chiang held troops in reserve to contain the Communist presence. Mao repaid the compliment to his former ally; as he distanced himself from his colleagues and centralized his personal power over his party and the districts he controlled, he too looked beyond the struggle against Japan towards a final confrontation with the Nationalists.

The war with Japan provided the mass of Chinese with a very palpable enemy 'other', but neither the Nationalists nor the Communists solved the problem of creating a national identity. Both Chiang and Mao personally, and the other leaders of the Nationalists and Communists as well, focused on the overwhelming necessity of a strong state. The state and its leaders, not the people as a whole, still constituted 'the nation' for them. The Nationalist regime suffered from 'systemic weaknesses' as well (Fairbank, 1992, pp. 289–93, 331–4). The party remained beset by internal factional struggles. Chiang relied on his personal allies and protégés to maintain his position as leader, but many of his key supporters were hopelessly corrupt. Many Nationalist functionaries had begun their careers under the Qing or under the warlords, and they continued to adhere to the old slogan 'become an official and become rich'. Many of the potential reformers among the younger generation had died during the massacre of the Communists in 1927.

The Nationalists mishandled their relations with farming families. Villagers learned they could expect far better treatment from the Communists. In addition, whereas the Nationalists had the reputation of favouring the property rights of landlords, the Communists declared themselves in favour of land reform, of 'land to the tiller' and a final end to the ancient exploitation of tenant farmers. The Nationalist government mismanaged the economy, allowing inflation to run out of control and dispossessing wealth-holders with a bungled currency reform in 1948. Finally Chiang committed irreparable political and military errors which ensured the Communist victory. His use of the military forces of Japanese puppet governments alienated many, and his insistence on an immediate campaign to regain Manchuria before securing his position in the central provinces proved to be a major strategic blunder.

Women played a decisive role in the Communist victory, both in their direct contribution and as a symbol of the superiority of the Communist Party over the Nationalists. The small number of women intellectuals in the first decade of the twentieth century had drawn on Western anarchist thinkers such as Kropotkin to criticize the inherited structure of the family. The emancipation of women from their position of subjection in the Confucian hierarchy and specifically from the practice of footbinding was one of the central demands of the larger numbers of women students who participated in the May Fourth Movement. Women were active in the urban Communist Party, and they died along with the men in the massacre of 1927. In the countryside, one of Mao's earliest works had analysed the position of the peasantry, and concluded that the families of small peasant households would provide the most promising basis for a Communist movement, because of their relatively democratic structure and the relatively equal position of husband and wife (Mao, 1927). In the districts where they gained power, the Communists recruited women actively. Women took the lead in the reorganization of village life, and especially in the 'struggle' meetings at which landlords and conservatives were denounced for their acts of oppression. As we will see in Chapter 11, after the establishment of the People's Republic the ideal of equality between the sexes proved to be a myth, but there is no doubt that the women who aided in the Communist victory believed in the ideal, and there is no doubt that in many districts the commitment of the Communists to the ideal tipped the balance in their favour.

However, despite his 'Sinification' of Marxism, his concern that Marxism should be applied 'concretely...so that its every manifestation has an indubitably Chinese character', Mao continued to conceive of individual Chinese as members of abstract classes, to be led by the elite and treated according to abstract and universally applicable principles. Under Communism as well as under the Nationalists, therefore, the result was a preference for central control, for dictatorship, and a postponement of the quest for a national identity. As seen in the following chapters, only in the 1980s did Chiang's heirs in Taiwan begin to integrate the mass of the population into the political process. In Beijing in the 1990s, Mao's heirs still could not conceive of the nation as including all the people. They continued, in the traditional manner of Chinese rulers, to view any dissent as disloyalty, and therefore protest could only be met with repression. Fifty years after the foundation of the People's Republic, still 'more than any event, the 1989 massacre reflected and affected a profound crisis of national self-definition' (Kim and Dittmer, 1993, p. 257).

Thailand

Which side do you think will be defeated in this war? That side is our enemy.

> Prime Minister Phibun Songkhram to the Thai Army
> Chief of Staff, at the outbreak of the Second World War

Thailand occupies a place somewhere between China and Japan as the one remaining independent country in Southeast Asia, and as a country whose indigenous form of government survived, but also as an Asian country which was subject to foreign pressures which limited its range of effective action. Chulalongkorn was succeeded first by Sonce Maha Vajiravudh (Rama VI, 1910–25), and then by Prajadhiphok (Rama VII, 1925–35), Chulalongkorn's seventy-sixth child. Both had been educated abroad, Westernized, and in the opinion of some historians 'to a deplorable extent, alienated from the cultural and political interests of their people' (SarDesai, 1994, pp. 168–9). The royal clan and their allies continued to monopolize office – of the fifteen prime ministers who served under Prajadhiphok, nine were royal princes. Some of the 'modernizing' thrust of Chulalongkorn's reign continued. Under Vajiravudh Chulalongkorn University was founded. The government began to expand compulsory primary education, and enrolments reached 40 per cent of the 7 to 14-year age cohort in the mid-1920s and rose further in the 1930s. Thailand sided with the Allies against Germany in the First World War, gained control of German railway interests, and joined the League of Nations. Under Prajadhiphok the privy council and council of state were expanded, an airport opened, and measures taken to improve public health.

However, opposition to royal absolutism spread and intensified. Vajiravudh alienated army and navy officers, although he survived attempted assassinations in 1912 and 1917. Under Prajadhiphok, the appointment of members of the royal family to high offices alienated commoner officials. During the 1920s hostility towards the large number of Chinese immigrants increased. Among the Chinese, higher numbers of female migrants provided Chinese men with marriage partners and reduced the previous tendency towards assimilation, and the victory of the Nationalists in China led to a new assertiveness among these 'overseas' Chinese. The Thai government pre-empted China's demands for special legal status for 'overseas' Chinese by revoking the existing extraterritorial privileges of Chinese immigrants in 1930.

Finally, during the depression the royal government revealed itself as both weak and incompetent. Addressing a meeting of military officers in February 1932, Prajadhiphok confessed,

The financial war is a very hard one indeed. Even experts contradict one another until they become hoarse. Each offers a different suggestion. I myself do not profess to know much about the matter and all I can do is to listen to the opinions of others and choose the best. I have never experienced such a hardship; therefore if I have made a mistake I really deserve to be excused by the officials and people of Siam. (Pasuk and Baker, 1995, p. 247)

In the event, Thailand remained on the gold standard, which hurt exports. The resulting decline in revenue led the government to cut its budget. The salaries of the bureaucracy and the military were slashed, and many were dismissed. Disgruntled government officials and army officers joined unemployed foreign-educated youth, and their resentment turned on the royal government.

Dissatisfaction led to revolution. Senior army officers led a coup on 24 June 1932. The plotters were intent on maintaining both the monarchy and the bureaucracy, but wanted to force the retirement of a large number of relatives and friends of the king. An attempted royalist restoration was thwarted, and Prajadhipok abdicated in 1935. As his successor the government selected his 10-year-old son Ananda, who was in school in Switzerland. Thailand had no resident monarch for the next 15 years. The princes were shut out of power, but in effect the governing elite expanded to include the victors in the revolution. The government suppressed any possible source of opposition, including newspapers, labour unions, and

Buddhist monks. Control of the government alternated between Pridi Bhanamyong, a professor of law with a leftist reputation, and Phibun Songkhram, an army officer supported by ultranationalist military leaders. Pridi had became prime minister following the 1932 coup. He called for an end to royal absolutism and broader participation in political life, and insisted that 'this country belongs to the people, not to the king as we have been deceived into believing'. Opposition to his political ideas and to his economic plans, which called for expropriation of large agricultural holdings, nationalization of major industrial and commercial enterprises, and a complete 'bureaucratization' of the economy, had contributed to the attempted royalist counter-coup. He was denounced as a Communist and forced to flee. However, he was recalled from exile by Phibun after the royalists had been suppressed and held a number of high offices. Pridi and Phibun both believed implicitly that the state must take charge of economic and social development. The tension between Pridi's technocratic but essentially civilian approach and Phibun's military emphasis remained latent until the end of the war. As foreign minister and finance minister Pridi renegotiated the unequal treaties with foreign powers, and British leases were renewed on terms more favourable to the government. Certain occupations were reserved for Thais, the government granted special assistance to Thai businesses, and government funds provided capital for joint government-private enterprises.

Through the 1930s the military and Phibun personally gained in influence. In his first major speech as minister of defence, Phibun argued that there were four fundamental political institutions in Siam: the monarchy, the Assembly, the bureaucracy, and the military. Of these only the military was 'abiding and permanent'; the Assembly could be 'abolished through various events and causes'. Drawing on German and Japanese models, Phibun and other army leaders argued that the military was the expression of the popular will because of its unique ability to build a stronger nation. Over the next years he consolidated his control of the military by placing his allies in key positions, and in December 1938 he pushed his rivals aside and assumed the post of prime minister.

The name of the country was changed from Siam to Thailand (land of the free) in 1939, and Phibun began to portray himself as the national 'leader'. The government adopted much of the rhetoric and symbolism of South American and European-style authoritarianism. Along with Western clothing went a new 'national' dance and pressure on non-Buddhists to convert to the 'national' religion, but the attempt to include a broader segment of the population in this new national community remained half-hearted at best. Problems were addressed by forming committees of high-ranking officials, often with overlapping membership. A plan to combine two major sects of Thai Buddhism was abandoned after opposition from segments of the monkhood, and the government's cultural decrees encountered much opposition. The young men's and young women's associations founded in 1935 remained small and confined to urban areas. A women's military unit was disbanded in 1944, along with most of the other creations of the 'Phibun movement' (Batson, 1980).

Thai army leaders admired Japan, and envied its successes in China. Thailand abstained from voting in the League of Nations' condemnation of Japan for the invasion of Manchuria. Contacts increased during the 1930s; Japan wanted access to Thai rice, rubber, and tin. Religious revivalism, ultranationalism, and militarism went together. An anti-Christian campaign ran parallel to a renewed anti-Chinese campaign. The government closed Chinese schools and newspapers, limited immigration, and deported 'illegal' migrants. Thailand demanded the return of the Cambodian provinces of Siem Reap and Battambang, ceded to the French in 1904. When war broke out, Phibun decided that Japan would be the winner, and Thailand declared war on France. Japan brokered an agreement with the Vichy administration in Indochina, which returned the provinces to Thailand. Thailand granted the Japanese transit rights and supplies, and in return received further gains in Laos, northern Malaya, and the Shan region of Myanmar.

As an ally of Japan, Thailand enjoyed relative independence, but discontent increased over martial law and high prices. In the background, Pridi, who had withdrawn from the government when the Japanese arrived and now served as regent for the young king, organized the Seri Thai (Free Thai) movement. Seri Thai was a disparate alliance of provincial dissidents – Lao and northeastern Thai politicians and business interests who resented the power of Bangkok – together with labour activists, radical intellectuals, and the Bangkok Chinese community. In mid-1944 Phibun resigned in favour of a civilian government, because of a profiteering scandal and the rejection in the Assembly by a coalition of Pridi supporters of his grandiose schemes for the construction of a new capital and a world centre of Buddhism (though his wife later said he had resigned because the postwar situation would be easier with the new prime minister, since 'he had declared war on the Allies, and the Allies were going to win'). Pridi negotiated with the Allies, and he managed to adapt Thai policy to the new situation. Thailand agreed to surrender its territorial gains, established relations with the Nationalist government in China, granted most-favoured nation status to the United States, and also legalized the Communist Party to please the Russians (Batson, 1980).

Conflicts within the government carried over from the prewar period, but they remained confined within the elite, between the followers of Phibun and Pridi on the one hand, and between both groups and a resurgent royalist party on the other. In 1946 Pridi became prime minister. 'Siam' was restored as the country's name, and the government pursued a rather anomalous leftist foreign policy. However, the War Criminals Act passed in 1945 was declared unconstitutional in 1946, pending charges were dropped, and many wartime leaders returned to office. A period of cooperation between Pridi and the royalists ended when Pridi insisted on an elected Senate rather than the appointed body favoured by the royalists and succeeded in packing the Senate with his supporters. The king was murdered in 1946 and Pridi was accused of complicity. In 1947 came a military coup, backed by royalists, demobilized soldiers, and followers of Phibun. In 1948 Phibun returned to power as prime minister, and despite attempted counter-coups by Pridi supporters, he held office until 1957.

The military–royalist government introduced a new constitution with an appointed senate, permission for military officers and civilian bureaucrats to sit in Parliament and hold cabinet office, and increased powers for the king. Pridi supporters in the government and army were retired, and the navy was purged in the aftermath of the counter-coup. Regional protest in the northeast and in the south was crushed, and a number of opposition leaders were murdered or disappeared. Suspected leftists, particularly Chinese with contacts in China, were arrested and occasionally murdered. Having secured its position, the army gradually reduced the power of the royalists. With generous aid from the United States, Phibun encouraged the centralization of the army under Sarit Thanarat. To balance the army Phibun also fostered the expansion of the police under Phao Siriyanond. By 1955–6 the police numbered some 48 000, including an elite corps under Phao's personal control, and actually outnumbered the 45 000 soldiers in the regular army. In 1957 Phibun attempted to secure his position over these two powerful subordinates. Returning to the 'leader' approach he had taken 20 years before, he staged an election featuring himself as a 'Peronist' popular leader, and used Phao's police to organize his campaign, break up opposition rallies, and stuff ballot boxes. On 14 September Sarit responded with a coup which took only one hour. Phibun and Phao fled, and in 1958 Sarit became prime minister (SarDesai, 1994, pp. 169–72; Pasuk and Baker, 1995, ch. 8).

Drawing on the formulations of Wichit Wathakan, an intellectual who had served as an ideologist to governments from the 1930s onwards, Sarit claimed to represent a 'Thai form of democracy'. He justified the appointment of military officers and bureaucrats to serve in Parliament because, he said, 'we work with honesty, scholastic competence, and just decision-making which is not under the influence of any private party and does not have to demonstrate personal heroism for purposes of future elections'. In the tradition of Meiji Japan, Sarit viewed the army as 'the army of the king' and the king in turn as the source of the 'one national spirit', but he insisted that the role of the king was passive. The king was to provide spiritual and moral headship while the government played the active role of determining and implementing policy. The state, said Sarit, consisted of three strata, the government, the bureaucracy, and the people, and it was the function of the government to make policy, of the bureaucracy to implement it, and of the people to accept it (Pasuk and Baker, 1995, pp. 284–5).

All told, since 1932 Thailand has experienced 13 revolutions, 8 constitutions, and over 30 changes of administration. Periods of rule by decree have alternated with experiments in constitutional rule. Military officials have dominated, but they have had to balance alliances among the royalist party, nobility, and senior bureaucrats. Although the forms of government responsible to parliament have generally been retained, the actual operation of government has remained in the hands of the elite. As seen below, economic growth has been rapid, but the Thai revolution has remained 'passive' in Chatterjee's sense, both in the equation of the state with the nation and in the continued dependence on foreign capital, first American and then Japanese.

Colonial Southeast Asia

You would understand better if you could see what is happening here, if you could feel the desire for independence which is in everyone's heart and which no human force can any longer restrain. Even if you come to re-establish a French administration here, it will no longer be obeyed: each village will be a nest of resistance, each former collaborator an enemy and your officials and colonists will themselves ask to leave this atmosphere which they will be unable to breathe.

Vietnamese Emperor Bao Dai to Charles de Gaulle, 1945

Following the First World War, the attempts to reconstruct the international economy, the international depression in agriculture, the model of League of Nations Mandates, and the sporadic and inconsistent attempts by the imperial powers to reform their colonial regimes and introduce some form of self-government, all reinforced the increasing dissatisfaction of colonial peoples and increased their receptiveness to nationalist appeals. Independence movements and uprisings, from the Philippines in the early 1900s to Indonesia in the 1920s and 1930s, can be placed against this background. In the depression of the 1930s, declining revenues led colonial government to cut social services; the 'home' government offered little or no aid.

The nationalist movements, however, were movements of elites. Thus, although 'the Filipinos carry the distinction of being the first people in Asia to successfully launch an anticolonial nationalist movement for independence' (SarDesai, 1994, p. 139), as we saw in Chapter 4, the old gentry families probably improved their position under the United States, and leaders such as Sergio Osmena and Manuel Quezon emerged out of their circles and depended on their support. On continental Southeast Asia, in Cambodia, Laos, and Malaya colonial governments retained native rulers but deprived them of power; there was little education except for members of the elite who went abroad, and the nationalist leadership emerged from these groups. In Myanmar, in contrast, the British had deeply offended the Burmese elite by reducing their country to the status of a province of India. The General Council of Buddhist Associations (the former Young Men's Buddhist Association) led protests against the British, and when reforms were granted in 1921, the GCBA increased its demands and boycotted the subsequent elections. By 1935 suspicion of the British had become so intense that the act which created a separate government – seen by the British as a concession to longstanding Burmese demands – was viewed by Burmese leaders as a plot to ensure perpetual British rule. Saya San, a former leader of the GCBA, led a rebellion in Lower Myanmar in 1935, and numerous parties emerged among the educated intellectuals, all for land reform, restrictions on Indian immigrants and money-lenders, and 'revival' of Burmese-Buddhist traditions.

In Vietnam, members of the Confucian landholding elite passed through the small French educational system and emerged as the leadership of the nationalist movement. Many of the 100 000 Vietnamese who served in France during the First World War also returned to join the nationalists. Young Vietnamese revolutionaries travelled to Japan and to China. Many nationalist organizations emerged in the 1920s, the largest of which was the Viet Nam Quoc Dan Dang (VNQDD, Vietnamese Nationalist Party), modelled on the Chinese Nationalist Party, which adopted Sun Yatsen's 'people's principles' of nationalism, democracy, and socialism.

Ho Chi Minh (one of many aliases) emerged from this milieu. Born in 1890 into a mandarin family, he travelled to London and to Paris. He joined the French socialist party and presented a petition for Vietnamese self-determination to the Versailles conference in 1919. He joined the Communist Party, went to Moscow in 1923, was sent to Canton 1924, and organized a small party of about 250 members, some of whom trained at the Nationalist military academy under Chiang Kaishek. In 1930, Ho united three groups into a single Indochina Communist Party (ICP). Uprisings followed in 1930 and 1931, first by the VNQDD and then by the ICP. The French introduced some reforms with a new monarchy under Prince Bao Dai, but he had no substantial power, and his chief minister Ngo Dinh Diem resigned in 1933.

In Indonesia, nationalist sentiment emerged from the frustration of the *priyayi* aristocrats and the *santri*, the indigenous commercial community who had hoped for opportunities under the 'Ethical Policy' after 1900, but found their ambitions blocked by the Dutch, and by Chinese entrepreneurs, with their greater capital and connections elsewhere in Southeast Asia and China. In 1902, Raden Adjeng Kartini, the daughter of the *priyayi* regent of Japara, founded a school for the daughters of Javanese officials, the inspiration for 'Kartini schools' throughout Java. Her published letters brought her fame among the Dutch, and she became a 'nationalist icon' when she died at age twenty-four in 1904 following childbirth (Kratoska and Batson, 1992, p. 267; Tiwon 1996). One of her associates, Dr Waidin Dudira Usada, founded Boedi Utomo (high endeavour) in 1908. The organization included many graduates of Kartini schools and enjoyed wide support among the *priyayi*. Officially nonpolitical because open opposition to Dutch rule would invite repression, Boedi Utomo advocated Western education to open avenues for individual and national progress, combined with a 'revival' of Javanese culture.

Sarekat Islam (Islamic Association or SI), founded in 1912, had a more economic and therefore anti-Chinese emphasis, and appealed more to *santri* and lower *priyayi*. SI's leader Umar Sayed Tjokroaminoto was a charismatic speaker with a broad appeal to farmers as well as the elite. Sukarno, at the time a young engineer, lived in his house for several years and married his daughter. Umar's aims remained moderate – to promote a commercial spirit among Indonesians, to protect Indonesian merchants against Chinese competition, and to protect Islam against Christian missionaries. SI claimed 2 million members throughout Indonesia by 1919, but avoided overt political activity and concentrated on education and economic issues. The Taman Siswa (garden of pupils) education movement, begun in 1921, advocated a development of 'Indonesian' culture as well as a blend of Indonesian and Western, fostered nationalist consciousness, and created a cadre of educated young people who joined nationalist organizations later. The Dutch introduced some reforms in response to SI demands, but without yielding effective power, and dissatisfaction and SI's heterogeneity led to conflict over goals and methods.

In 1914, the Indies Social Democratic Association (ISDV) had been founded within SI by Henrik Sneevliet, the later leader of the Dutch Communist Party. ISDV's Indonesian leaders Semaun and Tan Malaka insisted that SI should openly advocate political action, the overthrow of Dutch rule, and the establishment of a socialist state, and in 1920 they broke away and founded the Partai Kommunis Indonesia (PKI). In 1921, SI prohibited members from belonging to other organizations and expelled known Communists, and many young SI members moved to the PKI. The growth of the PKI also resulted from Dutch budget cuts in 1921, the discharge of junior (mostly Indonesian) officials, and increased taxes for Indonesians – Indonesians with incomes of 225 guilders paid 10 per cent, while Dutch only paid that rate if their incomes were over 9000 guilders. A survey of arrested Communists showed a literacy rate of 76 per cent among PKI members, compared to the 5 per cent average, and long periods of unemployment despite diplomas from Dutch native schools (Van Niel, 1960, pp. 233–4). The PKI grew to 50 000 members, with affiliated labour organizations. In 1923 a railway strike paralysed Java, and a series of strikes, lockouts, and demonstrations followed, culminating in an attempted revolution in November 1926. However, the movement found little response in the countryside, and was repressed.

In the aftermath of the failed revolution, Sukarno founded the Perserikatan Nasional Indonesia (PNI) on 4 June 1927. The PNI attempted to unite all non-Communist nationalist groups in a 'non-cooperation' movement along the lines of the Indian National Congress. In 1928, a Youth Congress adopted the red and white flag, Bahasa Indonesia ('the Indonesian language'), and the anthem 'Indonesia Raya' ('Greater Indonesia'). The Dutch in turn introduced a new Volksraad in 1925 with 30 Indonesian, 26 Dutch, and 5 'Asiatic' members. They also promised partly elected councils with non-European majorities at the provincial level, but the promise was not fully implemented. In 1936 the Volksraad called for an imperial conference to discuss ways and means of introducing

self-government. Nationalist leaders remained divided. The PNI failed to
convince the more pious Muslim groups. Mohammad Hatta and Sutan
Sjahir formed a 'PNI Baru' (New PNI), and Sukarno joined a rival
'Partindo' (Indonesia Party) founded in 1931 by R. M. Sartono.

The Second World War and the Postwar Era in Southeast Asia

Zero hour is near. Germany is almost beaten, and her defeat will lead to
Japan's. Then the Americans and the Chinese will move into Indochina
while the Gaullists rise against the Japs. The latter may well topple the
French fascists prior to this and set up a military government. . . . Indochina will reduce to anarchy. We shall not need even to seize power, for
there will be no power.

Ho Chi Minh, September 1944

I addressed 50,000 at one meeting, 100,000 at another. Sukarno's face,
not just his name, penetrated the Archipelago. I have the Japanese to
thank for that.

Sukarno, An Autobiography, 1965

There was widespread hostility to the rule of the colonial states by the end
of the 1930s. This hostility was portrayed in later nationalist writings as an
irresistible flood which would have swept the imperialists away, but this is
excessively optimistic. The colonial states had proved very effective in
suppressing dissent. Colonial governments maintained pervasive police
surveillance, continually harassed nationalist leaders and their organizations, and used military force when necessary. The Dutch repressed the
Indonesian uprising in 1926, and 13 000 PKI members were arrested,
imprisoned, and exiled to concentration camps in New Guinea. In turn,
Sukarno and other leaders were arrested and the PNI outlawed in 1930.
In 1932 Hatta and Sjahrir returned from the Netherlands, and joined
Sukarno founding a new Partai Indonesia, but all were arrested in 1933,
and remained in prison until released by the Japanese in 1942. The
Vietnamese uprisings in 1930 and 1931, first by the VNQDD and then
by the ICP, were suppressed by the French police, hundreds were killed,
and hundreds of others arrested. The 1935 Myanmar rebellion was put
down by police and militia units, and Saya San was executed in 1937.
Remaining nationalist leaders in Myanmar joined Gandhi and Congress

in withholding support from the British at the outbreak of war in 1939, and they were promptly imprisoned by the British.

Not all members of the native elites supported the nationalist movements; as seen above many profited under the rule of colonial states. At lower levels, educated natives found their most important source of employment in the growing bureaucratic administrations of the colonial states. And lower still, sons of farming families found employment as soldiers in colonial armies. Support for nationalist movements, though continually renewed, generally remained confined to the urban centres. Unrest in the countryside tended to be sporadic and traditionalist or millenarian (Ileto, 1992). In addition colonial governments adroitly played on the ethnic divisions in their possessions, for instance the employment of Karens and other minorities by the British in the administration of Myanmar. These divisions, and simple greed or economic necessity, also made it possible for police agencies to employ native agents for surveillance and penetration of nationalist organizations. Of course, colonial states sometimes discovered that their native agents were not reliable – the Vietnamese uprising in 1930 began when the military garrison at Yen Bay killed their French officers. On balance, however, the colonial states proved amply capable of maintaining themselves, and with the exception of the United States none of the colonial powers intended to surrender power willingly.

The defeat of the European powers by Japan, and the subsequent collapse of the Japanese occupying forces, provided the opportunity which had been lacking, a chance for would-be native leaders to seize power. It is important to recognize that Southeast Asian elites regarded the war in purely pragmatic terms, and worked first to ensure their own survival and secondly to advance the national, factional, or communal interests which they aimed to lead. The war against Japan was not a crusade for Southeast Asians; their enemy was imperialism. As we saw in Chapter 7 the Japanese occupation brought hardship but did not alter economic structures significantly; similarly the war did not cause major social transformations. Elite groups generally retained power, and individuals and groups who were influential in the postwar period were already powerful prewar. Politically, there was substantial continuity in nationalist leadership. For political leaders, the war provided the opportunity to move towards independence; there was no question that when independence was achieved, these groups would take power in the new states.

The Philippines appears the most straightforward. Quezon died in 1944, the Commonwealth was re-established under Osmena following the Japanese surrender, and independence came on 4 July 1946. Much of central Luzon had fallen under the control of the guerilla People's Anti-Japanese Army (abbreviated as Hukbalahap, and shortened to Huk), a mixture of farmers discontented by Japanese food seizures and inflation, Filipino troops who had refused to surrender, Communist-inspired social revolutionaries, unemployed youths, and professional bandits. The Huks were led by Juis Taruc, and although the movement was diverse, the general thrust was directed against the Filipino landlord class. Many old grudges were settled in the name of resistance; it has been asserted that 'the Huks killed fewer Japanese than they did Filipino landlords' (SarDesai, 1994, p. 194). In the areas they controlled, the Huks seized large estates and redistributed the land to small farmers. Branded simply 'Communist' by the landowning elite, they were deeply suspect to the Americans in the context of the Cold War, civil war in China, and Communist-influenced movements elsewhere in Southeast Asia. In particular, the Americans intended to retain control of their huge military bases at Subic Bay and Clark Air Field, held on 99-year leases from the new government, and saw the Huks as a threat.

Elite families typically had maintained the lowest possible profile during the war, waiting for the Americans to return. Most accommodated themselves to the Japanese occupation; there were few cases of open resistance among the elite, but apart from scattered accusations there was no attempt to pursue collaborators. With independence, well-connected individuals began to manoeuvre for political power. Manuel Roxas, a wealthy landowner who had served the Japanese without breaking his connections with the Americans, was pronounced free of any guilt by American General Douglas MacArthur, received American encouragement to campaign against Osmena, and became president. The regime which emerged was corrupt, and well-connected individuals siphoned much of the American aid intended for reconstruction into their own pockets. There was no social reform, and the Huks, now calling themselves the People's Army of Liberation, continued their insurgency into the early 1950s.

In the context of continued guerilla conflict with the need for armed protection and bitter election battles which determined the distribution of spoils, violence became institutionalized. Osmena's son Sergio, Jr maintained a private army of armed supporters to intimidate his political opponents in the 1950s, and numerous others did as well. Some have argued that Philippine politics has been dominated to the present by 'rent-seeking' family oligarchies able and willing to use violence as they contend for political office and for the favour of the current president. Because 'a president can create vast wealth for a favoured few by granting a *de facto* monopoly or approving low-interest loans . . . interaction between powerful rent-seeking families and a correspondingly weak Philippine state has been synergistic' (McCoy, 1994, pp. 19, 517; McCoy, 1980). Others have argued that the use of violence has not been systemic but exceptional, and have questioned the assumption that elite families function coherently as political factions, but the continuity of elite families, combined with the role of the state and the continued influence of the United States, mark the Philippines revolution as 'passive' in Chatterjee's sense.

Independence for Myanmar also came relatively quickly, but for different reasons. In 1943 the Japanese declared Burma independent. The new Burmese government occupied the administrative machinery left by the British and declared war on the Allies, but was quickly disillusioned by forced labour and requisitions of cattle and rice, the greed of Japanese war contractors, humiliations such as face-slapping of village officials, and symbolic issues such as the use of pagodas as latrines and burning of Buddhist scriptures. A coalition Anti-Fascist People's Freedom League (AFPFL) emerged under army commander Aung San which combined and extended the prewar independence movement. In this case independence would have come in any case. The British had always seen their policy towards Burma as supporting their primary interest in India – and the Indian Army had provided the force to hold Burma. Burma had already been separated from India and promised dominion status before the war. Now, the rise of the Indian national movement made the use of the Indian Army outside of India virtually impossible. In August 1945, British Indian military authorities in fact warned that the Indian Army could not be used to repress a nationalist uprising in Burma because of the effect this would have on Indian public opinion.

A massive campaign of strikes and demonstrations for independence followed the end of the war. The new governor invited Aung San and other non-Communist members of the AFPFL to join his council. They agreed even without a guarantee of independence and repressed the strikes. The Communists, excluded from power, denounced the AFPFL and Aung San as 'lackeys of imperialism'. In turn, the fear of a Communist revolt was used by the AFPFL to force the British to promise independence. The British requested that Aung San form a council of ministers in October 1946. Elections in January 1947 saw a complete victory for the AFPFL, in particular over the Communists. However, in July Aung San and seven other leaders were murdered. His successor, the devout Buddhist U Nu, led the country to independence on 4 January 1948, but did not command the confidence of any of the main factions contending for power. In addition to the split between the army leaders and the Communists, the government faced demands by minority peoples for self-government or independence. A Communist uprising in March 1948 was followed by a revolt of the Karen National Defense Organization which threatened the capital at one point. Communists and separatists remained in control of some 10 per cent of the country until the late 1980s (Taylor, 1980; Steinberg, 1987, p. 397; SarDesai, 1994, p. 221).

In Indochina in March 1945 the Japanese seized power from the French colonial administration, who had been moving to a 'Free French' position for fear of being too closely identified with the Japanese and weakening their case for retaining Indochina after the war. The Japanese encouraged Cambodian King Narodom Sihanouk to proclaim independence. They also told the Laotian king to declare independence; he refused, and they turned to a prince, who did. In Vietnam, eliminating the French in effect began the Vietnamese revolution, though this was not the intent of the Japanese. In Cambodia and Laos the native elite were able to contain popular unrest and work out arrangements with foreigners before, during, and after the war. In Vietnam, in contrast, the previous four decades had produced a revolutionary intelligentsia, a land-poor peasantry, a propertyless class of workers, and the eventual leaders of the revolution, who had developed their strategies and tactics in the 1930s. Significantly, the non-Communist VNQDD party structure had been destroyed by French repression, but the ICP had survived, helped by its tighter discipline and by the French Popular Front amnesty for political prisoners. In the countryside the Communists gained support because of their uncompromising demand for independence and specific policies directed towards subsistence needs and reform within the rural community (Marr, 1980; Luong, 1992; SarDesai, 1994, pp. 176–7).

In Cambodia the Japanese had also supported a Free Khmer movement led by commoners. When the French returned Sihanouk was satisfied with a grant of local autonomy within the French union. Then in 1953, after repressing dissident groups, Sihanouk suddenly demanded independence, a claim which aroused sympathy particularly in the United States, and the French devolved authority to him. In Laos the prince told the returning French he intended to remain independent, but the king deposed him. The king in turn was overthrown by the Lao Issarak (Free Lao) movement of virtually all the Western-educated elite including members of the royal family and nobility. They declared independence, but were defeated by the French in 1946. Lao Issarak split; the Pathet Lao

(Land of the Lao) was formed in 1949 in Vietnam, and the Laotian Communist Party followed in 1952. In 1954, the Pathet Lao controlled two provinces, and Laos was used as a staging area by the Viet Minh – the strategic importance of Dien Bien Phu was its position close to the Laotian border and supply routes. Laos became independent with the French withdrawal from Vietnam; the 'special position' of the Pathet Lao in their two provinces was recognized, and they were supposed to dissolve and participate in a new national government.

Ho Chi Minh, returning from the Soviet Union, convened an ICP Central Committee meeting in southern China in May 1941. The small Communist party by itself had no hope of winning power, and so an organization known as the Viet Minh (an abbreviation for Vietnam Independence Brotherhood League) was established to bring all groups together for immediate independence. Vo Nguyen Giap became the military leader of guerilla forces in mountainous regions. Ho was detained by the Chinese Nationalist government for two years, but was released at Chiang Kaishek's orders to lead the resistance against Japanese–French administration. When the Japanese deposed the French in March 1945, the well-organized Viet Minh spread out from areas which they already controlled, and by August had become a presence in virtually every village in Vietnam. With the Japanese surrender on 14 August the Viet Minh formed a National Liberation Committee with Ho as president and a nationalist programme. They occupied Hanoi, Bao Dai abdicated in favour of a provisional government, and the Democratic Republic of Vietnam was proclaimed. In the meantime the Allies had decided to restore French rule and had requested Nationalist China to occupy Vietnam north of the sixteenth parallel and Britain south of it. However, the Chinese, British, and American forces arrived in September to be confronted with a *fait accompli*. On the other hand the Viet Minh were strongest in the north, and weakest in the south, where by 1949 some of their earlier allies were siding with the French or neutral (Marr, 1980).

The Democratic Republic of Vietnam of course did not receive international recognition. The Chinese army, 180 000 strong, arrived in the north in early September, accompanied by copious amounts of worthless Chinese wartime currency and a 'disorderly crowd' of camp followers. They treated northern Vietnam 'as if it were a conquered country' and 'rampaged the countryside in a campaign of loot, plunder, and rape'. The British forces in Saigon released the French from prison and gave them arms. Ho, arguing that 'it is better to sniff the French dung for a while than to eat China's all our lives', dissolved the ICP, offered to share power with the VNQDD, and signed an agreement with the French: French troops would replace the Chinese forces, in return for recognition of the DRV as a 'free state... forming part of the Indochinese Federation and the French Union' and referendum votes in Cochin China to determine whether the south would join the north, and whether French troops should be withdrawn (Steinberg, 1987, p. 359; SarDesai, 1994, pp. 179–81).

The French were determined to reassert control (see Lewis, 1995). They hedged and then reneged on their guarantees, and on 23 November 1946 the cruiser *Suffren* bombarded Haiphong and killed 6000 people, the signal for general hostilities. The DRV army of 40 000 deployed into the countryside and opened a multi-front war. In 1949 France created a Republic of Vietnam, which along with Laos and Cambodia was to remain within the French union and firmly under French control. In the emerging Cold War world, the United States and Britain recognized the French creation while the Soviet Union and China recognized the DRV. The Viet Minh were supplied from China, and the French from the United States. The war produced blunders and heavy losses on both sides. The French were not good at guerilla tactics, and the Viet Minh were poor at conventional pitched battles. Finally in 1953 the French attempted to lure the Viet Minh into a last major battle at Dien Bien Phu, but Giap's forces surrounded them and cut them off. United States Secretary of State John Foster Dulles saw nuclear weapons as the only way to prevent defeat, but would not act without the British, and they refused because of the danger of Soviet retaliation and another world war.

Dien Bien Phu fell in 1954 just before an international conference in Geneva, and that should have sealed Vietnam's independence, but it did not. The French regime ended, but the Viet Minh, under pressure from the Russians and Chinese, who were then in favour of 'peaceful coexistence' with the West, accepted a division along the seventeenth parallel pending elections to be held in 1956. In the south a new government under Ngo Dinh Diem emerged with American support and enjoying 'the best possible American political thinking', in the words of CIA adviser Edward Lansdale (Steinberg, 1987, p. 361). Diem, a member of the Confucian elite, found any opposition intolerable as it called into question his moral superiority as ruler; the police state he established soon had incarcerated tens of thousands of political prisoners of all shades of opinion. He himself died in a coup in 1963. In 1959 the Communists began a series of 'synchronized uprisings'; in 1960 the southern Viet Minh was restored under the new name of National Liberation Front, and by

1962 they controlled or 'influenced' two-thirds of the villages in the south. To forestall a Communist victory, the United States began direct involvement, and by 1967 there were 525 000 United States troops serving in Vietnam. The resulting destruction disrupted the southern NLF, but the South Vietnam government could not survive without American military support and collapsed in 1975 when that support was withdrawn.

Ho Chi Minh had died in 1969, and the general secretary of the Vietnamese Communist Party, Le Duan, came to exercise a decisive influence over the Soviet-style Politburo. The party 'bore a striking resemblance to the elderly male Confucian oligarchy that had traditionally ruled Vietnam' and made up only 3 per cent of the population in 1976. Its members were typically far from young, and despite its official role as 'proletarian vanguard' fewer than 10 per cent were workers. In addition, only 17 per cent were women. Finally, during the 1980s, another aspect of the older elite culture re-emerged, as relatives of Le Duan and another powerful Politburo member, Le Duc Tho, came to occupy the strategic offices just below the Politburo (Steinberg, 1987, p. 367).

In Malaya and Singapore the Chinese community had become more cohesive and encapsulated because of more equal sex ratios in the prewar period. As in Thailand, many had come to consider themselves more 'Chinese' than before and supported China against Japan in the 1930s. Hurt by the depression, many had left the urban areas and became squatters, where some had adopted the Communist ideology. As seen in Chapter 7 the Japanese considered the Chinese as their enemies and treated them exceptionally harshly. They arrested and executed thousands in 1942, forced the Chinese community to pay a $50 million indemnity to atone for 'crimes' against Japan, and forcibly settled further thousands of urban Chinese in the countryside to increase food production. The Chinese predominated in the Malay People Anti-Japanese Army (MPAJA) guerilla struggle, but they as well as the Japanese requisitioned food from the Malay farming villages. In the prewar period rice production only covered 40 per cent of consumption and was paid for with rubber and tin exports, which had now ceased, and their activities therefore reinforced Malay hostility towards the Chinese.

The Japanese occupation was frankly imperialist, and intended to last forever. The Japanese considered Malays not ready for independence because of their 'political immaturity' and only ordered preparations for independence in July 1945, a month before Japan's own surrender. However, the Japanese did recruit Malays into the police because they did not trust the Chinese. They also favoured Malays in elite track schools where cadres of Japanese teachers trained students in the proper 'spirit' (*seishin*: 'nobody cries in pain in this school!'), self-reliance, Asian solidarity, and anti-Western and therefore anti-colonial attitudes. Most Malay civil servants were re-employed, though at reduced salaries, and they were required to engage in agricultural activities, which injured their sense of status but forged links with commoners which proved important in the independence movement. The Japanese also retained the sultanates. They had wanted to limit the sultans to a religious role and denied their theoretical claim to sovereignty because they intended to incorporate Malaya into their empire, but they were forced to change, and in effect returned to the British situation.

Previously, Malays had shown little national consciousness. The British attempted to hold the Malays in their villages, freeze social relations, and cut them off from the other communities and from the outside world. The Malays were to grow rice in their villages, while Indians and Chinese worked in the export sectors producing rubber and tin. The Japanese differed from the British in the thoroughness and completeness of their mobilization. All segments of society were affected. The Japanese demanded increased food production to meet the severe shortages, they demanded labour, they demanded service in military and paramilitary units, they demanded increased production of raw materials. And, as in the schools, they demanded that Malays absorb the Japanese 'spirit'. They aimed to Japanize Malays and create a desire to 'unite with Japan' and 'share hardships' with Japan to create an 'Asia for the Asians'. In effect, however, they awoke a 'new consciousness', a more broadly based desire for independence (Akashi, 1980).

At end of war, the MPAJA emerged as victors and moved against Malay collaborators. A year of racial violence ensued to mid-1946, and then the Malayan Union issue focused Malay hostilities on the British. The British attempted to create a new Malay Union with common citizenship. Malays interpreted this as reduction in their power and organized the United Malay National Organization (UMNO). The British scrapped the plan and in 1948 a new Federation of Malaya restricted citizenship to Malays. Malay aristocrats who had become civil servants under the British formed the leadership of the UMNO, and the first three prime ministers came from the aristocracy. It became common for influential figures with aristocratic pedigrees to straddle the public and private spheres as company directors, trust managers, and officials of public corporations, earning themselves the ironic title of 'administocracy' (Jomo, 1986).

The former strategic reasons for holding Malaya had disappeared with the British withdrawal from India and Myanmar, but the 'emergency' lasting from 1948 to 1960 delayed independence. In June 1948 the Malayan Communist Party (MCP) had risen in revolt. The 8 to 10 000 guerrillas were overwhelmingly ethnic Chinese, supported by possibly 500 000 squatters. The MCP did occupy some districts, but received no support from the Malay population, and no outside help. Combined police, intelligence, and military operations had eliminated any serious threat from the MCP by 1954, although some 2000 guerillas were still in existence on the Thai–Malay border in the late 1980s. The British won Malay support with a commitment to independence, won many Chinese with the introduction of a new organization to represent Chinese interests, and laid out 600 fenced 'new villages' to contain the squatters.

Although the British remained until 1960, officially power in Malaya passed to a Malay-dominated Alliance Party government under Abdul Rahman in 1957, under a constitution which gave power to the Malay sultans and made Malay the official language – clearly leaving the Chinese (36 per cent of the population) and Indians (11 per cent) at a disadvantage. In 1963 a new Federation of Malaysia included Malaya, Sarawak and Sabah (non-Malay, but Muslim), and Singapore (75 per cent Chinese). However, the ambitious head of the Singapore government, Lee Kuan Yew, aimed to unite all the non-Malay elements in the federation and then secure control of the federation government. To forestall this threat Abdul Rahman expelled Singapore from the federation in 1965.

The effects of the short Japanese occupation of Indonesia were extensive and lasting. The Japanese victories, especially the fall of Singapore, had a profound psychological impact, and Indonesians at first received the Japanese enthusiastically. The conquest brought no destruction; the Dutch abandoned the major cities following the fall of Singapore, and in Aceh (Sumatra) and Gorontalo and Bone (Sulawesi) the Indonesians themselves 'liberated' cities which they handed over to the Japanese. Japanese authorities promoted natives to higher administrative positions than they could have attained under the Dutch. They also drafted young men into the army, which numbered more than a million by 1945.

The schools reopened after six months, and as in Malaya the Japanese teachers attempted to create a new identity amongst their pupils through the inculcation of Japanese 'spirit' (*seishin*) and a brutal assault on Western colonial values – as one teacher said, 'I know how lazy the Westerners are, and the laziness they have taught you for hundreds of years is going to be wiped out' (Reid, 1980, p. 24). Elite tracks for the brightest students encouraged self-esteem. In the officer training programmes in the army self-esteem passed over into arrogance, as young Indonesian officers modelled their attitudes and behaviour on the exaggerated *samurai* posturing of the occupation army.

The Japanese introduced neighbourhood organizations patterned on those in Japan, with ten households in each group and ten groups in a district, for surveillance and control. They also created a national women's association (Fujinkai) based on the Japanese system, centrally controlled with neighbourhood branches. The system was not complete; the Fujinkai existed largely on paper, and in the neighbourhood of Yogyakarta, Java, studied by Norma Sullivan, there was neither a branch of the Fujinkai nor apparently any individual members (Sullivan, 1995, p. 59). However, the Japanese model was retained and extended by the new nationalist government. Until reforms introduced in 1989 altered the system, neighborhood associations (*rukun tetangga*) made up of groups of ten households formed the basic unit of local government in the urban areas of Indonesia. They were combined into district (*rukun kampung*) units with 'functional sections' with universal compulsory membership based on age, sex, and marital status. The youth and women's sections, which served as channels for national associations, are particularly reminiscent of the Japanese model.

In the cultural sphere, the break with the past was sharp and decisive. In the 1920s and 1930s Indonesian literature reflected Dutch influence over the native elite. Most writing was in High Malay, as opposed to the Bahasa of commerce, and was intended as reading for the class of subaltern clerks. Learning Dutch was discouraged – it was considered too difficult, and of course knowledge of Dutch lessened the difference between ruler and ruled – but nevertheless Dutch was the official language. The Japanese eliminated Dutch. Indonesian became the official language in 1942, and Dutch was wiped out, more completely than any conceivable independent Indonesian government could have done. In October 1942 the Japanese established an Indonesian Language Committee. They intended to replace it with Japanese, but Japanese was still a foreign language in the schools, and 'for the present' they used the Malay which had been the language of the nationalists since 1928 and became the basis of Bahasa Indonesia. The Indonesians had three and a half years to develop a 'national' language. The committee opened new areas where previously only Dutch had been used, sponsored new textbooks in all fields, and in October 1945 published a dictionary. A Centre for Monitoring and Development of Language remained as a legacy of the wartime period.

The development of a new language had an important and lasting impact on the creation of a new literature. In addition, a new history played a key role in the creation of a new 'national' consciousness. Nationalist historians portrayed a glorious pre-colonial past, followed by three and a half 'dark centuries' of Dutch rule, punctuated by heroic resistance to Dutch oppression. This resistance in turn was seen as laying the basis for the emergence of a single, unified Indonesian 'nation'. Texts written during the war remained standard for the next twenty years. As part of their anti-colonial campaign, the Japanese encouraged public manifestations of this new historical consciousness. Streets were renamed in honour of national heroes, ceremonies were held in honour of historical persons and events, and in September 1944 the national flag and national anthem were made mandatory at public functions.

Many Japanese quickly wore out their welcome, and on some outer islands there were gruesome atrocities. In general, the Japanese occupation attempted to encourage 'religious' organizations while repressing 'political'. Thus SI was banned, but the Islamic Federation was used to aid in recruiting for the army and requisitioning food supplies. But the leaders of the Islamic Federation became exasperated with the Japanese, as the requirement to bow towards Tokyo and recognize the divinity of the emperor offended Muslims, and the harsh treatment of farmers alienated the countryside. Indonesia was split into three divisions, and as we saw in Chapter 7, this damaged the economy severely. There were significant policy differences as well. On the crucial island of Java, General Imamura Hitoshi decided that a pragmatic 'soft' policy, emphasizing positive benefits to the local population, would build on the initial goodwill. He was opposed by other Japanese leaders, who insisted that 'a forceful administration like that in Singapore is the way to make the coloured people obey us'. But Java contained most of the prominent prewar nationalist leaders, and since Java alone was permitted to develop an island-wide leadership, when regional leaders who had been sponsored by the Japanese were named residents or governors of their areas after the declaration of independence, the Javanese leadership under Sukarno and Hatta became the accepted 'national' leadership.

The Japanese freed Sukarno and other nationalists and established Putera, a puppet political organization, and a government headed by Sukarno and Hatta. Nationalists, and possibly Sukarno and Hatta personally, also supported a new underground resistance movement organized by Sjahrir and Amir Sjarifuddin. The Japanese became suspicious and abolished Putera, but they kept Sukarno and Hatta as heads of government to secure as much cooperation as possible. Nationalist leaders played an ambivalent and potentially dangerous role. Under the Dutch, nationalists could say what they liked, as long as they were ineffective – any party which developed a mass following was repressed. Under the Japanese, nationalist leaders were restricted in what they could say, but they had a captive audience, often trucked in from surrounding areas by the Japanese army. As seen in the passage quoted at the beginning of this section, Sukarno recognized that these huge rallies organized by the Japanese had the effect of identifying him personally as 'our leader'. In addition, he and Hatta were accepted by the Indonesian elite during the Japanese occupation because of the very dangerous nature of their exposed position.

With the promise of independence in September 1944 Sukarno and his colleagues emerged as the leadership which would take over government. The Japanese attempted to grant independence to Indonesia in the summer of 1945, but Sukarno did not want to accept independence from them, and declared independence instead. However, the declaration was drafted in the house of Japanese Admiral Maeda, with representatives of both Japanese and Indonesian groups present, a controversial point, because the returning Dutch denounced the republic as a Japanese creation, so Indonesian leaders denied the Japanese influence (Reid, 1980). In 1941 the Dutch government in exile had promised an 'imperial conference' to discuss Indonesian self-government at the end of the war, but they returned in 1945 determined to stay. The Dutch intended to use Indonesia's resources for the reconstruction of the Netherlands – as Belgium was using revenues from the sale of uranium mined in the Congo to the United States. There were divisions within the nationalist movement, as some rejected any compromise with those who had collaborated with the Japanese, and the Islamic party denounced the Marxist-oriented socialists. Communists attempted to overthrow the government in June 1946 by kidnapping cabinet members, and attempted another revolt in 1948, which was suppressed.

All factions opposed the restoration of Dutch rule. The British released 200 000 Dutch prisoners of war, and the Dutch recruited soldiers among the native Christian minority. The islands divided into those areas controlled by the nationalists and those occupied by the Dutch with the aid of Allied troops. Negotiations led to an agreement in 1947 for a union of the United States of Indonesia within a larger union of Dutch colonies. The USI would have United Nations membership, but the Dutch would remain the only sovereign power. Accusations of bad faith and violations of the agreement followed. The Dutch then launched a 'police action', an attack on Nationalist territories. Intervention by the United Nations led to a cease-fire resolution by the Security Council in August 1947 and planned plebiscites. Further fighting and another Dutch 'police action' ensued. In January 1949 Indian prime minister Jawaharlal Nehru convened an Asian Conference on Indonesia in New Delhi, which denied the Dutch refuelling facilities for their aircraft and shipping. The Dutch also faced further pressure from the United Nations and especially from the United States, and finally yielded to the demand for independence on 27 December 1949.

The process of the creation of a new national community proceeded through the occupation and the war of independence. The Japanese did not contribute anything positive to the formation of the emerging national symbol system, but they did provide military training, created opportunities for publicity for nationalist leaders, and encouraged anti-Western sentiments. An interesting difference from the prewar situation is the high degree of unity shared by the nationalist leadership on their preferred 'values'. Most SI members had been agreed on the need for modernization, self-government, and socialism. They shared a hostility to 'capitalism' because it was considered 'sinful', because it was 'European' and 'Chinese', and because they considered it responsible for Indonesia's miseries. Socialism, they said, seemed to suit the Indonesian temperament of a 'group spirit' (*gotong rojong*), which they claimed was the 'traditional' outlook favouring mutual cooperation as against Western individualism.

In a speech in 1945 Sukarno presented his 'five principles' or *pancasila*: nationalism, internationalism, the principle of consent, social justice, and belief in God. These had the effect of staking out broad claims for the state. They also covered over the divisions between pious and nominal Muslims on the one hand and between secularist radicals and Marxists and anti-Marxists on the other. Nationalism, he said, meant the establishment of one national state 'based on the entity of one Indonesian soil from the tip of Sumatra to Irian'. Internationalism meant the mutual recognition of independent nations. Consent, representation, and consultation formed the proper basis of the state. Social justice promised political-economic democracy, but the state clearly would act as mediator between contending groups. And finally the right of every Indonesian to believe in their own God in effect limited the competing claims of Muslim religious leaders.

Professor Supomo, the leading judicial official on Java during the Japanese occupation and a leader in drafting the 1945 constitution, delivered a speech in May 1945 to the Body to Investigate Measures for the Preparation of Indonesian Independence which encapsulated the emerging consensus. Supomo thought Western individualism and liberalism 'invariably gave rise to imperialism and exploitation'. In contrast, he argued,

> The inner spirit and spiritual structure of the Indonesian people is characterized by the ideal of the unity of life, the unity *kawulo-gusti*, that is of the outer and the inner world, or the macrocosmos and microcosmos, of the people and their leaders. All men as individuals, every group or grouping of men in a society... is considered to have its own place and its own obligations according to the law of nature, the whole being aimed at achieving spiritual and physical balance... So it is clear that if we want to establish an Indonesian state in accordance with the characteristic features of Indonesian society, it must be based on an integralist state philosophy, on the idea of a state which is united with all its people, which transcends all groups in every field. (Reid, 1980, p. 26)

Accordingly, the draft constitution gave strong powers to the president, no rights to individuals except education and freedom of religion, and asserted that 'the economy shall be organized as a common endeavour based upon the principle of the family system'. That legacy persisted in subsequent constitutions. Added to this of course was the fact of widespread military mobilization, not only in its direct impact on society, but in the process of myth-making. It was easy for army officers to take credit for defeating the Dutch, and to move beyond this and envision the army as the epitome of the 'integralist state' and the 'unity of the outer and the inner world'. That legacy has persisted as well in subsequent disputes over the content of Indonesia's 'imagined community' (see Van Langenberg, 1993).

9

ECONOMICS, POLITICS AND ASIAN DEVELOPMENT IN THE POSTWAR WORLD

> ... despite the sloganeering about 'winds of change', 'the awakening East', or 'the revolution of rising expectations', and despite, too, the real possibility of a totalitarian triumph in Djakarta, there is no evidence that the major outlines of the Indonesian pattern of adaptation, of the plurality of diverse cultural cores which compose it, are likely to alter in the foreseeable future.
>
> Clifford Geertz, 1963

Through the 1950s and 1960s it was not clear that the economies of East and Southeast Asia would grow rapidly; on the contrary, they were universally regarded as part of the 'underdeveloped' world. The impact of the war and political instability placed a cloud even over Japan. Elsewhere war and civil war continued. The victory of Mao Zedong and the Communists in 1949 brought peace, but also cut mainland China off from the international economy. The defeat of the Nationalists transplanted their corrupt government to Taiwan. The division of Korea led to a new war and new dictatorships. As seen in Chapter 8, for Southeast Asia the end of the war against Japan merely opened the way for the wars of independence, the Indonesian war against the Dutch, the Malayan insurgency against the British, and the Vietnamese war first against the French and then against the Americans. The Vietnamese war involved Laos and spread into Cambodia, devastating that country as well. Conflict over the form of 'Malaysia' led to the expulsion of Singapore, and conflict within Indonesia to a massacre of 'Communists' and Chinese, and another dictatorship. None of the new regimes appeared likely to foster rapid development.

In the background the world economy entered an unprecedented upswing, but this too was not obvious until the late 1960s (see Tipton and Aldrich, 1987b). In the 1950s economics took a back seat to politics. The diplomatic division between 'East' and 'West', the superpower confrontation between the Soviet Union and the United States, and the overarching sense of competition between totalitarianism and democracy, all combined to colour debate over the possible consequences of different modes of economic organization. The gulf between socialism and capitalism appeared unbridgeable, and any regime which announced itself as socialist encountered the implacable hostility of the United States but gained little from the Soviet Union. Western capital withdrew from these 'unstable' areas, cutting them off from new technologies and managerial expertise, leading to widely expressed concern that limited economic development would be swamped by rapid increases in population.

Japan: Occupation and After

To Our good and loyal subjects: After pondering deeply the general trends of the world and the actual conditions obtaining in Our Empire today, We have decided to effect a settlement... to pave the way for a grand peace for all the generations to come by enduring the unendurable and suffering what is insufferable.

Recorded radio broadcast by Emperor Hirohito, 14 August 1945

In 1945, Japan lay in ruins, with 3 million dead, 5 million demobilized soldiers, and further millions of refugees from the lost empire. Three quarters of the merchant marine had been sunk, and Allied bombing had destroyed one quarter of all the buildings in Japan, along with perhaps one third of all industrial machinery. In addition, the Allies intended that Japan's unconditional surrender would be followed by a military occupation to ensure 'that Japan will not again become a menace to the peace and security of the world'. The official directive continued that this would be accomplished through the 'abolition of militarism and ultra-nationalism ... disarmament and demilitarization ... strengthening of democratic tendencies and processes in governmental, economic, and social institutions', and finally 'encouragement and support of liberal political tendencies' (Beasley, 1990, p. 214).

Authority rested firmly in the hands of the Americans, and power firmly in the hands of the American commander General Douglas MacArthur. He was assisted by a large number of military and civilian advisers, most of whom had no previous experience in Japan, and virtually none of whom spoke the language. They tended to recommend the adoption of institutions and programmes which were familiar from their own experience. Because they themselves often disagreed, and because they were forced to rely on the existing Japanese bureaucracy to implement their plans, the results frequently diverged from their intentions. Specialist scholars still debate the extent to which the 'new' Japan created by the American occupation in fact differed from the 'old' Japan the Americans hoped to replace.

Militarily, the occupation authorities certainly succeeded. The Japanese armed forces were destroyed. Twenty-eight leading politicians and 20 senior military commanders were tried for war crimes, and nine condemned to death. Several thousand individual junior officers and soldiers stood trial for specific atrocities, and many were executed or sentenced to prison terms. Around 200 000 individuals were 'purged', in that they were banned from further participation in public life. The capstone of the demilitarization process was embodied in Article 9 of the new constitution, which stated that 'the Japanese people forever renounce war' and that Japan would maintain no 'land, sea, and air forces' or any other 'war potential'.

Politically, the Americans made a conscious decision to rule through existing Japanese institutions in order to minimize the number of troops required to maintain order. MacArthur insisted that this must include maintaining the emperor as head of state, and he rejected demands that Hirohito be tried as a war criminal. Instead, the emperor publicly renounced his divine status, and Article 1 of the constitution declared him to be 'the symbol of the state and of the unity of the people, deriving his position from the will of the people in whom resides sovereign power'. The 'feudalistic' peerage was abolished, and the House of Peers replaced by an elected upper house. The Home Ministry was abolished and government powers decentralized. The judiciary was made independent under a new Supreme Court, which was also charged with protecting the basic rights written into the constitution – notably the provision for full equality between women and men.

The purge of former political leaders weakened conservatives relative to socialists and Communists, many of whom the Americans had freed from prison. The socialists won a plurality in 1947 and formed a coalition government, but were forced to implement a severe deflationary policy dictated by the Americans and bore the blame when Occupation authorities banned a general strike planned in protest. They lost office after only six months (see Seiyama, 1989). The left divided, and the conservative party, the Liberal Democrats, came to office. They were to rule continuously until 1993, but this could not be seen at the time, and their hold on power seemed precarious. They pressed through a peace treaty and a security treaty with the United States directed against the Soviet Union and the new People's Republic of China, but only over violent opposition, including a riot in the Diet chamber when opposition members attempted to seize the speaker's podium. A revision of the 'purge' regulations extended their scope to include left-wing radicals and allowed the government to review individual cases. Many purged conservative leaders returned to office, and some 22 000 socialists and Communists lost their jobs. The conservatives also undid many of the democratizing and decentralizing reforms. Local governments had not been given the power to levy taxes, and central agencies recaptured government functions one after another – thus, for instance, in 1951 most local police forces came under a new rural police agency.

Economically, the occupation authorities had abolished the *zaibatsu* and broken 83 companies into smaller units, which were intended to compete under the terms of the 1945 Antimonopoly Law modelled on American antitrust legislation. In 1947, a Law for the Elimination of Excessive Concentration of Economic Power envisaged the dissolution of an additional 323 companies. Further laws guaranteed minimum working conditions and provided for health and accident insurance. Unions were legalized and given the right to strike, and by 1948 there were 34 000 unions with nearly 7 million members, more than 40 per cent of the industrial labour force. Agricultural landlords were forced to sell their land above a certain small minimum to the government at artificially low prices, in order that the government in turn could sell it to the previous tenants on favourable terms. The government purchased some 1.8 million *chô* (1 *chô* = approximately 1 hectare) of land from 2.3 million landlords, and sold it to 4.7 million tenants. The share of land farmed by tenants dropped from 40 per cent before the war to 10 per cent.

However, under the Liberal Democrats the *zaibatsu* quickly re-emerged, although more loosely organized than before. Of the so-called 'big six', Mitsubishi, Mitsui and Sumitomo descended from the old Meiji *zaibatsu*, while Fuji, Dai-ichi and Sanwa were descendants of 'new' or 'second rank' *zaibatsu*. As horizontal alliances, they were held together by presidents' committees, cross shareholdings, interlocking directorships, and close connections to a single leading bank. The government applied the 1947 law to only 18 corporations, allowed purged members of *zaibatsu* families to return to public life, ended the prohibition on the use of their old names and trademarks, and drastically weakened the Antimonopoly Law in revisions passed in 1949 and 1953 (Sumiya, 1989). Meanwhile the labour movement was severely weakened by the 'red purge', new laws restricting 'subversive activities', the repression of several large strikes by the police, and prohibition of strikes by civil servants, workers in public enterprises, and employees of local governments.

At the peak of the new political system, the emperor reigned successfully as a constitutional monarch until his death in 1989 (Large, 1992). However, though some observers admired the capacity of the Liberal Democrats to adapt themselves to change (Curtis, 1988), many others saw Japanese democracy as a façade, behind which corrupt deals were done among powerful interest groups (Woronoff, 1986). Campaigning in Japan's large multi-member constituencies was expensive, and 70 per cent of the Liberal Democratic Party's income was reputed to come from big business sources (Sumiya, 1989). Japan was originally peripheral to United States plans, and intended to become a 'Switzerland of Asia', while China played the role of major United States ally in Asia. The defeat of the Nationalists in China and the outbreak of the Korean War led American leaders to view Japan as a major bastion against communism in East Asia, which led in turn to American acquiescence for the political and economic measures taken by the Liberal Democrats.

As for the new economic system, recovery to prewar levels of output was followed by an inflationary boom during the Korean War, and then by a severe recession in 1953 and 1954. Although Japan's direct military spending was limited to the compromise figure of 1 per cent of GNP, the expenses of supporting the occupation forces and American bases laid a heavy burden on the economy (Seiyama, 1989, p. 41). The land reform was a radical change, but it created an intensely conservative class of inefficient small farmers whose votes were critical to the Liberal Democrats, and whose interests had to be protected through tariffs and expensive subsidy programmes. In industry, the reimposition of monopolies controlled by the *zaibatsu* seemed likely to inhibit technological change. Low wages and low levels of living limited the domestic market. Japan's domestic coal resources were nearly exhausted. The Cold War cut Japanese industries off from China, formerly their most important source of raw materials and their largest foreign market. To pay for imported energy and raw materials Japan would have to export, but in the crucial United States market, 'made in Japan' was a joking synonym for 'shoddy'. Therefore, when the economy recovered strongly in 1956, there was no reason to suspect that this was the beginning of the famous 'period of high-speed growth' which would last until 1973.

China: The People's Republic and Mao

Let a hundred flowers bloom together, let a hundred schools of thought contend.

Hundred Flowers Campaign slogan, May 1956–May 1957

Study Chairman Mao's writings, follow his teachings and act according to his instructions.

Lin Piao, *Quotations from Chairman Mao Tse-tung*, 1966, frontispiece

Having defeated the Nationalists, the leaders of the new People's Republic faced the problem of establishing control, especially in the south and southwest. Initially, serving government officials (some 2 million, compared to at most 750 000 Communist cadres) were left in their offices. Inflation was reduced by seizing all banks, by establishing national trading corporations in all commodities, and most importantly by paying salaries in 'market-basket' terms, calculating amounts not in money but in terms of specified amounts of basic commodities. This made salaries independent of inflation, so although prices continued to rise by some 15 per cent annually, most urban wage earners did not suffer. General relief at the end of war turned to euphoria when the soldiers of the victorious People's Liberation Army, instead of raping and looting, devoted themselves to cleaning streets, repairing public works, and improving sanitation, and when the new authorities moved to round up and 're-educate' opium addicts, prostitutes, petty criminals, and beggars.

Mass campaigns operating through new national organizations for workers, youth and women mobilized support for the government's goals, identified actual and potential opponents, and equally importantly revealed especially devoted or talented supporters (Bennett, 1976; Teiwes, 1979). The 'three antis' campaign of 1951–2 against corruption, waste, and 'bureaucratism' aimed to stamp out inefficiency. Party membership increased from 2.7 million in 1947 to 6.1 million in 1953, and as qualified party cadres became available, the old officials were systematically replaced. The decision to intervene in the Korean War in 1950 proved costly. More than 2.3 million soldiers fought against the Americans and South Koreans, and casualties were heavy. The effort of maintaining these forces (about two-thirds of the army) in the field drained resources which could have been used at home. However, domestically the war provided the government with an opportunity to pursue its aim of reorganizing society along socialist lines under the cover of another campaign to 'resist America, aid Korea'.

Although initially the new government did not disturb private business interests, capitalists clearly had no place in a socialist society. Along with the 'three antis' and 'resist America, aid Korea', the 'five antis' campaign attacked capitalists, who were denounced for bribery, tax evasion, theft of state assets, cheating in their dealings with their workers and suppliers, and 'stealing of state economic intelligence'. The net was wide enough that any employer could be prosecuted. Eventually the government nationalized and collectivized all organizations – the term 'corporation' was limited to state enterprises and foreign businesses, but even these had no legal basis until the reforms following 1978. Because of the large role the Nationalist government had played in the economy, nationalization did not represent much change in the heavy industrial sphere; overwhelmingly, the firms taken over by the government were individual proprietorships, family firms, or small partnerships (Kirby, 1995), and for millions of men and women the change was abrupt and painful.

In the countryside a parallel process of land reform extended from the north and northeast into the south and southwest. The campaign aimed to eliminate landordism and redistribute land to poor peasants and landless labourers. As we have seen in previous chapters, however, there were many gradations and interconnections among farmers. The Land Reform Law of 1950 demonstrated the difficulties of distinguishing among 'landlords' (those who depended mainly on rent for their living), 'rich peasants' (those who hired one or more year-labourers), 'middle peasants' (those who supplied most of the labour on their farms themselves), 'poor peasants' (those who worked for others, usually as day-labourers, in addition to cultivating their own or rented land), and 'agricultural labourers' (those who worked for others for their living). The law specified calculations for the percentage of income derived from 'exploitation' to make the crucial distinction between 'rich' and 'middle' peasants, between those who would lose their land and those who would keep it – the dividing line of 15 per cent in the civil war period was increased to 25 per cent after 1950. The measures were sometimes inconsistent. One rule defined a rich peasant as someone who hired more labour than he and his household supplied, but another specified that 'income from exploitation' should be doubled if the household owned more than twice as much land as the average per-capita amount held by middle peasants, which in effect placed any family which hired a single year-labourer in the rich peasant class. This would have placed far too many peasants in the upper class, and the law was amended to raise the line above a one year-labourer (Huang, 1985, pp. 69–70).

The process in fact was far less rational and far more violent than implied by the careful distinctions written into the legislation. Following their military victory, the Communists sent teams of cadres into villages, where they organized the 'peasants' to attack the 'landlords'. The cadres encouraged women to participate in the campaign, particularly in the local 'speak bitterness' and 'struggle' meetings where grievances were aired. Because of the complexities of economic arrangements, anyone with an enemy in the village could be branded a 'landlord', denounced, publicly humiliated, and then tried, dispossessed, and quite possibly killed. The number of executions reached into the millions. Despite the pervasive atmosphere of crisis and terror, the government did secure the support of the poorest families by redistributing land in their favour, at least initially (Oi, 1989; Friedman et al., 1991).

The government intended that China would become an industrial power, and in the early years Soviet models were influential. Many of the economic planners who had worked for the Nationalist government elected to remain following the Communist victory. Central ministries decided priorities and allocated resources, passing their orders to provincial, regional, and local agencies, and finally to individual enterprises. The first five-year plan of 1953–7 reported impressive increases in industrial output. The government concentrated its efforts on large, capital-intensive plants. About half of the new investment in heavy industry was concentrated in 156 projects supported by the Soviet Union with technical assistance and loans. Some 10 000 Soviet experts worked in China and nearly 30 000 Chinese received technical training in the Soviet Union.

One way in which Chinese planning departed from the Soviet model from the beginning was in its emphasis on regional self-sufficiency. Part of Mao's vision was a China which would be able to defend itself by withdrawing into the interior provinces. Every province therefore required its own industrial base. Nearly all the Soviet-aided plants were located inland.

Disregard of locational factors, comparative advantage, and economies of scale led to a wasteful 'tendency toward regional autarky'. Lower level planning offices were organized on geographical rather than industrial lines as in the Soviet Union. Further, the Chinese planning mechanism never achieved the same degree of control over the economy which Soviet planners exercised, and the unplanned 'subeconomy' remained quite large and also fragmented along regional lines. Attempts to 'naturalize' economic relations and discourage the use of money enhanced the value of goods, but also led agencies into a battle over their control. This created confusion and tension between central and regional interests (Lyons, 1987).

Economic statistics were either not published or of dubious quality, and debate over economic policy was concealed from the outside world. Western scholars worked in a frustrating vacuum, struggling to reconcile the announcements of victories in campaigns and successful completion of projects with what appeared to be inconsistent shifts in policy. Subsequently it has been argued that policy in any given period reflected the relative strengths of representatives and advocates of three main tendencies – a bureaucratic line favouring control through the plan, a strategy favouring individual rewards and greater market influence, and a radical line favoring mass participation both in planning and administration – all of which led to dysfunctional consequences when carried to extremes. This has been offered as a possible explanation of the habitual reversion to bureaucratic solutions when market or radical disruptions occurred – as they were bound to, given China's technological backwardness, poor transportation, and poor communications (Solinger, 1984; Lee, 1987).

However, Mao Zedong's overriding concern was not economic development, but the creation of a society which would not be based on class divisions. Therefore, at the highest levels of government there was always some hostility to the use of material incentives or reliance on 'experts' to achieve economic growth (Perkins, 1983, p. 355). It was always better to be 'red' than 'expert', but in the last analysis, the crucial factor in any decision was the will of the leader. In his emphasis on the peasantry, on the role of women, on the flexibility of class analysis, and on pragmatic adaptation to changing conditions, Mao seemed to be extending and developing the tradition of Marxist social thought. For many hopeful social reformers and would-be revolutionaries around the world, 'Marxism-Leninism' became 'Marxism-Leninism-Maoism'. However, Mao came increasingly to believe in his own infallibility and in the power of his own will and the collective will of his followers to overcome any physical obstacle, and eventually he took leave not only of any recognizable Marxist analysis, but also of his senses.

The small peasant proprietors who had survived or gained land at the expense of landlords soon discovered that Mao, the party, and the government did not favour private property in agriculture any more than in industry and commerce. Using cadres and activists from the anti-landlord campaign, the government first moved peasants into mutual-aid teams, then organized them in agricultural producers' cooperatives, and then between 1954 and 1956 pressed them into 'higher level' collective farms where they would all work for wages. In 1958 collectivization was completed with the establishment of the communes, making six layers of administration, from province to prefecture, county, commune, brigade, and production team. China's 2000 counties were divided into 70 000 communes, each roughly equal to Skinner's 'standard marketing area'. Under the communes were 750 000 brigades, each the size of a village and containing on average 220 households or 1000 people, and finally 5 million production teams of 33 households or 145 persons, each responsible for the cultivation of some 20 hectares.

Under the new system, grain went first to the state. The state purchased this 'surplus' at a low fixed price, and used it to provide food for the urban centres. The remainder went to the 'three retained funds', for seed, for animal feed, and finally for the individual villagers' rations. Members of production teams received a basic grain ration, plus additional amounts based on 'work points' earned for their labour. Effort was encouraged by competition among the teams, and by the fact that the basic grain ration was set well below subsistence. Control was assured by eliminating the free market in grain. Villagers could only obtain the grain they had earned in their own village; their ration cards would not be honoured anywhere else in the country.

Within the villages the activist cadres quickly entrenched themselves as a new elite. Power went to those who were the most energetic in their support of the government, and the most ruthless in their pursuit of anyone who could be labelled an enemy of the state. For a time, faith in Mao and in the future allowed an extraordinary degree of mobilization. Soon, however, it became obvious that the surest way to advancement was through the party, and the cadres began to use their access to scarce resources to gain advantage over their neighbours. Cadres and administrators received bonus work points, for instance. Although mouthing the slogans of socialist egalitarianism, the cadres used networks of connections and patronage to secure power and preference, and the system rapidly became corrupt (Oi, 1989; Friedman et al., 1991).

The system also made no provision for improvements in productivity. Agricultural production rose only some 2 to 3 per cent per year from the 1950s to the late 1970s, barely keeping even with population (Perkins, 1983; Lardy, 1983). Output per hour may have declined from the 1950s to the 1970s (Rawski, 1983). Involution and the 'high level equilibrium trap' had continued (Huang, 1990, p. 16). The system froze population in the countryside, and the collective farm therefore 'shared a key characteristic with the prerevolutionary family farm: its labour supply was a given that could not be adjusted to changing labour needs in the manner of a capitalist farm'. The collective therefore responded to subsistence pressures or state demands by further intensifying labour inputs – extending the working day, or intensifying the efforts of the least powerful members of the community – 'even when the marginal returns to such labour input diminished sharply' (Huang, 1991, p. 631). As we will see in Chapter 11, the consequences, especially for women, were negative.

When planning agencies discussed the proposed second five-year plan in 1956, they concluded that while heavy industry was still important, Soviet aid had proved expensive and the Soviet model inappropriate. The loans had to be repaid. In addition it was argued that Chinese conditions, and especially the relatively large rural sector, differed greatly from the Soviet Union, and therefore smaller plants in decentralized locations would be more effective than large plants because they would reduce transport costs and use the labour available in each region. In addition, it was clear that the first steps of collectivization had not increased the output of the agricultural sector. Population had risen in the countryside and even more rapidly in the cities, but state grain procurements had remained static. More rapid progress in agriculture was essential.

At the same time, the 'hundred flowers' campaign of 1956 and 1957 aimed to integrate trained intellectuals into the new socialist state. Debate was encouraged: 'let a hundred schools of thought contend'. Mao apparently believed that there was no real opposition to his policies, and that the 'contending schools' would not disagree on fundamentals. However, after a few months of caution the campaign resulted in an outburst of severe criticism of the government and of the role of the party. The campaign was closed down immediately, and replaced by the 'anti-rightist' campaign of 1957–8, which led to widespread attacks on intellectuals of all kinds. Some 300 000 to 700 000 writers, publishers, teachers, administrators and skilled workers lost their jobs. As general secretary of the party, Deng Xiaoping played an active role in this purge.

Mao had decided to dispense with the services of intellectuals and 'experts' entirely, to abandon the 'fetish' of technology, and to rely on the energy and enthusiasm of youth to create his vision of a classless socialist society. His close associates and the new rural cadres supported him. The second five-year plan was never published. Instead, in late 1957, economic planning and control were radically decentralized, with even the central statistical bureau broken up into local units, and in the spring of 1958 Mao launched the 'great leap forward'. As the system of communes was being imposed on the agricultural population, local and regional cadres mobilized millions of men and women, who performed heroic feats of labour, working without rest to build roads, canals, dams and factories, to lay out new fields and forests – to do indeed anything they were ordered to do, and to do it by hand. The famous campaign to produce steel by smelting farm implements and household utensils in backyard furnaces began in July, and by October it was reported that a million tiny furnaces were in operation in the 'battle for steel'.

The results, although in large part concealed from the outside world, were disastrous. Local cadres reported their projects completed and their new industrial quotas fulfilled, and in addition reported huge increases in grain production. The reports were grossly optimistic; the steel produced in the backyard furnaces was useless, and the new dams and canals often damaged the local environment. And tragically, the reports of increased agricultural production were false. The weather in 1958 was good, but the weather in 1959 was poor. The dislocation caused by collectivization was often worsened by arbitrary directives, such as the order to plant seedlings closer together, since under a socialist system this would encourage co-operation among the plants rather than competition. The withdrawal of millions of workers from the farms for the multitude of projects of the 'great leap forward' meant that the crops which did grow could not be properly tended or harvested. But the government – and especially Mao himself – would not hear bad news. While agricultural output dropped, government requisitions remained high. The cities could be fed, but in the countryside somewhere between 20 million and 30 million people starved to death (Lavely et al., 1990, p. 813; Becker, 1996).

Many in government such as Deng Xiaoping concluded that economic planning would have to be placed on a rational basis once again, and that more positive incentives would have to be introduced to motivate farmers to produce more. For several years a more technocratic 'expert' line determined policy. Urban workers employed in the large state enterprises, though privileged in salary, food rations, housing, and social services, were placed under strict control. To reduce the population of the cities, which had grown rapidly during the 'great leap forward', millions of unemployed people were moved to the countryside. A system of complete household registration was introduced, along with a new food-rationing system. Some senior planners called for the reintroduction of private plots in agriculture, arguing that 'individual responsibility' would lead to increased output.

Mao, however, concluded not that he had been wrong, but that an even greater effort of will was necessary. In 1966 he launched another campaign, the 'great proletarian cultural revolution', and encouraged groups of young 'red guards' to take direct action to oust anyone who opposed the 'thought of Chairman Mao'. Deng and others were denounced as 'capitalist roaders' who were plotting to undermine the revolution. Schools and universities closed, because the only learning needed was contained in the *Quotations from Chairman Mao Tse-tung*, the 'little red book' which the red guards brandished aloft as they marched through the streets. Violent clashes ensued when the red guards attempted to displace local political and military authorities, and several provinces descended into something like civil war. The disorder continued past the official end of the campaign in 1969 as Mao attempted to dismantle the party he had created and rebuild it and China from scratch. The red guards and their successors were equally contemptuous of intellectuals and engineers, and they were virulently anti-foreign. To display any kind of expertise, any touch of intellectualism or foreignism, was to risk denunciation, disgrace, and possibly death. Some 400 000 persons did die of maltreatment, many thousands more committed suicide, and further hundreds of thousands suffered crippling physical or mental injury.

Economically as well as intellectually, the years from 1966 to Mao's death in 1976 were a 'lost decade'. As the cultural revolution spread to the countryside, farmers were forbidden to engage in any private 'capitalist' activity, such as raising pigs or chickens, and many starved as a result. Mao launched a further effort to decentralize China's industry, a 'third front' which would be safe from foreign attack. Remote areas in the northwest and southwest were selected as the sites for new factories, with new railways through the mountains and new hydroelectric dams. Local authorities again were given control over planning, and they channelled their own and the central government's resources into small manufacturing plants and power stations. Although total investment and industrial output rose rapidly, the net gain was small, for 'third front' projects

produced at very high cost, and the lack of control over regional authorities led to wasteful duplication (see Joseph et al., 1991). Mao himself, a
victim of chronic insomnia now haunted by evidence of his mortality,
disrupted railway schedules for weeks on end with his sporadic journeys
about the country in his private train, attended by young women whose
sexual attentions he believed would prolong his life (Li, 1994).

Korea: Independence and Division

On 15 August 1945 the Japanese offered the Korean nationalist leader Yo
Un-hyong the opportunity to establish an interim administration which
would preserve order and protect the lives and property of Japanese
citizens. He agreed, but instead of acting as the pliable figurehead for
which the Japanese hoped, he established an independent Committee for
the Preparation of Korean Independence. Provincial branches of the
Committee were formed within days, in two weeks there were already
145 branches covering most cities and towns, and within months village
'people's committees' had taken control of local government throughout
the country. On 6 September a representative assembly met in Seoul and
formed the Korean People's Republic.

The new government announced a land reform, under which the land
of Japanese and the Korean 'national traitors' who had collaborated with
them would be confiscated and redistributed to the tenants who worked it.
In addition, the government proposed to nationalize mines, large-scale
factories, railways, shipping, communications, and banks – most of these
had already been owned or controlled by the Japanese colonial state.
Small-scale industry and commerce would remain private, though subject
to state supervision. Minimum wages, an eight-hour day, and prohibition
of child labour fulfilled longstanding demands. Although the land reform
would have been a 'virtual death blow for the core of Korea's propertied
class', the overall thrust of the programme was moderate and reformist,
and there is no question that the new government enjoyed wide popular
support (Eckert et al., 1990, pp. 331–3).

In return for Soviet intervention in the war against Japan, the United
States had agreed to Soviet occupation of Manchuria and Korea. However, the atomic bomb and Japan's surrender made an invasion of the
Japanese home islands unnecessary, and the Americans began to consider
ways in which Soviet influence could be limited. In haste, they proposed a

division of Korea along the 38th parallel, a line drawn on a small-scale map of Asia by an American army officer in Washington because it divided the country more or less equally and placed Seoul in the proposed American zone of occupation in the south. The Soviets, who could have occupied the entire peninsula easily, instead accepted the American proposal.

Although they maintained a controlling presence in Pyongyang, the Soviets did not establish a formal occupation government. The land reform and nationalization measures of the People's Republic government suited their interests, as did the role of the Communists. In the north, therefore, a complete land reform came in March 1946. There was less bloodshed than in China, partly because many absentee owners lived in the south and partly because both the Japanese and many Korean landlords had already fled. In the south, however, the United States refused to recognize the People's Republic and instead set up a formal military occupation government. At first they attempted to rule through Japanese colonial officials, but Korean protests made this impossible. They then appointed Koreans, usually men who had served in the Japanese colonial administration who had been removed by the people's committees, and including thousands of members of the Japanese police. The Korean Democratic Party which gained United States support represented the interests of the property-owning classes, particularly the landlords, and the land reform finally announced in March 1948 was predictably modest, confined to rental lands formerly owned by Japanese, about 20 per cent of the total. In the meantime, in 1946 strikes had led to mass demonstrations protesting the policies of the occupation government. United States troops, Korean National Police, and a constabulary established by the occupation authorities repressed the protests and then moved against the people's committees. The last committee survived on Cheju island until 1949, when a full-scale military assault killed tens of thousands and destroyed three-fourths of the villages on the island (Eckert et al., 1990, pp. 337–9).

The escalating Cold War led to a series of more or less deliberate provocations by both sides. Both the Soviet Union and the United States backed a Korean leader as the head of a 'provisional' government. The Soviets supported Kim Il Sung, a young (thirty-three in 1945) man famous for his activities with Communist guerillas in Manchuria in the 1930s. The Americans favoured Syngman Rhee (Yi Sung-man), a much older (seventy in 1945) man with experience dating from the Independence Club, long residence in the United States, and rigidly anti-Communist opinions. By 1948 there were two separate Korean governments, the Republic of

Korea in the south and the Democratic People's Republic of Korea in the north. The Soviets withdrew in late 1948, and the United States in June 1949.

The brutal and bloody repression of the people's committees and labour organizations in the south, statements by Rhee and southern military leaders of their intent to retake the north by force, and a series of conflicts along the border, all seem to have contributed to the decision by North Korea to invade the south in 1950. Experienced veterans who had served in the Chinese civil war and equipment obtained from the Soviet Union gave the north the advantage. They pushed far to the south, but the United States, acting on the basis of a United Nations resolution, intervened and pushed the northern forces back to the Yalu River. This was the point at which Chinese forces attacked and pushed far to the south once again, only to be pushed back in turn, to a stalemate along the 38th parallel. A truce was finally signed in 1953.

The war brought appalling loss of life and destruction. Military and civilian deaths in the south totalled 1.3 million, and have been estimated in the north at 1.5 million out of a population only one half that of the south. Seoul changed hands four times, and Pyongyang and other northern cities were reduced to smoking rubble by American air raids. In the aftermath both north and south moved in increasingly authoritarian directions. Kim established a personal dictatorship which combined aspects of Stalin's Soviet model with an emphasis on his own personality as leader which resembled the cult surrounding Mao in China. North Korea was largely cut off from the outside world until Kim's death in 1995. Kim valued independence above all; the economy appears to have been geared towards maintaining a very large army, and doing so largely without either Soviet or Chinese aid.

In the south, Rhee organized a new Liberal Party in 1951 and secured increasing electoral majorities through the use of police surveillance and harassment of opponents, selective application of a National Security Law, and when necessary fraud and violence. With the end of the war this became more difficult, and in 1956, despite the death of his major opponent, Rhee still received only 55 per cent of the vote, down from 72 per cent in 1952, and his vice-presidential candidate was actually defeated. His response was to become more 'authoritarian' and to ignore the advice of economic technocrats in policy-making. This was the period of the 'import-substitution' strategy, but as observers noted at the time the policy was not in fact very coherent, nor was it pursued consistently. Rhee wanted as much discretion as possible, particularly over the distribution of

American aid. The financial weakness of the Liberal Party, and its declining popularity, made it reasonable for Rhee to maximize Korea's dependence on American aid, limit the range of public planning, and maintain direct control over policy instruments in order to build political support. The government under Rhee's direction distributed foreign exchange, bank credit, import licences, and privatized state firms (many of them former Japanese enterprises) to its supporters. The business leaders who profited then recycled a share of their gains to government officials, the party, and individual politicians. The Liberal Party was estimated to have a direct interest in half of all projects receiving US aid in 1960 (Haggard et al. 1991). The results were not promising: 'even in 1960, after the damage inflicted during the war had been repaired, ... few, if any, observers held out much hope of improvement for Korea's poverty-stricken economy' (Song, 1994, p. 57).

Independent Taiwan

In Taiwan, Chiang Kaishek remained president until his death in 1975, following a decision by the National Assembly to suspend the provision of the constitution which prohibited a president from serving more than two terms. Locked in the rhetoric of the Cold War, the United States continued to adhere to the fiction that Chiang's government was the government of 'China' until 1979. Taiwan received large amounts of American economic aid until 1965, and continued to receive military assistance in later years. The initial occupation of the island left the Nationalist government in control of Japanese public and private enterprises. This included large tracts of land owned by the colonial government, which had been reserved for future Japanese settlers. In 1951 the government sold some 180 000 hectares, about 20 per cent of all arable land, to 140 000 farm families. In 1953 the government forced all landlords to sell their tenanted land to it, and then resold the land to a further 190 000 farm families. Tenancy was reduced from 40 to 15 per cent of farmland, and the government gained the support of a substantial fraction of the population. As seen in Chapter 7, Taiwan already enjoyed extensive irrigation and other services developed by Japanese colonial authorities, and output rose rapidly.

In 1953 the government launched the first of several four-year plans for economic development. Former Japanese industrial plants were transferred to private ownership. New investment channelled through government agencies targeted small- and medium-sized plants producing primarily consumer goods, which were intended to replace imports. Cottage and handicraft industries were encouraged in the countryside. In 1956 the four-year plan could be declared a success, with over 600 new factories, industrial employment up from 274 000 to 340 000, and industrial production twice the 1951 level. The second and third plans also reported successes.

However, no one as yet had predicted that Taiwan was beginning to evolve into a tiger. In the late 1960s the economy depended on United States purchases for the war in Vietnam. As we will see in Chapter 11, development reflected the mobilization of cheap female labour. The division between Taiwanese and mainlanders remained deep. Government remained firmly in the hands of the Nationalist Party oligarchy which had accompanied Chiang. The legislature was dominated by men elected to represent districts on the mainland in 1947 – they still held 900 of the 1000 seats in the National Assembly 40 years later in the 1980s. Private business, wary of government, avoided corporate registration and remained individually owned or partnerships. When they reached the threshold of the size which required registration and government oversight, they very often created another firm alongside the old one. Part of the often-noted predominance of 'small' firms in Taiwan's economy reflected this feature of the company law, with groups of firms in 'parent–subsidiary' relationships, and single individuals chairing up to a dozen independent companies. Further, much of Taiwan's economic activity remained 'underground' in the sense of being unregulated – unregistered factories outside the regulated corporate sector, unmonitored credit clubs outside the regulated banking system, and other forms of activity – and these still accounted for possibly 40 per cent of all economic activity in the 1980s (Kirby, 1995).

Independent Southeast Asia

None of the emerging national regimes described in Chapter 8 appeared especially likely to achieve economic success, and some did not even have the opportunity. The war in Vietnam continued into the 1970s, and the fighting involved Laos and spread, tragically, into Cambodia. United States policy, framed in terms of the confrontation between 'socialism' and 'democracy', here intersected with the internal dynamic of Asian nationalist movements to create the conditions for a major disaster. Those countries nominally at peace suffered from internal instability. Further, in their emphasis on the power of the central government and on their determination to restrict participation in the new national community, ruling elites in fact placed economic development far down their real agendas, despite claims to the contrary.

Cambodia

Prince Norodom Sihanouk had proclaimed himself sole leader of the Cambodian independence movement in 1953. Because of the relative weakness of the Cambodian Communists, and because the Vietnamese Communists did not support their case, Cambodia was not divided as Vietnam and Laos were. However, although 'moderate' nationalists believed their aims had been fulfilled, Communists and others opposed to the monarchy remained dissatisfied. The nationalist movement divided, and the left divided further, into those who chose to move north to fight alongside the Vietminh in North Vietnam, those who remained underground in Cambodia, and those who supported a new radical socialist People's Party. Sihanouk abdicated and placed his father on the throne, leaving him free to rule as leader of his party, the Popular Socialist Community (Sangkum Reastr Niyum). The police pursued and imprisoned leaders and supporters of the People's Party, suspected Communists, and anyone else who opposed Sihanouk. Sangkum won 82 per cent of the vote and all of the national assembly seats in the first elections in 1955. Sihanouk's popular 'neutralist' foreign policy, a 'dictate of necessity' in his words, aimed to maintain Cambodian independence. Believing the North Vietnamese Communists would win, he moved towards them and away from the United States, but he balanced this with closer relations which China, to guard against a resurgence of Vietnamese expansionism. Army commander Lon Nol favoured a closer relationship with the United States.

In the late 1950s a group of radical students returned from France and took over the remnants of the Communist Party under the leadership of Pol Pot. Under attack from the police and army, they fled to the safety of the mountains in the northeast, hoping for support from the North Vietnamese. They waited in frustration for five years while the Vietnamese Communists pursued their own agenda – the Vietnamese found Sihanouk valuable, as his 'neutralism' allowed them the use of Cambodia as a transport route and staging area outside the reach of American air attacks. In the meantime the Cambodian economy passed from stagnation to crisis. Sihanouk's neutralism led to a break in relations with the United States, and an end to American aid. Cambodia depended on two exports, rice and rubber. The rice crop had been placed in the hands of a government monopoly, and the corrupt officials who gained control of the trade lowered the price paid to farmers in order to increase their own profits. However, dealing through Chinese merchants, the Vietnamese Communists had begun to purchase large amounts of rice, at prices higher than the government monopoly. Farmers refused to sell to the government, and government revenues declined drastically. Reforms in 1963 failed to overcome the problems.

Sihanouk's response to increasing criticism was to withdraw from politics, though he remained head of state. Elections in 1966 brought Lon Nol to power. The new government attempted to collect rice from the farmers by force to prevent its sale to the Vietnamese, and the predictable result was a rebellion centred in the western area of Samlaut, which the army suppressed brutally. Suspected communists were hunted down, and many fled to join Pol Pot in the mountains. In 1968 Pol Pot's reorganized Communist Party of Kampuchea (the Khmer Rouge, or 'Red Cambodians', a deprecatory term used by Sihanouk which became their public label) began an armed uprising, but the Vietnamese Communists still refused support. Then in 1970 Lon Nol deposed Sihanouk and allied himself with the United States and South Vietnam. The Vietnamese Communists now occupied northern Cambodia to secure their staging areas. Although suspicious of Vietnamese intentions, Pol Pot accepted this 'assistance'.

From 1970 to 1975 civil war raged, with heavy losses and few prisoners taken by either side. American aid for Lon Nol came in the form of a bombing campaign which caused heavy civilian casualties in Communist-held areas. The bombing intensified following the 1973 ceasefire in Vietnam and Laos, and eventually more bombs fell on Cambodia than had been dropped on Japan during the Pacific War. Lon Nol's regime demonstrated its incompetence as well as continuing the corruption of Sihanouk's government. In addition the deposed but still-popular Sihanouk now allied himself with the Khmer Rouge. Most importantly, however, the rural farmers accepted the Communist Party's assertions that Cambodia stood alone against the world in its struggle, and that the people of the cities were parasites, who existed only by draining away the wealth produced in the countryside.

In April 1975 the Lon Nol regime collapsed. The victorious Khmer Rouge ordered the expulsion of all Vietnamese and the sealing of the borders. They ordered the execution of all leaders of the Lon Nol government, administration and army. They abolished religion and ordered Buddhist monks to work. They 'naturalized' economic relations and eliminated the use of money and the operation of markets. Farmers were ordered into communes, which the Khmer Rouge believed would become self-sufficient centres of production, each producing for its own needs with no contact or trade with other centres. And, all of the people in all of the cities were ordered into the countryside to join the new rural commune organizations. Over three million people were marched out of the urban areas, carrying whatever they could with them. Thousands of the old, the very young, and the infirm died by the roadsides along the march. The communes were assigned projects such as dams and irrigation canals, to be constructed by hand as in China's 'great leap forward'. As 'new people' in the communes, the evacuees received the most meagre rations in return for the heaviest and most difficult work, and thousands died from overwork and undernourishment. Food output actually increased, but was siphoned off by the party to pay for imported Chinese weapons. Any opposition, any connection with the previous government or with the Vietnamese, any hint of 'intellectualism' or a foreign education, meant death. A million people may have perished under the Pol Pot regime.

Relations with Vietnam deteriorated rapidly into armed conflict. The Khmer Rouge government, fearing the 'contamination' of even its own cadres in the eastern border zone through contact with the Vietnamese, ordered them all to be killed, along with all of the 'new people' in the zone. Only those who fled into Vietnam escaped. The government launched new attacks into Vietnam, and in late December 1978 the Vietnamese responded with a full-scale invasion and overran the entire country in 17 days. Having undermined their support through their excesses, and now defeated militarily, the leaders of the Pol Pot government fled to the Thai border, and by mid-January 1979 a new People's Republic of Kampuchea had been proclaimed, led by those who had previously fled to Vietnam. Vietnamese and Soviet aid prevented a famine, as the survivors of the relocation flowed back into the cities. Reconstruction began, with the restoration of personal freedoms, of Buddhism, and of money and markets, but all with the assistance and under the guidance of the Vietnamese, who maintained an occupation force of some 160 000 soldiers.

China, to punish Vietnam for the destruction of its client state, invaded the northern provinces of Vietnam in February 1979, but withdrew after a costly and inconclusive campaign. Thailand, fearing Vietnamese domination of both the buffer states of Laos and Cambodia, brought every available diplomatic and military means to bear to force the Vietnamese to withdraw from Cambodia. American and Chinese pressure denied the PRK recognition by the United Nations. The Thai government refused to grant refugee status to some 300 000 people housed in huge camps along the border. These provided a continuing recruiting ground for opposition movements, including two anti-Communist organizations led by former prime minister Son Sann and by Sihanouk, who had survived years of house arrest, and also the Khmer Rouge, still the best organized and most powerful militarily, with 40 000 troops supplied and financed by China, with the arms and money channelled through the Thai army. These three formed an unlikely alliance opposed to the PRK and received international recognition. The Vietnamese attacked their bases in 1984–5, but they relocated across the Thai border. Under increasing economic pressure themselves as a result of the collapse of the Soviet Union, the Vietnamese announced that they would withdraw from Cambodia in 1989. In 1991 a cease-fire and a conference in Beijing finally confirmed Sihanouk as chairman of a new national council, with PRK prime minister Hung Sen as his deputy (Vickery, 1984; Evans and Rowley, 1990; Mackerras, et al., 1992, pp. 556–70; SarDesai, 1994, chs. 24–5).

Thailand

In Thailand, the coup which brought Sarit to power as prime minister in 1958 also entrenched an alliance of royalist noble families, bureaucrats, senior military officers, and business leaders: 'The economic nationalism of the businessmen was realized in government programmes to "develop" through private enterprise. The bureaucratic nationalism of the middle-rank officials was realized in the consolidation and extension of the bureaucratic state' (Pasuk and Baker, 1995, p. 287). The bureaucracy increased in size, from 75 000 'ordinary' officials in 1944 to 250 000 in 1965. Government departments multiplied and exfoliated, from 49 with 317 divisions in 1941, to 113 with 827 divisions in 1969. The military budget exploded from US$ 20 million in the early 1950s to US$ 250 million in the early 1970s. Power in Bangkok was centralized around those working in culture – virtually all higher education, for instance – commerce, industry, and was reinforced by the city's increasing size.

The interconnections among members of the privileged elite often began at Chulachomklao Military Academy or Chulalongkorn University and often involved intermarriage. Joint ventures between generals and civilian bankers and industrialists were also common. Individuals at the top of the pyramid profited from the opportunities for rent-seeking which were available for those with power in an authoritarian system. Construction contracts for the large hydroelectric projects of the 1950s, the right to fell the trees on the land which would be flooded, and the clearing and colonization of the areas opened for development by the new power sources and by new roads, all yielded handsome profits to those with the proper connections in the interior ministry, the army, and financial and industrial circles. While serving as prime minister Sarit himself sat on the boards of 22 companies. At his death he had amassed assets of 2.8 billion baht, much of it after becoming prime minister. An investigation resulted in the seizure of 604 million baht which appeared to have been 'looted' directly from the government, particularly from the government lottery which he administered (Pasuk and Baker, 1995, pp. 277–81, 285–8).

Senior officials in the Thai government involved themselves in the relocation and redirection of the opium trade. War disrupted old sources of supply in the 1940s. Remnants of the Chinese nationalist armies, fleeing southward after the victory of the Communists in the civil war, began to sponsor the production of opium in the mountainous upland areas of Burma, Laos, and northern Thailand. United States CIA officials supported them, in the hope of overturning the new People's Republic. Thailand retained a legal government opium monopoly, and Bangkok became the main port for export overseas. Thai army and police commanders, with their well-established local connections, lines of supply, and armed protection, came to dominate the trade. Both Sarit, as army commander, and his rival Phao, head of the police, became interested in the trade in the 1950s, and they became competitors. Phao allied himself with the CIA and seemed to have defeated Sarit, but then lost his position in the 1957 coup. As prime minister, Sarit outlawed opium, but not, it has been alleged, before he had acquired the entire crop for sale to reward his supporters (McCoy, 1972).

As a staunch ally of the United States, Thailand became an important base for American bombers. By 1969 there were 50 000 United States military personnel stationed in Thailand. Half of total Thai spending on the military came in the form of grants from the United States. In addition to financial aid the United States played a key role in training the Thai military. Because of Thailand's importance, the United States took an interest in Thailand's internal security, and therefore was also involved in the training of the Thai police. The United States presence offered further opportunities for influential officials to enrich themselves. A Thai air force officer gained control over the rest and recreation programme for American personnel, and one of Sarit's subordinates served as chairman of the firm which handled three-quarters of all internal shipments of United States military cargo (Pasuk and Baker, 1995, pp. 275–9).

Centralization of power in Bangkok required more direct administration of the provinces. New forestry regulations outlawed the mobile swidden pattern of cultivation typical of many hilly areas, and the prohibition of opium growing in 1958 destroyed another source of livelihood for rural villages. Opposition, notably in the same areas of the northeast which had resisted the central government in the early 1930s, led to police and military units launching 'pacification' campaigns. Their actions created support for the Thai Communist Party, which had adopted a strategy of 'encircling the cities from the rural areas' following the destruction of its urban-based organization after the 1957 coup. Thai Communists received support from China and Vietnam. In 1965 they announced the beginning of a guerrilla war. The brutality of the government forces – torture, rape, burning of entire villages – only served to spread and deepen opposition. An attempt to isolate villages as the British had done in Malaya and the United States was attempting in Vietnam failed, because military commanders refused to share their power with a new bureaucratic rival. An attempt to buy the support of insurgent villages with money provided by the United States USAID also failed, because neutral villages saw joining the insurgents as a way to attract funds. In 1969, districts in 35 of the 71 provinces were officially designated as 'communist-infested sensitive areas'. Two large-scale assaults on Communist base areas in 1972 ended disastrously.

Opposition to the military government increased in Bangkok as well, among the rapidly rising numbers of university students, but also among business leaders and other members of the elite, disappointed at a slowing of economic growth and increasingly dissatisfied and suspicious of the military's competence. In 1973 massive demonstrations by students led to a clash with riot police in which more than 100 students died. The military prepared to reassert its control by force, but the king intervened and ordered prime minister Thanom Kittikachorn and his deputy Praphat Charusathien to leave the country. In the aftermath the government seized

600 million baht from Thanom and Praphat, money it claimed had been directly stolen from the government.

However, the new government proved unstable. Renewed Communist agitation in Bangkok, the fall of Vietnam, a confrontation with the United States over the presence of American forces in Thailand, and a marked reluctance of foreign investors to risk their capital in the 'unsettled political climate' led to widespread fear of a Communist coup and a resurgence of support for the conservative bureaucracy and military. The king shifted his support to the right and granted Thanom permission to return to the country. The new alliance of conservative forces, and further instability caused by a campaign of right-wing terrorism, led to a series of violent incidents, culminating in late 1976 in a military assault on the campus of the leftist Thammasat University in which some 1300 died. The new government pursued its opponents, all of whom were labelled 'Communists', ruthlessly. Thousands of students and others fled to the countryside to join the Communist insurgents, and although the new government survived, at the time it seemed this increase in strength might bring the Communists to power (Pasuk and Baker, 1995, ch. 9).

Myanmar

Burma was approximately 75 per cent Burmese, virtually all Buddhists, mostly settled in the fertile southern and central river deltas. The largest of the groups making up the other 25 per cent were the Chins, Kachins, Shans, and Karens, who occupied the less fertile hilly areas in the east and north. The constitution of Burma provided for an upper house, the Chamber of Nationalities, to represent the non-Burmese minorities in proportion to their numbers. In addition, in 1952 U Nu launched a broadly based plan for economic development to transform Burma into a 'land of happiness' over the next four years, with increases in education, improved public health, subsidies for housing, and a series of measures to aid farmers including land reclamation, extended irrigation, redistribution of some 3.75 million hectares of land to new tenants, improved tenancy regulations, access to subsidized credit, and forgiveness of existing debts.

U Nu, though popular because of his reputation for personal honesty, was a rather doctrinaire socialist and also a devout Buddhist. The state remained paramount, and Buddhism was elevated almost to the status of a state religion – Burma played an important role in the 2500-year anniversary of the Buddha in 1956. Although there was no official discrimination, Indians were clearly unwelcome, and they left the country in large numbers. Previously they had provided commercial services, although as money-lenders and landlords they had been unpopular with Burmese farmers. They also made up a substantial fraction of the technically trained personnel in the country, and when they left, they were no longer available to administer the government's ambitious economic programmes. The cost of the civil wars against the Communists and the predominantly Christian Karens undermined the government's finances. The world price of rice dropped 25 per cent in 1955 and 1956. To aid the farmers, mostly Burmese, the domestic price of rice was supported by government purchases, resulting both in discontent among consumers and in increasing unsaleable surpluses held in government warehouses.

By 1956 the development plans had stalled, and the economy was in decline. The Communist Party had been outlawed in 1953, but Communists remained active in the opposition party, which gained a third of the popular vote in the elections of 1956. U Nu attempted to negotiate with opposition elements, which alienated members of his own party, the wartime alliance Anti-Fascist People's Freedom League. By 1958 the AFPFL had split, and the Communists re-emerged, sponsoring violent demonstrations and supporting the claims of Kachins and Shans for separate states. U Nu called on the army, under its commander Ne Win, to restore order. In 1960 new elections were held, but in the intervening two years Ne Win and other military commanders had acquired the taste for power, and in 1962 Ne Win seized control of the government. U Nu and other civilian leaders were interned, the legislature dissolved, and although the freedoms of speech, press, and assembly remained in theory, no criticism of the new administration was permitted.

The military government remained in control of Burma until 1988. Although the old constitution remained in effect until 1974, and elections were held periodically, a new party dominated by the military, the Burma Socialist Program Party, became the only legal party. Ne Win's control rested on a Revolutionary Council which provided him with his cabinet, and on Supreme State Councils with 'non-political' and military members at the state level. The Councils worked in cooperation with Security Administration Committees consisting of the regional heads of the civilian, police, and military administrations. Originally a small group, the BSPP expanded in the early 1970s and established parallel organs at state, district, subdistrict, and village levels, extending and broadening the central government's control. By 1981 there were some 1.5 million members, or around 5 per cent of the total population. Education, employment, promotion, and even paid holidays became increasingly linked to party membership.

The leaders of the old political parties and other members of the educated elite refused to cooperate with the military regime, and were shunted aside. The government's policies, outlined in 'The Burmese Way of Socialism' in 1962 and amplified in *The Correlation of Man and His Environment* in 1964, combined the analytical categories of a radical Marxism–Leninism with Buddhist philosophical ideas. In particular, the government emphasized the notions of impermanence and man's inherent greed as the source of all evil in this world. In consequence, according to the government, only a strong state can contain man's base instincts in the name of his higher spiritual needs. Concretely, this meant that although all farmers' debts were declared void in 1963 and all rents abolished in 1965, all land was formally owned by the state, and since all domestic and foreign trade was declared a government monopoly, farmers were forced to deliver their produce at whatever price the state chose to pay. It also meant the nationalization of virtually all businesses, which led to the forced migration of thousands of Indians, Pakistanis, and Chinese in 1963–4. It meant that all instruction in the schools had to be in Burmese. And it meant a self-imposed isolation and hostility to foreigners. Foreign firms were not allowed to invest, foreign individuals were discouraged from visiting, and Burmese rarely travelled outside their country (Steinberg et al., 1987, pp. 400–2).

The low prices which the government paid to rice farmers led to declining production, and Burma not only lost its position as one of the largest rice exporters in the world, but actually rationed rice. Foreign exchange earnings disappeared, along with foreign investment. The economy stagnated through the 1960s and early 1970s. Education declined as well, due in part to the stifling effects of government policy, but also because of a lack of adequate textbooks in Burmese. Even as they declined in numbers, however, students became demoralized, because the economy could not absorb the graduates as they emerged. Students, workers, and some soldiers became dissatisfied with limited opportunities and low levels of living, but their protests were repressed; in 1975 Rangoon was under martial law. Ethnic revolts continued; in 1981 the government itself identified four major and eleven minor armed opposition groups.

The Philippines

...to the Western mind, martial law by itself is outrageous...we in the Philippines have developed the new idea of a reform government under martial law...we are using it as the legal means to bring about badly needed and drastic reforms in our country...I believe that other democracies – especially in the poor countries – can use martial law in the same way.

Ferdinand Marcos, *Revolution from the Center: How the Philippines is Using Martial Law to Build a New Society*, 1978

Under the government of Ramon Magsaysay in the 1950s the Philippines seemed to be moving away from the inherited nexus of landholding, the professions, and political connections which generations of prominent Filipino families had used to maintain their wealth and power. Magsaysay came to prominence as the successful victor over the Huk rebellion. From a poor family himself, he was appointed defence minister by Elpidio Quirino, who had won the presidency in 1949 in an election marked by particularly extensive bribery, fraud, and violence. Despite this unpromising beginning, Magsaysay reinvigorated the army. His intelligence network enabled him to arrest the entire top leadership of the Communist Party, and captured documents yielded lists of members and sympathizers. Building on these successes, he moved against the Huks. Convinced that the majority of Huk supporters were land-hungry farmers rather than committed Communists, Magsaysay combined military repression with generous amnesties for those who surrendered. Former Huk rebels were settled on vacant land and provided with housing. He persuaded the army to guarantee that the 1951 elections would be honest, which restored confidence in the political system, and won easily when he stood for the presidency in 1953. An agricultural tenancy act brought greater security to tenants, as well as access to credit, technical advice, and better distribution of produce. A series of measures to respond to the needs of local communities, to create jobs, to move against corruption, and most importantly the beginnings of a genuine land reform, all seemed to promise even better things.

Unfortunately, Magsaysay died in a plane crash in 1957, and his successors lacked his personal authority. Politics returned to the hands of the old elite, who had no intention of yielding their position and the sources of their wealth. Corruption returned, and most importantly, land reform 'was much talked about but never implemented' (Steinberg et al.,

1987, p. 434). Campaigning against corruption, in favour of 'order', and for publicly financed economic development – 'rice and roads' – Ferdinand Marcos became president of the senate in 1963, won a landslide presidential victory in 1965 and an unprecedented re-election in 1969. Then in 1972, facing a constitutional ban on a third term, he declared martial law, announcing that he was acting 'to protect the Republic of the Philippines and our democracy'. Thousands were arrested, the media severely restricted, and the army tripled in size and given greater powers.

At first Marcos's philosophy of 'constitutional authoritarianism' seemed to bring positive results. Private armies were disbanded, and half a million weapons confiscated. He gained the support of the United States and international business interests. Tourism rose dramatically. The economy boomed, growing at 7 per cent annually. However, in the early 1980s both the economy and Marcos's hold on power weakened. The Philippines had announced an 'export-oriented' policy in the early 1970s, but export growth had not been sustained. There were policy failures; an overvalued exchange rate, extensive subsidies, and tariffs which distorted resource allocation (Hill, 1994). In contrast to more successful Asian economies, the Philippines had relatively highly capital-intensive industries which did not 'absorb' underemployed labour. There was almost no growth in real wages (Galenson, 1992). Centralization contributed to the further expansion of Manila. Urban real estate brought profits for private investors, but capital could have achieved higher total 'social' returns elsewhere. Slow overall growth meant that many who came to Manila found no jobs and drifted into the 'informal' sector and into the swelling slum areas – one-third of the population of Manila lived in Tondo and other slum areas in the late 1980s. And there was no land reform. Some 70 per cent of farmers were still tenants who turned over half of their produce to landlords. Urban unemployment, rural underemployment, and poverty restricted the potential for lasting growth.

The real problem, however, was Marcos himself. 'Cronyism' and corruption turned the Philippines into a notorious 'cleptocracy'. Under Marcos the state sector expanded substantially, and the boundary between state and private sectors blurred as control over these enterprises went to Marcos family members or friends. Government funds paid for monuments and palaces, or disappeared into bank accounts overseas. The government deficit rose, and was covered by inflation and by foreign loans. Foreign debt increased from US$ 600 million in 1965 to US$ 25.6 billion in 1985. There were new uprisings, of the Communist New Peoples' Army and of the Muslim Moros. Nevertheless, because he was 'anti-Communist' Marcos continued to have the support of the United States. Reformers remained suspect in the eyes of the Americans, whose overt and covert activities remained a background feature of political life (Shalom, 1981). In 1983 Benigno Aquino, who would most likely have become president if Marcos had not seized power in 1972, was shot to death by soldiers as he stepped off a plane at Manila airport, and Marcos, his health failing, began to lose the confidence of even his closest supporters. In 1986 Aquino's widow Corazon opposed Marcos in the presidential elections. Massive fraud brought victory to Marcos, but even United States president Ronald Reagan denounced the result. Defence minister Juan Enrile and chief of staff Fidel Ramos resigned and declared their support of Aquino, as did Catholic Cardinal Jaime Sin, and massive street demonstrations followed. Offered sanctuary in the United States if he resigned in favour of Aquino, Marcos left the country, leaving behind a legacy of economic problems created by his regime.

Malaysia

Independent Malaysia remained a 'dualistic' or 'plural' society, reflecting the specialization of ethnic groups in different areas of the economy. Malays remained mostly small farmers, mostly rural, and mostly poor. Chinese and Indians had moved from the tin mines and the large-scale rubber plantation industry into Singapore and other urban centres, into commerce and the professions, and they dominated those sectors of the economy not directly controlled by British interests. The Japanese occupation, as we have seen in Chapter 8, disrupted the colonial economy and exposed thousands of Malays to anti-colonial, anti-British, and anti-Chinese indoctrination, and the events of the anti-Communist 'emergency' reinforced anti-Chinese feelings further. With independence in 1957, political control passed to the majority Malays, but economic power remained in the hands of the Chinese and Indian minorities. Despite efforts by the government to foster Malay interests, economic inequality increased in the decade following independence, and Malay resentment finally culminated in the race riots of 1969 (Spinanger, 1986; Jomo, 1990).

In the aftermath of the riots, the government announced the New Economic Policy, which aimed to reduce economic inequality between the Malays and the other ethnic communities, particularly the Chinese. The Second Malaysia Plan 1971–1975 announced that,

the first prong is to reduce and eventually eradicate poverty, by raising income levels and increasing employment opportunities for all Malaysians, irrespective of race. The second prong aims at accelerating the process of restructuring Malaysian society to correct economic imbalance, so as to reduce and eventually eliminate the identification of race with economic function.

To build the 'first prong' the plan aimed to reduce Malaysia's dependence on primary products by encouraging labour-intensive light industries which would raise the share of manufactured goods in exports. Here Malaysian officials were following what they considered the Japanese model of development. To build the 'second prong' the government imposed quotas in education, employment, and access to capital to privilege Malays. Here Malaysian officials adopted the definitions of race imposed by the British on the very diverse Chinese, Indian, and Malay communities, because they suited the interests of the Malay political elite and conveniently glossed over the potentially dangerous divisions among Malays and between the mass of Malays and the elite (Lubeck, 1992, pp. 185–7). Places in schools and universities were reserved for Malays, and incentive schemes encouraged employers to prefer Malays in hiring new workers. The entire economy was to be restructured in ways which would improve the economic position of Malays. A new regional policy favoured poor regions with majority Malay populations. Government leaders particularly emphasized plans to reduce the proportion of Malays in agriculture, because they regarded the disproportionately large numbers of Malay farmers as both the cause and the main symptom of Malay backwardness.

The programmes were inconsistent, and they did not lead to either growth or equality. The share of Malays in agriculture did decline from around two-thirds in 1970 to 40 per cent in 1985, but in the meantime the government had also introduced programmes to improve the position of small farmers, mostly Malays. Along with regional subsidies and general programmes for rural welfare, these included an uneconomic attempt to promote self-sufficiency in rice, and expensive projects to encourage the processing of rubber produced by Malay small-holders. An attempt to create a heavy industrial sector was generally unsuccessful, producing a 'non-functioning' steel mill and an automobile, the Proton Saga, which depended entirely on Mitsubishi for parts and management, and on tariffs for sales (Lubeck, 1992, p. 183).

The New Economic Policy led to rent-seeking behaviour. Influential Malays used government quotas and incentive schemes to obtain preferential treatment for themselves and their families and friends. Trust agencies, which were intended both to provide capital for Malay enterprises and broaden ownership of assets in the Malay community, were in fact largely unaccountable to their shareholders, and they provided a conduit for the distribution of patronage and a source of funds for those in control. A few large corporations, mostly foreign-owned, controlled the major portion of financial assets and production in the mining, plantation, and manufacturing sectors. Local ownership of these corporations was highly concentrated in the hands of a few wealthy families, and the Malay directors (some 12 per cent of the total) generally had political or civil service backgrounds and held honorary or hereditary titles (Snodgrass, 1980; Hui, 1981). A frequently cited study concluded that around one hundred families owned nearly half of the capital of all Malaysian corporations. There was a large increase in income inequality within the Malay community, but on average Malays remained behind Indians and Chinese. Discriminatory hiring policies ensured that Malays enjoyed the lowest unemployment rate, but the professions remained overwhelmingly non-Malay. In 1985 Malays made up less than 25 per cent of architects, accountants, engineers, dentists, veterinary surgeons, and interestingly a similarly small proportion of lawyers. The major result of the New Economic Policy had been the development and consolidation of the Malay upper class (Faaland et al., 1991; Jomo, 1990; Hill, 1994).

Singapore

If you are going to have a planned economy, take over everything, plan your economy before you have got your technicians and your technocrats, how do you do it unless you have a really big power who says 'Look, let me help you and train these men for you'? Whereas if you take a more pragmatic approach and say, 'Well all right, let's build up these skills and this capacity for industrial production, half-socialist and half capitalist, and let the future be decided by the next generation', I think you will make better progress.

Lee Kuan Yew

Following the elections of 1959, Singapore became a one-party state ruled by Lee Kuan Yew and a small group of men close to him who shared his background in local elite schools and advanced education in Britain, such as economist Goh Keng-Swee. Their political vehicle, the People's Action Party, resting on the Chinese working and lower middle classes who made up three-quarters of Singapore's population, dominated the legislature with consistent large majorities. However, although the forms of the electoral and judicial processes were maintained, Lee and his henchmen harassed opponents and carefully controlled the media. Criticism of the government brought suits for defamation, convictions, fines, and possibly imprisonment. The National Trades Union Congress, under the umbrella of the PAP, which enrolled 90 per cent of union members, was headed by a government minister and staffed by government bureaucrats. There were no strikes or disturbances.

Its expulsion from Malaysia in 1965 cut Singapore off from its hinterland. The withdrawal of British troops 'east of Suez' in 1967 meant the loss of fully 10 per cent of national income and 40 000 unemployed workers. Singapore was forced to rely on its own resources. A small island, Singapore depends on imported food, raw materials, and energy – water supplies also have to be drawn from the mainland. In order to pay for these imports, Singapore must earn foreign exchange. In 1965 there was therefore no choice among policy options; Singapore was forced to pursue an 'export oriented' policy. On the other hand, the government also had to establish a reliable revenue base. Taxation, at the levels of income then prevailing, would have been insufficient and potentially dangerous politically. Again, there was no choice; the government would have to go into business itself.

Foreign investment was encouraged, and Singapore profited from a large entrepot trade. But the policy of open borders for trade and investment was combined with an expansion of government enterprises and with extensive intervention in the market. Statutory Boards and Government-Linked Companies (GLCs) proliferated. By 1980 the number of government-owned companies had risen to some 450, and their reported turnover of 8 billion dollars equalled around one-quarter of Singapore's total gross domestic product. A compulsory savings scheme was imposed, and the money channelled into heavy investment in government enterprises. The very large government sector included the provision of public housing, and the outward appearance of the city began to be transformed by massive apartment complexes. Housing policies had a political role as well. Construction projects broke up old neighbourhoods, and assignments to new housing were deliberately manipulated to prevent concentrations of Malays and Indians, in order to prevent them from electing their own representatives to the legislature. In addition the government operated all public utilities, transportation, and communications, but also financial services, trade, shipping, and a substantial number of manufacturing firms, notably in shipbuilding and armaments.

There was no reason to expect that this incoherent mix of programmes would be successful. Public housing was generally provided at subsidized rates, which drained resources from other uses. Although government enterprises ostensibly operated on performance criteria which ensured that returns were adequate, the financial details were secret, and management was accountable only to the government and Lee himself. Nothing particularly recommended Singapore to foreign investors in the environment of the late 1960s, and nothing guaranteed that foreign investment would aid the economy in the long run. The wealthy Chinese business classes, who might have been expected to provide the investment in export industries which Singapore required, were largely excluded from the government's sphere of economic activities, because Lee and his circle did not trust them (Vennewald, 1994). The frustrations of the minority Malay community added a further element of instability. Lee adopted the notion that Malays were inferior in intelligence, which provided a convenient explanation for their lower incomes, and the government manipulated population and education policies in ways intended to divide and disadvantage the minority communities.

Indonesia

In Guided Democracy the key ingredient is leadership. The Guider . . . incorporates a spoonful of so-and-so's opinions with a dash of such-and-such, always taking care to incorporate a *soupçon* of the opposition. Then he cooks it and serves his final summation with 'OK, now my dear brothers, it is like this and I hope you agree . . .' It's still democratic because everybody has given his comment.

Sukarno, *Autobiography*

Indonesia's political history divides into a period of parliamentary democracy from 1945 to 1959, a period of 'guided democracy' lasting from 1959 to 1965, and the 'new order' which followed. The 1945 constitution with its powerful president was announced on 18 August 1945, but suspended in favour of a parliamentary system several months later. A 'federal' constitution drawn up as part of the cease-fire agreement with the Dutch in 1949 was replaced in turn in 1950 by a 'provisional' constitution which provided for detailed guarantees of individual freedoms, a parliamentary system, a largely ceremonial presidency, and a constitutional assembly to create a permanent constitution. Elections were held both for the legislature and for the constitutional assembly in 1955. In 1959, however, Sukarno prorogued both the legislature and the assembly and decreed that the 1945 constitution would be the basis of government.

Sukarno insisted, and many agreed with him, that the very high level of political mobilization in fact made Indonesia ungovernable. The *pancasila* or five principles which he had formulated in 1945 – belief in one god, justice among peoples, unity of Indonesia, democracy through deliberation and consensus, and social justice for all – left Muslim parties and regional interests dissatisfied. Muslim leaders desired a more explicitly Islamic state, and many on the other islands resented the domination of Java. There were several rebellions against the central government in the 1950s, and the most serious combined regional and religious dissatisfaction, for instance the Darul Islam movement in West Java, the independence movement in the south Moluccas, and an army revolt in West Sumatra in 1958. Further, the government had not achieved social justice. The Dutch remained in control of major plantations and industrial enterprises, commerce remained in the hands of the ethnic Chinese minority, and small farmers remained under the domination of rural landlords. The Communist Party, with a membership claimed to be 3 million – the largest in the world outside the Soviet Union and the People's Republic of China – based its appeal on a call for land redistribution. The legislative elections in 1955 had produced a deadlock, with the two largest Muslim parties polling 20.9 and 18.4 per cent, Sukarno's own party 22.3 per cent, and the Communists 16.4 per cent.

Sukarno's solution was 'guided democracy', government by 'mutual cooperation' rather than majority rule. In practice this meant that Sukarno himself decided policy, balancing the interests of his supporters and potential rivals among army, religious, and Communist leaders. In retrospect, this seems an inherently unstable equilibrium. The army remained especially dissatisfied. Its leaders, trained by the Japanese, retained the arrogant mannerisms of their teachers. They considered themselves the conscience of the nation, superior to cowardly politicians, and they were morosely resentful that their central role in creating the new state had not been rewarded with an equally influential role in government and society. Sukarno pursued a confrontational foreign policy, pressing the Dutch for the surrender of Irian Jaya, the eastern half of New Guinea which they still occupied, and protesting the formation of Malaysia and independence for Brunei. Sukarno's anti-Dutch campaign climaxed in 1958 and included a ban on Dutch-language publications, refusal to permit remittances by Dutch expatriates followed by an order for the expulsion of 46 000 Dutch citizens, nationalization of Dutch property, abrogation of the diplomatic and economic agreements which had accompanied independence, and the repudiation of the entire Dutch colonial debt of US$ 1 billion. The *konfrontasi* with Malaysia in 1963–4 included an unsuccessful invasion of Sarawak by Indonesian forces. To punish Britain and the United States for supporting Malaysia, Sukarno nationalized British and American property and told the United States to 'go to hell with your aid'. Sukarno had established normal relations with the People's Republic of China in the 1950s, including a Dual Nationality Citizenship Treaty finally concluded in 1960, under which many of the 1.5 million ethnic Chinese gained Indonesian citizenship. China supported the Indonesian Communist Party, and possibly to balance this influence as well as to make up for the end of United States aid, Sukarno accepted large amounts of military and economic aid from the Soviet Union, as much as US$ 2 billion by 1965.

In the meantime the economy had stalled. Although it cannot quite be said that the Indonesian economy took off in the 1930s, it looks as though it was gathering speed down the runway. As we saw in Chapter 6, small-holder agricultural output rose substantially more rapidly than population from 1900 to 1940, and manufacturing output rose by four-fifths from 1920 to 1940 despite the depression. Wartime destruction returned the economy to levels not experienced for half a century, but the war did not destroy the potential for development, and recovery was rapid. Manufacturing output doubled from the low 1945 to 1950, and had risen another 50 per cent by 1960. However, the 1960 total was not exceeded until 1971. Further, although small-holder agricultural output increased, it only barely kept ahead of the very rapid rise in population (Van der Eng, 1992). That is, having resumed its acceleration down the runway in the 1950s, Indonesia returned to the terminal and postponed take-off for another ten years.

The policies of the new nationalist government clearly hampered development. In agriculture the very high quality agricultural research programme maintained by the Dutch was destroyed during the 1950s. The later acceleration of output resulted from imports of rice strains developed at the International Rice Research Institute in the Philippines, in part based on Dutch research (Van der Eng, 1994b). In manufacturing, the state sector had expanded greatly with the nationalization of some 800 Dutch, British, and American firms, but the departure of Dutch and other foreign managers left a mixture of bureaucrats and army officers in charge, most of whom were not technically trained, and many of whom were corrupt. Smuggling, often with the connivance and sometimes actually sponsored by corrupt bureaucrats and army officers, reached epidemic proportions. Soeharto was removed from his command in 1959 for being 'a shade too energetic' in his efforts to improve his own and his division's finances by such means (Schwarz, 1994, p. 28). Sukarno diverted a large fraction of the government budget to the construction of grandiose monuments and public buildings.

Sukarno believed political reform, mobilizing the people, and raising their consciousness to be more important than economic development, more efficient manufacturing, or the mundane details of bureaucratic reform, and he dismissed his critics as 'chicken-hearted souls with a grocer's mentality'. But 'guided democracy' in fact excluded the people from political activity, and national income probably declined in the mid-1960s. Foreign exchange receipts from plantation agriculture – still the major export – declined from US$ 442 million in 1958 to US$ 330 million in 1966. The government attempted to implement a rather confused and inconsistent policy of import substitution, which in part reflected the difficulty of attracting foreign capital following the nationalization of foreign enterprises, but as noted above manufacturing output stagnated. The large government deficits were covered by credit creation, leading to runaway inflation, with prices rising 100 per cent annually from 1961 through 1964 and 500 per cent in 1965. Lower-level government officials often resorted to second jobs, frequently driving pedicabs. An attempt to stabilize prices in 1963 – a requirement of an aid package from the United States and the International Monetary Fund following the settlement of the dispute over Irian Jaya, but before the dispute over Malaysia – involved budget cuts which hurt the army and interest rate increases which hurt small businesses. The Communist Party attracted support from unemployed youths and frustrated members of the educated elite in Jakarta and other urban centres, as well as from tenant farmers in the countryside. In addition to their 3 million members, the Communists claimed to have enrolled 5.7 million farmers in their peasant front, which would have given them the support of a quarter of all farming families.

The Communist Party, though far from being merely 'Chinese', did have a large Chinese membership, and leaned increasingly towards the People's Republic. The army, hostile to its Communist rivals, extended its hostility to Chinese in general. In 1959, even as negotiations were proceeding with the People's Republic, an official ban on 'aliens' engaging in rural trade provided regional army units with an excuse to begin forcibly moving Chinese from the countryside into the cities, and over 130 000 people were actually repatriated to China. Sukarno and of course the Communist Party opposed these actions. In 1963 the Communist Party launched a 'unilateral action' to implement land reform laws which had been passed in 1959–60. Farmers, especially in central and eastern Java, but elsewhere as well, began to seize land. Landlords, many of them supporters of the Muslim parties, resisted, and the Communist-inspired farmers came into conflict with regional military commanders as well. Violence spread through the countryside, with fights, burning of crops and buildings, kidnappings, and murder.

As the economy collapsed and political conflict escalated out of control, Sukarno's health began to fail, raising the possibility of instability at the top of the political pyramid as well. On 30 September 1965 a group of leftist army officers seized and murdered a group of senior generals, and announced that they had prevented a planned coup by the army. However, Soeharto, now the commander of the army's elite strategic reserve command, assumed control of the army, navy, and police, and the next night his troops overran the air base where the coup was centred. This was only the beginning, however. Army personnel and Muslims began to hunt and kill real and suspected Communists. Soeharto removed army units whose loyalty he doubted from some areas, and the 'loyal' units which replaced them often participated in the killings; in addition he seems to have encouraged continued violence in Jakarta so that in the end Sukarno would be forced to yield power to him to restore order (Ricklefs, 1993, p. 289). Some Muslim leaders declared the extermination of the Communists to be a holy war in which death would mean salvation. Landlords clearly often seized the opportunity to have the local leaders of tenant farmers' movements murdered, whether they were Communists or not. Religious, ethnic, and class hostilities combined to unravel the fabric of society. The killing began in mid-October 1965, raged into early 1966, and continued sporadically for a year thereafter. Estimates of the total number of dead range from a low of 100 000 to over 1 million; most place the number of victims between 300 000 and 400 000.

Because the violence was primarily rural, and because so many Chinese had already been driven out of the rural areas, most of the victims were not Chinese; nevertheless, the Chinese suffered as particular targets of hostility. Even though some Chinese led the demonstrations in favour of Soeharto, anti-Communist violence in Jakarta often took an anti-Chinese turn. They were driven out of Aceh and parts of North Sumatra, and the indigenous Dayaks attacked and expelled 45 000 Chinese from West Kalimantan over a year after the violence had abated elsewhere. At the end of 1966 Soemitro, serving as military commander of East Java, announced restrictions which would have obliterated the Chinese presence there: 'I didn't allow them to live in villages, I didn't want them to trade, I didn't even want them in business. No public use of the Chinese language, no Chinese books, no public speaking of Chinese, no Chinese shrines, nothing. We needed a comprehensive solution' (Schwarz, 1994, pp. 20–1, 105–6).

Soeharto adroitly exploited the violence to marginalize and then to replace Sukarno as head of the government. The new regime immediately received infusions of aid, first from Japan and then from a consortium of non-Communist creditors. In addition, the 'new order' at first seemed to have struck it lucky with a massive increase in revenue from oil sales. But, as in 1963 the conditions imposed by Indonesia's creditors were stringent, and the oil proved a mixed blessing. The money proved too much of a temptation, and flagrant corruption led to a scandal and a crisis in Pertamina, the state oil corporation, in 1975–6. For the rest of the economy, oil brought a variant of the 'Dutch disease', named after the economic malaise suffered by the Netherlands following the oil and natural gas discoveries at Groningen in the 1960s. Oil was a sort of enclave which provided relatively few jobs and used imported machinery, and therefore had little developmental impact on the rest of the economy. However, the money brought in by oil exports caused inflation, and as a result most of the non-oil export sector became uncompetitive. For the ruling elite, revenues from oil made it seem that the decline in other exports did not matter. Through the 1970s the government opted for a capital-intensive approach to development, investing in large-scale projects in oil refining, fertilizer, cement, aircraft, and other industries, projects which also favoured upper-income groups (Dapice, 1980). Many of these enterprises were poorly supervised, and some were corrupt, but until a sudden drop in oil prices in the 1980s brought a new crisis, reform seemed unnecessary (Hill, 1994). In 1981 a team of specialists concluded that 'no sympathetic observer can fail to be struck by the magnitude of Indonesia's development problems . . . while the 1970s was the best decade in Indonesia's recorded history for sustained growth, too many opportunities were missed . . . there is little reason to be sanguine about the future' (Booth and McCawley, 1981, pp. 321–2).

10

HOW MUCH IS THERE TO SHARE? POPULATION, RESOURCES AND PRODUCTIVITY

Although the debate over 'socialism' often overshadowed purely economic analysis, there was a good economic case for the pessimism expressed in the 1950s and 1960s regarding Asia's prospects for development. Asia seemed desperately short of the factors which economists identify as contributing to economic growth – the physical resources of land, labour, and capital, and the intangible resources of technology and entrepreneurship. Gunnar Myrdal's massive three-volume study, *Asian Drama* (1968), was a classic statement in its pessimistic, nearly despairing tone. Natural resources appeared inadequate, the labour force was overwhelmingly rural and uneducated, and capital seemed to be scarce. Modern technology seemed beyond the capacity of Asian societies, whether because of the shortage of capital, the insufficient supplies of skilled labour, or the inadequate knowledge of both government officials and private capitalists. Finally, Asian societies seemed traditional, unable to provide the supply of vigorous entrepreneurs required by a dynamic economy.

Underlying the pessimism regarding Asia's prospects was concern over the impact of rapidly rising population on economic development. Clifford Geertz's influential study of 'agricultural involution' in Indonesia argued that increases in rice output simply called forth additional increases in population, and conversely that increases in population could be absorbed by rice production even at very low levels of productivity. As a result, 'most of Java is crowded with post-traditional wet-rice peasant villages: large, dense, vague, dispirited communities – the raw material of a rural, non-industrialized mass society'. This might contribute to 'the real possibility of a totalitarian triumph', but Geertz could see 'no evidence' of significant change 'in the foreseeable future' (Geertz, 1963, pp. 129–30).

However, the subsequent history of East and Southeast Asia has demonstrated that, contrary to the forebodings of Myrdal, Geertz, and many others, the 'pattern of adaptation' could indeed alter. Childbearing habits, which seemed immutable, have changed. The dramatic declines in birth rates over the past generation show consistent patterns, under both capitalist and socialist regimes. Equally, the dramatic increases in national incomes have demonstrated that abundant natural resources are not a precondition for economic growth, that Asian labour is highly productive, that capital can be made available in sufficient amounts, and that modern technologies can be transplanted to and thrive in Asian environments. The values which a generation ago were proclaimed to be an insuperable hindrance to economic development are now counted as one of the secrets of rapid Asian growth.

Each of these factors provides a possible explanation of Asian growth. Nevertheless, as the sections below make clear, this is not simply a case of one group of experts having been proven wrong by another group. First, as seen in previous chapters, men, women, family groups and local communities had long experience in seizing economic opportunities. And, within each country, each of the factors evolved in its own complex way. The resulting patterns often appear quite similar to European experience, but this merely places Asian history into the same contentious realm as European studies. Thus analysis of the 'demographic transition' in Asia must balance the roles of changing economic conditions, individual choices, family choices, changing power relationships within families, and government policies, as has been the case in European demographic history. We feel on firmer ground looking at the extension of education and improvements in the quality of the labour force, but even here there is dispute. As in Europe, resource-poor Asian regions import raw materials, capital, and new technologies, but specialist scholars disagree over the ways in which these are translated into increases in national income. As in the cases of Chinese and Indonesian economic growth discussed in Chapter 6, although the debate is technical, it is far from merely 'academic'. The political stakes are high. As seen in other chapters, the governments of Asia are politically and socially repressive, but they justify their actions by claiming that they have delivered economic growth. Indeed, Asian political leaders rest their very legitimacy on the success of their economic policies and on the assertion that their policies will continue to succeed in the future. Leaders who have not delivered growth have lost power, and therefore discussions of the sources of growth are extremely sensitive and contentious.

Population Growth and the Demographic Transition in Asia

'Doomsday: Friday 13th November, A.D. 2026'.
H. v. Foerster, et al., *Science* 132 (1960): 1291

The historical development of Asian populations, their size today, and their future development, especially relative to the ageing populations of Europe and the United States, are all topics with obvious economic and political relevance. Historical demographers of Asia have encountered the same problem as students of European population history, namely that the relationship between population and food supplies is not a simple one. Malthus was correct insofar as we require food to live and reproduce, but beyond that truism lie complex relationships. It may be that population growth stimulates improvements in agricultural technology, for instance, and it is not clear what impact changes in food supplies will have on fertility. Further, famines and other major mortality crises seem to have little long-term effect on population growth, because numbers 'recover' rapidly in the aftermath. The famine of 1959–61 may have caused 20 to 30 million deaths in China, but demographically the losses were made good by a rebound in birth rates in the early 1960s (Lavely et al., 1990). Finally, the 'demographic transition' has spread to Asian societies, and although its causes are disputed, it cannot possibly have resulted from changes in nutrition (see Li, 1982, with references to European population history).

Although accurate estimates of China's population were impossible before the 1982 census, most observers agreed that the number of Chinese was accelerating towards one billion. The population of Japan was known to have begun to grow sometime in the nineteenth century, reaching 50 million in the 1860s, 75 million in the 1940s, and 100 million in 1967. Similarly, though each of the populations of Southeast Asia had its own history, all began to participate in a large overall increase from 1800 or 1850. The population of the Philippines, for example, rose 1.63 per cent per year from 1818 to 1918 and 2.46 per cent per year from 1918 to 1975 – but with a further acceleration to 2.89 per cent per year from 1948 to 1975.

Figures such as these, particularly the awesome figure of one billion Chinese, led in the 1960s to scenarios in which the growth of Asian populations would swamp whatever efforts might be made to raise the world's standard of living. Popular accounts employed the metaphor of the 'population bomb', a picture with particular impact in a post-nuclear world (Erlich, 1969). Economic historians portrayed the rise in human numbers as a line on a graph which rose gently for millennia and then turned ominously vertical in the twentieth century (Cipolla, 1965). Population growth, and particularly the acceleration of rates of increase, was one of the major problems cited by Myrdal in his analysis of the 'Asian drama', and one of the major sources of his pessimism regarding the potential for Asian development (Myrdal, 1968, vol. 1, ch. 10). The sources of his concern can be seen in Table 10.1.

Table 10.1 Rates of Growth of Population, 1800–1960 (per cent)

	1800/1850	*1850/1900*	*1900/1950*	*1950/1960*
Burma	0.6	1.1	1.2	1.4
Malaya and Singapore	1.0	2.9	2.2	3.2
Thailand	0.0	0.6	1.8	3.1
Vietnam, Cambodia, Laos	0.3	1.4	1.3	1.9
Philippines	1.4	1.4	2.1	3.1
Java and Madura	1.8	2.1	1.1	2.0 (all of Indonesia)
Rest of Indonesia	0.6	1.0	1.9	

Source: Myrdal, 1968, vol. 1, p. 435.

Clearly these rates could not continue to increase forever. In 1960 a group of scientists projected the accelerating rates of increase forward and calculated 'doomsday' – the day on which the human population would become infinite, and the entire universe would fill with living human flesh – Friday the Thirteenth, November 2026 (Foerster et al., 1960, cited in Pirie, 1969, p. 22).

However, the demographic doomsday has been postponed. Asian populations have undergone a fertility transition similar to the pattern of declining death and birth rates which moved across Europe from northwest to southeast in the nineteenth and early twentieth centuries. The declining birth rates can be seen in Table 10.2. However, and again as in Europe, death rates tended to decline sooner and more rapidly than birth rates, and the excess of births over deaths led to substantial increases in population. The balance can be seen in the rates of population increase shown in Table 10.3. In the 1960s rates of increase did indeed accelerate compared to the 1950s, but since then the rates of increase have declined in almost all Asian countries, and in most cases the decline has been substantial. We cannot be frivolous about the very real problems of unconstrained population growth combined with increasing levels of affluence. Neo-Malthusians (Erlich, 1991) and environmentalists (Suzuki, 1993) emphasize the problems that an exponential rate of growth in demand poses for the future. Laos, Vietnam, Cambodia, and the Philippines showed slight increases in their rates of population growth in the early 1990s, as death rates dropped more rapidly than birth rates. Even the new lower rates of growth are unsustainable in the long run, and some provinces of China and some countries such as Laos, Malaysia, and the Philippines still have rates of population growth high enough to make it very difficult for them to improve average levels of living significantly. But there has been a tendency, extending back to Malthus himself, for demographic pessimists to fail to take improvements in technology into account. In addition, Asian families have proven far more flexible in their demographic habits than most observers considered possible a generation ago.

Table 10.2   Birth Rates, 1950–95 (per 1000)

	1950	1960	1970	1980	1985–90	1990–5
Cambodia	–	–	–	–	42	39
China	37	21	33	18	21[1]	18[2]
Indonesia	–	–	–	–	29	27
Japan	28	17	19	14	11[1]	10
Malaysia[3]	42	41	38	30	32	29
Philippines[4]	32	24 (46)	26 (39)	30 (34)	33	30
Singapore	46	38	23	17	17	16
Taiwan	43	40	27	23	17[1]	12
Thailand	–	–	–	–	23	21
Vietnam	–	–	–	35[5]	32	29

Notes
1   1988.
2   1993.
3   Peninsular Malaya to 1980, then Malaysia.
4   Publication of revised statistics (in parentheses) indicates that the figures before 1980 were considerably understated, but it is not known whether the degree of understatement changed over time.
5   1980–5.
Sources: Hirschmann, 1994; Mitchell 1995; Institute for International Studies, University of Technology, Sydney, *Provincial China*, No. 1, March 1996.

Table 10.3 Rates of Growth of Population, 1950–95 (per cent)

	1950–9	1960–9	1970–9	1980–8	1990–5
Cambodia	2.29	2.49	(-0.90)	2.32	2.50
China	1.99	2.00	1.75	1.18	1.12[1]
Hong Kong	4.16	2.34	2.21	1.29	<1
Indonesia	1.84	2.30	1.81	1.96	1.81
Japan	1.10	0.93	1.06	0.54	<1
North Korea	0.46	2.53	2.38	1.70	1–2
South Korea	1.66	2.35	1.53	1.08	1+
Laos	1.59	2.16	2.23[2]	2.21	3.00
Malaysia	2.58[3]	2.19[3]	2.43[4]	2.39	2.35
Philippines	2.75	2.70	2.37	2.19	2.35
Singapore	4.50	2.18	1.40	1.03	1.04
Taiwan	3.19	2.83[5]	1.76	1.25	1+
Thailand	2.70	2.80	2.08[6]	1.73	1.47
Vietnam	1.52	1.88	na	1.66	2.07

Notes
1 1993–4.
2 1970–7.
3 Peninsular Malaya.
4 Malaysia 1975–9.
5 1961–9.
6 1974–9.
Sources: Calculated from figures in Hirschmann, 1994; Mitchell 1995; Institute for International Studies, University of Technology, Sydney, *Provincial China*, No. 1, March 1996. Recent figures are estimates from various sources. Variations in dates result from changes in estimation procedures or later revisions.

The available statistics are often inconsistent or incomplete. Nevertheless, the direction of development is clear. But why have Asian birth rates declined? Intuitively we feel that birth rates must have some relationship to economic development, and demographers have made elaborate attempts to correlate 'modernization' variables with fertility. These attempts have not been notably successful. A study of the demographic transition in Japan emphasized its 'practical political implications', for 'decreasing fertility is considered to be one of the most important strategies for economic development... Asians have expected Japan to be the most useful model for them'. Estimates suggested that death rates declined beginning in the 1880s, while birth rates may have risen from the 1880s to the 1920s and then begun to decline. However, because different estimates yielded different results with respect to timing, the author simply selected the estimates which fitted his preconceived notion that 'modernization generally reduced fertility, but economic take-off is accompanied by increasing demand for labour and rising levels of living, which may raise the birth rate' (Ohbuchi, 1976, pp. 330, 336–7). Similarly a more recent study continues to argue that the colonial regimes of Southeast Asia restricted modernization – defined as urbanization, industrialization, and increased education – and thereby perpetuated high birth rates into the 1960s, in contrast to Europe, where the birth rate was supposedly already moderate before industrialization and declined more rapidly than in Asia (Hirschmann, 1994, p. 414). In the first case, Japanese 'modernization' is now seen as extending well back into the Tokugawa period, and Japan does not seem to have had a take-off, and the argument therefore collapses; the second ignores both the high and rising birth rates across much of Europe in the first half of the nineteenth century, and the substantial increases in Asian urbanization, education, and even industrialization under the colonial regimes.

No general theory seems to cover all the cases. Thus rising income fails to explain why Malaysian Malays (the most prosperous) have experienced less of a decline in birth rates than Indonesian Malays and Muslims in southern Thailand. Increases in education do not explain the connection between high levels of education and a slow decline in the birth rate in the Philippines. And the influence of government policies fails to explain why the Burmese birth rate should have declined rapidly despite a strongly pro-natalist government policy and very restricted access to contraceptives (Caldwell, 1993).

In much demographic research, social and economic factors are no longer seen as having any direct effect on fertility, but rather as operating through a limited set of behavioural variables, the so-called 'proximate' determinants of fertility, which determine exposure to intercourse, control of conception, and rates of successfully completed pregnancies. Many studies therefore concentrate on showing how the proximate variables have changed over time, and the results predictably are largely descriptive. Further, many studies focus on the description and statistical analysis of government policies, a situation which reflects the fact that demographic research is expensive and has generally been funded by government agencies. One consistent relationship between demographic and social variables is the link between increasing levels of female education and declining birth rates, which suggests that an explanation must take gender relations into account. However, the dominant quantitative and 'scientific' mode of analysis often precludes critical analyses along gender or class lines. For instance, as seen below and in Chapter 11, the measurement of women's participation in the labour force depends on official definitions which often reflect the desires of ruling elites rather than what women actually do, and therefore observed relationships between these measures and fertility tell only a part of the story at best.

Across Asia, states have certainly attempted to influence families in their decision to have a baby. In China optimism and even pride in China's expanding population gave way to a concern for food supplies. The government launched a campaign to limit births in urban areas in 1963 and began the 'later, longer, fewer' campaign to reduce the rural birth rate in 1971. The 'one-child family' policy received high publicity in 1982, and was reportedly interpreted in most regions as permitting 20 births per 1000 population per year. Promised rewards included job security, promotion, and preference in housing and school enrolment for those who complied, and threatened penalties included demotion, fines, and food rationing for those who did not. Horrifying stories of abuses in the enforcement of the policy appeared, of districts where the menstrual periods of all women were monitored and women missing their period were routinely forced to undergo surgical abortions, of clinics where aborted foetuses piled on the floor, awaiting disposal. These reports were seized on by the American media, where they fed into the debate over abortion then raging in the United States. Some of the reports were exaggerated. Further, it is not clear whether the numerous reported examples of abuses represented evidence that local cadres were ordered to coerce women into compliance, or whether their publication was evidence of the central government's attempts to fight abuses (Mosher, 1983; see Diamond, 1985; Banister, 1987).

How effective was the one-child policy in causing the reduction in the birth rate? Overall, the birth rate did drop rapidly, from 37 per 1000 in the early 1950s, to around 30 in the early 1970s, 20 in the early 1980s, and 17 in the early 1990s. The birth rates of 20.9 and 18.0 per 1000 recorded in 1960 and 1961 reflected the effects of the famine; a recovery peak in 1963 (43.4 per 1000) was followed by a drop towards the declining trend. Between 1970 and 1980 rural fertility declined 60 per cent, an unprecedented rate for any large population (Lavely et al., 1990, p. 814). However, the decline had begun before the change in government policy. From the standpoint of modernization theory, the early decline in birth rates could be attributed to the changed institutional context under Communist rule. Work units, it was argued, now had the power to reward families who limited their offspring and penalize those who did not, while at the same time intermediate organizations established by party and state agencies provided a new counterbalance to the pull of traditional family ties

(Rozman, 1981). This, however, did not explain China's replication of the pattern of European population history, with high-income urban areas showing the earliest and sharpest declines, or the contrasting reported willingness of affluent families to pay the fines for extra children in the 1980s. The official relaxation of the one-child policy after 1984 was followed nationally by an increase in the proportion of women who had a second child. However, the aggregate birth rate continued to decline, because the proportion of women having a third or later child declined continuously over the entire period (Croll et al., 1985; Lavely et al., 1990, p. 814). The desire for large families declined, but the reasons remain obscure.

Many other Asian governments introduced policies to limit the growth of their populations, and as in China those policies interacted with the desires and plans of families to cause sharp declines in birth rates. In South Korea, family planning and the distribution of contraceptives, but also a continuing trend towards later marriage for women, caused a decline in fertility of both urban and rural women which cut the rate of population growth in half between the early 1960s and the early 1970s (Moskowitz, 1982, p. 78). In Singapore the development of a population control programme beginning in 1949 was followed by a rapid decline in fertility from the late 1950s. Family planning services were at first available through the Family Planning Association, but the decline accelerated after the institution of the more interventionist programmes of the Singapore Family Planning and Population Board. Through the 1960s and 1970s the government offered special priority for primary school enrolment to children from small families and to those whose parents had been sterilized before their fortieth birthdays. On the other hand, fertility decline was also correlated with changes in attitudes associated with a broad range of 'modernization' variables, such as education, female participation in the labour force, industrialization, declining numbers of domestic servants, 'breakdown of the extended family system', and 'a higher standard of living' (Saw, 1980, p. 182). In Thailand contraceptive use increased dramatically across classes and regions and the birth rate declined in the 1970s, with the encouragement of the Ministry of Public Heath and the high profile campaign of 'the minister for condoms' Mechai Viravaidaya (Krannich and Krannich, 1980; Knodel et al., 1987). As in Singapore, however, the impact of government policy is difficult to assess, because declining fertility was also accompanied by the beginnings of rapid income growth, and therefore policy intertwined with 'modernization' variables.

In Indonesia, Sukarno had proclaimed grandiloquently that the nation could support double or treble the 97 million people enumerated in the 1961 census. It has become one of the myths of the 'new order' that Soeharto reversed this pro-natalist policy unilaterally and single-handedly. Soeharto did indeed receive the United Nations Population Award in 1989 for his efforts, but at first he expressed no interest in birth control because of the danger of arousing the sensitivities of devout Muslims and accusations of 'immorality'. The pressure for family planning to become official policy came from the activist governor of Jakarta, Ali Sadikin, and the expansionist National Family Planning Coordinating Board (BKKBN). Sadikin was resented for his aggressive promotion of economic growth in Jakarta, and the BKKBN for its rapid expansion, access to foreign funding, and tendency to trespass on other agencies' areas of competence. Nevertheless, with Soeharto's support family planning for Java and Bali was included in the first five-year development plan, and eventually the BKKBN symbol and its slogans became ubiquitous. The government favoured particularly effective methods such as oral contraceptives, intrauterine devices, and injectibles (Dapice, 1980; McNicoll and Singarimbun, 1983). Policy was implemented through the coordinated efforts of several ministries, and through the Family Welfare Movement (PKK), the compulsory women's organization described in Chapter 11. Target-setting, periodic campaigns concentrating on particular target groups, and promotion of 'local autonomy' (at least to the extent of selecting names for programmes from local languages) have been cited as reasons for the 'success' of the BKKBN in reducing the birth rate.

However, the government's family planning policies were introduced at a time when the practice of parents arranging marriages for their young adolescent daughters with older men was declining. Therefore the age at marriage was rising, and these changes were already taking place before 1965. Infant mortality also declined, reducing the need for large families to ensure that some children survived. Further, surveys have shown that married people, increasing numbers of whom have chosen a marriage partner close to their own age, have altered their notion of the 'ideal' number of children from as many as five in the 1970s, to fewer than three in some regions in the 1990s. And finally, reported contraceptive use rose from a total of 18 per cent in 1976 to 50 per cent in 1991. The changes are greatest among the educated urban middle classes, and therefore are also correlated with rising housing prices and lengthening commuting times, especially for professional workers in Jakarta. Clearly the government has supported the desires of couples in making information and contraceptives available, but on balance it appears 'historical accident' has played at least as important a role as government policy (Hull, 1994).

In the Philippines, in contrast, government policies to reduce fertility were not especially successful up to 1975, despite favourable 'preconditions'. Further, they failed completely with the group of theoretically 'most ready' women, those under age thirty who stated they did not desire any more children. Analysts blamed poor coordination of public agencies, along with advocacy of relatively ineffective methods such as rhythm and condoms (Flieger and Pagtolun-an, 1981). Rhythm, the most unreliable, is the only method countenanced by the Catholic Church, which remains opposed to birth control in principle, and condoms of course depend entirely on the willingness of males for success. Under the Aquino government the Catholic hierarchy increased its influence and the government's commitment to birth control lessened. However, the entire government effort has been questioned; an analysis of the regional results of the 1978 population survey concluded that differing rates of economic development, rather than family planning, were the key to fertility decline (Hackenberg and Magalit, 1985). The statistical picture is clouded by new estimates which indicate that the birth rate before 1980 was seriously understated. It appears, however, that in the 1980s the birth rate and the rate of population growth both began to drop, quite apart from any change in policy.

In addition to the conceptual and practical problems of analysing fertility change, another difficulty in analysis is the interplay and potential conflict of population policy with other social, political, and economic goals. Government policy can be inconsistent, and it can change, depending on the interests of those in power. As we will see in Chapter 11, governments take an interest in women not only as mothers but also as workers, while trying at the same time to minimize their impact on political life, and these aims are frequently contradictory. In Indonesia, although there is no organized opposition to family planning, the government is concerned about devout Muslim opinion, and their opposition to 'immorality' has restricted access to condoms and limited public discussion of sexual issues such as AIDS. In Malaysia, President Mahathir Mohamed announced in 1984 that Malaysia required a population of 70 million by the year 2100 in order to create a sufficiently large domestic market to support the desired level of industrialization. Although the new goal would in fact have required a substantial reduction in the then current rate of population growth of some 2.4 per cent per year, Mahathir and other government officials confusingly called for rapid and substantial increases in fertility rates based on the principle that every woman should have five children (Healy, 1994, p. 102). Sometimes the interests of those in power are transparently political. Nationalist elites become nervous when birth rates decline close to replacement levels, for instance in Thailand. In the case of Singapore, projections showed that in the absence of significant migration, the population would stabilize by 2040, at 3.7 million. In response the government reversed course and began to encourage families to have more children, but only when the parents had a university education. President Lee Kuan Yew asserted in 1983 that the failure of tertiary-educated women to have as many children as less-educated women meant that 'levels of competence will decline. Our economy will falter, the administration will suffer and the society will decline'. The 'Graduate Mothers Policy' included tax incentives, insurance benefits, and preferential school registration for the children of tertiary-educated women, and conversely offered cash payments to poor and less-educated women who agreed to sterilization. The Social Development Unit, a state matchmaking agency, aimed to ensure that all tertiary-educated women married. The policy clearly favoured the Chinese, and proved so offensive that it was dropped in 1985. The government then resorted to 'less conspicuous' policies such as early streaming and programmes for 'gifted' students in the schools, and measures intended to encourage the immigration of Chinese (Rahim, 1994, ch. 7). The real problem, from the government's perspective, was that the birth rate of the Malay population in Singapore had not fallen as rapidly as that of the Chinese population, and existing trends would see the Malays become the majority ethnic group early in the next century.

Education and Investment in 'Human Capital'

Why isn't the whole world developed? . . . The answer, I suggest, has to do in important part with differences among countries in the extent of their population's formal schooling.

Richard Easterlin, 1981

Japan trains students to a high average level, but Japan does not encourage the really excellent student.

Teacher, elite private school, Tokyo, 1996

Assuming that population does not grow so rapidly as to swamp increases in income, then rising numbers of people mean that more workers will be available. However, in modern economic growth it is not only the number of workers which matters, but also their quality. Educated workers are more productive than uneducated workers. In Japan the relatively high level of both male and female literacy before the Meiji Restoration is commonly cited as a cause of rapid Japanese growth. Other countries have tended to experience surges in growth following a spread of basic education: Korea and Taiwan in the 1960s and 1970s, and Malaysia, Indonesia, and Thailand in the 1970s and 1980s. Education and training are expensive, and economists therefore refer to 'investment' in 'human capital'. The costs of education interact with other variables as well. Increased investment in female education, for instance, is correlated with declining birth rates. Education is expensive, not only for governments but for individual families as well, but education raises the value of girls. Educated girls and women in turn are more likely to take paid employment outside the home. This kind of employment decreases the time available for child-bearing and child-rearing, but it also increases the power of women within the family.

Education began to expand in the colonial period, as we saw in Chapters 7 and 8, and growth continued in the postwar period, especially secondary and tertiary enrolments, as shown in Tables 10.4, 10.5, and 10.6. The newly independent governments generally performed better than their colonial predecessors. Colonial governments certainly laid the foundation of primary education systems, but they hesitated to educate 'natives' above a certain level. The new national governments worked to extend primary education to all children, and they also substantially expanded education at the secondary and tertiary levels. There is still much to be accomplished. In the early 1990s in Indonesia, for instance, primary education had become nearly universal, but despite a doubling of secondary enrolments over the previous decade, a child still only had a one in three chance of enrolling in a secondary school, and then again only a one in three chance of moving on to tertiary education.

China lagged behind, and the figures show the influence of politics. After a substantial increase in the 1950s, primary enrolments stagnated, then rose, then declined in subsequent decades. The figures for secondary enrolments show a similar pattern, and the numbers remained very small relative to population in the late 1980s. The effects of the 'cultural revolution' and the attacks on intellectuals of all sorts are clear in the figures for tertiary enrolments. In addition, the 1982 census revealed that an entire cohort of the rural population had been deprived of schooling of any kind during the 'great leap forward'. There were substantial increases in the 1990s, but China remained a generation behind the rest of Asia, with only 2.8 million students enrolled in universities and a total of only 637 000 university graduates in a population of 1.2 billion in 1994.

The contrast between the People's Republic and Taiwan, the 'other' China, is revealing. In Taiwan, primary education became nearly universal in the mid-1970s, and schooling extended beyond basic primary instruction. Enrolments of people aged 12–14 rose from 23 per cent in the early 1950s, to 85 per cent in the early 1970s, and 100 per cent in the early 1980s. For the 15–17 age group, enrolments rose from 24 per cent in the early 1960s to 68 per cent in 1985–7. By the early 1990s over half of secondary students continued on to tertiary study. The large increases in enrolments and rates of enrolment were matched by substantial increases

Table 10.4   Asia: Enrolments in Primary Education, 1950–88, in Thousands, and as Percentage of School-Age Population

	1950	(%)	1960	(%)	1970	(%)	1980	(%)	1988	(%)
Cambodia	173		561		338		na		na	
China	28920	(24)	93790		105000		146000	(60)	125000	
Indonesia	5318[2]		8953	(38.1)	14870	(45.3)	22487	(57.8)	26725	
Japan	11202	(61.5)	12608	(62.4)	9493	(58.6)	11827	(62.1)	9873	
South Korea	2370[3]		3621	(58.1)	5749		5658	(63.9)	4820	
Laos	35		99		245		479		559[5]	
Malaysia[1]	677[2]		1273	(62.8)	1685	(56.0)	2009	(59.0)	2328	
Myanmar	358		1512		3249		4148	(47.9)	5202	
Philippines	3883	(70.5)	4200	(53.8)	6969	(71.9)	8290	(66.0)	9972	
Singapore	122		286		364		292		259	
Taiwan	907		1889		2445		2234	(59.6)	2407	
Thailand	2782		3586	(50.7)	4860	(49.3)	7393	(62.9)	6518	
Vietnam	590		1335[2]		2718[4]		8122		11387	

Notes
1   Enrolments including Sabah and Sarawak; percentage relates enrolment to population in Peninsular Malaysia only.
2   1951.
3   1952.
4   South Vietnam only.
5   1987.
Source: Calculated from data in Mitchell, 1995. Census years not always exactly the same as enrolment figures. 'School age' population is taken to mean ages 5 to 14, and therefore 60 to 70 per cent is the maximum possible, depending on the age children enter primary school, and the age at which they move to secondary school. The figures listed by Mitchell for China are apparently incorrect by a factor of 10.

Table 10.5   Asia: Enrolments in Secondary Education, 1950–1988, in thousands

	1950	1960	1970	1980	1988
Cambodia	3.5	34	83	na	na
China	1300	10 260	26 420	55 080	47 610
Indonesia	178[2]	744	1261	4365	8946
Japan	7279	9158	8948	9716	11 429
South Korea	424[3]	834	1634	3405	3981
Laos	0.7	2.9	10	79	119[6]
Malaysia[1]	43[2]	170	571	1076	1320
Myanmar	27	223	792	1046	1421
Philippines	485	670	1719	3019	3737
Singapore	7	58	137	174	202
Taiwan	80	263	978	1256	1298
Thailand	127	605/231[4]	512	1617	1735
Vietnam	31	212[5]	734[5]	3973	na

Notes
1   Enrolments including Sabah and Sarawak.
2   1951. 3   1952. 4   Changed definition. 5   South Vietnam only. 6   1987.
Source: Calculated from data in Mitchell, 1995. The figures listed by Mitchell for China are apparently incorrect by a factor of 10.

in expenditure and expenditure per student. Spending on education rose from 10 to 16.5 per cent of the government budget and from 1.7 to 5.1 per cent of national product from 1950–5 to 1984–7. Girls' educational participation rates increased faster than boys' rates, and their rising levels of education led to increasing measured women's participation rates in the labour force. Observers traced a clear link between increased skills and mobility – especially of women – and export growth (Chen and Hou, 1989, pp. 378–87).

It might seem obvious that investment in education was one of the 'secrets' of Asian growth. Non-Marxist economists and economic historians have argued that low levels of investment in education explain both 'why the whole world isn't developed' and 'why capital doesn't flow from rich to poor countries' (Easterlin, 1981; Lucas 1990). Presumably low levels of education result in low levels of productivity, perpetuating poverty and discouraging foreign investors, and therefore increasing educational levels would have the opposite effect. However, scholars are far from united in their view of the role of education and training in the ongoing process of development. The relationship between the educational system and economic growth is not direct, but complex and often coincidental. The expansion of education did not lead to increases in foreign investment

Table 10.6   Asia: Enrolments in Higher Education, 1950–88, in thousands

	1950	1960	1970	1980	1988
Cambodia	na	2	10	na	na
China[1]	137	962	48	1144	2066
Indonesia	na	29	248	566[8]	1179[9]
Japan	400	712	1670/1407[7]	1835	1995
South Korea	33[4]	101	201	648	1387
Laos	na	0.1	0.5	1.4	5.3[9]
Malaysia[2]	na	0.7	8	61	121
Myanmar	3[5]	13	50	162	222
Philippines	189	301	637	1276	1580
Singapore	0.8[6]	9	14	23	47
Taiwan	6.7	35	203	343	497
Thailand	25	51	55	599	703
Vietnam[3]	1.8	11	57	146	128

Notes
1   Universities.
2   1960 and 1970 peninsular Malaya only; 1960, 1970, 1980 universities only.
3   1960 and 1970 South Vietnam only; 1950, 1960, 1970 universities only.
4   1952.
5   1949.
6   1951.
7   Students in colleges and universities only after 1970.
8   1981.
9   1987.
Source: Calculated from data in Mitchell, 1995.

in Asia in the 1960s, for Western investors still did not consider Asian workers reliable and productive. The behaviour, attitudes, and lack of skills of local labour were cited in surveys of United States firms as the reason they had decided against an investment in every single East and Southeast Asian country, including Japan (Hanson, 1996).

It is not clear that all education is of equal value. Some of the advertisements for schools and courses which crowd Southeast Asian newspapers simply pander to the demand for paper qualifications regardless of quality. At the other end of the spectrum genuinely elite national universities such as Tokyo, Seoul, or Chulalongkorn are often competitive precisely because they offer entry into the guaranteed security of the bureaucracy. And there is the question of content, in the sense of specific knowledge imparted, the values and attitudes inculcated, and the general attitude towards the acquisition of knowledge fostered. World Bank economists congratulate the 'high performance Asian economies' for concentrating on expanding primary and secondary education, 'leaving demand for tertiary education to be largely met by a self-financed private system', and also for the success of their students in international comparative tests of cognitive skills, particularly mathematics. However, as they note, not all Asian students do well on standardized tests, and those that do well may benefit from the fit between the test and their curriculum as well as from 'teaching to the test' (World Bank, 1993, pp. 16, 45, 70–2). Further, an emphasis on primary-level, testable cognitive skills may not be the best basis for either short-term or long-term development. In the short term, industry-specific skills may be essential; in the longer term, higher levels of critical thinking may be more important than skill at solving set mathematical problems. The concern expressed by the Japanese teacher quoted above, that the system may bring students to a certain level but fail to foster genuine original talent, is shared by thoughtful educators elsewhere in Asia as well.

International fashion plays a role in the evaluation of educational systems – the authors of the World Bank study obviously felt bound to cite educational systems as a cause of Asian growth, despite the contradictory nature of the evidence. It was not always so. In Korea, for instance, in the 1970s observers worried that the educational system did not teach workers the skills required by industry. Rather, they noted, at all levels the system emphasized memorization, rote learning, and heavy-handed moral education. At the time this did not seem the best basis for modern economic development, although it was argued that by encouraging discipline and acceptance of social roles the educational system might have contributed to social integration and stability, and therefore, possibly, indirectly to the rapid rise in industrial output (McGinn et al., 1980, pp. 219–30; Mason et al., 1980, p. 378). Twenty years later, the 'new Confucian ethic', with its emphasis on 'spiritual and psychological discipline of the self', the aggregate expenditure of 13.3 per cent of national product on education, and in addition the fact that 'it is very common in Korea for parents to sacrifice their lives solely for the education of their children', were confidently cited as reasons for Korea's economic success (Song, 1994, p. 51). More sceptical observers noted that increases in university enrolments had matched the increase in the size of the government bureaucracy, that family saving and spending on education continued even in periods of over-supply of graduates in the 1960s and again in the 1980s – and that despite the high levels of education of the labour force, Korea suffered a continuing shortage of skilled workers, compared to university graduates (Robinson, 1991, pp. 222–3).

Education continues to be contentious in another sense. In all countries, education has an intimate connection to politics, to the power and prestige of social groups, and to the definition of the national community. Singapore's unsuccessful attempt to introduce 'Confucian' values into the school curriculum is of particular interest, because of the role which 'Neo-Confucian' ethics – considered in Chapter 12 – are often asserted to have played in economic development. In fact before 1970 Confucianism was not a topic of discussion in Singapore. Then in 1979 Deputy Prime Minister Goh Keng Swee, widely regarded as the architect of Singapore's successful economic policies, was placed in charge of the education ministry. The ensuing Goh Report recommended that a course in Moral Education replace the existing Education for Living and Civics courses, and that it be linked with religious instruction. In 1982 the government announced that Religious Knowledge courses would be compulsory from 1984. 'Confucianism' was added as an option, Goh travelled to the United States to consult with Chinese–American Confucian scholars as to which parts of Confucian ethics to introduce into the programme, Americans were retained as consultants, and an Institute of East Asian Philosophies was opened.

The Religious Knowledge course did not fulfil the government's hopes. In five years only about one-quarter of ethnic Chinese students opted for the Confucianism strand, and only half of the numbers of ethnic Chinese enrolled in Buddhism. 'Confucianism' faced problems as a philosophy of life competing with religions backed up by institutions and ritual. Organized religions were enjoying a revival and expansion, but it was not religion which the government wanted to encourage, because of the danger that religious conviction might lead to political activism. In 1987 several Catholic social workers agitating on behalf of Filipino maids were detained under the Internal Security Act, the Christian Conference of Asia was dissolved, a number of Christian missionaries were expelled, and visas were denied to foreign Islamic ulamas. The government introduced a 'Religious Harmony Bill' which formalized the complete separation of religion from politics. As these events were occurring, the government announced that the Religious Knowledge course would be phased out and replaced by a secular moral education programme. The new course emphasized certain selected 'Asian values', especially uncritical acceptance of authority and respect for teachers, scholars, elders, parents, the family, and the state. In addition, the government redoubled its efforts to foster Mandarin, insisting that it was the only 'mother tongue' for all Chinese and discriminating against other Chinese dialects as well as other languages. Lee Kuan Yew himself had written in the Goh Report that 'the greatest value in the teaching and learning of Chinese is in the transmission of the norms of social or moral behavior. This means principally Confucianist beliefs and ideas, of man, society and the state' (Wong and Wong, 1989; Rahim, 1994, ch. 7).

The question is often not whether education will contribute to national welfare, but which groups of children will benefit in the next generation. In Singapore the government intends the beneficiaries to be Chinese. In 1996 Malaysia began debate on an education bill intended to cover all aspects of schooling from preschool to university. The Malay-dominated government described the bill as a key instrument for producing a skilled workforce to move the country towards industrialized status. The opposition accused the government of keeping the contents of the bill secret over a period of ten years, and then rushing it through the parliament to prevent discussion. The bill was expected to extend the scope of Islamic religious education and to increase the compulsory use of the Malay language. Although it retained the semi-independent status of Chinese and Tamil schools, the opposition claimed the bill in fact imposed new restrictions on them. In the eyes of the opposition the new bill would in fact work to privilege Malays and disadvantage Chinese and Indians.

The Labour Force and Labour Movements

HPAE [high-performing Asian economies] governments have generally been less vulnerable and less responsive than other developing-economy governments to organized labour's demands to legislate a minimum wage.

World Bank, *The East Asian Miracle*, 1993

It is worse than the military.

Blue collar worker, Poongsan Corporation,
Korea, late 1980s

The increase in the size of the labour force in late nineteenth- and early twentieth-century Asia shows aspects familiar to students of European social history, notably heavy migration, the persistence of traditional patterns of employment and social relationships, and various forms of coercion. With independence, coerced labour disappeared, and international migration declined. The three largest flows were cut off, and there was no further movement of Chinese out of China, Koreans out of Korea, or Indians out of India. Filipinos moved to high-growth urban centres in Hong Kong, Singapore, the Middle East, and elsewhere, a total of 4.2 million people in 120 different countries, some 25 per cent of the country's total labour force. Further tens of thousands of Indonesians moved to Malaysia, and in the mid-1990s foreign workers made up 20 per cent of the labour force in Singapore. But these movements were not large, compared to the colonial era, and most national governments imposed highly restrictive immigration policies, which played an important role in the creation of their new national identities.

However, the number of workers continued to rise dramatically. Rising populations increased the potential supply of young people. More important, these young people were increasingly mobile. Internal migration, particularly to the provincial and national capital cities, accelerated. Although the imperialist regimes have often been blamed for fostering urban centralization, the proportion of the population living in Chinese provincial capitals and in all national capitals has continued to increase since the 1950s. Often the migrants from rural areas found themselves eking out an existence in the 'informal' or 'traditional service' sectors of these expanding urban centres. And, although the migrants typically had fewer years of education than people born in the cities, they had usually passed through the first years of primary school in the expanding educational systems.

Instead of capital moving workers, capital tended to move to the workers. If various forms of contract, indentured, and forced labour marked colonial economies, low wages seem to have played a key role in the initial export success of Asian economies after the Second World War. In Japan in the 1950s and 1960s, in the four tigers in the 1960s and 1970s, in Malaysia and Indonesia in the 1980s, and in the coastal regions of southern China in the 1990s, labour-intensive manufacturing industries drew on a surplus of underemployed workers, often rural migrants working in the informal sector. The wages paid to these low-skilled workers typically did not keep pace with growth, but it can be argued that even if real wages in the 'formal' sector had not risen at all, this still meant improved welfare, because employment here was superior to alternatives. Further, real wages for unskilled workers were unlikely to rise until the supply of 'surplus' labour had been exhausted. After this point, market forces have pushed up wages, as happened in Japan in the 1960s, in the four tigers and particularly Singapore in the late 1970s, and possibly in Malaysia in the late 1980s (Galenson, 1992; World Bank, 1993, p. 19; Hill, 1994).

The increasing size of Asian labour forces was only partly the result of population increase and internal migration; it also reflected increasing participation rates for women. This structural change is important, but difficult to measure. Census results measure what government statisticians have been told to do, not what workers do. Thus the recorded increases in female agricultural employment are probably largely spurious, representing not new women at work, but a new willingness of the government to count women as employed. In addition female employment is influenced by the 'additional worker' and 'discouraged worker' syndromes. Hard times may force women into employment to supplement their family's income. Conversely, extended periods of unemployment may cause women to drop out of the formal sector or even to withdraw from employment entirely. Male employment declines in hard times due to the 'discouraged worker' effect, but to a much smaller degree, and the male 'additional worker' effect is more often a response to economic upswing. Recorded male participation rates tend to fluctuate in a band from 75 to 85 per cent. The recorded female participation rates shown in Table 10.7 are likely to be underestimates. Similarly, as we will see in Chapter 11, the figures for female employment in manufacturing shown in Table 10.8 do not include the informal sector and are also probably underestimates. Even these figures show the rate of growth of female employment in manufacturing to range from equal to over twice the rate of growth of male employment, however. This 'feminization' of labour in the dynamic modern sectors of the economy certainly counts as one of the secrets of rapid growth (Lim, 1993).

Table 10.7 Asia: Female Participation Rates, 1960s–1980s
(per cent)

	1960	*1970*	*1980*	*1987*
Hong Kong	41.0	42.8	45.7	48.6
Indonesia	31.2	35.6	37.1	50.9
Japan	–	50.9	46.7	48.6
South Korea	31.4	38.4	–	44.9
Peninsular Malaysia	29.9	35.6	39.3	–
Philippines	27.2	34.1	–	20.0
Singapore	21.6	43.8	44.3	47.0
Thailand	81.4	73.2	62.3	76.3

Source: Lim, 1993, from International Labour Office, *Yearbook of Labour Statistics*.

Table 10.8   Asia: Male and Female Employment in Manufacturing, 1950–80 (thousands)

	1950		1960		1970		1980	
	Male	*Female*	*Male*	*Female*	*Male*	*Female*	*Male*	*Female*
Indonesia	–	–	1207	700	1575	1144	2644	2102
Japan	4243	1671	6644	3141	8974	4892	8745	4849
South Korea	–	83	373	129	957	522	1818	1016
Malaya	–	28	124	23	198	74	329	229
Philippines	246	207	398	453	672	763	–	–
Singapore	–	–	60	12	102	49	181	151
Taiwan	287	55	–	–	448	178	1183	893
Thailand	131	67	309	178	413	294	757	624

Source: Mitchell, 1995.

It has not been simply increasing skills, an increasing supply of workers, and low wages which have made life easy for Asian capitalists, however. The reputed docility of the workers has also smoothed the path of profits. In the bland phrase of the World Bank's economists, governments 'have generally been less vulnerable and less responsive' to labour's demands in Asia than elsewhere (World Bank, 1993, p. 19). The reasons for this are simple enough. Labour movements are weak, hampered both by pressure from the 'reserve army' of underemployed workers, and by government repression. Asian states have intervened continuously in labour relations to hold wages low and to minimize political opposition. This is as true of socialist as of capitalist regimes.

Following their victory in 1949, the Communist rulers of China developed a historiography of the labour movement which portrayed a linear development from imperialism to capitalist industrialization to the rise of a proletariat and a spontaneous flowering of class consciousness, leading to the revolution. Not surprisingly, this simplistic picture has been modified since the opening up of Chinese sources in the early 1980s. As in Europe, the industrial labour force in China evolved out of a long-term process of rural–urban migration, much of which was cyclical. Early industrial workers in Shanghai and Tianjin, for instance, returned to their home villages for major personal events or during economic downturns. Even after years in the cities, workers continued to identify themselves primarily as natives of their villages, often working and living with transplanted clusters of fellow villagers. Workers from different regions usually worked in separate areas of the mills, spoke different dialects, dressed differently, and rarely socialized. Most workers found jobs through personal contacts and retained them by establishing patronage ties with foremen and overseers. Criminal gangs played a central role in their lives, sometimes providing protection and assistance, but also ruthlessly controlling access to jobs, constantly threatening violence, and extorting substantial portions of the workers' incomes. A consciousness of themselves as a class emerged only after the Japanese occupation, and in particular only after the Communist Party recognized the need to identify with the special problems of the workers and began to campaign actively among them (Hershatter, 1986; Honig, 1986).

Support for the new regime in 1949 rested largely on the simple promise of stability and security which it offered after half a century of turmoil. As seen in Chapter 9, the government drew on and exploited these feelings, but the labour organizations which it established functioned primarily as instruments of mobilization, surveillance and control, and only secondarily as representatives of workers' interests and desires. In the state enterprise sector, workers were assigned permanent jobs when they completed their schooling. They had no right to quit or leave their assigned jobs; conversely, since allocations of labour formed part of the planning process, the party cadres who served as enterprise managers could neither hire nor fire workers. In practice this meant permanent tenure, an 'iron rice bowl' for workers to match the 'iron armchair' of the cadres. An implicit social contract evolved, under which the workers traded quiescence and compliance for a range of welfare provisions supplied by the enterprise, including insurance, housing, child-care, pensions, and even guaranteed jobs for their children. The system resulted in chronic overstaffing and low levels of efficiency, but it also provided security. Enterprises became in effect village communities or mini welfare states.

Reforms to state enterprises in the 1980s aimed to give managers more discretion but also to hold them more accountable for the profitability of the individual enterprise. Workers' efficiency was to be improved by eliminating permanent tenure and introducing short-term labour contracts. In 1984 new 'provisional guidelines' stated that 'an enterprise can decide its organizational and personnel matters at its discretion'. There was substantial opposition to these reforms at all levels, and they were not implemented thoroughly. Labour contracts were only applied to 'new' workers, and through 1988 covered only 8 per cent of workers in state enterprises (White, 1993, pp. 136–46). Nevertheless, to an extent they were 'successful', the reforms reduced job security, increased the intensity of labour, and drastically reduced the range of social services on which unemployed workers and their families could rely.

At the same time the government authorized the establishment of special economic zones in which workers were denied any right to collective representation. The administrative orders for the Shenzhen Special Economic Zone stated in 1984 that 'full management autonomy is given to an enterprise which is established by a foreign investor... the public administration... may not intervene in their activities', and that enterprises in the zone could recruit employees on the basis of 'individual examination' and pay them on whatever basis they chose, since 'prices in the specialized zones are, in principle, guided by market mechanism' (Watanabe, 1992, p. 140). The 'Preferential Policy and Rules of the Hainan Special Economic Zone' adopted in 1991 specified that 'the enterprise, in accordance with the seriousness of the case, has the power to take a variety of disciplinary measures, including dismissal, against staff members and workers who violate the rules and regulations of the enterprise with damaging consequences' (Chongyi and Goodman, 1995, p. 93).

Japan has developed its own mythical history of labour relations, which asserts that the characteristics of the 'Japanese employment system' – permanent lifetime employment, promotion and salaries based on seniority, and enterprise unions – sprang from a unique cultural disposition towards group loyalty on the part of workers, combined with a traditional yet rational paternalism on the part of managers. Scores of Western books on Japanese business practices have adopted this view (following Abegglen, 1958 and Dore, 1973), and in China opponents of the labour market reforms have cited the alleged success of the Japanese system as a reason for retaining permanent tenure for workers (White, 1993, p. 139). Others have seen the system not as a reflection of Japanese values, but as a rational response to the economic environment (following Taira, 1970). As in the West, however, labour relations in Japan involved bitter and frequently violent conflicts between workers and employers from the late nineteenth to the mid-twentieth century. The patterns of violence and confrontation in the coal industry (Allen, 1994) are very similar to those found in Europe and the United States. Senior government officials desired rapid economic development, but they also wanted social and political stability. Government employees enjoyed many of the features of permanent employment from an early period, and this became the preferred model. In the heavy industrial sector frequent intervention by the government eventually brought something resembling permanent employment to skilled male workers. These early forms, overlaid with allusions to 'traditional values', then provided models for the system as it developed after the Second World War (Crawcour, 1978; Gordon, 1985; Garon, 1987; Kinzley, 1991).

Those workers fortunate enough to work in government agencies or the largest private enterprises after the mid-1950s had indeed entered the 'middle class' as members of corporate 'families', and many clearly felt themselves as such (Gordon, 1985). However, they did so on their employers' terms, at the price of long hours, low wages, numbing conformity, and unions operated by the firm. Enterprise unions were typically headed by junior executives as one of their assignments on rotation through the branches of the firm's administration. All large firms possessed elaborate grievance procedures, but informal pressures ensured that they were never used (Galenson, 1976). In addition family resistance to changing jobs was often exploited by employers, combined with a general appeal to loyalty. These internal labour market policies bound workers to their employers. Further, only one out of every five Japanese workers ever enjoyed the benefits of permanent tenure. In the early twentieth century the government's concern did not extend to the girls and women in the textile industries, and in the postwar era the system never applied to female workers, even in large firms. The situation of the large majority of workers outside the enterprise system, many of whom worked for sub-contractors providing components to the large firms, was far less favourable. Sub-contractors paid wages driven down, for instance, by single women and by retired people struggling to add to inadequate pensions. They exercised absolute discretion over employment conditions, could dismiss workers at will, and had no obligation to provide insurance, retirement, or other benefits (Chalmers, 1989).

In the 1980s and 1990s the lifetime employment system came under increasing pressure. Increasing labour costs compared to other Asian countries led Japanese firms to relocate their production facilities overseas, in Korea, Southeast Asia and China. This affected sub-contractors first, but eventually the parent firms closed plants in Japan as well. This process of 'hollowing out' of Japanese industry meant for example that in the late 1990s Japan imported two and a half times as many television sets as it exported, all of them assembled in Japanese-owned factories in Southeast Asia and China. From the perspective of professionally qualified managerial employees, being tied to a single firm provided only limited scope for individual ambition. As some industries came to operate in internationally competitive environments, these workers might have a real choice of moving to foreign-owned firms, for instance banking and finance following the deregulation of 1988–9; in other industries where there still was a higher level of regulation and foreign firms were perceived as being at a disadvantage, there was less mobility, for instance pharmaceuticals. From the employers' perspective, the ageing labour force had created a 'diamond-shaped' hierarchy rather than a pyramid. In consequence top managers were motivated to eliminate middle-level managers and replace them with cheaper workers at the bottom (Beck and Beck, 1994). The balance depended on external factors. In the 1980s 'restructuring' affected mostly production workers, but in the 1990s it spread to the previously secure 'salarymen' as well.

Asian employers prefer to present their labour relations as harmonious and familial, another aspect of 'Asian', 'neo-Confucian', or 'traditional' values (see Song, 1994, ch. 11). This self-image has been disputed (Deyo, 1989). In Korea, for instance, although small firms may be more paternalistic and familial, large firms are notoriously authoritarian. Their close relations with government have encouraged an autocratic style within the firms, because business leaders may insist with impunity on their autonomy in decision-making. Families dominate these companies – the five sons of Hyundai's founder Chung Ju-yung are all senior managers in the firm – but that means that non-family members see younger family members placed over them, and the firm as a whole is not perceived as an extended family (Robinson, 1991, pp. 223–4). For example, the veneer of paternalism in Korea's Poongsan Corporation looks like a thin cover for authoritarianism, and is perceived as such. The company's relatively low turnover results from higher benefits paid. In the late 1980s the company ceased its previous open competitive recruitment and shifted to 'connection hiring' in order to ensure the exclusion of potential agitators. The bitter Angang strike of 1988–9 won support from radical students and other anti-government forces, but was suppressed. 'Korean workers are not particularly docile. Their apparent docility has been the result of governmental control, not the cultural tradition' (Kim, 1992, p. 198; Janelli and Yim, 1995).

Employers have reverted in some instances to updated versions of older patterns of mastership and bondage. A 1987 survey in Thailand revealed that workers in the private sector received almost half their earnings in kind. In Korea similar studies showed that 25 per cent of the earnings of white-collar workers, and 39 per cent of the earnings of blue-collar workers, were in the form of 'allowances' instead of basic wages (Galenson, 1992, pp. 88–9). Employers can also rely on the state to act in their interests (Deyo, 1989). Singapore controls the entire labour force through compulsory savings schemes and access to housing, as well as direct repression when necessary. Singapore reported exactly one labour dispute between 1978 and 1988 (Mitchell, 1995, p. 123). In Indonesia in 1985 the government obliged all labour unions to join the All-Indonesia Workers' Union (SPSI), dominated at the top by government appointees and members of the ruling party, and staffed at its middle levels by military personnel. In the early 1990s fewer than half the large enterprises which should have SPSI units had established them, and of those fewer than half had negotiated collective bargaining agreements. Over half of over 1000 firms surveyed in 1989 paid less than the minimum wage, which ranged from US $ 0.50 to US$ 1.50 per day, levels which the government's own calculations showed would cover only a fraction of a worker's 'minimum physical needs'. The reported strikes – fewer than 100 per year in the 1980s, but rising – were almost all illegal, having violated the procedures for settling disputes (Schwarz, 1994, pp. 258–60; Wolf, 1996).

Capital

Asia seemed short of capital, because of poverty and low savings, because local institutions were not capable of mobilizing what savings there were, and because 'traditional' values led potential investors to avoid the modern sector. Foreign capital can substitute for domestic savings, but these sources often depend on political considerations. The level of direct foreign investment in Asia was low in the late 1960s, compared to other less-developed regions, because foreign investors feared political 'instability' or did not trust the quality of Asian labour (Hanson, 1996). The socialist governments of China, North Korea, Vietnam and Burma, and 'neutralist' regimes such as Sihanouk's Cambodia and Sukarno's Indonesia, were cut off both from foreign aid and private investment by Western countries. United States aid to Taiwan and Korea was intended to shore up these two anti-Communist bastions. From 1953 to 1961 the United States financed 70 per cent of imports and 75 per cent of total fixed capital formation in Korea, figures sufficiently large that some of the slowdown often blamed on the alleged 'failure' of Korea's import-substitution policy can in fact be attributed to reductions in aid from the United States (Haggard et al., 1991).

Foreign aid and foreign loans can lead to 'dependence' in the sense that the recipient country is no longer independent to determine its own policies. International agencies have been accused of perpetuating a kind of 'neo-colonialism'. The World Bank traditionally favours large infrastructure projects which promote exports, usually of primary products. Assistance from the International Monetary Fund is conditional, meaning that in addition to repayment of the loans, the recipient must implement a package of policies intended to stimulate exports in order to bring the balance of payments back to equilibrium. The details of the agreements are usually secret. Typically, however, the policies include measures to encourage foreign investment, to reduce wages, and to reduce the government budget through cuts in spending on welfare, health, education, and local infrastructure. The IMF has often been harshly criticized for the obvious political bias in its preferred mix of policies (Körner et al., 1986). Further, theoretically there is no reason to expect that these policies will lead to growth, but it is almost certain that they will create discontent and lead to political instability. On the other hand, although agencies such as the IMF and the World Bank may influence policy and the selection of projects, the problems frequently result from mismanagement and corruption (Hill, 1994).

The Philippines, for example, borrowed to cover a deterioration in the terms of trade beginning in 1975, but much of the money went to unproductive investments and to cronies of the president, Ferdinand Marcos. In 1983 the Philippines defaulted on this debt. The International Monetary Fund and a consortium of aid-granting countries and agencies arranged further loans. In return, they required the government to adopt a range of policies including severe cuts in spending. The new loans and the accompanying conditions imposed on the government did not lead to growth. The economy stagnated, and slow growth and cuts in government spending led to political unrest, providing the background to the popular uprising which led to the end of the Marcos regime. The new 'people's power' government of Corazon Aquino continued to struggle under the burden of debt repayment, however. The economy continued to stagnate, the government was threatened by a new Communist uprising and six attempted military coups, and Aquino declared a state of emergency in 1989 before losing power in 1992. Obviously in this case international aid led to neither growth nor stability, but whether the weight of blame should fall on foreign international agencies, or on corrupt domestic elites, will depend on the perspective of the observer.

Private investment, often termed 'foreign direct investment' and abbreviated as FDI, has mostly flowed into manufacturing, partly because foreign investment in agriculture and services is often restricted. It is also highly export-oriented, even when standardized for industry and the size of the firm. The multinational corporations which make such investments have not always met with a friendly reception. Japan has always severely limited the options of foreign investors. Korea and Taiwan were quite closed at first but then became more open, particularly to Japanese firms. Singapore has always been quite open, Malaysia more so than others. Thailand has been more cautious, and perhaps surprisingly so has the Philippines because of a nervous fear of domination by the United States. Indonesia nationalized many foreign firms from 1957 to 1965, then became open to foreign investment in the late 1960s, shifted to a very restrictive policy from 1974 to 1984, and then shifted again to a much more open policy in the early 1990s. And of course socialist regimes remained outside the sphere of foreign investment until they changed or reformed.

On balance, Asian governments generally have became much more receptive to foreign investment. Given the more open environment, theory predicts that in oligopolistic industries leaders will set the pace, and therefore that once a new area is opened to foreign investment by one well-known multinational firm, others will follow. This is partly a follow-the-leader phenomenon, partly strategic investment to avoid being shut out of a potentially profitable field, and sometimes firms are exploiting the experience of previous entrants in order to learn from their mistakes and minimize costs. In addition there is a form of serial migration of firms, with companies entering foreign markets to provide goods and services to other firms from their own country which have already established themselves in the foreign market, for instance, branches of Japanese banks to provide facilities for Japanese manufacturing firms in foreign countries (Goodhart and Sutija, 1990; Hill, 1990; Tri and Booth, 1992).

From the late 1960s the source of private investment shifted from Europe and North America to Japan. Japanese authors have argued that Japanese investment was 'trade creating' and better adapted to local environments in business organization and factor proportions. Japanese firms in Southeast Asia tended to be organized in smaller plants, they concentrated in more labour-intensive industries, and they showed greater willingness to engage in joint ventures with local partners than their Western competitors (Kojima, 1978; 1985). However, this now appears to have been a passing phase related to differences in industrial organization in Japan compared to the United States and Europe. As the Japanese economy has matured, Japanese firms operating in Southeast Asia have come to resemble their American and European competitors more closely.

The characteristics of so-called 'Japanese-style' investment are now found in investment by firms from the new group of foreign investors, the four tigers – Hong Kong in Guangdong, Taiwan in Fujian, and Korea in North China and in Indonesia. The earlier surge of Japanese investment, and the more recent waves of capital from the four tigers, have resulted from the relocation of labour-intensive 'low end' manufacturing by firms as wages rise in their home economies (Hill, 1990; 1994).

Most of the nations of Asia have established special economic zones to encourage foreign investment. Inducements include exemption from tariffs on imported machinery and raw materials, exemptions from export duties, tax holidays followed by special low rates of tax, provision of land, and freedom from a broad range of government regulations. As noted above in the case of China, labour organizations are actively discouraged or expressly forbidden. National governments compete in the generosity of the terms offered. In addition, provincial authorities in the Philippines and China have joined the race. In Korea 'free export zones' (FEZ) were opened to foreign investors in the 1960s and 1970s. Much of the resulting investment was Japanese – 90 of 110 firms with 25 000 employees in the Masan FEZ in the early 1990s, for instance. Most provinces in the Philippines have established special economic zones, and again investment is largely Japanese, supplemented by American firms. Taiwan, Malaysia, Indonesia and Thailand have followed suit. Between 1972 and 1982 Malaysia's exports increased ten-fold, and the share of the 'free trade zones' rose from 1 per cent to over 60 per cent (Rasiah, 1993, p. 137). In China in 1980 an ordinance for establishing special economic zones was issued in Guangdong province, and zones were opened at Shenzhen, Zhuhai, and Shantou. Fujian and Hainan followed, and the Beijing authorities named a string of 'coastal open cities' and several large 'open economic regions' as well (Watanabe, 1992, pp. 137–42). In 1993 the capital in 'foreign invested enterprises' totalled US$ 38.0 billion, and they produced over 10 per cent of China's industrial output. In addition to Western and Japanese firms, much of the investment in coastal China has come from Hong Kong, Taiwan and Chinese firms in Southeast Asia.

As seen in Table 10.9, Asian economies enjoyed massive increases in investment from the 1960s onwards. Rising investment was clearly another of the secrets of Asian growth (World Bank, 1993, pp. 40–3). As output and income rose, the proportion saved and invested increased. This added to the large amounts of foreign investment. The ratios of capital formation – investment in plants, machinery, and infrastructure – compared to output are high. In 1988 the ratio in Australia (a high-income country in the Pacific region) was 23.7 per cent, in Brazil (a potential high-growth economy in Latin America) 22.2 per cent, in West Germany (the pre-eminent economy of Western Europe) 20.5 per cent, and finally in the United States 14.7 per cent.

Table 10.9   Asia: Ratio of Gross Fixed Capital Formation to Gross Domestic Product, 1950–88 (per cent)

	1950	1960	1970	1980	1988
Hong Kong	–	28.4$^{'63}$	19.3	33.6	24.6
Indonesia	5.9$^{'51}$	7.3	13.6	21.7	25.9
Japan	17.6	30.3	35.5	31.6	29.9
South Korea	7.4$^{'53}$	11.1	23.0	32.1	29.2
Malaysia	6.2	11.0	17.7	31.1	24.1
Myanmar	10.3	15.9	11.3	18.7	11.5
Philippines	12.9	13.6	15.8	27.2	17.8
Singapore	–	9.5	32.5	40.6	35.0
Taiwan	10.8$^{'51}$	16.8	21.6	30.6	20.7
Thailand	14.1$^{'52}$	13.9	23.8	25.2	27.0

Source: Calculated from data in Mitchell, 1995.

Resources and Productivity

$$Y' = A' + WN' + RK'.$$

Robert Solow, 1957

The final outstanding characteristic of the HPAEs [high-performing Asian economies] is their rapid productivity growth . . . about two-thirds of East Asia's extraordinary growth is attributable to rapid accumulation . . . The remaining third of this growth cannot be explained by accumulation and is therefore attributable to increased efficiency.

World Bank, *The East Asian Miracle*, 1993

Asian growth, like that of the Soviet Union in its high-growth era, seems to be driven by extraordinary growth in inputs like labour and capital rather than by gains in efficiency.

Paul Krugman, 'The Myth of Asia's Miracle', 1994

There were many more workers in Asia by the 1990s than in the 1950s, they were on average substantially better educated, and each of them had far more capital to work with. But were they more efficient? At first glance it seems they must have been so. After all, the vastly larger capital stock of the 1990s embodied an astonishing array of new technologies, many of which had not even been conceived in the 1950s. This was most spectacularly the case with electronics, but new techniques also became available in agriculture, and in industry the application of electronic technologies spread and revolutionized entire other sectors of manufacturing as well. Clearly technical advance played an important and possibly crucial role in economic growth in general and in industrial growth in particular. Economists always suspected this, and even occasionally argued that technical change has somehow caused economic growth. But how great was the impact of technology? Until the past generation we were unsure how to measure technology's contribution systematically. What was required was a means to separate the effects of increasing numbers of workers and greater amounts of capital on the one hand, from the effects of genuinely new ways of doing things on the other.

In 1957 Robert Solow published a famous article in which he suggested a means of measuring the contribution of technical change to growth – one of those ideas which, like so many new technologies, seems simple after someone else has thought of it. Output, Solow reasoned, is a function of the amount of labour, the amount of capital, and another factor – the potential increase in output per unit of input. This 'other' factor can be thought of as multiplying potential output at any given time:

$$Y = Af(N, K),$$

Where Y is output, N labour, K capital, and A is technical change, the 'other' factor. Using some simple calculus and making the economists' standard assumptions about the way the economy works, Solow showed that the rate of growth of output equals the rate of growth of technical change, plus the weighted growth rates of labour and capital, and that the weights of the growth rates of labour and capital are their respective shares in national income, 'wages' (W) and 'rent' (R):

$$Y' = A' + WN' + RK'.$$

So growth in productivity or technical change is the rate of growth in output less the weighted growth rates of labour and capital. More recent studies add another term measuring changes in educational levels to account for improvements in the quality of the labour force. The necessary figures – national product, years of schooling, labour force, capital stock, and the shares of labour and capital in national income – are more or less easily observable in industrial economies where statistics are relatively complete, most prices are set by the market, and the share of government is not too large, although even in industrial economies the underlying data are often estimates whose accuracy may be questioned. Solow's application of his method to data for the United States showed that technical change accounted for a surprisingly large fraction of total growth. Measuring growth itself became something of a growth industry, and a standard work concluded that nearly half (46.6 per cent) of the increase in output in the United States in the twentieth century had resulted from the more efficient use of resources (Denison, 1974, p. 127). Broadly similar results were obtained for other industrialized countries – that is, if there had been no technical change, these economies could have grown, but only at a little over half the rate they in fact enjoyed. There might have been some increase in output per worker, because of the increasing amounts of capital, but given the substantial increases in population which have accompanied modern economic growth, there would have been little or no increase in output per person.

Can these techniques be applied to Asian economies? And do increases in productivity explain rapid rates of growth? Put another way, is the ultimate secret of Asian growth the rising efficiency with which resources have been used? The World Bank's economists believe so, but other economists such as Paul Krugman remain unconvinced. There are problems of both data and the underlying assumptions. The World Bank team found, for instance, that income share data were not generally available. They developed alternate estimates, but some of their assumptions contain elements of circularity. Further, Solow's approach rests on the assumption that the shares of income enjoyed by labour and capital are determined by market forces. As seen above, however, wages have been held down in Asian countries by government intervention. Other prices are controlled as well. Banking and capital markets have been highly regulated. In addition, in 1990 official figures showed central government spending as a percentage of domestic product ranged from a moderate 15 per cent in Hong Kong and Thailand, to nearly 20 per cent in China, South Korea, and the Philippines, to around 25 per cent in Indonesia and Singapore, close to 30 per cent in Vietnam, over 30 per cent in Japan and over 50 per cent in Malaysia (Lubeck, 1992, p. 183; Japan 1988 from Mitchell, 1995); the true figure was probably higher in several cases, notably Thailand, Singapore and Indonesia. That is, a large proportion of economic activity is determined by non-market forces, and this undermines the reliability of the estimates.

The performance of Asian economies in fact varied widely. Not all grew rapidly over the entire period, and the Philippines was a notorious under-achiever. In addition, the World Bank estimates showed that the 'high performing Asian economies' divided into two groups. Hong Kong, Japan, South Korea, Taiwan and Thailand showed relatively high rates of productivity increase, above 3 per cent over the period from 1960 to 1989. However, productivity in Indonesia, Malaysia and Singapore increased at only just over 1 per cent, about average for high-income countries and below many other developing countries; at least 80 per cent of their growth resulted from increasing inputs, not from increasing efficiency (World Bank, 1993, pp. 46–69). These results are quite sensitive to the assumptions made. The World Bank figures show that slightly different assumptions reduce the measure of productivity substantially, and other scholars have argued that, except for Japan, none of the Asian economies has achieved substantial increases in productivity.

In the case of Singapore a series of studies have shown that the main contributors to growth were increases in the stock of capital and the labour force. The inflow of foreign capital ranged between 10 and 20 per cent of total product during the 1970s. Singapore also had a very high rate of domestic savings, peaking at 42 per cent of total product in the mid-1980s. Nearly half of domestic savings was generated by the public sector, and in particular the Central Provident Fund, a social security scheme whose compulsory contributions could take half of a worker's income. In 1966 Singapore's labour force participation rate was 42 per cent, and unemployment stood at 9 per cent. In 1983 the participation rate had increased to 64 per cent, largely because of the rising numbers of women in employment, and unemployment was only 3 per cent. However, total factor productivity increased only slightly if at all (Yuan, 1986).

The rapid rise in wages engineered by the government in late 1979 in order to squeeze out firms relying on unskilled cheap labour caused a recession but did not slow Singapore's growth over the longer term. Although we might expect that rising educational levels and rising wages suggest that productivity must have increased as well, the failure of productivity to increase has been confirmed in later studies. Krugman concludes that 'the miracle turns out to have been based on perspiration rather than inspiration: Singapore grew through a mobilization of resources that would have done Stalin proud'. Krugman's point is that increases in the employed share of the population, education and investment cannot be repeated. The participation rate cannot double again, education cannot be improved much beyond the levels already achieved, and the investment rate cannot be increased further. Therefore in the absence of improvements in productivity, Singapore's economy cannot continue to grow at a high rate, and to a somewhat lesser degree this must apply to all the other Asian economies as well (Krugman, 1994).

In Hong Kong as well increases in output depended to a much greater extent on increases in capital and labour than on improved productivity, compared to the advanced industrial economies of Western Europe and the United States. Hong Kong's growth clearly depended on increases in exports of manufactured goods, but even more telling is the finding that Hong Kong's success relied on the differential between Hong Kong's relative prices and the level of income in the United States, the main export market for Hong Kong's manufactures. Since the level of prices for manufactured goods in Hong Kong was largely determined by wage levels in the labour-intensive industries which provided the bulk of the exports (textiles, clothing, shoes, plastics, and later consumer electronics), the ability of firms in Hong Kong to hold increases in their wage levels below the rate of increase of incomes in the United States was the key to their success. That is, Hong Kong depended on action in the realms of politics and labour relations rather than technology and economics (Chen, 1979; 1980; Lin et al., 1980).

Discussions of productivity tend to focus on manufacturing, but Asia also enjoyed the good fortune of increasing food supplies, produced domestically, combined with declining rates of population growth. Agricultural modernization became the 'green revolution'. High-yielding varieties of rice first introduced in the 1960s, along with new techniques of planting, fertilization and harvesting, allowed food supplies to increase substantially faster than population. Throughout, governments intervened to force the pace of agricultural development. Despite the pessimism still expressed in the late 1970s regarding the possibility of achieving self-sufficiency in rice production, Indonesia became the 'most notable success', with a 'heavily managed and generously funded programme of subsidies and extension services' which had succeeded by the mid-1980s despite ongoing problems of 'bureaucratic inertia', drought and pests. The Philippines also achieved surprisingly good results, given the depredations of the Marcos regime and the recession of the mid-1980s; the location of the International Rice Research Institute in Manila may have speeded the introduction of new varieties. Experience elsewhere was more mixed. Government intervention in Korea was not especially successful and state policy in Malaysia was tied to the attempt to boost Malay income under the New Economic Policy, for instance. The changes sometimes disadvantaged small farmers and women. On balance, however, in addition to the undoubted benefits of increased food supplies, it has been argued that the distributional effects were not as unfavorable as feared. Agriculture became more commercial, there was some concentration of holdings, and sometimes farms were excessively mechanized. But in general labour was not displaced, rural incomes and nutrition improved, and productivity rose significantly (Hill, 1994).

Improvements in agriculture freed resources – both capital and labour – for industry. For all countries in the modern world, however, early industrialization has required a process of technology transfer. Changing technologies mean that conditions have varied from decade to decade and place to place. It takes time to develop the expertise required to import and modify new techniques. Japan benefited from previous experience and the relative simplicity of late-nineteenth century techniques, but it was decades before Japan produced its first steam locomotive, and further decades before the motors for the subsequent generation of electric locomotives could be produced in Japan. Therefore, systematic explanations of the resulting patterns of technology transfer over the past generation have proved elusive. In Thailand in the 1970s, for example, Thai firms appeared relatively capital intensive, compared to foreign-owned firms. Thais were accused of 'buying technology as an end in itself', but in the textile industry where many of these firms clustered, some traditionally labour-intensive operations had been transformed during the 1960s into capital-intensive activities, and Thai firms may therefore merely have been following international trends (Santikarn, 1981). Size of firm also does not provide a reliable index. Small firms led Japan's industrialization in the 1930s. In Indonesia and the Philippines cottage industries maintained high levels of employment into the early 1980s, despite low measured levels of productivity, whereas in Singapore there were few productivity differences related to the size of establishment (Bruch and Hiemetz, 1984). Technology plays a key role, and it can be imported successfully, but beyond these rather general truisms lie very complex interactions.

As noted above, the special economic zones are the focus for foreign investment, and therefore they are also the focus for technology transfer. What role have they played? There is both an optimistic case and a more pessimistic view. On the one hand, the plants in the zones tend to be new, modern, up-to-date and competitive. The labour they employ is certainly highly productive. Continued growth here could lead to ongoing improvements in productivity of the sort which the World Bank team believes have driven Asian growth. On the other hand, the industries in the special economic zones are low-skill, assembly-line production plants. Their management is foreign. They use imported machinery and raw materials. Some plants simply assemble parts shipped in from the more advanced production facilities in the investing country. In the late twentieth century this sort of development may be a poor base for future development. As seen in Chapter 5, Japanese workers in the bicycle industry in the 1930s could understand and make improvements in the technologies they used, and these improvements contributed to the development of the Japanese machinery industry in the postwar period. It was far less likely, for example, that in the 1990s that Malaysian workers could understand or improve on the technologies in the electronics industry. This darker view leads to doubts about the longer term.

The pessimistic case argues further that technology transfer does not lead to autonomous development. Rather, recipient countries remain confined to the lower ends of 'product cycle' development, that is, to mature products whose technologies are relatively standard and whose production location is determined by the cost of inputs and especially by large supplies of cheap labour. This is 'development by invitation'. Firms, and therefore national economies, remain dependent on their more advanced partners, confined to the less profitable ends of 'commodity chains' where they supply 'selective and supplemental' inputs required by the firms in the advanced nations. Western Europe, the United States, and especially Japan remain in control. Thus, 'although Taiwan and Korea sought to escape dependency in the 1970s, what they succeeded in doing was exchanging one form of dependency for another' (Cumings, 1987, p. 77). And in the 1990s it is argued that the Japanese pattern of 'government–business cooperation', 'business–business cooperation', and 'management–labour cooperation' has been transplanted to Southeast Asia in a way which guarantees that the emerging industrial sectors of those countries will remain dependent on Japan. In the words of the president of the Japanese Chamber of Commerce and Industry in Singapore,

> In my personal opinion, we should keep the control in Japan. Once you lose that control, that power, it never comes back. It never returns. All you have to do is look at what happened to England in the late nineteenth century, or what is happening to the United States today. (Hatch and Yamamura, 1996, p. 19)

One way for a country to avoid dependence on foreign capital and move towards autonomous development, is for the government to sponsor the introduction of advanced technologies. Korea is a frequently cited example. The government encouraged borrowing by Korean firms rather than direct investment by foreigners. Except for the export processing zones, which were isolated from the Korean market, foreign investors were forced into joint ventures with Korean partners. The state guided investment through sequential stages, from textiles to petrochemicals, shipbuilding, electrical machinery and consumer electronics in the 1970s, and then automobiles, personal computers and microelectronics in the 1980s. There were some spectacular failures, but the government made good the losses (Castells, 1992, pp. 38–9). Further, the large government-supported groups or *chaebol* have used the profits generated by low-end manufacturing to develop their own technological capabilities and reduce their dependence on foreign technology. The domestic content of Korean video cassette recorders, for instance, rose from 55 per cent in 1982 to 80 per cent in 1988 (Lim, 1994, pp. 193–4).

On the other hand, the government rewarded firms with the highest volume of exports, not necessarily those with the highest value added. Therefore, exporters did not have any particular incentive to invest in plants which manufactured parts and intermediate products, which would have required large and long-term investment in capital, technical resources and training. Rather, they collected the bonuses available from the government by importing parts and assembling products for export. They became, in short, heavy importers of inputs. As a result, in aggregate terms Korea became 'import dependent as well as export dependent'. From 1962 to 1986 Korean exports increased from US$ 55 million to US$ 35 billion, but imports rose from US$ 442 million to US$ 35 billion. Until 1980 imports consistently exceeded exports, and the deficit was financed by an accumulating international debt, which had reached US$ 40 billion in the mid-1980s. The trade surpluses of the mid-1980s were something of an anomaly, the result of the 'three lows', low interest rates, low oil prices, and a low exchange rate of the won to the yen and dollar. In the early 1990s, although some industries had reduced their dependence on foreign technologies, others remained confined to the low end of their markets, struggling against competitors offering lower labour costs (Chon, 1992; Song, 1994, p. 213).

11

THE DARK SIDE: WOMEN IN ASIAN DEVELOPMENT

The gendered nature of much Asian development provides another possible explanation of growth, and another point of comparison with the Western experience. Nationalist movements recruited and relied on women for support. Once in power, the new national governments considered the redefinition of gender roles to be one of their most pressing tasks. The redefined 'private' sphere which resulted had the effect of severely limiting the accepted role of women in the public life of the new national communities. At the same time, however, the requirements of economic development brought a more extensive deployment of women as workers. The contrasting goals of social and political stability and quiescence on the one hand, and economic and commercial dynamism and growth on the other, have created tension and conflict. The response of the ruling elites has frequently been to deny the tension and conflict, and in the shadow of that denial exploitation has grown and institutionalized itself. The exploitation of women makes up the dark underside of rapid development in Asia.

The labour force in the most rapidly expanding sectors of the economies of Asia has often been female. These women – often young unmarried girls – have been economically, socially, and often sexually mistreated. Their protests have been repressed, often violently. However, because the contradiction between the accepted 'private' role of women and the fact of their actual role in the economy is denied, repression can be denied, or justified as control of individual deviance. Because deviance is defined as individual and idiosyncratic, the systematic nature of female exploitation remains unidentified and often unreported. Repression of women as workers and as women reflects the stratified and gendered nature of the new national communities, and calling repression into question would be to call into question the rights of elite groups to govern.

Women in Politics

As a rule, a state without law-abiding families and reliable Gentlemen on the one hand, and, on the other, without the threat of foreign invasion, will perish. Only then do we learn the lesson that we survive in adversity and perish in ease and comfort.

Mencius, VI, B, 15

National communities are gendered. For obvious reasons, however, ruling elites find it convenient to ignore this fact. The emerging government elites of Asia naturally considered themselves 'reliable Gentlemen' in the sense referred to by Mencius. Further, they typically claimed to act under 'the threat of foreign invasion', whether we think of this in the narrow sense or in the broader sense of anti-imperialism or international economic competition. But in order to create their new national communities, the elites of emerging Asian nations discovered that they required 'law-abiding families' as well, and for this women were essential. If the state's authority was to extend to the control of the individual person, then inherited family structures had to be redefined. For this to occur, a new definition of what it meant to be a 'woman' also had to be created.

As seen in Chapter 5, the Meiji government in Japan redefined the family and redefined the social role of women, in order that families as groups and women as individuals could be enrolled in the service of the state. The elements of these new definitions were drawn eclectically from Japanese, Asian and Western sources, but the elite then asserted that they represented a unique 'Japanese' culture which had been inherited from the distant past. As seen in Chapter 8, nationalist movements in other Asian nations also claimed to be speaking in the name of ancient inherited traditions, but in fact had brought together disparate strands of thought and welded them into convenient wholes in the same eclectic manner as the Meiji oligarchs of the previous generation in Japan. As seen below, this frequently involved the creation of a new ideal female identity as well, and further, a definition of women's role which restricted them to a newly defined 'private' sphere. Most importantly, by defining and restricting their 'proper' realm, it excluded them from real power.

It can be difficult to trace these developments, because of the domination of the official ideology in the sources, and because of the complicity of many academics in the creation of the set of myths which enter into the new national identities. The strictures of feminist historians against Western historians and social scientists apply with even greater force in Asia. Judith Allen, for instance, argues that 'the agenda and values of most history, whether of the Right or the Left, serve to promote masculinism, thereby distorting the experiences and agency of women'. The 'commitment to an unexamined public/private split' leads to a 'privileging of public matters' and to positivist and empiricist approaches which insist, for instance, that only written records are evidence, and that the absence of evidence is to be taken as non-existence. Instead, Allen and other feminist scholars insist that we require 'theorizing' which will guide us to an explanation of 'silences'. Analysis based solely on economic class relations is not sufficient to capture the role of gender. Thus Marxist historians accept women's history only insofar as women are portrayed as part of the working class, and have no interest in conflict between the sexes. Indeed, 'Marxist historians employ notions of "the political" that are traditionally patriarchal'. They therefore are unable to see the 'centrality and autonomy' of relations between the sexes, and miss the 'inescapable fact' that women in the past 'existed and exerted agency' (Allen, 1986; Marshall, 1994, pp. 27–9).

Feminist social scientists emphasize that although ethnicity, gender and nationalism are markers of identity, particularly in developing societies, they do not constitute essences. In contrast to the claims of nationalist myth-making, they are created. They emerge from people's core experiences, yearnings and life plans, but they do so in a context where resources are scarce. As such, identities may be, and are, contested. The intersections of ethnicity, gender and nationalism can be traced across three areas – the realm of social and cultural reproduction, the realm of ideologies, stereotypes and practices, and nationalist politics and discourse. And, across a broad range of feminist studies, it is nationalist discourse in particular which is seen as tending to remove women from the public arena and construct an ideal of women's 'domesticity' (Wilson and Frederiksen, 1995; Marshall, 1994, pp. 122–7).

In Asia the division between public and private was the creation of central governments, part of their redefinition of gender roles to ensure power over families and individuals. The absence of records of violence against those who suffer or protest is the result of conscious policy not to collect information which does not support the power structure. As seen in Chapter 8, the nationalist revolutions were often 'passive' in Chatterjee's sense, and this was so not only in their relationship to capitalist modes of production, but also in their relationship to gender relations. Nationalist leaders emerged from pre-existing native elites which had not only continued to exist but had often actually prospered under foreign domination. They did indeed redefine the nation to extend it to all the 'people', including the lower classes the elite had previously despised. In addition, as seen in the case of Japan, the definition of the 'people' now also had to include women, previously invisible in public life. This inevitably led to attempts to redefine gender roles and family structures. In order for the new national identity to spread and become a political force, the elite required modern communications and an audience of literate people to whom they could direct their appeal, and as seen in Chapter 10 one of their responses was to extend education, especially to all girls as well as to all boys. The result has been a series of 'imagined communities' of individuals who may never meet but who can believe themselves to belong to a single nation.

But above all the members of the emerging national elite wanted to gain and retain power. Potential elements in the new national identity which did not contribute to their power were suppressed. This emphatically included claims by women not merely to support but also to share power in the national movement. Also as seen in Chapter 8, the elites also brought some of the preconceptions of their old elite status with them, first into the new nationalist movements, and eventually into the new national governments. Elements of Chatterjee's 'derivative discourse' therefore continued not only in the politics but also in the gender relations of the newly independent states. This is the origin of the pressure on workers and labour movements noted in Chapter 10, and it is the origin of the continual pressure on women to conform to the stereotyped roles dictated by a mythical national tradition and to confine themselves to a rigidly circumscribed private or domestic sphere. As seen below, however, the actions of the new states, notably in education, and their desire for economic development, inevitably lead women out of the purely private and domestic realms and into the public and contentious arena of economic relationships.

The mobilization of women by nationalist movements

As to the authority of the husband, it has always been comparatively weak among poor peasants, because the poor peasant women, compelled for financial reasons to take more part in manual work than women of the wealthier classes, have obtained more right to speak and more power to make decisions in family affairs. In recent years rural economy has become even more bankrupt and the basic condition for men's domination over women has already been undermined. And now, with the rise of the peasant movement, women in many places have set out immediately to organize the rural women's association . . . Where the political authority of the landlords is already completely destroyed, the peasants are beginning their attacks on the other three spheres, namely, the clan, the gods and the relationship between men and women.

Mao Zedong, 1927

Women were one of the key sources of support for nationalist movements. Indeed, one might say that the moment when most nationalist movements began to achieve success was the point at which they began actively to solicit support among women. This appears true of nationalist movements in the Middle East and North Africa, for instance, as well as in East and Southeast Asia (Moghadam, 1994). In order to recruit women to their cause, the leaders of the nationalist movements were forced to abandon portions of their traditionalist outlook and see women as active participants in the nationalist movements.

In China women played an important role in the anti-imperialist nationalist movement in the 1920s. Male Communist writers devoted considerable time and energy to discussion of the role of women, and women themselves were prominent in Communist intellectual circles (Gilmartin, 1995). The critical breakthrough came with Mao's identification of women as a potentially crucial force in the Communist Party's appeal to the lower stratum of the peasantry. His 'Report of an Investigation into the Peasant Movement in Hunan', quoted above, focused on the gender relations within the families of poor peasants. Poor peasant women, already relatively 'free' because of their poverty, led in the spontaneous struggle against landlords, lineages, religion and patriarchy. The decline of the rural sector meant that more and more peasant families would become poor, and therefore the number of such women would increase. 'At present, however,' Mao concluded, 'such attacks have only just "begun" . . . Hence at present our task is to guide the peasants to wage political struggles with their utmost strength' (Mao, 1927, pp. 46–7).

In the countryside, the Communists actively mobilized women, and they encouraged them to take part in the rural revolution in 'liberated areas' during the civil war. The Communists also only began to succeed in urban areas when they appealed directly to the interests of workers, especially women, and their success depended on their utilization of existing networks and 'sisterhoods' among women workers (Honig, 1986). The Communist appeal to women to throw off their traditional subjection contrasted starkly with the failure of the Nationalist ideology – an amalgam of Confucian traditionalism, a vague commitment to Sun Yat-sen's principles, and the fashionable trappings of interwar European fascism – to offer women anything, and this contributed significantly to their ultimate victory. In 1927 Nationalists hunted down suspected 'Communist' women, including some who had merely cut their hair short:

> ... intense political symbolism was associated with the women's deaths. Women's bodies were subject to mutilation as a statement against female activism, which had come to be viewed as a disturbing indicator of a world turned upside down ... in Hubei they reportedly 'cut open the breasts of the women comrades, pierced their bodies perpendicularly with iron wires, and paraded them naked through the streets'.
>
> (Gilmartin, 1995, p. 198–9)

Women were important in the development of Korean nationalism under the Japanese. Because of the continued impact of development – especially infrastructure – under Japanese rule, there was 'no strongly rooted insurgency' in the rural areas. Nevertheless, the uprooting of large numbers of peasants as part of the Japanese strategy of 'industrialization from above', especially in the 1930s, brought large numbers of people together in a context in which their hostilities would focus on the Japanese colonial authorities. Many of these people were women. Following their own 'model' of development, the Japanese recruited thousands of young farm girls and concentrated them in the textile factories, where the long hours, low wages, and harsh discipline led to dissatisfaction. Labour organizations emerged at an early date among these women, for instance the Chosen Women Fellowship in 1924 (Cumings, 1984, pp. 487–9). The tradition of women's involvement in labour organizations with nationalist agendas spread and deepened during the 1930s and into the war years. Women industrial workers played an important role in the national liberation movement. In 1946 Chun-Pyung (the All Korea Labour Council) claimed to have nearly 600 000 workers as members, including a high proportion of women (Ogle, 1990).

In Southeast Asia, as seen in Chapter 8, the Japanese occupation provided the opportunity for nationalist movements to expand into areas previously closed to them by the repression of the colonial regimes. The

Japanese also stimulated the mobilization of women in order to spread their anti-Western rhetoric more widely and effectively, and more immediately to involve them in the economy to increase output. In Indonesia, Japanese policies intersected with the existing nationalist movement. Women educated in the Kartini schools were an early focus of nationalist sentiment, and during the 1930s women's organizations such as the Union of Indonesian Women (abbreviated PERWANI) supported the nationalist underground as cooks, nurses and liaison officers. During the occupation, the mass political mobilization organized by the Japanese brought Sukarno and other nationalist leaders into contact with tens of thousands of women. The neighbourhood organizations and the national women's organization provided organizational support for the nationalist movement. Former leaders of PERWANI such as Mrs D. D. Susanto led in the formation of a new national women's organization, the Union of the Women of the Indonesian Republic (PERWARI), at a conference held in December 1945, only four months after the declaration of independence (Sullivan, 1994, pp. 58–60).

In Malaya, the Japanese mobilized previously secluded Malay women to replace men recruited into labour gangs or military units. In addition they mobilized women through the new women's movement. They banned the existing women's journal and dissolved the women teachers' organization. However, the new Malay-language magazines contained women's sections, and carried exhortations by women leaders for women to give up their preoccupation with jewellery, to engage in useful work and propaganda, and to serve their country and their race to the best of their ability – to 'give up their age-old seclusion and indifference and to take a keener interest in public affairs', and to 'take advantage of the splendid opportunity that is being given to them by the wise and farsighted administration'. In August 1943 the Japanese authorities launched a broad campaign to bring women into the labour force, and many women began to work in factories, restaurants, schools, shops and telephone exchanges. The effect, especially in urban areas, was to weaken the notion that work outside the home lowered a woman's status. In 1944 Women's Associations were active in cities, towns and districts, bringing women into contact with welfare activities, auxiliary police work, war relief, first aid, and food crop cultivation.

The continuity of these developments into the postwar era and their connection with the Malay nationalist political movement is well documented, as are the links among wartime organizations, the nationalist movement, and the traditional aristocratic elite. The women's movement campaigned to improve the social status of women, in alliance with women from the traditional elite. The leaders of the wartime Women's Associations joined with aristocratic women to sponsor new women's organizations which became the Kuam Ibu or Women's Section of the United Malays National Organization. The UMNO Women's Section aimed for 'the unity of women, an improvement of their status particularly in marriage, the promotion of secular and religious education and adult literacy, and the collection of relief and scholarship funds'. The techniques were the same ones learned from the Japanese, especially the staging of mass rallies of women, for instance to oppose the Malayan Union scheme, and night classes, now teaching literacy in Bahasa instead of Japanese (Akashi, 1980, pp. 70–7).

In Vietnam, women provided support for the independence movement and for the armed struggle against the French and then against the Americans. In reaction to the 'racial dyarchy' of the French colonial government, anti-colonial activists used the hierarchical structure of the village, as well as kinship and communal ties, to mobilize individual villagers. Both activists and followers understood equality and liberty as collective rights, not individual benefits, both in the 1920s Vietnam Nationalist Party and later under the Communists. Also, and crucially, the Vietminh had policies directed towards subsistence needs and reform within the local community (Luong, 1992). Particularly in the north, the Communist Party's strength lay in their rural base areas. Women's organizations mobilized support, provided food, nursing, and communication services, and many women served in combat – to the amazement, frustration, and even disgust of first the French and then the Americans.

It is significant that following the creation of the new states, oppositional and insurgent movements also appealed to women for support. In this they repeated the strategy of mobilization of female discontent which had been so important for the anti-imperialist nationalist movements of the previous generation. Among opposition parties, representation of workers' interests was often broadened into a programme of more nearly equal relations between the sexes. This sometimes led to the emergence of distinct organizations for women. In Indonesia, in contrast to the 'middle class' orientation of PERWARI, the programme of the competing Indonesian Women's Movement (GERWANI) associated with the Communist Party was overtly political and aimed to support the Party and its organizations, both by mobilizing masses of women and by locating and training female party members and cadres (Sullivan, 1994, pp. 58–60).

In the Philippines in the early 1980s, the ideology of the insurgent Communist New People's Army (NPA) also emphasized equality between the sexes. The NPA consisted of between 15 000 and 30 000 combat troops; in some districts as many as one in three may have been women. The NPA denounced 'feudal' sexual relationships such as arranged marriages and dowries, and 'bourgeois' sexual relationships such as family pressures to marry for financial reasons and the obligation to bear children in order to pass on private property. The NPA promoted the equal right of female comrades to court male comrades, and of all comrades to choose their love partners, as 'freedom of love and marriage' and 'equality between the sexes'. Promiscuity, usually attributed to and blamed on men, was frowned on as 'bourgeois indulgence'. Marriage was seen as a partnership, undertaken within and with the support of the Party. The Party advocated planned parenthood, conceived of as a combined political and personal decision to raise children in a 'proletarian way, scientifically and collectively'. In contrast to their public propaganda, which portrayed guerilla fathers and mothers cradling babies in one arm while levelling their rifles with the other, the NPA in fact treated children as important 'second liners', and mothers left their units to have their babies and rear their children. Although the pressures of commitment to the Party and the danger involved in armed resistance obviously limited the numbers of active recruits, the appeal of these ideas generated widespread support for the movement (Hilsdon, 1995, pp. 72–6).

The domestication of women by national states

Be honest and diligent girls, tender and modest wives, wise mothers, and you will be good patriots. True patriotism consists of fulfilling one's duties and valuing only rights appropriate to each according to sex and age, and not wearing the [liberty] cap and pantaloons and not carrying pike and pistol. Leave those to men who are born to protect you and make you happy.

Prudhomme, 1793

1. Woman's duty as wife. 2. Woman's duty as mother. 3. Woman's duty as procreator. 4. Woman's duty as financial manager. 5. Woman's duty as a member of society.

The 'five major duties' of women, Family Welfare
Development Program (PKK), Indonesia, 1977

The reason for the appeal of oppositional and insurgent movements to women is clear – although the revolutionary nationalist movements had appealed to women for support in the struggle to gain power, once in power the new national governments refused to share that power with the women who had supported them. European revolutions have shown a similar pattern. Revolutionary periods draw women out of the domestic sphere and are 'reinterpreted by women as a justification for entering the "masculine" public arena'. However, the mobilization of women and the upsurge of feminism in the revolutions of 1789, 1848, 1871 in France and 1848 in Germany were followed by repression and decline in subsequent periods of reaction (Bridenthal et al., 1987, p. 7; Anderson and Zinsser, 1988, p. 353). In the French Revolution, 'despite the unprecedented part women had played', even Jacobin journalists such as Prudhomme dismissed women's claims for equality 'as scarcely worthy of consideration'. The famous legal code introduced under Napoleon in 1802 significantly strengthened the rights of husbands and fathers over female family members and severely restricted the property rights of all women (Doyle, 1989, pp. 420–1). The Soviet Union legislated complete equality of women and men, instituted easy divorce, and legalized abortion. But regressive legislation under Stalin recriminalized abortion and reduced women to helpmates in the home who could support their husbands and sons in 'stakhanovite' efforts. Officially, women became 'mothers', and mothers became 'heroes', despite the fact that large and increasing numbers of women also worked full time outside the home (Stites, 1977; Goldman, 1993).

The Soviet Union in Europe, and China and Vietnam in Asia, are particularly significant examples, because of the explicit commitment of the Communist Party ideology to sexual equality and because of the repeated assertions that equality had been achieved in practice. In North Vietnam, it has been argued that the Party rested on the support of village communities. The local community could mobilize support around the 'primary objective' of national independence from the French 'despite the high cost of their action, the few foreseeable tangible benefits in the early years ... and the small odds of success'. Women and men supported the struggle for independence. After 1954 the policies of the government – land reform, cooperativization, the introduction of new village organizations – weakened the unity of wartime. As in China, the regime implemented these policies to dissolve previous class relations. But the persistence of the inherited male-centred hierarchy could be seen in the continued preference for sons, in male domination of family relations, and in the structure of organizations such as the local Party chapter. In the 1980s the introduction of the family contract system in agriculture and increased socio-economic differentiation appear to have reinforced these hierarchical social relations based on kinship units (Luong, 1992, p. 167).

Socialism did not bring equality for Chinese women. The myth of the role of women in the Communist revolution and of gender equality in the People's Republic was destroyed by works which appeared in the early 1980s. In the rural areas, although women were mobilized in the anti-landlord campaigns, collectivization did not do away with the patriarchal household. Rather, it created a 'democratic patriarchy' which allowed poor *male* peasants – the crucial base of support for the Communists in the countryside – to share more fully in control over land and its correlate, control over women. Membership in the new agricultural cooperatives was based on the household unit. Access to land and the distribution of income was structured on the basis of membership in family units, which were assumed to be headed by males. Cooperatives also were usually organized on the basis of existing villages in which most households were linked through male relatives. Women had less access to education beyond the primary level; the 1982 census showed that half of Chinese women age 12 and over were illiterate or semi-literate, compared with 21 per cent of men (Lavely et al., 1990). Women had less opportunity for Party or government employment. Women were paid according to lower pay scales for fewer work points, and their work points were paid not to them but to the male head of their household. In addition, they bore the double burden of outside work and household work. Families continued to arrange marriages and families continued to be patrilocal. Not surprisingly interview data show a resurgence of the stem family in both rural and urban areas after 1960 (Johnson, 1983; Stacey, 1983; Wolf, 1985; Croll, 1983).

In the urban areas, shifting economic policies directly affected women's employment opportunities. During the period of reconstruction women were encouraged to enter the industrial workforce. Here, however, they were concentrated in traditional female-dominated, low-wage sectors such as textiles. When urban unemployment became a problem in the mid–1950s the government encouraged women to withdraw from the labour force entirely. Articles appeared with titles such as 'How Housewives Can Serve Socialism'. During the 'great leap forward' in turn, urban women were again mobilized for factory employment, but this time to replace men who were to work at higher skill levels and for higher wages in heavy industry – 'the advancement of a large sector of the male labour force depended on the new female role' (Andors, 1983, p. 62).

Nor did the reforms of the 1980s help women. In the expanding industrial districts they provided the pool of cheap labour exploited by domestic and foreign entrepreneurs. In the countryside their position was also not improved by the transition to 'household responsibility' and 'contract' systems of production. The land and resources of the collectives were parcelled out not to individuals, but to household units, which of course were headed by males. Village women continued to suffer under the double burden of agricultural labour combined with household work (Myrdal, 1984; Honig and Hershatter, 1988). When farm families opened an additional small business, men worked in the business while the women 'specialized' in agriculture, especially younger 'junior' women, who might 'fill in' wherever they were needed by the family (Entwisle et al., 1995). The reform programme recreated 'Confucian' notions of women's subordination to the male head of the household. Further, woman's primary function was conceived as the maintenance of the household through their domestic functions as daughter, wife, and mother. This selective reading of Chinese tradition resolved the tension between the claim that the socialism of the People's Republic had led to gender equality and the fact that it had not. However, it did so only at the cost of a further paradox, the claim that women have no public role combined with the practice of a multiplicity of public roles. Public discourse ignored the specific roles of women, despite their important participation in agriculture, rural industry, and commodity production (Judd, 1994).

Nevertheless, the 'Chinese' family did not simply survive or re-emerge. The Confucian family values of the 1980s reform period did not replicate the family structures of the late Qing. Marriage laws emphasized the equality of the rights and duties of husbands and wives, particularly their right to work and their responsibilities towards their children; the detailed references to collateral relatives found in Qing legal codes disappeared (Wilson, 1993, pp. 108–11, 116–17). Although the patriarchal 'stem' family with several generations living under a single roof appeared to be an ideal, families in practice were portrayed and discussed in terms of two-generation 'nuclear' families of parents and children alone. Significantly, although as seen in Chapters 2 and 3 lineage groups played a key role in late Qing society and economic development, the government did not portray the lineage as the ideal 'Chinese' family. The public discourse of the 1980s and 1990s reforms gave lineages as such no public role – despite the fact that collateral relatives played an important role in the lives of many Chinese. As we have seen, villages frequently consist of households with male heads who are more or less closely related – a fact of primary importance to a young wife from another village. In both the countryside and in the cities observers report frequent use of 'family' connections to obtain employment and housing. As seen in Chapter 9, the emerging elite of village Party cadres used family connections to gain and retain power. During the reforms there were frequent reports of groups of relatives, sometimes former cadres, who gained control over collective lands, established rural industrial plants, or moved into urban real estate, commerce, and manufacturing in the open economic areas, especially in the south. These groupings would have been identified as 'lineages' in a previous generation.

The Chinese example is important to our understanding of the position of families, and therefore the position of women, elsewhere in Asia. Despite their public commitment to the family, the ruling elites in control of central state governments do not want to foster strong family groups if this means a lessening of their power. Although women are conceived of as subordinate in the domestic sphere, the family as such is not granted a political role, and certainly extended alliances of related families – lineage groupings – are not encouraged. Further, states in fact have no interest in a genuinely private sphere, despite the official definition of the family as a 'private sphere'. Such a sphere might become a basis for political organization (see Ginsborg, 1995).

Although the elite justifies its position with an appeal to national tradition, in family and gender relations as elsewhere the official reading and interpretation of 'tradition' is very selective. This is clearly the case in neo-Confucian thought. It is also true in Islamic societies, and the process is not confined to Asia. Algerian women before independence were represented as the 'woman freedom fighter', but following independence the Islamist movement abandoned references to war, wrote the woman freedom fighter out of history, and redefined women in accord with an 'Islamic projection of society', in which woman became the 'new woman' or 'Islamic sister', who must behave in accordance with Islamic principles, because if she does not, it 'will lead to *fitna*, moral or social turmoil' (Moghadam, 1994, p. 41). In Asia the question of who has the authority to define woman's role frequently leads in Muslim societies such as Malaysia and Indonesia to tensions between Islamic traditionalists and the state. Though the state wants support from traditionalists, the ruling elite does not want to share power with religious groups, and therefore typically does not support their claims for segregation of the sexes, regulation of dress and public appearance for women, multiple marriage, or divorce, for instance.

States – and the ruling elites which control them – want quiescent and docile populations which can be mobilized for political and economic goals but which do not contest the leadership of the elite. Therefore it is essential that the state be able to penetrate into the family. For the state's purposes, the best form of family is a relatively small unit, with family members publicly defined in terms of their 'private' family function, but in fact connected to state organizations, notably for youth and women. Further intrusions into the family sphere by institutions such as schools and employment, welfare, and regulatory agencies reinforce the state's power and restrict the autonomy of families and of individuals, particularly women (see Donzelot, 1980). The household registration system, residence restrictions, and food rationing introduced in China during the technocratic period following the 'great leap forward' can be seen in this way.

Similarly, though with less overt pressure than in China, 'Malaysian women are being groomed to take a sizeable role in producing modern culture', with consumption patterns aimed at 'the domestic construction of middle-classness' combined with an emphasis on motherhood as part of the '70 million' policy. In 1984 Prime Minister Mahathir Mohamed remarked that 'in a situation where there may be unemployment, it will be good for the girls to have babies and let others be employed', and Rafida Aziz, the chief of the Women's Section of the UMNO but also Public Enterprises Minister, said women should marry at age 19, in order that the five children the government recommended they bear could be spaced four years apart before they reached the age of 40. As an advertisement for the Selengor Development Corporation put it in 1991, 'We are building housing, you are building happy families.' In 1989 one state government introduced Islamic religious examinations for betrothed couples which required the bride-to-be to answer questions about the duties of a wife and to name five of the twenty-five prophets to demonstrate her religious knowledge. Nevertheless the cult of domesticity was combined with the expectation of continued employment, seen implicitly in the continued increase in the proportion of women working in the modern factory sector, and explicitly in advertisements portraying female professionals with their children, a sort of 'Malaysian superwoman' happily juggling her brood of children and her career (Stivens, 1994, pp. 87–8; 1996; Healy, 1994, pp. 102–3, 108–9).

Indonesia's New Order government has organized local politics through a particularly pervasive system of neighbourhood groups which are branches of national organizations. In 1973 the government established the Family Welfare Development Program (PKK) as the recognized, official, but 'non-political women's movement'. The minister of home affairs announced that whereas previously the development of the nation had been almost entirely the responsibility of the state, it was now time for all Indonesians to accept responsibility for and involve themselves in national development. In particular, married women were singled out as a group which would play a critical role in this new approach. New laws in 1974 specified links between the PKK and government at all levels, and provided for local units in all urban neighbourhoods and villages. The PKK pronounced the 'family' to be the fundamental social institution of the nation, and announced the 'five major duties' of women cited above, which obligated women to foster the values and behaviour on which the nation's development must be based. A new marriage law limited the minimum age of marriage and the freedom of men to repudiate their wives or take multiple wives – provisions which in fact appealed to upper class women's organizations, but which also promised to make the government's proposed family planning programme more effective.

Throughout, the 'practitioners' of the PKK have been exclusively female, and a parallel hierarchy of *ex officio* female officers ranges from the wife of the minister of home affairs down to the wives of local mayors. However, 'the theorists and ideologues of the PKK program are predominantly male'. Moreover, the ideology they have imposed on Indonesian women, though couched in the language of modernization, has in fact redefined and narrowed the domestic sphere by excluding areas of production and commerce which had previously been included as female activities related to the household. The PKK ideology now rigidly limits the domestic sphere to the home. Further, the officially accepted woman's 'place' has been restricted as well, confined to and made identical to the home. And finally, the home itself was redefined as a 'crucial arena of national development'. Within the home, the head of the household, always male, presides over 'the norm of a small, happy and prosperous family', according to an official statement in 1991. His wife is portrayed as the 'manager' of a 'separate but equal' sphere, and this 'equality' between the sexes is asserted to rest on 'traditional' Javanese/Indonesian values. In fact the domestic ideology does not accurately reflect either historical tradition or contemporary reality; however, it works to restrict women and ensures that they have no legitimate realm of public action – apart of course from the regular meetings of their Women's Section (Sullivan, 1994).

The repression of opposition by authoritarian governments has included the repression of women's organizations and labour organizations oriented towards women. In South Korea, Chun Pyung was allied with the

Communist Party, and was therefore seen as a threat by the United States as well as by the South Korean leadership, men with roots in the Japanese colonial era and the pre-colonial aristocracy. The South Korean government declared all 'social movements' illegal on 7 February 1948. Chun Pyung declined in the following campaign of coercion and organized right-wing terrorism (Ogle, 1990). In Indonesia, GERWANI became a prime target of the anti-Communist backlash following Soeharto's seizure of power in 1965. Macabre and patently false stories of the licentiousness of GERWANI members and of their alleged participation in the killing of the army officers which set off the coup were spread in the media. Leaders down to the local level were hunted down, many were killed, and even if only arrested and detained, these women were all blacklisted. They were banned from holding any official office, required to report regularly to local military officials, obliged to carry special identity cards identifying their 'suspect status', and severely restricted in their rights to travel within Indonesia (Sullivan, 1995, p. 60; Sears, 1996, p. 21).

Repression, though officially directed against particular targets, has clearly been intended to extend and reinforce the state's control over the entire population. The hostility of the new Indonesian government to the Chinese community and its organizations may have been only partly ethnic, and only partly political in being 'anti-Communist'; it may have been more deeply political in that family and community organizations not under the control of the ruling elite were seen as a threat to their power. In the Philippines in the late 1980s the later president Fidel Ramos, as army chief of staff and later as defence minister, developed the 'iceberg theory', an analogy by which the Communist Party and the NPA guerrillas were seen as merely the tip of the iceberg, whose much larger body was the submerged and therefore invisible support they enjoyed among the civilian population. The government sanctioned paramilitary and right-wing vigilante groups who assisted the army in identifying and arresting, but also in torturing and murdering, alleged dissidents and their families. 'Whole families or groups of villagers are killed together. Fanatical vigilantes who take part claim that children are killed because they are considered irreversibly affected by the alleged "godless communism" of their parents' (Hilsdon, 1995, pp. 107, 130 note 19).

Significantly, political repression has frequently involved overtly sexual violence against women. Having stepped outside their 'proper' sphere, women are punished not only as political opponents or protesting workers, but as women, to be degraded in ways which reinforce their sexuality. In Korea, male workers have often been used by employers and the government to repress female workers' protests, and the repression typically takes sexual forms − not only beatings and kidnapping, but sexual threats and rape of female kidnap victims. The pressure focused especially on women workers and women activists has been cited as a key factor in the decline of Chun Pyung (Ogle, 1990). When degradation proceeds to the point of torture it typically not only marks but physically obliterates women's sexuality. In the anti-NPA campaign in the Philippines the army and its allies treated torture victims differently, depending on their sex. Bodies of male political activists were found with eyes, ears, tongues and limbs removed, leaving them symbolically senseless and crippled, deprived of the organs with which they might criticize or resist. Women, however, had their genitals mutilated and their lower abdomens cut open, and pregnant women had the foetus cut out of their uterus. Torture is directed to the femaleness of the victim, and the mutilation symbolically punishes her for 'the crime of having transgressed the boundaries ascribed to womanhood' (Hilsdon, 1995, p. 130). The terror inspired by such horrifying victimization is intended not only to frighten potential opponents of the government directly, but also to bolster the gendered social order which the government hopes will minimize the very possibility of resistance.

Women in the Economy

Gender divisions

Singapore girl, you're a great way to fly.
Advertisement for Singapore Airlines

Feminist economists have argued that much of the labour performed by women in both Western and Asian economies is not only unpaid but also unrecorded, because it is defined as taking place in a 'private' sphere. When women do emerge from the private sphere to take paid employment, it is often part-time, casual, or home work, and the poor pay and conditions are justified as reflections of the flexibility which women allegedly need or demand, of the temporary nature of female employment, and of the supplementary role women's wages allegedly play in family incomes. Women are sometimes blamed for their lack of commitment to full-time employment. Alternatively, female employment patterns are seen as reflections of the 'natural' roles of women, particularly childbearing and childrearing (Benaria, 1985; Mies, 1986; Waring, 1988; Boris and Daniels, 1989).

Governments want workers, but they also want mothers; they want females in flexible roles in the labour force, but they also want females in circumscribed roles in the family. The 'conflation of the sexual division of labour with the public–private division' (Marshall, 1994, p. 46), which masks the contradiction between the role of mother and the role of woman worker, frequently leads to confusion and contradictions in state policies. This is demonstrated in Japan by the pervasive influence of the ideology of motherhood in Japanese labour legislation, which aims to protect not only the physical body of the potential mother, but also the social role of the mother, for instance in restrictions on overtime work for women, which it is believed will leave them too tired to do their housework. Provisions for maternity leave, menstrual leave, and breast-feeding breaks in the 1947 Labour Standards Law in fact resulted in thousands of female railway workers losing their jobs (Herold, 1980; Carney and O'Kelly, 1990).

Some of the problems of working women in Asia parallel conditions found in Europe and the United States, for instance segmented labour markets in the 'modern' sector. In most countries women are concentrated in disproportionate numbers in low-paying occupations; conversely, 'feminine' occupations are low-paying, and the 'feminization' of an occupation means a decline in its relative position. In Shanghai by the late 1940s women made up nearly two-thirds of the industrial labour force, and female cotton mill workers accounted for over a third of the total (Honig, 1986). These concentrations have continued and even been exceeded; in the electronics firms of the free trade zones in Malaysia in 1987, 76.4 per cent of the workers were female (Rasiah, 1993, p. 136). Table 11.1 shows the ratio of female to male wages over time in several

Table 11.1   Ratio of Female to Male Wages in Non-Agricultural Activities, 1980–94

	1980	1985	1990	1994
Hong Kong	77.7	79.2	70.0	64.7
Japan	43.6	42.1	49.9	51.5
South Korea	45.1	46.9	55.9	59.7
Singapore	61.5	63.4	–	–

Sources: International Labour Office, *Bulletin of Labour Statistics* (Geneva, various years); Lim, 1993.

countries. Much of the gap is explained by the concentration of women in low-paying jobs. However, as shown in Table 11.2, even in the very narrowly defined (and heavily feminine) categories of Electronics Equipment Assembler and Textiles Labourer, women still receive substantially less than men.

Table 11.2   Ratio of Female to Male Earnings, Textiles and Electronics, 1993–4

	Electronics Equipment – Assembler	Spinning, Weaving and Finishing Textiles – Labourer
China	46.1	75.5
Hong Kong	70.2	85.3
South Korea	69.0	68.4
Malaysia	73.6	84.1
Singapore	–	87.7

Source: International Labour Office, *Statistics on Occupational Wages and Hours of Work and on Food Prices, October Inquiry Results, 1993 and 1994* (Geneva, 1995). Ratios are either of wage rates or reported earnings.

In Asia as elsewhere the possibility of effective labour organization varies according to industrial structure and community groupings. These sometimes compromise and contain class solidarity and inhibit independent labour activism. When traditional and modern overlap, gender and economic modalities can come into conflict. Thus, in the Chinese silk industry the gender struggle against patriarchy may have restricted the growth of a specific working class consciousness (So, 1986). Also, as in Europe and the United States, mobilization of support for labour movements includes mobilization of women, but labour movements, once established, tend to support male interests. And, as in the Korean case, governments have adroitly exploited the differences between female and male workers. The United States occupation administration granted permission to continue low wages for women workers 'in accordance with the tradition of Asia', in effect defining women as an underclass, and as noted above male workers have been regularly mobilized to repress women workers' protests.

A relative absence of labour conflict has been cited as a distinguishing feature of Asian economic development. Development agencies in most of the rapidly growing Asian economies have attracted foreign capital with the promise of a docile labour force. This alleged docility has been attributed to traditionalism, but also to the large numbers of women in the labour force.

Asian women in particular are alleged by their governments to be quiescent, pliable and diligent workers, unlikely to protest or strike. The Philippines Department of Trade has produced a pamphlet which asserts that local women possess qualities of 'natural subservience' and a 'high tolerance for boredom', and the Malaysian government one which argues that,

> The manual dexterity of the oriental female is famous the world over. Her hands are small and she works fast with extreme care. Who, therefore, could be better qualified by nature and inheritance to contribute to the efficiency of a bench-assembly production line than the oriental girl. (Healy, 1994, p. 103)

Optimistically, some observers have attributed the absence of strikes to economic prosperity. Less optimistically, others have emphasized the weakness of labour organizations and blamed that weakness on political repression. In fact, as noted in Chapter 10 and below, there has been quite a lot of protest by both male and female workers, not all of it widely or accurately reported.

The varying fortunes of workers, both female and male, reflect a number of factors. Arguments based exclusively on traditionalism, prosperity or repression do not explain the differential ability of labour to resist state controls effectively across industries and countries. East Asian labour systems may be seen as non-proletarian (patriarchal, paternalistic, patrimonial), stable proletarian (largely male blue-collar workers in heavy industry), and 'hyperproletarian' (largely female factory workers in light industry). Only the stable proletarian blue-collar workers enjoy employment conditions which enable them to organize effectively and engage in overt collective action to improve their conditions. The non-proletarian workers are forced to resort to individualistic, covert protest, while the hyperproletarian female sector is marked by job turnover as the only avenue of redress (Deyo, 1989). As seen below, these categories in turn cut across the sectoral divisions of agriculture, the urban 'informal' sector, and the 'modern' industrial sector.

Agriculture

The wives and daughters of agricultural households are the source of the unlimited supply of labour.

W. Arthur Lewis

Across Asia for many centuries and well into the colonial period, most families mixed forms of agricultural production with the production of various kinds of non-agricultural products. The creation of a specialized, exclusively agricultural sector and a corresponding agricultural population is relatively recent. In a household which combined farming and non-farming activities, the role of women in production was open and obvious. Studies of the rural sector in developing Asian economies suggest that where household subsistence activities play an important role, patterns of equality within the household are maintained by patterns of responsibility and power of women, based on their monetary and non-monetary contributions to the family's livelihood (Rutten, 1982).

However, in the new specialized agricultural sector, the role of women, though significant, is often unrecorded. Governments and their statisticians have seen 'family' farms in terms of the activities of the male head of household. Women family members are seen as peripheral or part-time workers in the agricultural enterprise, and arguably the ideology of family domesticity militates against their being seen at all. Also, even in regions and cultures which accord relatively high status to women, employers favour men as heads of household, for example in the Philippines (Rutten, 1982). Particularly in Southeast Asia, married women in the countryside have often borne the burden of development programmes, mobilized when their labour was required, and then have been marginalized and excluded from the benefits of economic growth. The extensive debate over the benefits and possible negative consequences of the 'green revolution' often ignores the fact that the beneficiaries are often male and the victims often female (see Strange, 1981). Politics is involved as well. In agriculture as in industry, female labour has been occasionally mobilized to combat more militant male workers' movements, for instance in Indonesia. In the plantation sector, particularly on Sumatra, following the strikes and subsequent repression of the labour movement in the early 1960s, agricultural estates employed increased numbers of part-time workers. Many of these were women provided by a new class of labour contractors, and therefore 'labour retrenchment has been gender specific' (Stoler, 1985, p. 171).

When women's labour is recognized, it is often devalued; the definitions and boundaries between 'men's work' and 'women's work' change, but the lower value accorded the work done by women remains. In the 1930s and 1940s in the Yangzi delta, rice planting was assumed to be highly skilled work which only men could perform. Planters received twice the wages for weeding or harrowing, and three times the wages paid for 'women's work' such as pulling up paddy shoots. After the establishment of the People's Republic, women were mobilized to plant rice in order to raise output. They were paid on a piecework basis, and they regularly outperformed men. This was attributed to their more flexible wrists. In the early 1980s in these same villages, the gender division had reversed itself, and rice planting was now defined as exclusively women's work and no longer commanded a premium in pay (Huang, 1990, pp. 55–6).

As development proceeds, women in rural areas may find themselves increasingly narrowly defined as 'housewives' and their economic activities marginalized and confined to an informal sector of petty production and trade. As marginal, ancillary, and 'underemployed' workers, they provide the 'unlimited supplies of labour' which W. Arthur Lewis identified as the key resource in economic development in his immensely influential model of economic development. Lewis argued that such 'underemployed' workers are available to the modern sector for only a small premium over the wages paid in agriculture, and that their withdrawal from agriculture has no impact on either agricultural output or agricultural wages (Lewis, 1955). However, the rural 'traditional' sector is not simply static. Changes in agriculture have differential effects on men and women. In Korea, for instance, technical change in agriculture lowered employment opportunities for women, leading to a higher rate of migration for women, and larger numbers of women than men moving to cities. In Seoul and Pusan women made up 45 per cent of total employment in 1975. Over 60 per cent of female migrants were between 10 and 29 years old. Although better educated than young rural women who did not migrate, the migrants had a significantly lower rate of school enrolment than other young urban women, 13 per cent compared to 44 per cent for the 15 to 19 year-old age group. As workers migrants were confined to low-paying jobs, particularly in the industrial sector which had grown rapidly since 1960. They had not lost their connection with the countryside or with their families, however. In 1974, 55 per cent of single workers sent money home (Hong, 1984).

The urban informal sector

Outside of agriculture, development has also been segmented by gender. The informal trading sector in the rapidly growing cities employs primarily females, and as agriculture declines this sector provides the largest reservoir of labour. Rapid urbanization has resulted from both natural increase and migration from rural areas. Urbanization represents a structural change, and in several countries may be considered excessive, in that the growth of population has exceeded the availability of employment in the cities. The urban population also has run ahead of the provision of housing and infrastructure such as water, sewerage, schools and health facilities. Bangkok, Jakarta and Manila have large slum areas, estimated to contain 20, 26, and 35 per cent of the population respectively.

Because of the small number of full-time jobs in the 'modern' industrial or service sectors, compared to the increase in population, many people are forced to eke out a living in the informal sector. Of the range of employments, street vendors and peddlers are the most visible, but a broad range of small manufacturing activities, repair services, transportation of goods and people, and more or less intermittent or casual work as shop assistants and day-labourers is included as well. The common factor is the need for only a very small amount of capital for entry. A bicycle can be transformed by the addition of a sidecar into a vehicle for moving passengers or packages. A family can cook food for sale, or use a sewing machine, a simple stamping press, or some other 'adapted technology' operated in a makeshift squatter's house to produce goods which can be sold directly on the streets by children or other relatives, or possibly wholesale to other family groups who will sell them to others in turn. Such a family might also finish goods or produce parts or components for another manufacturer further up the network of subcontractors. Because wages are low – or non-existent for relatives – measured 'productivity' in the informal sector is low, and it is driven down further by the competitive pressure from the continual stream of new arrivals.

In this situation, families mobilize all members able to contribute. Males may be lucky and secure full-time employment in the 'modern' sector, leaving their wives and children to continue work in the informal sector. Alternatively, if as seen in the case of Korea the technical changes in agriculture press more women than men out of that sector, then substantial numbers of girls from the countryside will also seek work, and those unable to find work in the 'modern' sector may be absorbed into these small enterprises. Lines of contact often run through collateral relatives or acquaintances from the girls' home villages. In the late 1970s the share of workers in the informal sector was estimated at 45 per cent in Jakarta, 35 per cent in the cities of peninsular Malaysia, and 26 per cent in the cities of Thailand (Sethuraman, 1981).

The link between the informal sector and the modern sector, and the avenue which might be expected to open the way to higher incomes, is education. As seen in Chapter 9, this is one area where the new national governments expended considerable resources and made considerable advances. Here again we find a gap between women and men. Again, as in the case of Japan, the rise in school enrolments was at first confined to boys and only later included girls. And even after girls achieve more or less equal access to education, there remains the question of whether access to education and employment outside of the home improve women's position. The answer seems to depend in part on the class position of the household. Educated women from the middle classes have been entering the modern sector, because the demand for educated female labour has been rising, and either real family incomes have been declining or expectations and aspirations have been rising. Despite their inherited hostility to waged labour for women, these are the families which most often support advanced education for their daughters. Meanwhile, as noted above, uneducated and mostly poor women have tended to lose their traditional earning opportunities in agriculture, but suffer under intense competition in the urban informal sector. The poorest families, those which previously depended on income produced by the labour of their female members – labor which was often invisible in official statistics – have suffered (Papanek, 1984). Since the studies of the 1970s and early 1980s, industrial employment has expanded rapidly, but as seen below this has not benefited women greatly.

Prostitution, sex and gender

One simply had to – for the sake of the Company.
British business executive, offered the services
of a prostitute by his South Korean clients

Prostitution is pervasive in Asia. Notoriously, Japanese businessmen spend long evenings in hostess clubs surrounded by girls whose services can extend to sex, but only at prices which are prohibitively high for all but senior executives subsidized by their firms (Allison, 1994). In South Korea, business deals are often accompanied by the offer of a girl, as discovered by the British businessman quoted above. The same is true in Thailand, where the offer of particularly young girls to favoured clients is justified as 'traditional' Thai behaviour. In China, until the new People's Republic outlawed concubinage and slavery, girls could be sold. Girls as young as four or five were sold to work as household servants until they became old enough to become concubines, or to be sold again as wives or prostitutes – there were no restraints on how such girls and women were treated, because since they had no families, they had no status. The Hong Kong and Singapore colonial governments did little to discourage these practices, and they remained common there into the 1950s and 1960s (Jaschok and Miers, 1994). In the new 'reformed' Chinese economy, these traditional practices seem to be returning, and there are reports of abduction, forced prostitution and forced marriage. In Thailand and elsewhere in Southeast Asia virgins are now particularly prized because of the danger of AIDS, and girls have had operations performed on their vaginas to mislead customers.

Discussions and denunciations of prostitution are numerous, but tend to focus on the issue of the morality of exchanging sex for money, and on the obvious exploitation of the women. Nevertheless, prostitution has played a large role in the economies of Asia. Prostitution is linked to the informal sector, because women who have recently arrived in urban centres from the countryside, and urban women who have been thrown out of work, are two of the main groups who work as hostesses and whose work may slide over into prostitution. But prostitution is also connected to the modern sector, in two senses. It is itself a very large and well-organized industry, and it is a crucial component of the tourist industry in several countries, and therefore a significant source of foreign exchange earnings and of capital to finance the overall development of the economy.

The United States has been blamed for the spread of prostitution. It was endemic around American military bases in Korea and the Philippines and remains a problem on Okinawa. American soldiers in the Korean and Vietnam wars, during their periods of 'R&R' (rest and recreation), provided a lucrative market for organized prostitution in South Korea, Taiwan, Thailand, and elsewhere in Southeast Asia. From 1965 to 1972 United States soldiers may have spent US$ 111 million in Thailand alone on R&R packages organized by a travel agency established by a senior officer in the Thai air force which provided transportation, lodging, and money-changing facilities (Pasuk and Baker, 1995, p. 279). The end of the wars left a large industry seeking new customers. The United States also pushed tourism as a development strategy in Asian countries, as a 'peace-maintaining, harmony-producing industry', but these arguments were not enough to convince Asian nations to spend hundreds of millions of dollars on passenger aircraft, hotels, and other infrastructure. However, pressure from the United States convinced the World Bank, the United Nations, and other development agencies to make tourism projects eligible for financial and technical assistance grants. The resulting investment, and the following increase in tourism, directly benefited several branches of the United States economy, particularly the aircraft industry. The existing prostitution industry and the new tourism infrastructure meshed together to produce a very rapid increase in the number of 'tourists' seeking sex in South Korea, Taiwan, the Philippines, and Thailand (Truong, 1990).

In Taiwan the government began to promote tourism in the mid–1950s, following the end of the Korean War. The number of tourists increased from fewer than 20 000 annually in the late 1950s to over 1.5 million annually in the mid–1980s, and total annual revenue from tourism from around US$ 1 million to well over US$ 1 billion. Tourism was and remained largely centred on prostitution. Official statistics showed the number of sexually-oriented 'specialized businesses' increasing continuously until the government stopped listing them separately in the early 1970s. Unofficial estimates placed the number of prostitutes at over 300 000 in 1989. In 1957 Americans made up 70 per cent of the 18 000 tourists; by 1973 Americans were less than 20 per cent, and Japanese made up 72 per cent, of 580 000 tourists. Since then large numbers of overseas Chinese and others have been added to the continued stream of Japanese men. Despite periodic debate over the economic costs and benefits and the health and moral dangers of the industry, the government's support has continued. One government publication refers to the 'inexhaustible sources of pleasure' available to visitors, and critics note that the government's refusal to legalize prostitution fully has the effect of prohibiting women in the 'specialized businesses' from forming labour unions and therefore keeps the price of sexual labour low. Tourism is counted as an export industry, and as such has consistently ranked between fourth and sixth among all exports, and tended to rank highest during the period of rapid 'export-led' growth from 1956 to 1973 (Cheng and Hsiung, 1992, pp. 244–9).

There is an international 'frontier' dimension to prostitution as well, with poor regions and countries supplying girls and women (and less frequently, boys) and their sexual services to urban centres and to other countries. This repeats European experience; the large numbers of prostitutes in London in the middle decades of the nineteenth century, and in Berlin at the century's end, reflected the peaks of rural–urban migration in Britain and Germany. As the rural population has declined, scarcity has raised prices in Japan. Advertisements aimed at the Japanese market by Taiwanese and South Korean promoters emphasize the low prices they charge, compared to Japan. Significant numbers of the women in the Taiwanese prostitution industry come from other Southeast Asian countries. The Philippines has been a longstanding source of female labour for other countries, and many of these women have been employed as prostitutes. The emphasis on youth means many of the 'women' are in fact girls, some pre-pubescent. Estimates place the number of child prostitutes at 200 000 in Thailand, 60 000 in the Philippines, and 15 000 in Sri Lanka, for example. The business typically violates a number of international and local laws, and depends on police corruption for its existence.

More recently there has been a sudden boom in prostitution in Cambodia, financed largely by Thai business investment. Prostitution was forbidden under Pol Pot in the 1970s, but with the arrival of 20 000 United Nations troops in 1992 demand rose, and the industry is now firmly entrenched and 'exports' girls to other countries, especially Thailand. Observers estimate some 17 000 prostitutes in Phnom Penh, approximately one-third aged between 12 and 17 years. The girls are sold into prostitution by their families for an average of US$ 175. In rural Cambodia, the Khmer Rouge still hold much of the countryside hostage, landmines make farming difficult, and corruption diverts relief funds from districts where they are most needed. In 1992–3 more than 360 000 people were shifted from camps along the Thai border to 'resettlement sites', to build homes and resume an agrarian lifestyle. The plan failed because there was not enough arable land free of mines. In Battambang province in the northwest, 40 per cent of relocated people have no steady employment, no permanent housing, and no regular food supplies. They work for farmers who have land, or gather local plants such as morning glory which is eaten as a vegetable. In such circumstances, especially where an entire family faces starvation, selling a daughter to a Phnom Penh brothel may seem a reasonable alternative to the struggling parents.

The 'modern' sector and industry

Anybody's daughter will do.

Janet W. Salaff, 1992

The distinction between the agricultural and informal sectors of the economy, and the modern and industrial sectors, is often unclear. As seen above, individuals in the so-called 'traditional' sectors have been very responsive to market opportunities for a very long time. On the

other hand, the interest of governments in the sorts of economic development that contribute to the power of the state has led to resources being
made available to the 'modern' sector in very 'unmodern' ways. This has
particular relevance for women, for they have provided the largest number
of workers in the modern sector, and they have frequently been mobilized
in ways which reflect power relationships rather than the operation of the
market.

Japan pioneered the exploitation of young women in modern factories.
As seen in Chapter 5, the girls were recruited from farm families which
often desperately needed the wages they would earn in order to pay the
rent which would allow them to hold onto their land. The new model of
the nuclear family and the submissive values inculcated by the schools
endorsed their employment for the family's benefit until marriage. They
endured long hours, crowded housing in company barracks, miserly food,
and sexual harassment. Their health suffered in comparison with other
occupations. Attempts to escape were punished brutally by the employers,
and organized protests were repressed by the police. Yet, because there
were so many suffering families and because the government valued
export income more than the girls' well-being, they suffered for very little
return (Tsurumi, 1990).

Today the Japanese economy is marked by large pay differentials
between men and women, based on the assumptions that women will
not work after marriage, and that if they do, their income is not crucial to
their families' welfare. The famous lifetime employment system of the
large firms includes virtually no women. In such large companies young
women are employed as 'office ladies' or 'OL'. They serve as receptionists,
typists and general clerical staff, and one of their main functions appears
to be to make tea for their male colleagues as required. The positions
are terminal, in that they are seen as lasting for no more than a few years
at most. The firms expect the girls to resign if they marry, and opinion
surveys show that in fact many female university students expressly
intend to work for only a few years after graduation and to stop
work after marriage. Japan passed an Equal Employment Opportunity
law in 1986 but there has been no real attempt at enforcement. Some
firms hire women as window dressing at higher levels but give them no
work. A number of firms now have two employment tracks for women,
the OL positions and a promotion ladder, but in the latter case women
are expected to work the same long hours as male employees, which
they and their families assume means that they will not be able to
marry.

Most Japanese working women are employed by the dense network of subcontractors which supply the large firms – in the late 1980s there were 868 000 manufacturing firms with 300 or fewer employees, and two-thirds of these served as subcontractors to larger firms. During the 1970s the percentage of women employed part-time rose from 12 to 17 per cent of all female employees (Herold, 1980). The proportion and the absolute numbers were highly volatile, showing the expansion and contraction of subcontracting firms in response to the rise and fall of demand from the large firms, and demonstrating the insecurity of employment for most women. The period of slower growth since 1973 has borne particularly heavily on women, because in all firms, large and small, female workers are the first to be laid off in a decline (Chalmers, 1989). In this blue-collar manufacturing sector, harsh work rules and rigid discipline, boredom, long hours, and exhaustion make working conditions difficult. Here too there is strong pressure on women to resign when they marry and especially when they have children. Many do leave – turnover reaches 30 per cent annually. Those women who want to pursue continuous employment to retirement age must overcome the pressure of social roles dictated by gender ideology, that women are wives and mothers and female employment is temporary. Some succeed, because they have supportive family situations and 'put one's duty to one's job above one's right to take child-care hours or sick leave', but they are discriminated against, in that they cannot aspire to any sort of management position beyond line supervisor. Their horizons are limited and their definition of success circumscribed by the ideology they have internalized – having acquired and held a permanent position is enough for them (Roberts, 1994 , pp. 55, 104).

The Japanese case serves as an introduction to the position of women in the 'modern' industrial and service sectors of the urban districts elsewhere in East and Southeast Asia today. The economic and social structures which forced Japanese girls into the factories from the 1890s through the 1930s – rural poverty, high tenancy ratios, and the new family system – have had their analogues in the subsequent periods of rapid development in other countries. As noted above, in the mid-1970s a majority of young Korean women in urban centres sent a portion of their earnings home to their families in the countryside. In Taiwan during the same period the decision to seek factory work was a family, not an individual decision. The girls' incomes were seen as an opportunity to contribute to the family, not to improve their individual position. Few parents explicitly demanded that their daughters turn over their wages to them, but most expected that they would do so. The girls' earnings in turn were often channelled directly into financing the education of their brothers. Advanced education for girls – despite knowledge of both the girls and their parents that it was a prerequisite to entry into higher paying occupations – was not encouraged. The reason was that if girls continued to attend high school or college, they would be close to marriageable age by the time they were ready to begin work and therefore would not contribute much to their natal families. It was therefore not in parents' interest to encourage their daughters' educational aspirations (Kung, 1983).

A further element is added by a study of rural families in Java in the early 1980s. Here employers paid young women below the minimum wage, in the knowledge that their families would subsidize them. Employers justified these very low wages through appeals to gender ideology and with references to the 'equitable' rural agricultural family. Transport and lunches absorbed 40 per cent of commuters' wages. In contrast to the earlier Taiwan studies, the Javanese girls paid little or nothing to their families directly, but they did meet some of their own expenses, and their savings provided insurance against disasters. This suggests that here 'factory employment is useful for poor families less because it provides daily subsistence than because it ensures their existence in the long run and, at the very least, maintains the status quo' (Wolf, 1990a, 1990b).

The ideology of domesticity plays a role as well. In Indonesia (Sullivan, 1994), Malaysia (Healy, 1994), and Taiwan (Cheng and Hsiung, 1992), the opposition to women's work 'outside the home' seems to apply in practice only to their employment in traditional sectors of the economy, in agriculture, fishing, artisan production, and the urban informal sector. By devaluing these forms of work, the ideology fostered by government makes women available to the 'modern' manufacturing sector, though in some cases this in fact means bringing manufacturing into the home.

The Taiwan government introduced a Community Development Programme in 1968, to 'improve the people's material as well as spiritual lives'. Planned to last a decade, it was extended several times. Intended to deal with problems of food, clothing, living, transportation, and leisure, it also aimed to enhance 'traditional' Chinese moral values and social norms in the community. Women were crucial to the programme, both as a target group for training and as 'essential implementers' of the programme's activities. However, women were systematically excluded from the decision-making processes at all levels. A hierarchical structure of committees parallel to the state bureaucracy was supplemented by elected Community Councils, one of whose members served as local director. Committee members and chairs were overwhelmingly male, and since the

Community Councils were elected by male 'heads of households' rather than by individual members of the community, women had virtually no chance of election. It is worth noting as well that even this modest degree of democratization was considered potentially dangerous by the government through the 1970s, and until 1983 some one-fourth of Community Council members and directors were appointed directly by the state.

The programme sponsored basic engineering and construction projects, production and social welfare programmes, and initiatives to improve ethics and morale. Responding to surveys which had revealed that there were many 'idle women' in local communities, the government proposed a scheme of 'living-room factories' (*Keting gongchang*). Special loans were made to families to purchase machinery to set up in their homes, allowing female family members to undertake contract work for manufacturing firms. Families did indeed earn additional income, but employers were spared the minimum wages and health insurance to which factory workers were entitled, as well as saving other costs of formal factory employment, such as buildings, machinery, energy, supervision, and possibly dormitories and food – 'many "living rooms" were converted into "factories", housewives became workers, and work became "housewifeized"' (Cheng and Hsiung, 1992, p. 256).

In addition, at the initiative of Xie Dongmin, then governor and later vice-president, the government sponsored a parallel programme of 'mother's workshops' (*Mama jiaoshi*). As one official enthused in 1984, '*Mama jiaoshi* is a sound idea and a wonderful institution. To educate a woman into a good mother is equal to educate the whole family as well. If every family lives in comfort and happiness, the society will be peaceful and prosperous, united and harmonious. Ultimately, the whole country will be strong and well-off.' On the other hand, the official guidebook stated that the most important aim was 'to propagate government orders . . . Taking care of mother's interest and need is only secondary.' A broad range of workshops, held usually at weekends, covered the four areas of ethics and morality, sanitation and public health, homework and productive skills, and leisure activity and social services. 'Homework and productive skills' focused on the living-room factory programme; 'leisure activity and social services' included 'visit the aged, orphans, the handicapped, the mentally retarded, and military and poor families'. Not everything went exactly as the government hoped; folk dancing classes proved very popular, and local communities which focused on such 'trivial activities' received harsh criticism (Cheng and Hsiung, 1992, pp. 254–62).

Programmes such as Taiwan's depend on the willingness of families to make female labour available at very low rates of pay. It is now generally accepted by social historians – though not always by economists – that family structures determine the supply of labour and the distribution of income in ways that may not follow dictates of neoclassical economics. Rather than behaving in a manner analogous to a competitive firm, the family may distribute its resources along lines which reflect the relative bargaining strengths of family members and 'both cooperative and conflicting elements in family relations' (Sen, 1983). To this we may add that state policies, by patterning the choices available to families, also affect family structures. Family strategies have not been simply 'traditional'.

In Hong Kong and Singapore, as well as Taiwan, studies of the 'Chinese family' showed working women's contributions to family income were critical and unquestioned, but that these female workers were not accorded privilege and power within the family commensurate with their crucial input (Salaff, 1981; 1988). The family is defined, both by state policy and by its members, as patriarchal and patrilocal; however, it tends not to be extended beyond grandparents and occasionally in-laws. Therefore families go through phases of lower and higher 'dependency ratios', and the sorts of employment for which the family makes its female members available fluctuates accordingly. Thus to supplement inadequate earnings of the male head of household, unmarried daughters were the first to enter the labour force, and parents tried to lower the age of entry and raise the age of marriage of their daughters. Dependence on their daughters' incomes leads to the hesitancy regarding education mentioned above. The tendency for married women to withdraw from waged work depends on the balance of their earnings against the cost of housekeeping and childcare, with those having the most education able to negotiate the most flexible arrangements. Those who have withdrawn return when the dependency ratio improves, as their daughters begin to work first in the home and then outside, and as they acquire daughters-in-law (Salaff, 1992).

Special economic zones

Marsinah was murdered because she asked for too much. The 25-year-old Indonesian factory worker was dissatisfied with the pay she received for working a 12-hour day hunched over an assembly line performing tedious, eye-damaging work. So she led her fellow workers out on strike to demand a better deal: an increase in daily wages from the equivalent of $1.20 to $1.50, and a 30-cent lunch allowance. Marsinah didn't think her request was too unreasonable.

She was wrong. The day after the strike, which took place on Java, Marsinah disappeared. Her barely recognizable corpse was later found in a shallow, mud-swamped grave. She had been tortured, raped and stabbed; her stomach was ruptured and wooden splints had been rammed up her vagina. An independent Indonesian legal group believes the slaying was the work of the local military, which was being paid by the jointly owned Indonesian and European factory to intimidate unruly workers.

Abigail Haworth, 'Worked to Death,'
Marie Claire Australia, October 1995, pp. 26–32

We try to ensure the factories which make our product implement best practices for the people working in them.

Megan Ryan, spokeswoman for Nike Australia,
Sydney Morning Herald, 22 February 1997

As seen in Chapter 10, much of the direct foreign investment, and therefore much of the growth of Asian economies, has been concentrated in the special economic zones. With grants of land and subsidized infrastructure, largely free of taxes, and free as well from government regulations, foreign firms are left to produce goods for export as efficiently as they can. Efficiently means as cheaply as possible, and this means that labour costs must be held low. Competition among countries and among zones is intense and increasing, and cheap labour is the key factor in the decision to locate in one zone as opposed to another. Xiamen, the special economic zone in Fujian province, for instance, has been a particular focus of Taiwanese investment because of proximity and linguistic links, signing some 250 contracts per year until 1995, when the number dropped sharply. Observers say the reason is simple: average wages in Fujian are now 10 per cent higher than in central Sichuan province. One Taiwanese electrical appliance maker moved production from Taiwan to the mainland to take advantage of lower costs, especially wages, but now, the deputy manager says, 'wages are increasing and the standard of living is increasing, so costs are increasing', and the firm's net profit is down by 20 per cent compared to 1994. The firm is considering relocation to lower cost areas further inland. Interviews indicate other Taiwanese firms are contemplating leaving China and moving production to Vietnam.

The industries in the special economic zones are low-skill assembly line production plants – most commonly textiles and clothing, but also including a broad range of other consumer goods such as toys, household appliances, and electronics. The work is intense, stressful, repetitive and mind-numbingly boring. The wages are shockingly low. The labour force is overwhelmingly female. In some firms 80 to 90 per cent of the workers are young women. And, from Korea to Indonesia, foreign investors have been lured by access to a labour force which the host government guarantees will be not only cheap, but also flexible and above all passive. Of course many Asian governments restrict labour organizations throughout their economies, but in the special economic zones, restriction becomes outright prohibition, the assurance given to foreign investors that there will be no unions and no strikes. The women are controlled by their employers through confiscation of their identity cards, substantial 'deposits' or pay held in arrears to make the threat of dismissal more effective, confinement, and corporal punishments, and by the police or military through harassment, arrest, imprisonment, and sometimes torture and death. Discipline and harassment often takes specifically sexual forms, reinforcing women's identity as women and thereby emphasizing their dependent status.

Western, Japanese, Korean, and Taiwanese companies benefit, and claim they have no control over local labour practices. At the lowest end of the technology spectrum, textiles, clothing, shoes and toys, where competition is keenest and costs largely dependent on wages, American and European firms often subcontract their production to Taiwanese- or Korean-owned factories in Indonesia or China. In early 1997, Anita Chan published some of the details of conditions in the Yu Yuan shoe factory in Dongguan City north of Hong Kong (Taiwanese-owned, 40 000 workers producing 10 brands of shoes prominently including Nike and Adidas, 70 per cent female, harsh military discipline, earnings around US$ 80 per month, and a monthly average of 80 hours of overtime, well over the legal maximum of 35). In response, the spokeswoman for Nike Australia quoted above insisted that Nike 'did not own factories in Asia', and that they try to ensure best practices in the factories which produce their shoes.

Recruitment of girls and young women to work in the factories is often a family decision. Poor families in rural areas often depend on the wages of their daughters. A 22-year-old woman who had been sewing labels on shirts for seven years in the Kaohsiung special economic zone in Taiwan had been brought to the factory with 70 other girls from her village: 'I didn't have any choice. My parents needed me to start earning and they signed the contract with the factory for me.' She had in fact been under the legal age to begin work, but the firm circumvented regulations by providing a 'school' in the factory. In the Philippines, employers prefer single, childless women, because single women can work 'flexible' hours, and so it has become common to subject applicants to a medical examination to determine if they are still virgins. Also in the Philippines the mandatory annual medical examinations for workers are used by the firms to weed out unfit workers, for instance in the electronics industry, where firms routinely fire women whose eyesight has deteriorated.

The pay is held low, and further reduced by the conditions of employment. The woman in the Kaohsiung special economic zone in Taiwan is paid on a piecework basis, avoiding the official regulations which set minimum wages; her pay is docked when quotas are not met. On the other hand, the firm imposes overtime to fill large orders, and she remembers one five-week period of 16-hour days. In the Philippines firms prefer to hire workers on a series of short-term contracts rather than on the legally defined 'permanent' basis, because contract workers can be paid less than the legal minimum wage, and have no benefits such as sick leave entitlement. The minimum legal wage is US$ 5.00 per day, and many women earn only half that. The Yu Yuan factory in Dongguan requires unpaid hours of preparation before the workers' shifts officially begin and further unpaid hours if quotas are not met, but imposes a penalty for lateness equal to half a day's pay.

As in Japan a century ago, these women are often accommodated in dormitories provided by the employers. These range from dormitories with three-person rooms to sleeping halls with each bunk shared by two workers on different shifts. The accommodation at the Yu Yuan factory is 10 to a room, but relatively low-density for the district. Yu Yuan is better than some; other firms in southern China do not permit workers to leave the compound after work, and one Taiwanese factory employs 100 guards to watch over its 2700 workers. Even the better quality dormitories reinforce the firm's control over the women, however. A firm in the Bataan special economic zone in the Philippines forbids male visitors in the dormitory and only allows visits with relatives in a single visiting room. The firm justifies these rules as 'protecting the girls', but many of the women are in their late twenties and early thirties. They would like to marry, but cannot meet men; but they cannot leave the factory because there are no jobs elsewhere, and so they cannot stop work unless they marry.

The work is not healthy, and is often dangerous and made more so by inadequate safety measures. Muslim conservatives have expressed concern

over the morality of the girls employed in the special economic zones of
Malaysia, but firms have attempted to counter these complaints by instal-
ling prayer rooms in the factories. They have not improved wages or
working conditions, however. There have been many studies of Malay
women and the physical and psychological costs which factory employment has imposed on them (Strange, 1981; McGee, 1986; Ong, 1987).
Other examples abound. In the Philippines, a chemical firm using dip
processes stored chemicals in unlabelled containers, had poor ventilation,
did not provide masks or protective clothing, and did nothing when the
women suffered vomiting, skin rashes, headaches and internal bleeding. A
toy factory in the special economic zone near Bangkok burned down in
1993, and 174 women and 14 men died. The building had no fire escapes,
no alarms, and no fire extinguishers. The factory doors were locked and
the stairwells blocked with materials. Many died jumping from third-
storey windows. This firm had been officially warned after a fire three
years previously; nevertheless the owners at first refused to pay even the
small statutory compensation, though they eventually were forced to pay
by public outrage.

Discipline and repression are overtly sexual. Supervisors are male.
Taiwanese factories in China such as Yu Yuan employ former Taiwan
army officers to drill and discipline their workers, marching and counter-
marching them as part of their training. In Java, many of the personnel
managers in foreign-owned factories are retired soldiers or policemen
(Wolf, 1996). As noted, the supervisors even of the better dormitories
portray themselves as the 'protectors' of the girls. In the Philippines an
underwear factory forces workers to show their underwear as they start
work, so the male guards can note colour and brand, and check them
again as they leave. In Thailand a gem factory subjects women to random
strip searches by male guards, who harass and abuse them sexually.
Occasionally protest is framed in sexual terms as well. In a famous
incident in Korea in the 1970s, 70 women from a textile factory protested
by standing naked in front of riot police, and were pelted with human
excrement by male strike-breakers.

And what of Marsinah, the Javanese girl murdered in May 1993? The
Indonesian military often depend on the income earned from arrangements with businessmen in their districts to supplement their salaries
(Schwarz, 1994, pp. 28, 135–9, 260 note 85). Her protest almost certainly
threatened one such arrangement. But in addition she had transgressed
the permitted bounds of femininity, stepping into the public sphere – and
in so doing illuminating not only the systematic economic exploitation of

workers inherent in the policies of 'export promotion', but also the hypocrisy of the officially sanctioned definition of man and woman. For that
crime she, just as the suspected Communist rebels in the Philippines, had
to be punished in a way which would terrify and intimidate others, by
having her femininity not only marked, but obliterated.

12

THE DEVELOPMENTAL STATE IN ASIA: JAPAN AND THE FOUR TIGERS

The Role of the State

The Master said, 'The common people can be made to follow a path but not to understand it.'

Confucius, *The Analects*, VIII.9

Little else is requisite to carry a state to the highest degree of opulence from the lowest barbarism, but peace, easy taxes, and tolerable administration of justice; all the rest being brought about by the natural course of things.

Adam Smith, *The Wealth of Nations*, 1776

What is the role of the state in economic development? In today's Asia no one would deny that the state plays a large role in the economy (Alam, 1989; Wade, 1990; Weiss and Hobson, 1995). However, the content, quality and extent of government intervention have been the objects of extended and intense controversy. The rapid growth of the successful Asian economies can be interpreted from a neo-classical economic perspective as the predictable outcome of market-oriented policies, the minimalist programme of 'peace, easy taxes, and tolerable administration of justice' which Adam Smith argued would allow 'the natural course of things' to lead to 'opulence' (for instance World Bank, 1993). On the other hand, growth can be interpreted from a statist perspective which emphasizes the need for and central role of governments in guiding development, the path which Confucius argued the common people could be made to follow but not to understand (for instance Johnson, 1982; 1987; Amsden, 1989).

404

But what, indeed, is the state? Not only have social scientists debated state policy; there has been extensive debate over the very structure of the state in Asia. Many political scientists argue that the governing state in Asian nations is not only an actor in its own right, but also a set of interrelated institutions that exhibits continuity over time, providing varying incentives for groups to organize. An active state can provide opportunities for gain; where the state intervenes to promote or regulate, the line between public and private may blur (Haggard, 1990). In addition, observers tend to confuse positive with normative judgement, 'is' with 'ought'. Both neo-classicists and statist writers insist that their preferred policy mix will lead to more rapid growth, but neo-classicists also argue for less intervention in the economy on moral libertarian grounds, while many statist writers and Asian nationalists insist that government must intervene to defend the nation and create a 'better' society. Confucius and Smith both believed that their vision of government not only reflected the best policy in practical terms, but also prescribed the best policy in moral terms. Nevertheless, in the quotations cited above, both were being slightly disingenuous. Elsewhere, Confucius says the essence of policy is to populate the people, make them rich, and educate them, and implies that the natural abilities and interests of the people will ensure that the three aspects of policy fit together as a harmonious whole; on the other hand Smith looks to the state both to provide a broad range of services such as education and to prevent greedy merchants from conspiring against the public interest. Thus despite their differences Confucius and Smith might agree that the range of public policy and therefore the realm of the state can vary from time to time and place to place.

We can view the possible range of public actions and evaluate their consequences along a number of different axes. Neo-classical criticism of the role of activist states in the economy is frequently based on the expectation that state-led development and state intervention will create and perpetuate conditions for rent-seeking activities, with losses which surpass those resulting from any misallocation of resources which might otherwise occur. But others insist that the state does have a role to play in the absence of established markets or in cases of market failure, and that such action is crucial in the structural process of transformation to a more developmental model (Mann, 1986). The experience of East Asia shows that 'the key issue is not whether the states are interventionist but rather the quality of their intervention in the economy' (Evans, 1992, p. 84).

Another point of debate has been 'state capacity', meaning not only the abilities and commitment of government officials, but also durable and effective institutional structures. Clearly these play a crucial role, but evaluation varies depending on the perspective of the observer. There does appear to be a kind of logic of the 'developmental state' in Asia. Asian economies are by definition 'late developers', and in such countries the role of the state in development may be to substitute for the factors which served as preconditions of economic growth in the more fortunate earlier industrializers. In latecomers the state may provide the 'post-conditions' of growth, in Alexander Gerschenkron's famous phrase (Gerschenkron, 1952). In the context of competitive international economic development, the state's task may be to tame domestic and international market forces and harness them for national interests (Önis, 1991).

The key to development in this context may be a strong and autonomous state providing directional thrust to the operation of the market mechanism. The market can be guided by a long-term national investment policy formulated by government officials. A synergy of market and state can be provided by 'contests' (World Bank, 1993) among private firms instituted and supervised by state agencies. The government must mediate between interest groups competing for scarce resources, and to do this the state must create a space for itself in which state elites manoeuvre and play off interests against each other (Mann, 1986). Vested interests of course support the existing equilibrium, which limits the state's access to resources, and therefore it is also argued that the state requires high levels of internal cohesion and centralization to overcome potential 'principal/agent' and 'collective action' problems (Doner, 1992). As seen in Chapters 10 and 11, however, the social and political correlates of such developmental economic policies are interventions in family life, attempts to create national unity through the school system, repression of organized labour movements, and the imposition of a gendered ideology which allows mobilization of women for work but does not admit them to participate in public life.

How did the bureaucracies within successful developmental states acquire their autonomy? And, why did they use their autonomy to pursue economic development rather than rent-seeking or predatory goals, as has been common elsewhere? Initially, it seems, meritocratic recruitment procedures play an important role. Rigorous standards of selection generate competence, and they also create a sense of unity and identity among members of the bureaucratic elite. The sense of sharing a mission in the service of the nation is maintained even when senior government officials move to positions in politics or business. Keeping the size of the bureaucracy small maintains its identity as an elite and makes control and accountability easier. In the successful states, certain agencies have emerged as the primary institutions in the implementation of industry policy – the Ministry of International Trade and Industry (MITI) in Japan, the Economic Planning Board (EPB) in South Korea, and the Council for Economic Planning and Development (CEPAD) in Taiwan. Although different, they share general features, including their elite status within the bureaucracy, their acknowledged technical expertise, a clear focus, and insulation from political and interest group pressures. They are not too powerful because they do not control too many sectors, but they possess control over enough areas to achieve their goals. These are contingent factors as well, especially the relationship between the bureaucracy and the executive, sometimes phrased as a 'division of labour' between the tasks of ruling and reigning. In the successful states, it is argued, politicians provide space for bureaucrats by warding off interest groups which might deflect the state from its developmental priorities (Önis, 1991, pp. 114–15; Evans, 1992, 1995; Weiss, 1995).

'Asian Values': Neo-Confucianism as an Ideology of Development

The heart of Confucianism lies in 'the emphasis on the people and virtue' which is different from capitalism that 'lays emphasis on wealth or money and belittles morality'. It is also different from Communism which 'stresses material and shortchanges the people'. Both capitalism and Communism have their own base and both deviate from their own root. They do not have an optimistic future. Only the Chinese culture is indeed able to work for the well-being and peace of the people and promote the world to a state where harmony, equality and justice prevail.

> Chen Li-fu (Senior Adviser to the President of Taiwan) and
> Hou Chi-ming (Professor at ColgateUniversity, USA), 1989

An important aspect of Confucianism is that its precepts are vague enough to allow flexible interpretation.

> Australia, Department of Foreign Affairs and Trade, East Asia
> Analytical Unit, *Overseas Chinese Business Networks in Asia*, 1995

The success of any government policy depends on the willingness of the people to accept and act on it. If Asian states have succeeded, then their policies must have struck a responsive chord in their subjects. What was that chord? Gerschenkron argued that the further behind the state was, the stronger the ideology required to mobilize resources for development. Thus in Europe in his view liberalism in England was followed by an elitist St. Simonianism in France, nationalism in Germany, and Stalinist Marxism in Russia. Many have looked to the role of values, or religion, or culture in fostering growth in Asia, and much of the discussion has revolved around the contribution which Confucian or Neo-Confucian values have made to economic development. Tu Wei-ming, for instance, has defined Neo-Confucian values as 'an amalgam of the family or collectively oriented values of the East and the pragmatic, economic-goal oriented values of the West' (Tu, 1984, p. 110). He is convinced that 'values people cherish or unconsciously uphold provide guidance for their actions', particularly in the economic sphere. Confucian 'habits of the heart', he insists, are 'pervasive' in the East Asian 'Sinitic sphere', including Korea, Japan and Vietnam as well as Singapore in addition to China, Hong Kong, and Taiwan, and 'overseas' Chinese everywhere (Tu, 1989, pp. 70–1).

The Confucian concept of the individual differs from that of the West. The extension of the five relationships learned in the extended family setting gives East Asians a much more sophisticated ability to relate to others. The Confucian ethic,

> ...seems to have centred in an efficacious location much more generative and dynamic than the lonely self: the self that is not an island but an ever-expanding stream of interconnectedness...The Confucian conception that the self is a centre of relationships and that, as a dynamic centre, it constantly evolves around an ever-expanding network of human-relatedness seems to have helped East Asians to develop a form of modernization significantly different from that achieved by Western individualism...The ability of East Asian entrepreneurs to take full advantage of the human capital, be it family loyalty, a disciplined work force, or supportive staff is not an accident. They are the beneficiaries of the Confucian way of life. (Tu, 1989, pp. 74–5)

The Confucian concept of society also differs from that of the West: 'East Asian societies are in essence "fiduciary communities" which take internal cohesiveness as a precondition for long-term well-being of the people'. This leads in turn to a different definition of the state and of politics from that of the West. Political leadership rests on the recognized excellence of the ruler: 'authority is achieved by superior personality traits'. Personal excellence is revealed and fitness to govern is demonstrated in competitive examinations, especially in the recruitment of the Japanese bureaucracy. The elite status of government officials makes the mobilization of resources and the organization of 'development states' relatively easy. Abuses of power are certainly possible, but the Confucian notion that the ruler should be a moral exemplar means that revelations of corrupt behaviour lead to a crisis of legitimacy (Tu, 1989, pp. 74–6).

Nevertheless, Neo-Confucian scholars themselves note that although Confucian values dominated Chinese culture for two thousand years, they acted as an obstacle to the development of capitalism, modern science, technology, and modernization generally until their authority was overthrown by the West. Specifically, there was 'no modernization nor Western-type capitalism until the last thirty or forty years', and in Taiwan 'the economic miracle only started from the 1950s on' (Cheng, 1989, pp. 24–5). As Chapter 3 demonstrated, this is not in fact true, and Neo-Confucian scholars tend to distinguish between the high culture of the elite and the 'little tradition' shared by farmers, artisans, and merchants. For them, Confucian ethics mingled with Ch'an Buddhism and popular Taoism, and in the eighteenth and nineteenth centuries an expanding merchant class regulated their mercantile activities and personal lives according to Confucian ethical values (Cheng, 1989, pp. 34–5). For the elite, however, in contrast to Meiji Japan, the core values of Confucianism in China came under stress as a result of the ferment of the 1911 revolution and the May Fourth Movement. 'One result of this total rejection of Confucian values is that Confucianism becomes de-ideologized and set on a journey of intellectual reflection. This leads to a process of reinterpretation, rediscovery and reconstruction which would make the transformation of Confucian ethics possible' (Cheng, 1989, p. 37).

In Korea, Taiwan, Hong Kong and Singapore, 'Confucian ethics forms a component of the total forces toward transformation and development and has thus becomes absorbed as an organic part of the driving forces behind the successful launching and sustaining of economic development in East Asia' (Cheng, 1989, p. 24). Confucian ethics could 'open up' a way toward democracy and science, two basic values of the May Fourth Movement, but also 'modern Chinese have to understand modern life and the modern world'. A series of stages links with the principle of 'learning'. First, intellectuals' consciousness of 'misgivings' or 'profound care' are matched by the masses' virtues of patience and stamina. Second comes appreciation of creativity and flexibility. Third are efforts to absorb Western knowledge and values, a stress on learning, and emphasis on education. This leads to the fourth, to a new valuation of all Confucian virtues according to their potential contribution to 'maintaining individual integrity and social harmony or national coherence' – thus even 'feudalistic' precepts such as 'loyalty' or 'filial piety' can support nationalism or act as motivating forces in economic development. Others, such as 'thriftiness', 'hard-working', and 'arduousness', 'are actually powerful virtues of the Chinese people as a whole and they may actually derive from past agricultural social experience', and they lead directly to willingness to work hard and to save a high proportion of income, crucial for the early stages of economic development. Fifth, 'benevolence' and 'righteousness' can serve as the basis for supportive government policy. Sixth, 'wisdom' can receive a 'cognitive' orientation. Seventh, 'popular pragmatism of profit-seeking' is 'highly significant' in development. Confucius says the 'small man' seeks profit, but he does not denounce profit-making itself as base, and 'the fact remains that the general public will have profit-seeking as their goal'. But profit must be sought through 'right means', and one should always have the 'public good' in mind. So 'the productiveness of common people motivated by self-interest and the policy-making of superior men motivated by interest for the public good' in combination 'constitute the spiritual resources and abilities to make the right decisions and coordinate the right actions for modernization' (Cheng, 1989, pp. 38–43).

Thus Confucius' injunction to populate the people, make them rich, and educate them (*Analects* 13.9) leads to an analysis of periods in Taiwanese development: 1) 1952–63, enforcing the land-to-the-tiller policy and reaping the results of this policy so that agricultural development could be used as a basis for industrial development; 2) 1964–76, development of international trade and build-up of infrastructure for industrial development; 3) 1977–81, accelerated development of industry, especially manufacturing; 4) 1982–87, enhancement of commerce and service industries, consolidation of the economic system, and continued investment in heavy industry; 5) 1988–present [1989] upgrading of industry, precision industries, and the beginning of liberalization and internationalization of financial laws and policies. The five stages of Taiwanese development thus reflect the five powers. First, 'earth' stands for the 'policy of development in totality and mutuality', the first ten years when government planning was important, and 'benevolent policies' combined with cheap labour, willingness to work hard, diligence, and frugality. Second, 'metal' stands for 'conscious and consistent use of timely development strategies'. Third, 'water' stands for 'opening up to the international economic system', the export-oriented policy. Fourth, 'wood' stands for the 'wide and wise use of manpower and the synergic coordination and harmonization of labour and management', the increased use of educated and skilled workers reflecting the virtues of learning and education. And fifth, 'fire' stands for 'recruitment and exploration of skilled and expert manpower' and 'cultivation of the information and knowledge industry' (Cheng, 1989, pp. 48–50).

Clearly there is an element of chauvinism at work in claims for 'Chinese culture' such as the one cited above. The economic success of Chinese minority communities in Southeast Asia results from self-selection, access to capital, and political connections, rather than from Confucian values (EAAU, 1995, pp. 121–30). Further, as seen in Chapter 10, the failure of the Religious Knowledge course showed that Confucian values were far from pervasive in Singapore, for instance. In Taiwan as in Singapore, the assertion that Chinese or Confucian values had aided development was bound up with an effort by government officials to propagate certain selected aspects of Confucian thought, often in partnership with American academics. The emphasis on the role of superior men in divining the proper policy served to reinforce the position of ruling elites. The emphasis on the five relationships and the family served to justify the continued subordination and exploitation of women.

Further, appeals to Neo-Confucian values do little to explain rapid economic growth in non-Confucian societies. As seen in Chapter 8, the non-Confucian states of Southeast Asia produced articulate and sophisticated versions of their 'national' traditions, notably the portrayal of the interlocking roles of king, government and people in Thailand, or the ideal of the *pancasila*, the five principles, in Indonesia. And despite a tendency for Chinese authors to include Korea, Japan and Vietnam in the 'Sinitic' realm, writers from those nations tend to emphasize the distinctiveness and differentness of their indigenous traditions. Even Korean and Japanese authors who attribute growth to Confucian or Neo-Confucian values tend to emphasize the distinctiveness of their values. It is claimed that Koreans are 'the most homogeneous people in the world' who 'by nature are known to be future-oriented and optimistic' (Song, 1994, pp. 46, 53), or that Japanese Confucianism was unique, that it differed from other forms in significant ways which allowed it to function as a substitute for Western Protestantism and contribute to economic growth (Morishima, 1982). Those who are more sceptical have noted that the Korean government has in fact been quite ambivalent about its Confucian heritage, because of the connection of Confucianism with dependence on China, with the Yi dynasty, and with the Japanese colonial period (Robinson, 1991). In Japan there may be some resonance of Confucian values with popular tradition, in appeals to diligence, sincerity, frugality, or in the claims that the examination system leads to the selection of the best leaders and that bureaucratic guidance of the economy reflects the moral tutelage of the ruler; but these appeals are not the cause of development, and portrayals of consensual decision-making and ethical reciprocity are an 'ex post facto beautification of industrial relations' (Davis, 1987; Collcutt, 1991, pp. 153–4).

Nevertheless, the variants of nationalist discourse have in common that they are propagated by the schools and by the media, and therefore they may become the 'values people cherish or unconsciously uphold', which 'provide guidance for their actions' and in so doing become the glue which holds societies together. Thus *pancasila*, Indonesia's five principles, 'represent a search...for broadly inclusive principles to bind together the diverse groups of an extremely pluralistic society' (Liddle, 1992), and despite the embarrassing failure of the Confucianism course in the schools, in the late 1980s most of Singapore's citizens did identify with Singapore in a way which must be described as 'nationalistic' (Wong, 1993). Further, the debate itself may take on a life of its own, to the point where the ongoing discussion of what it is to be Confucian, for instance, itself becomes the essence of Confucianism. As seen below, something like this seems to have happened in Japan.

Japan: Managing an Advanced Economy

The era of high speed growth: one of many miracles?

The Emerging Japanese Superstate (Herman Kahn, 1970).

Asia's New Giant: How the Japanese Economy Works (Hugh Patrick and Henry Rosovsky, 1976).

Japan As Number One: Lessons for America (Ezra Vogel, 1979).

From 1956 to 1973 Japan's economy grew very rapidly. The rate fluctuated, but averaged 10 per cent annually during the 1960s. This was faster than any economy had grown before. Japan's 'economic miracle' stimulated intensive discussion of its possible causes, and equally intensive efforts to discover which of those causes could be exported to other countries. What lessons were there in the Japanese experience, not only for the developing economies, but for the advanced Western economies as well? (Ohkawa and Ranis, 1985; Vogel, 1979) One lesson, many argued, was the role of the state. In a very influential book Chalmers Johnson emphasized the continuities of Japanese government policy from the creation of the Ministry of Commerce and Industry in 1925, through the Second World War when many bureaucrats joined the military to control the economy, to the direction of investment towards selected growth industries by the Ministry for International Trade and Development (MITI) in the postwar period. In his view wartime planning was the ancestor of postwar economic planning (Johnson, 1982). He extended his analysis of Japan to a more general view of the 'developmental state', which has provided much of the stimulus for the discussion summarized above and in Chapter 13 (Johnson, 1987).

Johnson has been criticized for his over-emphasis of the continuity, consistency, and success of government policies. In broad outline the role of the state in the postwar Japanese economy does not seem so very different from the growth of government economic planning in Western Europe, notably the pre-history of the European Coal and Steel Community. The impression of infallibility derived from popularizations of Japanese policies such as the Income Doubling Plan of the 1960s or the activities of MITI needs to be balanced by appreciation of the failures of Japanese policy. Tariffs and non-tariff barriers propped up uncompetitive sectors, especially agriculture, the manipulation of financial markets distorted investment patterns, and the discrimination against consumers restricted the growth of the domestic market. In the key area of energy policy, the emergence of petroleum as the leading component of Japanese energy consumption diverged significantly from the intentions of both government and business planners, as the result of political conflict and economic competition rather than as the result of state intervention (Hein, 1990). Also, and again as in Europe, there has been extensive debate in Japan questioning the effectiveness of the government in managing postwar economic growth, with 'modern' economists and even some career bureaucrats arguing that rapid growth from 1945 to the late 1970s was mainly market driven and owed relatively little to policy, government guidance, or the peculiarities of Japanese culture (Nakamura, 1981; Kosai, 1986).

The era of high-speed growth parallelled the 'great boom' in Western Europe and the United States (Tipton and Aldrich, 1987b). The parallels with the 'economic miracle' in Germany were particularly close, but the Spanish and Italian 'miracles' also shared many of the same features. At the end of the war over half of the Japanese labour force still worked in agriculture. The rapid shift of labour from agriculture to industry – especially women working for low wages – meant that workers moved from a sector with relatively low productivity to one where output per worker was much higher. Further, a large backlog of technology lay ready to be exploited. Similar to Western Europe, but a generation ahead of most other Asian economies, Japan moved relatively easily into new processes in steel production, and into aluminum, petrochemicals and machinery. Imports of raw materials rose, but so did exports of finished products.

Domestic markets expanded. Wartime destruction, inflation and land reform all worked to reduce the previous concentration of wealth. Despite generally low wages compared to Western Europe or the United States (Seiyama, 1989), more Japanese had relatively more to spend. Although housing remained cramped, Japanese families equipped their homes with an array of products previously beyond their means, such as radios and then televisions, electric stoves, refrigerators, and then air conditioners, and bicycles, motorbikes, and then automobiles. This initial outfitting created an exponential increase in demand, a 'consumer durables revolution' again parallel to developments in Western Europe. As in Western European countries, in Japan the demand for consumer durables was met by domestic firms. As seen below, this contrasted sharply with the later experience of Southeast Asia and China, where rising incomes led to increased imports of consumer durables, notably of course from Japan. Export markets were also expanding. The incomes of consumers in the United States were rising rapidly, and this huge market was relatively open. The growth of exports contributed to the increasing scale of manufacturing, to further efficiency, and to the ability to move into new or more advanced areas. Thus in the mid-1960s the Japanese automobile industry passed the threshold size for the competitive production of cars with automatic transmissions, a crucial element in gaining acceptance in the American market.

The massive investment required by the expansion of industrial employment and production was made easier by the very high rate of savings, and by a host of government regulations which ensured that the bulk of those savings went into manufacturing plants and machinery and not for instance into housing. Here Japan differed from West Germany, where the government channelled investment into housing construction as well as manufacturing. In Japan the high rate of national savings reflected the tendency of Japanese workers to save a very high proportion of their incomes, over a quarter compared to less than a fifth in Western Europe and less still in the United States. The high rate of personal savings in Japan has defied easy explanations. Through the 1960s Japan's welfare system remained quite backward, and Japan has continued to spend far less on welfare than other developed countries. The Japanese, therefore must save for illness and retirement. In addition, consumer credit is limited, and so the Japanese must also save for the purchase of the consumer durables they desire. The very high cost of housing means they must save further large amounts for down payments when they purchase an apartment or a house, and those who rent must have a half-year's rent available for the required deposit. Education is a further expense, and both prep schools drilling students for university entrance exams and private universities charge high fees.

The low growth era and the 'bubble economy'

Japanese are only happy when they're being overcharged.
Real estate agent, Honolulu, late 1980s.

The Failed Miracle: Rarely has a country fallen so far so fast as Japan has in the past five years.
Time Magazine, 22 April 1996

Since 1973 the Japanese economy has grown far more slowly than during the era of high-speed growth, an average of 4 per cent annually through the 1970s and 1980s, followed by a recession and very low growth in the early 1990s. Again lessons are drawn, though now the lessons are that 'Japan's secret formula does not work any more', and that 'neither its economy nor its society enjoys a special dispensation from misery'. Ezra Vogel now sees 'malaise, a deep recognition that they are no longer on the way up ... There are no easy answers and, unlike the past, no unified response' (*Time Magazine*, 22 April 1996). Again, there are parallels with Western Europe and the United States, in slower growth, the apparent ineffectiveness of government intervention in the economy, and in the absence of consensus, but it needs to be remembered that Japan's growth has still been impressive when compared to the other developed countries. In particular, through the 1980s Japan continued to improve average levels of productivity. Paul Krugman argues that in contrast to the other rapidly growing economies of Asia, Japan since the 1950s has grown both through increasing inputs and through increasing efficiency, and that while 'today's fast-growth economies are nowhere near converging on US efficiency levels', Japan 'is staging an unmistakable technological catch-up' (Krugman, 1994, p. 73).

Lacking in natural resources, Japan obviously requires continued technological advance to maintain its position. This is a problem. Having caught up, Japan can no longer enjoy the advantage of borrowing advanced technology from the West. Japan does invest large amounts in 'research and development' (R and D) and ranks among the leaders in a number of 'knowledge intensive' industries (Morris-Suzuki, 1994). But there have been embarrassing failures, such as 'high-resolution' television and 'fifth-generation' computers. Japan produces relatively few PhD-level researchers, and lags badly in basic research. The government does not support basic research, and the rigid and hierarchical Japanese educational establishment does not encourage originality, particularly among young researchers. Most research is in applied fields, undertaken by large private firms, who do not share their ideas among themselves. It is also not clear how efficiently large firms deploy the research they sponsor, for numbers of studies have shown that firms connected with the major industrial groups are less efficient than smaller independent firms, and that the groups support their weaker members at the expense of the strong (Lincoln et al., 1996). The small-scale family enterprise segment of the economy, which spreads across distribution, services, low-end manufacturing, and agriculture, is inefficient, but unlikely to decline and extremely likely to increase its already potent rent-seeking activities in the political realm.

Agriculture poses particular problems. Despite impressive increases in productivity, Japanese farmers beginning in the 1960s progressively lost comparative advantage, not only to the domestic manufacturing and service sectors, but also relative to agriculture both in more land-extensive regions and in countries of intensive farming. In 1990 the net value added in Japanese agriculture was negative. One reason is the government's policy, embodied in the 1961 Agricultural Basic Law, to achieve parity in living standards between farm and non-farm workers. Government officials expected that declining birth rates and the shift of workers out of agriculture and into industry and services would facilitate this policy. Instead, rising life expectancy in rural areas and government subsidies together worked to provide the labour force to perpetuate a small-scale and largely part-time system of agricultural production. In order to meet its income parity goals, the government was forced to raise the prices of commodities, particularly rice, by several multiples, and the average level of agricultural protection rose from less than 20 per cent in 1955 to over 200 per cent in 1986, higher than any country other than Switzerland. Although movement towards an agricultural system resembling that of Denmark or the Netherlands might be feasible, the powerful position of the part-time farmers in Japanese politics and the entrenched interests of the Ministry of Agriculture, Forestry and Fisheries do not offer much hope (Simpson et al., 1985; Hayami, 1988; Van der Meer and Yamada, 1990).

As in Europe and the United States, the decline in birth rates means the Japanese population is ageing, which has already led to a steep increase in social security expenditures, placing the government budget under pressure. Like Europe and the United States, Japan needs to find ways of coping with an ageing population which will demand social services but not provide sufficient numbers of workers in the labour force. Current levels of contributions are insufficient to cover the expected pension payments, and the deficit will rise sharply following the year 2000 (Noguchi and Wise, 1994; Leibfritz and Roseveare, 1996). One obvious measure would be to reform the immigration law to allow larger numbers of foreign workers to live and raise families in Japan, and also to acquire Japanese citizenship (Shimada, 1994). This seems unlikely, for as seen below a widespread opinion among the Japanese people is that they themselves are incapable of accepting foreigners into their society.

Over the past decade, observers have noted sharper competition among interest groups and correspondingly greater difficulty in achieving consensus (see Yamamura and Yasuba, 1987). In 1993 the Liberal Democratic Party lost its absolute majority in the Diet, and splintered along internal factional lines into several competing parties. Also weakened by internal divisions and tarnished by revelations that its members had accepted payments from business interests similar to those collected by the LDP, the Socialist Party did not provide a credible alternative. Since the collapse of the LDP hegemony, successive unstable coalition governments have failed to provide strong leadership. Outside of parliament, there is no radicalism apparent among, for instance, female factory workers (Roberts, 1994).

In the absence of either firm parliamentary leadership or extraparlia-
mentary pressure for reform, one might expect the guiding hand of the
bureaucracy to become more evident. However, during the period of the
'bubble economy', the asset price inflation in the 1980s, the government
appears to have lost control of the economy. Financial deregulation
allowed large corporations to change their traditional method of fundrais-
ing. Previously they had borrowed up to 80 per cent of their capital from
banks, but now they began to issue convertible bonds and warrants, which
were purchased by investors in the hope of capital gains. Some of the
money raised was then employed by the corporations to purchase high-
yielding financial assets, a ploy which became known as 'zai-tech' or
financial engineering. In addition, the banks now needed customers for
the funds which large corporations had previously absorbed. The banks
lent large amounts to real estate investors, and these funds became the
source of the inflation of land prices. Government regulations intended to
restrict lending to the real estate industry failed to stem the flow.

At the same time, a macroeconomic policy of 'easy money, tight budget'
meant an 'unprecedented' easy money policy combined with 'excessive'
reductions in the budget deficit (Noguchi, 1994). The discount rate was
dropped to its lowest level ever between January 1986 and February 1987.
External pressure played a role – the need to cope with the appreciation of
the yen, United States desire for Japan to lower rates, and postponement
of a possible tightening of policy following the October 1987 stock market
crash. In addition, financial deregulation allowed corporations to raise
funds at 2 per cent and deposit them at 6 per cent. Financial institutions
did not raise rates on loans generally, but rather targeted increasingly risky
customers and especially the real estate industry.

As monetary policy loosened, fiscal policy tightened. Budget deficits had
appeared in the mid-1960s, as the costs of subsidies mounted and the
government spent to stimulate continued growth. They increased following
the first 'oil shock', the sudden increase in oil prices imposed by producing
countries in 1973. By 1980 Japan had one of the highest levels of public debt
in the world. The Ministry of Finance pressed for reductions in spending,
particularly on infrastructure projects, and for increases in taxes, including a
contentious new consumption tax in 1989. Tax receipts also rose because of
the surge in asset prices, but public investment declined relative to national
product, leading to a budget surplus and reduction of public debt. As a
result, financial institutions in effect were forced to lend more, and since they
could not lend to their traditional large corporate customers, they again
shifted to speculative lending. Prices of shares and real estate mounted to

astronomical heights, and Japanese investors went on an overseas shopping spree, snapping up 'trophy' properties at high prices.

Having created the conditions for the boom, the government intervened to burst the bubble. Between May 1989 and August 1990 the discount rate was raised well above its 1986 level. Rising interest rates caused a rapid decline in the stock market from early 1990. 'Total quantity restrictions' imposed on lending institutions by the Ministry of Finance during 1990 cut off new loans on real estate, and caused an equally rapid decline in real estate prices from late 1990 (Noguchi, 1994). However, both the mass of convertible bonds and warrants issued by corporations and the huge loans made by the banks (secured by inflated share and real estate prices) remained. As the recession deepened, bonds and warrants burdened both the issuers who were obligated to redeem them and the purchasers who faced rising interest charges on depreciating assets. Since they had often been bought with borrowed money, they burdened the banks as well. In addition the decline in real estate prices left the banks holding further bad debts of possibly US$ 1 trillion. Some banks failed, and some were merged into others; attempts to prop up the financial system caused heated debate in the Diet. Overseas, smaller economies such as Australia suffered as Japanese investors withdrew, and the dependence of the United States Treasury on Japanese purchases of its bonds meant that the Japanese financial crisis could involve the United States as well.

Japan faces problems in the late 1990s. Attempts to stimulate the economy by lowering interest rates had not succeeded in late 1996, in part because of the closer connection with the world economy created by financial deregulation. A long list of structural reforms remains to be addressed. As noted above, reform in agriculture or immigration policy seems unlikely, and in the aftermath of the bubble, reform of real estate and tax laws seems equally difficult. Politics remains largely a matter of money, and in labour relations conditions have worsened – a 'super ice-age' for female graduates especially. On the other hand, the 'flexible rigidities' of the Japanese approach to 'organized capitalism' may prove successful. State-supported oligopolies, bureaucratic influence over investment decisions, and the coordination of markets through administration, all are seen by both private and government elites as aspects of the modern economy which must be made to work efficiently, not opposed as deviations from a preconceived norm, and this makes planning potentially easier (Dore, 1986). The Ministry of Finance, though its reputation is somewhat tarnished and though there have been calls for its abolition, remains in place. MITI has moved strongly in the direction of sponsoring high-technology industries, and although financial deregulation has eliminated some of its most effective instruments, its expertise and guidance still command respect (see Huber, 1994; Weiss, 1995). The habits of cooperation among government, business, and labour could still be cited as the basis for continued Japanese expansion and penetration of the other growing economies of Asia (Hatch and Yamamura, 1996).

Japanese cultural nationalism in the contemporary world

Japan had no choice 'but to advance into Asia to defend itself.

A Comprehensive Study of the
Greater East Asia War, 1995

What Japan will do depends on how the Japanese view themselves. Because of the role of Japan in the Pacific War, Japanese nationalism remains a topic of concern. As in the case of Germany, both Japanese and foreign observers worry about any hint of a revival of the values that led to war (see Baruma, 1995). In addition we may inquire as to whether the ongoing development of Japanese nationalism might provide some hint as to possible future directions of other Asian nationalisms. In 1995 a committee of 105 LDP parliamentarians, including the then trade minister and later prime minister Hashimoto Ryutaro, approved the publication of an apologetic work insisting that Japanese aggression was defensive, and that the Rape of Nanking was 'a fabrication based on photo montages', and created an international scandal. Despite such incidents, however, there seem grounds for cautious optimism. Some writers have argued that nationalism in its early 'primary' form emphasizes history in creating a belief in community, and this would be the sense of nationalism in Meiji Japan, colonial Korea, or pre- and postwar Southeast Asia. At a later stage of 'secondary' nationalism, the existence of the national community can be taken for granted. The weight of emphasis is now given to the difference of the national community from others, to culture rather than history. Periods of concern may mark the later histories of all nationalisms, for instance the worry in England and the Netherlands in the 1970s about the influx of other races and attempts to define what was distinctively English or Dutch, or the periodic French concern with American influence, especially in language. The contemporary emphasis means that poets and historians are replaced by 'popular sociologists' (see Hutchinson, 1987).

Japan's version of secondary or 'cultural' nationalism is an ongoing debate over the distinctiveness of the Japanese people, or *nihonjinron*. The debate surfaces periodically in the mass media, and has been labelled 'the commercialized expression of modern Japanese nationalism'. Further, 'since competition for the *nihonjinron* market is fierce, writers have used one attention-catching key concept after another to describe Japanese uniqueness in a way that appeals to the general educated public'. Commercial imperatives therefore have called forth a multiplicity of definitions, but most writers share a 'culturalism', in that they see culture as 'infrastructural' and economic and political structures as outgrowths of that immanent culture. They tend to define Japanese culture by its difference, but not the difference of the 'other' but 'our' difference. It is Japan that is seen as different, often because of its position on the periphery of a normative central civilization, earlier China, and now the West.

The specific features cited as the defining characteristics of Japan tend towards the banal. Japanese communication is asserted to be non-logical, empathetic, and non-verbal – 'understanding with one's belly'. Japanese social structure is held to be based on groupism, verticality, dependence, or other-directedness. The authors tend towards a kind of race thinking. Japan is assumed to be uni-racial ('pure blood') and homogeneous. Finally, culture is assumed to be determined by race. The Japanese tend to emphasize not the superiority of their race (as in Western racism), but that complete possession of Japanese culture requires one to be born Japanese. 'Our own realm' is defined as an area where foreigners cannot penetrate, and which remains constant despite borrowings from foreigners. Things which foreigners can learn are usually objectifiable, such as knowledge of the language, art or everyday life; but the 'underlying culture' is inaccessible to them. The social, interpersonal, intuitive, empathetic aspects of interaction are not exportable – in contrast for instance to greater emphasis on the group in the sense of teamwork and cooperation, which is.

Businessmen, particularly executives in large firms, are the most avid consumers of the literature of cultural nationalism, and much of the writing is indeed connected to the study of business organizations. Businessmen see their reading as having an instrumental value in improving efficiency, and as preparation for actual or possible international contacts. Business leaders in Japan are widely considered to be a 'thinking elite', and there is a large market for their reminiscences, for instance those of Morita Akio of Sony, who said his goal was to 'create a family-like relationship', that 'consensus is natural to the Japanese', and that 'sometimes logic has to take a back seat to understanding'. In interviews, businessmen said such books did not tell them anything new, but confirmed knowledge they already thought they possessed, in a more precise or organized way.

Is the dissemination of cultural nationalism voluntary or compelled? Many companies have recommended reading lists, circulate books on the lists for employees, and produce their own in-house publications which recycle the same ideas. According to a company president, 'it's not easy to maintain good human relations in the company. Reading literature on Japanese social characteristics written by distinguished business leaders gives us a sense of direction.' However, a 34-year-old bank employee said, 'I try to read literature on Japan's business culture out of an instinct to defend myself in the organization. Our managers study organizational theory very well. So, I feel we have also to supply ourselves with the same kind of knowledge they have.'

Cultural nationalism could be a management ideology, but we would have to explain why business leaders also read the books for clarification of what they think they already know. It could be either an ideology or an explanation of economic success, but in fact the books are not always written with the purpose of explaining success, and they are often critical of Japan. The literature might represent a response to a threatened identity, but although some of the authors feel this way, most of the readers do not feel threatened by Westernization. Consumers of cultural nationalism texts do not have any particular feelings of veneration for the emperor, a strong contrast with the prewar period. Further, small, genuinely 'family' businessmen were not informed or interested – except for those who had previously worked in large companies. Japanese nationalism in the 1990s appeared fragmentary, because different groups held different attitudes about the content and ways of constructing a national identity. A school headmaster said, 'it is the national character of the Japanese to be obsessed with the question of what is unique about the Japanese' (Yoshino, 1992).

The Four Tigers

Our policies were not novel, innovative, or path-breaking ... The general policy line follows what had already been attempted in many developing countries. What was different was perhaps that our policies produced results. This could be because they were implemented more thoroughly, and with a high standard of integrity....But more important than what *we* did was the generally favourable background of the world economy.

Goh Keng Swee, Deputy Prime Minister of
Singapore, 1972, 1973

The Japanese case shows the difficulty of managing the growth and development of an advanced economy over any extended period of time, and also the contested nature of the definition of the national identity, even in a society as nominally 'homogeneous' as Japan. If there are lessons to be learned from Japan, they seem much more ambiguous and difficult than in the 1970s. But the search for models of development continues. Attention has turned to the 'newly industrializing countries' (NICs), and in particular to the four tigers, Korea, Taiwan, Hong Kong and Singapore. The sources of growth in the four tigers have been considered in Chapters 10 and 11. As in Japan and as elsewhere in Asia, these four economies benefited from high rates of savings and investment, increasing supplies of labour, and increasing levels of education, but also from relatively low wages enforced by political repression and a gendered public realm which allowed the exploitation of women in particular. However, whether their growth reflected improvements in aggregate efficiency and whether they have moved upward in the 'industrial product cycle' both remain disputed questions.

The four tigers, and the other successful Asian economies, have enjoyed spectacular success in export markets, and interpretation of their rapid growth has focused on the role of the state in fostering exports. International agencies tend to view development from a market-oriented neo-classical perspective. The Organisation for Economic Co-operation and Development (OECD) argues that the origins of rapid growth lie in 'trade liberalization' and 'an open trade regime' (Richards, 1993, 1994). The World Bank argues that when the governments of high performance economies do intervene, they do so in ways that in fact cause their economies to behave as if they were freely operating market economies (World Bank, 1993). In contrast, as noted above, many see the tigers' development from a government-centred statist perspective, and argue that successful export promotion resulted from continuous and active state intervention and guidance. As seen in the case of Japan and below, however, even successful states have their failures. An eclectic position might argue that no one approach will adequately cover all cases, and the truth must lie somewhere between the opposing views (for instance Chowdhury and Islam, 1993).

Two cheers for democracy: Taiwan and Korea

Aside from Japan, the archetypal 'developmental state', Taiwan and Korea have probably been cited most often as the Asian states in which the government agencies responsible for economic development have possessed the characteristics necessary to foster rapid growth (Amsden, 1989; Wade, 1990, 1993; Weiss, 1995; Weiss and Hobson, 1995). Further, both have moved away from authoritarianism and towards much more open, democratic political systems. However, the emergence of these effective economic agencies, let alone functioning parliamentary democracies, out of the situation of the 1960s and 1970s was anything but inevitable. In Korea the corrupt government of Syngman Rhee fell before popular and student protests in 1959, but an obvious weakness of the new 'second republic' was that many of its leaders saw Rhee's fall simply as an opportunity to enrich themselves. An upsurge of labour unrest also raised the spectre of communism. A subsequent coup, the military 'revolution' of 16 May 1961, in turn was followed by the restoration of nominal civilian rule under Park Chung Hee in 1964. Splits within the military almost proved fatal, but Park won a narrow victory in a referendum amid charges of election fraud, and once in power he established a presidential system which allowed him to select the cabinet and prime minister, and gave him powers over the judiciary, the press, public assembly and speech. A Political Party Law restricted political organizations and weakened all parties, including the ruling party (see Sung and Plein, 1995).

The leaders of the military coup considered themselves reformers, and they showed a puritanical and anti-urban bias which reflected their rural origins (Haggard et al., 1991). The first task of the new KCIA was screening 41 000 government employees, and almost 2000 were found guilty of corruption and anti-revolutionary activities. Over 120 businessmen were investigated following the coup, under a new definition of 'illicit' wealth which covered a range of activities common under the Rhee regime such as insider purchases of government properties, profiteering from access to government funds and licences, and corrupt contributions to political parties. The government nationalized the banks, cancelled all 'usurious' debts owed by farmers and fishermen, placed limits on interest rates, and promised that agricultural and fishery prices would be guaranteed through subsidies. The subsidies led to inflation, and the money supply rose 60 per cent in a year.

However, despite their hostility to big business, a group within the military wanted to coopt business leaders because of the danger of paralysing the economy. The result was a compromise. About 30 major industrialists were forced to refund their illicit wealth, but were found officially to have gained smaller amounts illicitly than initially thought. Park told the large corporations that their property was not their own but really belonged to the nation, and the government's initial development plan referred to 'state capitalism'. Businessmen were obliged to reinvest profits and were explicitly admonished to be frugal in their lifestyle – a generation later in the early 1990s a public dispute erupted over the propriety of business executives playing golf.

Thus, although the businessmen escaped punishment and indeed continued their privileged connection with the government, new economic policies subjected them to tests of efficiency and reduced rent-seeking. Therefore, somewhat paradoxically, 'state power and political insulation proved important for achieving a more market-conforming strategy' (Haggard et al., 1991, p. 851). Through the 1970s the government controlled about two-thirds of all investible funds. Resources were mobilized through the nationalized banks and direct allocations, credit policy and differential interest rates were used to channel investment in the directions selected by the government. Park used his position to dispense patronage in much the same way as Rhee. However, the government also adopted the proposal of a group of 'technocratic' or 'reform' bureaucrats to create a new 'super ministry' modelled on 'the Indian Planning Commission, which would combine centralized planning functions with control over the budget and inflows of foreign capital. Announced days before the military seized power, their proposal became the origin of the Economic Planning Board. The military needed to retain elements of the bureaucracy to maintain government functions, and the reform bureaucrats and their plans for centralized control fitted with the prejudices of the military leaders. Chang Key Young, the deputy prime minister, served as head of the EPB from 1964 to 1967. The pattern of weekly briefings, 'planning and control offices', and quarterly reports on the status and implementation of projects spread from the EPB to other agencies. The purge of potential opponents led, again somewhat paradoxically, to reforms in government recruitment and examination systems. Tax collection was an important example. Reorganization of the Taxation Bureau led to an increase in collections of 18.6 per cent in 1964, 44.5 per cent in 1965, and 68.7 per cent in 1966, with little change in the structure or rates of taxation.

The military intended these measures to buttress their power, but economic growth became an important element in legitimating their position. Park announced in 1962 that 'the key factor in the May 16 Military

Revolution was to effect an industrial revolution in Korea' (Haggard et al., 1991, p. 857). He told interviewers that he had consciously attempted to follow the economic pattern set by Japan in the Meiji period. The new institutional arrangements outlasted the military 'interregnum' and led to greater coherence of policy. At the famous monthly Export Promotion Meetings chaired by President Park and including relevant ministers, trade association leaders, and chief executives of major firms, sectoral plans and targets could be assessed, and obstacles to export development could be identified and dealt with on the spot. Park possessed the means both to reward and to punish – the meetings could result in immediate decrees with the force of law. Favoured firms received subsidies, especially in the form of cheap credit, and also tariff protection. However, continued subsidies and protection in domestic markets were linked to export performance, monitored monthly by the EPB. Politically, Park could both reconstitute his alliance with business interests and extract resources from them (Haggard et al., 1991; Sung and Plein, 1995). Economically, the system also provided the basis for 'discipline' of the private sector in that productive investment was rewarded and poor performance was penalized (Amsden, 1989, p. 14).

Exports rose of course, but as noted in Chapter 10, state intervention favoured firms which satisfied the government's demand for increased exports not by improving technology but by importing components for assembly. Further, domestic markets for successful exporters and for consumer goods were always protected. The government attempted to take advantage of international markets while at the same time pursuing policies which would minimize dependence on those markets. Thus, in order to ensure self-sufficiency in food, the government virtually forced the adoption of new rice varieties despite scientific doubts and the opposition of Korean farmers (Burmeister, 1988). And, fearing the loss of competitive advantage in light manufactured goods and a weakening of the security commitment of the United States following the end of the Vietnam war, the government also launched a Heavy Chemical Industrialization (HCI) drive in the 1970s. This attempt to skip stages of technological development has been seen as a partial return to an import substitution strategy. It led to closer links between government and *chaebol* groups, a far higher level of direct intervention in the economy, and serious misallocations of investment resources in major undertakings in heavy industry (Mason et al., 1980; Sakong, 1993).

Government policy pursued economies of scale regardless of regional consequences. Five of the six largest *chaebol* groups, which together produced some 50 per cent of South Korea's national product in the early

1990s, are located in the southeast. Many government leaders came from the southeastern districts of North and South Kyongsong and Taegu – in the 1980s over 40 per cent of high-level government officials had been born here, far more than would be expected on the basis of population – and they fostered the growth of their home region (Chon, 1992). As a result Korea became a dual economy. On the one hand there are large private enterprises and regions which have benefited from subsidized credit and which have been the major exporters of manufactured goods. On the other hand there are less-favoured regions and numerous small- and medium-sized firms which do not receive preferential loans and which do not have much direct contact with the government. In the early 1960s these smaller firms accounted for nearly 80 per cent of employment in mining and manufacturing, and 65 per cent of value added. Their share declined to 40 per cent of employment and 25 per cent of value added in 1973. With financial deregulation in the 1980s the share of small firms rose again, which suggests that as in the case of Japan the large firms favoured by government policy are not necessarily the most efficient. Phrased in more general terms, even in successful cases such as Korea, the developmental state, while correcting perceived market failures or guiding development, may find that the solutions to the problems create client groups determined to preserve their rents, and units within the government which act as their advocates (Krueger, 1990).

As seen in previous chapters, South Korea has been a very repressive state. Park said in 1971 that 'Asian peoples want to obtain economic equality first and build a more equitable political machinery afterward' (Haggard et al., 1991, p. 858). Park was assassinated in 1979. His death unleashed widespread protests, and another military coup in 1980 placed Chun Doo Hwan in the presidency. The imposition of martial law and arrest of opposition leaders sparked a 10-day uprising in the southwestern city of Kwangju. Paratroopers fired on the crowds, leaving 240 dead and over 1600 injured. Chun appealed to 'order' and 'Korean values'. He identified the 'good aspects' of Confucianism as the basis of Korean culture, especially 'discipline' and 'public interest', and argued that Koreans needed to maintain discipline in the name of economic development and national security in order to uphold their 'traditional' values. The bad things were 'foreign':

> The prevalence of toadyism, a blind admiration for all things foreign, a pervasive notion that money is everything, unbridled egoism and the like is indicative that for some, at least, spiritual and cultural interests

have taken a back seat to monetary ones. We must rectify perversion and confusion in values ... only then can a new era be forged. (Chun Doo Hwan, 'The 1980s Meeting a New Challenge' [1981], cited in Robinson, 1991, p. 219)

Chun ruled until 1988. Growth continued, but without Park, 'Korea, Inc.' did not seem to work as efficiently (Moskowitz, 1982, pp. 72–3). Under pressure from political dissidents and economic reformers, in June 1987 the government conceded the major demands of the opposition – direct presidential elections, amnesty for dissident leader Kim Dae Jung and other prisoners, respect for human rights, free speech, local autonomy and freedom for political parties. One of Chun's 1980 supporters, Roh Tae Woo, won the ensuing elections and became president of the new 'sixth republic'. Roh's regime has received credit for transforming Korea from an authoritarian military regime to a constitutional democracy (Bedeski, 1994), but criticism intensified, possibly because of the greater freedom of expression permitted. Dissidents pointed to a range of problems, including a general distrust of political leaders arising from pervasive corruption, claims of a breakdown of ethical norms, and a declining work ethic. Economic problems included a slowdown in economic growth, the uncontrolled growth of Seoul, conflict between the southeast and southwest regions, and rising labour unrest.

In 1993 Kim Young Sam, a former dissident and reformer favouring an open economy, elected local governments, and 'same name' bank accounts to make corruption more difficult, became the first non-military president in thirty years. In late 1995 Chun and Roh were arrested for their role in the 1980 coup and subsequent corruption. Roh admitted accumulating a US$ 653 million slush fund through massive bribes in return for government contracts. Also indicted were a group of former generals who participated in the coup, civilian and military aides accused of taking bribes, and a dozen business leaders accused of paying bribes, including the chairmen of Daewoo and Samsung. One senior prosecutor said, 'the investigation was conducted with a national call to cut off traditional collusive ties between politics and business'. On the other hand, another admitted that 'to minimize the economic impact, leniency has been given to businesses whose chairmen are doing a lot of work overseas, or which are doing large-scale projects overseas that if suspended could cause diplomatic problems'. Kim Young Sam's party, despite accusations that it had received illicit support and suspicions that Kim was pursuing his predecessors to deflect possible criticism from himself, won the parliamentary election in 1996, though with a reduced number of seats and a very low turnout (63.9 per cent, the lowest ever). The transition to democracy does not mean that South Korea will live happily ever after. Kim Young Sam's victory was shadowed by accusations of bribery, vote-buying, and hints that the prosecution of Chun and Roh was merely a smokescreen to conceal Kim's complicity. The economy slowed and many blamed rising wages. In late December 1996 in a secretive pre-dawn session of parliament attended only by members of Kim Young Sam's party, the government rushed through new laws which would make it easier for employers to lay off workers, to replace union members with non-union labour, and to impose flexible working hours. Promised new legislation which would have legalized a range of labour union activities was 'postponed', and security agencies were given more extensive investigative powers. The government argued the new laws were necessary to make the economy more competitive and to guard against threats from North Korea. Widespread strikes ensued, and in early 1997 the government delayed implementation of some provisions of the new laws and recognized the outlawed union confederation which had organized the strikes. In addition members of the government were implicated in another major bribery scandal, and Kim Young Sam's approval rating plummeted from 90 to less than 20 per cent.

Taiwan, despite its unpromising beginnings in the aftermath of the war and the Communist victory in China, possessed some features which in the longer run contributed to growth, including some which appeared to be disadvantages. Taiwan was relatively small, which meant a limited domestic market, but also that over time the gulf between Taiwanese and mainlanders could be overcome and a high degree of cultural homogeneity achieved. Taiwan was fortunate to receive 2 million migrants from the mainland. These included the remnants of the corrupt Nationalist regime, but also a large number of professionals, skilled workers, and former managers of commercial and manufacturing enterprises. Partly because of the influx, Taiwan had a very high population density, but the infrastructure laid down under Japanese colonial rule and the land reform increased productivity in agriculture. Therefore the rural and urban sectors merged socially and economically. The government worked to provide medical care, and as seen in Chapter 10 education expanded. The education system was open to all with ability and was Western in encouraging acceptance of new ideas, but it also attempted to reinforce those 'Confucian' values considered useful to economic development and political stability, and to suppress those not considered useful. This was true in public life as well. Thus savings were encouraged, but spending for traditional ceremonial purposes was discouraged. A Confucian emphasis on the family was allied with a 'Chinese' (but of course violently anti-Communist) patriotism.

Further, despite its 'dependent' or 'semiperipheral' role in the world capitalist system (So and Chu, 1995), Taiwan was not hurt by its client status or by the need to import both raw materials and technology. United States aid and diplomatic support provided capital and ensured access to imported technology. Despite being poor in resources, Taiwan obtained access to sufficient raw materials because of foreign demand for Taiwanese products, and access was easier because of the relatively small size and high geographical density of Taiwan's population. The growth of the economy kept unemployment low. Government policy held inflation low, and the government also must receive some of the credit for Taiwan's relatively equal distribution of income. On a more mixed note, Taiwan was politically stable, but this reflected the fact that it was a one-party state, ruled under martial law by the Nationalist Kuomintang (KMT). Taiwanese officials prided themselves on widespread social consensus and the relative absence of social 'deviancy', but this reflected the heavy hand of social and political repression, particularly of workers and women.

Taiwan's success obviously rested on export growth. Observers generally agree on a longish list of causes of success in export markets, but it is important that these causes were 'effective in combination with each other' (Metzger, 1989, pp. 151–66). In Taiwan as in Korea, it was not a dogmatic market 'liberalization', but the combination of market relations with a broad array of government interventions, which pushed the economy towards rapid growth. These included direct state investment in industry and other forms of sectoral targeting, import restrictions, export promotions, discretionary controls over foreign investment, strict controls over the banking system, and government-supported institutions to channel technology into favoured areas. The 'ten major projects' launched in 1973 included roads, railways, harbours, a nuclear power plant, and an airport, but also a steel mill, a shipbuilding facility, and a petrochemical complex. The following 'twelve new projects' begun in 1979 and the 'fourteen key projects' begun in 1985 continued the development of transport, nuclear power, and other infrastructure, but also expanded government manufacturing enterprises, notably the China Steel Corporation, the China Ship Building Corporation, and petrochemical plants. Though as in the case of Korea these initiatives were not always successful, 'government intervention cannot be dismissed as having made a negligible difference to outcomes' (Wade, 1990, pp. 305–6).

In addition to a high rate of domestic savings, Taiwan encouraged foreign investment in capital-intensive and high-technology industries with tax holidays and exemptions followed by preferential income tax rates. Three Export Processing Zones were opened in the 1960s, two in the south near Kaohsiung and one near the central city of Taichung, which offered a range of exemptions from duties and government regulations. Further inducements were offered under the Statute on Technical Cooperation; during the 1960s and early 1970s some three-quarters of the projects approved were agreements between Taiwanese and Japanese firms. In terms of total investments, however, overseas Chinese led with 31 per cent, followed by the United States with 30 per cent, and Japan with 17 per cent.

Taiwan developed an institutional equivalent of Japan's MITI and Korea's EPB, the Economic Stabilization Board of the 1950s which evolved into the Council for Economic Planning and Development (CEPAD). The relationship between government and industry differed somewhat, however, partly because of the greater importance of small- and medium-sized firms in Taiwan, and partly because of the suspicion with which private entrepreneurs regarded the Nationalist government. Over time, both CEPAD and government-sponsored trade organizations such as the Taiwan Textile Federation and the Taiwan Electrical Appliances Manufacturer Association have developed effective working relationships with private firms. Government agencies rely on a very efficient supply of information (for instance, statistics on imports and exports available within 48 hours), the elite status of officials, technical training which ensures 'good' decisions, and a civil service generally insulated from pressure from the legislature or interest groups. Even before political liberalization began, the press was fairly free to criticize the government in the economic sphere. This has proved useful as a further 'insulating' mechanism, and also provides information, because officials read the business press. Assistance offered to firms is conditional on their success, and conditions apply to the responsible officials as well as to the firms which receive aid. Officials know that decisions will be evaluated and criticized. Crudely, this reduces opportunities for kickbacks; more importantly, over the longer term the continuity of institutions ensures a generally high quality of decisions (Wade, 1993; Weiss, 1995).

The Neo-Confucian thinkers discussed above claimed their emphasis on consensus could be combined with cultivation of the individual. As long as the KMT monopolized power, such claims remained merely ideological, empty attempts to justify oligarchical rule. The significant thing about Taiwan's Neo-Confucian official ideology, is that the elite proceeded to act on its democratic implications. Chiang Kaishek died in 1975 and in 1978 his son, Chiang Ching-kuo, became president. Serving as premier during his father's last term as president, Chiang had sponsored the appointment of an unprecedented number of Taiwanese to senior government positions and the expansion of the legislature to allow the election of more Taiwanese representatives. In 1980 the first competitive national elections were held, though still within the framework of the single ruling party. Chiang pressed for liberalization of the KMT, including election of officers for fixed terms and inclusion of more Taiwanese. In 1986 he appointed a commission which recommended the lifting of martial law, legalization of political parties, greater power to the legislature, and greater local autonomy. Six of the previously 'illegal' parties filed for official status, and the electoral reforms led in 1986 to the first multi-party election.

Chiang Ching-kuo died in 1988, and vice-president Lee Teng-hui became Taiwan's first native-born president. In 1989 the opposition Democratic Progressive Party (DPP) 'defeated' the KMT by winning 30 per cent of the popular vote, but because of the continued presence of the surviving members of the legislature elected to the national parliament before 1949, the DPP still gained only a tiny minority of seats. Lee continued the movement towards a Taiwanese majority in the leadership of the KMT and in the government, but he also continued the development of the KMT from a 'revolutionary party' and towards a 'regular party', willing to surrender power if defeated at the polls. From 1989 to 1991 a reduction in the size of the legislature and phased retirement of the surviving mainland-elected members culminated in the general elections of 1991. The KMT won convincingly, with 71 per cent of the vote in the National Assembly. As the capstone of democratization, the presidency was made an elective office, and Lee himself was elected with a 54 per cent majority in 1996.

There is no question that Taiwan is a functioning democracy, but that does not mean living happily ever after. First, the KMT can expect to win elections because they are by far the best-financed party, and their opponents regularly accuse them of bribery and vote-buying. Opposition parties have difficulty gaining exposure because the KMT controls all three free-to-air television stations and many of the main newspapers have strong KMT affiliations. This leads to spectacular stunts to gain media coverage, for instance a candidate throwing eggs at the finance minister's office, and a retired erotic dancer whose campaign slogan has been 'let Taiwan be as strong as my breasts and let politics be as pure as my body'. Secondly, Taiwan, in contrast to Korea, does not have a national identity. The split between indigenous Taiwanese and mainlanders remains. Although overt ethnic friction and conflict appear to have virtually disappeared, ethnic identity has become a defining characteristic of political identifications. Conflict over political power appears to have polarized the community along ethnic lines, and indeed democratization appears to have encouraged this division by making competition for political power possible. Looming in the background is the question of reunification with China, and ethnic identity, party affiliation, and attitude towards China are closely aligned. Identification as 'Chinese', whether or not one is a mainlander, means voting for the KMT or for the breakaway New Party which maintains something like the old commitment to 'saving' China. Identification as Taiwanese, in contrast, means voting for the DPP. The ambiguity of Lee's position on unification clearly appeals to the majority, but the combination of 'money politics' and ambiguity covers both 'sub-ethnic strife' and the possible compulsion 'to seek an alternative identity', which could lead to a disastrous confrontation with China (Wachman, 1994; Wu, 1996).

Both South Korea and Taiwan face problems. South Korea's growth slowed along with the transition to democratic government. Labour costs were reported to have doubled from 1988 to 1995. Korean firms, attempting to maintain profits, established plants first in Southeast Asia and then in China. However, in implicit contrast to the Japanese, it was argued that 'the surge of Korean FDI in recent years has often been made on an ad hoc basis, unsystematic, and in a "gypsy pattern" seeking short-term profits' (Lee, 1993). At home, doubts were raised about South Korea's scientific capability, and about the continued effectiveness of economic policy. Significantly, Korea's trade deficit with Japan rose to US$ 10 billion in 1995. The imports continued to be overwhelmingly manufactured goods, not only parts for assembly and re-export, but also the machines used in the production processes. The widely recognized solution was an improvement in Korea's relative position regarding the development of new technologies. However, the Ministry of Education 'paid scant attention to university research', and the Ministry of Science and Technology did not have the budgetary or bureaucratic power needed to force through ambitious high-tech projects. Small and medium enterprises, the major suppliers of 'infra-industrial' goods such as machine tools, remained under-capitalized, neglected by government agencies, and often exploited by the large *chaebol* groups. The Economic Planning Bureau was merged with the enlarged Ministry of Finance and the Economy; having lost its autonomy it was not clear whether it could continue to play the guiding role attributed to it over the preceding three decades (Aubert, 1996). Those who attributed Korea's previous success to its 'presidential' system now expressed doubts as to whether the office still gave its incumbent sufficient power for effective action (Sung and Plein 1995).

North Korea also poses a looming threat to South Korea. In the decade before his death in 1995, Kim Il Sung had moved towards opening the economy to foreign investment and reforming the planning mechanism to allow greater flexibility. A Joint Venture Law was introduced in 1984. However, the new policy direction remained very limited. There was little new investment, and observers doubted if the changes in internal policy would meet the requirements of productivity improvement and economic growth. North Korea adopted neither Deng's Chinese policy of market-oriented reform and an open door for foreign investment, nor Gorbachev's Russian policy of a restructuring of the internal planning mechanism to achieve greater efficiency. Rather, reforms remained piecemeal. Official announcements continued to emphasize 'self-reliance' (*juche*) as a central ideological principle – for the nation, for localities, for enterprises, and for individuals (see Lee and Yoo, 1991).

The problem arises from the apparent failure of the reforms. Although Kim's son, 'Dear Leader' Kim Jong Il, seems to have consolidated his power without serious challenge, the economy has continued to decline. Although the North Korean industrial sector may actually have outperformed South Korea through the 1960s, like other socialist regimes it missed the electronics and computerization revolutions, and it is now reported to be outmoded and inefficient. Agricultural output declined to the point where international agencies warned of a possible famine (see EAAU, 1992, pp. 46–55). Floods in 1995 and 1996 led to particularly poor harvests, and there were reports of rations of as little as 400 grams of rice per day. State finances were reported in disarray, causing factories, hospitals, and schools to close. Occasional border incidents have fuelled South Korea's concern that a desperate North might launch an attack. Alternatively, hunger might drive unmanageable numbers of people southwards. Or finally, the North Korean regime might simply implode as the socialist regimes of Eastern Europe did in 1989. A possible reunification under those circumstances, with little chance of substantial foreign aid, could easily overwhelm the capacities of the South Korean economy. On the other hand, it has also been argued that indirect evidence such as fertility and urbanization ratios show a broad similarity between the North and South Korean economies, which suggests that reunification might not be so difficult after all (see Eberstadt, 1995).

The question of reunification poses a threat to South Korea's internal stability as well, because the well-organized student groups, heirs to previous generations of protesters, have focused on reunification as their next demand. A week of violence and rioting in August 1996 led to escalating repression by Kim Young Sam's government, and finally to the storming and closing of the faculty buildings where the students had barricaded themselves. Drawing on an old Korean literary tradition, and in striking parallel to the nationalist authors of the 1920s, contemporary radicals in Korea have linked the yearning for reunification symbolically to the self-sacrifice of a virtuous woman, in which 'the promise of conjugal conciliation becomes the allegory of hope for restored national legitimacy' (Jager, 1996, p. 19). However, there was no evidence of widespread support for the students' position among workers.

Taiwan's problem is China. Through the 1960s and into the 1970s, in the context of the superpower stalemate between the Soviet Union and the United States, Taiwan's threats to reconquer the mainland from the Communists and China's threats to liberate Taiwan from the nationalists remained shadowy reflections of the civil war. However, with the collapse of the Soviet Union, rapid economic growth and possible changes of leadership in China, and democratization in Taiwan, China's demand for the reunification of Taiwan with the mainland took on a different quality. In the 1980s, as Chiang Ching-kuo and the KMT leadership proceeded with democratization, China threatened it would invade if Taiwan declared independence. These threats may have affected the legislative elections of 1991, for the Democratic Progressive Party which favours independence lost votes. Most voters opted for the middle position advocated by president Lee Teng-hui and the KMT, that reunification was a desirable goal to be postponed until sometime in the future. Public opinion surveys showed that 76 per cent of Taiwan's population believed broadly in 'one China, but not now', which corresponded closely to the KMT's 71 per cent of the popular vote.

China increased the pressure during the presidential elections in 1996. Lee was denounced as the 'harlot of history', a 'traitor', 'villain', and 'splittist' who would lead Taiwan to declare independence and trigger the threatened invasion. Troops were massed in the coastal districts opposite Taiwan, and 'tests' of four ballistic missiles were conducted which targeted the waters off Taiwan's major ports. The United States intervened, moving naval vessels into the region and protesting to China. The threats appear to have helped Lee to his comfortable 54 per cent victory. Second in the voting was Pen Ming-min, the leader of the DPP committed to independence, with 21 per cent. For the future, the increasing economic power of Taiwan makes it difficult to ignore, but the increasing economic power of China makes it a major force in the region. Opinion polls say the Taiwanese would resist forcible unification, but there are large numbers of applicants for visas to emigrate, and large amounts of capital have been shifted to other centres – though this could be simply a reflection of the fact that Taiwan has a lot of foreign investment, particularly across the strait in Fujian. Another straw in the wind may be that Chiang Kaishek's family home in Zhejiang province has recently become a major tourist attraction, with reported visitors rising from 1 to 1.5 million from 1992 to 1994, and authorities claim that 90 per cent are mainlanders. In the spirit of the times regional authorities hope to use the attraction as a way of winning investment from Taiwan.

A tale of two cities: Hong Kong and Singapore

Again, as seen in Chapters 10 and 11, and again as in the cases of South Korea and Taiwan, the sources of growth in Hong Kong and Singapore have included large increases in savings and investment, in the size of the labour force, and in average levels of education, but also low wages and the exploitation of women. However, in contrast to South Korea and Taiwan, there appears to have been relatively little improvement in productivity. This seems particularly the case of Singapore, even on the most favuorable assumptions, but also appears to be true of Hong Kong.

There are striking similarities between the two island city states. Both began as colonial outposts of the British empire, and both became predominantly Chinese communities. Both served as entrepots for the surrounding regions. Both were cut off from their hinterlands and forced to find other means of survival. Both did so under highly centralized and authoritarian regimes, an indigenous one-party system in the case of Singapore and a colonial administration with very little scope for local self-government in the case of Hong Kong. Both have been portrayed as having profited from 'the fruits of free trade' (Richards, 1994) or even in the case of Hong Kong from being 'a study in economic freedom' (Rabushka, 1979). In fact, however, in both the state played a continuous and active role in the economy.

Hong Kong's initial problem was how to cope with masive immigration following the Communist victory in China. From around 600 000 in 1945 the population grew to over 2 million in 1950 and 2.6 million in 1956. Housing and social services were inadequate. There was little manufacturing industry, and Hong Kong's previous role as entrepot for trade flowing into and out of southern China had virtually ended. Still, the migrants did make up a potential supply of cheap labour. They also included a large number of owners, managers and skilled workers from the urban commercial and industrial centres of southern, central and northern China. Particularly prominent were the 'Shanghainese', a loose designation for all those from the lower Yangzi region. With their knowledge, plus what little capital and equipment they had been able to salvage and bring south with them, they recreated their firms in Hong Kong. In this case, 'overseas Chinese' settled in another Chinese community and repeated the success of immigrant Chinese communities elsewhere in Southeast Asia. They concentrated particularly in the cotton and textile industries; in the 1980s possibly 80 per cent of the cotton spinning mills in Hong Kong were majority Shanghainese enterprises (Wong, 1988). Hong Kong has also become the home for 'returnee' Chinese from Southeast Asia, especially from areas where they have suffered discrimination such as Indonesia and Myanmar/Burma. Partly because of this, Hong Kong has benefited from an expanding role as a provider of services linking Chinese communities throughout the Pacific basin (EAAU, 1995, pp. 90–9).

Through the 1970s and into the 1980s, the Hong Kong government used control of housing development, rent control, education and training, as well as its influence over investment and an emphasis on external trade to promote growth (Youngson, 1982). The government controlled all land as 'crown land' and leased it on terms which maximized its revenue on the one hand, and allowed it to subsidize housing projects and guide industrial development through the creation of industrial estates and 'flatted' factories on the other. While total output grew rapidly, total government expenditure grew twice as fast, and government welfare expenditures – including housing and education – six times as fast. The state's share of the increasing rate of capital formation rose from some 14 per cent in the 1960s to a peak of 23.4 per cent in 1983, and then settled at some 16 per cent of the high and rising totals in the later 1980s. In addition to classic infrastructure development, much of this investment was in public housing. Eventually nearly half of the population was accommodated in towering public housing blocks which, despite their initially low quality, did provide homes at far lower cost than would have been possible through private construction. The state also provided the education system, health services and transportation at preferential rates, and also controlled food prices. Estimates for data from the early 1970s indicated that the effect of government subsidies could add from 50 to 70 per cent to the incomes of working-class households.

Government subsidies reduced pressure for wage increases. Following riots in 1956, 1966 and 1967, Hong Kong enjoyed a long period of industrial peace. This meant that 'small business could concentrate on competitive pricing, shrinking and expanding their labour force according to variations in demand'. This was important, because small business predominated in the manufacturing sector of Hong Kong. Over 90 per cent of manufacturing firms in 1981 employed fewer than 50 workers, and in fact the average size of manufacturing establishment had declined substantially from the 1950s to the 1980s. Further, these many small firms were connected to world markets by a further large number of equally small firms specializing in export/import. Small firms had a predictably high mortality rate, but the subsidy system also 'created a safety net for low-risk entrepreneurialism'. Most firms were established by workers who 'bet their small savings', but could rely on public housing and other benefits if they failed. This dense network of small firms, many of them in subcontracting relationships, has been cited as the basis of the ongoing flexibility of Hong Kong's response to world market opportunities (Castells, 1992, pp. 47–9).

State policy in Singapore has passed officially through several stages. The government promoted import substitution from 1959 to 1965, then shifted to an emphasis on exports following the crisis of Singapore's ejection from the Federation of Malaysia. The government favoured the export of labour-intensive products in the late 1960s, but then decided to move to higher value-added goods in the 1970s. In the late 1970s the government deliberately increased labour costs to discourage low-skill, labour-intensive investment and lay the foundation for a 'second industrial revolution' – not entirely successfully, as foreign investors failed to respond. In the early 1980s the restructuring of the economy required by the shift away from labour-intensive exports in fact caused one of Singapore's few recessions. The government changed course again, turning the emphasis towards the services sector and away from industry altogether (Rodan, 1989).

Throughout, the government's policy aimed to reduce Singapore's traditional entrepot trade and create an economy based on manufacturing and tradeable services. This has been broadly successful. Entrepot trade dropped from 43 per cent in 1960 to 24 per cent in 1970 and 17 per cent in the late 1980s. Manufacturing rose from 11 per cent of total output in 1960 to 20 per cent in 1970 and 30 per cent in 1988. Exports of machinery and equipment increased from 11 to 38 per cent of total exports from 1965 to 1986 (Chowdhury and Islam, 1993). The electronics industry in particular has moved from labor-intensive assembly activities to capital-intensive manufacturing; employment has declined substantially, but output has continued to increase (Richards, 1994, p. 33).

Another constant has been the encouragement of foreign investment. The Economic Development Board (EDB) was established in 1961 to seek out and smooth the path of foreign firms wishing to establish plants in Singapore. The EDB has been praised for its pragmatic approach and its ability to learn from failures and mistakes (Schein, 1996), but it is not a 'planning' agency with the powers of Korea's EPB or Taiwan's CEPAD, nor has it fostered the creation of domestic technological capabilities, as MITI has in Japan. However, foreign firms have certainly found Singapore congenial. In the late 1980s foreign establishments employed over half of manufacturing workers and produced 70 per cent of industrial output and 80 per cent of manufactured exports. Foreign firms completely dominate electronics production, for instance. With the range of tailored benefits offered to foreign firms and the guaranteed absence of any form of labour organization, Singapore resembles a sort of large export-processing zone.

A final constant has been the direct role of government investment. Much of the manufacturing output not produced by foreign firms has been produced by the large state enterprise sector. The complex interlocking maze of government-linked companies (GLCs) includes six of seven listed marine industry companies, four of five listed defence firms, and the only listed petroleum refinery, as well as both international and domestic transport and communications. In total, GLCs control half of Singapore's economy. The government provides housing for a remarkable 87 per cent of the population, plus a range of subsidized services. As noted in Chapter 10, the capital needs of the government sector have been met largely through savings mobilized through the compulsory social insurance contributions made by workers to the Central Provident Fund.

Singapore's government is acclaimed for its efficiency, its meritocratic recruitment, and the absence of corruption. It is not, however a government of 'virtuous officials' on the Confucian model, but rather a 'British' public service in its technocratic and legalistic emphasis. Most officials are English-language educated; many do not read or write Chinese (Wong and Wong, 1989). Lee Kuan Yew and the small group of Western-educated professionals around him in 1959 had no military to rely on, and no family or ethnic networks to provide patronage. Possessing only their own skills and political abilities, they managed to hold power by solving the critical problems of unemployment and housing to the satisfaction of the mass of the population. Many of them were migrants themselves, members of the Anglicized *baba* and *nonya* Chinese communities of the Straits Settlements. They refused to share power with Singapore's indigenous Chinese business leaders. 'These men regarded traditional Chinese ways as outdated and superfluous to the task of modern nation building. Rather, they set about building on the institutional legacy left by the British' (EAAU, 1995, p. 70). Their economic development programme led to the creation of a group of bureaucratic administrators centred on the state enterprise system. The number of GLCs has continued to increase despite another shift in the government's rhetoric to 'privatization'. A pyramid of control begins with the prime minister's cabinet and a special committee, the Directorship and Consultancy Appointments Council. The second tier is the ministries, with the Ministry of Finance controlling four large holding companies and each of the other ministries in charge of the relevant statutory boards. Next is the group of directors and chairmen of the holding companies, who typically also sit on the boards of a number of the larger individual GLCs. Finally, directors of the larger GLCs also sit on the boards of smaller GLCs. The number of directors increased to close to 1000 in the early 1990s, of whom some 20 served as directors of 10 or more GLCs (Vennewald, 1994).

High positions come only to those whose loyalty has been tested by long service. The longstanding personal relations among senior officials, a complex rotation system, high salaries, and harsh punishments for corruption have worked to prevent the establishment of the sort of patronage and clientele networks which might allow individuals to transform economic control into political power. Appointments do depend on personal connections, but personal control by the group at the very top has ensured both technical competence and honesty. However, the government's administrative efficiency and the increasing affluence of the population have not translated into any lessening of the authoritarianism of the ruling elite. Regulation is notoriously obsessive and petty, for instance in the prohibitions on chewing gum, spitting or littering.

The ruling People's Action Party suffered a decline in its share of the vote from 76 per cent in 1980 to 61 per cent in 1991, but control over residence and legal harassment have continued to hold potential opposition in check. When J. B. Jayaretnam, leader of the opposition Workers' Party, successfully appealed against a conviction to the Privy Council, the government moved to outlaw such appeals in the future. In 1996 Lee Kuan Yew and his son were revealed to have received discounts on purchases of luxury apartments in new private developments. They donated the discounts to charity, but in addition new prime minister Goh Chok Tong not only cleared the Lees, but also threatened legal action against anyone accusing them of wrongdoing. Goh had his sights on the 1997 elections. The PAP increased its vote only slightly to 63.5 per cent, but the careful management of housing assignments, and the threat that refractory neighbourhoods would lose funding and be placed last in line for upgrading, meant that PAP candidates won 81 of 83 seats in the legislative assembly. Still not satisfied, the government launched a new series of defamation suits against its defeated opponents. In February 1997 oppsition leader Tang Liang Hong faced 13 writs for defamation. His home and office had been raided, his legal practice closed, his property and bank accounts frozen, limits placed on his family's spending, and a fund set aside for legal costs and damages.

Are there lessons to be learned here? Any lessons learned from Hong Kong will have to be absorbed quickly, for Hong Kong reverted to China in July 1997. Hong Kong will now be watched for clues as to the direction of development in China. Korea, Taiwan, and Singapore remain, but the lessons are disputed. In the political and social realm, Lee Kuan Yew has become one of the most eminent spokesmen for 'Asian values', but his attempt to foster Neo-Confucianism through the schools failed. Korean dissident Kim Dae Jung has attacked Lee's assumption that 'Western-style democracy is not applicable to East Asia', and cites not only the spread of democratic regimes but also the existence of longstanding democratic traditions on which those regimes can rest themselves (Kim, 1994). On the other hand, the transition to democracy in Korea and Taiwan was not inevitable. In the economic realm, the state has clearly played a large role, but the nature and degree of success of government action has varied, as indeed has the structure of the state itself. Debate continues. It is not yet clear whether any of the tigers will move successfully up the product cycle to autonomous development. Sceptical observers have dismissed Singapore as 'a *sui-generis* city-state ... a kind of glossy international service-sector shopping mall' (Frank Gibney, Pacific Basin Institute, *Foreign Affairs*,

March/April 1995, p. 171). On the other hand again, growth has continued, and others enthuse that 'Singapore now seems like the leading edge of the future' (Lester Thurow, Massachusetts Institute of Technology, foreword to Schein, 1996).

13

New Tigers, New Dragons, New Giants? The State And Development In China And Southeast Asia

I keep in mind that, historically, authoritarian regimes have tended to outlive their usefulness.

Ferdinand Marcos, 1978

Those who fail cannot be made examples to follow.

Mahathir Mohamed, 1982

Can the successes of Japan and the four tigers be replicated? Looking at states which hope for success, market-oriented reformers recommend liberalization of production, prices, interest rates and wages to allow them to find their 'natural levels', deregulation of financial markets and opening of restricted sectors to private investment, dismantling of restrictive legislation, lower and simpler systems of direct and indirect taxation, privatization of state-owned enterprises and liquidation of 'sick' units, and elimination of industrial licensing systems and foreign exchange controls. Where government intervention is required, they continue, the state should prefer policies which require a minimum of administrative and bureaucratic input, because once in place, policies divert scarce administrative resources, and of course the state should prefer policies whose costs are transparent and which minimize opportunities for rent-seeking (Krueger, 1990, pp. 20–1). Others find a continuing case for state intervention. It is not clear that either foreigners or domestic private firms will invest in the areas with the highest returns to the economy as a whole. If local entrepreneurs are coopted by foreign interests, the state must take up the burden, and if local entrepreneurs are inefficient, the state must encourage the most efficient among them (Doner, 1992, p. 99).

The successful developmental states of Asia all created institutional structures intended to foster and guide the growth of the economy. Both market reformers and statist writers often see this as one of the lessons of growth in Japan and the four tigers, and recommend the creation of similar state structures in their would-be imitators. Whereas statist writers view the role of government agencies as to intervene and direct development, market reformers emphasize the need for a strong state and insulated state agencies which will have the power to implement market-conforming reforms. There is a danger here. Durable and effective institutions may be deflected towards the defence of rent-seeking coalitions, after all. No less an authority than Ferdinand Marcos noted that authoritarian regimes tend to 'outlive their usefulness' (Marcos 1978, p. 92). Whatever its form, the state is not neutral, because it has its own interest in maximizing its own revenues, especially in areas where it holds a monopoly, in administration, protection, and justice. Further, state officials are themselves an interest group. The state's conflicting commitments, to maintain and defend property rights on the one hand, and to foster economic growth and equity on the other, may overlap and possibly conflict with the interests of powerful elites, and these may include individuals in the state apparatus (see Evans, 1992; 1995).

Observers have contrasted 'predatory' with 'developmental' states – the former extract resources, but do not provide public goods in return, for instance infrastructure investment or a legal environment which stimulates and supports entrepreneurial activity. Incumbents can use their position to create rents for their supporters, and if those groups become dependent on rents, even if their original influence was based on entrepreneurial activity, they may become a hindrance to further development. Such patronage politics becomes more of a problem as the range of state activities increases (Evans, 1989; Yahya, 1995). It also poses a problem when the line between public and private blurs, for instance when formerly socialist governments begin to privatize state enterprises, as in China and Vietnam, or when non-socialist states authorize major projects but exercise discretionary control over the bidding process, as in Indonesia and elsewhere, or when economic opportunities are granted to defined ethnic groups on a preferential basis, as in Malaysia.

Significantly, neither neo-classicists and market reformers on the one hand, nor statists and nationalists on the other, are enthusiastic about democracy, and the literature on the state only rarely considers the role of women. A political system which permits the easy organization of interest groups and the staging of mass protests makes things more difficult, both for state planners and for market reformers. Policies developed by bureaucratic experts may damage existing interests; market reforms do so almost by definition. Allowing labour organizations to press for significant increases in wages would lower profits, and raising the issue of gender would question the very legitimacy of the existing state. Mobilization is not always good. In extreme cases, public protests may paralyse government, as in Indonesia in the early 1960s, or a 'criminalization of politics' can occur, where money and the threat of violence determine policy, as has happened periodically in Thailand and the Philippines. Specific historical factors also play a role. States are relatively free of restraint during periods of national crisis, or during the 'honeymoon' period of a new administration. External threats in the postwar period allowed states to benefit from general nationalistic sentiments and created a consensus on the need for economic growth, and because of their strategic significance, some of the successful states benefited disproportionately from capital and technology imported from core countries (Önis, 1991; Yahya, 1995).

Equally significantly, the efforts of governments, and much of the debate over the effectiveness of their efforts, may be irrelevant. The records of even the successful states are in fact quite mixed. As seen in previous chapters, Asian women and men as individuals and as family groups have been active for centuries in seeking ways to improve their position. The attempts of successive states, whether pre-colonial, colonial, or post-colonial, to guide development have hampered these efforts as often as they have helped them. Two things appear to stand out about governing elites. One is their remarkable continuity over time. The other is the fact that their primary motive is to gain and retain power. The policies they pursue may or may not contribute to economic growth and to the well-being of the mass of the population; whether they do or not often depends on circumstances beyond the elites' control.

China: Asia's Next Giant?

The death of Mao and the rise of Deng

Practice Is the Only Criterion for Verifying Truth.
Guangming Ribao, Beijing, 11 May 1978

Whoever wins the battle for state power gets to occupy the throne.

Deng Xiaoping, June 1989

As Mao aged potential successors began jockeying for position. Army leader Lin Biao had used the end of the cultural revolution as an opportunity to place supporters in positions of influence in industry, agriculture, and education. By 1969 he was Mao's acknowledged heir. Mao, however, became suspicious of Lin and began to undermine his position. Lin in turn seems to have plotted a military coup, but the plans were discovered, and Lin and his wife died in September 1971 in a plane crash, apparently fleeing towards the Soviet Union. His supporters disappeared from public life. One of Lin's rivals was Deng Xiaoping, a protégé of premier Zhou Enlai but under a cloud since being denounced as a 'capitalist roader' during the cultural revolution. Zhou, one of Mao's oldest supporters, read the speech which branded Lin as a traitor, and then moved to place Deng and others of his supporters in key posts in the army, party, and provincial administrations. Mao's wife Jiang Qing led another group, largely centred in Shanghai and with support in the media and the paramilitary militia, dedicated to transforming the cultural revolution into an ongoing process. This 'cultural revolution group' became the notorious 'gang of four' following their defeat.

The year 1976 opened on an ominous note. Zhou Enlai died in January. Zhu De, one of the architects of the Communist military victory in the civil war, and another who had been attacked during the cultural revolution, died in July. The Yellow River flooded seven times during the summer. On 28 July an earthquake measuring 8.2 on the Richter scale levelled the mining centre of Tangshan, southeast of Beijing, killing 240 000 of the city's 1.6 million inhabitants and injuring another 164 000. 'After such an overwhelming portent, Mao could only die' (Fairbank, 1992, p. 405). Weakened by Parkinson's disease and a stroke, he did indeed die, on 9 September 1976.

The gang of four had prohibited public mourning following Zhou Enlai's death. Mass demonstrations orchestrated in March and April by their opponents were suppressed, and Deng was again stripped of his official positions. Mao named a compromise candidate, Hua Guofeng, as premier, hoping, it seems, that this would pave the way to power for Jiang Qing and her allies. For army, party, and government officials, however, the cultural revolution group posed an obvious threat. Many of them had suffered insults and disgrace during the cultural revolution and after, but had no recourse as long as Mao lived. Following Mao's death, however, Hua gained the support of army leaders and allies of Deng, and the gang of four were arrested on 5 October. Their followers were systematically removed from office. Hua was confirmed as Mao's successor, and Deng was restored to all his former offices.

Four years later in 1980 the gang of four and their main supporters were brought to trial. They were convicted, of course, but only after an elaborate and time-consuming procedure representing both the desire of the new leaders to establish their credibility on the basis of legalistic principles and their hesitancy to attack Mao too openly for fear of undermining the ultimate basis of their legitimacy. In the interval Deng had extended his base of support. The trial in effect undermined Hua's position as well, for despite his role in 'smashing the gang of four', he had been a 'whateverist' who had supported 'whatever' decision Mao had made and followed 'whatever' orders Mao had given, and he therefore bore some responsibility for the perpetuation of the 'leftist errors' of the gang of four. As Hua was deprived of his offices, supporters of Deng replaced him, and these men tended to be economic reformers. Zhao Ziyang, for instance, who had introduced pilot reform projects in Sichuan in 1978, became the new state premier in 1980. In 1981 Hua resigned as chairman of the party central committee and accepted a respectable but powerless retirement as the most junior of the six vice-chairmen. Deng emerged as China's new leader.

It is tempting to attribute the economic 'reforms' and the rapid growth of the Chinese economy since 1978 to a preconceived, consistent plan, implemented by Deng and his supporters (for instance Fairbank, 1992, ch. 21; Stevens, 1996). Deng said in an interview in 1979 that China possessed the same number of lathes as Japan had in 1960, and therefore should be able to attempt a similar economic take-off. Slogans such as 'economics takes command' or 'practice is the only criterion for verifying truth' reflected the adoption of economic development as a goal, but they also represented attempts to create the appearance of effective power over the economy. In fact, however, 'there was no "plan" of reform in the sense of a clear idea of some ultimate end-state and a series of steps or phases to reach it' (White, 1993, p. 49). As seen below the central government's control over the economy was often tenuous at best. Indeed, there was no guarantee that reform would be pursued at all. Above all, Deng and his allies desperately desired to retain power. Economic policy therefore remained political in the fundamental sense that it reflected the interests of those contending for power, and the economy in turn often moved in directions which the elite had neither foreseen nor desired.

The new orientation did not begin with Deng. Zhou Enlai had advocated both an opening of China to the outside world and economic restructuring. In the early 1970s he had pursued *détente* with the United States and a rapprochement with Japan. This was directed against the Soviet Union, but also against his rival Lin Biao, who favoured a Soviet-oriented foreign policy. One of the key elements in Zhou's policy was increased trade. The United States agreed to end its longstanding embargo on trade with China, and total trade trebled from US$ 5 billion to US$ 15 billion from 1971 to 1974. In one of his last public appearances in 1975, Zhou delivered a speech which outlined the 'four modernizations' of agriculture, industry, defence, and science and technology, a programme which would place China in the front ranks of world economic powers by the end of the century. This required the import of advanced technologies, paid for by earnings from trade. Zhou's protégé Deng, already branded a 'capitalist roader', inevitably became an advocate of trade and modernization. Equally inevitably, Deng and his supporters were forced to assume that technological change would be politically neutral and 'classless'. New techniques, they hoped, could be imported and applied without damaging Chinese social and cultural institutions, and without undermining the position of the Communist Party and its leaders (Dean, 1980).

Jiang Qing and the cultural revolution group opposed Zhou's policies as 'wholesale Westernization', and argued that in the nineteenth century this 'slavish comprador philosophy' had led politically to 'loss of sovereignty and national humiliation', ideologically to 'praise what was foreign and belittle what was Chinese', and economically to 'spreading a blind faith in the Western capitalist material civilization so as to turn the Chinese economy into a complete appendage of imperialism' (Liang Hsiao in *Historical Research*, 1975, quoted in Hsü, 1995, p. 813). By analogy this is what would happen if 'wholesale Westernization' were again pursued. Mao had argued 'politics takes command', that China could rely on its own resources, that the party should seek egalitarianism, and that to pursue economic growth for its own sake would lead to inequality, elitism, and bureaucratism. He had also argued on nationalist lines that foreign investment had crushed China's indigenous 'capitalist sprouts' and killed the potential for autonomous development. Jiang and her allies clearly had Mao and his authority on their side, and while they remained influential, 'reform' remained impossible. Symptomatically, China's foreign trade stagnated, at less than US$ 15 billion, from 1974 to 1977 (Lardy, 1992, pp. 11–12).

Reform and growth

> Our planning should combine relative centralism with a certain measure of flexibility.
>
> Xue Muquiao, 1980

The fall of the gang of four meant an immediate return to the policy of increasing trade. The State Council issued a series of directives permitting the establishment of joint ventures and establishing the first of the special economic zones. Control over foreign trade was decentralized by permitting increasing numbers of central agencies and regional governments to establish their own trading corporations. A dozen national corporations handled all foreign trade in the 1950s, but there were over 5000 trading companies by 1990. The official rate of exchange was lowered and import subsidies reduced, changes intended to bring the prices of imports closer to their economic costs. Preferences for export processing firms, licensing measures, and permission to retain a share of foreign exchange earnings aimed both to stimulate and to guide the growth of foreign trade. Trade in fact quadrupled in the ten years from 1978 to 1988 (Lardy 1992, ch. 3).

In February 1978 Hua Guofeng announced a ten-year plan, dated as having begun in 1976 with Mao's death and scheduled for completion in 1985. The programme embodied Zhou's four modernizations. Agriculture, the key problem area identified by Deng and others in the 1960s, remained the basis of the economy, but had lagged behind badly. Rural incomes had stagnated. The government proposed to increase agricultural output by increasing capital intensity, spreading the use of electrical power, mechanizing 85 per cent of all tasks, expanding irrigation facilities, and greatly increasing the use of chemical fertilizers. Pay for individuals in new, larger 'production brigades' would depend on the amount of work each performed. At the same time families would be given the right to farm communally owned lands on their own account, and sideline production by families was encouraged, particularly where it might lead to increased exports.

In the industrial sector the government proposed to match the entire increase in output since 1950 in eight years. From 1950 to 1980 industrial output had increased as much as 10 per cent per year. As seen in Chapter 9, however, many of the new plants were inefficient and poorly located. Further, as in other socialist systems the emphasis on heavy industry and on autarkic self-sufficiency meant that continued growth required increasing amounts of capital per unit of additional output, and to maintain growth the government had been forced to divert an increasing share of national income to investment. This – and the slow growth of agriculture – in turn was reflected in the failure of real wages to rise from 1957 to 1975, a development inconsistent with the interests of the expanding working class (Rawski, 1980; Perkins, 1983). The government's solution was a massive new round of investment. Hua announced 120 major industrial projects, including steel plants, oil refineries, coal mines and electric power plants.

Defence was a sensitive subject after the unimpressive showing of the Chinese forces in Vietnam in 1979. Upgrading China's very large but poorly equipped forces with foreign weapons would be prohibitively expensive and would make China dependent on foreign suppliers. Acquisition of foreign technologies for local production might take years without significantly reducing the gap between China and more advanced countries. In fact this aspect of 'modernization' appears to have been subsumed under the final one, science and technology. The number of researchers was to rise to 800 000, new centres would open, and projections placed China only a decade behind the most advanced nations by 1985.

Industrial investment was popular with regional cadres, for it meant spending and employment in their districts. But the plan was not completely coherent. Electrical power generating capacity as foreseen in the ten-year plan would not even have covered the planned increases in industrial output, and left nothing for the intended increase in agricultural electrification. Most important, there was not enough money to fund all the projects. The expenses of the Vietnam invasion were heavy. Hopes for large increases in oil production and earnings from oil exports were disappointed. Increases in wages and procurement prices for farm products and other raw materials drove up the general price level, possibly by 15 per cent in 1979 and more in 1980. Government budgets showed heavy deficits in 1979, 1980 and 1981.

The first round of reform had failed. In June 1979 Hua announced a three-year commitment to 'readjustment, reform, streamlining and upgrading'. The government slashed investments in heavy industry and construction, including joint ventures with foreign firms – Japanese losses were estimated at US$ 1.5 billion. Observers noted optimistically that policy appeared to be shifting away from the command economy and emphasis on heavy industry and towards market incentives and light industry, and that policy was also moving away from self-sufficiency and towards export promotion (Barnett, 1981; Solinger, 1984). Nevertheless, divisions remained between those who favoured a transition to 'market socialism' and those who wanted to retain central control over the economy and therefore over market relationships. Specific prescriptions remained vague and often contradictory. Xue Muquiao, the senior economic adviser quoted above, might indeed want to combine 'relative centralism' with 'a certain measure of flexibility' (in Wang, 1982, p. 23), but what this meant in practice was far from clear.

The government attempted to draw on the reserves of the agricultural sector, but without the promised increases in capital and technology. In 1979 the government offered some farm families the opportunity to work independently as contractors for their communes. Land would remain public property, but the communes would allocate plots to families in return for a promise to deliver a specified quantity of crops at the end of the season. In return, families received 'full responsibility' for all aspects of production, including the crucial areas of labour allocation and work schedules, and they were permitted to sell their surplus production in private markets. The government in fact intended the scheme as 'a concessionary measure appropriate only to poorer communes' (White, 1993, p. 100), but once introduced the new system spread irresistibly. Voting with their feet, farm families abandoned the communes in droves. By 1984 virtually all farm households throughout China were operating under the 'household responsibility' system. The number of private markets nearly doubled, from 33 000 to over 61 000.

The reforms were followed by rapid increases in output and rising rural incomes (see Perkins, 1986). By 1984 grain production had doubled, more specialized crops had increased even more dramatically, and television antennas had begun to sprout from rural roofs. The effectiveness of the household responsibility system in stimulating growth has been debated. Interviews with local cadres in the late 1980s indicated that they considered market forces to be very effective in motivating farmers to increase output (Nee and Su, 1990). However, in the absence of any change in technologies, the increases in output merely reflected higher levels of intensity of labor in the forms of greater enthusiasm and longer hours devoted to the family enterprise, a further stage of involution (Huang, 1990, pp. 17–18). Nevertheless, encouraged by the bumper harvests in 1984, the government pressed ahead with further reforms. Compulsory state procurements were to be phased out. Prices in the private markets were rapidly decontrolled, with the number of commodities subject to price controls declining from 111 to 17, accounting for only 30 per cent of sales. Land assignments were extended to fifteen years to encourage long-term planning and investment by farm families, and diversification into cash crops and non-agricultural employment was encouraged.

Increased motivation could only carry China so far. The slowdown came suddenly in 1985, and agricultural output stagnated in the late 1980s. Having nearly doubled from 1978 to 1987, rural per capita income failed to rise further in the late 1980s (Nee and Su, 1990, p. 5). The central government hoped that agriculture would muddle through on its own, and the share of the government budget devoted to agriculture declined through the 1980s. Local authorities favoured industry over agriculture, because industrial enterprises promised more immediate increases in their revenues, and because individual officials and their families saw opportunities for profit. Capital invested in 'cooperative' manufacturing plants by local governments was often appropriated by the senior managers, who came to regard themselves and their families as the 'owners' of the factories (Ho, 1994; Walder, 1995; Sargeson, 1996). In addition, as families left the farming collectives, they became less willing to devote their energies to maintaining 'public' facilities such as irrigation. The amount of irrigated land actually declined slightly from 1979 to 1988. And much grain still had to be delivered to the state. The government held these prices relatively low, for to raise them would not only have increased the already high rate of inflation in the cities, but would also have worsened the budget deficit. In fact, the government's budget crisis left procurement departments short of money, and farmers often had to accept 'white slips' promising them payment at some future date (White, 1993, ch. 3).

The government also faced a foreign exchange crisis in the mid–1980s. As the number of authorized trading enterprises increased, the government loosened controls over foreign exchange. However, the budgets of these enterprises were not controlled. Aiming to maximize their foreign exchange earnings, enterprises bid up the prices they paid for imported materials on the domestic market, but then attempted to undercut other enterprises when offering their goods for sale to foreign buyers. Exports rose, but the domestic currency costs of imports soared. In some cases export incentives, combined with low domestic prices set by state agencies, stimulated exports of some products even when they were in short supply, and Chinese factories were forced to re-import at higher prices the very goods which Chinese exporters had just sold abroad (Lardy, 1992, p. 113). In addition, trade liberalization led not only to imports of machinery and raw materials, but also to imports of consumer durables – automobiles, motor cycles, colour televisions, refrigerators, and washing machines.

The government attempted to regain control over foreign exchange. In 1985 foreign exchange earnings of public enterprises were first frozen and then 'borrowed' by the central government to finance its own imports. Nevertheless, the controls began to erode almost immediately. In 1986 many of the previous restrictions on foreign direct investment were removed, and the number of 'open' areas where such ventures enjoyed autonomy and preferential treatment was increased. In the south especially, local governments without special economic zones had been clamouring for permission to establish them in order to compete for foreign investment. Among the key benefits enjoyed by 'foreign invested firms' in the zones were the right to import machinery and materials, and the right to repatriate their profits. In 1987 individual overseas Chinese gained access to foreign exchange centres, a measure intended to encourage remittances to relatives living in China, but one which could be used by businesses to finance their imports as well. And in 1988 the central government abolished the controls imposed on public enterprises in 1985. The net result was negative. Although exports increased, imports rose again as well (Lardy 1992, pp. 58–61; Chai and Sun, 1993).

The government also attempted to master its fiscal problems. Budgets at all levels were cut repeatedly through the early 1990s, and as noted in Chapter 10 'reform' in the state enterprise sector meant loss of jobs. However, this led lower-level officials to sponsor their own 'development' programmes. At the local and regional levels government agencies sought foreign partners for investment, and the proliferation of such joint venture enterprises both blurred the distinction between public and private enterprise and created a very large sector over which the central government had little if any control. Some 400 special economic zones had been approved by local government authorities by the mid-1990s. The share of the central government in total tax revenues reportedly declined from 57 per cent in 1981 to 31 per cent in 1993.

The flood of foreign investment – a ten-fold increase from 1985 to 1993 – softened the impact of the government's financial difficulties by creating jobs and stimulating growth. By the end of 1994 over 220 000 'foreign invested enterprises' had been approved, total realized foreign investment amounted to US$ 95.5 billion, and foreign invested enterprises employed 3.2 million people nearly 4 per cent of the entire labour force (Sun, 1996). However, the pattern of investment also exacerbated the existing inequality between urban and rural districts and reinforced the concentration of growth in the cities and in the south. This was a long-standing problem. Despite the decline in urban population engineered by the government from 1960 to 1976 to reduce the demand for 'unproductive' urban expenditures, the gap between city and country had been 'aggravated, ossified even, by the wage and welfare standards which the regime early on bestowed on the urban-industrial sector' (Kirkby, 1985, p. 22). Now, foreign investment concentrated in urban areas in the south. Half of all employees in foreign invested enterprises were in Guangdong and Fujian alone, and nearly 10 per cent in Shanghai. From 1978 to 1991 the average ratio of urban to rural incomes rose slightly to about three to one, but the *absolute* gap doubled, and as rural incomes stagnated the gap widened in the following years. The favouritism shown the special economic zones reinforced the trend. The ratio of incomes in Shanghai to those in the poor province of Guizhou increased to over nine to one, and in Guangdong the wealthiest district had an average income 34 times greater than the poorest.

Income inequality increased not only among regions but also within both the agricultural and the industrial sectors. The government had accepted the growth of inequality and stratification as an unavoidable side effect of economic growth (Myrdal, 1984). The impact of the reforms was partly to blame. In rural districts, the 'implicit rent' of more productive land, which the government had previously siphoned off through the communes, was now retained by families under the 'household responsibility system'. In urban areas both 'incentive' pay and property income increased dramatically after 1985 (Chai and Chai, 1994). The remaining inconsistencies of specific government policies also had an impact. Until the mid-1990s, officially registered urban residents still had privileged access to rationed food at subsidized prices, for instance, and they often sold their ration coupons to illegal migrants from the countryside (Aubert, 1993). In the countryside a disproportionate number of the newly rich were former cadres and party members who allocated the best resources on contract to their own households and collateral relatives (Myrdal, 1984). The outright appropriation of public and communal assets by cadres led to the emergence of an entrenched 'property owning' class who could use government powers in their own interests – 'a million millionaires . . . with close links to the old bureaucracy' (Wright, 1994). This could take the form, for instance, of levying unauthorized taxes, whether to support local 'development' projects or simply to benefit themselves directly.

Rapid growth brought rising prices. The government announced an austerity programme in 1993, including further budget cuts, compulsory bond purchases, increased interest rates, and cancelled loans for 'speculative' projects, but prices continued to spiral upward, 22 per cent in 1994 and 15 per cent in 1995. The 1996–2000 Five-Year Plan called for slower growth and optimistically projected annual inflation limited to 10 per cent. In industry, population growth and 'restructuring' in the state sector meant that an estimated 19 million new jobs would be needed every year through the year 2010. To achieve this China needs technological innovation, but organizational fragmentation limits cooperation between research and production units. Despite the reforms, tension remains between the need to import the latest foreign technologies and the desire to protect existing domestic enterprises, and there is an additional tension between state enterprises and expanding non-state enterprises (Simon and Rehn, 1988).

Resource and energy constraints may hamper growth. China's goal is to quadruple 1980 energy output by the year 2000, a very difficult task in view of the poor product quality, high consumption of raw materials, outdated technology, and poor management in the sector (Smil, 1988). Key government figures remain committed to massive and possibly wasteful and environmentally damaging projects such as the Three Gorges Dam on the Yangzi (see Barber and Ryder, 1993). Air and water pollution are serious and worsening in the expanding industrial centres. In agriculture, although grain output covered demand in the mid-1990s, projections indicated a chronic deficit would open by the year 2000 and worsen thereafter. Affluent consumers were eating increasing amounts of meat (per capita pork consumption more than doubled between 1978 and 1991), and rising meat production required more than proportional inputs of grain. Only substantial price rises seemed likely to bring forth significant increases in domestic grain output; although tariffs could achieve this, they would do so only 'at large sacrifice of economic welfare' (Garnaut and Ma, 1992, p. 111). The more 'rational' solution, to import from low-cost regions, implied competition for Chinese farmers and loss of self-sufficiency. Further, the continued need for investment capital combined with the need to pay for imported grain required further increases in exports, but consumer spending and the pattern of foreign investment in the special economic zones had led instead to rising imports.

Nationalism and the failure of political reform

We must strictly ban the cultural trash poisoning the people and social atmosphere ... We cannot sacrifice culture and ideology merely for a short period of economic development.

Jiang Zemin, January 1996

Many observers, both in the West and in Asia, argue that the growth of market economies will lead to the emergence of an autonomous 'civil society' and eventually to demands for democratization of political life. Others insist that 'Asian values' do not lead either to a Western-style civil society or to Western-style democracy (see White, 1993, chs. 7–8). As seen in previous chapters, Asian economies have been market economies for a long time, and local communities have often been relatively egalitarian, but Asian central governments have not usually been democratic. More recently, as seen above in the cases of Japan and the four tigers, the record is mixed; though democracy does not seem inevitable in Asia, neither does it appear impossible. The outcome depends on the willingness of the elite to share power. Economic growth by itself does not force changes in the political system. In China, by the late 1990s, economic reform had not led to political reform. The ruling elite resisted any lessening of their control over political life, and indeed revealed an almost hysterical need to crush any hint of opposition. As seen in the quotation above, president Jiang Zemin seemed quite willing to sacrifice economic growth if it posed a threat to 'culture and ideology'.

Debate has continued among China's leaders over the continuation and form of economic reform. 'Hardliners', usually identified as elderly veterans of the Long March, have resisted the extension of market relationships and argued for reimposition of central control. Their opponents, typically younger, have insisted that economic reform must continue, and as long as Deng lived they had the support of the 'paramount leader'. Anyone advocating political reforms, however, found Deng implacably opposed. Deng himself argued in 1985 that 'building socialism with Chinese characteristics' required both the extension of market relationships and an 'open door' to foreign capital, technology and managerial expertise. Development would mean that some regions and some people would become rich before others. However, Deng emphatically denied that economic development would lead to the growth of a new capitalist class. He insisted that socialist principles of distribution would continue to be followed, and that the state would still control basic economic structures. Nor would foreigners dominate, for even joint ventures would be at least 50 per cent Chinese (Deng, 1985).

Deng supported hardliners in their attack on 'bourgeois liberalism' in 1986, which effectively quashed discussion of possible political reforms within the Party, but then in 1987 he denounced 'leftism' and forced the retirement of a number of old hardliners. He gradually extended the principle of limited tenure in senior offices. These moves could be seen as his consistent advocacy of reform limited to the economic sphere, but they could also be interpreted more cynically as manoeuvres intended to maintain his own position. As senior figures fought for power, cadres at lower levels of the party hierarchy exploited the reforms to enrich themselves. Groups of intellectuals and students protested against the spreading corruption and in favour of a more open political system. Demonstrations in December 1986 against the 'anti-bourgeois liberalism' campaign led to the fall of Hu Yaobang, general secretary of the party and a possible successor to Deng, on the grounds that he had been too lenient. In May 1989 students demanding political reform and action against official corruption occupied Tiananmen Square in Beijing. The number of demonstrators swelled towards a million, and demonstrations broke out in over 20 other cities as well. Zhao Ziyang, Hu's successor and like him a possible successor to Deng, temporized and was attacked by hardliners aiming to oust him, to repress political dissent, and possibly to derail economic reform as well. Deng withdrew his support from Zhao, and he was replaced by Jiang Zemin. Following consultations between Deng and military leaders, the government mobilized large numbers of troops across the country, and on 4 June army units attacked the unarmed demonstrators. Foreign estimates of the number of deaths ranged from hundreds to thousands. A wave of arrests followed.

In resisting calls for political change, China's elite found it difficult to call on 'national' tradition. Although Confucian family values could be deployed against women, the leadership still remained in theory committed to socialism and therefore to equality. Party leaders could not be virtuous Confucian rulers, because Confucius himself had been denounced in one of the larger Maoist campaigns, and because 'Neo-Confucianism' was clearly the product of Taiwanese intellectuals and Western Confucian scholars. Nevertheless China enjoyed substantial advantages over other authoritarian regimes. In contrast to the Soviet Union, no national groups were prepared to break away. Some Western political scientists speculated that the central government might lose control over emerging 'natural economic territories' in Liaoning–South Korea, Fujian–Taiwan, or Guangdong–Hong Kong–Taiwan (Scalapino, 1993, p. 234). Many in the south viewed the northern identity fostered by Mao and his successors as alien (Friedman, 1994). Many members of the minority nationalities resisted the official equation of 'China' with the Han majority (Gladney, 1994). None of these developments had coalesced into a separatist movement, however. Even in Tibet, though there was opposition to Chinese rule, there was no insurgency.

Compared to Eastern European socialist states and to the four tigers, there had been only minimal exposure to Western models. The demonstrations of 1986 and 1989 were led by students and aimed at the West. Across the country, however, levels of education remained low, and the government monopolized control over information. Further, no alliance of students with workers emerged, as happened in Korea. Deng's commitment to the 'open door' and to economic development remained. The inflow of foreign capital generated sufficient new jobs to absorb the decline in the workforce of state enterprises. Foreign invested firms often paid higher salaries than state enterprises, and as long as the boom lasted, the absence of the safety net of social services previously enjoyed by state employees was not missed.

How does the elite see China's role in the world? In 1979 China launched an invasion of Vietnam, to 'teach the Vietnamese some necessary lessons', according to Deng. The campaign failed to save the Pol Pot regime in Cambodia. In seventeen days China suffered 46 000 casualties, and the monetary cost severely damaged the ten-year plan. In the 1990s China called stridently for 'reunification' not only with Hong Kong and Macau, but also with Taiwan. The Taiwanese presidential election of 1995 was conducted in the shadow of massive army manoeuvres and 'tests' of ballistic missiles which made it plain that China could deliver nuclear warheads anywhere on Taiwan if it chose. China has also announced claims for sovereignty over the South China Sea. The resulting disputes with Taiwan, the Philippines, Malaysia, Brunei, Indonesia and Vietnam have ebbed and flowed, but they have been pressed by the Chinese government with strident (and manifestly false) assertions that the entire area has been inhabited by Chinese since 'time immemorial'.

There is a racist thread in Chinese nationalism as well. A tradition in China has regarded foreign 'barbarians' as racially different from Chinese 'humans', as well as culturally inferior, and historically this mode has become more common when China has been threatened by external forces, whether nomads, Buddhists, Manchus, or Westerners. In the eyes of nineteenth-century Chinese, Europeans were racially as well as culturally defective – their 'ash white' skin signified their 'demonic' spirit. Chinese racial theorists of the 1890s thought in terms of a supranational pan-Asian identity, but they became recognizably nationalist in the 1900s, and there is much evidence of racist thinking in the popular literature of the Republican period (Dikötter, 1992). Today discussions of Chinese culture can easily take a racial turn.

In addition, the deep divisions within China – country opposed to city, province opposed to province, north opposed to south – are often defined in 'racial' terms. In Shanghai the 'Subei' descend from nineteenth-century migrants from northern Jiangsu. Confined to expanding slum areas and low status employment, they were victimized during the Nationalist period, and they continue to suffer discrimination and inequality today, despite the rise of individual Subei within the local and national Communist Party, notably Zhou Enlai and Jiang Zemin, a former mayor of Shanghai. Many Shanghainese hide their Subei identity if they can. The Subei function as a negative 'other', perceived in ethnic terms. The Shanghai elite has consistently represented them as a collective, undesirable ethnic underclass – vagabonds, refugees, squatters, rickshaw drivers, night soil collectors. They are therefore different from the positively-valued Shanghai 'natives', who are portrayed as culturally refined, modern, and Western. But in fact this elite are themselves migrants, from south of the Yangzi river. That is, an ethnic identity has been created and imposed on one group of Han Chinese by another:

> In Shanghai, native place identity assumed ethnic meanings ... Only by understanding Subei natives as constituting an ethnic group, analogous to African-Americans or Chicanos in the United States, do the structures of inequality and processes of social construction bound to native place emerge. (Honig, 1992, p. 129)

One of the classic tactics of a leadership losing control over a divided society is to blame 'outsiders' for fomenting discontent. It seems to suit the ruling elite to portray China as under threat, both from within and from without. The Great Wall has become an icon, symbol of external defence and internal unity (Waldron, 1990). China nurses the humiliations of the imperialist age; a major historical work devoted to the oppression of China by foreigners was announced to coincide with the reclaiming of Hong Kong in 1997. In the present, China is in fact surrounded by heavily armed states, several of which dispute territory claimed or occupied by China. China may desire peace and stability, but Chinese observers view the international situation as fluid, inconsistent and uncertain (EEAU, 1996, p. 87).

Even more worrying for the elite, perhaps, is the insidious 'poisoning' of the 'cultural trash' imported from the West – the same 'wholesale Westernization' which the gang of four had warned against. Combating Western culture is not easy. Neo-Confucianism has been pre-empted by Taiwanese intellectuals, and to return to a genuinely socialist ideology would conflict with the interests of the new class of wealthy officials and would also frighten foreign investors. Instead, the formula 'stability and unity' has been deployed to discredit the defeated protesters of Tiananmen Square, and by implication the excessive openness and permissiveness of Western culture. In a speech to party propaganda officials in January 1996, Jiang Zemin warned of the dangers of moral and ideological laxity. He called on Chinese journalists to be 'engineers of the mind' and to 'safeguard the image of socialist China and create a favourable international environment for its reforms and opening up'. More concretely, all foreign economic news was to pass through the state-run Xinhua news agency, and access to the Internet was to be severely limited.

The treatment of Hong Kong is widely regarded as a test both of China's relations with the outside world and of the leadership's ability to cope with the consequences of reform and economic growth. In negotiations with the British, the Chinese government promised 'one country, two systems', and that Hong Kong's assimilation into China would extend over decades. The British in turn introduced a belated series of reforms giving a greater role to elected representatives on the Legislative Council, and members of the 'pro-democracy' movement were overwhelmingly elected. The Chinese authorities excluded pro-democracy advocates from the Preparatory Committee which organized the transition, replaced the Legislative Council with a 'provisional legislature' with appointed members and removed supporters of the pro-democracy movement following the handover. Chinese officials had already begun to take over sectors of the economy before the handover, and a series of 'shotgun marriages' forced Chinese partners on more or less unwilling Hong Kong firms.

Most of the 'foreign' investment in Guangdong is from Hong Kong, and Hong Kong's financial markets provide access to international financing for infrastructure projects. Therefore to a substantial degree China's economic development depends on Hong Kong. If China retains Hong Kong's legal system and allows individuals the same rights they enjoyed under colonial rule, then presumably the economy will continue its rapid development. Because Hong Kong is crowded and expensive, this would see a continued extension of Hong Kong capital into southern China. Most observers believe a leadership struggle lies ahead following the death of Deng, and aspiring leaders may be tempted to adopt a hard line on Hong Kong. The central government has wide latitude for interference in Hong Kong's internal affairs. China's leaders have made Hong Kong the pre-eminent symbol of China's humiliation by the imperialist powers in the nineteenth century, and they may therefore be tempted to force Hong Kong to conform to the same standards as the rest of China, or even to use Hong Kong as a demonstration of the central government's power. There seems a genuine fear of Hong Kong as a source of instability. One official was quoted as saying that 'one country, two systems' will apply to Hong Kong only, whereas 'Shanghai will always be a socialist city'. Although they might not appear in the form of a 'crisis', the consequences of Chinese mistakes in Hong Kong could be severe. A crackdown on political dissidents, excessively rapacious demands by corrupt officials, or failure to allow the legal system to operate (to enforce contracts for instance) could trigger a large migration and flight of capital. An estimated 1.1 million Hong Kong residents have at least one family member with a foreign passport, and another 3 million have relatives abroad who could sponsor their emigration if they felt their interests threatened. More than half of the companies listed on the Hong Kong Stock Exchange are legally domiciled outside of Hong Kong, and there are repeated reports of capital being shifted to safe havens around the world. A serious threat to these economic interests would choke off the flow of capital from Hong Kong into southern China. It could also choke off the flow from Taiwan, the most important source of capital in Fujian, and it would certainly make current and potential investors from Korea, Japan, Europe, and the United States nervous as well. As seen above, China depends on foreign capital not only for continued growth but equally importantly to cushion the negative consequences of growth.

Domestic opinion is also important, because the government has to reassure the Chinese people, and especially the newly wealthy cadres, that it can continue to deliver economic development. This requires maintaining and extending the openness of the country – in short, a commitment to further 'reform'. Nevertheless, leaders such as Jiang may not care about economic growth if it threatens their power. A fear of a collapse similar to the Soviet Union has led to an emphasis on sovereignty and national unification which overrides economic arguments. Therefore business interests hopeful that Beijing will simply allow Hong Kong to continue as it has may be disappointed. In response to the argument that crushing Hong Kong could be killing the goose which lays the golden egg, Chinese point out that 'our history is littered with dead geese'. (See Yahuda, 1996; Skidmore, 1996).

Southeast Asia: New Tigers, New Giants, New Dragons?

Of course you have to pay bribes in Thailand, even to traffic cops for instance. But at least there you know Thais will deliver. In Indonesia you have competing people you have to pay, and you don't always know where you stand. And the Philippines – even after you pay, you don't get results.

Australian businessman, 1995

Corruption in our country is not the result of corrupt minds but of economic pressures. Eventually, when economic development has gone so far as to produce a good overall standard of living, government employees will receive adequate salaries and have no reason to practice corruption.

Soeharto, 1991

There are several more would-be 'tigers' in Southeast Asia, notably Malaysia and Vietnam, Thailand has been labelled Asia's 'new dragon' (Kulick and Wilson, 1992), and Indonesia has been seen as 'Southeast Asia's emerging giant' (Hill, 1996). Here, however, rather than lessons, observers are especially keen to discover and popularize the next emerging economies. There are some patterns common to most Southeast Asian states. First is the continuing heritage of authoritarian rule by narrow elites, and the recurrent fact that particular groups contending for power advocate policies which support their position, whether these tend in the direction of 'reform' and 'market relations', or 'state autonomy' and 'guidance'. Further, Southeast Asian states have shared a tendency for the government sector, and the numbers of government officials, to grow. A 'runaway bureaucratization' occurred during the 1970s and 1980s in Indonesia and Malaysia, for instance. Spurts of bureaucratization have tended to follow political unrest or revolution. Bureaucratic control over the economy and the direct involvement of civil servants in business together have caused a blurring of the boundaries between state, economy, and society, a 'bureaucratic capitalism' (Evers, 1987). In addition, most Southeast Asian states possess relatively large armed forces, and the military has often played an important role, not only in politics but in the economy as well.

Outside of Singapore, governments are inefficient and corrupt. Bribery is common, from the petty level of avoiding an arbitrary traffic fine to substantial payments for government favours. Evidence for bribery is typically anecdotal, as with the experiences of the Australian businessman quoted above. However, the fact that choice government contracts, mining concessions, or logging rights go to domestic and foreign firms with the best connections is a matter of public record. Legal systems are often opaque and courts overburdened. Most governments have attempted to broaden their tax base, adding indirect, value-added, and capital gains taxes in addition to the traditional levies on commodities and international trade. However, again with the exception of Singapore, the complexity of the taxation systems has run ahead of the capacities of government officials, and 'tax evasion remains rife' (Hill, 1994, p. 845). Diane Wolf found that exploitation of young female workers and official corruption intersect when government inspectors allow firms to report higher wages than they in fact pay, raising their reported costs and reducing their taxable incomes (Wolf, 1996).

It has been argued that domestic firms in Southeast Asia find it difficult to innovate or introduce advanced technologies, not because of the external constraints imposed by the region's dependent position in the world economy, but because they are unwilling to do so. In this view the most successful domestic firms are in fact rent-seeking groups, whose success depends not on their economic efficiency, but on their contacts with government. This 'ersatz capitalism' has not created an independent technological capability, the ability either to transfer foreign methods or to develop new techniques. In the absence of technologically effective domestic firms, foreign firms provide the major technological thrust for growth. Rather than laying the basis for long-term industrial development, domestic firms have been content to exploit short-term advantage. Rather than seeking excellence, ersatz capitalists have been content to exploit their political connections to enrich themselves and their families. Their profits go to spending on consumption, and when they do invest, their money goes overseas or into urban real estate. In effect they have remained compradors of foreign firms (Yoshihara, 1988; see Doner, 1991).

On the other hand, in the decade since the theses of 'bureaucratic capitalism' and 'ersatz capitalism' were propounded, several of the Southeast Asian economies have continued to grow rapidly. The size of the government sectors has not impeded growth; on the contrary there is a positive correlation between size of government and economic performance. And, though the evidence is disputed and often turns on the technical details of particular industries, domestic firms have introduced new technologies. In response to external shocks, both government and private firms have proved responsive and flexible. Governments have cut expenditure or reoriented policy, as in Indonesia and Malaysia in the mid-1980s, and have proven sufficiently 'insulated' to continue these politically unpopular policies until fiscal and external balance had been restored.

Private firms have been equally responsive. The record of success suggests that either these firms are not merely rent-seeking, or that they are in fact increasingly efficient. Even the Philippines, typically the laggard, has grown substantially under the Ramos government, and even over the longer run has managed a fiscal policy 'tighter than many other developing countries' (Hill, 1994, p. 845).

However, there is one area where corruption, rent-seeking, and future growth intersect, and that is in the management of natural resources. The granting of mining and petroleum concessions is highly politicized, but often without sufficient checks to protect against environmental degradation or to maximize revenues. Forest resources are 'underpriced' in most countries, and the granting of logging licences is frequently simply corrupt (Hill, 1994). This is particularly tragic, because properly managed forests are renewable, but the clearfelling which is often practised leaves the hillsides bare and leads to erosion which can make regrowth impossible. Often high-quality timber is wastefully used because of the low prices which have been paid for logging rights. In Sarawak, connections among local politicians, Malaysian central government officials, and foreign companies, mainly Japanese, have led to the felling of rainforests and the use of the timber in Japan for cheap composition board (Colchester, 1995; Aiken and Leigh, 1992). The exploitation of timber and other resources in Mindanao and elsewhere in the Philippines has been widely reported (Turner et al., 1992; Broad and Cavanagh, 1993). In Indonesia a mix of corruption and poor policies has 'created a sector which has become totally dependent on highly subsidized log prices'. Prohibitive taxes on exports and arbitrary administered prices result in prices as much as 75 per cent below international levels. The resulting rate of felling is unsustainable: 'By any criteria, a crisis exists in Indonesia' (Thompson, 1996; Peluso, 1992; see Hill, 1996, pp. 144–6).

The socialist governments of Southeast Asia have performed rather indifferently in the economic sphere, but of course they have had to contend with war and its after-effects, and with the hostility of the United States and the hesitancy of foreign investors. Both Laos and Cambodia opened their economies to foreign investment in the 1990s. Laos remained something of an exotic mystery, even for international advisers. In Cambodia politics revolved around the machinations of factions in the extended royal family of the king Norodom Sihanouk. The Khmer Rouge, though apparently in decline, continued to control some border areas, and their presence prevented systematic development of natural resources or tourism. It was asserted by Global Witness, a British environmental group, that a properly managed forest industry could net the government over $US 100 million annually, for instance, but a series of corrupt deals among Cambodian, Thai, and Khmer Rouge officials in effect opened virtually all of the forests to exploitative stripping without replacement, leading to erosion. In the meantime much of Cambodia's farmland remained unusable because of anti-personnel mines.

Myanmar under Ne Win continued in isolation until the 1980s, and internal dissent was repressed. However, the government's attempts to control the economy largely failed, and a 'parallel economy' based on smuggling across the Indian and Thai borders expanded to control possibly half of all transactions. In 1988 the government cancelled large numbers of banknotes, hoping to stamp out smuggling and reduce inflation, and large public protests resulted. The police opened fire, killing some 300, and then raped and tortured arrested demonstrators. Continued protests led Ne Win first to call an early party congress and then to resign. His successor proved unacceptable, protests continued, and the army intervened, seizing power and establishing the State Law and Order Restoration Council (SLORC), chaired by army leader Saw Maung. Elections in 1990 resulted in an overwhelming victory (392 of 485 seats) for the opposition National League for Democracy (NLD). The SLORC rejected the result, arrested NLD leaders, and suppressed continued dissent. Thousands have disappeared into prisons and labour camps. However, international attention has limited the extent of repression, and the SLORC also has been embarrassed that one of the leaders of the opposition, Aung San Suu Kyi, is the daughter of national hero Aung San. In 1991 she was awarded the Nobel Peace Prize while under house arrest for her non-violent opposition to the regime. In 1995 and 1996 the SLORC and NLD were locked in a struggle over a proposed constitutional convention which the army leaders hoped would preserve their hold on power while diffusing discontent sufficiently to reassure potential foreign investors.

The United Nations has provided a forum for the NLD. The United States has pressed for a tougher stance against the military government because of its human rights violations. However, the SLORC has the support of some foreign economic interests. Japan has a plan to write off Myanmar's entire debt to Japan, and France's Total oil company is building a pipeline from southern Myanmar into Thailand. Thailand supports the military, and made only formal protests when Myanmar army units attacked Karen refugee camps in Thailand in late 1996 and early 1997. As some Western firms pulled out, companies controlled by Indonesian president

Soeharto's children moved into the communications, construction, pretro-chemical, logging, and animal food industries, often in partnership with firms controlled by the government. The Association of South East Asian Nations was reported to be planning to admit Myanmar to full membership, and in early 1997 Indonesia's foreign minister said ASEAN 'have never and will not make as a precondition or a criterion for membership the internal situation of a country'. The SLORC was also negotiating with the International Monetary Fund for new loans to rebuild the capital district's decaying infrastructure. Positive signs can be seen in the building boom in Rangoon and reported increases in small-scale commerce. However, army leaders have ignored the problems of forced labor, widespread poverty, and very low health standards (see Maung, 1991, 1992). The price of rice rose tenfold between 1988 and 1995, well above increases in average earnings.

The SLORC regime is also implicated in the drug trade. Following the outlawing of opium growing and processing in Thailand, the centre of production moved to northern Myanmar, in the Shan district. Khun Sa, the leading heroin dealer, also became the leader of a 20 000-strong Shan militia, one of the many insurgent groups confronting the government. The government gradually reached agreements with the other insurgents and launched a major offensive against the Shan separatists in 1995. In 1996 Khun Sa 'surrendered' and ended the insurgency, but he openly admitted to reporters that he would continue to grow and process opium. The government officially condemns the drug trade, but the amnesty granted Khun Sa is only one among many, and nothing has been done either to prevent the export of heroin or to reduce the domestic drug trade. The boom in construction is reportedly often financed by profits from the drug trade. Heroin addiction is widespread, and critics have accused the government of tacitly encouraging drug use to pacify young people who might otherwise support the NLD.

Vietnam's Second Five-Year Plan of 1976–80 failed because of a dogmatic attempt to force the capitalist south into conformity with the socialist north. Party leaders through the 1980s remained unwilling to modify their approach to the economy (Vo, 1990; Tri and Booth, 1992). Continued emphasis on the creation of a heavy industrial sector resulted in under-investment in agriculture and slow growth of food supplies. Clearly, however, the slowness of development partly reflected Vietnam's increasing international isolation. A generation gap similar to that in the Chinese Communist Party led to a split between the ageing generation who led the struggle against the French and Americans, and a younger more 'technocratic' group committed to more or less radical 'market reform', and the struggle between these groups has continued. Both groups have immediate roots in the prewar elite landowning class of Confucian scholars, and although both sides employ Marxist terminology, the debate is conducted in moralizing terms, for instance in the notion that monopolies are corrupt and that free competition leads to 'distribution according to work' (Elliott, 1993).

Better results were achieved during the Third Five-Year Plan of 1981–4, in part because of the pragmatic introduction of incentives to reward performance. Conservatives regained the upper hand in the mid-1980s, but the economy slowed and unemployment rose. The reform group regained their momentum at the Sixth Party Congress in 1986, with promises of new policies for agriculture, decentralization of planning, more emphasis on light industry, and exports based on private initiative and free markets (Kimura, 1989). The north typically was regarded as 'socialist' and the south 'capitalist', but there remained widespread variations in agricultural organization even in the north. In the south in the mid-1980s, although officially collectivization had reached its peak of success, in fact farmers had refused to form functioning cooperatives, and informants reported there was no real difference between private and collective property. In addition, shortages and the growth of 'parallel markets' created strong incentives for those who could to use state resources for their own and their families' benefit, effectively privatizing them (Beresford, 1989).

The collapse of the Soviet Union cut off aid and trade. Reformers insisted on the need to open the economy further and pressed through a devaluation of the currency, which reduced the role of the black market and cut the rate of inflation (see Ronnas and Sjöberg, 1990). Debate at the Seventh Party Congress in 1991 led to privatization of a limited number of state enterprises and an end to subsidies for the rest. Singapore replaced the Soviet Union as Vietnam's most important trading partner, and foreign investment began to flow in. The economy appeared to take off, growing at over 8 per cent annually for four years. However, growth brought inflation and worsened the gap between urban and rural incomes, and a growing trade deficit quickly led to an external debt equal to more than half of total national product. The debate over 'corruption' continued – not only the continued appropriation of state property, but also 'social evils' connected with Westernization. The army worried about the United States using the opening of the economy to 'bring Vietnam to its knees', and the government banned foreign language signs and billboards. The confusion reportedly led to a sharp drop in foreign investment in 1996, which if continued would place both infrastructure and industrialization projects at risk.

Of the non-socialist regimes in Southeast Asia, the Philippines has disappointed observers the most deeply. As seen in Chapter 9, the hopeful beginning of the Magsaysay government gave way to the corruption of Marcos, and in turn to a new hopeful beginning under Aquino. Aquino, however, inherited not only massive public debt, decrepit infrastructure, stagnant exports and urban unemployment, but also the existing power structure. Marcos himself had identified the 'politics of dependence' as the Philippines' most intractable problem. The poor masses, he said, had come to depend on 'the benefits − jobs, handouts, help in dealing with an often lazy and corrupt bureaucracy − that they could get from the rich and the powerful in exchange for their loyalty and courteous respect' (Marcos, 1978, pp. 19–20). Marcos argued that only martial law could combat these entrenched relationships, but martial law in fact merely provided the cover for the depredations of Marcos and his 'cronies' among the elite. Aquino relied on 'people power', and on the support of the Catholic Church hierarchy and military leaders such as Fidel Ramos. However, she also represented a faction within the elite, and she proved unable to create a genuinely new power base. In particular, land reform proved too difficult (Riedinger, 1995). Government contracts continued to be awarded on the basis of political connections. There was no attempt to reform the state sector. To please the Church the government abandoned any attempt at birth control. The military proved unreliable, and there were several attempted coups. In elections the old pattern of vote-buying and influence-peddling returned. Aquino initially offered amnesty to Communist and Muslim insurgents, but then adopted Ramos' uncompromising attitude and his support of right-wing vigilante groups. The economy continued to drift, and there was no growth at all in 1990 and 1991.

In 1992 Aquino's former supporter Ramos became president, but with less than a quarter of the votes cast. He established his authority over the army, and he benefited from splits in the Communist movement which had opened following the collapse of the Soviet Union. A campaign against corruption in the police and judiciary linked with a parallel campaign to end government monopolies; a supreme court judge who wanted to maintain the monopoly in long-distance communications was forced into retirement, for instance. The national power company was to be reorganized, and the previously subsidized power rates increased. Foreign debt at least did not increase further. Growth was slow in 1992 and 1993, but then increased with an inflow of foreign capital. However, some of the recorded increase may also have resulted from better reporting of the large 'underground' economy. There was still no land reform, and some observers have dismissed the anti-corruption and privatization campaigns as superficial attempts to placate the international agencies who hold the Philippines' debt.

The successful Asian economies have very high levels of savings and investment, and fiscal policies which ensure that these are channelled into productive investment. Compared to other Asian countries, the Philippines has a very low ratio of investment compared to total product, and there is no evidence of a spurt in investment (Table 10.9). The Philippines also has a very poor record of improving productivity (World Bank, 1993). The government has not gained control over sources and flows of capital. Tax evasion is reportedly high, particularly of course in the 'underground' economy, which some believe includes half of all economic activity. Growth has tended to result in consumer booms, with money spent on imported foreign products – designer clothes, Italian furniture, American household appliances. Investment not only remains low, but also goes into unproductive areas, for instance the new hotels along Ayala Avenue in Manila.

In Thailand the government survived the insurgency of the 1970s and rode a conservative wave to power. From 1976 to 1991 periodic elections failed to produce a majority, but all prime ministers were in fact army generals, notably Prem Tinsulanond, the most successful of the 'counter insurgency' generals and the longest-serving prime minister during the 1970s and 1980s. Agreement with China on citizenship for Chinese in Thailand made possible a more complete assimilation of several million Chinese immigrants, a development often cited as an important background factor in Thai economic success. In the provinces a boom in cash crops led to alliances between local military commanders and notables. In part sponsored by the military, large numbers of successful provincial businessmen entered political life. This required money to buy votes and provide patronage for supporters. Rapid growth and a proliferation of infrastructure projects provided further opportunities. The increasingly open corruption, dissatisfaction among senior bureaucrats when the government first bypassed them and then removed a number of them from positions in state enterprises, and acrimonious disputes over proposed cuts in the army budget, led to another military coup in 1991.

The new government did not ban political parties, nevertheless. An appointed civilian government pursued policies favoured by the Bangkok business community such as tax reform, while the military administration at the same time attempted to reassert the army's control over Thai society. A new constitution maintained much of effective power in the

Senate, whose members were nominated by the government. Elections to the new House of Representatives in 1992 did not produce a majority, but the largest party was the vehicle of the military, who clearly intended to solidify their control. Demonstrations began in April and continued into May. The army moved to suppress them, and possibly several hundred people died. However, the king demanded a halt to the violence, and international reporting of the riots and repression damaged Thailand's credit rating and choked off tourism and the flow of foreign investment. The alliance between military and business broke. New elections in September 1992 gave the opposition party a narrow plurality, although the 'electoral arithmetic' meant that reformers and liberals centred in Bangkok could not hope to dominate, and in 1995 the more conservative provincial-based parties returned to power (Pasuk and Baker, 1995, ch. 10).

In the meantime, Thailand has enjoyed substantial economic success. Predictably, international agencies attribute growth to private enterprise and the opening of the economy to world markets (Richards, 1993). In addition credit often goes to 'far-sighted bureaucrats' who pursued fiscal and monetary restraint, controlled foreign borrowing, and devalued the currency despite opposition from vested interests (Kulick and Wilson, 1992). The boom of the late 1980s was led by foreign investment. Growth depended at first on commodity exports, and then on low-end technology manufacturing, which in turn depended on low wages. But other countries now compete with Thailand in export crops such as rice and offer lower wages. Thailand needs to move to higher value-added production, but to do this will require changes in institutions, and this will be difficult. Growth and wealth have concentrated in Bangkok. The provinces have been left far behind, and politicians need to provide for their clients in the rural areas. The need for this patronage – which is of course corrupt, but is nevertheless redistributional – means that elected governments often damage the interests of urban groups such as the business associations, and this is one of the sources of the political instability and fragility of elected governments.

Thailand's future success depends on the balance between the state and private capitalists. This balance is disputed, as indeed is the question of whether there is in fact a 'national' capitalist class at all, in view of the continued role of the military, the Chinese community, and foreign interests. The role of private capitalists tends to be obscured by the fact of military dominance of the government. It has been argued that the 'symbiotic' relationship between local capitalists and the state can be seen in the shift from direct state investment to an import substitution strategy emphasizing the private sector in the 1950s, and towards an export-oriented strategy in the early 1970s (Hewison, 1989). More positive analyses see Thai politics as a 'moving equilibrium' with several power centres balancing each other so none gains permanent supremacy – military, political parties, king as mediating force between them, and business as an 'increasingly important participant' (Kulick and Wilson, 1992, p. 3). Since the 1970s Thai business associations have grown to play a leading role in state–business relations. Associations have shaped state sectoral policies and even overall strategies, most importantly the shift to export-oriented industrialization in the 1980s. Some argue that Thai business can force its demands on the bureaucracy, in contrast to 'developmental states' such as Japan (Laothamatas, 1992). On the other hand, emerging groupings of interrelated family-controlled companies have often depended on foreign sources of funds, and foreign capital has dominated in a number of key areas, with the notable exception of financial conglomerates (Suehiro, 1989).

In his 'Vision 2020' Malaysian prime minister Mahathir Mohamed predicted that Malaysia would become a developed country early in the twenty-first century. There are similarities with other successful Asian economies, notably a high rate of growth, rising per capita income, and a rising share of manufacturing in output and exports (see Brookfield et al., 1994). Mahathir has modelled 'Malaysia Inc.' and 'Look East' policies on Japan and the four tigers, particularly in allowing state agencies to mix market and intervention to achieve export growth. The Malaysian Industrial Development Authority (MIDA) has the task of ensuring that investment doubles from 1991–5 levels in the 1996–2000 period, for instance. Through the 1980s insufficient jobs were being created to absorb the rapidly increasing Malay labour force (Faaland et al., 1991), but the relaxation of the requirements of the New Economic Policy led to a boom in foreign investment in the late 1980s (Bowie, 1991). Malaysia in the mid–1990s has a labour shortage, especially of skilled workers. Wages have risen, and the demand for workers has attracted 700 000 to 1 million illegal migrants from Indonesia, the Philippines and Thailand to work in the plantation sector, services, and also manufacturing.

Malaysian manufacturing output rose sixfold from 1965 to 1985, and productivity increased in agriculture, so that real gross national product rose 6.8 per cent per year from 1973 to 1985, raising per capita income to over US$ 2000 (McGee, 1986). Between 1970 and 1990, manufacturing value added rose 10.3 per cent per year and increased from 14 to 27 per cent of gross domestic product. Manufacturing employment rose from 243 000 (8.7 per cent total employment) to 1.1 million (19.5 per cent), and in 1990 Malaysia exported US$ 19.2 billion worth of manufactured goods (60.4 per cent of exports), and manufacturing replaced both traditional primary commodities and oil and gas as the country's chief earner of foreign exchange (Bowie, 1991).

However, although a number of state enterprises were privatized in the 1980s (Hill, 1994), Malaysia has a very large state sector which is not operated on 'market-like' principles. Although some protected infant industries have achieved significant increases in productivity with relatively low domestic resource costs (Alavi, 1996), in general the import substitution sector is not linked to the export-oriented sector (an attempt to export the Proton automobile to Australia failed in 1996). In the advanced sectors capital is foreign not indigenous (the Proton's technology is exclusively Japanese). Manufacturing development concentrates in enclaves. Malaysia's semiconductor industry, which produces a third of manufactured exports, is completely dominated by multinational firms located in the export-processing zones (McGee, 1986; Jomo, 1990). In addition to heavy industry and import substitution, money has been poured into development schemes, the investment trust agencies, and loans to Malay businessmen. The planners are not autonomous, and decisions reflect 'interethnic bargains' and money politics (Jesudason, 1989; Jomo, 1990).

The government's New Economic Policy, by discriminating against the Chinese minority, hampered the development of domestic entrepreneurship and distorted growth patterns in favour of foreign-controlled, low technology enclaves and unprofitable state corporations (Jesudason, 1989). And the policy failed:

> It is now clear that the key relationship between technocratic state elites and Malaysian industrialists is aborted by the separation of economic and political power: the Malays control the state apparatus and the Chinese still, even after 20 years of the NEP, dominate the domestic commercial and manufacturing sector. (Lubeck, 1992, p. 184).

Even authors favourable to the NEP note that the government abandoned its anti-poverty goals. Though there was some shifting of ownership to Malays (EAAU, 1995, pp. 53–6), the benefits went to the Malay elite, often bureaucrats and members of the old aristocracy – in Jomo's phrase, the 'administocracy' (Jomo, 1986). Further, 'rather than aligning with the domestic bourgeoisie, the Malay-dominated state elite have, until now, aligned themselves with foreign capital in exchange for directorships, joint ventures, and other passive, essentially rentier rewards' (Lubeck, 1992, p. 184; see Faaland et al., 1991). The NEP officially expired in 1991, to be replaced by a new National Development Policy. However, the discrimination in favour of Malays has remained, in admission and graduation from schools and university, in employment, and in access to government benefits. Some technocratically inclined officials in the government advocate policies which would foster growth without regard for ethnic factors, but the interests of the 'oppressed majority' of Malays and of the wealthy Malay political and administrative elite militate against any reduction in their privileges.

Indonesia has grown rapidly under Soeharto's New Order, despite what appeared to be missed opportunities in the 1970s and the crisis triggered by declining oil prices in the early 1980s. Growth has resulted not merely from the oil boom, but also from the expansion of the labour force, increasing educational levels, and rising investment (see Booth, ed., 1992). Indonesia has emerged as yet another successful Asian exporter of manufactured goods. The government's macroeconomic policies have been praised by market-oriented observers. The decision in the 1980s to cut investment and reduce the size of the government sector in response to the sudden drop in oil revenues, and the concomitant shift away from import substitution and towards export promotion, are seen as decisive policy initiatives which paved the way for growth over the subsequent decade (Woo et al., 1994; Hill, 1994; 1996, chs. 3–4). The close connection of the military with the government bureaucracy has been widely recognized, but can be seen as a kind of 'managed pluralism', a very narrow oligarchy which nevertheless is able to allow the representation of new interests on a pragmatic basis (Bresnan, 1993).

Others have accused the Indonesian state of acting as an ally of foreign capitalists. The Inco Mining Company's nickel mining project in South Sulawesi, with central government support and in apparent collusion with local government officials, appropriated the most productive farmland in the district for the new company townsite, in effect forcing the local population to depend on wage labour with the company (Robinson, 1986). The United States-owned Freeport gold and copper complex on Irian Jaya is one of world's largest and provides a very substantial share of Indonesia's total foreign exchange earnings. The firm employs its own armed forces to repress dissent and calls on the army as necessary. Not only is it a focus of separatist attacks; the provincial governor has complained bitterly that 'the people in the house called Irian Jaya feed those in other houses but are themselves starving' (Schwarz, 1994, p. 64). The connection between primary products and manufacturing has not been established. The state oil corporation, Pertamina, despite a high degree of formal control over foreign oil corporations, generally failed to develop the hoped-for backward and forward linkages with indigenous industry, due in part to the internal structure of the corporation and in part to the lack of skilled managerial and technical staff (Oon, 1986). Rather, manufacturing exports remain confined to low technology areas dependent on foreign capital and low wages. The capital is often Korean, and in turn the Korean firms are often subcontractors of Western companies; as seen in Chapter 11 the workers are usually young women who are denied the right to organize and often paid below even the legal minimum wages.

There has not been a consistent economic policy under Soeharto. For example, praise for macroeconomic policies has been tinged with regret that sectoral policies and public-sector project selection have often been 'less than optimal' (Woo et al., 1994). Through the Presidential Instruction (INPRES) programmes, large grants flowed to regional and local governments to finance roads, schools, and health clinics, but the central government refused to give up authority even to its own local agents, and the excessive centralization greatly reduced the programmes' effectiveness (MacAndrews, 1986). Despite privatizations, the state sector remains large, and a number of private firms enjoy government-enforced monopolies. Three groups have contended for influence over policy. A circle of American-trained economists, the 'Berkeley mafia' or 'technocrats', have pressed for market-oriented reforms. They usually receive credit for the success of macroeconomic policies, but except for control over the central bank their position has never been institutionalized, and after their triumphs of the late 1980s their influence appears to have declined. B. J. Habibie, state minister for research and technology, leads those who feel government enterprises can lead Indonesia past dependence on raw materials and low-end manufacturing towards a position as a technologically advanced nation. Rather than relying on 'comparative advantage', Indonesia should develop 'competitive advantage' by fostering high-technology sectors as rapidly as possible. The third group consists of Chinese businessmen close to Soeharto and members of Soeharto's family. Their influence has been rising, and their wealth increasing. Soeharto's second son Bambang Trihatmodjo went into business in 1982 at the age of 29 with funds provided by middleman arrangements with Pertamina, the government petrochemical monopoly. By 1994 his group included over 100 companies with assets of some US$ 1.4 billion. The group's greatest asset, however, 'is Bambang's ability to ride roughshod over the bureaucracy'. 'Collectively, the family forms by far the most powerful economic dynasty in the country' (Schwarz, 1994, pp. 141–2; see Hill, 1996, ch. 6; EEAU, 1995, pp. 39–45).

One consistent element in policy, however, has been the unwillingness to share power. Opposition has been brutally suppressed, most tragically in the repression of resistance to the invasion and annexation of East Timor in 1975. Of a pre-invasion population of 650 000, at least 100 000 and possibly over 200 000 have died at the hands of the army. Opposition has not disappeared. In 1991 demonstrators in Dili were shot, bayoneted, and beaten to death. Although the numbers of victims are smaller, separatist movements in Irian Jaya, Sulawesi and Aceh have also called forth the worst in the army.

The preference for centralization and the obsession with control extends directly to the top. Soeharto personally prefers to remain free of institutional constraints, and appears unable to treat opposition as anything but disloyalty. The People's Consultative Assembly (MPR), which meets every five years to select the president, has never held a vote. Rather, a single candidate who has been duly nominated by all of the parties is 'chosen' by consensus. The suggestion that the opposition Democratic Party (PDI) might nominate someone other than Soeharto caused a major crisis in 1993. In the aftermath Megawati Sukarnoputri, daughter of first president Sukarno, became the leader of the PDI despite an attempt by the government to block her. In 1995 the government sponsored a breakaway congress of PDI members which elected a 'leader' suggested by the government. In 1996 demonstrations by the PDI in Jakarta were suppressed by the army, hundreds were arrested, and Sukarnoputri was placed under virtual house arrest while the government investigated those 'responsible' for the demonstrations.

The harassment of the PDI clearly points to the government's concerns over the 1997 elections, but it appears a bit excessive when we consider that the party received only 15 per cent of the vote in 1992. Golkar, which considers itself not a political party but a 'development agency', has won all elections since 1970 by landslide margins. Its 68 per cent of the vote in the 1992 elections was down 5 per cent from 1987, but its advantages remain formidable. There are no political party organizations at the village level, except for a limited period at election time. Between elections, however, Golkar alone among the parties can rely on the support of the bureaucracy, 6 million government officials and their families. Civil servants are required to belong to Korpri (Korps Pegawai Republik

Indonesia, or Civil Servants Corps), an organization founded in 1971, and their wives are obliged to belong to Dharma Wanita (Women's Duty), a parallel organization in which the women occupy positions which correspond to their husband's civil service rank (Suryakusuma, 1996). In early 1997 a ruling by the Minister for Home Affairs confirmed that public servants were bound by Korpri rules, which say they must vote for Golkar, despite constitutional guarantees of freedom of political association. Because the bureaucracy is 'all Golkar' the party can reach down to the village level whereas the two opposition parties cannot. Golkar has virtually exclusive access to the electronic media. It receives full coverage of its activities by the state-owned television network (TVRI), and the four private television channels are required to relay all TVRI news broadcasts. And of course Golkar has the support of the military, which continues to regard itself as the embodiment of the nation. Army leader Feisal Tanjung disappointed hopes of military disengagement from politics in October 1995 when he stated that the army could never be politically neutral.

Although he surprised supporters when he decided to stand for re-election in 1993, the ageing (born in 1921) Soeharto appears certain to stand again in 1998. He and the government may face increasing pressure from a more assertive civil society (Schwarz, 1994, chs. 9–10). However, in the absence of legitimate channels for political grievance, civil protest has taken the form of riots directed against the Chinese community, seen by 'native' *pribumi* Indonesians as having benefited unfairly from government favours, and against Christian and Buddhist religious minorities. Politics, family connections, and economic policy overlap. Indonesia will certainly face the problem of high costs in the subsidized and government-owned sectors. Competitiveness must increase if the economy is to continue to grow and in particular if it is going to diversify, but the most sensitive areas are precisely the ones in which Soeharto's cronies and family members have concentrated themselves.

Energy poses particular problems. Oil still contributed one third of export income in the mid-1990s, but increasing demand and declining output mean that Indonesia will become a net oil importer by the year 2000. Forward projections show electricity demand will outstrip conventional generating capacity by 2005. Plans for a dozen nuclear power plants along the north coast of Java raise serious environmental issues and reportedly were opposed by a large majority, although the government was unlikely to consult its opponents on the issue. Foreign firms and governments support the expansion of nuclear power – the United States company Westinghouse, but also Japan, Canada and Australia, which would supply much of the uranium. Aside from safety considerations, as elsewhere, nuclear plants are expensive, at least $US 17.5 billion for the construction of these twelve plants. The first plant alone would generate 40 tons of radioactive waste a year, which the government intended to store on site initially, and after that on uninhabited islands. As elsewhere as well, it was not clear whether any consideration had been given to the costs of decommissioning the plants at the end of their useful lives, nor was it clear whether the power would be priced to cover all the costs. However, the regime has already adapted to one potentially disastrous decline in oil revenues, and in addition, possession of natural resources has emphatically not been a necessary condition of growth in Asia (Hill, 1996, p. 252).

A further problem is the exploitation of mineral and timber resources. As elsewhere, these have been 'underpriced'. In the case of timber, the World Bank estimated that rainforests were being felled at a rate 50 per cent above that which might be sustainable, and that the government's inability to increase royalties as a result of the connections of logging interests to Soeharto was causing a loss of potential revenue of US$ 500 million per year (Schwarz, 1994, p. 140; Peluso, 1995; Thompson, 1996). The problem of regional disparity is another area of concern, particularly the relatively slow growth of per capita income outside of Java caused by the relatively small proportion of regional product retained in the regions for either consumption or investment (Booth, ed., 1992). The favouritism shown to migrants from crowded Java and Madura has caused resentment and led to rioting in Kalimantan. The resulting lack of employment opportunities could lead recruits to separatist movements, in East Timor, Irian Jaya, Sulawesi and Aceh.

14

EPILOGUE: CAN GROWTH CONTINUE?

Having concluded roundly, let us conclude squarely, with a concluding conclusion.

Joseph Levenson, *Confucian China and Its Modern Fate*

It is the historian's task to explain the past, not to predict the future, but this is the question which hovers in the background of discussion of economic development in Asia. A few of the considerations which may affect future growth have been suggested in Chapters 12 and 13, as well as a few areas where a future historian might look for explanations of growth or its absence. In general, it is clear that the structure of Asian states and the desires of key elite groups and individuals to retain power will pose problems for future growth by restricting the mobility of resources, for instance by protecting inefficient domestic producers, by allowing corrupt but influential individuals to affect policy, or through racist legislation discriminating against minority communities. They will also find it difficult to respond to the increasingly pressing need to satisfy the demands of their more affluent and better educated populations. Partly as a result of the slower population growth and increased education discussed in Chapter 10, and partly as a result of development itself, there will be upward pressure on wages. There will be further pressure especially from women, for the gendered structures considered in Chapter 11 will not contain the educated and mobile generation of women emerging in the next generation.

Preceding chapters have noted repeatedly that development does not depend on endowments of natural resources, and Chapter 10 argues the fears of neo-Malthusians that population growth will continue out of

478

control (Erlich, 1991) appear unfounded. Technological change will continue to make more efficient use of resources possible. Nevertheless, there are limits to sustainable rates of development, and there are serious environmental costs arising from previous development which will have to be addressed (Suzuki, 1993). Japanese public opinion is only beginning to come to terms with environmental degradation in Japan, and much Japanese foreign investment in fact exports the negative environmental consequences of Japanese growth elsewhere (McCormack, 1996). Some indication of the size of the problem looming across Asia may be seen in the Taiwan government's announced intention to devote 3.5 per cent of its expenditure during the 1991–6 plan period to environmental protection – more than for the entire agricultural sector and more than for science and technology.

The desperate drive for growth has often led to wasteful use of forest and mineral resources. The demand for power has led to massive increases in coal consumption and atmospheric pollution particularly in China. Hydroelectric projects bring upstream flooding as well as downstream damage. The Three Gorges project on the Yangzi, the proposed dam on the Batan Rajang in Sarawak, and a series of dams on the upper reaches of the Mekong and its feeders, for example, all pose serious environmental dangers. The nuclear reactors planned for the north coast of Java have also caused concern. Power is frequently underpriced, to subsidize farmers and domestic consumers, or to attract industrial investment, and the pricing almost never includes the cost of repairing environmental damage. In the longer run, this is inefficient, with the costs clearly outweighing the short-term benefits of rapid growth. Solutions, however, require not only the will of domestic leaders to confront the problems, but are almost by definition international in their ramifications. Wealthy countries – in East and Southeast Asia this means primarily the United States and Japan – will have to contribute as well (Tisdell, 1990, ch. 4; 1991).

China is crucial because of its size. After a long illness and three years after his last public appearance, Deng died in February 1997. His death, as an economist might say, had therefore been 'factored in' to Chinese government policy for some time. No expert expected sudden changes in policy. Nevertheless, possible changes in leadership in the near future add an element of instability to the entire Asian region. It seems likely, whatever shifts in leadership there may be, and indeed despite the possible wishes of the new leaders, that changes in economic and social structures will continue. Economically, the demand for resources which this will entail will place heavy pressure on China's domestic supplies of food, energy and raw materials. As emphasized in Chapter 13 China will be obliged to import more, and these increased imports will have to be paid for. Politically there appears no one among the likely successors to Deng who would foster the sort of reforms which Chiang introduced in Taiwan. None of these men will support calls for 'democracy'. However, a 're-former' among them might find a constituency in the newly rich cadres who will be seeking guarantees that their gains can be transformed into genuinely private property. The central government's policies in Hong Kong will provide an important clue as to future developments.

Japan's problems are detailed in Chapter 12. Despite those problems and a period of very slow growth in the 1990s, Japan remains the wealth-iest and the only undisputedly developed country in Asia. Therefore Japan's role in Asia and the relationship between Japan and China have been widely debated. To see 'Asia in Japan's embrace' (Hatch and Yama-mura, 1996) seems overdrawn. Though still poor compared to Japan, China is huge and growing rapidly. Their two economies are linked, and the links are growing. By 2015 Japan–China trade may be a larger fraction of world trade than Japan's trade with the United States. Japanese investment in China has grown rapidly in the 1990s and surveys indicate that it will continue to grow. Japan is currently China's major source of development assistance, and much of this is being used to develop infra-structure which will benefit Japanese firms wishing to invest in China. Currently both China and Japan must consider that the United States remains the hegemonic power. However, 'the future of US strategic engagement in the region has become a subject of speculation', and relations between China and Japan therefore could become competitive rather than complementary. Some Japanese leaders would like to see Japan exercising political and diplomatic leverage commensurate with its economic power, but Japanese forces are entirely defensive. As noted in Chapter 13 and above, the death of Deng has added an element of instability to Chinese policy, but there are those who might believe they could profit from a more aggressive stance. On balance, 'it is appropriate to be extremely cautious in making predictions' (EEAU, 1996).

The survey of the role of the state in the economies of Southeast Asia suggests that although they have displayed a considerable degree of pragmatism, the elites in control have difficulty in sharing power. They also have problems with political succession, an aspect of Southeast Asian life which some historians trace to the distant past (Van Niel, 1990b, p. 110; Wolters, 1982). An aspect of this elite authoritarianism is the heritage of instability and ethnic conflict after independence, for instance the turbulent conditions in Singapore in the 1950s which made up the background for the emergence of the People's Action Party, the desperate violence in Indonesia in 1965, or the 1969 riots which preceded Malaysia's adoption of the New Economic Policy. 'It has been in the urban areas (and perhaps secondly in other areas of modern economic development) that the newly independent states have generally found it necessary to revert to patterns of rigid authoritarian control that remind many persons of colonial days, but which also could be likened to precolonial patterns of hierarchy and control' (Van Niel, 1990b, p. 122). The question a future historian of Southeast Asia, and of Asia generally, may ponder is this: if the region's most progressive areas and groups are placed under the most restrictive control, can economic dynamism be maintained? And can authoritarian regimes continue to satisfy their increasingly highly educated and sophisticated subjects?

As in the case of China, another area in which all Asian nations will have to respond to sophisticated new demands is in trade. The development of the international economy will dictate the parameters within which Asian leaders will operate. There are two broad possibilities. The first is that international economic development proceeds in a series of long cycles of some fifty years' duration. If this is so, and if the period from 1950 to 1973 was an 'upswing' and the succeeding twenty-odd years a 'downswing', then the late 1990s might see the beginning of a new long upswing (Goldstein, 1988; Tylecote, 1993). Having survived and indeed prospered during the difficult 1970s and 1980s, Asia's exporters might find even greater opportunities in the first decade of the twenty-first century. If this were the case, then elites in growing economies could both provide for their own clienteles and buy off new groups which emerged out of the process of development. Additionally, the profits from foreign trade would provide the capital to advance to higher levels of development and possibly make good some of the environmental damage which has been done in the past generation.

Alternatively, the changes the world economy is undergoing may be structural rather than cyclical. Immanuel Wallerstein, the doyen of world systems theory, argues that the capitalist world economy whose history he has traced since the sixteenth century is coming to an end. A survey of the main problems confronting society today, according to Wallerstein, reveals that the assumptions on which the modern capitalist world system has been based no longer hold. First 'de-ruralization', the uncontrolled growth of urban agglomerations, signals an end to the pattern of capitalist development based on the incorporation of new groups of rural workers 'outside' the system, with phases of economic expansion at low wages followed by periods when workers organized to demand higher wages. Secondly, 'ecology', the demand for protection of the environment, signals an end to the process of capitalist accumulation based on the externalization of costs. Capitalist development has led to ecological waste, but now governments, confronted by the necessity either to raise taxes or to reduce profits, find they can do neither. Policy drifts, and Wallerstein sees no political constellation able to overcome this dilemma. Thirdly, 'democratization', the gradual increase in the rights of people to demand more (especially education and health) from their governments, confronts the inability of states to pay, leading to an ongoing fiscal crisis. Fourthly, the 'increase in the power of states', a truism for five hundred years until the 1970s, has been reversed. States are in decline. An anti-state rhetoric has accompanied a decline in efficacy. Those who can afford to, attempt to provide themselves with private police forces, schools, hospitals, communications and transportation, and refuse to pay for public provision of these services. But state structures are the heart of the 'liberal system', the glue that holds the system together (Wallerstein, 1996).

Are states becoming weaker? Kenichi Ohmae argues that the rise of 'regional' economies means 'the end of the nation state'. Investment, industry, information technology and individuals – the 'four Is' – have become more mobile and hence more global in their orientation. Borders are increasingly permeable. This makes it possible for economic units in any part of the world to acquire whatever they need for development. This in turn makes the traditional 'middleman' function of the state unnecessary, for 'growth depends on inviting the global economy in, not keeping it out'. However, national governments – or more precisely, governing elites – cling to power in the new situation by buying support from interest groups, usually through subsidies. The result is economic stagnation. Ohmae believes this is the cause of sluggish growth in Japan, and he blames bureaucrats for attempting to protect existing interests rather than encouraging change (Ohmae, 1995).

In contrast, Richard Rosecrance shares many of Ohmae's opinions, but concludes that the 'virtual states' which seize the opportunities of globalization and mobility will become stronger, not weaker. 'The virtual state is a country whose economy is reliant on mobile factors of production.' Its role is to encourage, stimulate and coordinate the activities of the 'virtual corporations' whose headquarters it houses. Product design, marketing and financing take place here, in the 'head' countries; production will occur wherever it is convenient and inexpensive, most likely in 'body' countries such as China or Russia. Several of Rosecrance's examples of 'virtual states' are small, notably three of the tigers, Hong Kong, Singapore, and South Korea. However, size does matter. Singapore is a 'negotiating entity' which 'depends as much or more on economic access abroad as it does on economic control at home', but in the United States 'major foreign trade and investment deals command executive attention as political and military issues did two decades ago', and diplomatic pressure is used to open the way for commercial advantage (Rosecrance, 1996).

How well will Asian economies cope with changes in the international economy? Structural changes lead to a much less optimistic scenario. No state appears willing to surrender its sovereignty; participation in international and transnational organizations appears less a commitment to 'globalization' and more an attempt to increase state power through collective action. A commitment to international cooperation and market regulation does not mean that states and the elites who govern them are committed to the welfare of their subjects. Charles Tilly argues that workers depend on the national state for protection and that 'globalization threatens labour's rights' (Tilly, 1995). National states may become less able, or less willing, to guarantee their workers a decent living, but they may use their public commitment to globalization and market forces as an excuse to increase their arbitrary power. The labour laws introduced by the South Korean government at the end of 1996, for instance, combined with proposed new powers for security agencies, would have strengthened the state in its dealings with workers, but were justified as necessary to hold labour costs down and make Korean industry more internationally competitive.

Because many of the Asian states are small, they may find their corporations shouldered aside by overseas competitors, backed by diplomatic pressure from their home governments. They may find themselves confined to the lower end of the manufacturing product cycle. They may find themselves dependent on foreign capital, with its demands for resources and labour, and its unwillingness to bear the costs of protecting the local environment or to pay decent wages. They may, in world systems terminology, be 'semiperipheralized' (see So and Chiu, 1995). Still relatively poor, they may not be able to satisfy the demands of emerging social groups without damaging the interests of existing elites and their clients. The resulting conflicts could easily destabilize the existing balance, with the most likely outcome a series of new and harsher authoritarian regimes, the sort which, as Ferdinand Marcos said in 1978, 'tend to outlive their usefulness'. Asian leaders may succeed in squaring these particularly intractable circles; if they do, they will have earned admiration and possibly deserve emulation. But if they do not, as Mahathir Mohamed remarked in 1982, 'those who fail cannot be made examples to follow'.

BIBLIOGRAPHY

Abegglen, James C. (1958) *The Japanese Factory: Aspects of Its Social Organization*, Glencoe: The Free Press.

Abeyasekere, Susan (1987) *Jakarta: A History*, Singapore: Oxford University Press.

Adas, Michael (1974) *The Burma Delta: Economic Development and Social Change on an Asian Rice Frontier, 1852–1941*, Madison: University of Wisconsin Press.

Aiken, S. Robert and Leigh, Colin (1992) *Vanishing Rain Forests: The Ecological Transition in Malaysia*. Oxford: Clarendon Press.

Akashi Yoji (1980) 'The Japanese Occupation of Malaya: Interruption or Transformation', in McCoy, ed., pp. 65–90.

Alam, M. Shahid (1989) *Governments and Markets in Economic Development Strategies: Lessons from Korea, Taiwan, and Japan*, New York: Praeger.

Alavi, Rokiah (1996) *Industrialization in Malaysia: Import Substitution and Infant Industry Performance*, London and New York: Routledge.

Allen, Judith (1986) 'Evidence and Silence: Feminism and the Limits of History', in Pateman and Gross, eds., pp. 173–89.

Allen, Matthew (1994) *Undermining the Japanese Miracle: Work and Conflict in a Japanese Coalmining Community*, Melbourne: Cambridge University Press.

Allison, Anne (1994) *Nightwork: Sexuality, Pleasure, and Corporate Masculinity in a Tokyo Hostess Club*, Chicago: University of Chicago Press.

Amsden, Alice H. (1989) *Asia's Next Giant: South Korea and Late Industrialization*, Oxford: Oxford University Press.

Anderson, Benedict (1991) *Imagined Communities: Reflections on the Origin and Spread of Nationalism*, revised edition, London: Verso.

Anderson, Bonnie S., and Zinsser, Judith P. (1988) *A History of Their Own*, New York: Harper and Row.

Andors, Phyllis (1983) *The Unfinished Liberation of Chinese Women, 1949–1980*, Bloomington: Indiana University Press.

Appelbaum, Richard P., and Henderson, Jeffery, eds. (1992) *States and Development in the Asian Pacific Rim*, Newbery Park: Sage Publications.

Aubert, Claude (1993) 'Agricultural Reform in China', *OECD Observer* 183 (August/September): 30–3.

Aubert, Jean-Eric (1996) 'Science and Technology in Korea', *OECD Observer* 200 (June/July): 35–9.

Baker, Christopher (1981) 'Economic Reorganization and the Slump in South and Southeast Asia', *Comparative Studies in Society and History* 23: 325–49.

Baldwin, Frank (1973) 'Missionaries and the March First Movement: Can Moral Men Be Neutral?' in Nahm, ed., pp. 193–219.

Banister, Judith (1987) *China's Changing Population*, Stanford: Stanford University Press.

Barber, Margaret and Ryder, Gráinne, eds. (1993) *Damming the Three Gorges: What Dam-Builders Don't Want You to Know*, Toronto and London: Earthscan.

Barnett, A. Doak (1981) *China's Economy in Global Perspective*, Washington, D. C.: Brookings Institution.

Baruma, Ian (1995) *Wages of Guilt: Memories of War in Germany and Japan*, New York and London: Meridian/Penguin.

Baskin, Jonathan B. (1988) 'The Development of Corporate Financial Markets in Britain and the United States, 1600–1914: Overcoming Asymetric Information', *Business History Review* 62: 199–237.

Batson, Benjamin A. (1980) 'Siam and Japan: The Perils of Independence', in McCoy, ed., pp. 267–302.

Baum, Richard, ed. (1980) *China's Four Modernizations*, Boulder: Westview.

Beasley, W. G. (1972) *The Meiji Restoration*, Stanford: Stanford University Press.

Beasley, W. G. (1987) *Japanese Imperialism, 1894–1945*, Oxford: Oxford University Press.

Beasley, W. G. (1990) *The Rise of Modern Japan*, London: Weidenfeld and Nicolson.

Beck, John C., and Beck, Martha N. (1994) *The Change of a Lifetime: Employment Patterns among Japan's Managerial Elite*, Honolulu: University of Hawaii Press.

Becker, Jasper (1996) *Hungry Ghosts: China's Secret Famine*, London: John Murray.

Bedeski, Robert E. (1994) *The Transformation of South Korea: Reform and Reconstruction in the Sixth Republic Under Roh Tae Woo, 1987–1992*, London: Routledge.

Benaria, Lourdes, ed. (1985) *Women and Development: The Sexual Division of Labor in Rural Societies*, Westport: Praeger.

Bennett, Gordon (1976) *Yundong; Mass Campaigns in Chinese Communist Leadership*, Berkeley: University of California Center for Chinese Studies.

Beresford, Melanie (1989) *National Unification and Economic Development in Vietnam*, New York: St Martin's Press.

Berger, Mark T. (1996) 'Yellow Mythologies: The East Asian Miracle and Post-Cold War Capitalism', *Positions: East Asia Cultures Critique* 4 (1): 1–37.

Bergère, Marie-Claire (1989) *The Golden Age of the Chinese Bourgeoisie 1911–1937*, Cambridge: Cambridge University Press.

Bernhardt, Kathryn (1992) *Rents, Taxes, and Peasant Resistance: The Lower Yangzi Region, 1840–1950*, Stanford: Stanford University Press.

Bernstein, Gail Lee, ed. (1991) *Recreating Japanese Women, 1600–1945*, Berkeley: University of California Press, pp. 217–38.

Blake, C. Fred (1994) 'Footbinding in Neo-Confucian China and the Appropriation of Female Labor', *Signs* 19 (3): 676–712.

Booth, Anne (1990) 'Foreign Trade and Domestic Development in the Colonial Economy', in Booth, et al., eds.

Booth, Anne (1991) 'The Economic Development of Southeast Asia: 1870–1985', *Australian Economic History Review* 31: 20–52.

Booth, Anne (1995) 'Real Domestic Income of Indonesia, 1880–1989: A Comment and an Estimate', *Explorations in Economic History* 23: 350–64.

Booth, Anne, and McCawley, Peter (1981) 'Conclusions: Looking to the Future', in Booth and McCawley, eds., pp. 315–22.

Booth, Anne, ed. (1992) *The Oil Boom and After: Indonesian Economic Policy and Performance in the Soeharto Era*, Singapore: Oxford University Press.

Booth, Anne, and McCawley, Peter, eds. (1981) *The Indonesian Economy During the Soeharto Era*, Oxford: Oxford University Press.

Booth, Anne, O'Malley, W. J., and Weidemann, Anna, eds. (1990) *Indonesian Economic History in the Dutch Colonial Era*, Yale University Southeast Asia Studies Monograph Series 35. New Haven: Yale Center for International Area Studies.

Bordo, Michael D., and Kydland, Finn E. (1995) 'The Gold Standard As a Rule: An Essay in Exploration', *Explorations in Economic History* 32 (4): 423–64.

Boris, Eileen, and Daniels, Cynthia, eds. (1989) *Homework*, Urbana and Chicago: University of Illinois Press.

Bowen, Roger (1988) 'Japanese Peasants: Moral? Rational? Revolutionary? Duped? – A Review Article', *Journal of Asian Studies* 47: 821–32.

Bowie, Alasdair (1991) *Crossing the Industrial Divide: State, Society, and the Politics of Economic Transformation in Malaysia*, New York: Columbia University Press.

Bowie, Katherine A. (1992) 'Unraveling the Myth of the Subsistence Economy: Textile Production in Nineteenth-Century Northern Thailand', *Journal of Asian Studies* 51 (4): 797–823.

Brandt, Loren (1985) 'Chinese Agriculture and the International Economy, 1870–1930s: A Reassessment', *Explorations in Economic History* 22: 168–93.

Brandt, Loren (1987) 'Farm Household Behavior, Factor Markets, and the Distributive Consequences of Commercialization in Early Twentieth-Century China', *Journal of Economic History* 47 (3): 711–37.

Brandt, Loren (1989) *Commercialization and Agricultural Development: Central and Eastern China, 1870–1937*, New York: Cambridge University Press.

Breman, Jan (1983) *Control of Land and Labour in Colonial Java: A Case Study of Agrarian Crisis and Reform in the Region of Cierbon in the First Decades of the Twentieth Century*, Dordrecht: Foris Publications Holland.

Bresnan, John (1993) *Managing Indonesia: The Modern Political Economy*, New York: Columbia University Press.

Bridenthal, Renate, Koonz, Claudia, and Stuart, Susan (1987) *Becoming Visible: Women in European History*, 2nd ed., New York: Houghton Mifflin.

Broad, Robin, and Cavanagh, John (1993) *Plundering Paradise: The Struggle for the Environment in the Philippines*, Berkeley: University of California Press.

Brookfield, Harold, ed. (1994) *Transformation with Industrialization in Peninsular Malaysia*, Kuala Lumpur and New York: Oxford University Press.

Brown, Aajeswary Ampalavanar (1994) *Capital and Entrepreneurship in South-East Asia*, New York: St Martin's Press.

Brown, Ian (1986) 'Rural Distress in Southeast Asia During the World Depression of the Early (1930s): A Preliminary Examination', *Journal of Asian Studies* 45 (5): 995–1026.

Bruch, Matias, and Hiemetz, Ulrich (1984) *Small- and Medium-Scale Industries in the ASEAN Countries: Agents or Victims of Economic Development?* Boulder: Westview Press.

Burmeister, Larry L. (1988) *Research, Realpolitik, and Development in Korea: The State and the Green Revolution*, Boulder: Westview.

Bush, Richard C. (1982) *The Politics of Cotton Textiles in Kuomintang China, 1927–1937*, New York: Columbia University Press.

Caldwell, John C. (1993) 'The Asian Fertility Revolution: Its Implications for Transition Theories', in Leete and Alam, eds. pp. 299–316.

Calman, Donald (1992) *The Nature and Origins of Japanese Imperialism: A Reinterpretation of the Great Crisis of 1873*, London: Routledge.

Caoili, Manuel A. (1988) *The Origins of Metropolitan Manila: A Political and Social Analysis*, Quezon City: New Day Publishers.

Carney, Larry S., and O'Kelly, Charlotte G. (1990) 'Women's Work and Women's Place in the Japanese Economic Miracle', in Ward, ed., pp. 113–45.

Castells, Manuel (1992) 'Four Asian Tigers With a Dragon Head: A Comparative Analysis of the State, Economy, and Society in the Asian Pacific Rim', in Appelbaum and Henderson, eds., pp. 33–72.

Chai, J. C. H., and Sun, Haishun (1993) 'Liberalizing Foreign Trade: Experience of China', University of Queensland, Department of Economics Discussion Papers, No. 135.

Chai, J. C. H., and Chai, K. B. (1994) 'Economic Reforms and Inequality in China', University of Queensland, Department of Economics Discussion Papers, No. 141.

Chalmers, Norma J. (1989) *Industrial Relations in Japan: The Peripheral Workforce*, London: Routledge.

Chao, Kang (1986) *Man and Land in Chinese History: An Economic Analysis*, Stanford: Stanford University Press.

Chatterjee, Partha (1986) *Nationalist Thought and the Colonial World: A Derivative Discourse*, London: Zed Books.

Chee, Changboh (1973) 'Korea Artiste Proletarienne Federation: A Case for Literature as a Political Movement', in Nahm, ed., pp. 231–48.

Chen, Edward C. Y. (1979) *Hypergrowth in Asian Economies: A Comparative Analysis of Hong Kong, Japan, Korea, Singapore, and Taiwan*, London: Macmillan.

Chen, Edward C. Y. (1980) 'The Economic Setting', in Lethbridge, ed.

Chen, Li-fu, and Hou, Chi-ming (1989) 'Confucianism, Education and Economic Development in Taiwan', in Chung-Hua Institution for Economic Research, eds.

Cheng, Chung-ying (1989) 'Totality and Mutuality: Confucian Ethics and Economic Development', in Chung-Hua Institution for Economic Research.

Cheng, Lucie, and Hsiung, Ping-chun (1992) 'Women, Export-Oriented Growth, and the State: the Case of Taiwan', in Appelbaum and Henderson, eds., pp. 233–66.

Chon, Soohyun (1992) 'Political Economy of Regional Development in Korea', in Appelbaum and Henderson, eds., pp. 150–75.

Chongyi, Feng, and Goodman, David S. G. (1995) *China's Hainan Province: Economic Development and Investment Environment*, Asia Paper 5, Asia Research Centre, Murdoch University. Nedlands: University of Western Australia Press.

Chowdhury, Anis, and Islam, Iyanatul (1993) *The Newly Industrializing Economies of East Asia*, London: Routledge.

Chu, Samuel C., and Liu, Armonk, eds. (1994) *Li Hung-chang and China's Early Modernization*, Armonk and London: M. E. Sharpe.

Chung-Hua Institution for Economic Research, eds. (1989) *Conference on Confucianism and Economic Development in East Asia, May 29–31 1989*, Conference Series No. 13. Taipei.

Cipolla, Carlo M. (1965) *The Economic History of World Population*, 3rd edition, Harmondsworth and Baltimore: Penguin.

Coble, Parks M. (1980) *The Shanghai Capitalists and the Nationalist Government, 1927–1937*, Harvard East Asian Monographs 94. Cambridge: Harvard University Council on East Asian Studies.

Cochran, Sherman (1980) *Big Business in China: Sino–Foreign Rivalry in the Cigarette Industry, 1890–1930*, Cambridge: Harvard University Press.

Cohen, Paul A. (1988) 'The Post-Mao Reforms in Historical Perspective', *Journal of Asian Studies* 47: 519–541.

Colchester, Marcus (1989) *Pirates, Squatters, Poachers: The Political Ecology of the Dispossession of the Native Peoples of Sarawak*, London: Survival International.

Collcutt, Martin (1991) 'The Legacy of Confucianism in Japan', in Rozman, ed., pp. 111–54.

Conroy, Hilary (1960) *The Japanese Seizure of Korea: A Study of Realism and Idealism in International Relations*, Philadelphia: University of Pennsylvania Press.

Cornell, Laurel L. (1996) 'Infanticide in Early Modern Japan? Demography, Culture, and Population Growth', *Journal of Asian Studies* 55 (1): 22–50.

Crawcour, Sydney (1978) 'The Japanese Employment System', *Journal of Japanese Studies* 4: 225–45.

Croll, Elisabeth J. (1983) *Chinese Women Since Mao*, London: Zed Books and Armonk: M. E. Sharpe.

Croll, Elisabeth J., Davin, Dalia, and Kane, Penny, eds. (1985) *China's One-Child Family Policy*, New York: St. Martin's Press.

Cumings, Bruce (1984) 'The Legacy of Japanese Colonialism in Korea', in Myers and Peattie, eds., pp. 478–96.

Cumings, Bruce (1987) 'The Origins and Development of the Northeast Asian Political Economy: Industrial Sectors, Product Cycles, and Political Consequences', in Deyo, ed., pp. 44–83.

Curtis, Gerald L. (1988) *The Japanese Way of Politics*, New York: Columbia University Press.

Cushman, Jennifer W. (1991) *Family and State: The Formation of a Sino–Thai Tin-Mining Dynasty, 1797–1932*. Edited by Craig J. Reynolds, New York: Oxford University Press.

Dapice, David (1980) 'An Overview of the Indonesian Economy', in Papanek, ed.

Dayer, Roberta A. (1981) *Bankers and Diplomats in China, 1917–1925: The Anglo-American Relationship*, London: Frank Cass & Co.

Davis, Winston B. (1987) 'Religion and Development: Weber and the East Asian Experience', in Weiner and Huntington, eds., pp. 221–80.

Dean, Genivieve C. (1980) 'A Note on Recent Policy Changes', in Baum, ed.

Deng, Xiaoping (1985) *Building Socialism with Chinese Characteristics*, Peking: Foreign Languages Press.

Denison, Edward F. (1974) *Accounting for United States Economic Growth*, Washington, D.C.: The Brookings Institution.

Deyo, Frederic C. (1989) *Beneath the Miracle: Labor Subordination in the New Asian Industrialism*, Berkeley: University of California Press.

Deyo, Frederic C., ed. (1987) *The Political Economy of the New Asian Industrialism*, Ithaca: Cornell University Press.

Diamond, Norma (1985) 'Rural Collectivization and Decollectivization in China – A Review Article', *Journal of Asian Studies* 44: 785–92.

Dikötter, Frank (1992) *The Discourse of Race in Modern China*, London: C. Hurst & Co., and Stanford: Stanford University Press.

Dittmer, Lowell, and Kim, Samuel S., eds. (1993) *China's Quest for National Identity*, Ithaca and London: Cornell University Press.

Dixon, Chris (1991) *Southeast Asia in the World Economy: A Regional Geography*, Cambridge: Cambridge University Press.

Doeppers, Daniel F. (1984) *Manila, 1900–1941: Social Change in a Late Colonial Metropolis*, Yale University Southeast Asian Studies. New Haven: Yale University Press.

Doner, Richard F. (1991) 'Approaches to the Politics of Economic Growth in Southeast Asia', *Journal of Asian Studies* 50 (4): 818–49.

Doner, Richard F. (1992) 'Limits of State Strength: Toward an Institutionalist View of Economic Development', *World Politics* 44 (3): 398–431.

Dong, Wonmo (1973) 'Assimilation and Social Mobilization in Korea: A Study of Japanese Colonial Policy and Political Integration Effects', in Nahm, ed., pp. 146–82.

Donzelot, Jacques (1980) *The Policing of Families*, London: Hutchinson.

Dore, Ronald P. (1973) *British Factory – Japanese Factory: The Origins of National Diversity in Industrial Relations*, London: George Allen and Unwin.

Dore, Ronald P. (1986) *Flexible Rigidities: Industrial Policy and Structural Adjustment in the Japanese Economy*, Stanford: Stanford University Press.

Dower, John (1986) *War Without Mercy: Race and Power in the Pacific War*, London and Boston: Faber and Faber.

Doyle, Michael W. (1986) *Empires*, Cornell Studies in Comparative History. Ithaca: Cornell University Press.

Doyle, William (1989) *The Oxford History of the French Revolution*, Oxford: Clarendon Press.

Dreyer, Edward (1982) *Early Ming China: A Political History, 1355–1435*, Stanford: Stanford University Press.

Duus, Peter (1984) 'Economic Dimensions of Meiji Imperialism: The Case of Korea, 1895–1910', in Myers and Peattie, eds., pp. 128–71.

Duus, Peter (1989) 'Introduction – Japan's Informal Empire in China, 1895–1937: An Overview', in Duus, Myers, and Peattie, eds.

Duus, Peter (1995) *The Abacus and the Sword: The Japanese Penetration of Korea, 1895–1910*, Berkeley: University of California Press.

Duus, Peter, Myers, Ramon H., and Peattie, Mark R., eds. (1989) *The Japanese Informal Empire in China, 1895–1937*, Princeton: Princeton University Press.

EAAU (1992) *Korea to the Year 2000: Implications for Australia*, Canberra: Australia, Department of Foreign Affairs and Trade, East Asia Analytical Unit.

EAAU (1995) *Overseas Chinese Business Networks in Asia*, Canberra: Australia, Department of Foreign Affairs and Trade, East Asia Analytical Unit.

EAAU (1996) *Asia's Global Powers: China–Japan Relations in the 21st Century*, Canberra: Australia, Department of Foreign Affairs and Trade, East Asia Analytical Unit.

Easterlin, Richard A. (1981) 'Presidential Address: Why Isn't the Whole World Developed?' *Journal of Economic History* 41: 1–19.

Eberstadt, Nicholas (1995) *Korea Approaches Unification*, Armonk: M. E. Sharpe.

Ebrey, Patricia (1991) 'The Chinese Family and the Spread of Confucian Values', in Rozman, ed., pp. 45–83.

Eckert, Carter J. (1991) *Offspring of Empire: The Koch'ang Kims and the Colonial Origins of Korean Capitalism, 1876–1945*, Seattle: University of Washington Press.

Eckert, Carter J., Ki-baik Lee, Young Ick Lew, Michael Robinson, and Edward W. Wagner (1990) *Korea Old and New: A History*, Cambridge: Harvard University Press.

Eichengreen, Barry (1992) *Golden Fetters: The Gold Standard and the Great Depression, 1919–1939*, Oxford: Oxford University Press.

Elliott, David W. P. (1993) 'Dilemmas of Reform in Vietnam', in Turley and Seldon, eds.

Elson, Robert E. (1984) *Javanese Peasants and the Colonial Sugar Industry: Impact and Change in an East Java Residency, 1830–1940*, New York: Oxford University Press.

Elson, Robert E. (1992) 'International Commerce, the State and Society: Economic and Social Change', in Tarling, ed., pp. 131–96.

Elson, Robert E. (1994) *Village Java Under the Cultivation System, 1830–70*, Sydney: Allen & Unwin.

Elvin, Mark (1973) *The Pattern of the Chinese Past: A Social and Economic Interpretation*, Stanford: Stanford University Press.

Eng, Robert Y. (1986) *Economic Imperialism in China: Silk Production and Exports, 1861–1932*, University of California, Berkeley, Institute of East Asian Studies, China Research Monograph 31. Berkeley: University of California Press.

Entwisle, Barbara, Henderson, Gail, Short, Susan, Bouma, Jill, and Zhai Fengying (1995) 'Gender and Family Business in Rural China', *American Sociological Review* 60 (1): 36–57.

Erlich, Paul R. (1969) *The Population Bomb*, San Francisco: Sierra Club.

Erlich, Paul R. (1991) *Healing the Planet: Strategies for Resolving the Environmental Crisis*, Reading: Addison-Wesley.

Esherick, Joseph W., and Rankin, Mary B., eds. (1990) *Chinese Local Elites and Patterns of Dominance*, Berkeley: University of California Press.

Evans, Grant, and Rowley, Kelvin (1990) *Red Brotherhood at War: Vietnam, Cambodia and Laos since 1975*, revised edition, London: Verso.

Evans, Paul M. (1988) *John Fairbank and the American Understanding of Modern China*, New York: Basil Blackwell.

Evans, Peter (1989) 'Predatory, Developmental and Other Apparatuses: A Comparative Political Economy Perspective on the Third World State', *Sociological Forum* 4 (4): 233–46.

Evans, Peter (1992) 'The State as Problem and Solution: Predation, Embedded Autonomy and Structural Change', in Haggard and Kaufmann, eds., pp. 139–81.

Evans, Peter (1995) *Embedded Autonomy: States and Industrial Transformation*, Princeton: Princeton University Press.

Evers, Hans-Dieter (1987) 'The Bureaucratization of Southeast Asia', *Comparative Studies in Society and History* 29 (4): 666–85.

Faaland, J., Parkinson, R, and Saniman, Rais (1991) *Growth and Ethnic Inequality: Malaysia's New Economic Policy*, Kuala Lumpur: Dewan Bahasa Dan Pustaka.

Fairbank, John K. (1992) *China: A New History*, Cambridge: Harvard University Press.

Fawcett, James T., Khoo, Siew-Ean, and Smith, Peter, C., eds. (1984) *Women in the Cities of Asia: Migration and Urban Adaptation*, Boulder: Westview Press.

Feeney, Griffith, and Hamano, Kiyoshi (1990) 'Rice Price Fluctuations and Fertility in Late Tokugawa Japan', *Journal of Japanese Studies* 16: 1–30.

Feeny, David (1982) *The Political Economy of Productivity: Thai Agricultural Development, 1880–1975*, Vancouver: University of British Columbia Press.

Fernando, M. R. (1993) 'Growth of Non-Agricultural Indigenous Economic Activities in Java, 1820–1880', in Lindblad, ed., pp. 89–109.

Fewsmith, Joseph (1985) *Party, State, and Local Elites in Republican China: Merchant Organizations and Politics in Shanghai, 1890–1930*, Honolulu: University of Hawaii Press.

Fieldhouse, D. K. (1984) *Economics and Empire, 1830–1914*, London: Macmillan.

Flieger, Wilhelm, and Pagtolun-an, Imelda (1981) *An Assessment of Fertility and Contraception in Seven Philippine Provinces: 1975*. Papers of the East–West Population Institute, 77. Honolulu: East–West Center.

Francks, Penelope (1984) *Technology and Agricultural Development in Pre-War Japan*, New Haven: Yale University Press.

Francks, Penelope (1992) *Japanese Economic Development: Theory and Practice*, London: Routledge.

Friedman, Edward (1994) 'Reconstructing China's National Identity: A Southern Alternative to Mao-Era Anti-Imperialist Nationalism', *Journal of Asian Studies* 55 (1): 67–91.

Friedman, Edward, Pickowicz, Paul, Selden, Mark, and Johnson, Kay A. (1991) *Chinese Village, Socialist State*, New Haven: Yale University Press.

Fruin, W. Mark (1983) *Kikkoman: Company, Clan, and Community*, Cambridge: Harvard University Press.

Galenson, Walter (1976) 'The Japanese Labor Market', in Patrick and Rosovsky, eds., pp. 587–672.

Galenson, Walter (1992) *Labor and Economic Growth in Five Asian Countries*, New York: Praeger.

Gardella, Robert (1992) 'Squaring Accounts: Commercial Bookkeeping Methods and Capitalist Rationalism in Late Qing and Republican China', *Journal of Asian Studies* 51 (2): 317–39.

Garnaut, Ross, and Ma, Guonan (1992) *Grain in China*, Canberra: Australia, Department of Foreign Affairs and Trade, East Asia Analytical Unit.

Garon, Sheldon (1987) *The State and Labor in Modern Japan*, Berkeley: University of California Press.

Geertz, Clifford (1963) *Agricultural Involution: The Process of Ecological Change in Indonesia*, Berkeley: University of California Press.

Gerschenkron, Alexander (1952) 'Economic Backwardness in Historical Perspective', in *Economic Backwardness in Historical Perspective: A Book of Essays*, Cambridge: Harvard University Press, 1962.

Gilmartin, Christina Kelley (1995) *Engendering the Chinese Revolution: Radical Women, Communist Politics, and Mass Movements in the 1920s*, Berkeley: University of California Press.

Ginsborg, Paul (1995) 'Family, Civil Society and the State in Contemporary European History: Some Methodological Considerations', *Contemporary European History* 4 (3): 249–73.

Gladney, Dru C. (1994) 'Representing Nationality in China: Refiguring Majority/ Minority Identities', *Journal of Asian Studies* 53 (1): 92–123.

Gluck, Carol (1985) *Japan's Modern Myths: Ideology in the Late Meiji Period*, Princeton: Princeton University Press.

Godley, Michael R. (1981) *The Mandarin-Capitalists from Nanyang: Overseas Chinese Enterprise in the Modernization of China, 1893–1911*, Cambridge: Cambridge University Press.

Goldman, Wendy Z. (1993) *Women, the State, and Revolution: Soviet Family Policy and Social Life*, Cambridge Russian, Soviet, and Post-Soviet Studies 90. Cambridge: Cambridge University Press.

Goldstein, Joshua S. (1988) *Long Cycles: Prosperity and War in the Modern Age*, New Haven: Yale University Press.

Goldstone, Jack A. (forthcoming) 'Gender, Work, and Culture: Why the Industrial Revolution came Early to England but Late to China', *Sociological Perspectives*.

Gomes, Alberto, ed. (1994) *Modernity and Identity: Asian Illustrations*, Bundoora: La Trobe University Press.

Goodhart, Charles A. E., and Sutija, George, eds. (1990) *Japanese Financial Growth*, London: Macmillan.

Gordon, Andrew (1985) *The Evolution of Labor Relations in Japan: Heavy Industry, 1853–1955*, Harvard University Council on East Asian Studies, Harvard East Asian Monographs 117. Cambridge: Harvard University Press.

Gragert, Edwin H. (1994) *Landownership under Colonial Rule: Korea's Japanese Experience, 1900–1935*, Honolulu: University of Hawaii Press.

Greenfeld, Liah (1992) *Nationalism: Five Roads to Modernity*, Cambridge: Harvard University Press.

Gullick, J. M. (1987) *Malay Society in the Late Nineteenth Century: The Beginnings of Change*, East Asian Historical Mongraphs. Singapore: Oxford University Press.

Hackenberg, Robert A., and Magalit, Henry F. (1985) *Demographic Responses to Development: Sources of Declining Fertility in the Philippines*, Boulder: Westview.

Haggard, Stephan (1990) *Pathways from the Periphery: The Politics of Growth in the Newly Industrializing Countries*, Ithaca: Cornell University Press.

Haggard, Stephan, Kim, Byung-Kook, and Moon, Chung-in (1991). 'The Transition to Export-led Growth in Korea: 1954–1966', *Journal of Asian Studies* 50 (4): 850–73.

Haggard, Stephan, and Kaufmann, Robert, eds. (1992) *The Politics of Economic Adjustment*, Princeton: Princeton University Press.

Hall, John A., ed. (1986) *States of History*, Oxford: Basil Blackwell.

Hamilton, G. G. (1985) 'Why No Capitalism in China? Negative Questions in Historical Comparative Research', *Journal of Developing Societies* 1: 187–211.

Hamilton, G. G. (1990) 'Patriarchy, Patrimonialism, and Filial Piety: A Comparison of China and Western Europe', *British Journal of Sociology* 41: 77–104.

Hane, Mikiso (1991) *Premodern Japan: A Historical Survey*, Boulder: Westview.

Hanley, Susan B. (1997) *Everyday Things in Premodern Japan: The Hidden Legacy of Material Culture*. Berkeley: University of California Press.

Hanley, Susan B., and Yamamura, Kozo (1971) 'A Quiet Revolution in Tokugawa Economic History', *Journal of Asian Studies* 30: 373–84.

Hanley, Susan B., and Yamamura, Kozo (1977) *Economic and Demographic Change in Preindustrial Japan, 1600–1868*, Princeton: Princeton University Press.

Hanley, Susan B., and Wolf, Arthur P., eds. (1985) *Family and Population in East Asian History*, Stanford: Stanford University Press.

Hanson, John R. (1980) *Trade in Transition: Exports from the Third World, 1840–1900*, New York: Academic Press.

Hanson, John R. (1988) 'Third World Incomes Before World War I: Some Comparisons', *Explorations in Economic History* 25: 323–36.

Hanson, John R. (1991) 'Third World Incomes Before World War I: Further Evidence', *Explorations in Economic History* 28: 367–79.

Hanson, John R. (1996) 'Human Capital and Direct Investment in Poor Countries', *Explorations in Economic History* 33 (1): 86–106.

Hardacre, Helen (1989) *Shintō and the State, 1868–1988*, Studies in Church and State, Princeton: Princeton University Press.

Hartmann, Jörg (1981) *Subsistenzproduktion und Agrarentwicklung in Java/Indonesien*, Bielefelder Studien zur Entwicklungssoziologie, 13. Saarbrücken: Verlag Breitenbach.

Haskell, Thomas L., and Teichgraeber, Richard F., eds. (1994) *The Culture of the Market: Historical Essays*, Cambridge: Cambridge University Press.

Hatch, Walter, and Yamamura, Kozo (1996) *Asia in Japan's Embrace: Building a Regional Production Alliance*, Cambridge: Cambridge University Press.

Hauser, William B. (1974) *Economic Institutional Change in Tokugawa Japan: Osaka and the Kinai Cotton Trade*, Cambridge: Cambridge University Press.

Hayami, Yujiro (1988) *Japanese Agriculture Under Siege: The Political Economy of Agricultural Policies*, New York: St. Martin's Press.

Headrick, Daniel R. (1981) *The Tools of Empire: Technology and European Imperialism in the Nineteenth Century*, New York: Oxford University Press.

Healy, Lucy (1994) 'Modernity, Identity and Constructions of Malay Womanhood', in Gomes, ed., pp. 96–121.

Hein, Laura E. (1990) *Fueling Growth: The Energy Revolution and Economic Policy in Postwar Japan*, Council on East Asian Studies. Cambridge: Harvard University Press.

Herold, Renate (1980) *Die Blume am Arbeitsplatz: Japans Frauen im Beruf*, Tübingen: Horst Erdmann Verlag.

Hershatter, Gail (1986) *The Workers of Tianjin, 1900–1949*, Stanford: Stanford University Press.

Hewison, Kevin (1989) *Bankers and Bureaucrats: Capital and the Role of the State in Thailand*, Yale University Southeast Asia Studies, Monograph Series No. 34. New Haven: Yale University Press.

Hill, Hal (1990) 'Foreign Investment and East Asian Economic Development', *Asian-Pacific Economic Literature* 46(1): 21–58.

Hill, Hal (1994) 'ASEAN Economic Development: An Analytical Survey – the State of the Field', *Journal of Asian Studies* 53 (3): 832–66.

Hill, Hal (1996) *The Indonesian Economy since 1966: Southeast Asia's Emerging Giant*, Cambridge: Cambridge University Press.

Hill, Hal, ed. (1994) *Indonesia's New Order: The Dynamics of Socio-Economic Transformation*, Sydney: Allen & Unwin.

Hilsdon, Anne-Marie (1995) *Madonnas and Martyrs: Militarism and Violence in the Philippines*, Asian Studies Association of Australia, Women in Asia Publication Series, Sydney: Allen & Unwin.

Hirschmann, Charles (1994) 'Population and Society in Twentieth-Century Southeast Asia', *Journal of Southeast Asian Studies* 25 (2): 381–416.

Hirschmeier, Johannes, and Yui, Tsunehiko (1981) *The Development of Japanese Business 1600–1980*, 2nd ed., London: Allen & Unwin.

Ho, Samuel P. S. (1984) 'Colonialism and Development: Korea, Taiwan, and Kwantung', in Myers and Peattie, eds., pp. 347–98.

Ho, Samuel P. S. (1994) *Rural China in Transition: Non-Agricultural Development in Rural Jiangsu, 1978–1990*, Oxford: Clarendon Press.

Hong, Lysa (1984) *Thailand in the Nineteenth Century: Evolution of the Economy and Society*, Singapore: Institute of Southeast Asian Studies.

Hong, Sawon (1984) 'Urban Migrant Women in the Republic of Korea', in Fawcett, et al., eds. pp. 191–210.

Honig, Emily (1985) 'Socialist Revolution and Women's Liberation in China – A Review Article', *Journal of Asian Studies* 44: 329–36.

Honig, Emily (1986) *Sisters and Strangers: Women in the Shanghai Cotton Mills, 1919–1949*, Stanford: Stanford University Press.

Honig, Emily (1992) *Creating Chinese Identity: Subei People in Shanghai, 1850–1980*, New Haven: Yale University Press.

Honig, Emily, and Hershatter, Gail (1988) *Personal Voices: Chinese Women in the 1980s*, Stanford: Stanford University Press.

Hou, Chi-ming (1965) *Foreign Investment and Economic Development in China, 1840–1937*, Cambridge: Harvard University Press.

Hou, Chia-chu (1989) 'The Influence of Confucianism on Economic Policies and Entrepreneurship in Taiwan', in Chung-Hua Institution for Economic Research.

Howell, David L. (1992) 'Proto-Industrial Origins of Japanese Capitalism', *Journal of Asian Studies* 51(2): 269–86.

Hsu, Cho-yun (1980) *Han Agriculture: The Formation of Early Chinese Agrarian Economy (206 B.C. – A. D. 220)*, Seattle: University of Washington Press.

Hsü, Immanuel C. Y. (1995) *The Rise of Modern China*, 5th edition, New York and Oxford: Oxford University Press.

Huang, Philip C. C. (1985) *The Peasant Economy and Social Change in North China*, Stanford: Stanford University Press.

Huang, Philip C. C. (1990) *The Peasant Family and Rural Development in the Yangtzi Delta, 1350–1988*, Stanford: Stanford University Press.

Huang, Philip C. C. (1991) 'A Reply to Ramon Myers', *Journal of Asian Studies* 50: 629–33.

Huang, Ray (1974) *Taxation and Governmental Finance in Sixteenth-Century Ming China*, Stanford: Stanford University Press.

Huber, Thomas M. (1994) *Strategic Economy in Japan*, Boulder: Westview Press.

Huenemann, Ralph W. (1984) *The Dragon and the Iron Horse: The Economics of Railroads in China, 1876–1937*, Cambridge: Harvard University Press.

Hugill, Peter J. (1988) 'Structural Changes in the Core Regions of the World-Economy, 1830–1945', *Journal of Historical Geography* 14: 111–27.

Hui, Lim Mah (1981) *Ownership and Control of the One Hundred Largest Corporations in Malaysia*, New York: Oxford University Press.

Hull, Terence H. (1994) 'Fertility Decline in the New Order Period: The Evolution of Population Policy 1965–90', in Hill, ed., pp. 123–44.

Hunter, Janet, ed. (1993) *Japanese Women Working*, London: Routledge.

Hutchinson, John (1987) *The Dynamics of Cultural Nationalism: The Gaelic Revival and the Creation of the Irish Nation State*, London: Allen & Unwin.

Ienaga, Saburô (1968) *The Pacific War: World War II and the Japanese, 1931–1945*, New York: Random House/Pantheon Books, 1978.

Ikegami, Eiko (1995) *Taming of the Samurai: Honorific Individualism and the Making of Modern Japan*, Cambridge: Harvard University Press.

Ileto, Reynoldo (1992) 'Religion and Anti-Colonial Movements', in Tarling, ed., pp. 197–248.

Irokawa Daikichi (1985) *The Culture of the Meiji Period*, Princeton: Princeton University Press.

Iwata, Masakazu (1965) *Ôkubo Toshimichi: The Bismarck of Japan*, Berkeley: University of California Press.

Jackson, James C. (1986) *Planters and Speculators: Chinese and European Agricultural Enterprise in Malaya, 1786–1921*, Kuala Lumpur.

Jager, Sheila Miyoshi (1996) 'Women, Resistance and the Divided Nation: The Romantic Rhetoric of Korean Unification', *Journal of Asian Studies* 55 (1): 3–21.

James, Harold (1992) 'Introduction: Central Bank Cooperation in the Interwar Period', *Contemporary European History* 1 (3): 227–31.

Janelli, Roger L., and Yim, Dawnhee (1995) *Making Capitalism: The Social and Cultural Construction of a South Korean Conglomerate*, Stanford: Stanford University Press.

Janetta, Ann Bowman (1987) *Epidemics and Mortality in Early Modern Japan*, Princeton: Princeton University Press.

Jansen, Marius B. (1984) 'Japanese Imperialism: Late Meiji Perspectives', in Myers and Peattie, eds., pp. 61–79.

Jaschok, Maria, and Miers, Suzanne (1994) *Women and Chinese Patriarchy*, London: Zed and Hong Kong: Hong Kong University Press.

Jesudason, James V. (1989) *Ethnicity and the Economy: The State, Chinese Business and Multinationals in Malaysia*, Singapore and New York: Oxford University Press.

Johnson, Chalmers (1982) *MITI and the Japanese Miracle: The Growth of Industrial Policy*, Stanford: Stanford University Press.

Johnson, Chalmers (1987) 'Political Institutions and Economic Performance: the Government–Business Relationship in Japan, South Korea, and Taiwan', in Deyo, ed., pp. 136–64.

Johnson, Kay Ann (1983) *Women, the Family, and Peasant Revolution in China*, Chicago: University of Chicago Press.

Jomo, Kwame Sundaram (1986) *A Question of Class*, Singapore: Oxford University Press.

Jomo, Kwame Sundaram (1990) *Growth and Structural Change in the Malaysian Economy*, New York: St Martin's Press.

Jomo, Kwame Sundaram, ed. (1993) *Industrializing Malaysia: Policy, Performance, Prospects*, London: Routledge.

Jones, Eric (1993) *Growth Recurring: Economic Change in World History*, corrected edition, Oxford: Oxford University Press.

Jones, Leroy P. and SaKong, Il (1980) *Government, Business, and Entrepreneurship in Economic Development: The Korean Case*, Cambridge: Harvard University Council on East Asian Studies.

Jones, Susan Mann (1981) 'Misunderstanding the Chinese Economy: A Review Article', *Journal of Asian Studies* 40: 539–57.

Joseph, William A., Wong, Christine P. W., and Zweig, David, eds. (1991) *New Perspectives on the Cultural Revolution*, Cambridge: Council on East Asian Studies, Harvard University.

Judd, Ellen R. (1994) *Gender and Power in Rural North China*, Stanford: Stanford University Press.

Juhn, Daniel Sungil (1973) 'The Development of Korean Entrepreneurship', in Nahm, ed.

Kaur, Amarjit (1985) *Bridge and Barrier: Transport and Communications in Colonial Malaya, 1870–1957*, Singapore: Oxford University Press.

Kelley, Allen C., and Williamson, Jeffery G. (1974) *Lessons from Japanese Development: An Analytical Economic History*, Chicago: University of Chicago Press.

Kerkvliet, Benedict J. (1977) *The Huk Rebellion: A Study of Peasant Revolt in the Philippines*, Berkeley: University of California Press.

Keyes, Charles F. (1983) 'Peasant Strategies in Asian Societies: Moral and Rational Economic Approaches – A Symposium. Introduction', *Journal of Asian Studies* 42: 753–68.

Kheng, Cheah Boon (1980) 'The Social Impact of the Japanese Occupation of Malaya (1942–1945)', in McCoy, ed., pp. 91–124.

Kim, Choong Soon (1992) *The Culture of Korean Industry: An Ethnography of Poongsan Corporation*, Tucson: University of Arizona Press.

Kim, Dae Jung (1994) 'Is Culture Destiny? The Myth of Asia's Anti-Democratic Values', *Foreign Affairs* 73 (6): 189–94.

Kim, Samuel S., and Dittmer, Lowell (1993) 'Whither China's Quest for National Identity?' in Dittmer and Kim, eds., pp. 237–90.

Kimura, Tetsusaburo (1989) *The Vietnamese Economy, 1975–86: Reforms and International Relations*, Tokyo: Institute of Developing Economies.

Kinzley, W. Dean (1991) *Industrial Harmony in Modern Japan: The Invention of a Tradition*, London: Routledge.

Kirby, William C. (1995) 'China Unincorporated: Company Law and Business Enterprise in Twentieth-Century China', *Journal of Asian Studies* 54 (1): 43–63.

Kirkby, Richard J. R. (1985) *Urbanization in China: Town and Country in a Developing Economy, 1949–2000*, New York: Columbia University Press.

Knodel, John, Chamratrithirong, Aphichat, and Debavalya, Nibhon (1987). *Thailand's Reproductive Revolution: Rapid Fertility Decline in a Third-World Setting*, Madison: University of Wisconsin Press.

Körner, Peter, Maass, Gero, Siebold, Thomas, and Tetzlaff, Rainer (1986) *The IMF and the Debt Crisis: A Guide to the Third World's Dilemmas*, London: Zed Books.

Kojima, Kiyoshi (1978) *Direct Foreign Investment: A Japanese Model of Multinational Business Operations*, New York: Praeger.

Kojima, Kiyoshi (1985) 'Japanese and American Direct Investment in Asia: A Comparative Analysis', *Hitotsubashi Journal of Economics* 26 (1): 1–35.

Kondratieff, Nikolai D. (1926) 'The Long Waves in Economic Life', in Haberler, Gottfried, ed., *Readings in Business Cycle Theory*, Philadelphia: Blakiston, 1951.

Kosai, Yutaka (1986) *The Era of High-Speed Growth: Notes on the Postwar Japanese Economy*, Tokyo: University of Tokyo Press.

Krannich, Ronald L., and Krannich, Caryl R. (1980) *The Politics of Family Planning in Thailand: A Case of Successful Implementation*, University of California Center for

South and Southeast Asia Studies, Monograph Series 19. Berkeley: University of California Press.

Kratoska, Paul, and Batson, Ben (1992) 'Nationalism and Modernist Reform', in Tarling, ed., pp. 257–324.

Kriedte, Peter, Medick, Hans, and Schlumbohm, Jürgen (1981) *Industrialization Before Industrialization: Rural Industry in the Genesis of Capitalism*, Cambridge and New York: Cambridge University Press.

Kristol, William, and Kagan, Robert (1996) 'Toward A Neo-Reaganite Foreign Policy', *Foreign Affairs* 75 (4): 18–32.

Krueger, Anne O. (1990) 'Government Failures in Development', *Journal of Economic Perspectives* 4 (3): 9–24.

Krugman, Paul (1994) 'The Myth of Asia's Miracle', *Foreign Affairs* 73(6): 62–78.

Kulick, Elliott, and Wilson, Dick (1992) *Thailand's Turn: Profile of a New Dragon*, New York: St. Martin's Press.

Kung, Lydia (1983) *Factory Women in Taiwan*, Ann Arbor: UMI Research Press.

Kuznets, Simon S. (1966) *Modern Economic Growth: Rate, Structure and Spread*, New Haven: Yale University Press.

Landes, David S. (1969) *The Unbound Prometheus: Technological Change and Industrial Development in Western Europe from 1750 to the Present*, Cambridge: Cambridge University Press.

Laothamatas, Anek (1992) *Business Associations and the New Political Economy of Thailand: From Bureaucratic Polity to Liberal Corporatism*, Boulder: Westview.

Lardy, Nicholas R. (1983) *Agriculture in China's Modern Economic Development*, Cambridge: Cambridge University Press.

Lardy, Nicholas R. (1991) *Foreign Trade and Economic Reform in China, 1978–1990*, Cambridge: Cambridge University Press.

Large, Stephen S. (1981) *Organized Workers and Socialist Politics in Interwar Japan*, Cambridge: Cambridge University Press.

Large, Stephen S. (1992) *Emperor Hirohito and Shôwa Japan: A Political Biography*, London and New York: Routledge.

Larkin, John A. (1982) 'Philippine History Reconsidered: A Socioeconomic Perspective', *American Historical Review* 87: 595–628.

Lavely, William, Lee, James, and Wang, Feng (1990) 'Chinese Demography: The State of the Field', *Journal of Asian Studies* 49: 807–34.

Lee, Chong-Sik, and Yoo, Se-Hee, eds. (1991) *North Korea in Transition*, Berkeley: Institute of East Asian Studies, University of California.

Lee, Peter N. S. (1987) *Industrial Management and Economic Reform in China, 1949–1984*, Hong Kong: Oxford University Press.

Lee, Robert (1989) *France and the Exploitation of China: A Study in Economic Imperialism*, East Asian Historical Monographs. Hong Kong: Oxford University Press.

Lee, You-Il (1993) 'Korean Investors in Southeast Asia: A Critical View', *Asiaview* 3 (3): 7–8. Asia Research Centre, Murdoch University.

Leibfritz, Willi, and Roseveare, Deborah (1996) 'Ageing Population and Government Budgets, *OECD Observer* 197: pp. 33–7.

Lethbridge, David, ed. (1980) *The Business Environment of Hong Kong*, Hong Kong: Oxford University Press.

Levenson, Joseph R. (1968) *Confucian China and Its Modern Fate*, Berkeley and Los Angeles: University of California Press.

Lewis, James I. (1995) 'The French Colonial Service and the Issues of Reform, 1944–8', *Contemporary European History* 4 (2): 153–88.

Lewis, W. Arthur (1955) *The Theory of Economic Growth*, London: Allen and Unwin.

Li, Lillian M. (1981) *China's Silk Trade: Traditional Industry in the Modern World, 1842–1937*, Harvard East Asian Monographs 97. Cambridge: Harvard University Council on East Asian Studies.

Li, Lillian M. (1982) 'Introduction: Food, Famine, and the Chinese State', *Journal of Asian Studies* 41: 687–707.

Li, Zhisui (1994) *The Private Life of Chairman Mao*, London: Chatto and Windus.

Liddle, R. William (1992) 'Indonesia's Democratic Past and Future', *Comparative Politics* 24 (4): 443–62.

Lim, Chong-Yah, and Lloyd, Peter, eds. (1986) *Singapore: Resources and Growth*, Singapore: Oxford University Press.

Lim, Lin Lean (1993) 'The Feminization of Labour in the Asia-Pacific Rim Countries: From Contributing to Economic Dynamism to Bearing the Brunt of Structural Adjustments', in Ogawa, Jones, and Williamson, eds.

Lim, Timothy C. (1994) 'Explaining Development in South Korea and East Asia', *Korean Studies* 18: 171–202.

Lin, Tsong-biau, Mok, Victor, and Ho, Yin-ping (1980) *Manufactured Exports and Employment in Hong Kong*, Hong Kong: The Chinese University Press.

Lincoln, James R., Gerlach, Michael, and Ahmadjian, Christina L. (1996) 'Keiretsu Networks and Corporate Performance in Japan', *American Sociological Review* 61 (1): 67–88.

Lindblad, J. Thomas, ed. (1993) *New Challenges to the Modern Economic History of Indonesia*, Leiden: Programme of Indonesian Studies.

Little, Daniel, and Esherick, Joseph W. (1989) 'Testing the Testers: A Reply to Barabara Sands and Ramon Myers's Critique of G. William Skinner's Regional Systems Approach to China', *Journal of Asian Studies* 48: 90–9.

Liu, Ts'ui-jung (1980) *Trade on the Han River and Its Impact on Economic Development, 1800–1911*, Taipei: Academia Sinica.

Lockard, Craig Alan (1987) *From Kampung to City: A Social History of Kuching Malaysia, 1820–1970*, Monographs in International Studies, Southeast Asia Series 75. Athens: Ohio University Press.

Lubeck, Paul M. (1992) 'Malaysian Industrialization, Ethnic Divisions, and the NIC Model: The Limits of Replication', in Appelbaum and Henderson, eds., pp. 176–98.

Lucas, Robert E. Jr. (1990) 'Why Doesn't Capital Flow From Rich to Poor Countries?' *American Economic Review* 80: 92–6.

Luong, Hy V. (1992) *Revolution in the Village: Tradition and Transformation in North Vietnam, 1925–1988*, Honolulu: University of Hawaii Press.

Lyons, Thomas P. (1987) *Economic Integration and Planning in Maoist China*, New York: Columbia University Press.

MacAndrews, Colin, ed. (1986) *Central Government and Local Development in Indonesia*, East Asian Social Science Monographs. New York: Oxford University Press.

Mackerras, Colin, et al. (1992) *Eastern Asia: An Introductory History*, Melbourne: Longman Cheshire.

Maddison, Angus (1982) *Phases of Capitalist Development*, Oxford: Oxford University Press.

Maddison, Angus (1987) 'Growth and Slowdown in Advanced Capitalist Economies', *Journal of Economic Literature* 25: 649–98.

Maddison, Angus (1989) *The World Economy in the Twentieth Century*, Paris: Organization for Economic Cooperation and Development.

Maddison, Angus (1995) *Monitoring the World Economy 1820–1992*, Development Centre Studies. Paris: Organization for Economic Cooperation and Development.

Malinvaud, E. (1986) 'Catching Up, Forging Ahead and Falling Behind', *Journal of Economic History* 46: 285–306.

Maloney, Barbara (1991) 'Activism Among Women in the Taishô Cotton Textile Industry', in Bernstein, ed., pp. 217–38.

Mann, Michael (1986) 'The Autonomous Power of the State', in Hall, ed.

Mann, Susan (1987a) *Local Merchants and the Chinese Bureaucracy, 1750–1950*, Stanford: Stanford University Press.

Mann, Susan (1987b). 'Women in the Kinship, Class, and Community Structures of Qing Dynasty China', *Journal of Asian Studies* 46 (1987): 37–56.

Mao Zedong (1927) 'Report of an Investigation into the Peasant Movement in Hunan', *Mao Tse-tung: Selected Works*, 5 vols, New York: International Publishers, 1954, vol. 1, pp. 21–59.

Mao Zedong (1939) 'The Chinese Revolution and the Chinese Communist Party', *Mao Tse-tung: Selected Works*, 5 vols, New York: International Publishers, 1954, vol. 3, pp. 72–101.

Marcos, Ferdinand (1978) *Revolution from the Center: How the Philippines Is Using Martial Law to Build a New Society*, Hong Kong: Raya.

Marr, David G. (1980) 'World War II and the Vietnamese Revolution', in McCoy, ed., pp. 125–58.

Marshall, Barbara (1994) *Engendering Modernity: Feminism, Social Theory, and Social Change*, Cambridge: Polity Press.

Mason, Edward S., et al. (1980) *The Economic and Social Modernization of the Republic of Korea*, Cambridge: Harvard University Council on East Asian Studies.

Maung, Mya (1991) *The Burma Road to Poverty*, New York: Praeger.

Maung, Mya (1992) *Totalitarianism in Burma: Prospects for Development*, New York: Paragon House.

McCormack, Gavin (1996) *The Emptiness of Japanese Affluence*, St. Leonards: Allen & Unwin.

McCoy, Alfred W. (1972) *The Politics of Heroin in Southeast Asia*, New York: Harper and Row.

McCoy, Alfred W. (1980) 'Introduction', in McCoy, ed., pp. 1–13.

McCoy, Alfred W. (1994) 'Introduction', and 'Rent-Seeking Families and the Phililppine State: A History of the Lopez Familiy', in McCoy, ed.

McCoy, Alfred W., ed. (1980) *Southeast Asia Under Japanese Occupation*, Monograph Series 22. New Haven: Yale University Southeast Asia Studies.

McCoy, Alfred W., ed. (1994) *Anarchy of Families: State and Family in the Philippines*, Madison: University of Wisconsin Center for Southeast Asian Studies.

McGee, T. G., ed. (1986) *Industrialisation and Labour Force Processes: A Case Study of Peninsular Malaysia*, Research Papers on Development in East Java and West Malaysia 1. Canberra: Australian National University, Research School of Pacific Studies.

McGinn, Donald R., et al. (1980) *Education and Development in Korea*, Cambridge: Harvard University Council on East Asian Studies.

McNicoll, Geoffrey, and Singarimbun, Masri (1983) *Fertility Decline in Indonesia: Analysis and Interpretation*, Committee on Population and Demography, Report No. 20. Washington, D.C.: National Academy Press, and Yogyakarta: Gadjah Mada University Press, 1986.

McVey, Ruth, ed. (1992) *Southeast Asian Capitalists*, Cornell Southeast Asia Program. Ithaca: Cornell University Press.

Mendels, Franklin (1972) 'Proto-industrialization: The First Phase of the Industrialization Process,' *Journal of Economic History* 32: 241–61.

Metzger, Thomas A. (1989) 'Confucian Culture and Economic Modernization: An Historical Approach', in Chung-Hua Institution for Economic Research.

Mies, Maria (1986) *Patriarchy: Accumulation on A World Scale*, London: Zed Books.

Mitchell, B. R. (1992) *International Historical Statistics: Europe 1750–1988*, 3rd edition, Basingstoke: Macmillan, and New York: Stockton Press.

Mitchell, B. R. (1993) *International Historical Statistics: The Americas 1750–1988*, 2nd edition, Basingstoke: Macmillan, and New York: Stockton Press.

Mitchell, B. R. (1995) *International Historical Statistics: Africa, Asia & Oceania 1750–1988*, 2nd revised edition, Basingstoke: Macmillan, and New York: Stockton Press.

Mizoguchi Toshiyuki (1989) 'The Changing Pattern of Sino–Japanese Trade, 1884–1937', in Duus, Myers, and Peattie, eds. pp. 10–30.

Moghadam, Valentine M., ed. (1994) *Gender and National Identity: Women and Politics in Muslim Societies*, United Nations World Institute for Development Economics Research. London: Zed Books, and Karachi: Oxford University Press.

Mokyr, Joel (1990) *Lever of Riches: Technological Creativity and Economic Progress*, New York: Oxford University Press.

Morishima, Michio (1982) *Why Has Japan "Succeeded"? Western Technology and the Japanese Ethos*, New York: Cambridge University Press.

Morris-Suzuki, Tessa (1989) *A History of Japanese Economic Thought*, London: Routledge.

Morris-Suzuki, Tessa (1994) *The Technological Transformation of Japan: From the Seventeenth to the Twenty-First Century*, Cambridge: Cambridge University Press.

Morris-Suzuki, Tessa, and Seiyama, Takuro, eds. (1989) *Japanese Capitalism Since 1945: Critical Perspectives*, London: M. E. Sharpe.

Mosher, Steven W. (1983) *Broken Earth: The Rural Chinese*, New York: Free Press.

Moskowitz, Karl (1982) 'Korean Development and Korean Studies – A Review Article', *Journal of Asian Studies* 42: 63–90.

Murray, Martin J. (1980) *The Development of Capitalism in Indochina, 1870–1940*, Berkeley: University of California Press.

Myers, Ramon H. (1980) *The Chinese Economy: Past and Present*, Belmont: Wadsworth.

Myers, Ramon H. (1989) 'Confucianism and Economic Development: Mainland China, Hong Kong and Taiwan', in Chung-Hua Institution for Economic Research, eds.

Myers, Ramon H. (1991) 'How Did the Modern Chinese Economy Develop? – A Review Article', *Journal of Asian Studies* 50: 604–28.

Myers, Ramon H., and Peattie, Mark R. eds. (1984) *The Japanese Colonial Empire, 1895–1945*, Princeton: Princeton University Press.

Myrdal, Gunnar (1968) *Asian Drama: An Inquiry into the Poverty of Nations*, 3 vols. New York: Pantheon for the Twentieth Century Fund.

Myrdal, Jan (1984) *Return to a Chinese Village*, New York: Pantheon.

Nahm, Andrew C., ed. (1973) *Korea Under Japanese Rule: Studies of the Policy and Techniques of Japanese Colonialism*, Center for Korean Studies, Institute for International and Area Studies, Western Michigan University.

Nakagane, Katsuji (1989) 'Manchukuo and Economic Development', in Duus, Myers, and Peattie, eds. pp. 133–57.

Nakamura, Masanori, ed. (1994) *Technology Change and Female Labour in Japan*, Tokyo: United Nations University Press.

Nakamura, Takafusa (1981) *The Postwar Japanese Economy: Its Development and Structure*, Tokyo: University of Tokyo Press, and New York: Columbia University Press.

Neal, Larry (1994) *The Rise of Financial Capitalism: International Capital Markets in the Age of Reason*, Cambridge: Cambridge University Press.

Nee, Victor, and Su, Sijin (1990) 'Institutional Change and Economic Growth in China: The View from the Villages', *Journal of Asian Studies* 49: 3–25.

Nelson, Richard R., and Wright, Gavin (1992) 'The Rise and Fall of American Technological Leadership: The Postwar Era in Historical Perspective', *Journal of Economic Literature* 30: 1931–64.

Nishida, Yoshiaki (1989) 'Growth of the Meiji Landlord System and Tenancy Disputes after World War I: A Critique of Richard J. Smethurst, *Agricultural Development and Tenancy Disputes in Japan, 1870–1940*', *Journal of Japanese Studies* 15: 389–415.

Noguchi, Yukio (1994) 'The "Bubble" and Economic Policies in the 1980s', *Journal of Japanese Studies* 20 (2): 291–330.

Noguchi, Yukio, and Wise, David A., eds. (1994) *Aging in the United States and Japan*, Chicago: University of Chicago Press.

Nolte, Sharon H., and Hastings, Sally Ann (1991) 'The Meiji State's Policy Toward Women, 1890–1910', in Bernstein, ed., pp. 151–74.

Nørland, Irene (1991) 'The French Empire, the Colonial State in Vietnam, and Economic Policy: 1885–1940', *Australian Economic History Review* 31 (1): 72–89.

Ogawa, Naohiro, Jones, Gavin W., and Williamson, Jeffrey G., eds. (1993). *Human Resources in Development Along the Asia-Pacific Rim*, Singapore: Oxford University Press.

Ogilvie, Sheilagh C. (1993) 'Proto-industrialization in Europe', *Continuity and Change* 8 (2): 159–79.

Ogilvie, Sheilagh C. and Cerman, Markus, eds. (1996) *European Proto-Industrialization*, Cambridge and New York: Cambridge University Press.

Ogle, George (1990) *South Korea: Dissent Within the Miracle*, London: Zed Books.

Ohbuchi, Hiroshi (1976) 'Demographic Transition in the Process of Japanese Industrialization', in Patrick, ed., pp. 329–62.

Ohkawa, Kazushi, and Rosovsky, Henry (1976) *Japanese Economic Growth: Trend Acceleration in the Twentieth Century*, Stanford: Stanford University Press.

Ohkawa, Kazushi, Shinohara, Myohei, and Meisner, Larry (1979) *Patterns of Japanese Economic Development*, New Haven: Yale University Press.

Ohkawa, Kazushi, and Ranis, Gustav, eds. (1985) *Japan and the Developing Economies: A Comparative Analysis*, International Development Center of Japan and Economic Growth Center of Yale University. Oxford and New York: Basil Blackwell.

Ohmae, Kenichi (1995) *The End of the Nation State: The Rise of Regional Economies*, New York: Free Press.

Oi, Jean C. (1989) *State and Peasant in Contemporary China: The Political Economy of Village Government*, Berkeley: University of California Press.

Ôkubo, Toshimichi (1873) 'Reasons for Opposing the Korean Expedition', in Tsunoda, Ryusaku, et al., eds., *Sources of Japanese Tradition*, vol. 2. New York and London: Columbia University Press, pp. 151–5.

Ong, Aihwa (1987) *Spirits of Resistance and Capitalist Discipline: Factory Women in Malaysia*, Albany: State University of New York Press.

Önis, Ziya (1991) 'The Logic of the Developmental State', *Comparative Politics* 24 (1): 109–26.

Oon, Khong Cho (1986) *The Politics of Oil in Indonesia: Foreign Company–Host Government Relations*, Cambridge: Cambridge University Press.

Owen, Norman G. (1984) *Prosperity Without Progress: Manila Hemp and Material Life in the Colonial Philippines*, Berkeley: University of California Press.

Pan, Ming-te (1996) 'Rural Credit in Ming-Qing Jiangnan and the Concept of Peasant Petty Commodity Production', *Journal of Asian Studies* 55 (1): 94–117.

Papanek, Gustav F., ed. (1980) *The Indonesian Economy*, New York: Praeger.

Papanek, Hanna (1984) 'False Specialization and the Purdah of Scholarship – A Review Article', *Journal of Asian Studies* 44: 127–48.

Pasuk, Phongpaichit, and Baker, Chris (1995) *Thailand: Economy and Politics*, Kuala Lumpur: Oxford University Press.

Pateman, Carole, and Gross, Elizabeth, eds. (1986) *Feminist Challenges: Social and Political Theory*, Sydney: Allen & Unwin.

Patnaik, Utsa (1995) 'On Capitalism and Agrestic Unfreedom', *International Review of Social History* 40: 77–92.

Patrick, Hugh, ed. (1976) *Japanese Industrialization and Its Social Consequences*, Berkeley and Los Angeles: University of California Press.

Patrick, Hugh, and Rosovsky, Henry, eds. (1976) *Asia's New Giant: How the Japanese Economy Works*, Washington, D.C.: The Brookings Institution.

Peluso, Nancy Lee (1992) *Rich Forests, Poor People: Resource Control and Resistance in Java*, Berkeley: University of California Press.

Perkins, Dwight H. (1969) *Agricultural Development in China, 1368–1968*, Chicago: Aldine.

Perkins, Dwight H. (1983) 'Research on the Economy of the People's Republic of China: A Survey of the Field', *Journal of Asian Studies* 52: 345–72.

Perkins, Dwight H. (1986) *China: Asia's Next Giant?* Seattle: University of Washington Press.

Pirie, N. W. (1969) *Food Resources Conventional and Novel*, Harmondsworth and Baltimore: Penguin.

Popkin, Samuel L. (1979) *The Rational Peasant: The Political Economy of Rural Society in Vietnam*, Berkeley: University of California Press.

Rahim, Lily Zubaidah (1994) 'The Singapore Dilemma: The Political and Educational Marginality of the Malay Community', Ph.D. Dissertation, University of Sydney.

Rabushka, Alvin (1979) *Hong Kong: A Study in Economic Freedom*, Chicago: University of Chicago Press.

Ramseyer, J. Mark, and Rosenbluth, Frances M. (1995) *The Politics of Oligarchy: Institutional Choice in Imperial Japan*, Cambridge: Cambridge University Press.

Rasiah, Rajah (1993) 'Free Trade Zones and Industrial Development in Malaysia', in Jomo, ed., pp. 118–46.

Rawski, Thomas G. (1980) *China's Transition to Industrialism: Producer Goods and Economic Development in the Twentieth Century*, Ann Arbor: University of Michigan Press.

Rawski, Thomas G. (1983) 'New Sources for Studying China's Economy', *Journal of Economic History* 43: 997–1002.

Rawski, Thomas G. (1989) *Economic Growth in Prewar China*, Berkeley: University of California Press.

Reid, Anthony (1980) 'Indonesia: From Briefcase to Samurai Sword', in McCoy, pp. 16–32.

Reid, Anthony (1988) *Southeast Asia in the Age of Commerce, 1450–1680*, vol. 1: *The Lands Below the Winds*, New Haven: Yale University Press.

Reid, Anthony (1996) 'Flows and Seepages in the Long-term Chinese Interaction with Southeast Asia', in Reid, ed., pp. 15–50.

Reid, Anthony, ed. (1996) *Sojourners and Settlers: Histories of Southeast Asia and the Chinese*, Asian Studies Association of Australia, Southeast Asia Publication Series 28. St Leonards: Allen & Unwin.

Reynolds, Craig (1995) 'A New Look at Old Southeast Asia', *Journal of Asian Studies* 54 (2): 419–46.

Richards, Anne (1993) 'Korea, Taiwan and Thailand: Trade Liberalisation and Economic Growth', *OECD Observer* 184: pp. 24–8.

Richards, Anne (1994) 'Hong Kong, Singapore, Malaysia and the Fruits of Free Trade', *OECD Observer* 185: pp. 29–33.

Ricklefs, M. C. (1993) *A History of Modern Indonesia since c. 1300*, 2nd ed., Basingstoke: Macmillan.

Riedinger, Jeffrey M. (1995) *Agrarian Reform in the Philippines: Democratic Transitions and Redistributive Reform*, Stanford: Stanford University Press.

Roberts, Glenda S. (1994) *Staying on the Line: Blue-Collar Women in Contemporary Japan*, Honolulu: University of Hawaii Press.

Robinson, Kathryn M. (1986) *Stepchildren of Progress: The Political Economy of Development in an Indonesian Mining Town*, Albany: State University of New York Press.

Robinson, Michael E. (1984) 'Colonial Publication Policy and the Korean Nationalist Movement', in Myers and Peattie, eds. pp. 312–43.

Robinson, Michael E. (1991) 'Perceptions of Confucianism in Twentieth-Century Korea', in Rozman, ed.

Rodan, Garry (1989) *The Political Economy of Singapore's Industrialization: National State and International Capital*, New York: St Martin's Press.

Rodd, Laurel R. (1991) 'Yosano Akiko and the Taishô Debate over the "New Woman"', in Bernstein, ed., pp. 175–98.

Ronan, Colin A. (1980–94) *The Shorter Science and Civilization in China*, 4 vols., Cambridge: Cambridge University Press.

Ronnas, Per, and Sjöberg, Örjan, eds. (1990) *Dô'i Mô'i: Economic Reforms and Development Policies in Vietnam*, Stockholm: Swedish International Development Authority.

Rooth, Tim (1993) *British Protectionism and the International Economy: Overseas Commercial Policy in the 1930s*, Cambridge: Cambridge University Press.

Rosecrance, Richard (1996) 'The Rise of the Virtual State', *Foreign Affairs* 75 (4): 45–61.

Rowe, William T. (1984) *Hankow: Commerce and Society in a Chinese City, 1796–1889*, Stanford: Stanford University Press.

Rozman, Gilbert (1973) *Urban Networks in Ch'ing China and Tokugawa Japan*, Princeton: Princeton University Press.

Rozman, Gilbert, ed. (1981) *The Modernization of China*, New York: The Free Press.

Rozman, Gilbert, ed. (1991) *The East Asian Region: Confucian Heritage and Its Modern Adaptation*, Princeton: Princeton University Press.

Rutten, Rosanne (1982) *Women Workers of Hacienda Milagros: Wage Labor and Household Subsistence on a Philippine Sugarcane Plantation*, Amsterdam: Antropologisch-Sociologisch Centrum, Universiteit van Amsterdam.

Saitô, Osamu (1983) 'Population and the Peasant Economy in Proto-Industrial Japan', *Journal of Family History* 8: 30–54.

Sakong, Il (1993) *Korea in the World Economy*, Washington, D.C.: Institute for International Economics.

Salaff, Janet W. (1981) *Working Daughters of Hong Kong: Filial Piety or Power in the Family?* Cambridge: Cambridge University Press.

Salaff, Janet W. (1988) *State and Family in Singapore: Restructuring an Industrial Society*, Ithaca: Cornell University Press.

Salaff, Janet W. (1992) 'Women, the Family, and the State in Hong Kong, Taiwan, and Singapore', in Appelbaum and Henderson, eds., pp. 267–88.

Sands, Barbara, and Myers, Ramon H. (1986) 'The Spatial Approach to Chinese History: A Test', *Journal of Asian Studies* 45: 721–43.

Santikarn, Mingsarn (1981) *Technology Transfer: A Case Study*, Singapore: Singapore University Press.

SarDesai, D. R. (1994) *Southeast Asia: Past and Present*, 3rd edition, Boulder: Westview, and Basingstoke: Macmillan.

Sargeson, Sally (1996) 'Localising Globalisation: Industrial Relations in a Chinese Joint-Venture Factory', Communications With/In Asia: 20th Anniversary Conference, Asian Studies Association of Australia, Latrobe University.

Saw, Swee-Hock (1980) *Population Control for Zero Growth in Singapore*, Singapore: Oxford University Press.

Scalapino, Robert A. (1993) 'China's Multiple Identities in East Asia: China as a Regional Force', in Dittmer and Kim, eds., pp. 215–36.

Schein, Edgar H. (1996) *Strategic Pragmatism: The Culture of Singapore's Economic Development Board*, Cambridge: MIT Press.

Schumpeter, Joseph A. (1934) *The Theory of Economic Development*, New York: Oxford University Press/Galaxy Books, 1961.

Schwarz, Adam (1994) *A Nation In Waiting: Indonesia in the 1990s*, Boulder: Westview Press.

Scott, James C. (1976) *The Moral Economy of the Peasant: Rebellion and Subsistence in Southeast Asia*, New Haven: Yale University Press.

Sears, Laurie J. (1996) 'Introduction – Fragile Identities: Deconstructing the Feminine in Indonesia', in Sears, ed., pp. 1–46.

Sears, Laurie J., ed. (1996) *Fantasizing the Feminine in Indonesia*, Durham and London: Duke University Press.

Seidensticker, Edward (1991) *Tokyo Rising: The City Since the Great Earthquake*, Cambridge: Harvard University Press.

Seiyama, Takurô (1989) 'A Radical Interpretation of Postwar Economic Policies', in Morris-Suzuki and Seiyama, eds.

Sen, Amartya (1983) 'Economics and the Family', *Asian Development Review* 1: 14–27.

Sen, Amartya (1987) *On Ethics and Economics*, Oxford: Basil Blackwell.

Sethuraman, S.V., ed. (1981) *The Urban Informal Sector in Developing Countries: Employment, Poverty and Environment*, Geneva: International Labor Office.

Shalom, Stephen, R. (1981) *The United States and the Phililppines: A Study in Neo-Colonialism*, Philadelphia: Institute of the Study of Human Issues.

Shimada, Haruo (1994) *Japan's 'Guest Workers': Issues and Public Policies*, Tokyo: University of Tokyo Press.

Silverberg, Miriam (1991) 'The Modern Girl as Militant', in Bernstein, ed., pp. 239–66.

Simon, Denis Fred, and Rehn, Detlef (1988) *Technological Innovation in China: The Case of Shanghai's Electronics Industry*, Cambridge: Ballinger Publishing Company.

Simpson, James R., et al. (1985) *Technological Change in Japan's Beef Industry*, Boulder: Westview.

Skidmore, Max J., ed. (1996) *The Future of Hong Kong*, Special issue of *Annals of the American Academy of Political and Social Science*, Volume 547 (September).

Skinner, G. William (1964–5) 'Marketing and Social Structure in Rural China' (3 parts), *Journal of Asian Studies* 24: 3–43, 195–228, 363–99.

Skinner, G. William (1977a) 'Regional Urbanization in Nineteenth-Century China', in Skinner, ed., pp. 211–52.

Skinner, G. William (1977b) 'Cities and the Hierarchy of Local Systems', in Skinner, ed., pp. 275–351.

Skinner, G. William, ed., *The City in Late Imperial China*, Stanford: Stanford University Press.

Smail, John R. W. (1961) 'On the Possibility of an Autonomous History of Modern Southeast Asia', *Journal of Southeast Asian History* 2: 72–102.

Smethurst, Richard J. (1986) *Agricultural Development and Tenancy Disputes in Japan, 1870–1940*, Princeton: Princeton University Press.

Smethurst, Richard J. (1989) 'A Challenge to Orthodoxy and Its Orthodox Critics: A Reply to Nishida Yoshiaki', *Journal of Japanese Studies* 15: 417–37.

Smil, Vaclav (1988) *Energy in China's Modernization: Advances and Limitations*, Armonk: M. E. Sharpe.

Smith, Anthony D. (1986) *The Ethnic Origins of Nations*, Oxford: Blackwell.

Smith, Robert J. (1983) 'Making Village Women into "Good Wives and Wise Mothers" in Prewar Japan', *Journal of Family History* 8: 70–84.

Smith, Thomas C. (1959) *The Agrarian Origins of Modern Japan*, Stanford: Stanford University Press.

Smith, Thomas C. (1988) *Native Sources of Japanese Industrialization, 1750–1920*, Berkeley: University of California Press.

Smith, Thomas C., and Eng, Robert Y. (1977) *Nakahara: Family Farming and Population in a Japanese Village, 1717–1830*, Stanford: Stanford University Press.

Snodgrass, Donald R. (1980) *Inequality and Economic Development in Malaysia*, New York: Oxford University Press.

So, Alvin Y. (1986) *The South China Silk District: Local Historical Tradition and World-System Theory*, Albany: SUNY Press.

So, Alvin Y., and Chiu, Stephan W. K. (1995) *East Asia and the World Economy*, Thousand Oaks: Sage Publications.

Solinger, Dorothy J. (1984) *Chinese Business Under Socialism: The Politics of Domestic Commerce, 1949–1980*, Berkeley: University of California Press.

Solinger, Dorothy J. (1991) *From Lathes to Looms: China's Industrial Policy in Comparative Perspective, 1979–1982*, Berkeley: University of California Press.

Solomou, Solomos (1987) *Phases of Economic Growth, 1850–1973: Kondratieff Waves and Kuznets Swings*, Cambridge: Cambridge University Press.

Solow, Robert (1957) 'Technical Change and the Aggregate Production Function', in Rosenberg, Nathan, ed., *The Economics of Technological Change*, Harmondsworth: Penguin, 1971.

Song, Byung-Nak (1994) *The Rise of the Korean Economy*, updated edition, Hong Kong: Oxford University Press.

Spence, Jonathan D. (1982) *The Gate of Heavenly Peace: The Chinese and Their Revolution 1895–1980*, New York: Penguin.

Spence, Jonathan D. (1996) *God's Chinese Son: The Heavenly Kingdon of Hong Xiuquan*, New York and London: W. W. Norton & Co.

Spinanger, Dean (1986) *Industrialization Policies and Economic Development in Malaysia*, Singapore: Oxford University Press.

Stacey, Judith (1983) *Patriarchy and Socialist Revolution in China*, Berkeley: University of California Press.

Steinberg, David J., et al. (1987) *In Search of Southeast Asia: A Modern History*, revised edition, Honolulu: University of Hawaii Press and St Leonards: Allen & Unwin.

Stevens, Barrie (1996) 'China Enters the 21st Century', *OECD Observer* 201 (August/September): pp. 28–32.

Stites, Richard (1977) *The Women's Liberation Movement in Russia: Feminism, Nihilism, and Bolshevism, 1860–1930*, Princeton: Princeton University Press.

Stivens, Maila (1994) 'Gender and Modernity in Malaysia', in Gomes, ed., pp. 66–95.

Stivens, Maila (1996) *Matriliny and Modernity: Sexual Politics and Social Change in Rural Malaysia*, Asian Studies Association of Australia, Women in Asia Publication Series. St Leonards: Allen & Unwin.

Stoler, Ann Laura (1985) *Capitalism and Confrontation in Sumatra's Plantation Belt, 1870–1979*, New Haven: Yale University Press.

Strange, Heather (1981) *Rural Malay Women in Tradition and Transition*, New York: Praeger.

Suehiro, Akira (1989) *Capital Accumulation in Thailand, 1855–1985*, Tokyo: The Centre for East Asian Cultural Studies.

Sullivan, Norma (1994) *Masters and Managers: A Study of Gender Relations in Urban Java*, Sydney: Asian Studies Association of Australia, Women in Asia Publication Series. Allen & Unwin.

Sumiya Toshio (1989) 'The Structure and Operation of Monopoly Capital in Japan', in Morris-Suzuki and Seiyama, eds.

Sun, Haishun (1996) 'Macroeconomic Impact of Direct Foreign Investment in China 1979–93', Working Papers in Economics, Department of Economics, University of Sydney, No. 232.

Sung, Denk Hahm, and Plein, L. Christopher (1995) 'Institutions and Techno-logical Development in Korea: the Role of the Presidency', *Comparative Politics* 28 (1): 55–76.

Suryakusuma, Julia I. (1996), 'The State and Sexuality in New Order Indonesia', in Sears, ed., pp. 92–119.

Sutherland, Heather (1979) *The Making of a Bureaucratic Elite: The Colonial Transform-ation of the Javanese Priyayi*, Asian Studies Association of Australia, Southeast Asian Publications Series 2. Singapore: Heinemann.

Suzuki, David T. (1993) *Time To Change*, St Leonards: Allen & Unwin.

Taira, Koji (1970) *Economic Development and the Labor Market in Japan*, New York: Columbia University Press.

Takeuchi, Johzen (1991) *The Role of Labour-Intensive Sectors in Japanese Industrialization*, Tokyo: United Nations University Press.

Tarling, Nicholas, ed. (1992) *The Cambridge History of Southeast Asia*, vol. 2: *The Nineteenth and Twentieth Centuries*, Cambridge: Cambridge University Press.

Taylor, Jean G. (1983) *The Social World of Batavia: European and Eurasian in Dutch Asia*, Madison: University of Wisconsin Press.

Taylor, Robert H. (1980) 'Burma in the Anti-Fascist War', in McCoy, ed., pp. 159–90.

Teiwes, Frederick C. (1979) *Politics and Purges in China: Rectification and the Decline of Party Norms, 1950–1965*, London: M. E. Sharpe.

Thomas, Stephen C. (1984) *Foreign Intervention and China's Industrial Development, 1870–1895*, Boulder: Westview Press.

Thompson, Herb (1996) 'Deforestation and Non-Sustainable Wood Production', Murdoch University, Department of Economics Working Papers, No. 152.

Thurow, Lester (1993) *Head to Head: The Coming Economic Battle Among Japan, Europe, and America*, St Leonards: Allen & Unwin.

Tilly, Charles (1995) 'Globalization Threatens Labor's Rights', *International Labor and Working-Class History*', 47 (Spring): 1–23.

Tilly, Charles, Tilly, Louise A., and Tilly, Richard (1991) 'European Economic and Social History in the 1990s', *Journal of European Economic History* 20: 645–71.

Tipton, Frank B. (1990) 'The Role of Government in the Economic Development of Germany and Japan: A Skeptical Reevaluation', in Tolliday, Steven, ed., *Government and Business*, International Library of Critical Writings in Business History, London: Edward Elgar.

Tipton, Frank B. (1996) 'Neuere Arbeiten zur Wirtschafts-und Sozialgeschichte Asiens', *Geschichte und Gesellschaft* 22 (2): 267–98.

Tipton, Frank B., and Aldrich, Robert (1987a) *A Social and Economic History of Europe, 1890–1939*, London: Macmillan.

Tipton, Frank B., and Aldrich, Robert (1987b) *A Social and Economic History of Europe from 1939 to the Present*, London: Macmillan.

Tisdell, C. A. (1990) *Natural Resources, Growth and Development*, New York: Praeger.

Tisdell, C. A. (1991) *Economics of Environmental Conservation*, Amsterdam: Elsevier.

Tiwon, Sylvia (1996) 'Models and Maniacs: Articulating the Female in Indonesia', in Sears, ed., pp. 47–70.

Totman, Conrad (1980) *The Collapse of the Tokugawa Bakufu 1862–1868*, Honolulu: The University Press of Hawaii.

Tri, V. N., and Booth, A. (1992) 'Recent Economic Developments in Vietnam', *Asian-Pacific Economic Literature* 4(2): 16–40.

Trocki, Carl A. (1992) 'Political Structures in the Nineteenth and Early Twentieth Centuries', in Tarling, ed., pp. 79–130.

Trompf, Garry, ed. (1993) *Islands and Enclaves: Nationalisms and Separatist Pressures in Island and Littoral Contexts*, New Delhi: Sterling Publishers.

Truong, Thanh-Dam (1990) *Sex, Money and Morality: Prostitution and Tourism in Southeast Asia*, London: Zed Books.

Tsurumi, E. Patricia (1984) 'Colonial Education in Korea and Taiwan', in Myers and Peattie, eds., pp. 347–98.

Tsurumi, E. Patricia (1990) *Factory Girls: Women in the Thread Mills of Meiji Japan*, Princeton: Princeton University Press.

Tu, Wei-ming (1984) *Confucian Ethics Today: The Singapore Challenge*, Singapore: Federal Publications.

Tu, Wei-ming (1989) 'The Confucian Dimension in the East Asian Development Model', in Chung-Hua Institution for Economic Research.

Turley, William S., and Seldon, Mark, eds. (1993) *Reinventing Vietnamese Socialism: Doi Moi in Comparative Perspective*, Boulder: Westview.

Turner, Mark, et al., eds. (1992) *Mindanao: Land of Unfulfilled Promise*, Quezon City: New Day Publishers.

Tylecote, Andrew (1993) *The Long Wave and the World Economy: The Current Crisis in Historical Perspective*, London: Routledge.

Van der Meer, Cornelis L. J., and Yamada, Saburo (1990) *Japanese Agriculture: A Comparative Economic Analysis*, London: Routledge.

Van der Eng, Pierre (1992) 'The Real Domestic Product of Indonesia, 1880–1989', *Explorations in Economic History* 29: 343–73.

Van der Eng, Pierre (1993) 'The "Colonial Drain" from Indonesia, 1823–1990', Economics Division Working Papers on Southeast Asia, No. 93/2. Canberra: Research School of Pacific Studies, Australian National University.

Van der Eng, Pierre (1994a) 'Assessing Economic Growth and Standards of Living in Asia, 1870–1990', *Proceedings of the Eleventh International Economic History Congress*, Milan, pp. 95–108.

Van der Eng, Pierre (1994b) 'Development of Seed-Fertilizer Technology in Indonesian Rice Agriculture', *Agricultural History* 68 (1): 20–53.

Van der Eng, Pierre (1996) 'Some Broad Features of Long-Term Economic Growth in Modern Southeast Asia', Communications With/In Asia: 20th Anniversary Conference, Asian Studies Association of Australia, Latrobe University.

Van Langenberg, Michael (1993) 'Importing Nationalism: The Case of Indonesia', in Trompf, ed., pp. 151–74.

Van Niel, Robert (1960) *The Emergence of the Modern Indonesian Elite*, The Hague: W. van Hoeve.

Van Niel, Robert (1990a) 'The Legacy of the Cultivation System for Subsequent Economic Development', in Booth et al., eds.

Van Niel, Robert (1990b) 'Colonialism Revisited: Recent Historiography', *Journal of World History* 1: 109–24.

Vennewald, Werner (1994) 'Technocrats in the State Enterprise System of Singapore', Asia Research Centre, Murdoch University, Working Paper No. 32.

Vermeer, Eduard B. (1988) *Economic Development in Provincial China: The Central Shaanxi since 1930*, New York: Cambridge University Press.

Vickery, Michael (1984) *Cambodia 1975–1982*, London: Allen & Unwin.

Viraphol, Sarasin (1977) *Tribute and Profit: Sino-Siamese Trade, 1652–1853*, Cambridge: Harvard University Press for the Council on East Asian Studies.

Vo, Nhan Tri (1990) *Vietnam's Economic Policy Since 1975*, Singapore: Institute of Southeast Asian Studies, ASEAN Economic Research Unit.

Vogel, Ezra F. (1979) *Japan as Number One: Lessons for America*, Cambridge: Harvard University Press.

Wachman, Alan M. (1994) *Taiwan: National Identity and Democratization. Taiwan in the Modern World*, Armonk and London: M. E. Sharpe.

Wade, Robert (1990) *Governing the Market: Economic Theory and the Role of Government in East Asian Industrialization*, Princeton: Princeton University Press.

Wade, Robert (1993) 'Managing Trade: Taiwan and South Korea as Challenges to Economics and Political Science', *Comparative Politics* 25 (2): 147–68.

Wakeman, Frederick (1966) *Strangers at the Gate: Social Disorder in South China, 1839–1861*, Berkeley: University of California Press.

Wakeman, Frederick (1977) 'Rebellion and Revolution: The Study of Popular Movements in Chinese History', *Journal of Asian Studies* 36: 201–37.

Wakita, Shigeru (1994) 'The Formation of Rational Expectations in the Rice Futures Market of Dojima, Osaka, in the Tokugawa Era', *Annals of the Institute of Social Science, University of Tokyo*, No. 36, pp. 93–114.

Walder, Andrew G. (1995) 'Local Governments as Industrial Firms: An Organizational Analysis of China's Transitional Economy', *American Journal of Sociology* 101 (2): 263–301.

Waldron, Arthur (1990) *The Great Wall of China: From History to Myth*, Cambridge: Cambridge University Press.

Wallerstein, Immanuel (1974–89) *The Modern World System*, 3 vols., New York: Academic Books.

Wallerstein, Immanuel (1996) *After Liberalism*, New York: New Press.

Wang, George C., ed. (1982) *Economic Reform in the PRC*, Boulder: Westview.

Ward, Kathryn, ed. (1990) *Women Workers and Global Restructuring*, School of Industrial and Labor Relations, Cornell University. Ithaca: ILR Press.

Waring, Marilyn (1988) *If Women Counted: A New Feminist Economics*, San Francisco: Harper and Row.

Warren, James F. (1981) *The Sulu Zone, 1768–1898: The Dynamics of External Trade, Slavery, and Ethnicity in the Transformation of a Southeast Asian Maritime State*, Singapore: Singapore University Press.

Waswo, Ann (1977) *Japanese Landlords: The Decline of a Rural Elite*, Berkeley: University of California Press.

Watanabe, Toshio (1992) *Asia: Its Growth and Agony*, East West Center. Honolulu: University of Hawaii Press.

Weiner, Myron, and Huntington, Samuel P., eds. (1987) *Understanding Political Development*, Boston: Little, Brown & Co.

Weiss, Linda (1995) 'Governed Interdependence: Rethinking the Government-Business Relationship in East Asia', *Pacific Review* 8 (4): 589–616.

Weiss, Linda, and Hobson, John M. (1995) *States and Economic Development: A Comparative Historical Analysis*, Cambridge: Polity Press.

White, Gordon (1993) *Riding the Tiger: The Politics of Economic Reform in Post-Mao China*, Basingstoke: Macmillan.

Wicks, Robert S. (1992) *Money, Markets, and Trade in Early Southeast Asia: The Development of Indigenous Monetary Systems to A.D. 1400*, Ithaca: Southeast Asia Program, Cornell University.

Will, Pierre-Étienne (1980) *Bureaucratie et famine en Chine au 18e siècle*, Paris and the Hague: Mouton.

Wilson, Fiona, and Frederiksen, Bodil F., eds. (1995) *Ethnicity, Gender and the Subversion of Nationalism*, special issue of *European Journal of Development Research*. Ilford: Frank Cass.

Wilson, George M. (1992) *Patriots and Redeemers in Japan: Motives in the Meiji Restoration*, Chicago: University of Chicago Press.

Wilson, Richard W. (1993) 'Change and Continuity in Chinese Cultural Identity: The Filial Ideal and the Transformation of an Ethic', in Dittmer and Kim, eds., pp. 104–24.

Winichakul, Thongchai (1994) *Siam Mapped: A History of the Geo-Body of a Nation*, Honolulu: Hawaii University Press.

Wolf, Diane L. (1990a) 'Linking Women's Labor with the Global Economy: Factory Workers and their Families in Rural Java', in Ward, ed., pp. 25–47.

Wolf, Diane L. (1990b) *Factory Daughters: Gender, Household Dynamics, and Rural Industrialization in Java*, Berkeley: University of California Press.

Wolf, Diane L. (1996) 'Javanese Factory Daughters: Gender, the State, and Industrial Capitalism', in Sears, ed., pp. 140–62.

Wolf, Margery (1985) *Revolution Postponed: Women in Contemporary China*, Stanford: Stanford University Press.

Wolters, O. W. (1982) *History, Culture, and Religion in Southeast Asian Perspectives*, Singapore: Institute of Southeast Asian Studies.

Wong, John, and Wong, Aline (1989) 'Confucian Values as a Social Framework for Singapore's Economic Development', in Chung-Hua Institution for Economic Research, eds.

Wong, Loong (1993) 'The Invention of Nationalism in Southeast Asia: Some Theoretical Considerations of Nationalism in Singapore', in Trompf, ed., pp. 127–50.

Wong, R. Bin (1992) 'Chinese Economic History and Development: A Note on the Myers-Huang Exchange', *Journal of Asian Studies* 51: 600–11.

Wong, Siu-lin (1988) *Emigrant Entrepreneurs: Shanghai Industrialists in Hong Kong*, Hong Kong: Oxford University Press.

Woo, Wing Thye, et al. (1994) *Macroeconomic Policies, Crises, and Long-Term Growth in Indonesia, 1965–90*, Washington, D.C.: World Bank.

World Bank (1993) *The East Asian Miracle: Economic Growth and Public Policy*, Oxford and New York: Oxford University Press.

Woronoff, Jan (1986) *Politics the Japanese Way*, London: Macmillan.

Wray, William D. (1984) *Mitsubishi and the N.Y.K., 1870–1914: Business Strategy in the Japanese Shipping Industry*, Harvard University Council on East Asian Studies. Cambridge: Harvard University Press.

Wright, Mary C. (1957) *The Last Stand of Chinese Conservatism: The T'ung-chih Restoration, 1862–1874*, Stanford: Stanford University Press.

Wright, Tim (1984) *Coal Mining in China's Economy and Society, 1895–1937*, Cambridge: Cambridge University Press.

Wright, Tim (1994) 'China: What Will Happen after Deng?' *Asiaview* 4 (3): 1–2. Asia Research Centre, Murdoch University.

Wu, Yu-shan (1996) 'From a Clash of Ideologies to a Duel of Nation States: The Impact of the PRC's Missile Tests', *Asiaview* 6 (1): 1–4. Asia Research Centre, Murdoch University.

Wu, Yanrui (1995) 'How Wealthy Is China? Patterns of Household Spending', Asia Research Centre, Murdoch University, Working Paper No. 53.

Yahuda, Michael (1996) *Hong Kong: China's Challenge*, London: Routledge.

Yahya, Faisal (1995) 'The State in the Process of Economic Development: The Case of India', *Asian Studies Review* 18 (3): 83–94.

Yamamura, Kozo (1974) *A Study of Samurai Income and Entrepreneurship*, Cambridge: Harvard University Press.

Yamamura, Kozo, and Yasuba, Yasukichi, eds. (1987) *The Political Economy of Japan*, vol. 1: *The Domestic Transformation*, Stanford: Stanford University Press.

Yamazaki, Masakuzu (1996) 'Asia, A Civilization in the Making', *Foreign Affairs* 75 (4): 106–18.

Yen, Ching-hwang (1986) *A Social History of the Chinese in Singapore and Malaya*, Singapore: Oxford University Press.

Yonekura, Seiichiro (1994) *The Japanese Iron and Steel Industry, 1850–1990: Continuity and Discontinuity*, Basingstoke: Macmillan.

Yoshihara, Kunio (1988) *The Rise of Ersatz Capitalism in South-East Asia*, Singapore: Oxford University Press.

Yoshino, Kosaku (1992) *Cultural Nationalism in Contemporary Japan: A Sociological Inquiry*, London: Routledge.

Youngson, A. J. (1982) *Hong Kong: Economic Growth and Policy*, Hong Kong: Oxford University Press.

Young, Ernest (1977) *The Presidency of Yuan Shi-k'ai: Liberalism and Dictatorship in Early Republican China*, Ann Arbor: University of Michigan Press.

Yuan, Tsao (1986) 'Sources of Growth Accounting for the Singapore Economy', in Lim and Lloyd, eds. pp. 17–65.

Zelin, Madeleine (1984) *The Magistrate's Tael: Rationalizing Fiscal Reform in Eighteenth-Century China*, Berkeley: University of California Press.

Index

Where entries for countries have sub-divisions, historical periods are cited first, in chronological order, followed by individual and thematic sub-heads, in alphabetical order.

Index

DATE DUE